FIFTEEN AMERICAN AUTHORS
BEFORE 1900

FIFTEEN AMERICAN AUTHORS BEFORE 1900

Bibliographic Essays on

Research and Criticism

EDITED BY

ROBERT A. REES and
EARL N. HARBERT

THE UNIVERSITY OF WISCONSIN PRESS
Madison, Milwaukee, and London

3/1973
am. Lit.

PUBLISHED 1971
THE UNIVERSITY OF WISCONSIN PRESS
Box 1379, Madison, Wisconsin 53701
The University of Wisconsin Press, Ltd.
70 Great Russell Street, London, WC1B 3BY

First printing

Printed in the United States of America
NAPCO Inc., Milwaukee, Wisconsin

ISBN 0-299-05910-3; LC 77-157395

To HENRY A. POCHMANN
Teacher, Scholar, Friend

Contents

Preface

With the explosion of modern scholarship during the past several decades, students and teachers of American literature have sought to keep abreast of research and criticism on our national literature. The American Literature Group of the Modern Language Association sponsored a beginning effort in the early 1950s which resulted in *Eight American Authors* (New York, 1956; reprinted, with a "Bibliographical Supplement," New York, 1963; currently being revised), edited by Floyd Stovall. This volume was such an immediate success that scholars expressed the need for similar reviews on other American writers. The response to this need has been manifest in several ways.

Jackson R. Bryer felt there was as much a need for reviews of scholarly literature on the major modern American authors at the end of the sixties as there had been for major nineteenth-century American authors at the beginning of the fifties. Professor Bryer, in his *Fifteen Modern American Authors* (Durham, N.C., 1969), did for the moderns what Stovall's volume had done for earlier writers. Scholarly journals also have contributed to the matter of assessment and evaluation by sponsoring special issues and essays on individual writers.

In addition to these comprehensive reviews, the American Literature Group in 1963 began sponsoring annual reviews of scholarship. Since that time *American Literary Scholarship: An Annual* (first under the editorship of James Woodress and, since 1968, of J. Albert Robbins) has become a standard reference guide. Part of the value of this volume is that it includes reviews of literature arranged according to themes, topics, and, to some extent, periods, as well as individual authors.

Fifteen American Authors before 1900 represents a continuation of these efforts, and extends the range of informed discussion to a group of American authors who have not been previously evaluated but who deserve to be. The editors acknowledge their indebtedness to these earlier efforts, both by way of good example and, in some instances, by way of wise counsel and generous guidance from other editors and contributors.

In addition to discussions of individual authors, this volume includes two essays addressed to regional considerations: "The Literature of the Old South" and "The Literature of the New South." Different from the other essays in both design and manner, these essays constitute a response to a special problem, brought to the editors' attention by students of southern literature. For various reasons, they pointed out, reliance upon authors alone created an unfortunate imbalance in the book and left the South without the attention it merited. At the invitation of the editors, Professors C. Hugh Holman and Louis D. Rubin, Jr., have provided reviews of the South in literature which nicely complement Professor Rubin's *Bibliographical Guide to the Study of Southern Literature* (Baton Rouge, La., 1969).

The list of authors found in this volume represents the editors' consensus, made after consultation with numerous scholars of American literature. There was unanimous agreement that Crane, Dickinson, and Howells should be represented; in addition the editors have attempted to include as many of the writers of secondary importance as was possible in a necessarily limited space. Initially this book was designed to cover only nineteenth-century writers, but it finally was felt that any attempt to bring American scholarship up to date had to treat the three most important writers before 1800—Edward Taylor, Jonathan Edwards, and Benjamin Franklin—as well as those authors—like Henry Adams and Frank Norris—who flourished in the nineteenth century but who actually wrote some of their works in the twentieth century. Undoubtedly some readers might argue with our final list, which includes, if not all the writers who deserve review, at least those who seemed to us most deserving at this time.

Each contributor was selected on the basis of both knowledge about and interest in his subject. Once assigned, he was free to choose the materials he would consider; selection (and omission) of essays and books, and, in particular, the use of graduate dissertations and foreign criticism were considered matters of individual judgment. The editors insisted only that every contributor be familiar with all the material on his subject, including that listed in the 1969 *PMLA* Bibliography. Most contributors were able to bring their reviews closer to the actual date of publication of this volume. As a matter of overall form, it seemed desirable to divide each essay into five major divisions: Bibliography, Editions, Manuscripts and Letters, Biography, and Criticism.

The most complete citation of a book or article is found in its first appearance. Later citations appear in abbreviated form, unless the text requires a fuller description for clarity. Short titles for periodicals and some standard reference works are included in the Key to Abbreviations. Because of the profusion of reprints, the contributors generally have included reprint information only when the original publication might be difficult to obtain.

Several sources of bibliographical information deserve mention here. In addition to *American Literary Scholarship* (Durham, N.C., 1965–), which was discussed above, current bibliography is listed quarterly in *AL* (see Key to Abbreviations, pp. xv–xvii), annually in *AQ*, in the *Annual Bibliography of English Language and Literature* (issued by the Modern Humanities Research Association), and in the *PMLA* bibliography. Selective listings on special topics have appeared in the paperback series of Goldentree Bibliographies (New York), including: *American Literature through Bryant: 1585–1830*, compiled by Richard Beale Davis; *The American Novel through Henry James*, compiled by C. Hugh Holman; *The American Novel: Sinclair Lewis to the Present*, compiled by Blake Nevius; and *Afro-American Writers*, compiled by Darwin T. Turner. *American Literature, Poe through Garland* (Harry Hayden Clark) and *American Drama from Its Beginnings to the Present* (E. Hudson Long) are also promised but have not appeared at this writing. *CHAL* and *LHUS*, especially the bibliographical *Supplement* (1959), remain standard authorities for various authors and topics; a welcome recent addition, *A Bibliographical Guide to the Study of Southern Literature*, edited by Louis D. Rubin, Jr., supplements Clarence Gohdes's *Bibliographical Guide to the Study of the Literature of the U.S.A.* (3rd ed., Durham, N.C., 1970).

The contributors to this volume recognize also a general debt to the multitude of studies that have formed the foundations upon which this collection is raised. Jacob Blanck since 1955 has been issuing his monumental *Bibliography of American Literature* (New Haven, Conn.), describing according to modern principles the first editions and other separates of some three hundred American writers who died before 1931. More recently, *ALR* and *EAL* have begun to offer their readers essay reviews and bibliographical listings of scholarship on American authors, including some considered in this collection. *Abstracts of English Studies* and *American Literature Abstracts* regularly epitomize critical essays that might otherwise escape attention, and *American Literary Manuscripts* (Austin, Tex., 1960; currently being revised) brings together a sometimes useful (if often inaccurate and incomplete) listing of major library holdings in the United States.

Perhaps the story of American literature has grown too large for easy telling; nevertheless the value of *LHUS* (3rd ed., revised; New York, 1963) is secure. James Hart's *Oxford Companion to American Literature* (4th ed., New York, 1965; rev. 1971) provides a handy compendium of capsule information. Many of the larger literary problems are not easily defined in terms of individual authors, and broader studies of foreign influence or native philosophical movements are required to fill special needs. Harry Hayden Clark edited as long ago as 1954 a collection of essays by scholars of the American Literature Group which examined the rise and fall of the grand "isms" in American literary history, under the title, *Transitions in American Literary History* (Durham, N.C.). The reprinting of *Transitions* (Octagon, New York, 1967) is an event that deserves special mention.

Interest in literary criticism abroad and at home is clearly very high. Almost every essayist reported that his first problem was one of selection. Since there was space for evaluation of only the most significant studies, many of the items listed in the above bibliographies, as well as titles included in Lewis Leary's *Articles on American Literature, 1900–1950* (Durham, N.C., 1954) and Leary's *Articles on American Literature, 1950–1967* (Durham, N.C., 1970), could not be fitted into the essays that follow. The editors of this volume have demanded economy, even in the treatment of the most significant figures.

Robert A. Rees
Los Angeles, California

May 1971

Earl N. Harbert
New Orleans, Louisiana

Acknowledgments

THE following is a list of acknowledgments that contributors wish to make to individuals who have been helpful to them in the preparation of their essays and to institutions which have provided assistance and support.

Mr. Beard thanks Miss Marion Henderson and Miss Irene Walsh of the Reference Department of the Goddard Library, Clark University, for aid in obtaining materials; Mr. Milton Halsey Thomas and Professor Karl J. R. Arndt for scholarly assistance; Mr. Robins Best and Mrs. Sharyn Philcox for help in assembling materials and preparing manuscript; and Dean Saul Cohen of the Graduate School of Clark University for funds for clerical assistance.

Mr. Granger thanks Dr. Leonard W. Labaree, editor emeritus of the Papers of Benjamin Franklin, and Dr. Whitfield J. Bell, Jr., Librarian of the American Philosophical Society.

Mr. Harbert thanks Eric Partridge and Professors Roberta Reeder and Charles Vandersee for their help and the Tulane Council on Research for financial support of the entire project.

Mr. Keller thanks John B. Pickard and Roland H. Woodwell for reading his manuscript and making helpful suggestions and corrections.

Mr. Menikoff thanks Helen Hemmes, Genevieve B. Correa, and the Humanities Reference Staff, Hamilton Library, University of Hawaii.

Mr. Rees thanks Marjorie Griffin for research assistance and for many helpful suggestions in the preparation of his manuscript; Thomas Wortham for reading the manuscript and making helpful suggestions and corrections; and the Research Committee of the U.C.L.A. Academic Senate for a research grant which supported his project.

Mr. Rocks thanks Nancy C. Michael for her excellent work as a research assistant and the Tulane Council on Research for a grant to help with his study.

Mr. Rust thanks Professors Andrew Hilen, Lewis Leary, and Robert S. Ward, and the curators of the manuscripts at the Thomas Bailey Aldrich Memorial, Boston Public Library, Bowdoin College, Henry E. Huntington Library and Art Gallery, Houghton Library of Harvard University, Massachusetts Historical Society, Pierpont Morgan Library, University of Virginia Library, and Yale University Library.

In addition, both editors wish to express their special gratitude to Jackson R. Bryer for much helpful advice and criticism, and to Lynda Boose, whose index forms a valuable part of this volume.

Key to Abbreviations

AH   *American Heritage*
AHR   *American Historical Review*
AL   *American Literature*
ALR   *American Literary Realism*
AM   *American Mercury*
AN&Q   *American Notes & Queries*
AQ   *American Quarterly*
Archiv   *Archiv für das Studium der Neueren Sprachen und Literaturen*
ArQ   *Arizona Quarterly*
AS   *American Speech*
ASch   *American Scholar*
AtM   *Atlantic Monthly, Atlantic*
AWS   American Writers Series
BAL   *Bibliography of American Literature*
BB   *Bulletin of Bibliography*
BFHA   *Bulletin of the Friends Historical Association*
BJRL   *Bulletin of the John Rylands Library*
BNYPL   *Bulletin of the New York Public Library*
Bookman   *Bookman* (U.S.)
BuR   *Bucknell Review*
BUSE   *Boston University Studies in English*
Caliban   *Caliban* (Toulouse)
Carrell   *Journal of the Friends of the U. of Miami (Fla.) Library*

CE   *College English*
Century   *Century Illustrated Monthly Magazine*
CH   *Church History*
CHAL   *Cambridge History of American Literature*
CLAJ   *College Language Association Journal*
CMHS   *Collections of the Massachusetts Historical Society*
Col   *Colophon*
DA   *Dissertation Abstracts*
DAB   *Dictionary of American Biography*
Daedalus   *Daedalus (Proceedings of the American Academy of Arts and Sciences)*
DN   *Delaware Notes*
DVLG   *Deutsche Viertel jahrsschrift für Literatur Wissenshaft und Giestesgeschichte*
EA   *Études Anglaises*
EAL   *Early American Literature*
EALN   *Early American Literature Newsletter*
EIHC   *Essex Institute Historical Collections*
EJ   *English Journal*
ELH   *Journal of English Literary History*
ELN   *English Language Notes*

ESQ   Emerson Society Quarterly
Expl   Explicator
ForumNY   Forum (New York)
FR   French Review
The Friend   The Friend: A Quaker
Weekly Journal
HLB   Harvard Library Bulletin
HLQ   Huntington Library Quarterly
HM   Harper's Magazine, Harper's
New Monthly Magazine,
Harper's Monthly Magazine,
Harper's
HTR   Harvard Theological Review
IJHP   Iowa Journal of History and
Politics
JA   Jahrbuch für Amerikastudien
JAmS   Journal of American Studies
JEGP   Journal of English and Germanic Philology
JFI   Journal of the Franklin Institute
JHI   Journal of the History of Ideas
JRUL   Journal of the Rutgers University Library
KR   Kenyon Review
LHJ   Ladies' Home Journal
LHUS   Literary History of the United States
MagA   Magazine of Art
MF   Midwest Folklore
MFS   Modern Fiction Studies
MissQ   Mississippi Quarterly
MLA   Modern Language Association
MLN   Modern Language Notes
MLQ   Modern Language Quarterly
MLR   Modern Language Review
Monatshefte   Monatshefte für Deutschen Unterricht, Deutsche
Sprache und Literatur (Wisconsin)
MP   Modern Philology
N&Q   Notes and Queries
NAR   North American Review

NCF   Nineteenth-Century Fiction
NDQ   North Dakota Quarterly
NEHGR   New England Historical and Genealogical Register
NEM   New England Magazine
NEQ   New England Quarterly
NR   New Republic
NYH   New York History
NYHTBR   New York Herald Tribune Book Review
NY Review of Books   New York Review of Books
NYTBR   New York Times Book Review
Outlook   Outlook (U.S.)
PAAS   Proceedings American Antiquarian Society
PAPS   Proceedings American Philosophical Society
PBSA   Papers of the Bibliographical Society of America
PHR   Pacific Historical Review
PMASAL   Papers of the Michigan Academy of Science, Arts, and Letters
PMHB   Pennsylvania Magazine of History and Biography
PMHS   Proceedings of the Massachusetts Historical Society
PMLA   Publications of the Modern Language Association of America
PNJHS   Proceedings of the New Jersey Historical Society
PQ   Philological Quarterly
QH   Quaker History: Bulletin of the Friends' Historical Association
RR   Romanic Review
SAQ   South Atlantic Quarterly
SatR   Saturday Review
SB   Studies in Bibliography: Papers of the Bibliographical Society of the University of Virginia
SCraneN   Stephen Crane Newsletter

SELit   Studies in English Literature
(Eng. Literary Soc. of Japan,
U. of Tokyo)
SN   Studia Neophilologica
SoR   Southern Review
SP   Studies in Philology
SR   Sewanee Review
SSF   Studies in Short Fiction
*Sym   Symposium: A Quarterly
Journal in Modern Foreign Literature*
TLS   Times Literary Supplement
(London)
TSE   Tulane Studies in English
TSL   Tennessee Studies in Literature

*TSLL   Texas Studies in Literature
and Language*
TUSAS   Twayne's   United   States
Authors Series
*UKCR   University of Kansas City
Review*
UMPAW   University of Minnesota
Pamphlets on American Writers
VQR   Virginia Quarterly Review
WHR   Western   Humanities   Review
WMQ   William   and   Mary   Quarterly
YR   Yale Review
*YULG   Yale   University   Library
Gazette*

FIFTEEN AMERICAN AUTHORS
BEFORE 1900

Henry Adams

EARL N. HARBERT

MORE THAN half a century has passed since the death of Henry Adams and since the appearance of his classic personal testimony, *The Education of Henry Adams*. During these fifty years, friends, reviewers, biographers, historians, and literary critics have written voluminously about Adams. This essay attempts to identify the most useful studies of Henry Adams and his work.

BIBLIOGRAPHY

There is no comprehensive bibliography for Henry Adams. Much has been done, however, and the student can piece together a reliable working bibliography from a number of essays and checklists. Chief among these is the excellent retrospective review by Charles Vandersee, "Henry Adams (1838–1918)," in *ALR* (Summer 1969), which concentrates upon the last twenty years of scholarship. Vandersee divides his essay into criticism, bibliography, manuscripts, and other topics, and concludes with a usable index which makes his cross-referencing clear. I shall cite his study at several points in this discussion.

Jacob Blanck's standard *Bibliography of American Literature* includes Henry Adams in volume I and provides the usual description of editions, reprints, and "References." Of special interest is the illustration: "Syllabus. History II. Political History of Europe from the 10th to the 15th Century," which may surprise a present-day academic who does not look upon a course syllabus as imperishable literature. The most nearly complete chronology of Adams's writings is found in the three volumes of Ernest Samuels's biography: *The Young Henry Adams* (1855 to 1877); *Henry Adams: The Middle Years* (1878 to 1891); *Henry Adams: The Major Phase* (1892 and after). Samuels's list supersedes the "Bibliography of the Writings of Henry Adams" in

James T. Adams, *Henry Adams* (New York, 1933) and improves upon
the list of published writings in Elizabeth Stevenson, *Henry Adams: A
Biography* (New York, 1956). The selected bibliography in William
H. Jordy's *Henry Adams: Scientific Historian* (New Haven, Conn.,
1952) has been modernized and, with a preface, appears in the 1963
(Yale paperback) reprint; the result is a useful discussion of later work
pertinent to Jordy's topic. The *LHUS* and *Supplement* (1959) offer a
general list of older studies. George Hochfield, *Henry Adams: An
Introduction and Interpretation* (New York, 1962), Robert A. Hume,
Runaway Star: An Appreciation of Henry Adams (Ithaca, N.Y., 1951),
and Max I. Baym, *The French Education of Henry Adams* (New York,
1951, 1969) offer specialized bibliographies, the last directing attention
to Adams's reading and to the contents of his library.

A German essay, "Henry Adams: Ein Forschungsbericht 1918–1958"
by Bernhard Fabian (*Archiv für Kulturgeschichte*, 1959) is helpful—
the citations are mostly in English—but somewhat dated and not always
reliable. Current scholarship on Adams is included in the standard
bibliographies (see the preface, pp. ix–xii), and a nearly complete
list of dissertations may be found in *Dissertations in American Literature 1891–1966* (Durham, N.C., 1968). Some omissions and the special
values of theses and dissertations are discussed by Vandersee in *ALR*.
Several older studies are included in the somewhat unwieldy volume,
Bibliography of Comparative Literature (Chapel Hill, N.C., 1950),
compiled by Fernand Baldensperger and Werner P. Friederich; however, this book lacks an index. From the number and variety of these
sources, it should be clear that collecting all materials in a modern,
enumerative bibliography would be a major contribution.

EDITIONS

At a time when interest in authoritative editions of American writers
is high, the absence of any prospects for the Collected Writings of
Henry Adams seems noteworthy and regrettable. The need is obvious
to every student who looks at the publication histories of *Mont-Saint-
Michel and Chartres* (privately printed, Washington, 1904 and revised,
1912; published, Boston, 1913) or *The Education of Henry Adams*
(privately printed, Washington, 1907; published, Boston, 1918). Serious misprints, such as the *to* for *or* between *Newton* and *suffer* on page
496 of the *Education*, discussed by J. C. Levenson, in "Henry Adams
and the Art of Politics" (*SoR*, Winter 1968), occur in all current
printings; these should be corrected and the numerous changes between
the private printings and general publication accurately described.

Although many excerpts from Adams's well-known writings have appeared in popular anthologies, substantial works like the *Letters of John Hay and Extracts from His Diary* (3 vols., privately printed, Washington, 1908), with its confidential key to names and places, remain unavailable. Still, much of the writing is in print, although in the absence of a standard edition, individual titles must be sought from a confusing array of hard-cover and paperback editions, abridgments, and reprints.

The *Education* is available in a Modern Library reprint and a Sentry paperback with a superior introduction by Sir Denis Brogan. Ernest Samuels's forthcoming Riverside (Houghton Mifflin) edition promises to improve upon both of these, which use the 1918 text without explanation or commentary. *Mont-Saint-Michel and Chartres* can be found in many university libraries in the 1912 (private) printing, and the 1913 text has been reprinted in paperback, with introductions by various hands. After the appearance of several abridgments, the complete *History of the United States During the Administrations of Jefferson and Madison* (New York, 1889–1891) has been reprinted (Hillary House and others), although again, changes in the text from the first private printing (Cambridge, Mass.) are ignored. One particularly brilliant segment of the *History*—the six-chapter opening to Vol. 1— has been made available in a separate paperback: *The United States in 1800* (Ithaca, N.Y., 1955). Elizabeth Stevenson compiled *A Henry Adams Reader* (Garden City, N.Y., 1958); George Hochfield collected *The Great Secession Winter of 1860–61 and Other Essays* (New York, 1958; reprinted, Cranbury, N.J., 1962); and Edward Saveth added his own analysis of Adams's importance as a historian in *The Education of Henry Adams and Other Selected Writings* (New York, 1963). Both Henry Adams and Charles Francis Adams, Jr., are represented in *Chapters of Erie and Other Essays* (Boston, 1871, 1886), which has been reprinted in full (New York, 1966) and in a paperback abridgment (Ithaca, N.Y., 1956).

Democracy: An American Novel (anon., New York, 1880) and *Esther: A Novel* (pseud., Frances Snow Compton, New York, 1884) have also appeared in English editions (and the former in a French translation, Paris, 1883); both have been reprinted in paperback, most conveniently in a combined edition (Garden City, N.Y., 1961) introduced by Ernest Samuels. The Scholars' Facsimiles and Reprints edition of *Esther* (New York, 1938; now Gainesville, Florida) remains a bookman's favorite, even though Robert Spiller's pioneering introduction (see *Criticism*, below) has been reprinted elsewhere. *John Randolph* (Boston, 1882) and the collection of essays on history edited by Henry's brother Brooks Adams as *The Degradation of the Democratic Dogma* (New York, 1919) have also appeared in paperback editions. In a noteworthy introduction to the Harper Torchbook *Degradation*, Charles Hirschfeld discusses Brooks's "insensitivity" to Henry Adams's "work as a first-rate historian and conscious literary artist" and finds that the essays move toward a remarkably modern philosophy of scientific history. *The Life of George Cabot Lodge* (Boston, 1911) is combined with Edmund Wilson's commentary in *The Shock of Recognition* (Garden City, N.Y., 1943; reprinted with corrections, 1955). Much of Henry Adams's other work is now listed in reprint catalogues, including such previously hard to find items as *Memoirs of Marau Taaroa Last Queen of Tahiti* (privately printed, Washington, 1893), *Historical Essays* (New York, 1891), both the *Life* and *Writings of Albert Gallatin* (Philadelphia, 1879), and Adams's edition of *Documents Relating to New-England Federalism, 1800–1815* (Boston, 1877). Information about reprints is included in Vandersee (*ALR*, Summer 1969). For details concerning the poems and other short pieces, consult the appropriate section below.

MANUSCRIPTS AND LETTERS

Welcome news for all students of Henry Adams's life and work is the plan of Harvard University Press to collect and publish letters to persons outside the Adams family, in a series separate from the projected family correspondence. Many letters—numbered in the hundreds—have not yet been printed, including some directed to such close friends as Elizabeth Cameron and John Hay, who belonged to Adams's innermost circle. *American Literary Manuscripts* (Austin, Tex., 1960; currently being revised) contains a listing of important library holdings; it should be used along with the excellent account of letters and manuscripts in Vandersee's *ALR* bibliography. Many manuscripts, including letters, papers, and diaries, were destroyed by the author's own hand; others, notably the manuscript biography of Aaron Burr (1882), have simply disappeared. The massive collection of Adams Papers (microfilm, 608 reels) has been catalogued by the Massachusetts Historical Society (Boston, 1954–59), and Robert A. Hume, *Runaway Star*, includes in his bibliography a list of "Works Containing Letters of Henry Adams." Some of Adams's apprentice writing has never reached print (undergraduate essays and poetry, for example) but other incidental pieces are emerging: "Henry Adams Reports on a Trades-Union Meeting," edited by Charles I. Glicksberg (*NEQ*, Dec. 1942); "Henry Adams Reports on a German Gymnasium," edited by Harold Dean

Cater (*AHR*, Oct. 1947); and "Henry Adams Silenced by the Cotton Famine," edited by Joseph A. Boromé (*NEQ*, June 1960). Cater's inclusion in his *Henry Adams and His Friends: A Collection of His Unpublished Letters* (Boston, 1947) of "a hitherto unknown Henry Adams manuscript" brought to light an important essay in letter form, designed to accompany *The Rule of Phase Applied to History* (1909).

Previously unpublished letters will continue to appear. A volume of South Sea correspondence is expected to fill in details of Adams's travels with John La Farge, and Mme E. de Chazeaux is at work on a French translation of letters from the South Seas, 1890–91, in addition to the series of seven she has already printed, "Lettres de Henry Adams: Tahiti 1891" (*Revue de Deux Mondes*, Sept. 1968). Other scholars have reported that rich materials are being mined in Adams's correspondence with Bernard Berenson and in the Lodge collections at the Massachusetts Historical Society. Aside from Cater's volume, the standard published collections are *A Cycle of Adams Letters, 1861–1865* (2 vols., Boston, 1920), and *Letters of Henry Adams, 1858–1891* (2 vols., Boston, 1930, 1938), both edited by Worthington C. Ford. Deletions and omissions make the text somewhat unreliable by modern standards, but these volumes constitute the foundation of Henry Adams's considerable reputation as a letter-writer. Mabel La Farge in 1920 edited *Letters to a Niece and Prayer to the Virgin of Chartres* (Boston), the first printing of Adams's long poem. One critic's selection from these several collections (except for one letter) appeared in the "Great Letters Series" with an enthusiastic introduction by Newton Arvin as *The Selected Letters of Henry Adams* (New York, 1951). The editor's essay is reprinted, along with Arvin's review of Ford's *Letters*, "A Warning; not an Example," in *American Pantheon* (New York, 1967). A modern American estimate of Henry Adams's talent has been set down by Louis Kronenberger in "The Letters—and Life—of Henry Adams" (*AtM*, Apr. 1967; reprinted in *The Polished Surface*, New York, 1969), and a comparable British opinion is offered by Marcus Cunliffe, in *The Literature of the United States* (3rd ed., Baltimore, Md., 1967), who calls Adams "one of the best letter-writers in the language."

Henry Adams's marginalia have been summarized by Henry Wasser, *The Scientific Thought of Henry Adams* (Thessaloniki, 1956), and examined by Max Baym, "William James and Henry Adams" (*NEQ*, Dec. 1937), and *The French Education of Henry Adams*, and by Paul H. Bixler, "A Note on Henry Adams" (*Col*, Part 17, 1934). In addition, a microfilm reproduction of marked books in Adams's personal library is on deposit at the Massachusetts Historical Society, and a listing of his undergraduate holdings, "The 1858 Catalogue of Henry Adams'

Library," has long been available (*Col*, Autumn 1938), thanks to the industry of Mr. Baym. Among Henry Adams's personal papers, found neatly packaged after his death, was the bulk of the correspondence published as *The Letters of Mrs. Henry Adams 1865–1883*, edited by Ward Thoron (Boston, 1936), which includes a sample page from the Adamses Engagement Book.

BIOGRAPHY

Henry Adams's reputation has benefited from his biographers, who as a group have presented a portrait sympathetically drawn which yet avoids hero worship and mythologizing. Standard for every purpose is Ernest Samuels's three volume biography: *The Young Henry Adams, Henry Adams: The Middle Years*, and *Henry Adams: The Major Phase* (Cambridge, Mass., 1948, 1958, 1964). In the preface to the first volume, Samuels says he intends to correct the misrepresentation of Adams that emerges from the *Education*, and he threads a careful way through a massive accumulation of documents, including the Adams Papers. His biographical formula—"a coherent body of fact with a modicum of interpretation"—allows ample room for discussion while correcting past mistakes, especially those founded upon such unreliable documentation as bowdlerized letters. The volumes grow in size as the subject becomes more complex, but lucidity never disappears. The notes explain such matters as Samuels's use of quotations and provide, in addition, a prodigious collection of supporting detail for the core narrative. Appendix A in *The Major Phase* summarizes "The Travels of Henry Adams." More than its predecessors, this final volume demonstrates the limitations (often self-imposed, especially where psychological theorizing and literary interpretation are concerned) and the more numerous advantages of Samuels's method. Faced with a variety of seductive temptations that might have turned him toward pessimistic philosophy, popularized science, or historical determinism, Samuels manages to bring his man through it all. The treatment of Henry Adams's marriage and the tragic death of Marian Hooper Adams, who nowhere appears in the *Education*, triumphantly justifies Samuels's sobriety of manner that always rises above gossip yet refuses to romanticize.[1]

---

1. The definitive nature of Ernest Samuels's three-volume biography calls for further consideration of its critical reception. Generally, reviewers received each of the volumes with enthusiastic approval. Kenneth S. Lynn (*Reporter*, 17 December 1964) stressed Henry Adams's contemporaneity; in the *Education* Samuels exposes

A sprightly one-volume account, Elizabeth Stevenson's *Henry Adams: A Biography* (New York, 1956; reprinted, 1961) focuses upon the enigmatic relationship between Henry Adams the author and the subject of the *Education* and adds a feminine touch by highlighting the "private world of women" in which Adams lived. Something of the drawing room charmer, rather than the intellectual dynamo, emerges in this portrait of a "Satanic gentleman." Unfortunately, all the correspondence between Adams and his female friends was not available to this biographer; other letters must have added to the picture provided by the subject himself. About Henry Adams's writings, Elizabeth Stevenson is often perceptive, especially in matters of style, but she is also sometimes guilty of oversimplification, reducing the contents of the later works to a series of questions, themes, and outline summaries. Nevertheless, she makes the man worth looking for, even while the literary artist escapes.

Brief descriptions of Henry Adams's life are included in various anthologies of American literature, and many critical studies review at least some of the biographical details. The curious nature of the *Education* guarantees from the first reading a nearly automatic association of Adams's life with his writings. This situation, even if there were no other considerations, makes Ernest Samuels's commitment to a full-scale biography indisputably laudable. Brooks Adams showed the way in

---

"one of the truly meaningful figures of modern American literature, an anti-hero with whom all our intellectual losers from Quentin Compson to Herzog can claim relationship." James K. Folsom (*MP*, Nov. 1965), in a balanced, comprehensive review of all three volumes, finds no serious flaws; Samuels has written with "a sure eye for what parts of his subject's life are of real literary or biographical significance." Best of all, in Folsom's view, Samuels has not sought to impose a simplistic unity upon a complex subject: "He is the only major student of Adams to face squarely up to the fact that Adams' fascination for mid-twentieth-century readers lies precisely in the nature of his *failure* in his various attempts at synthesis; and that they seek in his work not a simple explanation for this fact of failure but a study of his mind which makes synthesis impossible." Almost alone among reviewers, Roger Sale found serious fault with Samuels (*Hudson Review*, Autumn 1965) because the biographer showed a "distrust" of the *Education*. Sale rates the *Major Phase* the "least satisfactory" of Samuels's three volumes, principally because Samuels fails to evaluate Henry Adams's writings properly and to recognize the playfulness of his method and style. The biography shows itself an old-fashioned, "philistine" essay in history; its subject becomes lost in "the welter of unshaped materials." A transatlantic demurrer was registered in *TLS* (28 October 1965); the reviewer believes that Samuels "has not lived up to the promise of his first volume" in part because he failed to treat candidly Adams's relationship with Mrs. Cameron. For a list of reviews selected by Samuels himself, see Charles Vandersee, "Henry Adams" (*ALR*, Summer 1969).

1919 when he wrote "The Heritage of Henry Adams" for the *Degradation of the Democratic Dogma*. Pointing to the Adams family as the most relevant frame of reference, Brooks fixed upon the intellectual kinship of "two powerful and original men, the grandfather and the grandson" (John Quincy Adams and Henry Adams). To understand Henry's *Education* (published a year before), the reader (according to Brooks) must know the history of the Adamses through four generations, so that he can understand where Henry fitted the family mold and where he did not. Other special qualities of family life were identified by James Truslow Adams (not a family member) in *The Adams Family* (New York, 1930), subtitled the "biography of a family," which was followed by his *Henry Adams* (New York, 1933). Cater's biographical introduction to his 1947 collection of letters added fresh material. A year later Robert Spiller brought together in his *LHUS* account (reprinted in *The Oblique Light*, New York, 1968) critical and biographical commentary, to form a well-balanced appreciation of Henry Adams and to warn readers against accepting the unauthorized subtitle of the *Education* ("An Autobiography") at face value.

The problem of evaluating Adams's inconsistent attempts at self-portraiture in books and letters is not, however, the only obstacle to a satisfactory understanding of the man. Much of his life was spent among the few friends and family members who could be classed as intimates, and their accounts of Henry Adams must be placed alongside his own. Brooks Adams's "The Heritage of Henry Adams" encouraged other critics to consider the Adams family history a kind of key to the writings of Henry and the other Adamses. Worthington Chauncey Ford's "The Adams Family" (*Quarterly Review*, Apr. 1922) reviews six books by family members (including the *Education, Chartres, Chapters of Erie*, and two by Charles Francis Adams, Jr.), finding in them evidence to support the general conclusion: "Exclusion from a public career fostered a family trait which has enriched American history and example—the habit of self-examination." V. L. Parrington preferred his own thesis concerning the family, which he labeled the "most distinguished in our history" (*Beginnings of Critical Realism in America*, New York, 1930). "Ancestral bias," according to Parrington, accounted for "the skepticism of the House of Adams" (particularly noticeable in Henry and Brooks) which prevented their understanding "men and measures." This view accepts without serious reservation the report of "failure" offered in the *Education*. More sympathetic evaluations of the Adams clan have lately been recorded: Stephen Hess celebrates the industry and energy of the Adamses in *American Political Dynasties: From Adams to Kennedy* (Garden City, N.Y., 1966), although he does not advance his case beyond the limits of popular biography. Cleveland Amory too has found room for the Adamses in his society trilogy, bringing the family story briefly but entertainingly up to date in *Who Killed Society?* (New York, 1960).

Looking more deeply into family history, in order to review Samuels's *Major Phase* ("Impressionist of Power," *NY Review of Books*, 14 January 1965), Alfred Kazin finds that Henry (and Brooks) personified, more than hereditary skepticism, a fascination with power as both a practical and an intellectual possession. A generation before Henry, Brooks, John, and Charles Francis, Jr., were active, the mantle of power was worn by their father, the subject of Martin Duberman's biography, *Charles Francis Adams, 1807–1886* (Boston, 1961). Henry was his father's favorite, and this volume shows that the younger man had in his father a model of intellectual and political achievement who suddenly became an example of senile incapacity, one powerful enough to frighten any student of heredity.

The relationship between Brooks and Henry Adams was special, even for this special family. Much of their correspondence is presently unavailable in print, and what we have must be used with great caution. Arthur Beringause draws heavily upon the letters (especially those of the 1890s) for his *Brooks Adams: A Biography* (New York, 1955). This book adds substantially to our understanding of their father's influence upon Henry and Brooks, the two sons who worked most closely with him, and of the intellectual exchanges between the brothers which led to Brooks's *Law of Civilization and Decay*. Still, many questions remain unanswered, as Marc Friedlaender makes clear in "Brooks Adams *en Famille*" (*PMHS*, 1968). A more narrowly defined examination, especially useful to students of historiography, is *Henry Adams and Brooks Adams: The Education of Two American Historians* (Norman, Okla., 1961); after systematically describing four "traditions" in family thinking, Timothy P. Donovan documents their potency. He is less successful, however, at showing how Henry Adams gave artistic expression to inherited ideas in his historical writing. A more informal and personal account of life among the four Adams brothers can be found in Abigail Adams Homans's *Education by Uncles* (Boston, 1966), which amplifies her essay "My Adams Uncles: Charles, Henry, Brooks" (*YR*, Spring 1966). Mrs. Homans remembers Uncle Henry as a kindly tutor and sage counselor, surrounded by a youthful entourage during the years after the death of his wife.

Almost a family member was Aileen Tone, the "secretary-companion and adopted niece," who shared Henry Adams's last years (1913 to 1918). Her story, gathered from notes, letters, and personal interviews, has been summarized by Louis Auchincloss, " 'Never leave me, never leave me' " (*AH*, Feb. 1970); it paints a difficult yet fascinating Henry Adams, thirty years Aileen's senior, who punctuated his pathetic expressions of loneliness with moments of fitful charm. Another unusual tribute, this one from a Harvard student who grew into a sometimes stormy friendship with his history teacher, is found in the pages of *Early Memories* (New York, 1913) by Henry Cabot Lodge. Lodge knew all the Adamses, and his comments about the family in the "Memorial Address," included as a preface to *Charles Francis Adams, 1835–1915: An Autobiography* (Boston, 1916), exhibit a New England understanding of the Brahmin mind. The *Education*, of course, sends us back again and again to think about New England, just as it requires us to ponder the characterizations of Henry Adams's friends. Several studies are helpful for the latter undertaking: *The Life and Letters of John Hay* (2 vol., Boston and New York, 1915), by William Roscoe Thayer, portrays the talented gentleman whose political career fascinated Adams. Hay's letters make this old-fashioned biography an especially valuable register of Adams's complex personality upon a sensitive, intelligent man of great good humor. Another symbolic figure in the *Education* is Clarence King, the thoroughly modern scientist. David H. Dickason's "Henry Adams and Clarence King: The Record of a Friendship" (*NEQ*, June 1944) recognizes the importance of learning more about the mysterious geologist; yet the essay depends too much upon a narrow selection of source materials. The Adams-King friendship must be studied in Thurman Wilkins's *Clarence King: A Biography* (New York, 1958) if the details of King's life (such as his secret marriage) and his influence upon Adams are to be grasped. Henry Adams's personal tribute to his recently dead friend, "King," in *Clarence King Memoirs* (New York, 1904), is also indispensable.

A number of sources touch upon one facet or another of Henry Adams's variegated life. In *Roman Spring: Memoirs* (Boston, 1934), Mrs. Winthrop Chanler devotes a short chapter to the "Friendship of Henry Adams" and discusses the vexing question of his attraction to Roman Catholicism. Indeed, Adams's travels—intellectual, spiritual, physical—have fascinated almost as many observers as has the grip of New England Puritanism on Henry and the Adams family. Louise Fant Fuller, "Henry Adams: Pilgrim to World's Fairs" (*TSL*, 1964), uses evidence from Adams's letters to study his responses "to the three fairs that he attended": the 1893 World's Columbian Exposition; an 1895 visit to Chartres cathedral, "where he met the Virgin"; and the Paris Exposition of 1900. The *Education* and *Chartres*, Mrs. Fuller finds, distort the chronology of sensibility established by the letters and confuse Adams's impressions of the moment. Motoshi Karita reports on "Henry Adams in Japan" (*SELit*, 1962), including books he read and places he visited, and concludes that Adams always remained "unable to penetrate to the inner life of the Japanese." Donald Richie's earlier essay with the same title (*Japan Quarterly*, Oct.–Dec. 1959) reached a similar conclusion. Perhaps the East was just too far from Boston. Louis Auchincloss, "In Search of Innocence" (*AH*, June 1970), looks at records of the second journey that Adams made with John La Farge (1890) to Hawaii, Samoa, and Tahiti, and finds that La Farge's watercolors display greater objectivity than Adams's writings. A bonus is the color illlustrations of work done by both La Farge and Adams.

Drawing upon an unsurpassed knowledge of the subject, Ernest Samuels has added some afterthoughts to his biography. "Henry Adams' 20th Century Virgin" (*Christian Century*, 5 October 1960) connects Adams's personal theology with nineteenth-century anthropology. Mariolatry offered an explanation for the natural superiority of women, a belief Adams had long held without being able to explain; since Adams's death, Samuels finds, the "Marian development" of Roman Catholic theology has assimilated Henry Adams's views. In another essay, "Henry Adams and the Gossip Mills" (*Essays in American and English Literature Presented to Bruce Robert McElderry, Jr.*, edited by Max F. Schulz, Athens, Ohio, 1967), Samuels answers an English critic (see footnote 1 above, p. 8) and then goes on to explain the hearsay rule used in the biography: "Whether a rumor deserved a page, a line, a footnote or charitable oblivion would depend on the credible evidence for it and not on its piquancy." Samuels dismisses claims of Henry Adams's paternity of Martha Cameron and labels "inconclusive" the evidence of any liaison between Adams and Martha's mother, Elizabeth Cameron, who, in modern terminology, cannot be labeled his "mistress."

Poetic and fictional representations of Henry Adams add a certain sparkle to his collected biography. Conrad Aiken, in Section 8 of *The Kid* (New York, 1947), "The Last Vision," pays a verse tribute to the courageous but ever dark and painful journey of an intellectual who engaged in a lifelong search for "godhead." A more acute characterization, which captures a very different, sunshiny side of Adams during the happy years of his marriage, comes from Henry James, who knew both Marian and Henry Adams well. As Mr. and Mrs. Bonnycastle of Washington, D.C., the Adamses appear in James's "Pandora," where Henry is described by an omniscient narrator: "Her husband was not in politics, though politics were much in him."

CRITICISM

The popularity of Henry Adams's writings as a subject for literary criticism has increased spectacularly since 1950. Once the fascinating puzzle of Adams's life had been put together definitively by Ernest Samuels, the way was cleared for exercises of another character, of many different kinds. The results of these critical investigations are before us now in profusion; and if they seem at times impressively masterful but too often uneven in quality, confused and partial in comprehension, and contradictory in conclusion, no experienced reader of literary criticism will be surprised. Perhaps commentary must be expected to mirror every feature of Henry Adams's personality that found its way into a single letter or sentence or line of poetry. The critical situation, in short, is lively. It can best be considered in a discussion of individual works, after a brief look at the most important general estimates.

General Estimates

Many readers first meet Henry Adams in one of the anthology introductions which are critical essays in their own right and deserve separate reprinting. Ernest Samuels's discussion in *Major Writers of America*, edited by Perry Miller (New York, 1962), places Adams in a New England literary tradition that prized dissent. Rebellion rather than conformity marked Henry Adams: "the question of fame and success haunted him more, perhaps, than it did any other American writer." Samuels rejects the label "sentimental pessimism" for Adams's philosophy and wisely insists upon crediting fully the ambiguities of a complex mind. Another anthology introduction concentrates on literary artistry: Charles R. Anderson, in *American Literary Masters* (New York, 1965), shows that Adams "uses language like a poet" throughout his work; he experimented as he searched for an adequate mode of self-expression to record the "meaning of history and man's place in it." A longer introductory evaluation appears in George Hochfield's *Henry Adams: An Introduction and Interpretation*, in the American Authors and Critics Series. It contains these basic materials: a chronology of Adams's life, brief but incisive discussions of the chief writings, and a selected bibliography. Robert Spiller's "Henry Adams" (*LHUS*) remains richly suggestive twenty years after its first appearance. A skillful mixture of biography and criticism yields a commanding overview of the subject; the discussion draws upon the well-known *Chartres* and *Education* to document the thesis: "Throughout his life Adams thought of himself as a man of letters rather than primarily as a historian, scientist or philosopher." Spiller also found a place for Adams in *The Cycle of American Literature* (New York, 1955; reprinted, Mentor, 1957) as "a literary man who could at least state the issues of the new order both in human and cosmic terms." An "ability to reconcile reality and myth by the use of symbols" forms the "secret" of Adams's considerable success. Other observers have carried Spiller's idea further but none holds a higher opinion of Henry Adams: "Adams laid the foundations for modern literature even more than for modern history by asking questions with which literature alone was competent to deal."

Among a younger generation of scholar-critics J. C. Levenson ranks as the chief interpreter of Adams's writings. *The Mind and Art of Henry Adams* (Boston, 1957; reprinted, Stanford, 1968) has become a critical touchstone. *Mind and Art* is neither an easy book nor a simplified introduction; it best serves a reader already familiar with Adams by laying down basic lines of inquiry and exploration and by documenting every assertion. More than most lengthy critical studies, this book achieves a unity and comprehensiveness which add formal completeness to its argument and make difficult any adequate representation in summary or quotation. Levenson traces the chronology of Adams's literary development, allowing for the influences of family, school, reading, and so on. We follow the artist and the thinker, stopping from time to time to measure his growth. The chief academic performance of Professor Adams, "Anglo-Saxon Courts of Law" (1876), for example, displays "his ability not only to test historical facts, but to organize his knowledge." An emphasis upon literary (rather than biographical) considerations does not, however, prevent the author's using explanations to illuminate dark corners: "While earlier Adamses wrote as public men even in their correspondence, Henry Adams wrote as a private citizen—whether he was a private secretary or a professional scholar who put his work before so limited an audience that publication served to conceal." Levenson's treatment of the major works offers a remarkable range of explications, designed not only to do justice to the peculiar qualities of individual genres and examples but also to show the place and importance in the larger pattern of Adams's thought and writing. Close reading and wide reference achieve a happy conjunction in *Mind and Art*, and as a result Levenson's whole achievement becomes something more than the sum of its parts.

Levenson has made other important contributions to critical understanding. "Henry Adams and the Art of Politics" (*SoR*, Winter 1968) turns an old biographical question decisively toward a literary answer: "The idea of politics as an art clarifies at once Adams's relation to twentieth-century estheticism and to his eighteenth-century political inheritance." In an earlier piece, "Henry Adams and the Culture of

Science," in *Studies in American Culture: Dominant Ideas and Images*, edited by Joseph J. Kwiat and Mary C. Turpie (Minneapolis, Minn., 1960), Levenson surveys Adams's intellectual approach to science and concludes: "His own way of taking action was to ask, more cogently than any of his countrymen then or since, the leading questions about science—in what spirit to cultivate it, in what ways to use it, how to relate it to other kinds of knowledge." By capturing the tentative and interrogatory qualities of Adams's thought, Levenson provides a necessary check against too literal interpretation of "scientific" history or philosophy.

One possible objection has been raised by Martin Green in *The Problem of Boston* (New York, 1966), which acknowledges a debt to Yvor Winters. Believing "that the history of nineteenth-century Boston is also the history of the American mind," Green finds in Adams's thought a spectrum of "prudish" attitudes, and "deterioration" overall. Because Levenson celebrates "the power of mind," he wrongly suggests, according to Green, that Henry Adams achieved transcendence over "fact" and "experience." This thesis reopens an old argument, which owes something to Van Wyck Brooks, who identified Henry Adams as a representative "New England Mind" in *The Flowering of New England* (New York, 1936, 1957). Another observer, T. K. Whipple, deserves more credit than he usually receives; his *Spokesmen* (New York, 1928) selected Adams as one of ten American writers whose "Poetic Temper" set them against "practical society." A provocative although irritatingly tentative consideration of Adams's cultural significance can be found in Ferner Nuhn, *The Wind Blew from the East: A Study in the Orientation of American Culture* (New York, 1942); his chapter "Henry Adams and the Hand of the Fathers" (reprinted in *Literature in America*, edited by Philip Rahv, New York, 1957) concentrates upon "the feminine element" in Adams's thought and the importance of polarities in his writing. Another weakness of the cultural approach shows itself in Nuhn's verdict: finally, Henry Adams remains "not quite the artist." Many readers do not agree.

The value of fitting Adams into the intellectual or (more recently) the psychological climate of his age has been demonstrated, even where consideration of his writings is reduced to a brief survey, as in Jay Martin's *Harvests of Change: American Literature, 1865–1914* (Englewood Cliffs, N.J., 1967). Martin nominates "Sages of Society," of whom Adams and Twain best illustrate a consciousness "of the push of history against human ideals." Warner Berthoff, *The Ferment of Realism: American Literature, 1884–1919* (New York, 1965), displays a very different literary persuasion. He classes Henry Adams among those realists who discovered that traditional forms "would not serve." Berthoff shows that Adams's major writings belong to a "Literature of Argument" which we have not recognized and do not fully understand.

As we have already noted, Henry Adams is often associated with a family political or social position. Perhaps the clearest short example, Lynn Hudson Parsons, "Continuing Crusade: Four Generations of the Adams Family View Alexander Hamilton" (*NEQ*, Mar. 1964), applies the idea of a family prejudice to Henry's chief works. Other observers have preferred to fit the views of the Adamses into a grander intellectual design—the usual designation is "conservative"—where the problem of accurate definition often remains unsolved. In *The Conservative Mind* (London, 1954; reprinted, Avon, 1968) Russell Kirk sketches a line of conservative thought from Edmund Burke to Henry Adams by way of John Adams, but Allen Guttmann, *The Conservative Tradition in America* (New York, 1967), refuses to accept the label "Conservative" for Henry Adams, who is called a "Liberal stripped of illusions." Other students of Adams's thought have insisted upon bypassing politics and finding the critical key in education, considered by several Adamses to be "a central business in life." Clarence K. Sandelin's dissertation (Wisconsin, 1956), "The Educational Philosophy of Henry Adams: A Brahmin Contribution to Critical Realism," brings all the evidence together but pushes the thesis too hard. A more balanced discussion, "Henry Adams: Educator" (*Serif* [Kent, Ohio], June 1967), by John L. Gribben, looks closely at the relationship between the life and writings. Henry Adams's education from books and his uses of an important literary heritage are the subjects of Max Baym's *The French Education of Henry Adams,* to which should be added Baym's "Three Moths and a Candle: A Study of the Impact of Pascal on Walter Pater, Henry Adams and Wallace Stevens," in *Comparative Literature: Proceedings of the Second Congress of the International Comparative Literature Association,* edited by Werner P. Friederich (Chapel Hill, N.C., 1959). The French influences have been studied by others as well, and Samuels surveys the situation with care; new material is added in André Monchoux, "Propos inédits sur la France dans les lettres de Henry Adams" (*Revue de Littérature Comparée,* Apr.–June 1967).

One of the first full-scale attempts to understand the complexity of Henry Adams's work, Robert A. Hume's *Runaway Star: An Appreciation of Henry Adams* (1951), remains a useful demonstration (even for those who do not distinguish three levels in "the sensibility of Henry Adams") of what had to be done to make Adams a respectable subject for literary criticism. Yvor Winters, for example, insisted with characteristic vigor (*The Anatomy of Nonsense*, Norfolk, Conn., 1943) that Adams's late works (including *Chartres* and the *Education*) represent "the radical disintegration of mind," probably brought on by an "accumulation of emotion." Winters's chapter "Henry Adams" (reprinted in *In Defense of Reason*, New York, 1947) raised its own emotional response, chiefly in William Jordy's fine book, *Henry Adams: Scientific Historian*, and in Stanley Edgar Hyman's *The Armed Vision* (rev. ed., New York, 1955). From 1931 on, an important general estimate of Adams emerged in the many essays by R. P. Blackmur, written as preliminary studies for a book that remained unfinished at his death. Their variety makes them an unsatisfactory basis for determining Blackmur's critical "stance"; fortunately, the most important pieces have been reprinted in *The Expense of Greatness* (New York, 1940) and *A Primer of Ignorance*, edited by Joseph Frank (New York, 1967).

A recent trend in general studies has encouraged revaluation and greater self-scrutiny among Adams's critics. Harry M. Campbell's short but provocative "Academic Criticism on Henry Adams: Confusion About Chaos" (*Midcontinent American Studies Journal*, Spring 1966) claims that Spiller and Winters (among others) have bent Adams to fit their own designs; the pessimistic prophet, rightly understood, belongs to a brotherhood of "atheistic existentialists," with Sartre, Camus, and their followers. Other critics have found that philosophy, science, history, and biography are finally secondary to the art of Henry Adams, whose irony, symbolism, and humor need further explanation. A more methodical charting of critical response up to the 1950s is contained in a Ph.D. dissertation, "The Reputation of Henry Adams" (Chicago, 1954), by Moreene Crumley. Her study testifies to the growth and development of criticism from the "vogue" of Henry Adams in the 1920s to his establishment as an author of international interest.

History of the United States of America during the Administrations of Thomas Jefferson and James Madison

"I never yet heard of ten men who had ever read my history," Henry Adams claimed, fifteen years after its publication, and the *Education* allows no room for doubt about the author's disappointment. Status as a classic of American historical writing has since been granted to the *History*, but only after the author's death, when almost everything he had written began to share the almost magical spell cast by the *Education*. The *History*, however, deserves to stand alone. Its volumes contain the best of Adams's political biographies (including the never-published life of Aaron Burr), and every page shows the technique and style of a master historian who had learned his art in a lengthy apprenticeship.

The value of such training is recognized in William Jordy's *Henry Adams: Scientific Historian*. In part because of its excellent bibliography, the book has become the chief resource for all students of Adams's thinking about history. The preface to the 1963 edition surveys recent scholarship and answers questions raised by Howard M. Munford, "Henry Adams and the Tendency of History" (NEQ, Mar. 1959), who views Adams's exposition of scientific history as a Delphic joke, full of "elaborate irony" and "grim humor." Jordy assures us that he considered that possibility before dismissing it from his book. However, Jordy claims that he did not ignore Adams's value as a seer, despite the accusations of Lewis Mumford in "Apology to Henry Adams" (*VQR*, Spring 1962), nor did he set out to demolish a set of half-baked, pseudoscientific notions. Jordy does try (with large success) to be fair to Adams, science, and history; if his efforts fail to satisfy every specialist, they succeed in combination (as narrower investigations have not done) by fixing the *History* and the historical essays within a workable biographical and literary frame. Adams was not merely a historian, even less was he a scientist. His "awareness of literary values," as Jordy understands them, "with all that such awareness implied for his personality, saved Adams from a blind faith in science." Jordy tells us where and why Adams failed, but also how he succeeded.

The Scientific Thought of Henry Adams by Henry Wasser includes much of the same material about Adams and science, without this useful frame. Wasser's "The Thought of Henry Adams" (*NEQ*, Dec. 1951) makes a case for the primacy of science. Two well-reasoned European accounts discuss the problem with special intelligence: Robert Mane, "Henry Adams et la science" (*EA*, Jan.–Mar. 1963) and Ursula Brumm, "Henry Adams als Historiker: Seine Bedeutung für die amerikanische Literatur- und Geistesgeschichte" (*Archiv*, Oct. 1962). Two essays in *JHI* provide a measure for a change in thinking about Adams's use of science: W. Stull Holt, "The Idea of Scientific History in America" (June 1940), surveys the sources, assumptions, development, and value of "scientific history," placing Adams among his contemporaries and asserting that "no generally accepted verdict can as yet be said to have been rendered." Joseph Mindel's "The Uses of Metaphor: Henry Adams and the Symbols of Science," published twenty-five years later (Jan.-Mar. 1965), applies modern scientific knowledge to correct not only Adams's mistakes but those made by Levenson (*Mind and Art*) and Jordy as well. Mindel studies his subject against a background of the "uses and misuses of metaphors in science"; Adams emerges as a knowledgeable (if amateurish) commentator, who imaginatively fashioned a "metaphorical link between history and science." Mindel's essay reminds nonscientists that Henry Adams (and how many others?)

could more easily misinterpret the "philosophy and methodology" of science than the meaning of laws and facts. Howard M. Munford, in "Henry Adams: The Limitations of Science" (*SoR*, Winter 1968), acknowledges that "Adams did know what he meant" when he wrote about science. Not "revealing objective truth" but making use of the opportunity science offered for "redoing, remaking, reforming the world" was Adams's goal.

Thomas N. Bonner opens his brief introduction, "Henry Adams: A Sketch and an Analysis" (*Historian*, Nov. 1957), with the declaration that Adams "is the one important American historian whose life is more significant than the history he wrote." Here, Bonner echoes Henry Steele Commager, who set his colleagues the task of explaining the why and how of the *History*, rather than simply accepting the text as "good history—better had not been written." Commager's chapter, "Henry Adams," in *The Marcus W. Jernegan Essays in American Historiography*, edited by William T. Hutchinson (Chicago, 1937), raises Adams's banner high: "Adams illuminates, better than any of his contemporaries, the course of American history." Commager goes on to explain: "All his life Henry Adams made it a rule to ask questions which he could not answer—questions which were, perhaps, quite unanswerable . . . his true function was to provoke speculation, not to satisfy it." Commager himself achieved something similar.

For the novice, a usable introduction to the *History* can be found in *The American Historian: A Social-Intellectual History of the Writings of the American Past* (New York, 1960); in it Harvey Wish devotes a chapter, "Henry Adams and the Dream of a Science of History," to surveying where Henry stands among historians, critics, and other Adamses, and where the *History* fits among his writings. Robert Allen Skotheim, *American Intellectual Histories and Historians* (Princeton, N.J., 1966), discerns few faults in the *History*; his emphasis upon "intellectual" content serves to disconnect the introduction and conclusion from the body of political history by judging the parts separately. This approach reverses conventional assessments, which weigh heavily all the materials of politics and diplomacy, even if the result is damaging to Adams's reputation. Ferdinand Schevill (*Six Historians*, Chicago, 1956) calls the political matter "too detailed"; he argues that the portrayal of character (rather than diplomacy or ideas), especially Jefferson's character, an "unquestioned masterpiece of the Adams gallery," is the real strength of a flawed classic.

One of the most serious questions raised about the *History* concerns Adams's objectivity; he has been examined on grounds of filial loyalty, regional bias, political persuasion, racism, and scientific accuracy, among others. Richard Beale Davis rubs an old sore with his suggestion that Adams is unfair to the South (*Intellectual Life in Jefferson's Virginia, 1790–1830*, Chapel Hill, N.C., 1964), and Peter Shaw adds specific accusations of family favoritism in "Blood Is Thicker Than Irony: Henry Adams' *History*" (*NEQ*, June 1967). The possibilities of political bias are explored by Edwin C. Rozwenc's "Henry Adams and the Federalists," in *Teachers of History: Essays in Honor of Laurence Bradford Packard*, edited by H. Stuart Hughes (Ithaca, N.Y., 1954). The chief measure of Adams's political attitudes has always been the intriguing figure of Thomas Jefferson, who is studied by Merrill D. Peterson in *The Jefferson Image in the American Mind* (New York, 1960, reprinted, Galaxy, 1962) and "Henry Adams on Jefferson the President" (*VQR*, Spring 1963). A defense of Adams's efforts to achieve historical objectivity can be found in Earl N. Harbert's "Henry Adams' New England View: A Regional Angle of Vision?" (*TSE*, 1968), which concentrates upon literary technique. Nathalia Wright looks at the problem created by Adams's "Puritan" mind in "Henry Adams's Theory of History: A Puritan Defense" (*NEQ*, June 1945).

Applying the rigorous requirements of modern social science, the *History* must be judged unscientific. "The Limits of Social Science: Henry Adams' Quest for Order" (*American Political Science Review*, Dec. 1956) reports the findings of Henry S. Kariel, who admits that Adams anticipated significant developments in social science, even though he could not keep himself from pushing his theories to hasty (and often unwarranted) conclusions. Yet Adams's thinking, unlike his writing, was never "dogmatic" in Kariel's view; Adams "actually accepted no law . . . as complete." He searched for an impossible answer, beyond the reach of both "positivist science and negativist art," one which even today "defies denotation and symbolization." This essay may be difficult reading for a nonscientist, but it uncovers a number of Adams's scientific missteps. A less tenable critique, based on an alleged failure of Adams to respond fully to the system of Karl Marx, is Richard Greenleaf's "History, Marxism, and Henry Adams" (*Science and Society*, Summer 1951); Greenleaf finds that Adams approached no closer to the truths of Marxian analysis than "impure materialism," which left him an apologist for capitalism.

Other readers such as Edward Stone use Adams's historical writings to classify him among the *Voices of Despair* (Athens, Ohio, 1966). Gerrit H. Roelofs's "Henry Adams: Pessimism and the Intelligent Use of Doom" (*ELH*, Sept. 1950) opened the theme to literary (as well as philosophical) considerations; and more recently the despair motif has figured in "The Lost America—The Despair of Henry Adams and Mark Twain" (*Modern Age* [Chicago], Summer 1961) by Tony Tanner, and Charles Vandersee's "The Mutual Awareness of Mark Twain and Henry Adams" (*ELN*, June 1968). The latter reviews previous scholarship and enters a dissenting conclusion: Adams *did* meet Twain and did become his model for the "unhappiest man" in *What Is Man?* Two essays by Harvey Gross comprise a highly eclectic attempt to show how Adams's conception of history influenced modern literature; "'Gerontion' and the Meaning of History" (*PMLA*, June 1958) and the less convincing "History as Metaphysical Pathos: Modern Literature and the Idea of History" (*Denver Quarterly*, Autumn 1966).

The larger matters of historiography lie beyond the scope of the present essay. Nevertheless, some attempt to locate Henry Adams among American historians has a place here. An examination of the subtle yet powerful "involvement" with life experienced by Adams as a historian can be found in Edward Lurie's "American Scholarship: A Subjective Interpretation of Nineteenth-Century Cultural History," in *Essays on History and Literature*, edited by Robert H. Bremner (Columbus, Ohio, 1966). Lurie sketches the elitist limitations of Adams and his peers, such as John Hay and Clarence King, who approached politics and culture with a serious handicap based upon preconceptions. Adams memorialized in prose both his failure to grasp the real value of Willard Gibbs's science and his ability to master the intellectual and moral "currents" in history and life, which his heritage had better prepared him to comprehend. Other historians, Lurie tells us, have followed Adams's lead, taking only what they please from him— Populist or Jeffersonian history or elitist "assumptions about cultural vapidity"—and in the process they have created an "irony of historiography" by which Adams is made to seem what he was not. Alfred Kazin agrees that it is Adams who "more than any other created our image of history; who in fact shapes our idea of history" ("History and Henry Adams," *NY Review of Books*, 23 October 1969, 6 November 1969), and he attributes Adams's attitude to a simply attraction to (perhaps an obsession with) power in every form.

Adams sought from first to last to bring the didactic potential of history under personal control, and specific literary techniques offer important clues to his success and failure. "Henry Adams' Paraphrase of Sources in the *History of the United States*" (*AQ*, Spring 1965) by Richard C. Vitzhum looks at "some 130 of the 190" published sources for the nine volumes; John S. Martin's "Henry Adams on War: The

Transformation of History into Metaphor" (*ArQ*, Winter 1968) treats the usefulness of metaphor as both literary and historical expression. Ralph Maud ("Henry Adams: Irony and Impasse," *Essays in Criticism* [Oxford], Oct. 1958) warns that "no amount of investigation into the irony will . . . reveal an answer that counteracts the surface despair." These studies can be used to document in their several ways Ernst Scheyer's thesis in "The Aesthete Henry Adams" (*Criticism*, Fall 1962) that Adams's "theory of history was primarily aesthetically conditioned." More recently, Scheyer has collected from this and four other of his essays a series of topical impressions about Adams's tastes in art objects, history, and artistic friends, and expanded them into *The Circle of Henry Adams: Art and Artists* (Detroit, Mich., 1970). Building upon the work of Robert A. Hume, Scheyer brings the training and knowledge of an art historian to the task of studying Adams the aesthetic historian (especially in *Esther, Chartres*, and the *Education*) against the background of the art movements that influenced his epoch.

J. C. Levenson has contributed in large measure to our understanding of the *History* in both *Mind and Art* and "Henry Adams and the Culture of Science." His treatment of family and cultural heritage and his informed interest in literary artistry make these discussions invaluable. More recently, Levenson has summarized his estimate in "Henry Adams," an important chapter in *Pastmasters: Some Essays on American Historians*, edited by Marcus Cunliffe and Robin W. Winks (New York, 1969). Reviewing Adams's whole career as a teacher and writer of history, Levenson notes an increasing "professionalization." Adams learned to use larger and larger quantities of historical evidence to reach progressively grander generalizations about history and life, which in turn required more sophisticated means for expression: careful selection of material, suppression of judgments in favor of "facts," skillful manipulation of a narrative point of view, reliance upon symbols rather than words. As he achieved mastery, Adams did not abandon political convictions, Levenson asserts; they remain hidden in the fabric of the *History*, to argue a case for "the primacy of foreign policy." Levenson's chapter strikes a note of serious reconsideration (rather than introduction) which will appeal to those who have read Adams's historical writings with care. It shows that the *History* has attracted readers for a variety of reasons but that, without exception, the best critics have discovered for themselves the truth of Henry Adams's remark to fellow historian Frederic Bancroft: "I doubt if there is a chapter in my history that I have written less than four or five times."

Poetry and Essays

Although the first appearance of "Prayer to the Virgin of Chartres" has been noted, it will be helpful to list other printings: Robert A. Hume, *Runaway Star*; *The American Poets 1800–1900*, edited by Edwin H. Cady (Glenview, Ill., 1966); and Elizabeth Stevenson, *Henry Adams Reader* (which also contains "Buddha and Brahma"). Three sonnets appear in Samuels's *Middle Years*, and there is an Adams jingle in Wasser's *Scientific Thought of Henry Adams*. No other poetry has reached print, although more does exist. Mrs. Jane Wilson Hipolito's dissertation, "The Secret World of Henry Adams" (UCLA, 1968), expands upon what was known about Adams as poet, and her discussion makes good use of previously unpublished material. Denis Donoghue adds some interesting speculations in *Connoisseurs of Chaos: Ideas of Order in Modern American Poetry* (New York, 1965).

Aside from general estimates, which usually treat the poetry as a helpful but clearly secondary evidence of Adams's art, several commentators have studied the poems closely. Yosal Rogat, "Mr. Justice Holmes: Some Modern Views" (*University of Chicago Law Review*, Winter 1964), makes "Buddha and Brahma" the core statement of a philosophical theme that unites Henry James and Oliver Wendell Holmes, Jr., with Adams. All three shared an "ambiguous" social position: "Distinguished" by birth, they nevertheless "had to achieve [further] distinction" by their own efforts in the separate spheres which satisfied their individual needs for "power" or "force." Although the essay concentrates upon Holmes, Adams's poem is used to speak for all three about their peculiar relationship with an unfriendly world—"both attached and detached." This well-documented excursion into cultural history corrects a popular misunderstanding that Adams was an exotic disciple of doom. The same poem receives detailed explication in Eusebio L. Rodrigues's "Out of Season for Nirvana: Henry Adams and Buddhism," in *Indian Essays in American Literature: Papers in Honour of Robert E. Spiller*, edited by Sujit Mukherjee and D. V. K. Raghavacharyulu (Bombay, 1969). The author finds that Adams "never did surrender himself completely to Buddhism," although "the way to the Perfect Life did provide Adams with a sense of direction." All the published verse is reviewed in Stephen Mooney's "The Education of Henry Adams (Poet)" in *TSL* (1961), which shows that Adams demonstrated the "imagination of a poet" even when he wrote prose. Mooney finds the verse to be "occasional" and Adams a "poet of ideas." Only the "Prayer to the Virgin of Chartres" emerges as an unqualified success, "a poetic microcosm" of *Mont-Saint-Michel and Chartres*.

Collective consideration of Henry Adams's essays unfortunately blurs important distinctions based upon chronology, type, subject, and value; convenience alone is served. The early nonhistorical essays have attracted less attention than they deserve; apart from introductions to reprint collections, the most helpful discussions are to be found in the appropriate volume of Samuels's biography. The question of social prejudices, especially anti-Semitism, remains unresolved (at least until publication of the Bernard Berenson–Henry Adams correspondence); the basic evidence is brought together in a chapter ("Henry Adams' Norman Ancestors") of Edward N. Saveth's *American Historians and European Immigrants* (New York, 1948), where the essays receive adequate attention. Additional information may be found in "Henry Adams and the Jews" (*Chicago Jewish Forum*, Fall 1966) by Abraham Blinderman, and "Henry Adams and the Invisible Negro" (*SAQ*, Winter 1967), in which Charles Vandersee measures Adams's "skepticism and indifference" about Negroes against the attitudes of Boston and finds that Henry was much less "racist" than his outspoken brothers, Brooks and Charles Francis Adams II.

Among the late essays, "The Rule of Phase Applied to History" (1909) and "A Letter to American Teachers of History" (1910) are often treated, along with the final third of the *Education* (and sometimes *Chartres*), as exercises in historiography. A separate discussion of these essays will not be attempted here, except to note that William H. Jordy's *Henry Adams: Scientific Historian* is the indispensable guide through the intricacies of scientific theory and speculation.

Biographies and Novels

Over a thirty-year period Henry Adams exercised his skills as biographer, completing four printed works and the manuscript of a fifth. *The Life of Albert Gallatin* (1879), *John Randolph* (1882), *Memoirs of Marau Taaroa: Last Queen of Tahiti* (1893), and *The Life of George Cabot Lodge* (1911) are different enough to discourage generalizations about their author's attitudes and techniques; taken together they prove at least his remarkable versatility. The never-printed, book-length life of Aaron Burr is generally believed to have been transferred from manuscript to the pages of the *History*. Of all these, the *Lodge* has received the least attention, although it has been attractively treated in Edmund Wilson's *The Shock of Recognition*, which reprints the text. Lodge's tragic story represented a deep personal loss to Adams, a much older friend of the young poet; this brief biography registers an authentically emotional response and one that helps us to locate the elusive figure of Henry Adams in his final years. The more exotic *Tahiti*,

too, has suffered unmerited neglect, as Robert E. Spiller testifies in the
introduction to his Facsimile reprint edition. The rarity of copies from
the 1893 (private) printing is explained by Ira N. Hayward in "From
Tahiti to Chartres: The Henry Adams–John La Farge Friendship"
(*HLQ*, Aug. 1958), which describes the author's presentation copy to
his artist friend. *Tahiti* is one of "the few sources of information on
pre-Christian society" in the Pacific, as Robert Langdon reminds us. In
"A View on Arii Taimai's Memoirs" (*Journal of Pacifc History*, 1969),
Langdon describes the circumstances of composition and reassesses *Tahiti*'s importance. The article is followed by a bibliographical note
describing "one of the only three known" copies of the 1893 *Tahiti*
which may have belonged to "Queen Marau herself"; this accounting
does not include the Huntington Library copy.

Adams's reputation as a biographer rests upon the volumes devoted
to American statesmen and the chief character portrayals in the *History*. The old-fashioned qualities of *Gallatin* are generally acknowledged; perhaps its author's admiration for his subject made for a dull
book. The most authoritative evaluation is that of Gallatin's modern
biographer, Raymond Walters, Jr. (*Albert Gallatin*, New York, 1957),
who found that Adams's version "was written with scholarly care"
although it showed less "literary skill" than the *History*.

Few critics have been as understanding about *John Randolph*. William Cabell Bruce devoted much of his preface to *John Randolph of
Roanoke* (New York, 1922) to "correcting" with fresh vitriol the portrait that Adams had fashioned: "He has fully availed himself of the
opportunity . . . to direct against the memory of Randolph the thrice-
refined venom which filtered into his own veins from those of his great-
grandfather, grandfather and father. The book is really nothing but a
family pamphlet, saturated with the sectional prejudices and antipathies of the year 1882." Henry B. Rule documents some of these accusations in "Henry Adams' Attack on Two Heroes of the Old South"
(*AQ*, Summer 1962), focusing upon "Captain John Smith" and *John
Randolph*, and concluding that both family pride and the Adamses'
antislavery views are as important as the pursuit of historical truth.

Henry Adams's two novels, *Democracy: An American Novel* (1880)
and *Esther: A Novel* (1884), have established his stature as an interesting "novelist of ideas," but they are generally regarded as too "thin" to
rank among the best of the genre. Neither was issued in the name of
Henry Adams; his publisher, Henry Holt, recounts the amusing secrets
of authorship in *Garrulities of an Octogenarian Editor* (Boston, 1923).
A discussion of Adams's politics can be found in Ernest Samuels's
Middle Years, and a good introduction to both novels is George Hoch-

field's *Henry Adams*. R. P. Blackmur ("The Novels of Henry Adams," *SR*, Apr. 1943; reprinted in *A Primer of Ignorance*) reminds us of a basic problem—"Adams' two novels . . . unlike those of a professional novelist, do not show their full significance except in connection with his life"—and concentrates upon the themes of social condemnation, prophecy, and feminine superiority which tie the novels together. A philosophical frame large enough to fit both is provided by Michael Colacurcio, "*Democracy* and *Esther*: Henry Adams' Flirtation with Pragmatism" (*AQ*, Spring 1967); while Robert I. Edenbaum prefers to consider the novels as a double answer to one (reductive) question, in "The Novels of Henry Adams: Why Man Failed" (*TSLL*, Summer 1966). "It is very easy to underestimate Henry Adams as novelist," D. S. R. Welland cautions ("Henry Adams as Novelist," *Renaissance and Modern Studies*, 1959) at the beginning of his well-informed discussion, which shows how the circumstances of Adams's life and the popularity of other writers prevented a fair reception of the novels in England. Welland reviews Adams's often-noticed debt to Hawthorne and enlarges the study of influences by making a good case for both George Eliot and the "comedy of manners."

Although we have yet to see the exaltation of Henry Adams as a prophet of women's liberation, R. P. Blackmur and Robert E. Spiller long ago pointed to the fascinating women in Adams's novels as the symbolic center of his thought. Adams believed, as Spiller explains, "that women still could supply the secret knowledge that men had lost, that they held the key to the ultimate mysteries" (*The Cycle of American Literature*). The quest for the "eternal woman" has been adopted by a covey of critics, who seem not to have advanced explanations very far. In "Henry Adams and the Influence of Women" (*AL*, Jan. 1947) R. F. Miller notes that "neither heroine can be convinced by reason." Edward N. Saveth, in two essays that cover much the same ground ("The Heroines of Henry Adams," *AQ*, Fall 1956, and "The Middle Years of Henry Adams: Women in His Life and Novels," *Commentary*, May 1959), finds that Adams's "prototype" women display a mixture of great strength and equally great destructiveness. Saveth sees Adams's "ideal women" as both "life-affirming" and "life-denying" and Adams himself as a victim of "bad luck" with a series of "cold comfort" heroines in his novels and his life. Leslie A. Fiedler (*Love and Death in the American Novel*, Cleveland, Ohio, 1962) agrees that the "divine ideal" imposed itself upon Adams's relationships with "actual ladies whom he knew" and declares further that Henry Adams "cannot imagine a truly sexual heroine."

Democracy holds an important place among "political novels." In a pioneer survey, *The Political Novel: Its Development in England and America* (New York, 1924), Morris Edmund Speare calls Adams's book "the first true political novel written in America." Joseph Blotner's *The Modern Political Novel: 1900–1960* (Austin, Tex., 1966) recognizes *Democracy* as an important "predecessor" of those novels (in his period) which "set national politics in an atmosphere of moral sickness." W. Gordon Milne in *The American Political Novel* (Norman, Okla., 1966) explains more of Adams's "expertise" and decides that *Democracy* appeals because of wit, urbanity, and polish and fails because "it is a novel *about* things rather than an imaginative recreation of things." Irving Howe also finds fault with Adams's inhibitions in *Democracy*, his refusal to allow "a little more of the original pain and anger" to break through the stylish veneer (*Politics and the Novel*, New York, 1957; reprinted, Fawcett, 1967). Granville Hicks, in the revised edition of *The Great Tradition* (New York, 1933; rev., 1969) reconsiders his earlier complaint, that Adams wrote "merely to amuse himself," without fully reneging: "I still think Adams was a strong combination of prophet and crybaby." Among more limited discussions, in "The *Democracy* of Henry Adams" (*The "Democracy" of Henry Adams and Other Essays*, Bern, 1950) H. Lüdeke sees "political practice in America" with the sharp eyes of a foreigner. C. Vann Woodward (*The Burden of Southern History*, Baton Rouge, La., 1960) locates in Adams's view of the South "ambivalent attitudes" that include admiration for those "antique values" preserved in Virginia. In "The Pursuit of Culture in Adams' *Democracy*" (*AQ*, Summer 1967), Charles Vandersee concentrates upon the first chapter of *Democracy*, to explain how Adams builds a satire which directs its attack not only against American "culture" but against Henry Adams himself.

Esther, of course, has a very different history, in part because of a close association with the tragic figure of Marian Adams and in part because the subject of religious faith discourages the sort of free-and-easy commentary that politics encourages. The historical importance of *Esther* as a document of disbelief has been established in two essays: Wallace Evan Davies, "Religious Issues in Late Nineteenth-Century American Novels" (*BJRL*, Mar. 1959), and Elmer F. Suderman, "Skepticism and Doubt in Late Nineteenth Century American Novels" (*Ball State University Forum*, Winter 1967). The latter pays tribute to Adams's use of "science" and "comparative religion" as innovations in theological debate. Millicent Bell, in "Adams' *Esther*: The Morality of Taste" (*NEQ*, June 1962), makes the novel into coterie literature, written only for "a private group of friends" who could supply the necessary "annotation from the record of Adams' life." Her sensitive reading rests upon the acceptance of an almost complete "biographical parallel" between Marian Adams and Esther; and the emphasis upon "private" readers conflicts with Henry Adams's declarations about *Esther* as a public experiment, as Ernest Samuels reports. In many ways the most satisfying discussion, Robert E. Spiller's introduction to the 1938 Facsimile edition (reprinted as "The Private Novel of Henry Adams" in *The Oblique Light*) has prevailed for more than thirty years. *Esther*, Spiller suggests, "probes to deeper levels of experience" than does *Democracy*; a "thoroughly good" novel, *Esther* must be read without undue emphasis upon Marian Adams's life but with a sense of history that allows appreciation of the "costume" quality which the novel has acquired "with the passing of time."

Mont-Saint-Michel and Chartres

From the moment it first appeared in the hands of those friends fortunate enough to receive a privately printed copy, *Chartres* has evoked from readers as literary as Henry James and as knowledgeable as the historian Ferdinand Schevill a stream of praise. In a letter James celebrated the charm of *Chartres;* Schevill's *Six Historians* pronounced it "the most penetrating book on the medieval spirit ever produced by an American." That "spirit" has sometimes puzzled Roman Catholic theologians and systematic historians, but *Chartres* rises above all controversy to enjoy nearly unalloyed approval. A relationship to the *Education* is often suggested, most notably by Samuels, Levenson (*Mind and Art*), Lyon, and Conder. (For the last two, see *Recent Criticism*, below.) A survey of the problems in *Chartres* (especially the treatment of St. Thomas Aquinas) may be found in Michael Colacurcio's "The Dynamo and the Angelic Doctor: The Bias of Henry Adams' Medievalism" (*AQ*, Winter 1965). In a very personal way Adams believed that "reason inevitably destroys faith"; and his own testimony, as Colacurcio demonstrates, never loses sight of the need for individual human conviction. John P. McIntyre, S. J., in "Henry Adams and the Unity of *Chartres*" (*Twentieth Century Literature*, Jan. 1962), allows for imaginative freedom in Adams's handling of philosophy and history; but Frederick J. Hoffman's chapter, "Nostalgia and Christian Interpretation: Henry Adams and William Faulkner," in *The Imagination's New Beginning: Theology and Modern Literature* (Notre Dame, Ind., 1967), insists that Adams's "rebellious irritation with Puritanism" leads to a theological distortion which raises the Trinity to an "Absolute" and "ignores the Incarnation." Comparative study can sometimes help us gauge similarities and differences that otherwise go unnoticed; Kermit Vanderbilt's *Charles Eliot Norton* (Cambridge, Mass., 1959) uses the attitudes of Adams and Norton toward Chartres Cathedral as a proof of the variety in New England thinking.

An earlier essay makes the feelings evoked by *Chartres* an important key to Adams's art. R. P. Blackmur, in "The Harmony of True Liberalism: Henry Adams' *Mont-Saint-Michel and Chartres*" (*SR*, Jan.-Mar. 1952; reprinted in *A Primer of Ignorance*), attempts to reconstruct the personal feelings about faith and intellectual equilibrium which underlie Adams's message: "Faith, to work, cannot be exacerbated; and yet, to work, faith seems always either to have persecuted the unfaithful or put them beyond the pale of faith's benefits." Accepting this, Adams knew that "unity was in the convergence of straight lines in the *general* mind and was most likely never unity at all in any single mind—unless in Saint Thomas'." Blackmur examines Adams's figures one by one, describing the role each plays out in a thematic drama and showing how "the emotion of incertitude is put against the emotion of conviction." During the final "phase" of Adams's art, this passion play "reaches into his own experience," Blackmur contends, and a goal of "organic unity" controls both the artist and the man.

The Education of Henry Adams

Since its publication the *Education*[2] has held first place as the central document upon which every broad consideration of Henry Adams is based. An unlikely best seller in 1919, the book first invited comparison with other autobiographies of the New England Puritan kind. When Ernest Samuels cleared away the confusion, readers were able to concentrate upon the nonbiographical possibilities of the *Education*—history, prophecy, pathos, and humor.

Adams tells of his literary debts to Rousseau, Augustine, and Gibbon, and critics have freely suggested additional sources and influences: Samuels's biography, Baym in the *French Education*, and Henry A. Pochmann, *German Culture in America* (Madison, Wis., 1957), whose conclusions are enlarged in "The German Education of Henry Adams," written by Foster Park for *Appalachian State Teachers College Faculty*

2. T. S. Eliot's early review of the *Education* deserves special attention. In the *Athenaeum*, 23 May 1919 (reprinted as "A Sceptical Patrician" in *Major Writers of America*, vol. 2), Eliot showed a lack of sympathy with both the matter and the manner of the *Education*, although he recognized its peculiar fascination: "The really impressive interest is in the mind of the author, and in the American mind, or that fragment of it, which he represents." Eliot also sounded a warning which all too few of Adams's readers have taken seriously: "It is doubtful whether the book ought to be called an autobiography, for there is too little of the author in it."

Publications (1962). Among essays which concentrate more narrowly upon possible sources, Gene H. Koretz, "Augustine's *Confessions* and *The Educaton of Henry Adams*" (*Comparative Literature*, Summer 1960), and Richard Ruland, "Tocqueville's *De la Démocratie en Amérique* and *The Education of Henry Adams*" (*Comparative Literature Studies*, Fall 1965), have special value. All together, the suggestions point up the many ways in which Adams read and used books; but even more clearly, sources and influences fall far short of explaining the *Education*, which simply cannot be dismissed as derivative. This caution applies to other studies of influence, beginning with Stuart P. Sherman's "Evolution in the Adams Family" (*Nation*, 10 April 1920), and includes two recent Ph.D. dissertations, "The American Adams" (Columbia, 1965) by Peter Shaw and "The Influence of the Family Tradition upon Selected Works of Henry Adams" (Wisconsin, 1966) by Earl N. Harbert. Sherman finds the *Education* to be "only the last or the latest chapter of a continued story" which began in the *Diary* of John Adams and ran its course in the writings of John Quincy and Charles Francis Adams. Shaw uses all available evidence to prove a reversal in literal meaning of failure, the term Adams habitually applied to himself when he meant something else. In "The Success of Henry Adams" (*YR*, Autumn 1969), Shaw interprets the idiom of self-condemnation as an ironic expression of success in the traditional (among the Adamses) arts of politics and diplomacy.

Meanwhile, other studies have muted the original accusations of philosophical pessimism and "sentimental nihilism" (in the words of Paul Elmer More, *Shelburne Essays*, Boston, 1921). Better understanding of the author has opened new ways to read the *Education*, making older views seem too simple, as in Richard Hofstadter's *Anti-Intellectualism in American Life* (New York, 1962). This influential historian of ideas concedes that the *Education* stands as a "towering literary monument" to post–Civil War reform; yet he rates the book "a masterpiece in the artistry of self-pity." Austin Warren comes to a different conclusion, after studying Adams as a regional spokesman, in *The New England Conscience* (Ann Arbor, Mich., 1966); caught between the conflicting demands of acting both as researcher and interpreter, Adams could reach no literary solution that satisfied his "conscience." Unfortunately, Warren's chapter stops short of showing how these polar possibilities work themselves out in the *Education*.

A favorite method of avoiding biographical impasse in interpretation is to turn from the author and to treat the *Education* as a window looking out upon the world. Ralph Gabriel's *The Course of American Democratic Thought* (New York, 1940) admitted Adams to an

official position as a witness to history, chosen "to illustrate trends in
the thinking of American historians." The *Education* has offered varied
testimony: Leo Marx finds that "a sense of the transformation of life
by technology dominates *The Education* as it does no other book";
accordingly he uses Adams's metaphorical measurement, the "Two
Kingdoms of Force" (the Virgin and the Dynamo), as an index of
attitude in *The Machine in the Garden: Technology and the Pastoral
Ideal in America* (New York, 1964). Marx always retains a sensitivity
to the literary merits of the *Education*, discussing the combined techniques of the "cool historian and the impassioned poet" which show
themselves in Manichean polarities, "technological determinism," and
a frenzied appeal for human response. "Doubleness" seems to Marx
characteristic of twentieth-century American "pastoralism," but Morton and Lucia White (*The Intellectual Versus the City: From Thomas
Jefferson to Frank Lloyd Wright*, Cambridge, Mass., 1962) insist that
Adams finds fault with the American city "out of concern for civilization" and not "in the name of nature." (Of special value is the Whites'
use of Adams's letters to point up once again how much the retrospective *Education* differs from other accounts of the author's feelings,
expressed at the time of the experiences themselves.) Alan Trachtenberg's *Brooklyn Bridge: Fact and Symbol* (New York, 1965) treats
Adams as a keen observer of politics in the Gilded Age. Borrowing, as
Leo Marx does, from the metaphoric possibilities of the two "Kingdoms
of Force," Trachtenberg shows that Adams was not alone in seeking a
symbolic reconciliation of conflicting cultural forces and that the bridge
may have greater symbolic value than the Virgin and the Dynamo.
This study also corrects Adams's view of Abram S. Hewitt. One other
broad evaluation, a controversial classic of its kind, W. J. Cash's *The
Mind of the South* (New York, 1941) registers a southerner's agreement with the portrayal of southern character in the figure of Roony
Lee.

    In a volume provocatively titled *Books That Changed Our Minds*,
edited by Malcolm Cowley and Bernard Smith (New York, 1939),
Louis Kronenberger shows how the "bitterly ironic tone" of the *Education* endeared it to post–World War I readers, while a "validity of
predicament" guarantees that it will speak to men and women of all
times. Clearly, the *Education* has become many different things to many
men, even though the "why" still seems far from being answered. F. O.
Matthiessen, in *American Renaissance* (New York, 1941), pointed to
the unlikely kinship between Walt Whitman and Henry Adams, built
upon their mutual awareness "of the power of sex." Adams's view was
simply larger than those of many contemporaries; his appreciations of

sex, science, history, politics, art, and education helped to make life interesting, as Robert Spiller shows (*Cycle of American Literature*). And J. C. Levenson ("Henry Adams and the Culture of Science") prefers to measure Adams's intentions and success by his interest in teaching: "assertion of mind" for the author and the reader become the only possible solution to the ultimate problem posed in the *Education*; Adams "shaped his comments to stimulate younger men and make them seek better answers than his own."

One special difficulty arises—how to grasp and assimilate the full symbolic value of Adams's narrative. Kenneth Burke acknowledges the problem in *A Grammar of Motives and A Rhetoric of Motives* (combined ed., Cleveland, Ohio, 1962), although "attenuated self-immolation" may not strike every reader as the result Adams seeks to achieve: "*The Education of Henry Adams* . . . exemplifies ritual transformation by a shift from personal images to impersonal ones," and an "imaging of a fall" dominates the sections of historical speculation. Burke's insistence upon mythic and imagistic interpretation (and vocabulary) allows no room for biographical discussion. His work has been a rich resource for critics concerned primarily with finding symbolic patterning in all of Adams's work. Their many-sided conversation has been neatly catalogued in Melvin Lyon's comprehensive volume (see *Recent Criticism*, below); nevertheless a few essays deserve attention here: Lynn White, Jr., "Dynamo and Virgin Reconsidered" (*ASch*, Spring 1958), applies to Adams a great familiarity with medieval history and technology, to show that the famous chapter in the *Education* is not necessarily a discussion of polar opposites. Various uses of symbols and images have been identified and discussed by Kenneth MacLean, "Window and Cross in Henry Adams' *Education*" (*University of Toronto Quarterly*, July 1959), and James K. Folsom, "Mutation as Metaphor in *The Education of Henry Adams*" (*ELH*, June 1963). A single issue of *ArQ* (Winter 1968) contained both William J. Scheick's "Symbolism in *The Education of Henry Adams*" and Charles Vandersee's study of animal imagery, "The Four Menageries of Henry Adams." Also helpful is the more general "Poetry and Language," contributed by Norman Holmes Pearson to *A Time of Harvest: American Literature, 1910–1960*, edited by Robert E. Spiller (New York, 1962); Pearson raises Adams to high station: "The book which, more than any other, represents the American writer's entrance into the twentieth century is *The Education of Henry Adams*." A look at the busy year when Henry Adams was elected to membership in the American Academy of Arts and Letters can be found in Charles Vandersee's "Henry Adams and 1905: Prolegomena to *The Education*" (*JAmS*, Oct. 1968).

The difficulty of "placing" the *Education* in some respectable literary tradition encourages comparative discussion. One valuable development has emerged—the recognition (if not yet definition) of American autobiography as a genre inclusive enough to contain the Mathers, Franklin, James, and Thoreau, as well as Adams. A. D. Van Nostrand, in *Everyman His Own Poet: Romantic Gospels in American Literature* (New York, 1968), matches the *Education* with the writings of Edgar Allan Poe without illuminating the former very much; another modest contribution, a brief note on narrative tone in *Walden* and the *Education*, is Taylor Stoehr's "Tone and Voice" (*CE*, Nov. 1968). By far the most satisfactory study of the *Education* as autobiography and a seminal discussion overall is Robert F. Sayre's *The Examined Self: Benjamin Franklin, Henry Adams, Henry James* (Princeton, N.J., 1964); Sayre compares and contrasts the autobiographical efforts of James and Adams, showing that both men relied upon Franklin's *Autobiography* as a kind of model. This common debt tells us less about Adams than does the examination of the relationship between the two Henrys: "from time to time they met until the time when, influenced to some degree by each other, they transformed . . . family traditions of personal narrative into their contrasting autobiographies." Adams took a larger role as teacher, a lesser as artist; he converted popular themes— religion, Darwinism, failure—into literary strategies which "connect" to his age. By mistreating himself in his account, Sayre contends, Adams bombarded his readers with a powerful kind of education, an "examination of life." Tony Tanner's "Henry Adams and Henry James" (*Tri-Quarterly* [Evanston, Ill.], Winter 1968) enlarges on Sayre's analysis, especially by pointing to the psychological gap between the self-satisfaction James knew from his art and the torment that haunts Adams (in the aftermath of theorizing about life), until "consciousness itself ceases to have any value for him." *Spiritual Autobiography in Early America* (Princeton, N.J., 1968), by Daniel B. Shea, Jr., identifies Quaker and Puritan modes of autobiography, both of which show up in a "late" form in the *Education*.

A final cautionary note may be useful. Three important essays warn against misreadings of various kinds and call for further attention to unresolved critical problems: the possible exaggeration of Adams's failure concerns Herbert F. Hahn in "*The Education of Henry Adams* Reconsidered" (*CE*, Mar. 1963); Max I. Baym, "Henry Adams and the Critics" (*ASch*, Winter 1945–46), sounds a similar alarm. Henry Wasser's brief footnote to the critical history of Adams's best known book, "*The Education of Henry Adams* Fifty Years After" (*Midcontinent American Studies Journal*, Spring 1969), confesses to critical inadequacies in the name of us all: we remain "still troubled by the problem of how to explain his mind."

Recent Criticism

Since this essay was begun, three important books have appeared, as if to prove the vitality of Adams criticism. Vern Wagner's *The Suspension of Henry Adams: A Study of Manner and Matter* (Detroit, Mich., 1969) follows his "The Lotus of Henry Adams" (*NEQ*, Mar. 1954); the book focuses upon "technique," especially "juncture" (which welds together "manner" and "matter"), and the "humor" of Adams's sardonic variety. Their effect, Wagner feels, is to create an "inconclusive, irresolute, uncertain, doubtful" silence—the philosophical and artistic "suspension" in his title. His thesis forces Wagner to make nonsense of too many passages, but he presents the best analysis yet of the "genuine humorist" in Adams. *Symbol and Idea in Henry Adams* (Lincoln, Neb., 1969) by Melvin Lyon combines detailed explications of six major works with a broad discussion of "eight or nine primary aspects" of Adams's thought, to form a remarkably complete treatment of "imaginative symbolism," its development, use, and meaning. More than forty pages of critical notes summarize other interpretations; and the introduction attempts to define with unusual precision the author's terms and method. Unfortunately, some repetitions between text and notes and between critical notes and footnotes bring the organization into question; but the comprehensiveness of Lyon's account makes his book valuable. John J. Conder's *A Formula of His Own: Henry Adams's Literary Experiment* (Chicago, 1970) is limited in size and scope, concentrating upon the literary form and technique of *Chartres* and the *Education*, which together form "a single unit of art." (For a contrasting view, which insists upon the aesthetic unity of the *Education* and which treats the book as an "apotheosis" of the autobiographical form and its author as both "orderer" and "interpreter" of a failure, see Chapter 6 in David L. Minter's *The Interpreted Design as a Structural Principle in American Prose*, New Haven, Conn., 1969.) Conder allows a place to other writings, but he emphasizes their secondary values, studying them for clues to Adams's developing artistry or as supporting evidence for interpretations of the "masterpieces." Whether such an approach is justified, each reader will have to decide for himself. Conder's method reveals the poetic possibilities in Adams's best prose, and it yields some surprises. Neither *Chartres* nor the *Education*, the author finds (unlike Lyon), "depends upon symbols to achieve a unity of form"; instead, "the various elements of historical and personal experience [are] united by a fictional persona and by recurrent methods of presenting material in a widely varying, often sharply opposed, set of contexts." Conder's closely reasoned explications defy summary treatment. Yet, by anatomizing the "works themselves," he almost certainly forces us to reconsider older readings, even if our notions of the "internal necessity" within "fictional" forms do not exactly correspond to his.

In the several sections of this essay, I have suggested a few of the directions which future research might take. Recent contributions show that interest has shifted away from Henry Adams's life and toward the methods and effects of the literary artist. Certainly, the appearance of additional letters from and to Adams and of authoritative texts in modern editions will improve the present situation. More generally, the experience of reviewing the accomplishments of the past leads me to consider with unwonted optimism the prospects for the future. Most of all at the half-century mark, it is pleasant to note that, however bright the future may be, Henry Adams already has provided a durable and rewarding subject for serious study.

William Cullen Bryant

JAMES E. ROCKS

WILLIAM CULLEN BRYANT's importance in the history of nineteenth-century American life and letters is unquestioned, yet the state of Bryant studies has not changed much in the last three decades. Some excellent work has been done recently, of course, but the situation as Herman Spivey described it in 1950 remains today about the same: Spivey pointed out that there was no complete edition of Bryant's letters, editorial writings, or poetry, and that no definitive scholarly or critical biography had ever been written on him. In fact, Spivey argued, in his "Manuscript Resources for the Study of William Cullen Bryant," most of the basic scholarship on Bryant, except for his early years, remained to be done (*PBSA*, III Quarter 1950). Bryant was a prolific writer, and the fact that his manuscripts are scattered and often difficult to decipher certainly helps to explain the lack of authoritative editions and scholarly studies. The forecast for the seventies looks better, however, for several scholars are undertaking projects that should result in definitive editions of the letters and poems and a critical biography. Necessary groundwork is still being prepared, based largely on the distinguished writings of the most important Bryant scholar of this century, Tremaine McDowell.

BIBLIOGRAPHY

A rather complete description of Bryant's works is in Jacob Blanck's *Bibliography of American Literature* (New Haven, Conn., 1955), which divides the listings into three sections: primary books and books containing first edition material, collections of previously published poems, and books that contain material reprinted from the books listed in the first section. Blanck admits that there must be errors in his compilation, since it is difficult to identify all of Bryant's poems because of the extensive number of reprintings and the revised titles in various anthologies. Many of Bryant's poems have never been accurately dated: Parke Godwin's *A Biography of William Cullen Bryant, with Extracts from His Private Correspondence* (2 vols., New York, 1883; reprinted 1967) is frequently erroneous. The only substantial bibliography of Bryant published before Blanck, and often in error, was Henry C. Sturges's *Chronologies of the Life and Writings of William Cullen Bryant, with a Bibliography of His Works in Prose and Verse* (New York, 1903; reprinted 1968), which appeared also as a part of the 1903 Roslyn Edition of Bryant's poetry. Sturges's compilation is divided into lists of the different kinds of writing that Bryant did and is "inaccurate and incomplete," according to Tremaine McDowell, in *William Cullen Bryant*, the American Writers Series volume of representative selections (New York, 1935); in the notes McDowell corrects some of Sturges's errors. In "The Chronology of a Group of Poems by W. C. Bryant" (*MLN*, Mar. 1917), A. H. Herrick points out errors in Godwin's and Sturges's dating of seven poems. Some of the articles discussed under *Biography* and *Criticism*, below, also correct the misdatings of poems, particularly of "Thanatopsis," which was written later than has been commonly thought. A full and accurate chronology of Bryant's poems needs to be done and will be served by the collecting of poems for a new edition.

The only important recent bibliography of secondary materials on Bryant is that included in Richard Beale Davis's Goldentree Bibliography, *American Literature through Bryant, 1585–1830* (New York, 1969). It updates the annotated listing in McDowell's AWS volume.

EDITIONS AND TEXTS

Since not all of Bryant's poems or prose writings have been identified or collected, none of the many editions of his works is complete or textually authoritative. The most important editions appeared in the late nineteenth century and have recently been reprinted. Although Bryant's poetry may not be his most important achievement, it is the poetry that would take priority in any new edition of his works. Richard E. Peck has begun collecting Bryant's poems for a possible new edition, and he indicates that the task will be large and complex.

Although many volumes of Bryant's writing were published during his lifetime and shortly thereafter, only a few can be regarded as in any way "standard." *The Poetical Works of William Cullen Bryant* (New York, 1876) is the last edition to have passed through the poet's hands. Parke Godwin's six-volume *Life and Writings of William Cullen*

Bryant includes the two-volume *Poetical Works of William Cullen Bryant* (New York, 1883; reprinted 1967); the two-volume *Prose Writings of William Cullen Bryant* (New York, 1884; reprinted 1964), which has additional materials not found in earlier editions and some textual revisions and notes by the editor; and the two-volume biography discussed below. The Roslyn Edition, *The Poetical Works of William Cullen Bryant* (New York, 1903; reprinted 1969), is an inclusive one-volume collection, without Godwin's notes. *Tales of Glauber-Spa* (New York, 1832), in which two of Bryant's prose tales and sketches appeared, has been reprinted in the American Short Story Series of Garrett Press (New York, 1969).

Bryant's early political satire, *The Embargo*, has been reprinted in a facsimile edition, with a short but comprehensive introduction by Thomas O. Mabbott (Gainesville, Fla., 1955). Previously uncollected poems are to be found in Seymour L. Gross's "An Uncollected Bryant Poem" (*N&Q*, Aug. 1957), which reproduces a poem written hastily for the fiftieth anniversary of Washington's inauguration, and in Tremaine McDowell's "An Uncollected Poem by Bryant" (*Americana*, July 1934), which reprints a mediocre gift-book poem entitled "To William." In "The Exhibition in the Palace: A Bibliographical Essay" (*BNYPL*, Sept. 1960), Earle E. Coleman includes the three drafts of a short ode that Bryant wrote for the New York Crystal Palace Exhibition in 1853. (Other uncollected poems can be found in essays discussed under *Criticism*.) Robert B. Silber, in his dissertation (State University of Iowa, 1962) "William Cullen Bryant's 'Lectures on Mythology'" (*DA*, xxiii, 4021–4022), edits the five unpublished lectures that were presented at the National Academy of Design in New York in 1827.

MANUSCRIPTS AND LETTERS

The only large collection of published letters is that in Parke Godwin's biography of Bryant (see *Biography*, below). Godwin, Bryant's son-in-law, extracted from rough drafts of the letters, most of which he did not have access to. Bryant's letters are at long last being collected and tabulated. The first volume (correspondence to 1833) of a proposed six-volume edition is currently under preparation by William Cullen Bryant II and Thomas G. Voss. William Cullen Bryant II reports that Bryant wrote more than 2,350 identifiable letters, of which perhaps all but about 200 are recoverable in whole or in large part. According to Voss, the largest holders of manuscript letters—and these repositories represent only about one-fifth of the number of libraries where such materials can be found—are the college or university libraries of Amherst, Brown, Columbia, Duke, Johns Hopkins, Princeton, Virginia, Williams, and Yale. The following historical societies hold manuscript letters: Bureau County, Princeton, Illinois; Chicago; New York; and Pennsylvania. Manuscript letters are to be found in these libraries: Huntington; New York Public (incompletely catalogued); New York State at Albany; Pierpont Morgan; Queensborough, New York, Public; and the Library of Congress (incompletely catalogued). Together these collections include about 550 letters.

The listing of manuscript holdings, including letters, in *American Literary Manuscripts* can be considered only a general guide for the scholar because in many instances the reports are inflated; in others they do not reveal new acquisitions. The major manuscript collections have been examined in the very helpful essay by Herman Spivey, "Manuscript Resources for the Study of William Cullen Bryant." Spivey provides brief descriptions of eighteen collections, thirteen of which he considers significant in extent and value; he also gives a partial list of correspondents. Six of the collections—the most important— are housed in the New York Public Library: the Bryant-Godwin Collection, the Bryant Family Papers, the Bryant Miscellaneous Papers, the Berg Collection, the Goddard-Roslyn Collection (including hundreds of manuscript versions of Bryant's poems), and the John Bigelow Collection. Other important holders are the New York Historical Society, the New York State Library at Albany, the Boston Public Library, the Massachusetts Historical Society, the Houghton Library at Harvard, the Williams College Library, and the Longfellow House in Cambridge, Massachusetts; smaller collections can be found in the Yale University Library, the Library of Congress, the Duke University Library, the William L. Clements Library of the University of Michigan, and the Huntington Library. Included in these major collections— there are over fifty other places that have Bryant materials, according to *American Literary Manuscripts*—are manuscripts, journals, letters to and from Bryant, and other documents relating to the poet, including a good collection of first editions at Yale. Most of this material has remained essentially untapped by Bryant scholars.

From these various collections some of the letters written to and from Bryant have been printed in a score of articles and notes in the past forty years. Many of the letters clarify biographical problems or add somewhat to our understanding of Bryant's opinions as a poet and editor. The first group of articles under consideration here offers information relevant to a discussion of Bryant's life. Tremaine McDowell's "William Cullen Bryant and Yale" (*NEQ*, Oct. 1930) contains letters to and from his former Williams roommate, John Avery, about his ill-fated determination to enter Yale. Bryant's stilted rantings in these letters are obviously made with tongue in cheek, and his praise of the legal profession might be compensation for a short-lived college career. The Sedgwick family's influence during his unhappy years as a lawyer in Great Barrington and later is revealed in an exchange of letters between Bryant and Charles, Henry, and Catherine Sedgwick, many published for the first time in C. I. Glicksberg's excellent essay, "Bryant and the Sedgwick Family" (*Americana*, Oct. 1937). Letters written from about 1833 to 1839 to his brothers Cyrus and Austin and to his mother concerning family matters are in Helen L. Drew's "Unpublished Letters of William Cullen Bryant" (*NEQ*, June 1937). Of greater importance are the fourteen letters (1831 to 1878), mostly from Cullen to his brother John, which reveal Bryant's plans to leave the *Post*, probably to devote himself to poetry; in "Bryant and Illinois: Further Letters of the Poet's Family" (*NEQ*, Dec. 1943), Keith Huntress and Fred W. Lorch point out that much of Bryant's wealth came from investments in Illinois farmland.

In "William Cullen Bryant Changes His Mind: An Unpublished Letter about Thomas Jefferson" (*NEQ*, Dec. 1949), Herman Spivey shows that Bryant changed from a strong anti-Jeffersonian attitude in his youth to a pro-Jeffersonian stance in his later years. Spivey has also written a significant study of Bryant's attitudes toward Lincoln during the Civil War; this essay, "Bryant Cautions and Counsels Lincoln" (*TSL*, 1961), includes previously unpublished letters—there are thirty-one to Lincoln—with Bryant's comments on slavery, the war, and, particularly, federal appointments. Spivey makes it clear that Lincoln read Bryant's letters, respected his opinions, replied in his own hand to some of them, and heeded his advice on a number of appointments. Some remarks on public affairs, particularly the Civil War, can be found in nineteen letters (1849 to 1866) to a close friend at Roslyn, Long Island; they involve personal matters of perhaps limited significance but reveal the warmth of Bryant's personality (William D. Hoyt, Jr., "Some Unpublished Bryant Correspondence," *NYH*, Jan. and Apr. 1940). Bryant's opinions on some major questions of his day are to be found in three letters printed in Paul Crapo's "Bryant on Slavery, Copyright, and Capital Punishment" (*ESQ*, III Quarter 1967).

Several essays collect for the first time letters to and from Bryant and editorials by Bryant that shed additional light on his relationships with important writers. C. I. Glicksberg reprints editorials and reviews by Bryant and letters by Cooper in "Cooper and Bryant: A Literary Friendship" (*Col*, Part 20, 1935); these materials reveal Bryant's admiration for and defense of Cooper during the novelist's "war with the press." Longfellow and Bryant were but casual acquaintances, as Glicksberg shows in "Longfellow and Bryant" (*N&Q*, 3 February 1934). Bryant's arduous trip to St. Augustine, Florida, is described in a letter to William Gilmore Simms, with whom he was friendly, in John. C. Guilds, "Bryant in the South: A New Letter to Simms" (*Georgia Historical Quarterly*, June 1953). Paul Hamilton Hayne also admired Bryant, as is shown in several letters Hayne wrote in 1873 requesting that Bryant write a memorial ode to Simms for the *Evening Post* (Edward G. Bernard, "Northern Bryant and Southern Hayne," *Col*, n.s., Spring 1936). Frank Smith's "Schoolcraft, Bryant, and Poetic Fame" (*AL*, May 1933) includes several letters in which Bryant criticizes a poem by William Hetherwold, presumably a protégé of Schoolcraft but who Smith thinks was actually Schoolcraft.

Correspondence that treats of random matters having to do with Bryant's poetic and editorial careers is extensive. Letters (1823 to 1825) to Theophilus Parsons dealing with Bryant's writing for the *Literary Gazette* are in Joseph George Ornato's "Bryant and the *United States Literary Gazette*" (*ESQ*, III Quarter 1967). Eight letters (1841 to 1874) covering a variety of topics, including Bryant's remarks on the genesis and publication of "Thanatopsis" and his response to South Carolina's secession, can be found in David R. Rebmann's "Unpublished Letters of William Cullen Bryant" (*ESQ*, III Quarter 1967). Three uncollected travel letters written in 1873 and subsequently published in the *Evening Post* appear in C. I. Glicksberg's "Letters of William Cullen Bryant from Florida" (*Florida Historical Society Quarterly*, Apr. 1936). Another Bryant letter (1848), concerning an obscure play by a woman's rights advocate, appears in Robert H. Woodward's "Bryant and Elizabeth Oakes Smith: An Unpublished Letter" (*Colby Library Quarterly*, Dec. 1959). Jay B. Hubbell's "A New Letter by William Cullen Bryant" (*Georgia Historical Quarterly*, Sept. 1942) reprints Bryant's review of a history of Georgia. Bryant's letter of regret that he cannot attend the Revolutionary War Centennial appears in Arthur Eugene Bestor, Jr.'s, "Concord Summons the Poets" (*NEQ*, Sept. 1933), and his refusal to write a poem on the battle of Oriskany is in Robert H. Woodward's "Bryant and the Oriskany Centennial" (*ESQ*, II Quarter 1963). Peter B. Morrill's "Unpublished Letters of William Cullen Bryant" (*ESQ*, II Quarter 1962) deals with personal matters that do not significantly supplement Godwin's biography, despite Morrill's argument to the contrary. Some miscellaneous personal letters (1838 to 1877) are in Edward J. Lazzerini's "Bryant as a Writer of Friendly Letters" (*ESQ*, III Quarter 1967). A brief letter in Benjamin Lease's "William Cullen Bryant: An Unpublished Letter" (*N&Q*, Sept. 1953) reveals Bryant's humorous side.

Many of the letters that have been published in the last few years add, finally, little dimension to our understanding of Bryant. The proposed edition of the letters, however, should provide important background necessary for future studies of Bryant's life and work; and examination of the manuscripts of Bryant's poetry and prose will be an essential step toward any future edition of his writings and any new evaluations of his poetic career.

BIOGRAPHY

There is no definitive biography of Bryant; until the last two decades, there were substantial gaps in our knowledge of his life. Many of the recent essays on Bryant have continued to address themselves to biographical questions as well as critical ones; and with the proposed edition of the letters under way, a new biography seems likely. William Cullen Bryant II intends to write a biography but will collect the correspondence first; according to him, his "life" will try to reestablish a balance between Bryant's poetic achievement and the other areas of Bryant's activities—journalism, the fine arts, public affairs, and literary and social criticism.

The "standard" biography of Bryant is by his son-in-law and *Evening Post* associate, Parke Godwin. *A Biography of William Cullen Bryant, with Extracts from His Private Correspondence* (2 vols., New York, 1883; reprinted 1967) is part of Godwin's six-volume edition of Bryant's writings. Godwin's study, which combines discussion of his subject's life with many lengthy letters, is a rather slow-moving if careful work. Godwin admires his subject to the extent that he is fundamentally uncritical, both of the man's life and his writings, although Godwin does on occasion allow characteristics of Bryant's personality to speak for themselves without intrusive evaluation. Chapter One of Godwin's book is Bryant's own autobiography, written in 1874 and 1875, that ends with the year 1811 and is full of chatty reminiscences but sparing of details; Bryant admitted a poor memory for particulars and an indifference to the task of writing down his own life. Beginning in the second chapter, Godwin provides a lengthy background of Bryant's parents but treats the Williams College period only briefly. Chapters Six and Seven, on the period from 1811 to 1815, incorrectly date some of Bryant's poems and thus are misleading on the development of his mind and art. (The biographical inaccuracies of these early chapters have been largely corrected by more recent scholars.) Although Godwin is understandably vague and incorrect regarding his father-in-law's early life, he is quite informative about the *Evening Post* years, particularly in his treatment of Bryant's European travels—he slights the

American journeys—and the letters Bryant contributed to the paper. In fact, the three volumes of travel sketches, *Letters of a Traveller* (New York, 1850), *Letters of a Traveller, Second Series* (New York, 1859), and *Letters from the East* (New York, 1869), provide information about Bryant that biographers and scholars have not utilized sufficiently. In addition, Godwin discusses the translations of the *Iliad* and *Odyssey* extensively. Throughout this rambling biography Godwin portrays honestly Bryant's public side; but Godwin offers little insight into the private man, a regrettable lack, but as he and others indicate, Bryant maintained a distinct separation between his two lives, finding in his family and books an escape from the discomforts of the editor's uneasy chair. Godwin, in a speech on Bryant published in his *Commemorative Addresses* (New York, 1895), sees Bryant's birth and life paralleling that of a young nation; but, unlike the official biography, this speech is highly sentimental. Godwin's major biography forms the basis of the chronology of Bryant's life by Henry C. Sturges which appears in the 1903 Roslyn Edition. Richard Henry Stoddard's short but inaccurate memoir is also included in this edition.

Many of the book-length biographies of Bryant are little more than reminiscences or scissors-and-paste redoings of Godwin's work. In the two concluding chapters of his life of Bryant, Godwin refers to the funeral oration delivered by Henry W. Bellows, *In Memoriam, William Cullen Bryant* (New York, 1878), and to subsequent commemorative addresses by G. W. Curtis, *The Life, Character, and Writings of William Cullen Bryant* (New York, 1879); Samuel Osgood, *Bryant Among His Countrymen* (New York, 1879); and Robert C. Waterston, *Tribute to William Cullen Bryant* (Boston, 1878). These eulogistic statements are minor additions to the record of Bryant's death. Five other book-length studies of Bryant are more ambitious but of varying worth. David J. Hill's *William Cullen Bryant* (New York, 1879), worthless to the modern scholar, is sketchy, uncritical, and overly appreciative, as is Andrew James Symington's *William Cullen Bryant; a Biographical Sketch* (New York, 1880), which can be readily cast into the same scholarly limbo. John Bigelow, an associate on the *Evening Post*, wrote the American Men of Letters biography, *William Cullen Bryant* (Boston, 1890), dividing his material by topic, rather than using the conventional chronological approach. Bigelow's recollections of Bryant are honest and valuable, although Bryant's early years receive rather sketchy treatment. Bigelow discusses both the poet (see particularly Chapter VII) and the editor, and he argues that Bryant saw few people in order to avoid compromises in the political opinions that inspired his editorials. William Aspenwall Bradley's English Men of Letters biography, *William Cullen Bryant* (New York, 1905), draws on earlier biographies but offers more astute and frequently critical judgments; this judicious book is marred, however, by Bradley's overemphasis on Bryant's Puritanism. Even if it offers no new material—Bradley admits as much—this book provides pleasant reading; objectivity with respect define the biographer's approach to his subject. The only "modern" lengthy work on Bryant's life is Harry H. Peckham's *Gotham Yankee* (New York, 1950), a derivative and effusive rehashing of earlier biographies that makes little if any attempt to incorporate the new scholarly materials and facts that have been revealed in the last half-century. Peckham senses the variety of Bryant's achievements but argues for his importance in American literary history in a style full of clichés and syrupy verbosity; unfortunately, Peckham's biography is more laudatory than are the hyperbolic nineteenth-century commemorations of Bryant.

Specific periods of Bryant's life, particularly his first thirty years, have been examined carefully by modern scholars, and their essays contribute to the fuller picture of Bryant's family background and of his intellectual and artistic development that is necessary for a comprehensive study of his life. Bryant was deeply influenced by his parents, Peter and Sarah Snell Bryant. Hallock P. Long, in "The Alden Lineage of William Cullen Bryant" (*NEHGR*, Apr. 1948), outlines his several Mayflower ancestors, while Tremaine McDowell, in "The Ancestry of William Cullen Bryant" (*Americana*, Oct. 1928), characterizes the individualism of the Bryant family and the practical, worldly temperament of the Snells. Dr. Peter Bryant wrote some passable verse before Cullen's birth; the possible influence (on, for example, *The Embargo*) of his father's Augustan poetry and political opinions is discussed in Donald M. Murray's "Dr. Peter Bryant: Preceptor in Poetry to William Cullen Bryant" (*NEQ*, Dec. 1960). Sarah Snell Bryant is still insufficiently known to determine the extent of her influence on her poet son, but in a chatty essay by Amanda Mathews, "The Diary of a Poet's Mother" (*Magazine of History with Notes and Queries*, Sept. 1905), some extracts from her diary suggest the strong-willed, stern, pioneer Yankee that George V. Bohman characterizes in "A Poet's Mother: Sarah Snell Bryant in Illinois" (*Journal of the Illinois State Historical Society*, June 1940). This interesting account relates Mrs. Bryant's property-minded move to Illinois in her late sixties to join her sons, Cyrus, John, and Arthur.

Although the character of the poet's mother still remains sketchy, the personality and development of her teen-age son has been rather fully chronicled in two highly informative and entertaining essays by Tre-

maine McDowell, "Cullen Bryant Prepares for College" (*SAQ*, Apr.
1931) and "Cullen Bryant at Williams College" (*NEQ*, Oct. 1928).
The former discusses Bryant's study of the classics at the home of his
severe and orthodox uncle, the Reverend Thomas Snell, and at a school
in Plainfield; the latter, his disappointing year at the recently founded
college in Williamstown. Here he confronted new and diverse religious
views, developed his ability as a versifier, and was stimulated generally
to more independent thinking; the strict rules of conduct at the school
annoyed the restive student body, including even Cullen, who was
always shy but did value close friendships. In his later life Bryant
always regretted that he had not continued his college work, and he
mistakenly attributed little indebtedness to his year at Williams. Between 1816 and 1821, when he married Frances Fairchild, he debated
the abandonment of poetry for law. But stimulated by the *North American Review*, he determined to continue writing, thereby winning the
approval of the Boston literati (particularly for his recitation of the
Harvard Phi Beta Kappa poem, "The Ages"), and published his first
volume of poems. These important years are recorded by Tremaine
McDowell in "Bryant and *The North American Review*" (*AL*, Mar.
1929). His residence in Great Barrington, Massachusetts, from 1816 to
1825, was a time of intellectual loneliness and dull legal work, until
he met Catherine Sedgwick, a member of a distinguished family, who
encouraged Bryant's literary life there and later in New York. The
years 1825 to 1827 are recorded in two excellent essays, Richard D.
Birdsall's "William Cullen Bryant and Catherine Sedgwick—Their
Debt to Berkshire" (*NEQ*, Sept. 1955) and C. I. Glicksberg's "Bryant
and the *United States Review*" (*NEQ*, Dec. 1934). These essays show
how arduous and uncertain were Bryant's early months as an editor
away from the New England region that had given him his early
reputation.

Bryant's half-century editorship of the *Evening Post* and his residence
in the New York area have been extensively chronicled, particularly
by his contemporaries. Although Godwin and Bigelow were Bryant's
associates on the newspaper, they did not provide as exhaustive an
examination of his editorial career as Allan Nevins does in *The Evening Post: A Century of Journalism* (New York, 1922). Nevins's book
is important because it compares the *Evening Post*'s editorial opinions
with those of other major New York newspapers and provides a rather
full view of the city as it was growing during those years; Nevins gives
lively accounts of William Leggett, John Bigelow ("a model American
gentleman"), John R. Thompson, Charles Nordhoff, and Parke Godwin, whose biography he occasionally corrects. Nevins delineates the

growth of Bryant's political liberalism and emphasizes the varying moods of the editor's personality, offering in Bryant's insistence on a regimen of diet, exercise, and sleep in order to keep his body fit one other reason for his supposed coldness and social aloofness. Nevins is concerned, of course, with Bryant's newspaper career and therefore slights his belletristic writings.

Most of the material in Curtiss S. Johnson's study, *Politics and a Belly-Full* (New York, 1962), comes from other books on Bryant, notably those by Godwin, Bigelow, and Nevins, but his study offers a conveniently short and readable survey, with a conclusion that summarizes and assesses Bryant's years as editor rather well. Frank L. Mott, in *American Journalism, a History: 1690–1960* (3rd ed., New York, 1962), briefly assesses Bryant's editorship and praises the man and his paper for distinguished publishing. In "William Cullen Bryant—Puritan Liberal" (*The Romantic Revolution in America*, New York, 1927), Vernon L. Parrington calls Bryant "the father of nineteenth-century American journalism." Understandably, Parrington's essay focuses upon Bryant's editorial career, as does Part II of Tremaine McDowell's introduction to the AWS volume, *William Cullen Bryant*; both summarize Bryant's political idealism judiciously. In an essay with a misleading title, "William Cullen Bryant and Communism" (*Modern Quarterly* [New York], July 1934), C. I. Glicksberg argues effectively that the editor, although a courageous liberal, was reactionary in his attitudes toward economic conflicts between labor and capital. Eva B. Dykes's "William Cullen Bryant: Apostle of Freedom" (*Negro History Bulletin*, Nov. 1942) generously praises the editor's liberal views on the black man's condition. Edward K. Spann examines a friendship divided over economics and politics in "Bryant and Verplanck, the Yankee and the Yorker, 1821–1870" (*NYH*, Jan. 1968).

Several other studies also treat Bryant's editorial years, and although they are in part critical the studies are further examinations of his opinions, his involvement in New York intellectual life, and his editorial practices. William Cullen Bryant II, in his 1954 Columbia University dissertation, "Bryant: the Middle Years; a Study in Cultural Fellowship" (*DA*, xiv, 1218), discusses Bryant's influence on American culture from 1825 to 1850; included is a list of works by Bryant that have not heretofore been credited to him. His relations with the South, both as traveler and editor, were always cordial, even though he was strongly antislavery and believed ardently in a determined prosecution of the war. In "Bryant and the South" (*TSE*, 1949), Max L. Griffin discusses in admirable detail Bryant's trips to the South, his friendships with southern writers, and the laudatory notices of his poems in southern reviews. Howard R. Floan, in "The New York *Evening Post* and the Ante-bellum South" (*AQ*, Fall 1956), covers much of Griffin's ground but looks more specifically at the *Post*'s extensive presentation of news about the South up to the 1850s. A 1966 University of Wisconsin dissertation by Thomas G. Voss, "William Cullen Bryant's *New York Evening Post* and the South: 1847–1856" (*DA*, xxviii, 698A–699A), examines closely the period from the newspaper's opposition to the Mexican War to its acceptance of the Republican party, and reviews Bryant's principles of government and the southern opposition to some of those views. Finally, three articles by C. I. Glicksberg further amplify Bryant's role as editor: "William Cullen Bryant and the American Press" (*Journalism Quarterly*, Dec. 1939) and "William Cullen Bryant: Champion of Simple English" (*Journalism Quarterly*, Sept. 1949) discuss his campaigning for an enlightened American press against the abuses of contemporary newspaper practices and his efforts to write in a simple, uninflated editorial style. Glicksberg's third essay is on the feminist Fanny Wright, whose New York lectures occasioned Bryant to write a satiric ode. The essay is "William Cullen Bryant and Fanny Wright" (*AL*, Jan. 1935). Bryant's New York is the subject of Chapter XI of Van Wyck Brooks's *The World of Washington Irving* (New York, 1944). In *The Raven and the Whale* (New York, 1956), Perry Miller makes cursory references to Bryant's aloof position as an editor in the midst of the Young America "movement." Miller's remarks would suggest that Bryant was less interested generally in the intellectual and artistic life of New York than we know he was. Bryant may have been reticent, but he was not indifferent to the quest for literary nationalism; he wrote friendly literary notices for his newspaper and knew several painters whose artistic ideas influenced his own poetry. In order to see the problem of Bryant and the New York milieu in its clearest perspective, one needs to read other studies, such as those discussed under *Criticism*.

Although Bryant's European travels during these years have been discussed in detail, only one essay has been written about his American journeys and his attitudes toward the country as expressed in the letters for the *Post*. Donald A. Ringe, in "William Cullen Bryant's Account of Michigan in 1846" (*Michigan History*, Sept. 1956), indicates that little use has been made of these documents and describes the last of three trips Bryant made to visit his mother and brothers in Illinois, including a journey of more than a week in northern Michigan which Bryant recorded in lively accounts. Ringe's essay suggests a direction for subsequent inquiry into Bryant's literary methods as an interpreter of the American scene and into his evaluation of it. (Since it is difficult to separate a man's life from his writings, some information pertaining to Bryant's biography will be found in books and essays that are largely critical and therefore are discussed below.)

The writing on Bryant's life has so far failed to create a complete or accurate picture of the man and his milieu; the different periods of his life have been studied principally in isolated fragments. However good the pieces, we lack a whole view—a study for which significant work has certainly been done.

CRITICISM

Although there is extensive critical writing on Bryant, major essays of a general evaluative nature are few in number. Despite their excellence in synthesizing his career and the themes and techniques of his poetry, no really long significant critical work, with the possible exception of Albert F. McLean, Jr.'s admirable Twayne United States Authors Series volume, *William Cullen Bryant* (New York, 1964), has been completed. For the student interested in the history of criticism on Bryant, there is a well-edited collection of essays and excerpts by his contemporaries—John Neal, Hugh Swinton Legaré, John Wilson, and Edgar Allan Poe—in Tremaine McDowell's AWS *William Cullen Bryant*. McDowell's important collection, which should be reprinted, is both well selected and handy, and it does offer a variety of critical reactions to Bryant's work; other nineteenth-century articles are listed in his evaluative bibliography. Together these essays offer a dialogue between those whose adulation of Bryant is unrestrained and those whose criticism finds him austere in temperament and deficient in intellect. Of more than simply historical interest are the following essays, most of which point out Bryant's limitations in a direct but judicious fashion: Thomas Powell, "William Cullen Bryant," in his *The Living Authors of America* (New York, 1850); E. S. Nadal, "William Cullen Bryant" (*Macmillan's Magazine*, Sept. 1878); E. C. Stedman, "William Cullen Bryant," in his *Poets of America* (Boston, 1885); Henry D. Sedgwick, Jr., "Bryant's Permanent Contribution to Literature" (*AtM*, Apr. 1897); W. R. Thayer, "Bryant," in his *Throne-Makers* (Boston, 1899); Augustus Hopkins Strong, "William Cullen Bryant," in his *American Poets and Their Theology* (Philadelphia, 1916); Fred Lewis Pattee, "The Centenary of Bryant's Poetry," in his *Sidelights on American Literature* (New York, 1922); and Rémy de Gourmont, *Deux Poètes de la Nature: Bryant et Emerson* (Paris, 1925). Harriet Monroe's attacks (*Poetry*, July 1915; *Dial*, 14 October 1915 and 25 November 1915) against Bryant, with blustery defense by John L. Hervey (*Dial*,

15 August 1915, 28 October 1915 and 9 December 1915), represent
the disillusionment caused by the apparent materialism of nineteenth-
century establishment writers and the reaction of a critic armed to protect the American pantheon. The exchange, a battle of rhetoric that
rarely concerns the evidence of Bryant's achievements, reveals more
about the critics than about their subject but is nevertheless a curiosity
in the history of Bryant studies.

Those general essays that offer praise tempered by balanced judgment and keen critical insight are not numerous, although they do
give the student a good background for his reading of Bryant; the best
of these essays were written primarily before the mid-forties, and since
then most Bryant scholarship, however good, has treated more specific
critical problems. The first of these broad assessments that remains
valuable is W. E. Leonard's "Bryant" in *CHAL*. Leonard does overstate
his arguments that Wordsworth and other poets were not an influence
on Bryant, and that the poet did not really develop over the years
because he experienced no moral or intellectual crises; but, despite
what some might consider his undervaluing of Bryant's imagination
and intellectual abilities, Leonard's survey is fair and perhaps painfully
honest. This essay treats Bryant as poet and disregards his work
as editor; the matter of balance is therefore faulty but does not create
a seriously disproportionate evaluation. Leonard's discussion is decidedly appreciative, as is Vernon L. Parrington's "William Cullen Bryant
—Puritan Liberal," in his *The Romantic Revolution in America*. Parrington's essay provides a good companion piece to Leonard's, for Parrington is interested mainly in Bryant's journalistic reputation, which
he finds to be of extraordinary dimensions. Parrington does not outline
much of Bryant's intellectual growth, with the exception of his readings
in political economy, saying incorrectly that the steps of his development cannot easily be traced, but Parrington does find in Bryant's
mature liberalism a rather good example of his own socioeconomic view
of American literary history. In "William Cullen Bryant: A Reinterpretation" (*Revue Anglo-Américaine*, Aug. 1934), C. I. Glicksberg
offers astute insight into the two halves of Bryant's creative life, the
poet and editor; he argues that the older Bryant had little more to say
about the subjects he had poetized in his youth and that, although
journalism provided him needed experience, he could not treat contemporary material in his poetry because of his view that art must
reveal the universal. (Glicksberg here suggests that Bryant wrote less
occasional verse than he actually did.) By giving himself to a business
career, Bryant, says Glicksberg, compromised his Romantic devotion
to art. Glicksberg's thoughtful and laudatory essay comes to the almost

inevitable conclusions about Bryant as a poet: had he been more intense and versatile, his writings would have been considerably enriched. Like the best critics on Bryant, Glicksberg does not take the apologist's tone but tries, rather, to show the strengths of Bryant's limited talents. These essays reveal the complexities of mind and art in a widely oversimplified nineteenth-century writer.

No critical and scholarly examination has done more to instruct modern students of Bryant than has Tremaine McDowell's introduction to the AWS volume; with the exception of some questionable dating of the poems before 1821, this assessment remains the best single work on the poet's whole career—as poet, critic, and editor. The discussion of Bryant's religion is especially strong; the treatment of his politics is overly concise and has been more amply articulated by others, notably Allan Nevins. McDowell's approach to his subject is both topical and chronological, and his footnotes and notes to the works amplify considerably and specifically the arguments in the introduction. McDowell readily acknowledges that Bryant was a poet of minor rank, as he does even more emphatically in his synopsis of Bryant in *LHUS*. For its length this discussion is quite inclusive; it summarizes Bryant's life and his ideas briefly but pointedly. McDowell emphasizes the twin streams of Calvinism and Unitarianism in Bryant's family heritage and his long years of fearing death that, along with readings in his father's library, lay behind the composition of "Thanatopsis." Also, McDowell argues that because Bryant was quite uncomfortable in New York society, he cultivated an austerity that many mistook for his real personality; furthermore, according to McDowell, his emotions did become smothered under the rigidity of his mask and he did become as cold and silent as the iceberg to which he has often been compared. With this explanation of Bryant's personality, McDowell offers one of many reasons for the man's patriarchal demeanor. Bryant, he goes on to say, was a hard-working but not brilliant editor, and his small output shows him to be a man of modest genius. In contrast to the AWS introduction, McDowell offers, in this *LHUS* essay, a tougher-minded analysis of his subject.

Another essay of similar scope but of less value is by Arthur Hobson Quinn in *The Literature of the American People* (New York, 1951). Quinn's appreciative essay is long on biography and quotation from the poetry but rather short on synthesis of Bryant's ideas or on the question of his growth as a thinker. A recent article of general evaluation by Benjamin T. Spencer, "Bryant: The Melancholy Progressive" (*ESQ*, II Quarter 1966), argues that Bryant was a believer in a qualified millenium. Although Bryant thought there was a possibility for a limited utopia, he saw it finally displaced by the vicissitudes of human life. Spencer's short essay makes interesting points that he does not elaborate or document as thoroughly as he might have. (Bryant's views of human perfection and the vanity of human effort have been presented in articles that will be discussed subsequently.) The most recent general essay—and one that shows Bryant studies alive and well—is Alan B. Donovan's "William Cullen Bryant: 'Father of American Song'" (*NEQ*, Dec. 1968). Donovan praises Bryant for assimilating the prevailing intellectual trends of his day: the Puritan perceptual process, the neoclassic appreciation for the order of nature, and the Romantic emphasis on feeling and imagination. From these disparate traditions, says Donovan, Bryant formulated a theory of verse that is "the first native articulation of the art of poetry."

Albert F. McLean, Jr.'s TUSAS *William Cullen Bryant* is the only lengthy critical study of Bryant ever published and the most complete discussion of his achievement since McDowell's AWS introduction. The book minimizes biographical fact, although the introductory chapter does present an outline of Bryant's life. Here McLean concentrates on the influences on Bryant's mind; and his device of the concentric circles of Bryant's expanding sensibility, although perhaps too neat, provides a workable approach. McLean argues that Bryant's thought and art did not really mature in any important way, yet his discussion at times belies this point. The strength of his study is his assessment of about thirty important poems, particularly "Thanatopsis." McLean brings much material to bear upon his analysis of the poems and his discussion of Bryant's limited intellectual development (in some instances, perhaps too much for the length of the work); the book is informative, challenging, and polished. In its freshness of approach and in its able and learned synthesis of Bryant's varied career, it should be considered one of the important studies in Bryant criticism.

The topic of Bryant as a theoretical and practical critic has been treated in a variety of essays and longer works of American criticism; several books mentioned earlier—Nevins's, McDowell's AWS introduction, and McLean's—have some relevant discussions of this important aspect of Bryant's career. Bryant was an important early critic in American literature, second only to Poe in the pre–Civil War period, even if many of his ideas were largely derived from his readings in late eighteenth-century estheticians. He bridged the change in literary taste from the Neoclassical to the Romantic periods, and in the four *Lectures on Poetry*, which have yet to be thoroughly analyzed or evaluated, he wrote the earliest important critical statements in America. A significant influence on his theory was that of Archibald Alison's *Essays on the Nature and Principles of Taste* (Edinburgh, 1790), a work which argued that esthetic pleasure arises through mental associations. According to William P. Hudson, in "Archibald Alison and William Cullen Bryant" (*AL*, Mar. 1940), the young poet read this work before he went to Williams College and was impressed with Alison's ideas about nature as a healing power and poetry as a suggestive rather that imitative art, all ideas that influenced his later thinking. John P. Pritchard's three studies of American criticism, particularly *Return to the Fountains: Some Classical Sources of American Criticism* (Durham, N.C., 1942), which shows how Horace's and Aristotle's poetics influenced American critics, help explain Bryant's relevance as critic to his age. According to Pritchard, Bryant was knowledgeable about Horace and inadequately read in the *Poetics*, and Pritchard illustrates Bryant's classical influences with appropriate quotations from Bryant's works. References to Bryant are much more cursory in Pritchard's *Criticism in America* (Norman, Okla., 1956); most of them concern the influence of Coleridge on Bryant's theory. In *Literary Wise Men of Gotham: Criticism in New York, 1815–1860* (Baton Rouge, La., 1963), Pritchard refers generally to the power of Bryant's critical voice as an editor. For a contrasting opinion about Bryant's possible importance, one might consult Perry Miller's *The Raven and the Whale* (see *Biography*, above).

Other significant books and essays refer, at times rather sketchily, to Bryant's criticism in the context of broader discussions and offer background for the study of Bryant as critic: William Charvat's *The Origins of American Critical Thought, 1810–1835* (Philadelphia, 1936); Floyd Stovall's *American Idealism* (Norman, Okla., 1943), which argues that Bryant's eighteenth-century roots kept him from becoming fully a Romantic; John Stafford's *The Literary Criticism of "Young America": A Study in the Relationship of Politics and Literature, 1837–1850* (Berkeley, Calif., 1952); M. F. Heiser's "The Decline of Neoclassicism, 1801–1848," in *Transitions in American Literary History*, edited by Harry H. Clark (Durham, N.C., 1953); Harry H. Clark's "Changing Attitudes in Early American Literary Criticism: 1800–1840," in *The Development of American Literary Criticism*, edited by Floyd Stovall (Chapel Hill, N.C., 1955); and Clarence A. Brown's editing of *The Achievement of American Criticism: Representative Selections from Three Hundred Years of American Criticism* (New York, 1954), which reprints Bryant's first and second lectures on poetry and has a very general introductory essay on the background of American criticism but a very helpful bibliography of primary and secondary works. Rebecca Rio Jelliffe's dissertation (Calif.-Berkeley, 1964), "The Poetry of William Cullen Bryant: Theory and Practice" (*DA*, xxv, 4148–4149), discusses the influence of English and Scottish associationism on his criticism and poetry. Bryant's critical evaluations of contemporary works have received some notice in books and essays dealing with his *Evening Post* years: C. I. Glicksberg's "New Contributions in Prose by William Cullen Bryant" (*Americana*, Oct. 1936) looks back to his work as a reviewer for the *United States Review and Literary Gazette*; topics covered range over the novel, South American literature, poetry, education, science, and the two short stories by Bryant that appeared in this journal. The related matter of the oral delivery of his poems, particularly "The Ages," is discussed in C. I. Glickberg's "From the 'Pathetick' to the 'Classical': Bryant's Schooling in the Liberties of Oratory" (*AN&Q*, Mar. 1947) and a minor correction is suggested in Louis S. Friedland's "Bryant's Schooling in the Liberties of Oratory" (*AN&Q*, May 1947). Bryant was "the forefather of American prosody," according to Gay Wilson Allen, in *American Prosody* (New York, 1935), an extensive review of Bryant's mechanics which shows that he was, nevertheless, rather conservative in his use of stanzaic devices.

Scholarship on Bryant as critic has certainly not been exhausted, but the picture becomes more complete if we examine the research done on Bryant's interest in art and his relationships with important American artists of the Hudson River School. He wrote extensively on art, particularly on what he saw during his European travels, and found in the landscape paintings of his friends Thomas Cole and Asher Durand a pictorial view of nature which corresponded directly with his own efforts to verbalize responses to nature. Donald A. Ringe has written three excellent essays on Bryant and art; the most general one, "Bryant's Criticism of the Fine Arts" (*College Art Journal*, Fall 1957), considers Bryant's interest in art and those characteristics he most prized—realistic depiction, the presence of light and shadow, the harmony of the unified whole, and moral significance (which Ringe calls a "critical blindspot"). After arguing that Bryant was limited by his judgment of the choice of subject in an art work, the essay moves to a consideration of Bryant and Cole, a relationship more elaborately examined in Ringe's earlier essay, "Kindred Spirits: Bryant and Cole" (*AQ*, Fall 1954). According to Ringe, the two men considered the external scene an intermediary between man and God and were aware of man's need for profound humility in nature; both in their knowledge of Volney's *Ruins* accepted the concept of inexorable time that destroys man's creations. The essay concludes with comparisons of several of Bryant's poems and Cole's paintings in respect to theme and technique. In "Painting as Poem in the Hudson River Aesthetic" (*AQ*,

Spring 1960), Ringe discusses again the influence on Bryant (also Cole and Allston) of the Scottish associationists; because beauty is in the mind of the beholder, the artist tries to suggest rather than to imitate. To Bryant, however, poetry is superior to painting because it more directly involves the imagination and because language can be more suggestive than painting; the weakness of the artistic tendency toward allegorization is, to Ringe, the decided emphasis on content over form.

Ringe's essays provide a fuller treatment of the topic than does Charles L. Sanford's "The Concept of the Sublime in the Works of Thomas Cole and William Cullen Bryant" (*AL*, Jan. 1957), which although informative covers no new ground. Of relatively little value, except that it appeared before the other articles, is Evelyn L. Schmitt's "Two American Romantics—Thomas Cole and William Cullen Bryant" (*Art in America*, Spring 1953). The most thorough history of the relationship between Bryant and artists is James T. Callow's recent study, *Kindred Spirits: Knickerbocker Writers and American Artists, 1807–1855* (Chapel Hill, N.C., 1967). Callow discusses extensively Bryant's acquaintance with many contemporary artists, and he offers abundant documentation to support his study, which although somewhat workmanlike represents impressive scholarship. Even though this book does not treat Bryant's esthetics, it adds significantly to the earlier work on Bryant and art, one of the more fully researched topics in Bryant studies.

Bryant's poetry has also been treated extensively, in the general works discussed above and in essays that look more directly at the techniques and themes of his poems and place him in the context of his age. The following group of essays provides some background for a reading and evaluation of Bryant's poems, particularly "Thanatopsis." Along with these essays one must consider, of course, the scholarship on Bryant's theories as a critic and his opinions on art. Although Bryant's poetry is usually considered humorless, C. I. Glicksberg finds some humor in the poet's satiric political poems; "Bryant, the Poet of Humor" (*Americana*, July 1935) also identifies some of Bryant's poems in the *Evening Post*. One essay that argues Bryant's fundamental inability to break with traditional rhetorical poetry and write in a more private and therefore less didactic tone of "pure" poetry is Marvin T. Herrick's "Rhetoric and Poetry in Bryant" (*AL*, May 1935), which seems to suggest that Bryant's poetry would have been better had he written in the style of Poe. It should be noted that Bryant's traditions and influences, particularly those of the associationist philosophers and the New York artists, determined his influences—for better or worse—and his limitations as a poet are more attributable to his modest genius. Herrick cites "Thanatopsis" as an example of rhetorical verse and "The Rivulet," "March," "Summer," "To a Fringed Gentian," and "The Death of the Flowers" as examples of "pure" poems; whether the latter, because they are "pure," are better than the earlier contemplation of death is decidedly an open question. Behind Herrick's essay is the usual suggestion of Bryant's deficiencies, which George Arms discusses in his prefatory essay to a selection from Bryant in *The Fields Were Green: A New View of Bryant, Whittier, Holmes, Lowell and Longfellow, with a Selection of Their Poems* (Stanford, Calif., 1953); this essay was a reprint, with some slight changes, of "William Cullen Bryant: A Respectable Station on Parnassus" (*UKCR*, Spring 1949). Arms does not present a particularly new view of Bryant; and he tends to damn by faint praise, particularly since he points out so many inconsistencies in Bryant's thought and action and argues that a lack of complexity, thin diction, and an indecisiveness about theory were among Bryant's faults. Arms's essay is not without insight, but he seems, finally, to suggest that Bryant's station is more precarious than secure.

Roy Harvey Pearce, in his distinguished study *The Continuity of American Poetry* (Princeton, N.J., 1961), refers to Bryant as a representative poet whose works were meant to reinforce and confirm the people's opinions and prejudices, in short their dreams. For Pearce, Bryant's poems and, particularly, his essays on poetry are cautionary, an opinion with which Bernard Duffey disagrees in his essential article on nineteenth-century American poetry, "Romantic Coherence and Romantic Incoherence in American Poetry" (*Centennial Review* [Mich. State Univ.], Spring 1963, Fall 1964). Duffey considers that the "coherent" poets, among them Emerson and Bryant, spokesmen for the Protestant spirit, used religion or something akin as a medium of analogy; for the poets of "incoherence" the dogmas of naturalism acted upon their Protestant tenets of deism and evangelicalism. Duffey deals at length with Bryant and offers one of the most effective explanations ever advanced of Bryant's important historical position.

Evans Harrington, in "Sensuousness in the Poetry of William Cullen Bryant" (*University of Mississippi Studies in English*, 1966), says that the sensuousness of Bryant's poetry reveals Bryant's capacity to respond emotionally to man and nature. This article, which offers nothing particularly new, discusses Bryant's sensory responses to the world in his poems and concludes that since the sense of sight is most outstanding he uses pictorial imagery extensively. The majority of Bryant's poems are animated by simple perceptions, feelings, and instincts, says Harrington, although it is death that elicits the keenest and most persistent response from Bryant. Sydney Poger's "William Cullen Bryant: Emblem Poet" (*ESQ*, II Quarter 1966) suggests the possibility of further work in Bryant and the tradition of the emblem. Norman Ferdinand Christensen's 1960 University of Wisconsin dissertation, "The Imagery of William Cullen Bryant" (*DA*, XXI, 195), classifies Bryant's leading images (earth and flowers are used most frequently) and finds that they represent a clearly ordered world view that reflects tension between change and permanence.

Bryant's themes are discussed, of course, in all the writings on him; however, some essays treat his thinking about important nineteenth-century ideas and movements and try to determine his response to changing intellectual fashions. One of the continual topics in Bryant studies, about which there are differing opinions, is the influence of Puritanism on his cast of mind. Most critics are rightly aware of his development away from this tradition, as they certainly are in the case of Hawthorne, but they often disagree about its residual effects. An overemphasis on Bryant's Puritanism can be found in Norman Foerster's essay, "Bryant," in *Nature in American Literature* (New York, 1923), reprinted—with some elaboration on the differences between Wordsworth and Bryant—from "Nature in Bryant's Poetry" (*SAQ*, Jan. 1918). Foerster was among the first to enumerate the variety of concrete images in Bryant's poetry and to suggest that the sensuousness prominent in his relation to external nature precludes the indictment that he was essentially a cold man. Even though Foerster deemphasizes the occasional echoes of Wordsworthian sentiment in Bryant's poetry, he still subscribes in the main to the traditional view that Bryant was vastly influenced by the English poet and therefore deserves the title the American Wordsworth. Foerster's essay is still valuable.

Bryant's use of the European past has been documented rather thoroughly in numerous works (although influence studies are certainly not exhausted), but, as Donald A. Ringe points out in "Bryant's Use of the American Past" (*PMASAL*, 1956), Bryant also looked back to the short history of his own country not merely to respond to the call for nationalistic poetry but to emphasize the moral that when man places faith in material success and disregards spiritual values he is doomed to fall through the sin of pride. The theme of "the march of the generations" is central to Bryant's poetry, says Ringe, even though Bryant's illustrations were limited by the lack of "ruins" in the United States. The culture of the mound-builders was important to him, as Ringe notes and as Curtis Dahl explains in his well-researched essay, "Mound-Builders, Mormons, and William Cullen Bryant" (*NEQ*, June 1961). Bryant's references to this extinct civilization in "Thanatopsis" and "The Prairies" are supported by highly respected contemporary archaeological works, which Dahl discusses at length. As Ringe indicates, Bryant thought of the displaced American Indians as the victims of American settlement and portrayed them as proud, fierce, and magnificent in the face of death. Bryant's Indians (unlike Cooper's) have been only cursorily treated in an early essay by Jason Almus Russell, "The Romantic Indian in Bryant's Poetry" (*Education*, June 1928).

Bryant's interest in science was more extensive than is usually thought, as Frederick William Conner argues in *Cosmic Optimism: A Study of the Interpretation of Evolution by American Poets from Emerson to Robinson* (Gainesville, Fla., 1949). Bryant encouraged the dissemination of scientific knowledge but had no sympathy with Darwinian evolution or the frequent reaction of agnosticism; he did, however, accept the ideas of process, flux, and amelioration—the impermanence of human life and the perpetual renewal of nature in the cycle of seasons were Bryant's themes of change. To what extent new discoveries in geology influenced his belief in the dynamic state of nature within an inflexible rule of order, which derives its purpose and direction from God, is problematical, according to Donald A. Ringe's "William Cullen Bryant and the Science of Geology" (*AL*, Jan. 1955), which builds on Conner's previous work. Ringe believes that these ideas were present in Bryant's earlier works (like "The Ages") and that new geological studies gave him evidence for his own beliefs. His interest in a variety of contemporary scientific questions is briefly examined by C. I. Glicksberg in "William Cullen Bryant and Nineteenth-Century Science" (*NEQ*, Mar. 1950).

Bryant emphasized the emotional origin of art, but although he usually composed in moments of inspiration he revised cautiously and carefully in order to find the right word, usually a simple one, to express precisely his original idea. Bryant's poems were usually improved in this manner, as Tremaine McDowell shows in his important study, "Bryant's Practice in Composition and Revision" (*PMLA*, June 1937). McDowell examines early drafts in manuscript and compares them with the printed versions, particularly of "Thanatopsis." In "The Juvenile Verse of William Cullen Bryant" (*SP*, Jan. 1929), McDowell examines Bryant's early career from 1803 to about 1811 and illustrates his development through five stages: the religious, the satirical, the pastoral, the political, and the classical. This essay adds to our understanding of Bryant's practice in composition and includes some previously unpublished juvenilia written before "Thanatopsis." Richard E. Peck's "Two Lost Bryant Poems: Evidence of Thomson's Influence"

(*AL*, Mar. 1967) studies two uncollected poems, "The Seasons" (1806) and "A Thunderstorm" (1807), which foreshadow themes and natural settings treated by the adult poet. These early poems, Peck argues, were not inspired by Grandfather Snell's suggested topics or by overtly religious or political themes.

"Thanatopsis," among the most important early works in American literature, has received rather wide analysis. Bryant has always been considered something of a child prodigy, for it has always been assumed that the poem was composed in 1811, after his one year at Williams; Bryant, moreover, was inclined to date the poem earlier as he grew older. Among the more important arguments advanced is William Cullen Bryant II's contention that the poem was composed in 1815, during the time in which "The Yellow Violet," "Inscription for the Entrance to a Wood," and "To a Waterfowl" were written. Bryant's "The Genesis of 'Thanatopsis'" (*NEQ*, June 1948) treats in detail, including the influences of the Graveyard poets, Byron, Cowper, and Wordsworth, the years 1811 to 1815, when the young poet was growing into maturity and when his religious doubts and fear of death were intensifying. Bryant's argument has the force of logic, clear exposition, and documentation; this essay has done more than any other to clarify the poet's early years. Two earlier essays on "Thanatopsis" have long been considered of historical value and should be noted for their early attempts to suggest sources and revisions. Carl Van Doren's "The Growth of 'Thanatopsis'" (*Nation*, 7 October 1915) attributes to the Graveyard school a significant influence; William Cullen Bryant II, however, dates the reading of these works as 1813, rather than 1811. Willis Fletcher Johnson's "Thanatopsis, Old and New" (*NAR*, Nov. 1927) contends that the original introductory four quatrains provide a logical introduction to the poem and are harmonious with it; the article compares this magazine's first published version in 1817 with the revised poem in 1821, which included an introduction and conclusion that Johnson considers must have been written at the time of its first draft; both opinions are decidedly dubious.

The only recent essay on Bryant's major poem is Albert F. McLean, Jr.'s "Bryant's 'Thanatopsis': A Sermon in Stone" (*AL*, Jan. 1960), which sees in the poem a tripartite division like the Puritan plain-style sermons, with a pattern of *doctrine, reasons,* and *uses*—one which Bryant did not necessarily imitate consciously. McLean also discusses the question of voice, which is that of nature, a voice that could be detached and universal. (McLean in addition writes at length about the poem, expanding this essay and discussing sources and revisions, in his Twayne volume.) Yvor Winters contrasts in some interesting ways "Thanatopsis" with Stevens's "Sunday Morning" in *The Anatomy of Nonsense* (Norfolk, Conn., 1943); Arthur I. Ladu suggests the influence of Byron on one passage in "A Note on *Childe Harold* and 'Thanatopsis'" (*AL*, Mar. 1939); in "A Passage in 'Thanatopsis,'" Charles Washburn Nichols finds in the poem an echo of the Book of Job (*AL*, May 1939); Thomas O. Mabbott discusses the allusions inherent in "the Barcan wilderness" in "Bryant's 'Thanatopsis'" (*Expl*, Dec. 1952); and Vernon F. Snow presents reasons for Bryant's mentioning the Oregon River in "'Where Rolls the Oregon . . .'" (*WHR*, Summer 1956).

In the light of his suggested redating of "Thanatopsis," William Cullen Bryant II, in "The Waterfowl in Retrospect" (*NEQ*, June 1957), argues that manuscript evidence places the composition of "To a Waterfowl" between 1812 and 1815, several months before "Thanatopsis" instead of four years after it. Bryant's second most famous poem receives a good explication in Donald Davie's essay, "Bryant: 'To a Waterfowl,'" in *Interpretations: Essays on Twelve English Poems*, edited by John Wain (London, 1955). Cecil D. Eby, Jr., corrects one of Parke Godwin's notes in "Bryant's 'The Prairies': Notes on Date and Text" (*PBSA*, III Quarter 1962). "The Prairies" as a refutation of Buffon and others who believed in the degradation of America is treated well in Ralph N. Miller's "Nationalism in Bryant's 'The Prairies'" (*AL*, May 1949); and in "Bryant and James Grahame" (*N&Q*, 14 December 1935), Thomas O. Mabbott finds in Grahame's "The Sabbath" a possible source of "A Forest Hymn." G. Giovannini explains the meaning of "the primal Curse" in "Inscription for the Entrance to a Wood" (*Expl*, Apr. 1946). Bryant's tales receive brief comment in Fred Lewis Pattee's *The Development of the American Short Story* (New York, 1923) and Arthur Hobson Quinn's *American Fiction: An Historical and Critical Survey* (New York, 1936).

Comparative studies of Bryant and other writers are rather extensive. Whitman and Bryant have been contrasted in two essays: C. I. Glicksberg, in "Whitman and Bryant" (*Fantasy*, 1935), shows that the two men, although vastly different in poetic practice, thought kindly of one another's work; Bryant objected to the form of *Leaves of Grass* but must have disapproved of the content as well, says Glicksberg. Donald A. Ringe goes more deeply into their related philosophical world views in "Bryant and Whitman: A Study in Artistic Affinities" (*BUSE*, Summer 1956); Ringe compares their themes as religious nature poets, their imagery, and their prosodic techniques. Bryant, the poet of universal themes, respected Whittier's crusading verse, according to C. I. Glicksberg's "Bryant and Whittier" (*EIHC*, Apr. 1936). Tremaine

McDowell's "Edgar Allan Poe and William Cullen Bryant" (*PQ*, Jan. 1937) recounts Poe's curious adulation of Bryant, both as poet and public figure, and Bryant's lack of sympathy for Poe. In "Bryant on Emerson the Lecturer" (*NEQ*, Sept. 1939), C. I. Glicksberg considers Bryant's admiration if not wholehearted enthusiasm for Emerson's philosophy. Jacob H. Adler's "A Milton-Bryant Parallel" (*NEQ*, Sept. 1951) points out several similarities between the poets. Bryant's interest in French literature and his possible debt to Gautier is discussed generally in Joseph S. Schick's "William Cullen Bryant and Théophile Gautier" (*Modern Language Journal*, Jan. 1933), and the likelihood that Mallarmé knew of Bryant in Poe's reviews is suggested by Henry A. Grubbs in "Mallarmé and Bryant" (*MLN*, June 1947). Bryant's enthusiasm for German culture is examined in A. H. Herrick's "William Cullen Bryants Beziehungen zur Deutschen Dichtung" (*MLN*, June 1917) and in Henry A. Pochmann's *German Culture in America* (Madison, Wis., 1957). J. Chesley Mathews's "Bryant's Knowledge of Dante" (*Italica*, Dec. 1939) and "Bryant and Dante: A Word More" (*Italica*, Sept. 1958) cover that topic well. Bryant's interest in Spanish and Spanish-American culture was most profound, as Stanley T. Williams discusses at length in *The Spanish Background of American Literature* (Vol. II; New Haven, Conn., 1955). The controversy surrounding the possible meeting of Bryant and José María Heredia and whether Bryant translated his "Ode to Niagara" is treated in numerous essays, the most important of which in English are E. C. Hills, "Did Bryant Translate Heredia's 'Ode to Niagara'?" (*MLN*, Dec. 1919); José de Onís, "The Alleged Acquaintance of William Cullen Bryant and José María Heredia" (*Hispanic Review*, July 1957); Manuel Pedro González, "Two Great Pioneers of Inter-American Cultural Relations" (*Hispania*, May 1959); and in Frederick S. Stimson and Robert J. Bininger, "Studies of Bryant as Hispanophile: Another Translation" (*AL*, May 1959). Recent essays in Spanish are Manuel Pedro González, "Bryant y Heredia" (*Revista Nacional de Cultura* [Caracas], Nov.-Dec. 1962); and Héctor H. Orjuela, "Revaloración de una vieja polémica literaria: William Cullen Bryant y la oda 'Niágara' de José María Heredia" (*Thesaurus: Boletín del Instituto Caro y Cuervo*, May-Aug. 1964).

Bryant's contemporary reputation in Britain, France, and Germany is surveyed or referred to briefly in William B. Cairns's *British Criticisms of American Writings, 1815–1833* (Madison, Wis., 1922); Clarence Gohdes's *American Literature in Nineteenth-Century England* (New York, 1944); Robert W. Duncan's "The London *Literary Gazette* and American Writers" (*Papers on English Language and*

Literature, Spring 1965), which corrects Cairns; Harold Elmer Mantz's *French Criticism of American Literature Before 1850* (New York, 1917); Sidney L. McGee's *La littérature américaine dans la "Revue des deux mondes" (1831–1900)* (Montpellier, 1927); and Harvey W. Hewett-Thayer's *American Literature as Viewed in Germany, 1818–1861* (Chapel Hill, N.C., 1958).

The most important scholarly and critical writing on Bryant has appeared in the last forty years; the best of it has focused on Bryant as a product of his heritage and his age and has made a valuable contribution to our knowledge of American cultural history in the nineteenth century. The way of future Bryant scholarship seems clear; although the bibliographical problems are complex, new editions of the letters and poems are being planned or edited. Bryant's reputation may never change, but our awareness of his importance can and will.

James Fenimore Cooper

JAMES FRANKLIN BEARD

RANKING COOPER with Hawthorne, Melville, and James in *The Eccentric Design* (New York, 1959) as "the four greatest novelists America produced in the nineteenth century," Marius Bewley expressed a personal judgment of Cooper shared by an increasing minority of readers. Whether or not Bewley's unconventional estimate of the novelist's importance achieves popular critical acceptance, Cooper scholarship and criticism have been moving in the last two decades towards a major revaluation.

BIBLIOGRAPHY

The most generally useful bibliography of Cooper's publications is still *A Descriptive Bibliography of the Writings of James Fenimore Cooper* (New York, 1934) by Robert E. Spiller and Philip C. Blackburn. Introduced by Spiller's pioneering essay on Cooper's publishing practices, this work provides information of first editions and printings, lists many subsequent American and British reprints, and cites some translations into French, German, and a few other languages. It identifies sets, including some foreign sets, and locates many Cooper titles published serially or miscellaneously. Jacob Blanck's *Bibliography of American Literature* supplements Spiller and Blackburn with publication dates drawn from contemporaneous trade journals and with details on states, bindings, and other variants. Warner Barnes (*Library Chronicle of the University of Texas*, Summer 1962) lists further variants in twelve first editions. Copies of numerous American printings are located in Lyle H. Wright's *American Fiction, 1774–1850* (2d rev. ed., San Marino, Calif., 1969), and other copies are located in *The National Union Catalog* of *Pre-1956 Imprints*, vol. 121. Warner Barnes has prepared a census and finding list of Cooper imprints in English to 1861, containing almost 900 individual titles and 12 sets, which the American Antiquarian Society in Worcester, Massachusetts, plans to publish in its *Proceedings*. The most nearly complete short title list of Cooper's published works, excluding items in the edition proper, is given in Volume VI of *The Letters and Journals of James Fenimore Cooper* (6 vols., Cambridge, Mass., I and II 1960; III and IV, 1964; V and VI, 1968), edited by James Franklin Beard.

A new descriptive bibliography of Cooper editions in English, exhaustive in its study of settings, states, issues, concealed impressions, and variants of all kinds, is much needed. Incomplete but helpful guides to individual printings and sets of the French translations are contained in appendixes to Margaret M. Gibb's *Le Roman de Bas-de-Cuir: Etude sur Fenimore Cooper et Son Influence en France* (Paris 1927) and Marcel Clavel's *Fenimore Cooper: Sa Vie et Son Oeuvre: La Jeunesse, 1789–1826* (Aix-en-Provence, 1938). The most extensive list of Cooper editions published in France in French and English during the nineteenth century appears in *Catalogue Général des Livres Imprimés de la Bibliothèque Nationale* (Paris, 1897). Preston A. Barba, finding no other nineteenth-century novelist so widely circulated in Germany in translation, supplies a partial calendar of German translations to 1911 (*Indiana University Studies*, II, 1914). After the 1820s, German translations of Cooper are reported in the cumulative volumes of Christian Gottlob Ranser's *Vollständiges Bücher-Lexikon* and its successors. John DeLancey Ferguson, declaring Cooper to have been the most frequently translated American writer in Spain, gives a preliminary bibliography of Spanish translations in *American Literature in Spain* (New York, 1916). In his initial investigation of Italian translations, James Woodress discovers 148 editions of Cooper published in Italy between 1828 and 1964, approximately half of which were published after World War II (*Studi Americani*, 1965). Curiously, Valentina A. Libman's *Russian Studies of American Literature* (Chapel Hill, N.C., 1968), translated by R. V. Allen and edited by Clarence Gohdes, refers to few early translations, though Cooper was widely read in Russia in the nineteenth century in French, translated there into Hebrew, and certainly into Russian. Joseph Sabin's *Dictionary of Books Relating to America*, IV (New York, 1870) lists tantalizing examples of translations of Cooper; but there has never been a comprehensive study of translations, though Cooper's books have been translated into Dutch, Danish, Norwegian, Swedish, Polish, Finnish, Hungarian, Greek, Czech, Persian, and other languages. Indeed, the incomplete evidence suggests that no nineteenth-century American writer, not even Whitman, has been so widely translated.

Robert E. Spiller's selective, annotated list of books and articles about Cooper in the AWS *James Fenimore Cooper: Representative Selections* (New York, 1936) supersedes all earlier compilations. Good selective bibliographies for later scholarship and criticism are supplied in the *Bibliography* of *LHUS* (1948), its *Supplement* (1959), and in studies of Cooper by Marcel Clavel, Dorothy Waples, James Grossman, Donald A. Ringe, Warren S. Walker, Thomas Philbrick, Kay Seymour House, and others. Various specialized bibliographies are more exhaustive: Lewis Leary, *Articles on American Literature 1900–1950* (1954), James Woodress, *Dissertations in American Literature 1891–1966* (1968), Thomas F. Marshall, *An Analytical Index to American Literature* (1954), the yearly bibliographies in *Annual Bibliography of English Language and Literature*, *AL* and *PMLA*, and, since 1963, *American Literary Scholarship: An Annual*.

EDITIONS

Although editions of Cooper—individual and collected—are innumerable, no work by Cooper edited according to the most exacting modern critical standards has yet been published; and no complete collection of his fiction or nonfiction exists. Until definitive texts can be prepared, readers must rely on texts of varying and uncertain quality embodying inaccuracies characteristic of most nineteenth-century American texts. By selecting modern editions based on the earliest authoritative texts, students can at least minimize accumulated corruptions and indiscriminate modernizations.

Despite his impatience of detail, Cooper was far more demanding in his habits of composition, revision, and supervision of printers than his detractors have implied. He often revised manuscripts and proofs extensively and frequently corrected first editions and texts in successive printings, particularly between 1820 and 1833. Two incomplete collections of his fiction published before his death in 1851 are especially important for his alterations: works revised between 1831 and 1833 for Richard Bentley's "Standard Novels" series, and the twelve volumes of the Author's Revised Edition (*The Ways of the Hour* was not revised) issued by George P. Putnam (1849–1851). Stringer and Townsend's "Choice Edition" (1856–1858) matched eight new titles to the Putnam plates, and W. A. Townsend's Darley-illustrated edition (1858–1861) matched twelve more, with a total of thirty-two titles. Other American sets of the 1850s derived from old, often original plates. The Household Edition, published by Houghton, Mifflin and Company (also Hurd and Houghton), 1876, 1881–1884, in thirty-two volumes, is useful mainly for introductions (to fifteen of the volumes) by Susan Fenimore Cooper. For several decades the Mohawk Edition, published by G. P. Putnam's Sons, 1895–1896, and reissued at intervals, was the most accessible edition. The Greenwood Press, Westport, Connecticut, has recently reissued in facsimile the old double-columned P. F. Collier edition, 1891–1893, with the usual thirty-two titles in ten volumes, but with texts appallingly corrupt.

The continuing appeal of the best of Cooper's fiction, especially of the Leatherstocking Tales, is illustrated by the multiple reprints, mostly paperbacks, currently available. *The Pioneers* (1823), *The Last of the Mohicans* (1826), *The Prairie* (1827), *The Pathfinder* (1840), and *The Deerslayer* (1841) are individually available in series published by the New American Library, Washington Square Press, Airmont, and Dodd, Mead, with afterwords or introductions by James Grossman, Robert Spiller, Allan Nevins, John William Ward, Thomas Berger, and J. F. Beard. Other editions readily available and deserving mention are *The Pioneers* (Rinehart) introduced by Leon Howard, *The Last of the Mohicans* (Riverside) by William Charvat, *The Prairie* (Rinehart) by Henry Nash Smith, and *The Pathfinder* (Modern Library) by Norman Holmes Pearson. For readers mainly interested in Natty Bumppo, Allan Nevins's *The Leatherstocking Saga* (Pantheon, 1954; Modern Library, 1966) excerpts from the Leatherstocking Tales in chronological order passages relating to the hero and summarizes the omissions. Nevins's long introduction is informed and warmly sympathetic.

Thanks to an increasing demand and to the resources of modern publishing, more than half the remainder of Cooper's fiction has reappeared in one or more discrete editions during the last two decades. The AMS Press has announced a facsimile of the 1820 edition of *Precaution*. At least five editions of *The Spy* (1821) have been published and others are in process. *Tales for Fifteen* (1823), of which only four first editions are known, was reproduced in facsimile in 1959 by Scholars' Facsimiles & Reprints with an introduction by J. F. Beard. *The Pilot* (1824) and *The Red Rover* (1827) have held their own with one new edition, and *The Wept of Wish-ton-Wish* (1829) and *The Water-Witch* (1830) have each been announced in facsimile editions by the AMS and Scholarly presses. *The Bravo* (1831), edited for Twayne by Donald A. Ringe, and *Home as Found* (1838), introduced for Capricorn by Lewis Leary, exemplify for modern readers some of Cooper's most pungent social and political criticism. As a tribute to Gregory Lansing Paine, George F. Horner and Raymond Adams published in 1949 a new edition of the *Autobiography of a Pocket-handkerchief* (1843); and Allen Knots, Jr., prepared in 1956 an introduction and captions for a specially illustrated edition of *Afloat and Ashore* (1844). *Satanstoe* (1845), introduced by Robert L. Hough, was reprinted in 1962 by the University of Nebraska Press with the text of an earlier edition introduced by Robert E. Spiller and Joseph D. Coppock. Its sequel, *The Chainbearer* (1845), second volume in the Littlepage trilogy, was recently announced in facsimile from the first American edition by the AMS Press. Thomas Philbrick's edition of *The Crater* (1847) in the John Harvard Library series by Harvard University Press is a model of thoughtful, careful scholarship, though the text is not definitive. *The Sea Lions* (1849) has been reissued by the University of Nebraska Press with an introduction by Warren S. Walker; and *The Ways of the Hour* (1850) has been reproduced in facsimile from the first American edition in Gregg's series of American Novels of Muckraking, Propaganda, and Social Protest. The miscellaneous origins of these editions help to explain the absence of some of Cooper's most interesting fiction.

Much of Cooper's nonfiction has also been reissued in the last twenty years. An entirely new entry in the Cooper canon, *Early Critical Essays (1822) by James Fenimore Cooper*, consisting of book reviews written for *The Literary and Scientific Repository, and Critical Review*, was published in facsimile by Scholars' Facsimiles & Reprints in 1956, with an introduction and headnotes by J. F. Beard. *Notions of the Americans* (1828), introduced by R. E. Spiller, was reissued in a facsimile of the first American edition by the Ungar Publishing Company in 1963. *A Letter to His Countrymen* (1834) was reprinted in *Jahrbuch für Amerikastudien* (1960). *Gleanings in Europe* [:*France*] (1837) and *England* (1837) are available from the Kraus Reprint Company in texts edited by R. E. Spiller in 1928 and 1930; and *The American Democrat* (1838), reprinted with an introduction by H. L. Mencken in 1931, was reissued by Vintage in 1956 with a supplementary introductory note by R. E. Spiller. The *Democrat* is also available from Funk and Wagnalls and from Penguin, the latter edition edited and introduced by George Dekker and Larry Johnston. *The Chronicles of Cooperstown* (1838) is included in histories of Cooperstown, New York, reissued at intervals by publishers of the *Freeman's Journal*. Facsimiles of the French first (in English) of the *History of the Navy of the United States* (1839) and of the American first of *Lives of Distinguished American Naval Officers* (1846) were published in 1969 by the reprint houses of Gregg and Garrett respectively. *New York* (1864), part of the introduction to Cooper's uncompleted *Towns of Manhattan* reprinted as a separate in 1930 by William Farquhar Payson and introduced by Dixon Ryan Fox, is supplemented by J. F.

Beard, "The First History of Greater New York: Unknown Portions of Fenimore Cooper's Last Work" (*New-York Historical Society Quarterly*, Apr. 1953). Though not recently reprinted, R. E. Spiller's *James Fenimore Cooper: Representative Selections, with Introduction, Bibliography and Notes* remains a useful anthology of Cooper's nonfictional prose.[1]

Temporarily helpful as they have been and are, these editions are obviously not substitutes for a comprehensive, critical, unmodernized, annotated edition of Cooper's fictional and nonfictional works. That part of the Cooper canon available today is available generally in expensive older editions, expensive facsimile editions, or modern editions corrupt and uncritically modernized. Cooper scholars, in repeated conferences held under the auspices of the Center for Editions of American Authors of the Modern Language Association, have agreed that an inclusive, definitive editions of his writings is a desideratum; and preliminary studies for the forty-eight-volume collaborative project, to which the Cooper family has reserved manuscript rights, have been in progress for some years. Work on the earliest projected volumes, announced by the State University of New York Press, is proceeding in various locations under the joint sponsorship of the American Antiquarian Society and Clark University in Worcester, Massachusetts.

LETTERS AND MANUSCRIPTS

With the generous assistance of the Fenimore Cooper family, librarians, collectors, scholars, institutions, and foundations, one part of the larger effort, *The Letters and Journals of James Fenimore Cooper*, has been edited by J. F. Beard and published by the Belknap Press of Har-

---

1. Other miscellaneous writings by Cooper introduced by Spiller but not recently reissued are: an article on slavery in the United States written for the *Revue Encyclopédique* (Apr. 1827) and originally published in French, but first printed from the English manuscript in *AHR* (Apr. 1930); *Letter to Gen. Lafayette . . . and Related Correspondence on the Finance Controversy* (1831–1832), published (New York, 1931) for the Facsimile Text Society; and *The Lake Gun*, an allegorical short story published in *The New York Parthenon* in 1850, issued as a separate (New York, 1932) by William Farquhar Payson. *The Home Book of the Picturesque* (1852), containing Cooper's essay "American and European Scenery Compared," has been published in facsimile by Motley F. Deakin (Gainesville, Fla., 1967). J. A. Kouwenhoven (*Col*, Autumn 1938) has located a scene from Cooper's lost play *Upside Down* in W. E. Burton's *The Cyclopædia of Wit and Humor* (New York, 1858).

vard University Press.² This edition provides full, annotated texts of all letters and journals known and available to the editor when the work was in preparation. The texts are arranged in convenient chronological units, and each unit is preceded by a brief introduction. Volume VI contains the index. Texts of additional letters are being collected for publication in significant supplementary groups as they surface in the files of autograph dealers, collectors, and libraries. *Correspondence of James Fenimore-Cooper* (New Haven, Conn., 1922), edited by Cooper's grandson James Fenimore Cooper, contains letters to Cooper not reprinted in *Letters and Journals* and also "Small Family Memoirs," an account of her childhood by Susan Fenimore Cooper, daughter of the novelist. Lafayette's letters to Cooper, so far as they were then available, were edited by Stuart W. Jackson (*YULG*, Apr. 1934). Other important or interesting letters to Cooper, often summarized or quoted in *Letters and Journals*, have been or are being published with the collected letters of his correspondents.

As Cooper's literary executor, J. F. Beard has been responsible since 1948 for collecting and assembling facsimiles of letters, documents, and literary manuscripts whose holographs have become widely scattered in the United States and abroad since the novelist's death in 1851. The four largest collections are papers owned by the Fenimore Cooper family; the Cooper Collection of the Beinecke Rare Book and Manuscript Library, Yale University; the Clifton Waller Barrett Library of American Literature, University of Virginia; and the Berg Collection of the New York Public Library. The list most nearly complete for locations of Cooper's letters (some letters have new owners and new locations are known) is provided in *Letters and Journals*, vi. Cooper's literary manuscripts, like his letters, are widely scattered. Some, indeed, were scissored to pieces for nineteenth-century autograph collectors. Many have yet to be located, and until they are, work on the definitive edition of Cooper's writings will be impeded.

BIOGRAPHY

The earliest significant biographical treatment of Cooper is William Cullen Bryant's "Discourse on the Life, Genius, and Writings of J.

---

2. Reviewed, among others, by Perry Miller (*NYHTBR*, 10 April 1960), Kenneth Lynn (*The Reporter*, 23 June 1960), Oscar Cargill (*SatR*, 16 April 1960), R. E. Spiller (*NYTBR*, 15 May 1960), Lewis Leary (*VQR*, Autumn 1960; Summer 1965; Summer 1968), Willard Thorp (*NYH*, Oct. 1960; *NYHTBR*, 24 January 1965), Marcel Clavel (*EA*, Oct. 1963), and James H. Pickering (*NCF*, Dec. 1968, *NYH*, Oct. 1970).

Fenimore Cooper." Brief as it is, this encomium by a friend and literary confidant, delivered at the Public Memorial Meeting at Metropolitan Hall, New York City, on 25 February 1852 and printed with
other tributes in G. P. Putnam's *Memorial of James Fenimore Cooper*
(New York, 1852), remained for thirty years the closest approach to
formal biography. Believing that living celebrities should eschew biographies of themselves, Cooper supplied the scantiest biographical data
during his life for brief essays by Samuel Carter Hall and Rufus Wilmot
Griswold (see *Letters and Journals*, II, 58–60; IV, 340–347, 459–462)
and, shortly before his death, enjoined his family emphatically not to
authorize a biography. His motive may have been modesty or reticence,
truculence, or a fear that rehearsal of his quarrels might create new
unpleasantness for his family. His injunction destroyed any possibility
of immediate use of his papers and discouraged efforts to collect reminiscences and biographical documentation.

Recognizing Cooper's prohibition as a form of literary hari-kari,
some members of his family wished to disregard it. A few months after
his death, his publisher son-in-law Henry F. Phinney proposed to reissue
The American Democrat with a biographical sketch of the author.
Mrs. Cooper objected to the sketch as violating "my Husband's earnest
charge, against any authorized biography" and suggested instead the
inclusion of Cooper's replies to invitations from literary societies and
printers' organizations. In 1854, after their mother's death, Cooper's
daughters, acting apparently with the novelist's closest friend, Commodore William Branford Shubrick, made tentative arrangements with
Dr. James Wynne for "a memoir of about 500 octavo pages, giving the
chief incidents of [Cooper's] life, illustrated by his own journals . . .
interspersed with views of his works." This project failed also, seemingly
because Paul, the novelist's only son, shared his mother's stricter attitude. Cooper's daughter Susan, an author who understood the delete-
rious effect of the ban on accurate information, was left to sustain her
father's literary reputation as well as she could through fugitive publications. *Pages and Pictures* (1861), her selection of passages and illustrations from his fiction with her brief introduction, was conceived as
"a substitute for a Life of him." She later revised and extended these
introductions for the Household Edition of Cooper's *Works* (1876–
1884), published several autobiographical documents from Cooper's
papers in *Putnam's Magazine* (1868–1869), and wrote two articles
reminiscent of her childhood for the *Atlantic Monthly* (1887). Her
"Small Family Memories," begun in 1883 at the instance of her nephew,
Cooper's grandson and namesake, and published in his *Correspondence
of James Fenimore-Cooper*, is an informal record of her life to 1828.

Susan Fenimore Cooper's accounts of her father and her family remain invaluable biographical sources, though she wrote from memory and must be constantly checked and supplemented.

When Yale's great Chaucer scholar Thomas R. Lounsbury agreed to write the American Men of Letters Cooper (New York, 1882), the family attitude had not relaxed. Some twenty years later, Lounsbury stated in a letter to DeWitt Miller (owned by the writer and dated New Haven, 9 January 1902):

The writing of the life of Cooper was . . . a sort of *tour de force*. I had little knowledge of him when I set about it, had no special interest in his writings, & had read but few of them. Warner [Charles Dudley Warner, editor of the series] stood over me with a club & said I must take the man's life; & so, like a good or a bad boy, I did.

Lounsbury's assassination of Cooper the man, unlike Mark Twain's assassination of Cooper the artist a bit later, was not intentional. Cut off from most documentary material, Lounsbury rummaged wherever he could find information, in a few files of letters preserved by Cooper's friends, but especially in newspapers and other ephemeral printed sources, many of them hostile to Cooper. His book was impressive for its wit, industry, and style; but no biography written under these circumstances could be satisfactory. Susan Cooper, always an unwilling agent in enforcing her father's restriction, complained to the publisher Houghton Mifflin in a letter quoted by James Grant Wilson in *Bryant, and His Friends* (New York, 1886):

Mr. Lounsbury's book has been a disappointment. While he has done justice to the high moral tone of the novelist, the sketch of his social character is absurdly distorted. He represents Cooper as a cold, gloomy cynic; in fact, he was generally considered a very agreeable companion, full of animated conversation. His social feelings were very strong. He was remarkably fond of children, and very indulgent to young people, entering with zest into their pleasures. Had Mr. Lounsbury known Cooper personally, he would have written a very different book. Some of his comments are absurdly erroneous, as for instance where he says Cooper was a "Puritan of the Puritans"; for never was there a nature more opposed to the narrow prejudices of Puritanism. And what could be more absurd than to say that he had a lingering weakness for poor George the Third!

Years later, reliving his chagrin when Houghton Mifflin showed him Miss Cooper's letter, the exasperated biographer wrote, in the letter to DeWitt Miller previously quoted:

Susan was a nice old lady, but not gifted with much penetration, which however had its compensation in a peculiar capacity to misunderstand. I represented Cooper as being by *nature* a Puritan of the Puritans: dear Susan thought I referred to his *beliefs*, not being aware that Puritans existed in England centuries before Puritanism, or special Puritanic views which we associate with the name. One has, however, to content himself with supplying knowledge: he can not supply comprehension.

In the absence of more satisfactory sources, subsequent Cooper scholars have accepted Lounsbury's scholarly distortions and Susan Cooper's unscholarly reminiscences, many of them shadowy memories from her childhood, as more authoritative than they are. Miss Cooper, despite Lounsbury, was an intelligent woman; and she understood her father better than his biographer, though she did not write about him as a scholar might. Lounsbury, though he lacked the intimate knowledge to portray Cooper as a complex human being, had sufficient scholarly aplomb to compose a "model biography," which, according to the *LHUS* in 1948, "is not yet superseded."

Actually, the task of correction was begun in the brief, admirably balanced Beacon Biography *James Fenimore Cooper* (Boston, 1900) by W. B. Shubrick Clymer, who inherited the holographs of Cooper's letters to Clymer's grandfather, Admiral Shubrick. Quoting generously from these letters to demonstrate Cooper's personal warmth and social and political acuteness, Clymer attributed much of the novelist's acerbity to his "Horatian hatred of the mediocrity which is a foe to excellence." Clymer's contribution was augmented by Mary E. Phillips, whose *James Fenimore Cooper* (New York, 1913) was designed as a "simply told *personal life*," profusely illustrated by pictures "of men, women, places and things" figuring in the story of the man. In her search for fresh biographical materials, Miss Phillips was greatly assisted by Cooper's grandnephew George Pomeroy Keese, who had known the novelist well during the last eighteen years of his life, had collected assiduously, and had published his own reminiscences (*Harper's Weekly*, Supplement, 29 July 1871). Though Clymer and Phillips owed much to Lounsbury (and were perhaps less exacting in details than he), they began at last to demonstrate that, despite Lounsbury's forbidding portrait, the author of the Leatherstocking Tales was an interesting, complicated, and, in many respects, delightful man.

Biographical study of Cooper entered a new phase with the publication of the *Correspondence of James Fenimore-Cooper*, edited by Cooper's grandson. Aware of the need for a fuller understanding of his grandfather, the editor selected from his collection of family papers letters he thought would contribute most to an understanding of Cooper and his times. However, he warned in his introduction, he considered *all* the sources then available to be inadequate for the purpose of satisfactory biography; and he expressed Victorian reservations about publishing details of a private life. His *Correspondence* contained letters to and from Cooper in about equal proportions, with many passages silently expunged. Without purporting to be comprehensive or cohesive, it afforded unsuspected glimpses of a fascinating social and intellectual life marked by extraordinary vigor, variety, and depth of involvement. One reviewer, Henry Seidel Canby, expressed amazement that "a great romancer, producing a shelf of books in his lifetime, of which a number attained the widest international reputation . . . did not take his work seriously except as a means of livelihood and reputation." Instead of cultivating aesthetic, critical, or stylistic refinements, Canby continued in *Definitions* (Second Series, New York, 1924), "the man's intellect turned always towards social criticism or politics."

The young Robert E. Spiller, whose publications were to have a decisive influence on Cooper scholarship and criticism, made the same discovery independently and unexpectedly at about the same time, while preparing a chapter on Cooper for his first book, *The American in England* (New York, 1926). Spiller recalls (*NYH*, Oct. 1954) that while examining Cooper's travel books in what he imagined would be a routine encounter he suddenly found in the novelist's "struggle to discover a meaningful relationship between literary expression and American life . . . the epitome of the birth-struggle of a national culture." This recognition of Cooper's unsuspected stature by Spiller, repeated soon after by Vernon L. Parrington, John F. Ross, and others, invested Cooper with a new and exciting importance as a Representative Man, a writer whose intellectual and emotional tensions tallied with peculiar sensitivity to the tensions of the evolving national culture. To study Cooper was to study American civilization at a crucial point in its development, to probe its contradictions, and to discern its past and future patterns. It is this emblematic, often enigmatic Cooper, responding profoundly and fearlessly to the challenges of his age, who attracted Spiller and his colleagues. The received image of Cooper today is, to a remarkable extent, an elaboration of the image they created.

Recovery of biographical detail was not, however, a primary consideration for scholars interested in Cooper's social and political ideas. John F. Ross referred to his *Social Criticism of Fenimore Cooper* (Berkeley, Calif., 1933) as a "study of American civilization as reflected in Cooper's work," and Parrington and Mencken relied on the biographical sources already available. Even Spiller presented his seminal study *Fenimore Cooper: Critic of His Times* (New York, 1931) as "a record of the evolution of a point of view" and "not biography in the ordinary sense." Nevertheless, Spiller displayed in this book, in his editions of

France (New York, 1928) and *England* (New York, 1930), in his introduction to *James Fenimore Cooper: Representative Selections*, and in numerous other introductions and articles, a full appreciation of the uses of biographical and cultural detail; and he extended factual knowledge at every opportunity, especially in his careful retracing of Cooper's European travels. Spiller's major contribution in the 1930s was his bold, imaginative comprehension of the intricate gyrations of Cooper's mind as it grappled with the significant issues of his times. These issues, Spiller saw, could be most effectively defined in a biographical matrix. If this emphasis neglected Cooper the artist, except as Cooper employed his art as a vehicle for his ideas, it seemed a valid and necessary reversal of Lounsbury's portrait of Cooper the irritable malcontent who forsook his art to meddle stubbornly and irresponsibly in social and political preachment. Most important, Spiller's approach opened a new, serious, timely dimension for other scholars.

In the wake of Spiller's early books appeared Henry W. Boynton's *James Fenimore Cooper* (New York, 1931), a biography that professed to be "not a book of criticism, but a study of a man whose genius stands beyond challenge while his personality, singularly complex, baffling, and deserving of study has been almost unregarded." Boynton was in fact less concerned to penetrate baffling complexities than to explore human interest in his subject. Shown mainly in action, his Cooper is the bluff, impulsive, good-humored sailor, tenacious in friendship or hostility, uxorious, combative, vain and tactless at times, but dedicated with peculiar fervor to his image of the United States, "the *patria*, the mystical entity for which men gladly die." The late Dorothy Waples credited Boynton with restoring Cooper "as a hearty, active, attractive man, inclined to argue, certainly, and loving to shine, but thoroughly kind, gay, and attractive." Boynton's breezy, almost garrulous style and his access, greater than that of earlier biographers, to manuscript sources enabled him to give vivid surface impressions; but the man Boynton portrayed with so much relish is hardly the "man whose genius stands beyond challenge." The distance between the two, measured in intellect and imagination, is immense.

Two potentially important studies of Cooper's reputation have a semibiographical focus: Ethel R. Outland's *The "Effingham" Libels on Cooper* (Madison, Wis., 1929) and Dorothy Waples's *The Whig Myth of James Fenimore Cooper* (New Haven, Conn., 1938). Drawing mainly on contemporaneous newspapers and magazines, Miss Outland attempted to document Cooper's complicated quarrels with the press, including his libel suits against Andrew Barber, William Leete Stone, Park Benjamin, Thurlow Weed, James Watson Webb, and Horace

Greeley. Though she reprinted useful materials, her sources were far less complete and more strongly biased than she realized; and her conclusion that Cooper's suits were influential in shaping New York State's libel laws has been contested by legal authorities. Miss Waples's more ambitious study sought to explain how America's most popular novelist, more through his virtues and circumstances than through his faults, became one of the most unpopular men of his time. Her thesis, that Cooper was an innocent victim of a cabal of Whig editors because he was more than a nominal party Democrat, proposed a drastic oversimplification. Cooper was undoubtedly victimized by the Whig press, but the nature of his involvement was far more complex than Miss Waples suggested. Her book is perhaps more valuable for the evidence she collected than for the restrictive logic of her argument.

Much the weightiest and most methodic biographical study is Marcel Clavel's *Fenimore Cooper: Sa Vie et Son Oeuvre, La Jeunesse, 1789–1826*, accompanied by *Fenimore Cooper and His Critics: American, British and French Criticisms of the Novelist's Early Work* (Aix-en-Provence, 1938). These works, which earned Clavel his *doctorat-ès-lettres* at the Sorbonne and a Montyon prize from the French Academy, deserve much more attention than they have received from American scholars. Their preparation, which Clavel has charmingly described in *À Propos du Centenaire de la Mort de Fenimore Cooper et du Congrès de Cooperstown de Septembre 1951: A French Tribute to James Fenimore Cooper* (Aix-en-Provence, 1956), required fifteen years of research in the United States, England, and France, and a personal devotion matched by few other Cooper scholars. While not definitive, even for the portion of Cooper's life treated, Clavel's work was encyclopedic in aim and scope and remarkably complete considering the sources available to him. His biographical volume contains long, appreciative, academic discussions of six of Cooper's early books, discussions that contravened the popular tendencies in the United States to belittle Cooper and his art. Though World War II interrupted Clavel's plan to complete his work on the same ample scale, he has remained an unabashed champion, describing Cooper in 1951 as "still one of my most constant and congenial companions." His contributions to Cooper scholarship have been impressive, all the more because so few American scholars have considered Cooper worthy of such sustained attention.

In the second American Men of Letters *James Fenimore Cooper* (New York, 1949; Stanford, Calif., 1967), James Grossman, a practicing lawyer of much taste, wit, and discernment, retold Cooper's story with interpretive comments on his works. The richness of this book lies mainly in its happy blend of curiosity, enthusiasm, sympathy, restraint, and intuition. Though his research in primary sources was limited, Grossman's psychological insights are rewarding. He recognizes, for example, that Cooper's most emphatic public gestures often contradicted his real feelings. Grossman is not, as an experienced barrister, dismayed by Cooper's legal squabbles. His critical remarks are also perceptive, though his final estimate of Cooper's art is ambivalent. Cooper "was a loose, slovenly writer throughout his entire career," says Grossman of *The Spy*, "but on great occasions, especially in his early work, he kept quiet so well that we can only wonder idly how he learned such restraint, or whether—and this is perhaps the highest form of critical praise—he really knew what he was doing." If so, Grossman never tells. Perhaps it does not matter. His often brilliant seriatim remarks, betraying the strong hold of Cooper's fiction on a highly sophisticated mind, may reveal more than Grossman is willing to admit explicitly. Despite some condescension, his book remains possibly the best one-volume introduction to Cooper the man and his writings.

Grossman pointed to the crux of the modern biographical problem when he commented that "too much is known about [Cooper] to accept the literary personality at face value, too little to create a man independently of it." Largely, one suspects, because of this crucial dearth of biographical information, subsequent book-length studies of Cooper have employed biographical detail mainly as a convenient framework for critical discussion. The disappointing state of our information is not the fault of Cooper's biographers or of the authors of the several valuable biographical articles,[3] but the inevitable result of the failure of his family and friends, who wished to respect his ban on a biography, to collect data and documents under systematic supervision. The loss is, of course, irreparable, but not total. Recent research confirms what earlier scholars had suggested—that much that was supposed irretrievably lost has, in fact, miraculously survived. The publication of Cooper's *Letters and Journals*, it should be noted, is the first phase of a necessarily slow, collaborative effort to increase the biographical store. The second phase, drawing on a very much larger quantity of documentation, should be the publication of a critical biography which the writer has had in progress for some years.

---

3. Among the more useful biographical articles are studies of Cooper's Otsego inheritance by Lyman H. Butterfield (*NYH*, Oct. 1949; Oct. 1954), of his naval career by Louis H. Bolander (*United States Naval Institute Proceedings*, Apr. 1940), and of the Bread and Cheese Club by Nelson F. Adkins (*MLN*, Feb. 1932) and Albert H. Marckwardt (*AL*, Jan. 1935).

CRITICISM

Source Studies

While source studies of Cooper have followed various patterns, reflecting his extensive knowledge of men, things, and books, all or almost all have had to depend on evidence in the fiction itself. No catalog of Cooper's reading or library could be complete, and information about his personal life sufficiently detailed to confirm suspected real-life sources is largely missing. This accidental incompleteness of the record does not prove Cooper naive or untutored. The student of sources and influences must, in fact, consider that he was an omnivorous reader (of fiction in his youth and of nonfiction in his maturity), that he collected and dispersed the equivalent of several private libraries, and that he registered sensitively and retentively in his writings impressions of an extremely varied life.

In *James Fenimore Cooper: An Introduction and Interpretation* (New York, 1962) and in articles (see especially *NYH*, Oct. 1954), Warren S. Walker shows how Cooper employed many familiar elements of folk culture: traditional character types, legends of the supernatural, Negro lore, folkways, and dialects. He lists (*MF*, No 2, 1953) several hundred proverbs from the fiction. He argues persuasively that much of the popular appeal of Cooper's frontiersmen, sailors, Indians, Yankees, squatters, and Negroes rests on the authentic folk flavor of their manners, habits, dialectal peculiarities, beliefs, and superstitions. James H. Pickering (*New York Folklore Quarterly*, Mar. 1966) comments on Cooper's skillful use of the folk festival of Pinkster in *Satanstoe*; and W. H. Bonner (*MLN*, Jan. 1946) shows how he drew variously on the legend of Captain Kidd in *The Red Rover*, *The Deerslayer*, *The Sea Lions*, and *The Water-Witch*. John H. Clagett (*Southern Folklore Quarterly*, Dec. 1966) and Thomas L. Philbrick (*James Fenimore Cooper and the Development of American Sea Fiction*, Cambridge, Mass., 1961) indicate Cooper's firsthand knowledge and use of folklore of the sea.

Even before Lewis Cass remarked (*NAR*, Apr. 1828) that Cooper's Indians followed "the book of Mr. Heckewelder, instead of the book of nature," the authenticity of Cooper's portrayal of Indian life had been questioned; and commentary on this subject still accumulates. Such fastidious Indian historians as Paul A. W. Wallace (*American Philosophical Society Proceedings*, No 4, 1952; *NYH*, Oct. 1954) and Arthur C. Parker (*NYH*, Oct. 1954) complain that Cooper was insufficiently expert as ethnologist to distinguish fact from bias in the Indian authorities he employed. That he was remarkably faithful to these authorities, nevertheless, Gregory L. Paine (*SP*, Jan. 1926), J. A. Russell (*Journal of American History*, First Quarter 1929), and John T. Frederick (*PMLA*, Dec. 1956) agree. Indeed Edwin L. Stockton, Jr., in his intensive investigation of *The Influence of the Moravians upon the Leather-Stocking Tales* (*Transactions of the Moravian Historical Society*, 1964) shows that such celebrated exploits as those involving "moccasin lore," "bent Twigs," and "animal-skin masquerades" derive not from Cooper's supercharged fancy but from Heckewelder, who, Stockton also suggests, influenced the presentation of religious and social ideas in the Leatherstocking Tales. In short, while Cooper obtained most of his information on Indian life at second hand, he was as faithful to his sources as his knowledge and the exigencies of his craft allowed. He did not, like many of his critics, confuse the boundaries of historical and imaginative truth.

Much heated, inconclusive, and doubtfully useful speculation has arisen from the search for real-life prototypes of two Cooper characters: Harvey Birch and Natty Bumppo. Tremaine McDowell in "The Identity of Harvey Birch" (*AL*, May 1930) explores thoroughly and dismisses the often-advanced claims of Enoch Crosby (subject of H. L. Barnum's *The Spy Unmasked; or, Memoirs of Enoch Crosby, Alias Harvey Birch*, New York, 1828) and other proposed models for the hero of *The Spy*. James S. Diemer (*AL*, May 1954) nominates a new candidate, John Champe. Warren S. Walker's "The Prototype of Harvey Birch" (*NYH*, Oct. 1956) dismisses Champe and suggests that Harvey's exploits were based on the combined adventures of the "Culvers" (Abraham Woodhull and Robert Townsend), secret agents described in Morton Pennypacker's *General Washington's Spies on Long Island and in New York* (Brooklyn, N.Y., 1939). Dispute concerning the prototype of Natty Bumppo involves claims of Nathaniel and David Shipman, both hunters whom the youthful Cooper may have known. When Nathaniel's protagonists planned a monument at his grave (behind the Baptist Church in Hoosick Falls, New York, not on the prairie), descendants of David (buried at Fly Creek, near Cooperstown) threatened suit. Edith Beaumont summarizes this hundred-year-long, mock-epic contest, fought in the local New York State press, in *The Valley Sampler* (Bennington, Vt., 24, 31 July 1969). Carl Suesser (*Westermanns Monatschefte*, May 1934) nominates a German prototype, Johann Adam Hartmann.

A more authentic genealogy of the Leatherstocking Tales, as Joel Porte suggests in *The Romance in America* (Middletown, Conn., 1969), would include Homer and Milton; for Cooper's writings are thoroughly indigenous to the western literary tradition. John J. McAleer (*NCF*,

Dec. 1962), identifying only a few of Cooper's Biblical analogies as "tentative experiments in symbolism," explains them as efforts to expose "the practices of Calvinism as they had survived in nineteenth-century America." E. P. Vandiver (*Shakespeare Assoc. Bull.*, Apr. 1940; *PMLA*, Dec. 1954) maintains that in 1,089 lines drawn from 36 plays Cooper displays thorough assimilation of Shakespeare, even of the lessser plays, revealing Shakespeare's influence in imaginative suggestions and characterizations as well as in functional use of quotations. W. B. Gates, "Cooper's Indebtedness to Shakespeare" (*PMLA*, Sept. 1952), finds in one-third of Cooper's fiction incidents and plot elements apparently derived from Shakespeare and many significant adaptations of character. The subtlety of these echoes, Gates notes, shows that Shakespeare's influence operated on a subconscious as well as a conscious level. Analogous investigations would disclose Cooper's heavy indebtedness to other earlier classic authors and also to such contemporaries as Wordsworth and Byron.

Commenting on Sir Walter Scott's assumed originality as a writer of romance, Cooper observed (*Knickerbocker Mag.*, Apr. 1838) that Jane Porter's *The Scottish Chiefs* (1810) was a work of Scott's "own country, class, and peculiar subject, differing from a Waverly [1814] merely in power." Cooper saw his pattern of romance, like Scott's, as a generic synthesis of earlier fictional idioms, including Scott's; and he was vexed, for other reasons as well, by his unflattering cognomen, "the American Scott." The most recent and perceptive treatments of this still-controversial subject are in Donald Davie's *The Heyday of Sir Walter Scott* (London, 1961) and George Dekker's *James Fenimore Cooper: The Novelist* (London, 1967; New York, 1968). Davie and Dekker both argue that one of the best approaches to an understanding of Cooper is through an understanding of Scott. An unpublished dissertation, "The Personal and Literary Relationships of Sir Walter Scott and James Fenimore Cooper" (North Carolina, 1950) by George W. Walker, also investigates the Cooper-Scott relationship. Barrie Hayne, "Ossian, Scott and Cooper's Indians" (*JAmS*, July 1969), mediates the seemingly conflicting demonstration of Georg Fridén in *James Fenimore Cooper and Ossian*, Essays and Studies on American Language and Literature, VIII (Upsala, 1949), that the rhetoric of Cooper's Indians derives from Byron and Ossian and the contention of John T. Frederick, "Cooper's Eloquent Indians" (*PMLA*, Dec. 1956), that it derives from transcriptions and translations of Indian speech by Heckewelder and other American authorities. Hayne explains the similarities of primitive elegiac speech in Ossian, Scott, Cooper, and American Indian sources by assuming that it expressed a contemporaneous concept of a decorous language for the melancholy contemplation of dying races.

Efforts to trace specific influences by adducing close parallels between Cooper's fiction and that of other novelists have not been notably successful. Thus, H. H. Scudder (*SR*, Apr.–June 1928), seeking to show that *Precaution* was written in imitation of Jane Austen's *Pride and Prejudice*, and G. E. Hastings (*AL*, Mar. 1940), that it was more probably Jane Austen's *Persuasion*, tell us more about Cooper's general indebtedness to the women novelists than they do about the specific inspiration for *Precaution*. The parallels between *The Headsman* and Balzac's *Jésus-Christ en Flandres*, described by Thomas R. Palfrey (*MP*, Feb. 1932), may or may not be accidental. Quite different is the case for Cooper's obvious and extended borrowings from *Gulliver's Travels* in *The Monikins*, fully investigated by Willi Müller in *The Monikins von J. F. Cooper, in ihrem Verhältnis zu Gulliver's Travels von J. Swift* (Rostock, 1900). As W. B. Gates remarks (*MLN*, June 1952) in considering Cooper's indebtedness to *Robinson Crusoe* in *The Crater*, Cooper deliberately invites comparison of his hero and Defoe's.

Following a regionalist approach, Joan D. Berbrick in *Three Voices from Paumanok* (Port Washington, N.Y., 1969) traces the influence of Long Island—its geography, people, history, folklore, and associations—on the writings of Cooper, Bryant, and Whitman.

Insofar as Cooper derived facts, details, and substantive suggestions for his fiction from printed sources, he usually preferred nonfiction, especially works of history, biography, travel, exploration, and social, economic, and political commentary. Students of these sources agree on the thoroughness of his assimilation. The borrowings present themselves, as James H. Pickering has accurately observed, as a conglomeration of bits and pieces. Since most such studies depend on direct or indirect disclosures by Cooper, who was characteristically coy on the subject, many of his printed sources may still be unidentified.

The more sensitive source studies demonstrate that Cooper used his materials freely as an artist, varying his method from book to book to obtain the total effect desired. Thus, as Thomas Philbrick indicates in "The Sources of Cooper's Knowledge of Fort William Henry" (*AL*, May 1964), Marcel Clavel in *Fenimore Cooper: Sa Vie et Son Oeuvre* and David P. French (*AL*, Mar. 1960) probably erred in ascribing to Cooper's treatment of historical events in *The Last of the Mohicans* the circumstantial care he lavished on them in *Lionel Lincoln* and *Mercedes of Castile*, works which were historical novels in a very special sense. E. S. Muszynska-Wallace's "The Sources of *The Prairie*" (*AL*,

May 1949) suggests the subtle imaginative process by which details from Cooper's Indian sources were intermingled and fused in the scenes of the fiction. Emilio Goggio (*RR*, July-Sept. 1929) asks implicitly the question as to how, if at all, Cooper's use in good faith of possibly misleading historical sources in *The Bravo* complicates the critic's task. Studies which inform and greatly enrich knowledge of Cooper's use of sources are articles by Horace H. Scudder (*PMLA*, Sept. 1947) on *Homeward Bound*, by Donald M. Goodfellow (*AL*, Nov. 1940) on *Mercedes of Castile*, by R. H. Ballinger (*AL*, Mar. 1948) on *The Two Admirals*, by Dorothy Dondore (*AL*, Mar. 1940) and James H. Pickering (*AL*, Jan. 1967) on *Satanstoe*, by James H. Pickering (*NYH*, Apr. 1968) on *Wyandotte*, by Horace H. Scudder (*AL*, May 1947) and W. B. Gates (*AL*, May 1951) on *The Crater*, and by W. B. Gates (*PMLA*, Dec. 1950) on *The Sea Lions*.

Influence Studies

No thorough, truly comprehensive study of Cooper's influence exists, though his writing had enormous immediate impact and left effects readily traceable in the patterns of American culture. The diversity and vagaries of his literary reputation have complicated and delayed even limited syntheses, though Willard Thorp's excellent brief paper "Cooper Beyond America" (*NYH*, Oct. 1954) gives a foretaste of their potential interest and value.

Curiously, since Cooper was the major shaper of American romance in the 1820s and 1830s, his influence even on such contemporaries as Catharine M. Sedgwick, James Hall, John P. Kennedy, Daniel Thompson, and John Esten Cooke seems not to have been systematically investigated, though Alexander Cowie in *The Rise of the American Novel* (New York, 1948) and Ernest E. Leisy in *The American Historical Novel* (Norman, Okla., 1950) point invitingly in this direction. C. Hugh Holman (*AL*, May 1951) differentiates carefully the influence of Scott and Cooper on the romances of William Gilmore Simms, suggesting that Cooper might have been a better model than Scott for Simms's Revolutionary romances; and Edward P. Vandiver, Jr. (*MLN*, Apr. 1955) concludes that Simms's Porgy in *The Partisan* was based, in part, on Cooper's Lawton in *The Spy* and his Polwarth in *Lionel Lincoln*. Nathalia Wright (*AQ*, Fall, 1952) traces a generic kinship between Cooper's Steadfast Dodge in *Homeward Bound* and Melville's Frank Goodman in *The Confidence Man*, and Morton L. Ross (*AL*, Nov. 1965) identifies Captain Truck's "mania of introducing" in *Homeward Bound* with that of Captain Boomer in *Moby-Dick*.

While more an accomplished essay in literary history than a study of influences, Thomas L. Philbrick's *James Fenimore Cooper and the Development of American Sea Fiction* documents admirably Cooper's formative influence on American nautical fiction. Philbrick shows how Cooper's early sea tales established an "idealized conception of maritime life" for novelists like Joseph C. Hart and short story writers like William Leggett in the 1820s and 1830s and how subsequent efforts by Cooper and his followers to construct a "meaningful alternative to that conception" included experiments by Edgar Allan Poe, Richard H. Dana, Jr., Robert M. Bird, and Charles J. Peterson. The imitations of Cooper's sea tales by E. Z. C. Judson ("Ned Buntline") and others in the 1840s parallel the early flood of imitations of Cooper's frontier fiction. Unfortunately, limits of scope do not permit Philbrick to compare Cooper's nautical romances to those of Frederick Marryat, Eugène Sue, Joseph Conrad, and countless other writers who profited from his example.

Curiosity about Cooper's British influence seems not to have progressed beyond George Wherry's reminder (*N&Q*, 16 September 1911) that Thackeray modeled Col. Newcome's death scene on Leatherstocking's. Selective summaries of contemporaneous British reviews are provided in William B. Cairns's *British Criticisms of American Writings, 1815–1833* (Madison, Wis., 1922) and Marcel Clavel's *Fenimore Cooper and His Critics: American, British and French Criticisms of the Novelist's Early Work.*

Cooper's early influence in France has been much more actively investigated, beginning with George D. Morris's *Fenimore Cooper et Edgar Poe: D'après la Critique Française du Dix-neuvième Siècle* (Paris, 1912), which surveys French criticism of Cooper in such periodicals as *Le Globe* and *La Revue Encyclopédique* and by such critics as Balzac, Sainte-Beuve, Charles Romey, Louis de Laménie, Philarète Chasles, and George Sand. Georgette Bosset's *Fenimore Cooper et le Roman d'Aventure en France vers 1830* (Paris, 1928) focuses on the high point of Cooper's popularity in France, between 1826 and 1830, and the period of his greatest influence on French fiction, between 1829 and 1836. Mlle Bosset finds much evidence of Cooper's influence on Balzac's first acknowledged work, *Le Dernier Chouan* (1829) or *Les Chouans*, and traces of intermittent influence on Balzac's fiction until his last, unfinished work *Les Paysans* (1844). She maintains that *The Pilot* (1824) and *The Red Rover* (1827) infected the French imagination with ideas of nautical glory and inspired the great vogue of French maritime fiction by Eugène Sue, Edouard Corbière, Auguste Jal, Jules Lecomte, and others, beginning with Sue's *Kernock le Pirate* (1830). Measuring influence more rigidly, Margaret Gibb in *Le Roman de*

Bas-de-Cuir minimizes Cooper's effect on Balzac and depreciates the importance of his effect on Alexandre Dumas père, Gabriel Ferry, and Gustave Aimard, since these writers addressed themselves at least partly to adolescents. Other students of Cooper's impact on French literature, E. Preston Dargan ("Balzac and Cooper: *Les Chouans*," *MP*, Aug. 1915), James L. Shepherd III ("Balzac's Debt to Cooper's *Spy* in *Les Chouans*" *FR*, Dec. 1954), Eric Partridge ("Fenimore Cooper's Influence on the French Romantics," *MLR*, Apr. 1925), and Regis Messac ("Fenimore Cooper et Son Influence en France," *PMLA*, Dec. 1928), take account of the possible indirection and intricacy of imaginative influences, especially on writers themselves strongly imaginative.

As the nineteenth-century American most often translated into German, Cooper rivaled Scott almost as equal in Germany and inspired numerous "German Fenimore Coopers." As early as 1826, *The Spy* apparently affected details (C. D. Brenner, *MLN*, Nov. 1915) in Wilhelm Hauff's *Lichtenstein*. A fascinated Goethe began reading Cooper methodically in 1826 and borrowed from *The Pioneers* for the setting and characterization of his *Novelle* (1827), according to Spiridion Wukadinović, *Goethes "Novelle": Der Schauplatz, Coopersche Einflüsse* (Halle, 1909), and would doubtless have borrowed further had he completed his *Wilhelm Meisters Meisterjahre* and brought his hero to America. After Goethe, Karl Postl ("Charles Sealsfield"), the Moravian ex-monk and *émigré*, was the best-known German writer to fall early under Cooper's spell. Postl was not uncritical of his model (Karl J. R. Arndt, "The Cooper-Sealsfield Exchange of Criticism," *AL*, Mar. 1943), which he sought to "improve" upon rather than repudiate. By the mid-1850s, four other German *émigrés* with personal experience of America (Friedrich A. Strubberg, Baldwin Möllhausen, Friedrich W. C. Gerstäcker, and Otto Ruppius) were producing voluminously in fiction strongly reminiscent of Cooper. The debts of these writers to Cooper are well documented in various studies, individual and collective, published and unpublished, listed in Lawrence M. Price's *The Reception of United States Literature in Germany* (Chapel Hill, N.C., 1966), a work which usefully digests Cooper's impact on German literature. Harvey Hewett-Thayer's *American Literature As Viewed in Germany, 1818–1861* (Chapel Hill, N.C., 1958) reviews Cooper's early critical reception in Germany. By the 1860s, even before his influence had yielded to the Mayne Reid's and the Karl May's, Cooper's books were being regularly abridged and edited for juveniles. Anneliese Bodensohn argues eloquently and persuasively in her *Im Zeichen des Manitu: Coopers "Lederstrumpf" als Dichtung und Jugendlektüre*

(Frankfurt am Main, 1963) that Cooper should be rescued from this plight.

For American readers, Maria Bobrova's appreciative *James Fenimore Cooper: An Essay on His Life and Creative Work* (Saratov, USSR, 1967) provides fascinating hints of Cooper's imaginative impact on the Russian and Soviet mind. Quoting the well-known critic V. Belinsky on Cooper ("Marvelous, mighty, great artist!"), Bobrova suggests that his influence in Russia much exceeded Sir Walter Scott's and that "Our Cooper" remains in the Soviet Union the most appealing of nineteenth-century American writers. Without approving "feudalistic" elements in his thinking, she praises his courage and merciless truth-telling and credits him with showing the role of the people in the creation of American society, with articulating the faults of bourgeois capitalism, and with opposing the racist and genocidal treatment of the Indian. Cooper overstepped the limits of his time and society, she argues, and serves and will serve humanity.

Study of Cooper's influence elsewhere abroad languishes, though Dorothy S. Vivian shows the Argentine novelist Domingo Faustino Sarmiento drawing on Leatherstocking for his hero of the *pampa* Facundo Quiroga (*Hispania*, Dec. 1965). Robert L. Johnson suggests that the Australian novelists Henry Lawson and Joseph Furpy owe something to Cooper (*Southern Review* [U. of Adelaide], no. 3, 1965), and Julian Krzyanowski rebuts earlier scholars who said Cooper's fiction did not visibly affect Adam Mickiewicz (*International Journal of Slavic Linguistics and Poetics*, 1961). Cooper's considerable impact on serious later American writing has also been largely ignored, though Gordon Mills notes similarities in the paradoxical values of the wilderness and civilization as represented by Cooper and Jack London (*NCF*, Mar. 1959), and Sacvan Bercovitch, "Hackleberry Bumppo: A Comparison of 'Tom Sawyer' and 'The Pioneers,'" volunteers the dangerous truth that Cooper's influence extends to Mark Twain (*Mark Twain Journal*, Summer 1968). If registered at all, Cooper's imaginative bequests to such giants as Conrad and Tolstoy have roused little curiosity.

Much more inviting, and obvious, has been Cooper's influence on the subliterary mass-entertainment media. Henry Nash Smith's classic study *Virgin Land: The American West as Symbol and Myth* (Cambridge, Mass., 1950) traces the Leatherstocking type from John Filson's archetypal Daniel Boone legend through its transfiguration in Cooper's imagination and on through the successive phases of its deterioration and perversion at the hands of professional dream merchants. Though he finds "the character of Leatherstocking . . . by far the most important symbol of the national experience of adventure across the continent," Smith denies the Leatherstocking Tales stature as "a major work of art" and fails to appreciate the ironic nightmare that knowledge of the so-called "sons of Leatherstocking" would have occasioned both to their imputed father and his creator. Though he takes Cooper somewhat more seriously as artist, James K. Folsom in *The American Western Novel* (New Haven, Conn., 1966) generally supplements Smith, observing that "every major theme of the Leatherstocking Tales is picked up by later writers about the West." Folsom maintains that, in addition to evident formulae, these novels derive their elegiac tone and their concern with the nature of law and justice, especially their distinction between rights of use and ownership, from Cooper. Unavoidably, many popular or semipopular articles, like Warren S. Walker's "Buckskin West: Leatherstocking at High Noon" (*New York Folklore Quarterly*, June 1968), associate Cooper with the symbols of mass culture. The possible danger of this kind of identification is illustrated in the distinguished social historian Henry Bamford Parkes's "Metamorphoses of Leatherstocking" (*Modern Writing*, no. 3, edited by William Phillips and Philip Rahv, New York, 1956), in which Parkes makes Leatherstocking a convenient "expression of some deep compulsion of the American spirit" to reject law and civilization and to accept the notion that "organized society is somehow antagonistic to individual integrity." No greater misinterpretation of Cooper is possible.

The full measure of Cooper's influence is untaken. If Cooper wrote, as Conrad asserted, "before the great American language was born," he undoubtedly shared in its creation. This phase of Cooper's influence seems totally unexplored, except in random articles like Joseph Slater's speculations about the phrase "Dutch treat" in *Satanstoe* (*AS*, May 1951). Though most of Cooper's early fiction was staged at home and abroad in plays, burlettas, and operas, the adaptations seem to have been investigated in only two articles: John D. Gordan's "*The Red Rover* Takes the Boards" (*AL*, Mar. 1938) and John McBride's "Cooper's *The Spy* on the French Stage" (*University of Tennessee Studies in the Humanities*, no. 1, 1956). While Warren S. Walker's studies have revealed Cooper admirably as both a user and fabricator of American folklore, much more remains in this vein, as George Monteiro's article on Billy Kirby as a possible source for Paul Bunyan suggests (*MF*, Winter 1962).

Cooper and His Age.

Following the example of Robert E. Spiller, an ever-increasing number of scholars have sought to define the reciprocal relationships between Cooper and his age. Since his thought and attitudes involve a multiplicity of ideas, assumptions, problems, and values, the effort has been necessarily complex. It has been further complicated, as Spiller notes in "Second Thoughts on Cooper as a Social Critic" (*NYH*, Oct. 1954), by Cooper's incorrigible experimentation with fiction as a medium for ideas and also, as James Grossman in "James Fenimore Cooper: An Uneasy American" (*YR*, Summer 1951) and Robert H. Zoellner in "Fenimore Cooper: Alienated American" (*AQ*, Spring 1961) attest, by the paradoxes and psychic depth of his commitment to his country's destiny. Despite apparent and sometimes real inconsistencies, closer scrutiny suggests an essential coherence that has been obscured by differences of presupposition and emphasis among his critics, as well as by inadequate information.

Cooper's socio-political ideas have elicited especially varied responses. In V. L. Parrington's *The Romantic Revolution in America* (New York, 1927), Cooper is a Platonic Jeffersonian, an anachronistic agrarian, defending a nonexistent republic in which self-restraint and disinterested intelligence can somehow be made to prevail. H. L. Mencken's introduction to *The American Democrat* (New York, 1931), Russell Kirk's *The Conservative Mind* (New York, 1953), and George J. Becker's "James Fenimore Cooper and American Democracy" (*CE*, Mar. 1956) portray Cooper as a superior mind resisting the threat to individuality from the ignorant and the irresponsible. Arthur M. Schlesinger, Jr., in *The Age of Jackson* (Boston, 1945) and John C. McCloskey in "Cooper's Political Views in *The Crater*" (*MP*, Nov. 1955) interpret his development as retrogression from a Jeffersonian-Jacksonian stance to a conservatism little short of Whiggery. The ease with which his meanings have been unconsciously warped to fit pre-existing critical categories is illustrated by Schlesinger's unintentional misquotation from *New York* (p. 56): ". . . we do not believe any more in the superior innocence and virtue of a rural population than in that of the largest capitals" as "We do not believe any more in the superior innocence and virtue of a rural population" (*The Age of Jackson*, p. 380). In short, Cooper was not so much a Hamiltonian, Jeffersonian, or Jacksonian as a political independent whose philosophic position, however eclectic, should be considered on its own terms.

The underlying unity of Cooper's thought is recognized in several useful studies which point significantly to earlier, mainly eighteenth-century origins for Cooper's key ideas. Examining *Notions of the Americans* as a commentary on democracy, Morton J. Frisch (*Ethics*, Jan. 1961) finds its Enlightenment assumptions thoroughgoing. Contrasting *Notions* and the Effingham novels as representatives of Cooper's thinking in the 1820s and 1830s, Marvin Meyers's *The Jacksonian*

Persuasion (Stanford, Calif., 1957) shows Cooper less a proper Jacksonian than an advocate of that Tory phase of Jacksonism which mourned the "Great Descent" from the Doric or First American Republic. Comparing Cooper's economic suppositions in his European trilogy of the 1830s and in his Littlepage trilogy of the 1840s, Marius Bewley, in *The Eccentric Design* (New York, 1959), discovers not a diametrical contrast or reversal but a dialectical continuity which stresses different aspects of the problem of a ruling elite and which provides repeated analogies to the writings of John Adams. In his detailed study of Cooper's various expressions of the interplay between the melioristic premise and the premise of "innate corruption," Frank M. Collins, "Cooper and the American Dream" (*PMLA*, Mar. 1966), reveals in still another dimension the pertinence of the eighteenth-century heritage. The conflict, Collins concludes, "did not so much end in an outright victory for either view as subside in a faltering synthesis."

Cooper's comments on European society and politics aroused Robert E. Spiller's earliest interest in Cooper; and, in a long series of books, articles, and introductions, beginning with the chapter in *The American in England* and extending to his UMPAW *James Fenimore Cooper* (1965), Spiller has established himself as the leading authority on Cooper's intellectual response to Europe. His most important statements on the subject are in *Fenimore Cooper: Critic of His Times*, (New York, 1931), in introductions to *France* and *England* from Cooper's *Gleanings in Europe*, and articles on Cooper's involvement with Lafayette in the Finance Controversy of 1831–32 (*AL*, Mar. 1931) and the struggle for Polish freedom in 1830–32 (*AL*, Mar. 1935). In other articles on Cooper's European interests, Russell Kirk ("Cooper and the European Puzzle," *CE*, Jan. 1946) argues that in his three European romances "Cooper was holding up the failings of European systems as a warning to America that her free institutions, too, could perish"; and Anne C. Loveland ("Cooper and the American Mission," *AQ*, Summer 1969) considers the attacks on these books and on Cooper's European political involvements generally as the conservative or Whig response to the effort to export American political principles.

The most comprehensive study of American society in Cooper's fiction is Kay Seymour House's *Cooper's Americans* (Columbus, Ohio, 1965). Regarding the American settings as a kind of Yoknapatawpha County, with its heartland in New York State, Mrs. House describes the inhabitants as defined either by the social characteristics of their group or class (women, aborigines, blacks, Dutch, New Englanders, gentry, sailors) or—for characters able to transcend these categories— by their responses to open experience. According to Mrs. House, characters of the second type, including Leatherstocking and other heroes of romance, "identify the uniquely American opportunity" and explore the limits and possibilities of democratic life, while characters of the first type reveal "America's connections with aboriginal and European cultures." Historically, the first type is important because it established the first persuasive images in American fiction of such groups as Indians, frontiersmen, blacks, and sailors.

Albert Keiser's *The Indian in American Literature* (New York, 1933) describes Cooper's intentions and accomplishments in presenting Indians in the thirteen tales in which they appear, finding the portrait "remarkably complete and faithful." Agreeing that Cooper tried to use his Indian materials responsibly, Roy Harvey Pearce in *Savagism and Civilization* (Baltimore, Md., 1965, first published in 1953 as *The Savages of America*) and "Civilization and Savagism: the World of the Leatherstocking Tales," in *English Institute Essays, 1949* (New York, 1950), sees Cooper's Indians shaped by "savagism," the concept that whatever the Indian's virtues in the wilderness, his inferiority and doom were irrevocably decided by his obstinate refusal to become civilized. However useful for intellectual history, this idea—which synthesized the conventions of "noble" and "ignoble" savages—is too abstract and reductive to account wholly for Cooper's intentions. Thus, the "doctrine of gifts," a corollary of "savagism," may explain difficulties in race-assimilation; but it also embodies, as Cooper employs it, a plea for ethnic self-respect and for warm human sympathies across ethnic barriers. Some Cooper Indians are—by design—more truly civilized than their white destroyers.

Lucy L. Hazard in *The Frontier in American Literature* (New York, 1927) and indeed all commentators on Cooper's frontiersmen remark that Leatherstocking mediates between savage and civilized worlds, while his other frontiersmen illustrate a variety of more likely combinations of qualities drawn from both worlds. Miss Hazard wonders how far actual frontiersmen shared Natty's love of Nature! In "The Frontiersman in Popular Fiction, 1820–60," in *The Frontier Re-examined*, edited by John F. McDermott (Urbana, Ill., 1967), Jules Zanger contrasts the popular images of Daniel Boone and Davy Crockett, showing Natty to be a mixture of the two, progressively dominated by characteristics of Boone and such Cooper frontiersmen as Hurry Harry and Ishmael Bush to conform more nearly to the Crockett image. Stressing Natty's closeness to the Boone legend, Henry Nash Smith's *Virgin Land* finds Leatherstocking's greatest profundity as symbol in his expression of the tension between social order and individual freedom, a tension that was endemic to frontier conditions but one that Cooper could not resolve satisfactorily. Kay Seymour House in *Cooper's Americans* and Edwin Fussell in *Frontier: American Literature and the American West* (Princeton, N.J., 1965) regard the frontier and its conflicts as a metaphorical field or microcosm in which Cooper achieved some of his happiest and most complex insights.[4]

Though W. H. Gardiner noted, in reviewing *The Spy* in 1822, the novelty and verismilitude of the black servant Caesar, the first detailed description of Cooper's gallery of sympathetically drawn blacks is apparently that by Mrs. House. Characters like Neb in *Afloat and Ashore* and *Miles Wallingford* are probably better guides to Cooper's understanding of black experience than such statements as his 1827 article on Slavery for the *Revue Encyclopédique* (printed in English by Spiller, *AHR*, Apr. 1930), where he was cast by circumstances as apologist for an institution he deplored. Tracing the evolution of his attitudes towards the South, Max L. Griffin (*SP*, Jan. 1951) shows that Cooper conceived of emancipation as a necessary but slow and complex process requiring education of blacks and compensation of owners. He at no time approved of violence or threat of violence by North or South, but he concluded early that if the issue had to be decided by force, the Union—and freedom—would be the victor.

"Cooper's was the first significant [American] literary mind," writes Edwin H. Cady in *The Gentleman in America* (Syracuse, N.Y., 1949), "stirred by the philosophy of gentility." Cady argues persuasively that Cooper's concept of the gentleman pervades his thought and fiction, informing even his treatment of Leatherstocking and Uncas.

Yet critics of Cooper's gentry, who usually confine themselves to the Effinghams and Littlepages, have seldom been kind from the time of Thackeray to the present. Granville Hicks in "Landlord Cooper and the Anti-Renters" (*Antioch Review*, Spring 1945) laments that the novelist's anachronistic notions of landed gentry led him to betray his talents and "his generous hopes for his fellow-countrymen" by waging a reactionary class warfare in the Littlepage trilogy. Donald A. Ringe, in "Cooper's Littlepage Novels: Change and Stability in American Society" (*AL*, Nov. 1960), points out that the Littlepage family undergoes progressive democratization from novel to novel and so may be regarded as advocates of an ordered change as opposed to the chaotic change threatened by the Newcome family. Telescoping author and fictitious narrator, Jesse Bier (*TSLL*, Winter 1968) complains that

---

4. S. B. Liljegren's *The Canadian Border in the Novels of J. F. Cooper* (Upsala, 1968) summarizes the tales and portions of tales set on or near the Canadian border.

Satanstoe (and presumably the entire Littlepage series) exudes a nox-
ious class consciousness that Cooper unconsciously parodies; and James
W. Tuttleton (*BNYPL*, May 1966) suggests that Cooper indulged a
strong private bias in creating his bigoted, greedy New Englanders as
offsets to his New York gentry. A balanced, comprehensive account
of Cooper's involvement in the Anti-Rent War on behalf of the landed
aristocracy is David M. Ellis's "The Coopers and New York State
Landholding Systems" (*NYH*, Oct. 1954).

As Howard Mumford Jones indicates in his introduction to *James
Fenimore Cooper: A Re-Appraisal*, several papers read at the Cooper
centennial observance sponsored by the New York State Historical
Association in Cooperstown in September 1951 and published as a
special issue of *New York History* (Oct. 1954) considered neglected
aspects of Cooper's relationship to his age. James Grossman reveals how
Cooper's struggle with the press in his no doubt ill-advised libel suits
was motivated by his deep conviction of the importance of a responsible
press. William Charvat explores authoritatively the relatively unknown
terrain of Cooper's relations with his publishers in a paper reprinted
in Charvat's *The Profession of Authorship in America, 1800–1870*,
edited by Matthew J. Bruccoli (Columbus, Ohio, 1968). Walter Muir
Whitehill brings his expertise as professional naval historian to bear
on Cooper's *History of the Navy* (1839), the first thorough, systematic
history of the United States Navy. James F. Beard discusses Cooper's
close personal and aesthetic associations with his artist contemporaries
emphasizing his affinity to Thomas Cole and painters of the Hudson
River Valley School.

Cooper's affinities with the Hudson River School artists have since
been reexamined and restated several times from slightly different
points of view. Regarding Cooper and the painters as *moralistes*, H. M.
Jones finds significant analogies both of technique and philosophic outlook (*TSE*, 1952, reprinted in *MagA*, Oct. 1952; *History and the Contemporary*, Madison, Wis., 1964; and *The Frontier in American Fiction*,
Jerusalem, 1956). Donald A. Ringe shows that Cooper, like Thomas
Cole, used patterned landscape series to convey themes beyond the
scope of a single landscape, actually borrowing for *The Crater* the motif
of the mountain peak in Cole's great cycle *The Course of Empire* (*AL*,
Mar. 1958); Ringe also finds that in various works, but especially in
The Bravo, Cooper, like the painters, employed chiaroscuro self-consciously as an expressive device (*PMLA*, Sept. 1963). James T. Callow's
*Kindred Spirits: Knickerbocker Writers and American Artists, 1807–
1855* (Chapel Hill, N.C., 1967) is chiefly useful for biographical and
cultural documentation.

Harry Hayden Clark's monograph-length "Fenimore Cooper and Science" (*Wisconsin Academy of Sciences, Arts and Letters*, 1959, 1960) was definitive at the time it was prepared, and it remains an exhaustive, richly informative study—impervious to summary. Clark concludes that Cooper was enthusiastic towards science as a means of advancing utilitarian ends and as an agency fulfilling Providential purposes, but that he rejected the notion that science could eradicate evil or compensate for irrational impulses in man.

Clark, H. M. Jones (*Belief and Disbelief in American Literature*, Chicago, 1967), and Ringe (*Papers of the Michigan Academy of Science, Arts, and Letters*, 1959; *PMLA*, Dec. 1960) have stressed the importance of Cooper's Episcopalianism, especially in the fiction of his later years. Ringe discusses, for example, the epistemological implications of his religious attitudes for such novels as *Jack Tier*, *The Crater*, *The Oak Openings*, *The Sea Lions*, and *The Ways of the Hour*. Cooper undoubtedly felt strong religious influences towards the end of his career, as these critics assume, but there may be some question as to how far he accepted personally the Episcopal dogmas he seemed to espouse.

Cooper as Artist

As Walter Sutton remarked, in "Cooper as Found—1949" (*UKCR*, Autumn 1949), at the nadir of Cooper's reputation as artist, the pattern of "sympathetic criticism . . . reveals a curious paradox." His preeminence as a writer of fiction was acknowledged, directly or indirectly, by all important American writers of his time and by most of his British and Continental peers, including Goethe, Balzac, Sand, and Trollope. With gentle disclaimer, he could repeat to his wife a story that Sir Walter Scott, "while at Naples, declared a person you love had more genius than any living writer." Conrad and Lawrence spoke eloquently of him to a later generation. Yet the first century and a quarter of Cooper criticism produced remarkably little in an idiom acceptable to mid-twentieth-century sophisticates to justify high claims for his art. Sutton recommended that readers, emulating Thoreau who flung out his three superfluous stones to avoid dusting them, "take fresh inventory and eliminate from our shelves books which only habit and traditional veneration have led us to regard as American imaginative literature of the first order."

Nineteenth-century criticism of Cooper, including representative and historically important reviews by William H. Gardiner (*NAR*, July 1822; July 1826), Francis Bowen (*NAR*, Jan. 1828), Francis Parkman (*NAR*, Jan. 1852), Henry T. Tuckerman (*NAR*, Oct. 1859), and George S. Hillard (*AtM*, Jan. 1862), reveals more about his position in

American literature than about his art. Even such writers of fiction as Balzac (*Revue Parisienne*, 25 July 1840), Simms (*Magnolia*, Sept. 1841), Poe (*Graham's Magazine*, Nov. 1843), Melville (*Literary World*, 28 April 1849; 16 Mar. 1850), and Sand (*Autour de la Table*, Paris, 1875) tell the modern reader remarkably little about Cooper's artistry. This criticism is, at its best, an impressionistic tapestry in which certain recurrent motifs emerge for comment: Cooper's unmistakable nationality in the selection of scenes, events, and characters; his similarity or dissimilarity to Scott; his powers of graphic observation and description; his "facility in inventing incidents and weaving them together in clear spirited narrative"; the probability or improbability of his plots; his uneven success in character delineation; his inequalities of style; and the appropriateness or inappropriateness of his modes of representation.

Properly noting that Cooper paid much attention to his theory of representation, Arvid Shulenberger in *Cooper's Theory of Fiction* (Lawrence, Kans., 1955) maintains that it was transformed over three decades from "a theory of realism arguing for literal truth of representation" to a theory "that the ideal rather than the literal truth should be presented," so that the fiction exhibits "a progress from realism to romance." This conclusion, based on emphases in the prefaces, is misleading. Cooper's early prefaces stressed "realistic" intentions because the fiction was closer to American realities than that to which readers were accustomed; his later prefaces insisted stoutly on his prerogatives as imaginative writer because literal-minded readers treated his fiction as autobiography or history. Actually, what Cooper sought more or less consistently was an effective fusion between the *real* (conceived as fidelity to human nature and to professional, social, and geographical peculiarities) and the *ideal* (conceived as aesthetic qualities deriving from the operation of the imaginative process). The major shift of emphasis in the fiction was, on balance, in the direction of realistic techniques.

Cooper never articulated his theory of romance fully or systematically, however; and when his vogue persisted into the 1880s and beyond, his forms now thoroughly debased by imitators, he became an inevitable target for attack by realists like Howells and Twain and, later, naturalists like Norris and Crane. Some dozen years after Lounsbury's book on Cooper, Twain took Lounsbury's incautious reference to the Leatherstocking Tales as "pure works of art" and other impressionistic nuggets as points of departure for his hilarious, but coldly calculated, "Fenimore Cooper's Literary Offenses" (*NAR*, July 1895). Cooper soon became, as Sydney J. Krause states in "Cooper's Literary Offenses: Mark Twain in Wonderland" (*NEQ*, Sept. 1965), "the realists' whipping boy, the visible symbol of defunct romanticism, and insofar as he falsified the life they would represent truly, he was its most vulnerable and appropriate symbol." The existence of at least two earlier versions of the Twain essay and the curtailment of the weaker parts of the third version (Bernard DeVoto, "Fenimore Cooper's Further Literary Offenses," *NEQ*, Sept. 1946) suggest the care with which Twain proceeded. To reply at all was to risk the damaging admission that one took the essay seriously (see D. L. Maulsby, *Dial*, 16 Feb. 1897); not to reply was to risk seeming to concur silently.

The Twain essay merely aggravated the dilemma of critics who attempted for the next half century to keep Cooper's reputation as artist alive. "On the one hand," as Walter Sutton declared, they "freely acknowledged that Cooper was a clumsy writer who never mastered the niceties of his craft, while on the other hand [they] asserted that he was a golden story teller, a true artist who somehow, through the exercise of a tremendous native energy, overcame his limitations and succeeded in creating the American epic." Even such discriminating critics as W. C. Brownell in *American Prose Masters* (New York, 1909), John Erskine in *Leading American Novelists* (New York, 1910), Carl Van Doren in *The American Novel* (New York, 1921), and Henry Seidel Canby in *Classic Americans* (New York, 1931) found it increasingly difficult during the heyday of realism to make a persuasive case for Cooper's artistry. Critics interested in Cooper primarily for his ideas and social criticism were not required to defend him as artist. The result, of which Marcel Clavel complained on his trip to the United States, was a virtual abandonment from the 1920s through the 1940s of even the pretense that Cooper was an artist. One distinguished professor is reported to have read the Twain essay to his classes with the admonition that it contained all his students needed to know of Cooper. Organizing the Cooper Centennial meetings in Cooperstown for 1951, the writer could find no reputable critic willing to speak on Cooper as artist. Sutton's proposal that Cooper's works be "flung out" seemed an honest recognition of accomplished fact.

Nevertheless, Conrad's disgusted comment on the Twain essay in a 1908 letter to Arthur Symons ("That dismal 'bajazzo' with his debased jargon . . . smirches whatever he touches.") is merely one indication that admirers of Cooper's art did not wholly abandon the field to Twain. D. H. Lawrence, in *Studies in Classic American Literature* (New York, 1923), attributes Cooper's peculiar power in the Leatherstocking Tales to his mythic evocation of the American past ("She starts old, old, wrinkled and writhing in an old skin") and future ("a gradual sloughing of the old skin, towards a new youth"). The spontaneity of Lawrence's enthusiasm is best shown in his original essays written for the *English Review* (Feb., Mar. 1919) and reprinted in *The Symbolic Meaning*, edited by Armin Arnold (London, 1962). Proceeding quite differently—collating texts of *The Spy*—Tremaine McDowell (*SP*, July 1930) reveals in Cooper an unexpected capacity for stylistic revision; and Yvor Winters (*Maule's Curse*, Norfolk, Conn., 1938), discovering variety and elements of distinction in Cooper's style, remarks that chapter VII of *The Deerslayer* "is probably as great an achievement of its length as one will find in American fiction outside of Melville." Moving beyond Winters, who sees Cooper as great only in fragments, Marius Bewley in "Revaluations: James Fenimore Cooper" (*Scrutiny*, Winter 1952–53; reprinted in *The Eccentric Design*) maintains in his provocative examination of *The Deerslayer* and other works that Cooper was a higher kind of storyteller than Scott, able to conceive action as a moral pattern "which becomes the form of the completed tale." Preferring to approach Cooper through Scott, Donald Davie writes warmly and at length of Cooper's art in *The Heyday of Sir Walter Scott*. "However much I may differ from Mr. Winters and Mr. Bewley at specific points," he confesses, "I am impenitently of their opinion that Cooper is a very great writer indeed."

While Richard Chase exaggerated in asserting in *The American Novel and Its Tradition* (Garden City, N.Y., 1957) that interesting criticism of Cooper "had to be in one way or another an elaboration or revision of Lawrence," the mythic approach provided a halfway station to Cooper as artist, where critics could explore his and their own cultural assumptions. Chase *does* elaborate on Lawrence. Henry Nash Smith, correlating Cooper's assumptions about the West with those from other sources, provides in *Virgin Land* an indispensable panoramic context for all nineteenth-century Western heroes. Roy Harvey Pearce, in "The Leatherstocking Tales Re-Examined" (*SAQ*, Oct. 1947), postulating that Cooper intended Leatherstocking as a tragic figure whose way of life has to be extinguished to permit the advance of civilized society, concludes that Cooper failed as artist because he did not represent that society successfully. R. W. B. Lewis, in *The American Adam* (Chicago, 1955), characterizes Natty Bumppo as the "Adamic hero unambiguously treated—celebrated in his very Adamism," an Adamism evoked largely in spatial terms. According to David W. Noble in *The Eternal Adam and the New World Garden* (New York, 1968), this mythic construction must be qualified by the realization that Natty is not wholly exempted from time, society, and human weakness. Charles A. Brady in "James Fenimore Cooper: Myth-maker and Christian Romancer" (*American Classics Reconsidered*, edited by

Harold C. Gardiner, New York, 1958) points to elements of classical and Christian myth in Cooper, especially in the Leatherstocking Tales; and Leslie Fiedler, in *Love and Death in the American Novel* (New York, 1960), finds in Cooper a congeries of mythic characters and relationships and ample confirmation of his theories of heterosexual-homosexual attitudes in American cultural history. Though these studies suggest, in their variety, the rich mythopoeic texture of Cooper's fiction, they presuppose, as R. W. B. Lewis notes, "an astonishing lack of co-ordination between the classical ingredients of narrative: plot and character and thought and diction."

Meanwhile, critics interested in rehabilitating Cooper's reputation as artist and in seeing his work as an organic whole began tentatively to follow Marius Bewley and Donald Davie in the direction of formal analysis and close thematic scrutiny. Donald A. Ringe, in *James Fenimore Cooper* (New York, 1962), examines carefully Cooper's ideas, settings, and characters to show the novelist, at his best, "a serious artist who could generate an important moral theme from the skillful handling of his materials." Quite properly considering Cooper a *moraliste*, Ringe contributes exceedingly perceptive interpretations of individual books, including some usually neglected, and demonstrates, in addition, the underlying unity in Cooper's developing moral vision. George Dekker's *James Fenimore Cooper* is, as the author says, basically "a critical survey of Cooper's fiction," in which he argues that Cooper, though "not a novelist of the very first rank," has "real strengths . . . great and richly compensating." Approaching Cooper, like Donald Davie, through Scott and in the manner of Georg Lukács, Dekker is concerned with patterns of tension created by large, impersonal social, political, and economic forces within the novelist's world. His method is eclectic and his conclusions, some refreshingly irreverent, are usefully calculated in this transitional period of Cooper criticism to challenge readers to think for themselves.

Recent criticism has gradually but unmistakably shifted its attitude towards the Leatherstocking Tales, confirming perhaps Cooper's prediction that these romances would decide the issue of his survival and artistry. Whereas Louise Pound's analysis of Natty's diction (*AS*, Sept. 1927) reinforced Twain's emphasis on its incongruities, Alan F. Sandy, Jr. (*ESQ*, Summer 1970) considers the levels of diction, in *The Deerslayer* at least, part of the total design. Among other sympathetic studies of individual tales not already cited in this survey are discussions of *The Deerslayer* by David Brion Davis in *Twelve Original Essays on Great American Novels*, edited by Charles Shapiro (Detroit, Mich., 1958), Edwin T. Bowden in *The Dungeon of the Heart* (New York,

1961), and Arthur Mizener in *Twelve Great American Novels* (New York, 1967). *The Pioneers* is discussed by Kay Seymour House in *The American Novel*, edited by Wallace Stegner (New York, 1965), Thomas Philbrick (*PMLA*, Dec. 1964), and E. Arthur Robinson (*PMLA*, Dec. 1967); *The Prairie* by William Wasserstrom (*American Imago*, Winter 1960; reprinted in *Psychoanalysis and American Fiction*, edited by Irving Malin, New York, 1965), Jesse Bier (*TSLL*, Spring 1962), William H. Goetzmann (*Landmarks of American Writing*, edited by Hennig Cohen, New York, 1969), and John William Ward (*Red, White and Blue*, New York, 1969). Such essays as these, some excerpted in Warren S. Walker's convenient *Leatherstocking and the Critics* (Fair Lawn, N.J., 1965), suggest a depth and complication in Cooper's art quite unrecognized in earlier criticism.

Yet, excellent as much recent criticism of the Leatherstocking Tales is, it contains all too little suggestion of the tightness of form requisite to classic art. The mythic approach, flexibly defined and oriented, is still preferred by Robert H. Zoellner in "Conceptual Ambivalence in Cooper's Leatherstocking" (*AL*, Jan. 1960); by D. E. S. Maxwell in *American Fiction: The Intellectual Background* (New York, 1965); and by Edwin Fussell in *Frontier: American Literature and the American West*. Klaus Lanzinger considers Cooper along with Herman Melville, Frank Norris, and Thomas Wolfe in *Die Epik im amerikanischen Roman* (Frankfurt am Main, 1965). A. N. Kaul's chapter, "The History and the Myth of American Civilization," in *The American Vision: Actual and Ideal Society in Nineteenth-Century Fiction* (New Haven, Conn., 1963), is an astute treatment of the Anti-Rent trilogy as an archetypal expression of Cooper's impossible demand on history and of the Leatherstocking Tales as a countervailing mythic expression of ideal—but useful because critical—moral and social values. David Howard, in *Tradition and Tolerance in Nineteenth-Century Fiction* (New York, 1967), comments perceptively on many elements of form in the Tales, especially in *The Last of the Mohicans*; and Joel Porte, in *The Romance in America*, deals sensitively with concepts and images of race, women, and nature as they are evoked in the series. Correlating the experience of discovering a landscape and of reading a Leatherstocking Tale, John F. Lynen acutely proposes in *The Design of the Present* (New Haven, Conn., 1969) that the "true action is the growth of awareness of a situation which pertains throughout the novel," "a continually deepening perception of what is always there." The long controversy over Cooper's stature as artist has not, surely, been decided; but the issue has been effectively joined.

Stephen Crane

DONALD PIZER

I HAVE ATTEMPTED to include all major work on Stephen Crane. However, a small number of important studies (particularly foreign) and a smaller number of 1969 articles have been unavailable to me. A special problem in citing articles about Crane is that many have been reprinted, often more than once, in texts designed for student use. Rather than attempt to note every instance of this kind of republication, I have noted the existence of collections of critical writings about Crane at appropriate points in my discussion. I have, however, listed other forms of republication.

MANUSCRIPTS

The two principal Crane manuscript collections are at Columbia University and the University of Virginia. The Columbia collection, some thirteen hundred items, consists essentially of material preserved by Cora Crane and acquired by the Library in 1952. Its greatest strengths are in manuscripts of Crane's poems, stories, and sketches, and in scrapbooks of his published journalism. Daniel G. Hoffman describes the collection in "An Unwritten Life of Stephen Crane" (*Columbia Library Columns*, Feb. 1953), but a fuller description and partial list can be found in Joan H. Baum, *Stephen Crane (1871–1900): An Exhibition of His Writings Held in the Columbia University Libraries* ... (New York, 1956). The collection has served as the basis for two important books, Daniel G. Hoffman's *The Poetry of Stephen Crane* (New York, 1957) and Lillian Gilkes's *Cora Crane: A Biography of Mrs. Stephen Crane* (Bloomington, Ind., 1960). Most of the material in the collection which was unpublished in 1952 has now been published, largely by R. W. Stallman. The University of Virginia manuscript holdings represent the collecting efforts of Clifton Waller Barrett.

97

The Barrett Collection boasts, above all, the manuscript of *The Red Badge of Courage* (the only surviving complete holograph of a Crane novel) and contains as well a sizable body of miscellaneous material, including Crane's notebook. Some of its most significant items are noted by Miss Baum in her 1956 catalogue (the exhibition was a joint one of the Columbia and Barrett collections), but no separate list or calendar of its holdings has appeared. Additional Crane collections of some importance are those in the Syracuse University and Dartmouth College libraries and in the private possession of Charles Feinberg and Melvin H. Schoberlin. The Arents Collection at Syracuse is described in an appendix to *Stephen Crane: Love Letters to Nellie Crouse*, edited by Edwin H. Cady and Lester G. Wells (Syracuse, N.Y., 1954); the Dartmouth collection is listed in Herbert F. West, *A Stephen Crane Collection* (Hanover, N.H., 1948). There is a sufficient amount of Crane manuscript material (particularly letters) in various other private and public collections to suggest that a census of Crane manuscripts would be helpful.

BIBLIOGRAPHY

Early Crane bibliographies were superseded by Ames W. Williams and Vincent Starrett, *Stephen Crane: A Bibliography* (Glendale, Calif., 1948). The Williams and Starrett bibliography played a major role in the Crane "revival" of the early 1950s, but in the more than two decades since its appearance many scholars have noted errors and gaps, particularly regarding Crane's journalism. Unfortunately, corrections and additions are scattered throughout Crane scholarship of the last twenty years, and any attempt to list or describe them would require a separate essay. Joseph Katz has promised a full-scale bibliography, but until its appearance the scholar is directed to Jacob Blanck, *Bibliography of American Literature*, II (New Haven, Conn., 1957), for Crane's separate publications and to the secondary bibliographies noted below for items which deal with Crane's periodical publications. (In particular, Joan H. Baum's exhibition catalogue lists journalistic publication in the Columbia collection which is not in Williams and Starrett.) It should be noted that almost every major Crane scholar since 1950 has made some contribution to the establishment of the Crane canon, and that the current University of Virginia edition of Crane's works will no doubt result in still further additions and corrections.

There have been surprisingly few attribution controversies in Crane scholarship despite his extensive anonymous journalism. His distinctive style has no doubt aided in the identification of all but the most severely copy-edited items. Nevertheless, two cruxes of recent years are "Veterans' Ranks Thinner by a Year" and "Stephen Crane's Pen Picture of the Powers' Fleet Off Crete." Although Thomas A. Gullason attributed the first item to Crane (*NCF*, Sept. 1957), Daniel G. Hoffman has convincingly dismissed the attribution (*NCF*, June 1959). The second item is the center of a running controversy between R. W. Stallman and Lillian Gilkes over whether or not Crane could have been in Crete at the time the article was written and filed. (See, in particular, Gilkes's *Cora Crane;* Gilkes and Stallman in *SSF*, Fall 1964; Stallman's *Stephen Crane: A Biography*, New York, 1968; and Gilkes in *AL*, May 1969.) The argument hinges on suppositions derived from tenuous biographical evidence and will therefore probably continue for some time.

The secondary bibliography section of Williams and Starrett has been superseded by later, fuller lists. The most useful compilations are those by Maurice Beebe and Thomas A. Gullason, "Criticism of Stephen Crane: A Selected Checklist with an Index to Studies of Separate Works" (*MFS*, Autumn 1959), and Robert H. Hudspeth, "A Bibliography of Stephen Crane Scholarship: 1893–1962" (*Thoth*, Winter, 1963). Two continuing bibliographies are "The *Thoth* Annual Bibliography of Stephen Crane Scholarship" (each Spring issue) and the "Quarterly Checklist" of Crane scholarship in the *Stephen Crane Newsletter*. R. W. Stallman has announced his plans for a complete, annotated bibliography of Crane scholarship and criticism. Many of the Crane editions and collections cited below contain secondary bibliographies of varying degrees of completeness.

EDITIONS, TEXTS, AND REPRINTS

Wilson Follett's edition of *The Work of Stephen Crane* (12 vols., New York, 1925–27; 6 vols., New York, 1963) made available a large body of Crane's work which had long been out of print. The collection is very much a creature of its time in its somewhat precious bookmaking, in its array of generally uninformed and irrelevant introductions by contemporary literary and journalistic lights, and in its haphazard and undescribed editorial methods. It will be superseded (except for a few of its biographical introductions) by the Virginia Edition of *The Works of Stephen Crane*, edited by Fredson Bowers, of which Volume I (*Bowery Tales*) and Volume VII (*Tales of Whilomville*) appeared in 1969. Sanctioned and supported by the Center for Editions of American Authors, the Virginia Edition is as much a product of the bibliography-conscious sixties as was the Follet edition of the celebrity-minded twenties. Each volume in the edition is armed with lengthy biographical-historical and textual introductions by distinguished scholars, and each bristles with the apparatus of textual criticism. The Virginia Edition will no doubt be a milestone in Crane criticism and scholarship, for it will bring together all of Crane's writing (except for his letters and memoranda) in a context which attempts to make immediately apparent the biographical and bibliographical facts of each work. Nevertheless, one might wish that Crane's work could have been edited for a scholarly audience without so complete a commitment to the formidable and often questionable methodology of Fredson Bowers. For example, Bowers's desire to achieve a single eclectic text results in a futile coalescing of two distinctive works—the 1893 *Maggie* and its 1896 revision—into what can only be called the Bowers *Maggie*. In addition, Bowers's faith in the Greg principle that authority lies in the text closest to the author (in practice almost always the earliest text) is frequently a handicap rather than an aid in the editing of Crane. Like many nineteenth-century authors, Crane often saved his manuscripts but seldom had an opportunity to preserve the authorially revised typescript or proof which served as printer's copy. But because Bowers is committed to the primary authority of the manuscript, he must attempt the almost impossible task of determining which variants between a printed text and a manuscript are the product of authorial revision and which are the result of unauthorized editorial change. The result is a text which must be used with close reference to the textual notes and which will be a hazardous text when it is reprinted without such notes. Finally, Bowers's full-scale grappling with the punctuation history of minor Crane hackwork is a depressing example of methodological absolutism. Perhaps there is a mean between the casual editing of the twenties and the present emphasis on critical texts and common sense be damned. But until that golden day the modern critic and scholar should be thankful that the Virginia Edition, with its excessive virtues, is in process.

Until the completion of the Virginia Edition, a number of modern editions which supplement and correct the Follett edition are indispensable. Among these are R. W. Stallman and E. R. Hagemann's *The War Dispatches of Stephen Crane* (New York, 1964) and *The New York City Sketches of Stephen Crane* (New York, 1966); Olov W. Fryckstedt's *Stephen Crane: Uncollected Writings* (Uppsala, 1963); and Thomas A. Gullason's *The Complete Short Stories and Sketches of Stephen Crane* (New York, 1963) and *The Complete Novels of Stephen Crane* (New York, 1967). Stallman and Hagemann bring together all of Crane's writing (some of it previously unpublished) bearing on two phases of his career. The phases—war and the city—are important, and Stallman and Hagemann not only collect a good deal of otherwise dispersed material but also provide much useful historical information. The two volumes, however, suffer from overediting and from padding. For example, the reader is solemnly informed in a footnote to "An Experiment in Luxury" that "Crane's own life was anything but an experiment in luxury," while the *War Dispatches* collection contains a number of well-known stories (not dispatches) readily available elsewhere. But in one sense the volumes are underedited as well as overedited. The editors apparently made little attempt to track down variants in the newspaper appearances of Crane's dispatches, and in several instances their choice of text is both questionable and undiscussed. Olov W. Fryckstedt's important edition includes almost all the significant items in the two Stallman and Hagemann volumes and considerable additional material. Fryckstedt is a less-obtrusive editor, since he has confined himself to the republication, without notes, of all of Crane's work not republished elsewhere. His textual editing, however, also leaves much to be desired. With some exceptions, he prints without annotation exactly what he has found in the original publication, a method which makes it impossible for the reader to determine whether Fryckstedt or the original is responsible for an obvious error or a nonsensical passage. It appears from the work of Stallman, Hagemann, and Fryckstedt that we need to know a great deal more about newspaper and syndicate editorial practices and about the significant substantive variants in Crane's newspaper publication before a reliable text of his journalism can be published.

The two volumes edited by Thomas A. Gullason complement those by Stallman, Hagemann, and Fryckstedt in that they concentrate on fiction rather than journalism. Gullason's long introductions to both volumes are not indispensable, and he too leaves many textual and bibliographical questions unanswered. For example, in general he chooses as text the last printing of a work in Crane's lifetime, a practice which has little relevance to Crane, who seldom supervised republication of his work. Moreover, it is often impossible to identify precisely what text Gullason has chosen. Nevertheless, both collections are extremely useful because of their completeness. (They are also, in these days of inflated book prices, remarkably good buys.) The *Complete Novels* is especially helpful, since it brings together the major variants in all of Crane's novels—that is, the 1893 variants in *Maggie*; the uncanceled passages in *The Red Badge of Courage* manuscript which are not in the published book; and the passages in the Columbia type-

script and the Heinemann edition of *Active Service* which are not in
the American edition.

It would be well to mention at this point four general collections
which have played and will play a major role in Crane studies. William M. Gibson's *Stephen Crane: "The Red Badge of Courage" and
Selected Prose and Poetry* (New York, 1950; rev. 1956 and 1968) and
R. W. Stallman's *Stephen Crane: An Omnibus* (New York, 1952)
helped to establish both the canon of Crane's major work and important areas of critical interest. Joseph Katz's *The Portable Stephen Crane*
(New York, 1969) and Maurice Bassan's *Stephen Crane: A Collection
of Critical Essays* (Englewood Cliffs, N.J., 1967) continue the unending
attempt to isolate the best in Crane's writing and in writing about him.

In addition to complete or special collections of Crane, there have
been major editions of specific works and of his poems and letters. I
propose to discuss these in the order of their composition by Crane,
beginning with the Sullivan County sketches. It was Melvin Schoberlin
who discovered and republished what he called *The Sullivan County
Sketches of Stephen Crane* (Syracuse, N.Y., 1949), with an important
introduction. Only three of the ten sketches had been previously known
or collected, and Schoberlin in his introduction noted the significance
of the sketches in their anticipation of many of Crane's later themes and
techniques. Almost twenty years later, six additional sketches were
found, again in the *New York Tribune*. As often happens, this second
discovery, though long delayed, was announced almost simultaneously
by Thomas A. Gullason in "A Stephen Crane Find: Nine Newspaper
Sketches" (*Southern Humanities Review*, Winter 1968) and by R. W.
Stallman in *Stephen Crane: Sullivan County Tales and Sketches*
(Ames, Iowa, 1968), though Stallman anticipated Gullason by a year
in republishing one of the new sketches (*AL*, Nov. 1967).

Crane's *Maggie* has received much editorial attention in recent years,
most of it stemming from the discovery that the 1893 *Maggie* is a significant work in its own right. In "Stephen Crane's Revision of *Maggie*"
(*AL*, Jan. 1955), R. W. Stallman discussed in some detail the differences between the 1893 and 1896 versions and stressed that future editions should include the paragraph from Chapter Seventeen which was
omitted from the 1896 edition. Joseph Katz, in "The *Maggie* Nobody
Knows" (*MFS*, Summer 1966), also emphasized the distinctiveness of
the 1893 edition, though his contention that the curtailing of profanity
in the 1896 version weakens the religious theme in the novel is unconvincing. In response to this interest in the 1893 *Maggie*, Joseph Katz
and Donald Pizer prepared facsimile editions of the 1893 text (Gainesville, Fla., 1966, and San Francisco, 1968), and Maurice Bassan pre-

pared a particularly useful edition—*Stephen Crane's "Maggie": Text and Context* (Belmont, Calif., 1966)—in which he republished the 1893 text and introduced the substantive 1896 variants in footnotes. Until recently almost all editors of general collections of Crane have used an unannotated text of the 1896 *Maggie*. A shift in direction, however, is suggested by Joseph Katz's choice of the 1893 text for his *Portable Stephen Crane* and by Thomas A. Gullason's inclusion of the 1893 substantive variants in his *Complete Novels*. Only Fredson Bowers, in the Virginia Edition, has attempted to produce a single eclectic text from the two versions. It remains to be seen whether future editors will prefer his method or that of Katz, Bassan, or Gullason.

The text of *The Red Badge of Courage* may prove to be a major crux in modern bibliographical studies. Until 1951, when John T. Winterich included unpublished material from *The Red Badge* manuscript in his London Folio Society edition of the novel, the 1895 Appleton text had sole authority. (Joseph Katz has recently republished the 1895 Appleton edition in facsimile [Columbus, Ohio, 1969]). A fuller description and use of the manuscript, including an important distinction between an early short version (SV) and a later long version (LV), were provided by R. W. Stallman in his 1952 *Omnibus* volume. Winterich and Stallman noted that not only did the long version bear the mark of significant revision by Crane, but also that a number of passages left uncanceled in the LV manuscript were not published in the Appleton text. Both Winterich and Stallman (and Gibson in 1956) printed this omitted material in brackets as part of their integral text. In recent years, however, most editors have concluded that Crane himself was responsible for the excision of this material and that the inclusion of it within the text is unjustified. Editors of *The Red Badge* have therefore either placed the omitted material in footnotes or appendices (Richard Lettis et al., in 1960; Sculley Bradley et al., in 1962; and Thomas A. Gullason in 1967) or have omitted it entirely (Daniel G. Hoffman in 1957; Richard Chase in 1960; Frederick C. Crews in 1964; and Joseph Katz in his 1969 *Portable Stephen Crane*).

The two most important discussions of the text of *The Red Badge* are by Stallman in his Signet edition (New York, 1960) and by William L. Howarth in "*The Red Badge of Courage* Manuscript: New Evidence for a Critical Edition" (*SB*, 1965). Stallman's Signet volume can best be described as a tentative critical edition. Relying on the Appleton version as copy-text, he supplies uncanceled LV passages in brackets within the text and canceled LV passages and "critically interesting [SV] variants" in footnotes. The attempt is useful in that Stallman includes more of the *The Red Badge* manuscript than any other editor, but its value is qualified by Stallman's reliance on two insufficiently discussed or verifiable editorial principles—that the LV uncanceled omissions should be included in the text and that certain SV substantive variants are more interesting than others. Howarth's article is the first full discussion of the physical state of the *The Red Badge* manuscript and of the relationship of its condition to problems bearing on the preparation of a critical edition. Howarth is particularly valuable in establishing the order and extent of Crane's revisions (he notes seven distinct writing states), in discovering several hitherto unknown corruptions in the Appleton text, and in correcting Stallman's account of the manuscript. He is probably on shaky ground, however, in his belief that the LV served as printer's copy for the Appleton text. This conclusion would be enormously helpful to an editor of a critical text of *The Red Badge*, since he could then eliminate from consideration the missing typescript posited by most editors. The weakness in this argument is that the manuscript, as Winterich noted, shows scarcely any sign of printshop handling. So despite the efforts of Stallman and Howarth, the textual problem of *The Red Badge* still seems a long way from a successful resolution. The key to the problem no doubt lies in the still obscure details of the publishing history of the novel.

Crane's poems were collected by Wilson Follett in his 1925–27 edition and in *Collected Poems of Stephen Crane* (New York, 1930). Neither volume is of bibliographical interest. An important modern critical edition is Joseph Katz's *The Poems of Stephen Crane* (New York, 1966). Katz includes every known Crane poem and supplies an elaborate textual apparatus. His edition will no doubt serve as the basis for the Virginia Edition text of the poems.

Most of Crane's uncollected and unpublished work which is not in the 1925–27 edition has been collected in the various editions by Stallman and Hagemann, Fryckstedt, and Gullason noted above. Significant items which have not as yet been collected appear in two articles by R.W. Stallman, "Stephen Crane: Some New Stories" (*BNYPL*, Sept., Oct. 1956; Jan. 1957) (various fragments from the Columbia and Barrett collections) and "Stephen Crane: Some New Sketches" (*BNYPL*, Nov. 1967) (three excellent Mexico City sketches).

The first major collections of Crane's letters were by Stallman in his *Omnibus* and by Edwin H. Cady and Lester G. Wells in *Stephen Crane: Love Letters to Nellie Crouse*. Stallman and Lillian Gilkes then published their invaluable *Stephen Crane: Letters* (New York, 1960), which remains the standard edition. Like much of Stallman's editorial work, the collection is occasionally faulty in its transcriptions and facts. But in this instance Stallman's tendency toward excessive editorial commentary has resulted in a volume which has an old-fashioned life-in-letters usefulness. Indeed, in some ways the edition` is a more satisfactory introduction to Crane's life than Stallman's full-scale biography. However, a new edition of Crane's letters is needed, since a sizable number of new letters has appeared since 1960 and since Stallman and Gilkes's annotation requires updating and correction. The principal additions to the collection of Stallman and Gilkes are William White's "A Stephen Crane Letter" (*TLS*, 22 September 1961) and the various letters published in almost every issue of the *Stephen Crane Newsletter* since its founding in the fall of 1966.

The *Stephen Crane Newsletter*, edited by Joseph Katz, is now the principal vehicle for the publication of bibliographical, textual, and biographical notes on Crane. It is occasionally not unlike other author-newsletters in its failure to distinguish between the trivial and the significant. (One group of letters from Crane's boarding school headmaster to Mrs. Crane is for the most part a collection of bills, including some for laundry.) But many of the enterprises of the *Newsletter* serve important functions—its census of 1893 *Maggie*s, for example, or such continuing features as its quarterly checklist, its reviews, and its work-in-progress reports.

BIOGRAPHY

There are at present four major biographical studies of Crane: Thomas Beer, *Stephen Crane: A Study in American Letters* (New York, 1923); John Berryman, *Stephen Crane* (New York, 1950); Edwin H. Cady, *Stephen Crane* (New York, 1962); and R. W. Stallman, *Stephen Crane: A Biography*. In addition, Stallman's long introductions in his *Omnibus* volume almost constitute a critical biography, and Louis Zara's *Dark Rider: A Novel Based on the Life of Stephen Crane* (New York, 1961), is what its subtitle says it is.

Beer's work has so often been called brilliantly impressionistic but faulty that I would like to approach it from another direction after noting the crux which it represents in Crane studies. Beer relied on many letters and interview notes which are no longer extant. (His most severe critics would argue that much of this material was never extant.) In the years since the publication of his biography, students of Crane's life have frequently found demonstrable errors in this presently unavailable but supposedly documentary base of biographical detail. Yet because Beer still remains our only source of knowledge about many phases of Crane's life, scholars must continue to rely upon him despite his proven untrustworthiness.

Beer's declared intent was to destroy the myth of Crane as a demonic artist, but his biography, though it achieved this end, created several new myths about Crane. First, his book is less a biography of Crane than a study of Crane and his time. Crane emerges from Beer's pages not as a fully realized personality but as "A Study in American Letters," that is, as an artist misunderstood and crushed by the philistine culture of the 1890s. This myth of Crane survived well into the 1950s when E. H. Cady and others revealed that Crane shared many of the popular assumptions and beliefs of his time. A second myth introduced by Beer was that of the role of fear in Crane's psychical makeup—an approach which immediately suggested the need for a Freudian reading of Crane's life and work. Beer's oft-noted impressionistic style is therefore less significant as a characteristic of the twenties than is his interpretation of Crane in terms of two widely held views of the American artist current during that decade—that our best artists are victimized by American life and that their work expresses above all the drama of their suppressed inner life.

Like Beer, Berryman is usually a delight to read. Beer's strength lies in his ability to gather seemingly disparate concrete details into a single ironic or (less often) pathetic effect. Berryman also has an ironic touch, but his sense of narrative pace is far superior to Beer's, since Beer, indeed, was not interested in narrative coherence. Moreover, Berryman, unlike Beer, was aware of his responsibilities as a literary biographer. So we are rewarded with graceful accounts of the sources, composition, publishing history, and reputation of Crane's major works. Some of this detailed information has proven to be faulty or incomplete, but the basic outline of Crane's life and work emerges firmly and, on the whole, authoritatively from Berryman's book.

Berryman's long final chapter, "The Color of This Soul," has had some notoriety in American literary criticism as an extreme example of Freudian biography. His thesis, that Crane's Oedipus complex was responsible for his lifelong interest in older, disreputable women, is open to question, since the early death of Crane's father would seem to preclude a heavy reliance upon on Oedipal interpretation of Crane. Moreover, Berryman's collage technique—that is, his gathering together of similar images and symbols from the entire corpus of Crane's work in order to "paste up" a Freudian reading of Crane—is ingenious at best. Horses, the color red, and Negroes do appear in Crane's work, but so do many other symbols. Although it is sometimes dangerous to call upon common sense as a guide when discussing a complex literary figure, A. J. Liebling's criticism of Berryman nevertheless rings true. As Liebling noted in "The Dollars Damned Him" (*New Yorker*, 5 August

1961), a highly intelligent, very young man is apt to get involved with women older than himself, and a man who liked horses is apt to include them in his work.

Although Berryman's final chapter has often been singled out for adverse criticism, many readers are apparently unaware that Berryman's Freudian thesis shaped his interpretation of works discussed at some length earlier in the book, for example, "The Monster" and "The Blue Hotel." In short, Berryman is very much an advance over Beer as a usable scholarly biography but his is still too much a "poetic" biography in a pejorative sense. That is, his imaginative response to his subject colors and controls the work more than most readers would prefer.

Although Edwin H. Cady's study is a critical biography, with more criticism than biography, his section on Crane's life is nevertheless a valuable contribution to Crane biography. Reacting no doubt to the single-thesis approach of Beer and Berryman in biography and Stallman in criticism, Cady refuses to categorize Crane or his work but rather views him as "an uncrystallized experimenter, a youthful pluralist." In two brief but cogent chapters, he defines the tone of the principal moments in Crane's life, confronts the major cruxes in Crane biography, and places Crane firmly in the context of his family, his time, and his friends. In short, Cady's fifty-odd pages constitute an excellent introduction to Crane's life.

In the years since Berryman's *Stephen Crane*, a great deal of Crane biographical material has become available. The Columbia and Barrett collections, the Stallman and Gilkes edition of the letters, and the Gilkes biography of Cora Crane, to name but a few such aids, all seemed to open the way for a definitive biography, with R. W. Stallman, the doyen of Crane scholars, the obvious biographer. Unfortunately, the best that can be said of Stallman's massive work is that it will do until a better book is written. It has all of Stallman's weaknesses and few of his strengths. It is discursive, repetitive, poorly organized, padded, overpolemical, and thesis-ridden. Almost every work by Crane, from the most familiar to the most obscure, is subjected to a pedestrian summary of its contents and to a cursory critical discussion, the latter often a rehash of standard Stallman opinions available in superior form elewhere. And after almost twenty years of berating Beer and Berryman for their errors, Stallman still feels obliged to note every point at which he corrects them.

Saddest of all, Stallman is simply not a good biographer. Important moments in Crane's life, such as the *Commodore* disaster or his Cuban war experiences, are narrated poorly, and Stallman often slips into the cardinal sin of the literary biographer, the too easy translation of biographical fact into literary event. For example, we are told of a college tug-of-war in which Crane participated and are then informed, "The Lafayette College tug-of-war became the flag that is wrenched from the enemy in *The Red Badge*."

There are flashes of Stallman at his best in character vignettes (Crane and Conrad) or in an occasional provocative remark, but all in all the biography is poorly written and, despite its over 100 pages of documentation, poorly researched. (Many reviewers noted its inaccuracies, and the *Stephen Crane Newsletter* seems to be running a quarterly check list of its errors.) In truth, it is a tired book: it should have been compressed, reorganized, rewritten, and checked fully for accuracy. Stallman has the knowledge and the intellect to produce a major Crane biography, and he was poorly served by those editors and readers who permitted what is essentially a draft to appear in print.

I will now discuss biographical studies which bear significantly on particular phases of Crane's career. In general, I omit reminiscences of Crane by friends and relatives. Such accounts have long been available and their pertinent information has been fully absorbed into later biographical studies.

Work on Crane's school years suffers from a paucity of knowledge about Crane himself during these years. Nevertheless, it is valuable to know that Crane attended institutions at which Methodism or military drill or sports were inseparable from his daily life. Some of the most important articles on Crane's school years are: Jean Cazemajou, "Stephen Crane: Pennington Seminary: Étape d'une éducation méthodiste" (*EA*, 1967) and Thomas A. Gullason, "The Cranes at Pennington Seminary" (*AL*, Jan. 1968) for Crane's first prep school; Lyndon U. Pratt, "The Formal Education of Stephen Crane" (*AL*, Jan. 1939) for Claverack, Lafayette, and Syracuse; and Claude Jones, "Stephen Crane at Syracuse" (*AL*, Mar. 1935). Crane's boyhood and young manhood in Asbury Park are well surveyed by Victor A. Elconin, "Stephen Crane at Asbury Park" (*AL*, Nov. 1948), with particular emphasis on the summer of 1892. But since Asbury Park's "precarious balance of pleasure and morality" (Elconin) undoubtedly played a major role in shaping Crane's ironic vision of life, this phase of his youth—that is, the social morality of Asbury Park—requires fuller study than it has received.

Crane's early years in New York are still obscure, despite the continuing effort by Crane scholars to answer such basic questions as what he was reading and writing, who his friends were, and where he was living. The most important sources of information about this period are Corwin K. Linson's *My Stephen Crane*, edited by Edwin H. Cady

(Syracuse, N.Y., 1958), and the various recollections of Hamlin Garland. Neither writer is completely dependable, though Garland's invaluable accounts have been more or less untangled and interpreted by a number of scholars. Donald Pizer, in "The Garland-Crane Relationship" (*HLQ*, Nov. 1960[1]), corrects Garland's confused and contradictory chronology by reference to his contemporary journals and letters, while Olov W. Fryckstedt, "Crane's *Black Riders*: A Discussion of Dates" (*SN*, 1962); Robert Mane, "Une recontre littéraire: Hamlin Garland et Stephen Crane (*EA*, 1964); and Stanley Wertheim, "The Saga of March 23: Garland, Gilder, and Crane" (*SCraneN*, Winter 1968) refine and correct Pizer's restructuring of Garland's account of the relationship.

Two other early literary associations which have been explored are those of Crane and William Dean Howells and Crane and Elbert Hubbard. The best discussion of Howells and Crane is in Edwin H. Cady's *The Realist at War* (Syracuse, N.Y., 1958), though Clara and Rudolf Kirk also present a useful summary in their edition of Howells's *Criticism and Fiction, and Other Essays* (New York, 1959). Crane and Hubbard are the subject of David H. Dickason's "Stephen Crane and the *Philistine*" (*AL*, Nov. 1943) and Joseph Katz's "How Elbert Hubbard Met Stephen Crane" (*SCraneN*, Spring 1968).

Most studies of Crane's early New York years have understandably concentrated on such verifiable matters as his friendships. Few scholars have attempted, as does Joseph J. Kwiat in "The Newspaper Experience: Crane, Norris, and Dreiser" (*NCF*, Sept. 1953), to discuss the impact of Crane's free-lance reporting experiences on his work and thought. But as Ellen Moers has recently demonstrated in her *Two Dreisers* (New York, 1969), the New York newspaper and magazine world of the 1890s was alive with ideas and enthusiasms and with personal intrigue and gossip. Crane was very much part of this life, and we will not fully understand this phase of his experience until we know more about his relationship to the journalistic subculture of the 1890s.

We know much more, of course, about Crane's post-1894 years, after *The Red Badge* brought him fame and notoriety. Saving his English experiences for later discussion, the most important events of this period were his trip west, his filibustering experiences in Florida, his rela-

---

1. Reprinted in Pizer's *Realism and Naturalism in Nineteenth-Century American Literature* (Carbondale, Ill., 1966). Other Pizer articles cited below which are reprinted in this collection are: "Late Nineteenth-Century American Naturalism: An Essay in Definition," "Romantic Individualism in Garland, Norris, and Crane," and "Stephen Crane's *Maggie* and American Naturalism."

tionship with Cora, his Tenderloin misadventure with Dora Clark, and his reporting of the Greco-Turkish and Cuban wars.

Crane's trip to the West and to Mexico in early 1895 has been insufficiently researched, but his filibustering experiences are fully documented. William Randel has filled in the Jacksonville background in "Stephen Crane's Jacksonville" (*SAQ*, Spring 1963) and "From Slate to Emerald Green: More Light on Crane's Jacksonville Visit" (*NCF*, Mar. 1965), supplemented by Joseph Katz, "Stephen Crane, 'Samuel Carlton,' and a Recovered Letter" (*NCF*, Sept. 1968). Crane's shipwreck adventure has occasioned a controversy over the accuracy of his later account, both in his news story and in "The Open Boat." The problematic issues are: was there treachery aboard the *Commodore*, how many men were in the boat, did the captain shirk his duty, and were the seas rough? Berryman in 1950 and Cyrus Day in "Stephen Crane and the Ten-foot Dinghy" (*BUSE*, Winter 1957) doubt the factual accuracy of Crane's accounts of these matters. Crane has been defended by William Randel, "The Cook in 'The Open Boat'" (*AL*, Nov. 1962); William T. Going, "William Higgins and Crane's 'The Open Boat': A Note About Fact and Fiction" (*Papers on English Language and Literature*, Winter 1965); and R. W. Stallman, "Journalist Crane in That Dinghy" (*BNYPL*, Apr. 1968). The controversy has served the useful purpose of reminding us that, as in most disasters, the *Commodore* shipwreck produced varying impressions on its participants and observers. Crane's brilliance, most critics would now agree, lay in his shaping of his own impressions into a work of art, whether the waves were high or low on January 1, 1896.

Crane's Jacksonville period also marked the beginning of his relationship with Cora. (He had apparently just escaped from a difficult entanglement with Amy Leslie; see Joseph Katz, "Some Light on the Stephen Crane-Amy Leslie Affair," *Mad River Review* [Dayton, Ohio], Winter 1965.) This all-important relationship, first hinted at by Beer and discussed at greater length in later biographies, is in part the subject of Lillian Gilkes in *Cora Crane: A Biography of Mrs. Stephen Crane*. Crane, however, is a somewhat shadowy figure in this study, for Miss Gilkes's interest is centered firmly on Cora. In the author's view, Cora was not the overblown, matronly figure recalled by Conrad, Ford, and James but a heroic late nineteenth-century New Woman riding full-tilt against Victorian conventions. Miss Gilkes's work is based on extensive research in Florida and England and among the Columbia Crane papers, but her biographical method is nevertheless suspect because of her close identification with her subject. (For example, she is confident enough of her material to create dialogue.) The principal value of her biography is not in increasing our understanding of Crane's inner life. Rather, her work is a fascinating account of late nineteenth-century Anglo-American social practice (as distinct from morality) and of the amazingly disordered circumstances of Crane's final years.

Crane's 1896 New York experiences and his adventures as a war correspondent are well surveyed in Stallman and Hagemann's two editions noted above. These may be supplemented by Olov W. Fryckstedt's "Stephen Crane in the Tenderloin" (*SN*, 1962), which is still the best account of the Dora Clark affair, and by Scott C. Osborn's "The 'Rivalry-Chivalry' of Richard Harding Davis and Stephen Crane" (*AL*, Mar. 1956).

Our knowledge of Crane's English years is based in part on excellent reminiscences and pen portraits by such friends as Conrad, Wells, James, and Ford. Their accounts, and the friendships themselves, are the subject of Eric Solomon's slight but useful *Stephen Crane in England: A Portrait of the Artist* (Columbus, Ohio, 1964). Of greater significance than Crane's personal relationships in England is the possibility that he overproduced and catered to popular taste in order to maintain the style of life represented by Brede Place. An acceptance of this possibility is implicit in Stallman and Gilkes's full accounts of the Cranes in England and it is also the explicit thesis of A. J. Liebling's "The Dollars Damned Him" and James B. Stronks's "Stephen Crane's English Years: The Legend Corrected" (*PBSA*, 1963). Daniel G. Hoffman's revelation, in "Stephen Crane's Last Novel" (*BNYPL*, June 1960), that Crane was planning to write a Revolutionary War novel in order to capitalize upon the vogue for such fiction also supports this view of his last years. And, finally, E. R. Hagemann's "The Death of Stephen Crane" (*PNJHS*, July 1959) is an exhaustive account, based largely on documents in the National Archives, of Crane's illness, death, and burial.

CRITICISM

General Estimates and Interpretations

Some of the early estimates of Crane remain among the best general introductions to his work. George Wyndham's "A Remarkable Book" (*New Review*, Jan. 1896); Edward Garnett's "Mr. Stephen Crane: An Appreciation" (*Academy*, 17 December 1898; reprinted, with additions, in Garnett's *Friday Nights*, New York, 1922); and H. G. Wells's "Stephen Crane: From an English Standpoint" (*NAR*, Aug. 1900; reprinted in *The Shock of Recognition*, ed. Edmund Wilson, New York, 1943) helped to establish such permanent areas of critical interest as Crane's irony and psychological realism, the canon of his best work, and the relationship of his technique and form to painting. Vincent Starrett's "Stephen Crane: An Estimate" (*SR*, July 1920; reprinted in Starrett's *Buried Caesars*, Chicago, 1923) played an important role in the "rediscovery" of Crane and continues to have intrinsic value. Alfred Kazin's pages on Crane in *On Native Grounds* (New York, 1942) and Grant C. Knight's section in *The Critical Period in American Literature* (Chapel Hill, N.C., 1951) have not weathered as well as the essays by Garnett and Wells. The best recent general estimates, most of which combine biographical and critical interpretation, are by Warner Berthoff, *The Ferment of Realism* (New York, 1965); Larzer Ziff, *The American 1890s* (New York, 1966); Jay Martin, *Harvests of Change* (Englewood Cliffs, N.J., 1967); and Jean Cazemajou, *Stephen Crane* (UMPAW, 1969).

I will now discuss, more or less in chronological order, the major critical approaches to Crane's work. My classification is, of course, in part arbitrary, but some classification is necessary if the basic tendencies in Crane criticism are to be made discernible.

In Crane's own day it was common to call him an impressionist and to associate his techniques with those of the studio. Garnett and Wells stressed this aspect of Crane, as did Ford Madox Ford in his later and influential article "Techniques" (*SoR*, July 1935). Impressionism, however, has often served merely as a vague description of Crane's color sense and of his highly distinctive narrative technique and prose style. More recent critics who are absorbed in the possibility of discussing Crane as an impressionist have refined their use of the term in several ways. One group has sought to define his impressionism by locating its source in Crane's contemporary world. Joseph J. Kwiat, in "Stephen Crane and Painting" (*AQ*, Winter 1952), builds valiantly on a base of scanty evidence to claim that Crane's association with various minor illustrators during 1891–93 led to his acceptance of impressionistic ideas and techniques. On the whole, it has been less difficult to find literary sources for Crane's impressionistic aesthetic. James B. Colvert, in "The Origins of Stephen Crane's Literary Creed" (*University of Texas Studies in English*, 1955), persuasively contends that Crane's voiced literary ideals ("I understand that a man is born into the world with his own pair of eyes," etc.) parallel those of the artist Dick Heldar in Kipling's *The Light That Failed*. Donald Pizer, in "Romantic Individualism in Garland, Norris, and Crane" (*AQ*, Winter 1958), and Stanley Wertheim, in "Crane and Garland: The Education of an Impressionist" (*North Dakota Quarterly*, Winter 1967), stress the impact of Garland's impressionistic beliefs on Crane during the vital 1892–93 period. Even Crane's color sense has been associated with a literary source, by Robert L. Hough, in "Crane and Goethe: A Forgotten Relationship" (*NCF*, Sept. 1962).

The difficult task of attempting to pinpoint what is meant by Crane's stylistic impressionism was first undertaken at any length by R. W. Stallman in his 1952 *Omnibus* volume. Stallman's belief that Crane's style is "prose pointillism" suffers from the inevitable fuzziness that results from the translation of brush and canvas terminology into literary practice and effect. Much more useful are the recent and important articles by Sergio Perosa, "Stephen Crane fra naturalismo e impressionismo" (*Annali di Ca' Fascari* [Venezia], 1964; translated and reprinted in *Stephen Crane: A Collection of Critical Essays*, ed. Maurice Bassan), and by Orm Øverland, "The Impressionism of Stephen Crane," in *Americana Norvegica*, edited by Sigmund Skard and Henry H. Wasser (Philadelphia, 1966). Both writers closely examine Crane's point-of-view technique, his episodic structure, his imagery and symbolism, and his syntax and diction. Although their essays are major contributions to our understanding of Crane's prose style and fictional technique, their critical insights are ultimately of value in spite of rather than because of their consideration of Crane as an impressionist. In short, the term "impressionist" has been useful as a way of placing Crane in a particular historical context, but it is of less worth as a means of describing the particulars of his style because of the obfuscating associations attached to the term.

A significant variation in the interpretation of Crane as an impressionist was first introduced by Charles C. Walcutt in *American Literary Naturalism, A Divided Stream* (Minneapolis, Minn., 1956) and pursued at greater length by David R. Weimer in *The City as Metaphor* (New York, 1966). Walcutt's remark that Crane is probably closer to expressionism than impressionism is fully and brilliantly explored by Weimer, who concludes that Crane's fragmentation and stylization of experience are less related to the eye of the impressionist painter than to the intellect of the expressionist playwright.

Although Crane's fellow writers have tended to consider him principally as an impressionist, academic criticism, with its ideological bent, has more frequently approached him as a naturalist. Much of this criticism straitjacketed Crane in an abstract definition of naturalism ("pessimistic determinism" or the like) and served little purpose except to pigeonhole him neatly. Two influential studies of this kind are Oscar Cargill's *Intellectual America* (New York, 1941) and Malcolm Cowley's "'Not Men': A Natural History of American Naturalism" (*KR*, Summer 1947; reprinted in *Critiques and Essays on Modern Fiction*,

1920–51, ed. John W. Aldridge, New York, 1952). This simplistic view of Crane persists even in such otherwise sophisticated works as Desmond Maxwell's *American Fiction: The Intellectual Background* (New York, 1963) and Edward Stone's *Voices of Despair* (Athens, Ohio, 1966). Occasionally it appears in somewhat disguised form, as in Gordon O. Taylor's *The Passages of Thought: Psychological Representation in the American Novel, 1870–1900* (New York, 1969), but is essentially the same old naturalistic wolf.

The three most important studies of Crane as naturalist are Lars Åhnebrink, *The Beginnings of Naturalism in American Fiction* (Uppsala, 1950); Charles C. Walcutt, *American Literary Naturalism*; and Donald Pizer, "Late Nineteenth-Century American Naturalism: An Essay in Definition" (*BuR*, Fall 1965). Åhnebrink seeks to place Crane fully in the European naturalistic tradition, particularly that of Zola. His critical method consists largely of the examination of parallel passages and themes in the work of Crane and such writers as Zola, Tolstoy, Turgenev, and Ibsen. His parallels, however, reveal primarily that descriptions of a slum tenement, for example, will often include odors, noise, and violence. They do not cast light on the distinctive qualities of mind that produced works as different as *Maggie* and *L'Assommoir*. Nevertheless, Åhnebrink's voluminous documentation convincingly establishes the pervasiveness of such subjects as alcoholism and slum conditions in the late nineteenth-century social and literary consciousness of both Europe and America. Walcutt's study of Crane as a naturalist appears to work at cross-purposes with his general thesis that American naturalism is a divided stream—that is, that the nineteenth-century currents of intuitional idealism and mechanistic determinism reach an uneasy and inconsistent union in the naturalistic novel. To Walcutt, Crane is the one major example in American naturalism of a complete and coherent determinist. Walcutt successfully discusses *Maggie* as a deterministic novel, but in his analyses of Crane's later work, including *The Red Badge*, he overemphasizes deterministic threads in a complex pattern of themes. Paradoxically, Walcutt's greatest impact on Crane criticism has probably been less his discussion of Crane than his general thesis in *American Literary Naturalism*. For since 1956 many critics have accepted his belief that American naturalism—including the work of Crane—must be approached as a complex literary phenomenon rather than as merely a weak-minded illustration of a particular philosophical doctrine. Pizer's article follows in the path blazed by Walcutt with two major differences. What Walcutt views as thematically and artistically inept (particularly the mixing of philosophical attitudes), Pizer views as a source of depth and power. And Pizer places Crane in a definition of naturalism which derives from the practice rather than the theory of late nineteenth-century American fiction and which therefore refuses to consider deviations from Zolaesque or other concepts of naturalism as aesthetically or thematically significant.

I have already noted the Freudian aspects of the biographies by Beer and Berryman. Maxwell Geismar, in *Rebels and Ancestors* (Boston, 1953); Daniel G. Hoffman, in *The Poetry of Stephen Crane*; and Stanley Wertheim, in "Stephen Crane and the Wrath of Jehovah" (*Little Review*, Summer 1964), also view Crane as a classic Oedipal case. Geismar in particular vigorously searches out Oedipal symbols in most of Crane's work. Hoffman, however, adopts this angle of approach as one of several critical methods, and Wertheim explores less blatantly than most Freudian critics the theme of guilt in Crane. Inevitably, *George's Mother* has attracted the greatest attention from Freudian-minded critics. Often, a Freudian reading of this novel is awkwardly applied to other major works by Crane, as in Norman Lavers's "Order in *The Red Badge of Courage*" (*University Review*, Summer 1966). Jungian readings of Crane tend to concentrate on *The Red Badge* and Crane's concept of the hero. John E. Hart's "*The Red Badge of Courage* as Myth and Symbol" (*UKCR*, Summer 1953) remains the best of such studies. Donald B. Gibson's *The Fiction of Stephen Crane* (Carbondale, Ill., 1968) is ostensibly a study of Crane in relation to Erich Neumann's Jungian *The Origins and History of Consciousness*. In fact, it is an amateurish reading of Crane in which the author mechanically applies a free will–determinism formula to the interpretation of work after work. Gibson lacks any "feel" for his subject (he can ask of the phrase "squat ignorant stables" in *Maggie*, "What are 'ignorant' stables?") and his book is best forgotten.

Crane's social themes are often mentioned in discussions of his New York slum writing, but there is little full-scale discussion of him as a critic of his society. (He appears only briefly, for example, in W. F. Taylor's standard *The Economic Novel in America*.) Two exceptions, both of which discover a strong sense of the reality of the class struggle in his work, are Russel B. Nye's "Stephen Crane as Social Critic" (*Modern Quarterly*, Summer 1940) and M. Solomon's "Stephen Crane: A Critical Study" (*Masses & Mainstreams*, Jan. 1956). Neither study is entirely persuasive, primarily because of the difficulty in separating Crane's social attitudes from other, more prominent aspects of his thought—his views of God and nature, for example. Moreover, it is obvious that his social ideas cannot be adequately described by summarizing the plots of his fiction, as Robert W. Schneider does in *Five Nov-*

elists of the Progressive Era (New York, 1965). Crane's idea of society is no doubt a significant element in his thought (most full-length studies of his work inevitably touch upon it), but a meaningful discussion of that idea awaits a critic who is willing to confront the full complexity of Crane's themes and techniques in pursuit of his subject.

Studies of Crane as religious symbolist tend to concentrate on *The Red Badge* and on his poetry. Since examination of religious themes in his poetry usually occurs within full-scale discussions of his poetic art, I will reserve commenting on these themes until later. More pertinent at this point is the controversial reading of *The Red Badge* by R. W. Stallman, a reading which implies that Christian symbolism is at the heart of all of Crane's work. Stallman's interpretation of *The Red Badge* as a story of Christian redemption first appeared in his 1951 Modern Library edition of the novel. Since then he has repeated it many times (with occasional variations in emphasis), most notably in his "Stephen Crane: A Revaluation," in *Critiques and Essays on Modern Fiction, 1920–51*, edited by John W. Aldridge, in his 1952 *Omnibus* volume, in his essays on Crane in *The Houses That James Built* (East Lansing, Mich., 1961), and in his Crane biography. Few readers of Crane would deny that Christian symbols and themes pervade his work, but most would probably echo Isaac Rosenfeld's early comment in "Stephen Crane as Symbolist" (*KR*, Spring 1953) that Stallman "is working his poor horse to death." I shall take up Stallman's reading of *The Red Badge* at greater length later, but it is appropriate at this time to note such major negative responses to his methods and thesis as Philip Rahv, "Fiction and the Criticism of Fiction" (*KR*, Spring 1956); Norman Friedman, "Criticism and the Novel" (*Antioch Review*, Fall 1958); and, in particular, Stanley B. Greenfield, "The Unmistakable Stephen Crane" (*PMLA*, Dec. 1958). The general import of these responses is that Stallman has woven a disparate group of images into a theme which is extraneous to or contradicted by the themes present in the plot and characterization of the novel. This debate on the validity of a predominantly Christian symbolist reading of Crane occurred primarily during the 1950s, when both New Criticism analyses of fiction and Christian myth interpretations of all literature were much in vogue. Except for Stallman, critics of the 1960s have turned to other interests, which suggests that an emphasis upon Crane as a Christian symbolist has had its day.

A more recent critical tendency has been to attempt to define Crane's moral position without recourse to the absolutes of pessimistic determinism or Christian redemption. In a series of closely reasoned articles which usually draw upon Crane's best work, a number of critics have discussed Crane's cosmic vision as a complex entity that defies easy classification. The first such writer was John W. Shroeder, in "Stephen Crane Embattled" (*UKCR*, Winter 1950); followed by Greenfield; by James B. Colvert, in "Style and Meaning in Stephen Crane's 'The Open Boat'" (*University of Texas Studies in English*, 1958) and "Structure and Theme in Stephen Crane's Fiction" (*MFS*, Autumn 1959); by George W. Johnson, in "Stephen Crane's Metaphor of Decorum" (*PMLA*, June 1963); and by Max Westbrook, in "Stephen Crane: The Pattern of Affirmation" (*NCF*, Dec. 1959), "Stephen Crane and the Personal Universal" (*MFS*, Winter 1962–63), and "Stephen Crane's Social Ethic" (*AQ*, Winter 1962). Most of these critics accept Greenfield's view that Crane's work exhibits a "balance between the deterministic and volitional views of life." Each, however, asserts this position somewhat differently. Colvert, for example, stresses Crane's ironic relationship to his characters, Johnson their role-playing, and Westbrook their ethical limitations yet ultimate responsibility. With the exception of Shroeder's early, tentative article, all are major efforts. Perhaps the essays of Colvert and Johnson will have the most influence on Crane criticism, since their study of Crane's technique as a means of describing his ethic avoids the usual hazards of attempting to apply such philosophically absolute terms as "free will" and "determinism" directly to the complex reality of a literary construct.

Our greater knowledge of Crane's life and times and the recent growth of American Studies as a discipline have encouraged critical studies which stress the American roots of his subjects and themes. A pioneer "Americanist" study of Crane was Marcus Cunliffe's "Stephen Crane and the American Background of *Maggie*" (*AQ*, Spring 1955). Cunliffe ably demonstrates that the sources of Crane's story are less attributable to Zola than to American social reform tracts of the 1880s and 1890s. In other attempts to dispel the notion that Crane was a "sport" on the American scene, Donald Pizer, in "Romantic Individualism in Garland, Norris, and Crane," notes the similarity between Crane's aesthetic beliefs and an Emersonian faith in the artist's private vision, and Daniel G. Hoffman, in *The Poetry of Stephen Crane*, locates the specific source of Crane's symbolic technique in an Emersonian aesthetic. Edwin H. Cady has opened up two rich areas of interest of Crane in an American context: Crane and the American enthusiasm for sports, in "Stephen Crane and the Strenuous Life" (*ELH*, Dec. 1961), and Crane and the code of the Christian gentleman, in *Stephen Crane*. And Crane has belatedly and unconvincingly been discussed by David W. Noble in connection with an American

Edenic myth, in *The Eternal Adam and the New World Garden* (New York, 1968).

Perhaps the most important study of Crane in relation to his American setting is Eric Solomon's *Stephen Crane: From Parody to Realism* (Cambridge, Mass., 1966). Solomon believes that many of Crane's themes have their origin in his conscious parody of late nineteenth-century popular literary formulas and subjects—slum reform and temperance writing, romantic war fiction, the dime western, and children's stories. His book is both the best study of the literary origins of Crane's fiction and one of the few full-length studies of Crane which discusses the various major divisions in his work with a coherent and acceptable analytical device, that of Crane as parodist. Nevertheless, this device is also the source of some of the book's weaknesses. Least significant of these is Solomon's neglect of his thesis when he is confronted by an essentially nonparodic work, such as "The Open Boat." More vital are his bypassing of a theoretical discussion of parody as a literary mode and his fuzzy and limited concept of "realism." For Solomon, realism seems to be merely the opposite of what Crane is parodying in particular works, and he concludes that most of Crane's major fiction moves from a parody half to a realistic half. In short, Solomon is often formulistic and he is weak on theory. But no student of Crane can neglect his discussion of the relationship between Crane's writing and the literature of his time.

Finally, Crane has come within the compass of the recent critical movement which finds most major writers to be existentialists. Two articles which adopt this view toward his work are William B. Stein's "Stephen Crane's *Homo Absurdus*" (*BuR*, May 1959) and Florence Leaver's "Isolation in the Work of Stephen Crane" (*SAQ*, Autumn 1962). Both critics find that Crane's work exhibits the existential themes of the absurdity of ethical values and the isolation of man in an amoral, Godless universe. Although these are by no means novel conclusions, both writers state their case persuasively.

Maggie *and Other Early Work*

Most critical discussions of Crane's early journalism have appeared in editions of the Sullivan County sketches (Schoberlin, Stallman, and Gullason) and in general studies of his work and career. Inevitably, almost all of this criticism is devoted to isolating those characteristics of Crane's early newspaper work which anticipate later themes and techniques. An excellent recent demonstration of the possibilities of this approach is Marston La France's "The Ironic Parallel in Stephen Crane's 1892 Newspaper Correspondence" (*SSF*, Fall 1968).

La France reveals that a basic Crane technique—the ironic juxtaposition of two seemingly diverse yet essentially similar moral climates—appears in his early accounts of Asbury Park and Ocean Grove. Although limited in scope, La France's discussion is probably more useful than the many analyses which attempt to locate complex philosophical positions in such slight and "clever" works as the Sullivan County sketches. Moreover, since we now have available a sizable amount of pre-*Maggie* journalism by Crane in addition to the Sullivan County sketches, there is a need for studies which consider all of Crane's early work as a single area of critical interest.

Crane's New York sketches and tales have attracted the special attention of Maurice Bassan: "Misery and Society: Some New Perspectives in Stephen Crane's Fiction" (*SN*, 1963); "The Design of Stephen Crane's Bowery 'Experiment'" (*SSF*, Winter 1964); and "Stephen Crane and 'The Eternal Mystery of Social Condition'" (*NCF*, Mar. 1965). Bassan's first article usefully places Crane's Bowery sketches in the context of the depression of 1893–94, but his final two studies are somewhat strident attempts to demonstrate the literary worth of "An Experiment in Misery" and "An Experiment in Luxury." Jean Cazemajou's "Stephen Crane et ses esquisses de vie New-Yorkaise" (*Caliban*, Jan. 1964) is an unanalytical survey of all of Crane's New York sketches.

Maggie is of course the early work by Crane which has received the greatest critical attention. The fullest and most useful introductions to the novel are in the editions by James Colvert, *Bowery Tales* (Charlottesville, Va., 1969), and by Donald Pizer, *Maggie: A Girl of the Streets*. Both Colvert and Pizer stress the native sources of the novel, as do Marcus Cunliffe in "Stephen Crane and the American Background of *Maggie*" and Thomas A. Gullason in "The Sources of Stephen Crane's *Maggie*" (*PQ*, Oct. 1959). The search for native roots, however, has occasionally resulted in straining analogous to earlier attempts to discover French sources for Crane's work. Two recent examples are Sholom J. Kahn, "Stephen Crane and Whitman: A Possible Source for *Maggie*" (*Walt Whitman Review*, Dec. 1961) and Donald B. Kuspit, "Charles Dana Gibson's Girl" (*JA*, 1962).

As with *The Red Badge*, critical opinion is divided in its belief as to what constitutes the main thrust of *Maggie*. Most early critics, and more recently David Fitelson in "Stephen Crane's *Maggie* and Darwinism" (*AQ*, Summer 1964), envision the novel as portraying above all an uncompromising Darwinistic determinism. Another group of readers, while accepting the conditioning force of environment as a principal theme, note the presence of other major themes as well, particularly those which suggest the continuing significance of character even in a slum world. Howells viewed *Maggie* in this light as early as 1896, in his introduction to the Heinemann edition (reprinted in *Prefaces to Contemporaries [1882–1920]*, edited by George W. Arms et al., Gainesville, Fla., 1957), when he noted that the novel resembled a Greek tragedy in its account of a soul "struggling vainly with inexorable fate." More recently Thomas A. Gullason in "Thematic Patterns in Stephen Crane's Early Novels" (*NCF*, June 1961) and Max Westbrook in "Stephen Crane's Social Ethic" have stressed that the characters of *Maggie* are either unfulfilled dreamers or do indeed have responsibility for their fates. Perhaps the most pervasive approach to the novel in recent years, however, is one which holds that Crane's satire is directed against middle class and romantic attitudes rather than against the slum dwellers who unwittingly ape these attitudes. Some critics reach this position by an analysis of Crane's ironic techniques: W. B. Stein, "New Testament Inversions in Crane's *Maggie*" (*MLN*, Apr. 1958); Joseph X. Brennan, "Ironic and Symbolic Structure in Crane's *Maggie*" (*NCF*, Mar. 1962); and Janet Overmyer, "The Structure of Crane's *Maggie*" (*UKCR*, Autumn 1962). Others have concentrated on such particulars as Crane's portrayal of the theater or of Maggie's mother to reach a similar conclusion: R. W. Stallman, "Stephen Crane's Primrose Path" (*New Republic*, 19 September 1955) and "Crane's *Maggie*: A Reassessment" (*MFS*, Autumn 1959); Donald Pizer, "Stephen Crane's *Maggie* and American Naturalism" (*Criticism*, Spring 1965); William T. Lenehan, "The Failure of Naturalistic Techniques in Stephen Crane's *Maggie*," in *Stephen Crane's "Maggie": Text and Context*, edited by Maurice Bassan; and Philip H. Ford, "Illusion and Reality in Crane's *Maggie* (*ArQ*, Winter 1969).

The aspect of *Maggie* which has received the least satisfactory criticism is its form. R. W. Stallman (in his *Omnibus*) has attempted to describe *Maggie* as a novel of alternating moods, but a description of this kind is applicable to most fiction. Edwin H. Cady (in his *Stephen Crane*) divides the work into four thematic sections, with alternating picture and scene in each unit, and maintains that the novel is flawed in structure because its climax (Maggie's death) occurs at the end of the third section. Malcolm Bradbury, in an offhand but suggestive article, "Sociology and Literary Studies. II. Romance and Reality in *Maggie*" (*JAmS*, July 1969), claims that Crane's ironic juxtaposition of deluded characters and a Darwinistic universe results in the breakdown of the traditional linear plot. Bradbury, however, does not attempt to describe what has replaced plot as a structural principle in *Maggie*. In short, as in criticism of *The Red Badge*, though many writers approach the theme of *Maggie* through its form, few have attempted a full formalistic description or analysis of the novel.

George's Mother has received surprisingly little critical attention other than passing comment in general studies of Crane. Joseph X. Brennan, in "The Imagery and Art of *George's Mother*" (*CLAJ*, Dec. 1960), analyzes the imagery of the novel and unconvincingly concludes that George's mother is one of the few "really sympathetic" figures in all of Crane's fiction and that the work is better than *Maggie*. James B. Colvert, in his introduction to the Virginia *Bowery Tales*, deals successfully with the complicated problem of the dating of the composition of the novel (see also Maurice Bassan, "An Early Draft of *George's Mother*," *AL*, Jan. 1965) but appears to be forcing his contention that Crane wrote the work as a "realistic" novel in the manner of Howells and Garland because of their criticism of *Maggie*. Colvert and many other critics have noted that *George's Mother*, because of its mother-son center and its temperance and religious themes, is the most personal of Crane's novels. This characteristic and the comparatively low-keyed techniques of the novel have perhaps deterred critics from full consideration of what is undoubtedly a major work.

The Red Badge of Courage

The best general introductions to *The Red Badge of Courage* are those by Richard Chase and Frederick C. Crews in their editions of the novel (Boston, 1960, and Indianapolis, Ind., 1964) and by Edwin H. Cady in his *Stephen Crane*. Two useful collections of criticism are *Stephen Crane's "The Red Badge of Courage": Text and Criticism*, edited by Richard Lettis et al. (New York, 1960) and *The Red Badge of Courage*, edited by Sculley Bradley et al. (New York, 1962). I have already discussed general textual studies of *The Red Badge*, but I should note at this point textual commentary which bears significantly on interpretation of the novel. Both Olov W. Fryckstedt, in "Henry Fleming's Tupenny Fury: Cosmic Pessimism in Stephen Crane's *The Red Badge of Courage*" (*SN*, 1961), and Edwin H. Cady (in his *Stephen Crane*) take up the thematic implications of the omission from the 1895 edition of several uncanceled passages which are present in the long version manuscript. Both agree that the passages are heavy-handed, ironic accounts of Henry's attempt to find a naturalistic explanation for his actions and that their omission is therefore an improvement. Joseph Katz, in his introductions to the facsimile edition of the December 9, 1894, *New York Press* syndicated version of *The Red Badge* (Gainesville, Fla., 1967) and to the facsimile edition of the 1895 Appleton text (Columbus, Ohio, 1969), seeks to demonstrate that

Crane's preparation of an abridged text for syndication represents a major and beneficial revision of his manuscript, since the syndicated text contains a number of important passages not in the long version but present in the 1895 edition. Until there is evidence, however, that Crane participated in the preparation of his novel for its December 1894 syndication, it can be maintained with equal probability that his revision of the long version occurred at some unknown time before late 1894.

At one stage in the history of Crane scholarship, *The Red Badge* was an active field for source hunters. Crane's reading of Zola and Tolstoy, his acquaintance with Civil War veterans, his knowledge of various Civil War novels and historical works—all were pursued with vigor and often with the intent of establishing a major source. Today, the tendency in general accounts of *The Red Badge* is to deemphasize the importance of sources and to acknowledge the existence of several different threads of influence without stressing one or the other. Nevertheless, some kinds of source study have undoubtedly been more fruitful than others, with the search for literary antecedents perhaps among the less productive because the least demonstrable.

Lars Åhnebrink's *The Beginnings of Naturalism in American Fiction* is the definitive study of Crane's possible debts to Zola's *La Débâcle* and to Tolstoy's war fiction. On the whole, however, V. S. Pritchett's comment in *The Living Novel* (New York, 1947) that the influence of European war novels on Crane was general rather than specific is more persuasive than Åhnebrink's detailed analogies. Crane's Homeric parallels have been discussed by Warren D. Anderson, in "Homer and Stephen Crane" (*NCF*, June 1964), and Robert Dusenberg, in "The Homeric Mood in *The Red Badge of Courage*" (*Pacific Coast Philology*, Apr. 1968). A group of Civil War novels are offered as sources by H. T. Webster, "Wilbur F. Hinman's *Corporal Si Klegg* and Stephen Crane's *The Red Badge of Courage*" (*AL*, Nov. 1939); Thomas F. O'Donnell, "De Forest, Van Petten, and Stephen Crane" (*AL*, Jan. 1956) (*Miss Ravenel's Conversion*); and Eric Solomon, "Another Analogue for *The Red Badge of Courage*" (*NCF*, June 1958) (Joseph Kirkland's *The Captain of Company K*). Recently, several critics have cited essays which contain ideas about war that appear to resemble Crane's. Eric Solomon, in "Yet Another Source for *The Red Badge of Courage*" (*ELN*, Mar. 1965), suggests Horace Porter's "The Philosophy of Courage," and Neal J. Osborn, in "William Ellery Channing and *The Red Badge of Courage*" (*BNYPL*, Mar. 1965), offers Channing's sermon on "War."

A much more profitable vein of source hunting is that which concerns Crane's use of Civil War material. Lyndon U. Pratt, in "A Possible Source of *The Red Badge of Courage*" (*AL*, Mar. 1939), and Thomas F. O'Donnell, in "John B. Van Petten: Stephen Crane's History Teacher" (*AL*, May 1955), note Crane's association with the Union veteran General Van Petten, his history teacher at Claverack. The most important study of this kind is Harold R. Hungerford's " 'That Was at Chancellorsville': The Factual Framework of *The Red Badge of Courage*" (*AL*, Jan. 1963). Hungerford demonstrates beyond doubt that Henry's "Various Battles" are those of Chancellorsville and that Crane's source was principally *Battles and Leaders of the Civil War*. Frederick C. Crews, in his edition of *The Red Badge of Courage*, supplements Hungerford's article by supplying several maps of the battle and by textual annotation which notes references and allusions to the Chancellorsville campaign.

R. W. Stallman's well-known discussion of the wafer image at the close of Chapter Nine has stimulated interest in the source of the image. Scott C. Osborn, in "Stephen Crane's Imagery: 'Pasted Like a Wafer' " (*AL*, Nov. 1951), locates the image in Kipling's *The Light That Failed* and believes that both Kipling and Crane intended a sealing wax rather than a communion allusion. Stallman came to the rescue of his reading in "The Scholar's Net: Literary Sources" (*CE*, Oct. 1955) but was answered in turn by Edward Stone, in "The Many Suns of *The Red Badge of Courage*" (*AL*, Nov. 1957), and by Eric W. Carlson, in "Crane's *The Red Badge of Courage*" (*Expl*, Mar. 1958). In "Stephen Crane's 'Fierce Red Wafer' " (*ELN*, Dec. 1963), Cecil D. Eby, Jr., indirectly defends Stallman when he claims that the presence of "fierce" in the manuscript does not invalidate a religious allusion. And undoubtedly we shall be hearing again about this "two-handed engine" of American scholarship.

Criticism of *The Red Badge* has been so varied in focus and method that it is difficult to shape a discussion of its major tendencies. One problem in particular, however, which has occupied almost all critics is that of Crane's relationship to Henry Fleming at the close of the novel. Does Crane wish us to accept at face value Henry's estimation of himself as a "man"; or is Crane once again ironically depicting Henry's capacity for self-delusion; or is his characterization of Henry consciously or unconsciously ambivalent? To emphasize this particular crux in the interpretation of *The Red Badge* is to oversimplify some critical discussions and to reorient the principal direction of others, but it is perhaps the only way to bring some order in brief compass to a large body of work.

The position that Crane is ruthlessly ironic toward Henry throughout the novel and that the book is therefore a study of man's ability to delude himself under any circumstances is best represented by Charles C. Walcutt in his *American Literary Naturalism, A Divided Stream.* With the principal exception of Jay Martin, in *Harvests of Change,* most critics have not accepted such an extreme view of Crane's attitude toward Fleming. They argue that evidence both within the novel and in such works as "The Open Boat" reveals Crane's belief that men can become "interpreters" of their experience. A position directly opposed to that of Walcutt can be closely identified with two schools of criticism—the religious and the mythic. If Henry undergoes a sacramental experience in the novel (either in connection with Jim Conklin or in relation to battle in general) or if he is initiated into manhood in any one of several mythic patterns, his final self-evaluation is lent authority, since it is the product of his maturation. The religious interpretation of *The Red Badge*—in particular the interpretation of Jim Conklin's death as a redemption experience—is of course closely associated with the work of R. W. Stallman, from the introduction to his Modern Library edition in 1951 to his 1968 biography. (It would be an interesting exercise, by the way, to trace the permutations in the tone of Stallman's discussions of the redemption theme in *The Red Badge,* from the certainty of the early 1950s to the willingness to hedge in 1968. But major critics, like major writers, should not be held to a foolish consistency, and the religious center of the novel has always been the principal focus of Stallman's interpretation.) The fullest endorsement of Stallman's redemption reading is by Daniel G. Hoffman in his introduction to *The Red Badge of Courage and Other Stories* (New York, 1957). The most elaborate and successful interpretation of the novel as an initiation myth is by John E. Hart, in *"The Red Badge of Courage* as Myth and Symbol." A rather weak echo of Hart's thesis can be found in David L. Evans, "Henry's Hell: The Night Journey in *The Red Badge of Courage"* (*Proceedings of the Utah Academy of Sciences, Arts & Letters,* 1967).

In other "affirmative" readings of *The Red Badge,* however, there is less of a sense that a particular critical method, such as symbolic imagery or myth criticism, has produced a predictable interpretation. A sizable number of critics have had the "felt response" that Crane wished to affirm some aspect of experience in his depiction of Henry and they have struggled manfully in order to define the nature of this theme. So James B. Colvert, Eric Solomon, and John Fraser—in "Structure and Theme in Stephen Crane's Fiction"; "The Structure of *The Red Badge of Courage"* (*MFS,* Autumn 1959); and "Crime and Forgiveness: *The Red Badge of Courage* in Time of War" (*Criticism,* Summer 1967)—

contend that Fleming matures during the novel in his understanding of social and moral reality and that this maturity takes the fictional configuration of his movement from isolation to group acceptance, loyalty, and duty. Other critics, though they also stress some growth on Henry's part, see his development in less positive terms. James T. Cox, in "The Imagery of *The Red Badge of Courage*" (*MFS*, Autumn 1959), and Marston La France, in "Stephen Crane's *Private Fleming: His Various Battles*," in *Patterns of Commitment in American Literature*, edited by Marston La France (Toronto, 1967), argue persuasively that Henry progresses from a romantic vision of the world to an awareness that man lives in a hostile and godless universe. A third group of critics often adopts Freudian ideas to maintain that Henry's maturity stems from his ability to exorcise the specter of fear in its various guises. Perhaps the best of such readings is Daniel Weiss's "*The Red Badge of Courage*" (*Pychoanalytic Review*, Summer, Fall 1965), though the articles by Bernard Weisberger, "*The Red Badge of Courage*," in *Twelve Original Essays on Great American Novels*, edited by Charles Shapiro (Detroit, Mich., 1958), and Kermit Vanderbilt and Daniel Weiss, "From Rifleman to Flagbearer: Henry Fleming's Separate Peace in *The Red Badge of Courage*" (*MFS*, Winter 1965–66), should also be noted.

The critical approach which stresses that purposeful ambivalence is the key to the close of the novel stems largely from Stanley B. Greenfield's influential article "The Unmistakable Stephen Crane." Greenfield argues that Crane portrays life as an experience in which the individual can both learn and remain deluded. Henry, for example, has gained from his experiences but he is nevertheless deluded in his understanding of what he has gained. Thus, Crane's tone is the mixed one of sympathetic identification and of irony. Ralph Ellison states this view of the novel succinctly in *Shadow and Act* (New York, 1964), when he writes that "although Henry has been initiated into the battle of life, he has by no means finished with illusion—but that, too, is part of the human condition." Further support of Greenfield's thesis can be found in Frederick C. Crews's introduction to *The Red Badge*; Donald Pizer, "Late Nineteenth-Century American Naturalism: An Essay in Definition"; Larzer Ziff, *The American 1890s*; and John J. McDermott, "Symbolism and Psychological Realism in *The Red Badge of Courage*" (*NCF*, Dec. 1968).

To some critics, however, the ambivalences (or ambiguities) at the close of the novel constitute major weaknesses either in Henry or in Crane's artistry. William B. Dillingham, in "Insensibility in *The Red Badge of Courage*" (*CE*, Dec. 1963), and John W. Rathbun, in "Structure and Meaning in *The Red Badge of Courage*" (*Ball State University Forum*, Winter 1969), believe that Henry's movement from introspective self-analysis to instinctive participation in group action is necessary and triumphant but that it also represents the loss of a distinctively human form of sensitivity. And Clark Griffith, in "Stephen Crane and the Ironic Last Word" (*PQ*, Jan. 1968), holds that Crane's belief that life is an insoluble puzzle led him to undermine, with a final ironic touch, our acceptance of any meaning which his characters think they have gained from experience. Griffith's position is not far from the view that the insoluble ambiguities at the close of *The Red Badge* stem from Crane's conscious or unconscious confusion. John Berryman writes more frankly than most readers who hold this view when he comments, in "Stephen Crane, *The Red Badge of Courage*," in *The American Novel*, edited by Wallace Stegner (New York, 1965), "I do not know what Crane intended. Perhaps he intended to have his cake and eat it too—irony at the end, but heroism too." Mordecai Marcus, in "The Unity of *The Red Badge of Courage*," in *Stephen Crane's "The Red Badge of Courage": Text and Criticism*, edited by Richard Lettis et al., and James B. Colvert, in "Stephen Crane's Magic Mountain," in *Stephen Crane: A Collection of Critical Essays* edited by Maurice Bassan, also adopt this position. Marcus asserts that Crane could not make up his mind whether Henry had matured or was deluded, while Colvert, in a probing and provocative essay, finds that Crane's joining of sentimental solipsism and ironic deflation in his own self-evaluation is the underlying source of the novel's flawed conclusion.

Studies of the form of *The Red Badge* have tended to concentrate on its imagery and symbolism, with Stallman's religious reading often serving as a starting point. Stallman's interpretation of the imagery and symbolism of *The Red Badge* (as well as his reply to critics of this approach) can best be found in *The Houses That James Built*. Edwin H. Cady states the position of those critics who reject Stallman's thesis when he writes in his *Stephen Crane*: "The decisive difficulties with the Christian-symbolist reading of *The Red Badge*, it seems, are that there appears to be no way to make a coherent account of the symbols as referential to Christian doctrine and then to match that with what happens in the novel." A number of critics other than Stallman have pursued various threads of imagery in the novel with less ambitious aims but often with more productive results. Among these are Claudia C. Wogan, "Crane's Use of Color in *The Red Badge of Courage*" (*MFS*, Summer 1960)(a simple listing); Mordecai and Erin Marcus, "Animal Imagery in *The Red Badge of Courage*" (*MLN*, Feb. 1959); James W. Tuttleton, "The Imagery of *The Red Badge of Courage*"

(*MFS*, Winter 1962–63) (pagan religious imagery); William J. Free, "Smoke Imagery in *The Red Badge of Courage*" (*CLAJ*, Dec. 1963); and John J. McDermott, "Symbolism and Psychological Realism in *The Red Badge of Courage*" (wound symbolism). Other than Stallman, the major reading of *The Red Badge* as a work in which theme and form arise out of a complex interaction of image patterns is James T. Cox's "The Imagery of *The Red Badge of Courage*." Cox's brilliant commentary on various imagistic threads (particularly those involving the sun) is a high point in the application of New Criticism techniques to *The Red Badge*. That is, his argument is persuasive but it is occasionally difficult to recall that he is writing about *The Red Badge*.

A secondary area of formalistic analysis has been the overall structure of the novel. R. W. Stallman has often called the form of *The Red Badge* "a repetitive alternation of contradictory moods." Thomas M. Lorch, in "The Cyclical Structure of *The Red Badge of Courage*" (*CLAJ*, Mar. 1967), also stresses repetitive change, though that of action and of Henry's thought rather than of mood. On the other hand, Eric Solomon, in "The Structure of *The Red Badge of Courage*," and John M. Rathbun, in "Structure and Meaning in *The Red Badge of Courage*," suggest that the key to the novel's form is its developmental structure. A good many of the significant aspects of the form and technique of *The Red Badge* have either been totally neglected or only tentatively sketched, perhaps because critical preoccupation with the imagery of the novel has obscured the need to examine other formalistic problems. However, Robert L. Hough, in "Crane's Henry Fleming: Speech and Vision" (*Forum* [Houston], Winter 1961), comments briefly on Crane's shifts in levels of diction; Mordecai Marcus, in "The Unity of *The Red Badge of Courage*," in *Stephen Crane's "The Red Badge of Courage": Text and Criticism*, edited by Robert Lettis et al., attempts to define the various kinds of irony in the novel; and Edwin H. Cady (in his *Stephen Crane*) and Robert C. Albrecht, in "Content and Style in *The Red Badge of Courage*" (*CE*, Mar. 1966), try to come to grips with the complex problem of Crane's point-of-view technique. Finally, Donald Pizer, in "A Primer of Fictional Aesthetics" (*CE*, Mar. 1968), uses *The Red Badge* to illustrate a number of ways in which formalistic analysis can be brought to bear upon a complex work of fiction.

Major Short Fiction: "The Open Boat," "The Monster," "The Bride Comes To Yellow Sky," and "The Blue Hotel"

There is substantial agreement among Crane critics that "The Open Boat" is his best short work (many would say his best work of any length) and that the story's central theme concerns nature's indifference to man, with a significant corollary theme that man is capable of a sympathetic union with his comrades in adversity, if not with nature. Critical attention has focused, therefore, on various ways of stating this theme and on Crane's mastery of technique. Richard P. Adams, for example, in "Naturalistic Fiction: 'The Open Boat'" (*TSE*, 1954), notes that Crane's covert nostalgia for a natural world of warmth and relatedness is responsible for the emotional and thematic power of the story. Peter Buitenhuis, on the other hand, in "The Essentials of Life: 'The Open Boat' as Existentialist Fiction" (*MFS*, Autumn 1959), looks forward rather than backward for a controling focus and finds that Camus's idea of the absurd can best describe the central vision of experience expressed by "The Open Boat." And Mordecai Marcus, in "The Three-Fold View of Nature in 'The Open Boat'" (*PQ*, Apr. 1962), notes that nature in the story is portrayed sequentially as malevolently hostile, as thoughtlessly hostile, and, finally, as indifferent.

On the whole, the best work on "The Open Boat" has dealt with Crane's craftsmanship. Caroline Gordon, in "Stephen Crane" (*Accent*, Spring 1949; reprinted in Caroline Gordon and Allen Tate, *The House of Fiction*, New York, 1950), and James B. Colvert, in "Style and Meaning in Stephen Crane's 'The Open Boat,'" concentrate on Crane's point-of-view technique, while Peter Buitenhuis, in "The Essentials of Life: 'The Open Boat,'" and John T. Frederick, in "The Fifth Man in 'The Open Boat'" (*CEA Critic*, May 1968), are particularly apt in analyzing Crane's language and imagery. Perhaps the best overall studies of the story are by Daniel G. Hoffman, in *The Poetry of Stephen Crane*, and Andrew N. Lytle, in "'The Open Boat': A Pagan Tale," in *The Hero with the Private Parts* (Baton Rouge, La., 1966). Hoffman revealingly demonstrates the close relationship between "The Open Boat" and Crane's best poetry, and Lytle discusses with sensitivity and clarity Crane's expert handling of point of view, plot, characterization, and imagery.

"The Monster" has grown in critical reputation during the last two decades but has still to receive full-scale attention. Unfortunately, it is not as short as "The Bride Comes to Yellow Sky" or "The Blue Hotel" and not as good as "The Open Boat" and is therefore seldom anthologized. The satiric portrayal of village morality in the story has been recognized from the beginning and has often been well described—see, for example, Wilson Follett's introduction to Volume III of *The Work of Stephen Crane* (New York, 1926)—but criticism which goes beyond this commonplace is often merely biographical or idiosyncratic. Thus, Sy Kahn, in "Stephen Crane and the Giant Voice in the Night: An Explication of *The Monster*," in *Essays in Modern American Litera-*

ture, edited by Richard E. Langford (DeLand, Fla., 1963), and J. C. Levenson, in his introduction to Volume VII of *The Works of Stephen Crane* (Charlottesville, Va., 1969), suggest somewhat irrelevantly that Crane's experiences with Cora led him to condemn middle class morality on its home grounds, the small town. And James Hafley, in "*The Monster* and the Art of Stephen Crane" (*Accent*, Summer 1959), is blatantly ingenious in his exploration of the imagery of the story. However, Thomas A. Gullason, in "The Symbolic Unity of 'The Monster' " (*MLN*, Dec. 1960), convincingly charts the ironic reversals which are central to the story's satiric thrust. And J. C. Levenson, in a discussion which has wide-ranging implications for Crane's mind and art (in Levenson's introduction to Volume VII of *The Works of Stephen Crane*), notes the two major interlocking themes of the story—Crane's portrayal of the "psychological landscape" of American life by means of the macabre, and his ironic juxtaposition of the pulls of ethical belief on the one hand and the practical requirements of "civilization" on the other.

The most useful extended discussion of "The Bride Comes to Yellow Sky" is in Eric Solomon's *Stephen Crane: From Parody to Realism*. Solomon establishes without doubt the relationship between Crane's parodic use of the dime novel and his satire of the cultural assumptions of both eastern and western readers. Many critics have more or less echoed this view of the story, with perhaps A. M. Tibbetts's "Stephen Crane's 'The Bride Comes to Yellow Sky' " (*EJ*, Apr. 1965) the best study aside from Solomon's. The principal crux in the story is the extent to which it is an allegory of the Death of the West—the West either as myth or as reality. Although Robert Barnes, in "Crane's 'The Bride Comes to Yellow Sky' " (*Expl*, Apr. 1958), and Jay Martin, in *Harvests of Change*, attempt to demonstrate the existence of this theme, the story's predominantly comic spirit (as well described by Tibbetts) appears to resist a neat allegorical formulation.

"The Blue Hotel" is a compelling work, which is more than can be said of most of its criticism. The story, particularly in recent years, seems to attract commentary which can most charitably be described as forced. (Joseph Katz has collected much of the significant writing on the story in *Stephen Crane: "The Blue Hotel,"* Columbus, Ohio, 1969.) With some exceptions the earliest extended criticism of the work is still the best. Walter Sutton, in "Pity and Fear in 'The Blue Hotel' " (*AQ*, Spring 1952), identified man's alien position in nature as a central motif, while Stallman (in his *Omnibus*) stated the case for considering the final section of the story superfluous. The best of these early studies, and still the most useful article on the story, is Joseph N. Satterwhite's

"Stephen Crane's 'The Blue Hotel': The Failure of Understanding" (*MFS*, Winter 1956–57). Satterwhite comes to grips with the two principal areas of interest in the story—its theme of complicity and its parable form—and he also takes a stand in a debate found in most criticism of the work when he finds that its ending is an appropriate gloss on its theme.

Much of the recent criticism of "The Blue Hotel" continues to be preoccupied with the themes of misunderstanding and alienation and with the relevance and success of the close of the story. Ray B. West, Jr., in "Stephen Crane: Author in Transition" (*AL*, May 1962); Eric Solomon, in *Stephen Crane: From Parody to Realism*; and Sister Mary Anthony Weinig, in "Heroic Convention in 'The Blue Hotel'" (*SCraneN*, Spring 1968), refine our appreciation of Crane's ironic themes and techniques, though their readings do not vary significantly from those of Sutton and Satterwhite. William B. Dillingham, however, in "'The Blue Hotel' and the Gentle Reader" (*SSF*, Spring 1964), does add a new note in his comment that Crane's refusal to permit the reader to respond sympathetically to the Swede includes us all in the ironic thrust of the conclusion, since we, too, have failed to understand. And H. Alan Wycherley, in "Crane's 'The Blue Hotel': How Many Collaborators?" (*AN&Q*, Feb. 1966), identifies the bartender as yet another contributor to the Swede's death.

But a great deal of the recent criticism of "The Blue Hotel" falls into the categories familiar to anyone who has "read through" the modern criticism of a "difficult" work. Robert F. Gleckner, in "Stephen Crane and the Wonder of Man's Conceit" (*MFS*, Autumn 1959); Hugh N. Maclean, in "The Two Worlds of 'The Blue Hotel'" (*MFS*, Autumn 1959); and Robert Van Der Beets, in "Character as Structure: Ironic Parallel and Transformation in 'The Blue Hotel'" (*SSF*, Spring 1968), trace elaborate threads of symbolic action in the story in order to announce themes readily available elsewhere in the work. James T. Cox and Edward Stone—in "Stephen Crane as Symbolic Naturalist: An Analysis of 'The Blue Hotel'" (*MFS*, Summer 1957) and in "Stephen Crane," in *A Certain Morbidness* (Carbondale, Ill., 1969)—concentrate on symbolism arising out of imagery. Stone's discussion of Crane's color symbolism is often helpful, but Cox's article is a classic of its kind. Centering on the stove as a key symbol, he examines the "symbolic substructure" of the story and concludes that the theme of "The Blue Hotel" is precisely the opposite of the Easterner's final words. Indeed, two other critics have reached a similar unconvincing conclusion. Marvin Klotz, in "Stephen Crane: Tragedian or Comedian: 'The Blue Hotel'" (*UKCR*, Spring 1961), reads the story as a deliberate burlesque of literary naturalism in which most apparent themes are ironic reversals of their true meaning, and Bruce L. Grenberg, in "Metaphysics of Despair: Stephen Crane's 'The Blue Hotel'" (*MFS*, Summer 1968), believes that the existential themes pervading the story cause the Easterner's final words to be Crane's "bitterest irony." All in all, Crane studies would profit from a ten-year moratorium on "Blue Hotel" explications. One way to achieve this end would be to require that each would-be explicator read every article published on the story.

Other Fiction

Crane's minor fiction has not attracted a large or significant body of criticism. I will discuss this commentary within the following divisions: Crane's western stories, his war stories, and his Whilomville tales; and his three last novels—*The Third Violet, Active Service,* and *The O'Ruddy.*

Criticism of Crane's western stories has of course centered on "The Bride Comes to Yellow Sky" and "The Blue Hotel." However, "Horses —One Dash," "The Five White Mice," and "A Man and Some Others" often receive passing criticism in general studies of Crane. Eric Solomon's chapter "The Gunfighters" in his *Stephen Crane: From Parody to Realism* is the fullest and best discussion of this otherwise neglected phase of Crane's writing.

Several scholars have worked on the sources of Crane's war fiction. James M. Gargano, in "Crane's 'A Mystery of Heroism': A Possible Source" (*MLN*, Jan. 1959), strains for a Biblical parallel, while Thomas A. Gullason, in "Stephen Crane's Private War Against Yellow Journalism" (*HLQ*, May 1959), notes a minor influence on Crane's war fiction, his distaste for the "new journalism" of Pulitzer and Hearst. Two discoveries of specific sources are by Hans Arnold, who in "Stephen Crane's 'Wyoming Valley Tales': Their Source and Their Place in the Author's War Fiction" (*JA*, 1959) cites Crane's reliance on his grandfather's *Wyoming* (1858), and by C. B. Ives, who in "'The Little Regiment' of Stephen Crane at the Battle of Fredericksburg" (*Midwest Quarterly*, Spring 1967) identifies both the battle and the regiment. Arnold, however, is less successful in arguing that Crane's Wyoming Valley stories are really early rather than late works.

Other critics have attempted to distinguish among various phases in Crane's depiction of battle and soldiers and to relate these phases to significant moments in the development of his literary imagination. E. R. Hagemann, in "Stephen Crane's 'Real' War in His Short Stories" (*AQ*, Winter 1956), and Thomas A. Gullason, in "The Significance of 'Wounds in the Rain'" (*MFS*, Autumn 1959), believe that Crane's first-hand experience of battle resulted in war fiction superior to his earlier, entirely imaginative depiction of war. Gullason also seeks to make the somewhat shaky point that the quality of *Wounds in the Rain* undermines the widely held belief that Crane's writing declined during his last years. Eric Solomon, in "Stephen Crane's War Stories" (*TSLL*, Spring 1961), adds a third phase to Crane's war fiction, that of the four Spitzbergen tales written in 1899. In these stories Crane's two earlier themes of the soldier's isolation or fear and of his professional pride give way to the theme of the mingled glory and horror of battle. Solomon has probably defined too neat a pattern for Crane's war fiction, but his article is nevertheless one of the best attempts to deal coherently with this aspect of Crane's work.

Finally, a number of critics have worked closely with particular war stories. Two unsatisfactory readings are Paul Witherington's "Stephen Crane's 'A Mystery of Heroism': Some Redefinitions" (*EJ*, Feb. 1969), and Neal J. Osborn's "The Riddle in 'The Clan': A Key to Crane's Major Fiction?" (*BNYPL*, Apr. 1965). Witherington imposes a myth and ritual interpretation upon "A Mystery of Heroism" and Osborn struggles to demonstrate that all of Crane's principal themes and techniques can be found in "The Clan of No-Name." A much more successful article is William B. Dillingham's "Crane's One-Act Farce: 'The Upturned Face'" (*Research Studies* [Wash. State Univ.], Dec. 1967), in which Dillingham studies the amalgam of the comic and the grotesque which is the particular effect of this story and of much of Crane's best work.

Crane's Whilomville stories have attracted attention both because of their intrinsic interest and because of their critical usefulness as a unified body of work late in his career. J. C. Levenson, in his introduction to Volume VII of *The Works of Stephen Crane*, has painstakingly detailed the publishing history of the stories. Levenson, as well as most other commentators on the stories, believes that they do not represent a major effort by Crane. Critics, however, have stated this position in varying ways and degrees, from Stallman's contention (in his *Omnibus*) that they are "lightweight stuff" to Solomon's belief (in his *Stephen Crane: From Parody to Realism*) that they are of uneven quality. Those who praise the stories usually base their evaluation on Crane's successful blending of nostalgia for and satire of village life and mores. This is more or less the position of Ima H. Herron, in *The Small Town in American Literature* (Durham, N.C., 1939); Grant C. Knight, in *The Critical Period in American Literature;* and Jean Cazemajou, in "Stephen Crane et la petite ville américaine" (*Caliban*, Mar. 1967). John C. Martin, in "Childhood in Stephen Crane's *Maggie*, 'The Monster,' and Whilomville Stories" (*Midwestern University Quarterly*, 1967), takes this view a step further and argues that the theme of the relationship of the individual to society is as well dramatized in these stories as in Crane's major work. Finally, George Monteiro, in "Whilomville as Judah: Crane's 'A Little Pilgrimage' " (*Renascence*, Summer 1967), examines the satiric theme of one of the better stories in the series.

Most Crane critics would not be too much disturbed if *The Third Violet, Active Service,* and *The O'Ruddy* disappeared from the face of the earth, and this sentiment is reflected in the nature and extent of the criticism of these works. An exception is Thomas A. Gullason, who, in "The Jamesian Motif in Stephen Crane's Last Novels" (*Personalist*, Winter 1961), unsuccessfully seeks to demonstrate that the presence of the Jamesian theme of sensitivity to class in these novels lends them significance. *The Third Violet* has of course often been mined for its autobiographical themes and implications; a good early example is Wilson Follett's introduction to Volume III of *The Work of Stephen Crane* (New York, 1926). In particular, Crane's inability to portray feminine characters (as well described by Edwin Cady in his *Stephen Crane*) has served as grist for various kinds of mills. *Active Service* has had few admirers (and probably few readers). All Carl Van Doren could muster in its favor in his introduction to Volume IV of *The Work of Stephen Crane* (New York, 1926) was some faint praise for its "incidental detail." Like *The Third Violet*, it will no doubt continue to interest biographers more than critics. Discussion of *The O'Ruddy* has concentrated on the tangled history of its authorship and publication. Thomas Beer supplied much useful information on these problems in his introduction to Volumes VII and VIII of *The Work of Stephen Crane* (New York, 1926). Lillian Gilkes and Joan H. Baum, in "Stephen Crane's Last Novel: *The O'Ruddy*" (*Columbia Library Columns*, Feb. 1957), identify those chapters written by Crane and those by Robert Barr and also describe the complicated negotiations which preceded the completion and publication of the novel. Bernard O'Donnell, in "Stephen Crane's *The O'Ruddy*: A Problem in Authorship Discrimination," in *The Computer and Literary Style*, edited by Jacob Leed (Kent, Ohio, 1966), confirms their authorship attributions with some slight refinement. And Jean Cazemajou, in "*The O'Ruddy*, Robert Barr, et *The Idler*" (*Caliban*, Jan. 1968), discusses Barr's serialization of the novel. Though most critics would probably echo Edwin Cady's comment (in his *Stephen Crane*) that the novel contains the seeds of a successful parody of the swashbuckling romance, few have found the work of sufficient interest to warrant extended discussion.

Poetry

Joseph Katz has incorporated earlier textual and bibliographical studies of Crane's poetry into his introduction and notes to *The Poems of Stephen Crane*. Still of independent interest, however, are Olov W. Fryckstedt's "Crane's *Black Riders*: A Discussion of Dates," for its authoritative account of the composition of the poems of Crane's first collection, and Thomas F. O'Donnell's "A Note on the Reception of Crane's *The Black Riders*" (*AL*, May 1952) and Jean Cazemajou's "A propos de quelques parodies de l'oeuvre de Stephen Crane" (*Caliban*, 1965) for their bearing on the influence of Crane's poetry on his reputation in the 1890s.

The problem of sources and influence has been as troublesome for critics of Crane's poetry as it has been for critics of his fiction. The Bible (for its parable form) and Emily Dickinson were frequently mentioned in early criticism. Daniel G. Hoffman, in *The Poetry of Stephen Crane*, added Ambrose Bierce and Olive Schreiner, with particular emphasis on Miss Schreiner's *Dreams*, an emphasis affirmed by Carlin T. Kindilien, in "Stephen Crane and the 'Savage Philosophy' of Olive Schreiner" (*BUSE*, Summer 1957). Hoffman also discounted Emily Dickinson's influence, finding the two poets dissimilar in theme and form. James M. Cox, in "*The Pilgrim's Progress* as a Source for Stephen Crane's *The Black Riders*" (*AL*, Jan. 1957), convincingly demonstrates the importance of Bunyan's parable form and techniques. Cox's essay is also an illuminating discussion of major tendencies in Crane's poetry as a whole. A number of critics, however, appear to be mining rather thin veins of possible influence: E. A. Gillis, "A Glance at Stephen Crane's Poetry" (*Prairie Schooner*, Spring 1954) (Aubrey Beardsley); Thomas A. Gullason, "Tennyson's Influence on Stephen Crane" (*N&Q*, Apr. 1958); and Richard E. Peck, "Stephen Crane and Baudelaire: A Direct Link" (*AL*, May 1965).

The best general introductions to Crane's poetry are Henry Lüdeke's "Stephen Crane's Poetry," in *The "Democracy" of Henry Adams and Other Essays* (Bern, 1950); Daniel G. Hoffman's *The Poetry of Stephen Crane*; and Joseph Katz's introduction to *The Poems of Stephen Crane*. Lüdeke, in an article which anticipates much later criticism, discusses with good sense such matters as Crane's irony and his religious themes and the relationship between his poetry and Emily Dickinson's. Katz is best for a solid introduction to the biographical setting of the poems. He is less successful in his attempt to demonstrate that *The Black Riders* volume has a coherent structure. Hoffman's study is of course one of the "basic books" (Cady's term) on Crane. Hoffman's forceful revelation that Crane wrote two kinds of religious poems—those involving a God of vengeance and those involving a God of love—is perhaps the best known aspect of his book, since his discussion made obsolete a great deal of earlier criticism which had pigeonholed Crane as an 1890s atheistic iconoclast. (See, for example, Carlin T. Kindilien's *American Poetry in the Eighteen Nineties*, Providence, R.I., 1956.) But Hoffman is perhaps most stimulating in his analysis of Crane's movement from allegorical to symbolic poetry and in his attempt to define and explore Crane as a symbolic writer in prose as well as in poetry. Moreover, though it is possible to quarrel with some of Hoffman's general ideas about Crane's life and work, his reading of individual poems is of a very high order.

Criticism of Crane's poetry both before and after Hoffman is overshadowed by his work. Harriet Monroe's "Stephen Crane" (*Poetry*, June 1919), in which she dismisses Crane as a sententious and often sophomoric moralist, still represents a sizable body of critical opinion, though the careful study of Crane's best poetry has tended to qualify that view. Recently, several critics have attempted to find a single "key" to Crane's poetry, particularly to *The Black Riders*. (*War is Kind* is usually admitted to be a hodgepodge.) Max Westbrook, in "Stephen Crane's Poetry: Perspective and Arrogance" (*BuR*, Dec. 1963), finds the key in Crane's adoption of seemingly opposite yet essentially complementary poetic "voices" to express a central creed of compassion. Much less persuasively, Yoshie Itabashi, in "The Modern Pilgrimage of *The Black Riders*: An Interpretation" (*Tsuda Review* [Tokyo], Nov. 1967), believes that the order of the poems in the volume is that of a spiritual journey culminating in an acceptance of a compassionate God. A larger group of critics have concentrated on Crane's poetic form. Harland S. Nelson, in "Stephen Crane's Achievement as a Poet" (*TSLL*, Winter 1963), unsuccessfully seeks to prove that Crane's parables are as powerful as his symbolic poems. Christof Wegelin, in "Crane's 'A Man Said to the Universe'" (*Expl*, Sept. 1961), and Mordecai Marcus, in "Structure and Irony in Stephen Crane's 'War Is Kind'" (*CLAJ*, Mar. 1966), work closely and well with the form of two of Crane's most reprinted poems. Perhaps it was Wegelin's comments on the device of the confrontation in "A Man Said to the Universe" which stimulated Ruth Miller to write what is probably the best and most important discussion of Crane's poetry since Hoffman's book. In her "Regions of Snow: The Poetic Style of Stephen Crane" (*BNYPL*, May 1968), she examines the various shapes that Crane gave to his basic structural device of the encounter. Her conclusion, that Crane's wisdom is adolescent but that his poetic constructs delight us, has often been felt but has never been so well stated.

Influence and Reputation

Discussions of Crane's influence have centered on Conrad and Hemingway, with the Crane-Hemingway relationship in particular receiving considerable attention. Criticism of Crane's influence on Conrad—R. B. Sewall, "Stephen Crane's *The Red Badge of Courage*" (*Expl*, May 1945) (on *The Red Badge* and *Lord Jim*); Guy Owen, Jr., "Crane's 'The Open Boat' and Conrad's 'Youth' " (*MLN*, Feb. 1958); Peter Baasner, "Stephen Crane and Joseph Conrad," in *Kleiner Beträge zur Amerikanischen Literaturgeschichte*, edited by Hans Galinsky and H. J. Lang (Heidelberg, 1961); and Bruce Johnson, "Joseph Conrad and Crane's *The Red Badge of Courage*" (*PMASAL*, 1963) (on *The Red Badge* and *The Nigger of the "Narcissus"*)—has been thin in substance and has often adopted Conrad's later, patronizing tone toward Crane. There is room for a major study of this relationship.

The best general discussions of the personal and literary parallels between Crane and Hemingway are those by Philip Young, in *Ernest Hemingway* (New York, 1952), and Daniel G. Hoffman, in *The Poetry of Stephen Crane*. Both critics note the importance of a personal code in the value systems of the two writers as well as similarities in subject matter and theme in various works. Other scholars have dealt in greater detail with the prose style of the two authors and with particular influences. W. Gordon Milne, in "Stephen Crane: Pioneer in Technique" (*Die Neueren Sprachen*, July 1959), comments on the tendency toward compression and simplicity in the prose style of both writers, characteristics which have also been noted by Harold C. Martin, "The Development of Style in Nineteenth-Century American Fiction," in *Style in Prose Fiction*, edited by Harold C. Martin (New York, 1959), and Richard Bridgman, in *The Colloquial Style in America* (New York, 1966). I confess that I am unconvinced by attempts to find links between two such distinctive prose styles. Philip Young's remark that "The Blue Hotel" probably influenced "The Killers" is well documented by J. A. Ward, in " 'The Blue Hotel' and 'The Killers' " (*CEA Critic*, Sept. 1959). But William B. Bache is less persuasive in his "*The Red Badge of Courage* and 'The Short Happy Life of Francis Macomber' " (*WHR*, Winter 1961). A somewhat different direction in Crane-Hemingway studies is taken by Earle Labor, in "Crane and Hemingway: Anatomy of Trauma" (*Renascence*, Summer 1959). Labor compares Frederic Henry and Henry Fleming and makes the useful point that Crane and Hemingway had divergent views about the meaning of war despite similarities in their depiction of the subject.

Crane's critical reputation is frequently commented on but has been inadequately documented. The best studies of the reception of his books in his own time are in the biographies by Berryman and Stallman, though there are also a number of articles on special aspects of this subject: Thomas F. O'Donnell, "A Note on the Reception of Crane's *The Black Riders*"; R. W. Stallman, "Crane's *Maggie* in Review," in *The Houses That James Built* (the 1896 *Maggie*); Eric Solomon, "Stephen Crane, English Critics, and American Reviewers" (*N&Q*, Feb. 1965) (*The Red Badge*); and Joseph Katz, "The 'Preceptor' and Another Poet: Thomas Wentworth Higginson and Stephen Crane" (*Serif* [Kent, Ohio], Mar. 1968). Crane's reputation in the 1920s, when he was often interpreted as a rebel against American puritanism, can best be studied in the criticism of the period itself, particularly in Beer's biography and in such estimates as Matthew Josephson's in "The Voyage of Stephen Crane," in *Portrait of the Artist as American* (New York, 1930). The most useful summary of tendencies in recent Crane criticism is Edwin H. Cady's "A Brief Essay on Basic Books" in his *Stephen Crane*, though Stanley Wertheim's annotated bibliography in *Stephen Crane: "The Red Badge of Courage" and Selected Prose and Poetry*, edited by William M. Gibson (New York, 1968) is more up to date. There are only two general surveys of Crane's critical reputation—John W. Stevenson's superficial "The Literary Reputation of Stephen Crane" (*SAQ*, Apr. 1952) and Maurice Bassan's brief but incisive account in the introduction to his *Stephen Crane: A Collection of Critical Essays*.

Emily Dickinson

JAMES WOODRESS

Since 1924 the reputation of Emily Dickinson has been growing steadily, and since Thomas H. Johnson's complete edition of her poetry in 1955 interest has increased spectacularly. The end does not yet seem to be in sight. In 1967 three books and six dissertations were devoted to her work, and in 1968 five books, five more dissertations, and two editions appeared, and a quarterly bulletin was launched. In 1969 another book joined the procession, and the annual MLA bibliography listed nearly three dozen Dickinson items representing scholarly activity in five countries outside the United States: Canada, France, Japan, Roumania, and India. That the interest has reached a high and apparently stable level seems apparent from the yearly MLA listings: thirty items in 1966, twenty-two in 1967, thirty-one in 1968, and thirty-four in 1969. As this book goes to press in 1971, a new and bigger bibliography and a book-length gathering of poetic tributes have come out so far this year. *Books in Print* (1968) listed no less than twenty-six available works about Emily Dickinson. Both quantitatively and qualitatively the attention Emily Dickinson has received in the past decade and a half makes her America's number one woman poet, and she now seems firmly placed in the firmament of the handful of major nineteenth-century figures who long have dominated our literary history. The chief problem that the student or teacher of American literature today has in confronting Emily Dickinson is in keeping up with the scholarly and critical explosion. All the essential manuscripts and scholarly tools are now available for studying her poems, and of the making of books and articles about Emily Dickinson there seems to be no end.

BIBLIOGRAPHY AND CONCORDANCE

The growing interest in Emily Dickinson finally has culminated in adequate bibliographical materials. The most important bibliography is Willis J. Buckingham's *Emily Dickinson: An Annotated Bibliography* [of] *Writings, Scholarship, Criticism, and Ana, 1850–1968* (Bloomington, Ind., 1970). This volume, containing about 2,600 items, is exhaustive in its coverage and a mine of accurate information. It lists all the materials one expects in such a work: earlier bibliographies, a guide to manuscript collections, publication data for both poems and letters, books and articles about Emily Dickinson. It also includes doctoral dissertations, M.A. and B. A. theses (the last two items of doubtful utility), creative tributes, recordings, broadcasts, films, data on commemorations and exhibitions, lists of unpublished papers delivered at scholarly meetings, and miscellanea. Nearly half of the listings (1,214) are in section six ("Parts of Books and Signed Articles"), although hundreds of these items are reviews rather than works of scholarship or criticism. The section on translations and foreign estimates and criticism (326 items) is especially thorough and goes far beyond any other compilation. Yet it must be said that in this *omnium gatherum* there is a lot of trivia. While it is clearly useful to include a large number of reviews of the early editions of the poems, it is hard to see who will have need for a listing of 64 reviews of Genevieve Taggard's *Life and Mind of Emily Dickinson*, and it seems hardly worth listing unpublished concordances based on the pre-Johnson text now that there is in print a good computer-made post-Johnson concordance.

Although Buckingham's bibliography casts its net more widely, it does not supersede Sheila Clendenning's *Emily Dickinson, A Bibliography: 1850–1966* (Kent, Ohio, 1968), which includes 951 well-organized, annotated, indexed, and cross-referenced items, both primary and secondary sources. Mrs. Clendenning's compilation includes some 1967 items so that it is almost as up to date as Buckingham's listings, which do not go beyond 1968. She ignores peripheral items such as poetic tributes and fictional portrayals and lists 12 pages of poetry explications, 585 articles about Emily Dickinson, and 45 books. There is, in additon to the usual information on editions and the publication of individual poems and letters, an annotated list of dissertations and an admirable introductory essay summing up the growth of Emily Dickinson's literary reputation. Furthermore, Mrs. Clendenning's bibliography is a beautifully printed letterpress book, bound attractively in what Emily Dickinson probably would have described as cochineal.

There are other recent bibliographies of less utility: Klaus Lubbers, *Emily Dickinson: The Critical Revolution* (Ann Arbor, Mich., 1968), contains about one thousand unannotated items arranged as a supplemental list of sources rather than as a bibliography. About half of his listings are reviews which appeared between 1890 and 1962. Another less complete list of reviews between 1890 and 1896 may be found in Millicent Todd Bingham's *Ancestors' Brocades: The Literary Debut of Emily Dickinson* (New York, 1945; reprinted, Dover, 1967). A general list of 436 items, now superseded by the Clendenning and Buckingham bibliographies, is found in Susan Freis's "Emily Dickinson: A Checklist of Criticism, 1930–1966" (*PBSA*, IV Quarter 1967). Jacob Blanck, in *BAL*, volume 2, besides describing the primary works in more detail than anyone else, also includes poems set to music, anthologies, and fiction. An extensive list of creative tributes to Emily Dickinson appears in the *Emily Dickinson Bulletin* (Jan. 1969).

Two pioneering bibliographies, now hard to come by, are of historic interest: Alfred Leete Hampson's *Emily Dickinson: A Bibliography* (Northampton, Mass., 1930), and *Emily Dickinson, December 10, 1830–May 15, 1886: A Bibliography* (Amherst, Mass., 1930). The latter, which was compiled by the Jones Library staff, contains a forword by George Whicher. These are subsumed into the more recent compilations but were the initial efforts to collect bibliographical information, along with the catalogue of a Yale University Library exhibition, also issued in 1930, the centennial year of Emily Dickinson's birth.

A final bibliographical item, although of peripheral importance, should be mentioned, because it appeared too late to be included in either the Buckingham or Clendenning bibliographies: Robert Fraser's *The Margaret Jane Pershing Collection of Emily Dickinson* (Princeton, N.J., 1969). It is a twenty-three-page pamphlet, with an introduction by Richard M. Ludwig, which describes a collection recently presented to the Princeton Library.

For current bibliography one should consult the annual volumes of *American Literary Scholarship* (Durham, N.C.), edited by James Woodress from 1965 to 1969 and by J. Albert Robbins from 1970 on, and the annual listings in *PMLA*. The former reviews briefly and evaluates the annual Dickinson scholarship.

At the beginning of 1968 Emily Dickinson joined the select group of authors to whom an entire journal has been devoted. The *Emily Dickinson Bulletin*, edited by Frederick L. Morey, 4508 38th Street, Brentwood, Md. 20722, appears quarterly in duplicated format and serves as newsletter, clearinghouse for notes and queries, serial bibliography, and repository of short articles.

One service that computer technology can perform for humanistic scholarship is the preparation of concordances. Emily Dickinson is the first American to benefit from the efforts of the Cornell Concordance Center with S. P. Rosenbaum's *A Concordance to the Poems of Emily Dickinson* (Ithaca, N.Y., 1964), an impressive 899-page volume that

indexes over one hundred thousand of Emily Dickinson's words. It gives
not only the word in context but also includes the first line of the poem
in which the work occurs and is keyed to the number of the poem in
Johnson's text. The appendix includes word-frequency lists (*heaven*
appears 143 times, *death* 141, *bride* 14, *husband* 1). Cornell has preserved the tape for the print-out so that future scholars can ask for
specific data not included in the concordance. This concordance already
is getting heavy use in specialized studies of style, diction, and imagery.

EDITIONS

Emily Dickinson has the most fascinating publication history of any
American author. The place to begin this absorbing story is with Mrs.
Bingham's *Ancestors' Brocades*, which tells how the poems originally
came to be edited by her mother, Mabel Loomis Todd, and Thomas
Wentworth Higginson (*Poems by Emily Dickinson* and *Poems . . . Second Series*, Boston, 1890, 1891). The story also has been told more
succinctly and objectively, and with some corrections, by a contemporary scholar, R. W. Franklin, in *The Editing of Emily Dickinson: A
Reconsideration* (Madison, Wis., 1967). Lavinia Dickinson found the
poems among her sister's effects after her death and engaged Mrs. Todd,
wife of an Amherst College astronomy professor, and Col. Higginson of
Boston to edit them. They labored to present twentieth-century poems
to a nineteenth-century audience. "The editors were wise enough to
think the poems good, and practical enough to realize that many of
their contemporaries would find the poetry offensive in style, if not in
content" (Clendenning, p. xii). The two editors tried to make the
meter scan and the lines rhyme. By nineteenth-century standards they
did not regularize enough; by present criteria, of course, they took
unwarranted and indefensible liberties. Mrs. Bingham tells this story
well, but she is an apologist for her mother's work, and she makes
Lavinia too much a villain. When the first two volumes came out, both
editors and, most of all, the publisher were surprised at the favorable
reception and excellent sales, and Mrs. Todd alone then edited two
volumes of letters to satisfy the curiosity about Emily Dickinson that
the poems had aroused. Later in 1896 Mrs. Todd alone brought out
Poems . . . Third Series. By this time 450 poems, less than half the number that Mrs. Todd had transcribed from the MSS turned over to her
by Lavinia Dickinson, had been published.

A celebrated feud between the Dickinsons and the Todds broke out
after the publication of *Poems . . . Third Series*. It occurred over a piece
of land Austin, Emily's brother, intended to give Mrs. Todd for her

editorial services. Sister Lavinia, however, filed suit to recover the property after Austin's death, testifying that she had been tricked into signing the deed of conveyance, and she won her case. The Todds appealed to the Massachusetts Supreme Court and lost. Thereupon Mrs. Todd, who was the only person besides Higginson able to edit the poems, put all the materials she had in a camphorwood chest, stored it away, and never spoke to Lavinia Dickinson again. The town of Amherst took sides, and the split was irrevocable. Thus ended the Todd-Higginson dynasty. For students who wish to see these early printings, a facsimile edition has been brought out by George Monteiro, *Poems (1890–1896)* (Gainesville, Fla., 1967), in which all three of the original volumes are reprinted.

The Middle Kingdom belonged to Martha Dickinson Bianchi, daughter of Emily's brother Austin and Susan Gilbert Dickinson. Emily Dickinson's poetry dropped out of sight from 1897 until Mrs. Bianchi published *The Single Hound* (Boston, 1914), which contained another 147 poems (only one of them had been previously published) chosen from among the 276 poems that Emily had sent her sister-in-law, who lived next door. During the succeeding years Mrs. Bianchi continued her editing with the aid of Alfred Leete Hampson and brought out *The Complete Poems* (Boston, 1924), which was far from complete but added five new poems; *Further Poems . . . Withheld from Publication by Lavinia Dickinson* (Boston, 1929), all of which were among those that Mrs. Todd had received from Lavinia, transcribed, and returned; *Poems* (Boston, 1930); and *Unpublished Poems* (Boston, 1935). *Further Poems* added 175 to the canon and *Unpublished Poems* presented another 131. All these, plus six more from *Poems* (1930) and *Life and Letters* (Boston, 1924), made a total of 908 poems published over a period of forty-five years. But this was by no means the total left by the poet.

Before this tangled publishing history moves into its next phase, however, the editorial work of Conrad Aiken should be mentioned. In the same year that Mrs. Bianchi brought out the so-called *Complete Poems*, he became the first outside editor and issued his own *Selected Poems* (London, 1924) chosen from the Todd-Higginson texts. He later began to attack Mrs. Bianchi's editorial work in a running skirmish that went on as late as 1945. Her editions, Aiken charged, except for *The Single Hound*, were full of distortions, misrepresentations, and stupidities, and when he reviewed *Further Poems* in 1929 he demanded a new, corrected edition. His attacks were perhaps too vigorous, but they were typical of the response of the academic and literary community to Mrs. Bianchi's editions.

During the thirties Mrs. Bingham opened the camphorwood chest
and resumed the work her mother had abandoned after the lawsuit.
Mrs. Todd had died in 1932, and there was no further reason for with-
holding unpublished poems. The third period in the publication history is the Bingham Dynasty, and it lasted from 1945 until 1955. During
this decade, besides publishing *Ancestors' Brocades* (she waited until
Mrs. Bianchi died before airing the feud), Mrs. Bingham edited one
important collection of poems and two volumes of letters. *Bolts of Melody* (New York, 1945), which also has Mrs. Todd's name on the title
page, was the work in progress at the time of the lawsuit. For the first
time in all the Emily Dickinson publishing history a carefully edited
text appeared, for Mrs. Bingham, trained as a scientist and interested in
literature, had a modern notion of an editor's responsibilities. *Bolts of
Melody* contained 668 new poems, bringing the total then published to
1,576. But even as late as 1945 no outside scholar ever had seen the
manuscripts of these poems.

In the fifties, however, the manuscripts became available, and the
Fourth Dynasty or the Age of Johnson began. Johnson issued his three-
volume edition of all the poems Emily Dickinson is known to have
written—1,775, together with the variants—as *The Poems of Emily
Dickinson* (Cambridge, Mass., 1955). The Johnson edition was a historic event in Dickinson scholarship and for the first time united the
papers that had been divided by the Todd-Bingham and Dickinson-
Bianchi feud. In addition to listing manuscript variants, the Johnson
edition also records previous publication data and the emendations of
earlier editors. For the first time Emily Dickinson's idiosyncratic punctuation—mostly dashes—is retained, and the edition attempts to date
the poems by studying their location in the packets as left by Emily
Dickinson and by a close study of handwriting changes over the years.
The front matter and appendices contain a great deal of information
about the creation and editing of the poems, the recipients of the poems,
and the manuscripts. The Johnson text has been reprinted as *The Complete Poems of Emily Dickinson* (Boston, 1960), in one volume, without critical apparatus (and with some silent textual changes). *Final
Harvest* (Boston, 1962) prints a selection of 575 poems from the Johnson text, both in hard-cover and in paper. Later printings added another poem (J-398) at the end of the collection. Another selection based
on the Johnson variorum edition is James Reeves, *Selected Poems of
Emily Dickinson* (New York, 1959). Reeves has standardized spelling
and punctuation in an intelligent way and equipped his edition with
an extensive biographical and critical introduction.

While the Johnson edition was a great landmark, careful scrutiny
of the manuscripts since 1955 has revealed a few errors and faulty read-

ings. Franklin's *The Editing of Emily Dickinson* finds that about 10 percent of the Johnson edition could be improved: "Mrs. Todd's transcripts, her typewriters, her diaries and journals, as well as the manuscripts themselves have fresh contributions to make to our understanding of Emily Dickinson's poetry and how we should edit it" (p. xvii). David Higgins, in "Twenty-five Poems by Emily Dickinson: Unpublished Variant Versions" (*AL*, Mar. 1966), supplements Johnson with variants taken from the Todd-Bingham Dickinson Papers at Amherst College and one poem at the Library of Congress.

MANUSCRIPTS AND LETTERS

Almost all the extant Emily Dickinson manuscripts are now available in two large institutional collections: the Houghton Library of Harvard University and the Amherst College Library. In 1950 the Harvard Library was given all the papers formerly owned by Martha Dickinson Bianchi and A. L. Hampson. This is a big collection, which includes not only the manuscripts of the poems but also letters by Emily Dickinson and a great many family papers. The library also has books from the Dickinson library and furniture and pictures from the home in Amherst. Many of the holograph poems were stitched into a series of forty packets, the identity of which has been preserved, and about two-thirds are fair copies. The Amherst College collection dates from 1956–57 when Mrs. Bingham gave the college the papers she had inherited from her mother. This too is a large holding, occupying twenty-seven feet of space and containing Mrs. Todd's transcripts, holograph poems, correspondence, ancillary manuscripts, and other papers. This collection has been made available on microfilm by the Folger Shakespeare Library (Washington, D.C., 1957), and Mrs. Bingham has written a *Guide to the Use of the Microfilm* . . . (Amherst, Mass., 1957). Anyone planning to study the manuscripts, which are filled with immense complexities, should first read Franklin's book. It describes the Harvard and Amherst Collections in great detail, suggests some reordering of the packets from Johnson's arrangement, corrects some of Johnson's slips in editing the mass of material which went into the variorum edition, and analyzes exhaustively the early editorial vicissitudes of the manuscripts. Franklin concludes with a thoughtful discussion of the future problems of editing a reader's edition of the poems.

Thomas H. Johnson's edition of the poems was followed by a companion three-volume edition of *The Letters of Emily Dickinson* (Cambridge, Mass., 1958). Aided by an associate editor, Theodora Ward, he managed to round up about 1,150 letters and prose fragments for this collection. The letters are accurately transcribed and arranged chrono-

logically, although dating was difficult and often could only be approxi-
mated. Two-thirds of the letters were published from holographs; the
rest derive from transcripts or earlier printed versions. The holograph
letters are widely scattered in the hands of libraries and individuals,
but the Johnson-Ward edition includes in its critical apparatus the location of the manuscript and the data, where appropriate, concerning
previous publication. Certainly additional letters will turn up in the
future, but since 1958 no significant additions to the letters have been
published. Richard Sewall, in "The Lyman Letters: New Light on
Emily Dickinson and Her Family" (*Massachusetts Review* [Univ. of
Mass.], Autumn 1965, published also as a monograph by the University
of Massachusetts Press), has found some excerpts from Emily Dickinson's letters in letters written by Joseph B. Lyman to his future wife
(see *Biography*, below).

All of the early letter collections have been subsumed into the Johnson-Ward edition, but it is worth while to point out Mrs. Todd's role as
editor of the letters as well as editor of the poetry. She published the
first collection (Boston, 1894), and if it had not been for her industry
in gathering letters within a decade after Emily Dickinson's death,
many would not have survived. Even so, there were other important
letters that Mrs. Todd was not able to trace, such as the letters to Benjamin Franklin Newton or to George Gould. Also many of the letters
which she collected and returned after transcribing have now disappeared. Mrs. Todd reissued her two-volume collection the year before
she died (New York, 1931) with previously suppressed passages restored
and six new letters to Charles Clark, which threw new light on the
relationship with Charles Wadsworth. Neither of the two letter collections issued by Mrs. Bianchi in 1924 and 1932 is reliable or of any use
today. On the other hand, Theodora Ward's edition of *Emily Dickinson's Letters to Dr. and Mrs. Josiah Gilbert Holland* (Cambridge, Mass.,
1951) is a carefully edited collection of letters to the editor's grandpar-
ents, and Mrs. Bingham's *Emily Dickinson: A Revelation* (New York,
1954) prints accurately the important letters to Judge Lord (see *Biography*, below). The last important letter collection, *Emily Dickinson's
Home: Letters of Edward Dickinson and His Family* (New York, 1955),
also Mrs. Bingham's work, is not incorporated in the Johnson-Ward
edition, except for the three "master" letters written by Emily.

BIOGRAPHY

Emily Dickinson's biography is just as snarled as the publication
history of the poems. As early as 1890 her love poems caused a writer
in the *Springfield Republican* to wonder what had inspired such pas-

sionate outbursts. Mrs. Todd, however, tried to forestall the search for a lover by writing in her introduction to *Poems . . . Second Series* that Emily Dickinson had "lived in seclusion from no 'love-disappointment' " and that her life was the normal blossoming of a nature "introspective to a high degree." Lavinia Dickinson before her death in 1899 apparently dragged a red herring across the trail, but when Mrs. Bianchi's introduction to *The Single Hound* (1914) and later her *Life and Letters* (1924) appeared, there were tantalizing hints about the man in her aunt's life. As biography, Mrs. Bianchi's work was myth-making, misleading, and downright erroneous. Public interest in Emily Dickinson grew in the twenties and produced, among other things, a search to find the missing man. The centennial of her birth brought two books which now have only historic interest: Josephine Pollitt, *Emily Dickinson: The Human Background of Her Poetry* (New York, 1930), and Genevieve Taggard, *The Life and Mind of Emily Dickinson* (New York, 1930). The former nominated Major Hunt, Helen Hunt Jackson's first husband, as the lover, and the latter accorded the honor to George Gould, an Amherst College student whom Emily knew fairly well. Neither candidate deserved the nomination. Both books are enthusiastic and tend to make a cult of Emily Dickinson; Miss Taggard's book attempts to trace intellectual growth and to discuss the poetry, but she lacks aesthetic distance.

The first reliable (and still valuable) biography was George Whicher's *This Was A Poet: A Critical Biography of Emily Dickinson* (New York, 1938; Philadelphia, 1952; Ann Arbor, Mich., 1957). At least, until recently, most students of Emily Dickinson have accepted Whicher's reconstruction of his subject's life. He identified Benjamin Franklin Newton, the young student who had read law in Squire Dickinson's office, and the Reverend Charles Wadsworth, a Presbyterian minister of Philadelphia, as central figures in her life. Newton had encouraged her to write, had introduced her to Emerson's poetry, had gone on to Worcester to continue his studies, and had died early. Wadsworth had been a sort of spiritual father to her and the object of her love, but he never had been aware of his effect upon her. These two men had a strong impact on her development as a poet, and with that, says Whicher, "posterity is legitimately concerned." Whicher also was the first scholar to warn biographers that the *I* in Emily Dickinson's poetry, as she wrote Higginson, "does not mean—me—but a supposed person." Finally, Whicher's book placed Emily Dickinson firmly in the context of her background: "The quintessence of the New England spirit was embodied in Emily Dickinson. She cannot be rightly understood except in terms of her heritage" (Whicher, p. viii).

Since Whicher's biography appeared, other men have shown up in

Emily Dickinson's life. The most sensational disclosure came in Mrs. Bingham's *Emily Dickinson: A Revelation* (New York, 1954), which brought to light the relationship with Otis Lord of Salem, judge of the Massachusetts Supreme Court and formerly Edward Dickinson's best friend. In this volume Mrs. Bingham published a biographical essay and a packet of love letters written to Judge Lord during the late seventies and early eighties. The letters show a deep attachment, reciprocated by the much older judge, not an attachment sublimated in poetry, like that which occurred about 1860–1861.

Another man in Emily Dickinson's life was Samuel Bowles, editor of the *Springfield Republican,* long known as a good friend of both Austin and Emily Dickinson. Winfield Townley Scott, "Errand from My Heart" (*Horizon,* July 1961), argues persuasively that Bowles, not Wadsworth, was the man who inspired the love poems. The same argument is developed more fully by David Higgins in *Portrait of Emily Dickinson: The Poet and Her Prose* (New Brunswick, N. J., 1967). This also is the view of Ruth Miller in *The Poetry of Emily Dickinson* (Middletown, Conn., 1968).

Still another candidate for Emily Dickinson's lover was produced by Rebecca Patterson, *The Riddle of Emily Dickinson* (Boston, 1951), in Kate Scott Anthon, a friend and occasional correspondent. This book reads a lesbian relationship that no other Dickinson scholar finds credible. Jay Leyda writes: "Unfortunately the real importance of ED's relation to Catharine Scott has been obscured by a work [*The Riddle*] that constructs a fictitious set of sexual circumstances" (*The Years and Hours of Emily Dickinson*, p. lxix). Kate Scott was an important friend who reacted with excitement when Emily Dickinson showed her some poems at a critical point in Emily's artistic development.

The interest in Emily Dickinson, which had reached a high level by the twenties, produced a number of personal reminiscences, such as Clara B. Green's "A Reminiscence of Emily Dickinson" (*Bookman,* Nov. 1924), Gertrude M. Graves's "A Cousin's Memories of Emily Dickinson" (Boston *Sunday Globe,* 12 January 1930), and MacGregor Jenkins's *Emily Dickinson: Friend and Neighbor* (Boston, 1930). Mrs. Bianchi also contributed a volume, *Emily Dickinson Face to Face: Unpublished Letters with Notes and Reminiscences* (Boston, 1932). Mrs. Bianchi was about twenty when her aunt died, and her reminiscences of life among the Dickinsons are useful if read cautiously. To these memoirs should be added the large collection of family letters in Mrs. Bingham's *Emily Dickinson's Home,* which add significant detail for understanding the context of Emily Dickinson's life, the town of Amherst, family relationships, and daily routine. In addition, the more recently discovered Lyman letters (see *Manuscripts and Letters,* above) give some valuable glimpses of the Dickinson family. Joseph Lyman was a distant Dickinson relative, a schoolmate of Austin's, one of Lavinia's beaus, and a good friend of Emily's. He had warm memories of the days he spent visiting in the Dickinson home. These letters also reveal that Emily's "terror—since September" probably was caused by eye trouble, not unrequited love.

The decade of the forties produced no biographies, unless one includes Henry W. Wells's *Introduction to Emily Dickinson* (Chicago, 1947), which is more criticism than biography. In the fifties, however, there were Richard Chase's volume in the American Men of Letters Series, *Emily Dickinson* (New York, 1951), and Thomas H. Johnson's companion volume to his edition of the poems, *Emily Dickinson: An Interpretive Biography* (Cambridge, Mass., 1955). Both are important critical biographies that deal intelligently with the relationship between Emily Dickinson's poetry and her background, friendships, and cultural context, but neither Chase nor Johnson adds biographical data to Whicher's account.

One of the most important sources of biographical material came out early in the sixties: Jay Leyda's *The Years and Hours of Emily Dickinson* (2 vols., New Haven, Conn., 1960). This is the raw material of biography—928 pages of entries from the letters and diaries of many people, from newspapers and other printed sources—all arranged chronologically. It begins with the announcement in 1828 of Edward Dickinson's intention to marry Emily Norcross and ends with a letter describing Emily Dickinson's funeral in 1886. The front matter includes a detailed biographical dictionary of "The People Around Emily Dickinson" and an extensive appendix locating sources.

Since Leyda's book came out, no new biographical discoveries have been made, although both Higgins and Miller have reinterpreted the old evidence to argue that Bowles was the object of Emily Dickinson's love and the man she addressed as "master." Higgins's *Portrait* is a competent book based on a close reading of all the letters, and while his evidence is no more conclusive than Whicher's, it is perhaps more plausible. Both Johnson and Chase and more recently Gelpi and Sherwood (see *Criticism,* below) accepted Whicher's identification of Wadsworth, but Mrs. Bingham, who was in a position to know as much as anyone, never advanced a candidate (*Emily Dickinson's Home*). When she first published the three impassioned "master" letters to their unknown recipient, she remained noncommittal. Both Theodora Ward (see below) and Jay Leyda think that neither Wadsworth nor Bowles was the addressee. Actually there were several other male friends in Emily Dickinson's life who have not been mentioned in this discussion, but she probably was stating a fact when she wrote Higginson that "my life has been too simple and stern to embarrass any." There is, of course, no doubt of Wadsworth's importance to her, for she referred to him specifically as "my dearest earthly friend."

Besides Newton, Wadsworth, and Bowles, the role played by Thomas Wentworth Higginson was of great significance. The facts about this relationship have never been obscure, for Higginson wrote the introduction to *Poems* (1890) and two articles about Emily Dickinson (*Christian Union*, 25 September 1890, and *AtM*, Oct. 1891). The latter article printed letters and recounted the friendship, which began when Higginson published "A Letter to a Young Contributor" in the *Atlantic* (Apr. 1862) and she wrote asking him to be her preceptor. He soon dropped the role of literary advisor but remained her friend and correspondent. This friendship is well treated by Whicher, Johnson, and others and fills a good portion of Anna Mary Wells's *Dear Preceptor: The Life and Times of Thomas Wentworth Higginson* (Boston, 1963). Miss Wells's view of Higginson is more favorable than the average estimate.

Most of the books on Emily Dickinson since 1960 have dealt primarily with her poetry, placing it in context, to be sure, but chiefly concerned with thematic development, ideas, imagery, poetic form, and explications. Theodora Ward, however, in *The Capsule of the Mind: Chapters in the Life of Emily Dickinson* (Cambridge, Mass., 1961), is an exception, as are Higgins's *Portrait* and Miller's *The Poetry of Emily Dickinson*. Mrs. Ward traces the inner story through the self-revelation found in the poems, but being aware of the serious danger of drawing false inferences, she proceeds carefully. As Johnson's assistant, she spent a great deal of time studying and ordering the manuscripts, and she writes with authority. She is especially good in her chapters devoted to Mr. and Mrs. Holland, Samuel Bowles, and Col. Higginson. Mrs. Miller's book in its early chapters is largely concerned with biography, the Dickinson-Todd relationship, the correspondence with Higginson (which she thinks Johnson misunderstood), and the Bowles friendship. Jack L. Capps, in *Emily Dickinson's Reading: 1836–1886* (Cambridge, Mass., 1966), expands the biographical information previously available on his special topic—but for the purpose of illuminating the art. This is a valuable study. John B. Pickard, in *Emily Dickinson: An Introduction and Interpretation* (New York, 1967), has written a good short study for college students, and he combines both biography and criticism. An even briefer but reliable introduction, prepared for British readers, is Douglas Duncan's *Emily Dickinson* in Oliver and Boyd's Writers and Critics Series (Edinburgh, 1965).

CRITICISM

Eighty years have passed since Roberts Brothers of Boston published *Poems by Emily Dickinson* in 1890. This period divides itself evenly into two eras: the period of judicial criticism and the period of academic criticism. For the first forty years Emily Dickinson's poetry was judged by writers and literary journalists who struggled to evaluate her work and to fit her into categories. The majority of reviewers liked her poems but were hard put to explain why she was good or to defend her violations of nineteenth-century poetic norms. Whether the puzzled reviewers created an audience or interested readers sold her poems by word-of-mouth praise is a moot point. At any rate, the poetry created a considerable stir in the nineties and went through repeated printings. Then there was a second wave of interest after 1914 when Mrs. Bianchi began editing her aunt's poems. Following the centennial year of her birth, 1930, the writing about Emily Dickinson began to be dominated by the academic critics. No longer was it necessary to evaluate her poetry. By that time it belonged to literature and could be treated with the same serious analysis that one applied to Milton or Keats.

There are three useful books that enable one to study the first seventy years of Dickinson criticism, both the judicial and the academic criticism: Lubbers, *Emily Dickinson: The Critical Revolution*; Caesar R. Blake and Carlton F. Wells, eds., *The Recognition of Emily Dickinson* (Ann Arbor, Mich., 1964); and Richard B. Sewall, ed., *Emily Dickinson: A Collection of Critical Essays* (Englewood Cliffs, N.J., 1963). The first traces with great thoroughness the growth of the poet's reputation from the time she first wrote Higginson in 1862 ("Are you too deeply occupied to say if my verse is alive?") until the end of 1962, a century later. It not only charts the vicissitudes of Emily Dickinson's posthumous fame, but it also succeeds in mapping the changing tastes and interests of a hundred years of literary history. The other two books are collections of essays that provide abundant documentation (without much overlap) for Emily Dickinson's developing reputation. Among the forty-five selections in the Blake-Wells volume and the seventeen in Sewall's collection, only four are duplicated. The former volume concentrates on Emily Dickinson's reception before 1930 and the latter, which is one of Prentice-Hall's Twentieth Century Views Series, prints only one essay written before 1932.

The Growth of a Reputation: 1890–1930

Higginson's essay in *The Christian Union* and his introduction to *Poems* (1890) were designed to prepare the way for the poetry. He wrote Mrs. Todd when the volume came from the printer: "I am *astounded. . . .* How could we have doubted them." In his preface, however, he had to defend the irregular meter, lack of rhymes, ellipsis, and compression: "In many ways these verses will seem to the reader like poetry torn up by the roots, with rain and dew and earth still clinging to them, giving a freshness and a fragrance not otherwise to be conveyed." He also argued that she had a "rigorous literary standard" of her own and a "tenacious fastidiousness" in her choice of words. He concluded that "when a thought takes one's breath away, a lesson in grammar is an impertinence." Even with Higginson as coeditor, however, Thomas Niles of Roberts Brothers was reluctant to publish the poems and asked the writer-critic Arlo Bates to give an opinion. Bates's report stated: "There is hardly one of these poems which does not bear marks of unusual and remarkable talent; there is hardly one of them which is not marked by an extraordinary crudity of workmanship." He insisted on cutting the proposed selection in half, and the first volume came out with only 116 poems. These "yes, but" reactions to Emily Dickinson's poems were rather typical of the large number of reviews that the volume received.

Only William Dean Howells (*HM*, Jan. 1891) was unequivocal in his praise and unruffled by the apparent lack of form. Where Higginson's preface tried to fit Emily Dickinson into a tradition by comparing her with Blake, Howells noted that it was an Emerson who had read Blake who had influenced her. He also thought there was a bit of Heine in her poetry, but he did not suppose she ever had read the German poet. Although most of the poems were short, Howells thought each "a compassed whole, a sharply finished point" and he believed Emily Dickinson had "spared no pains in the perfect expression of her ideals." Even the poems that seemed to have been left rough or rude gave the impression that "the artist meant just this harsh exterior to remain."

Andrew Lang, the most formidable of the British reviewers, found nothing to admire in the poems. He launched an anonymous diatribe in angry rebuttal to Howells and found fault with the lack of rhyme, the faulty grammar, and general incomprehensibility of the metaphors. He summed up with "balderdash" and wondered if Howells really was serious in praising "this farrago of illiterate and uneducated sentiment" (*London Daily News*, 2 January 1891). Later Thomas Bailey Aldrich, who had succeeded Howells as editor of the *Atlantic*, gazed into a cloudy crystal ball when he predicted that "oblivion lingers in the immediate neighborhood" of Emily Dickinson's verse (*AtM*, Jan. 1892). He was reviewing *Poems, Second Series*, and apparently felt a need to help stamp out "Miss Dickinson's *disjecta membra*" which Howells and Higginson thought so highly of. He was not nasty, like Lang, but he could not take seriously a poet who eschewed rhyme and meter, and in answer to Higginson's preface wrote that "an eccentric, dreamy, half-educated recluse in an out-of-the-way New England village (or any-where else) cannot with impunity set at defiance the laws of gravitation and grammar."

By the time Mrs. Todd alone edited *Poems, Third Series* (1896) Emily Dickinson's verse no longer was a novelty. The reviewers had her pegged generally as poet *manqué* and fewer notices appeared than before. Higginson, who reviewed the volume in the *Nation* (8 October 1896), still was fond of the poetry "in spite of all its flagrant literary faults." But there were several essays in 1896 which summed up all of Emily Dickinson's poems then published and looked ahead toward the twentieth-century estimate of her place in American literature: Bliss Carmen, "A Note on Emily Dickinson" (Boston *Transcript*, 21 November 1896); Harry Lyman Koopman, "Emily Dickinson" (*Brown Magazine*, Dec. 1896); and Rupert Hughes, "The Idea of Emily Dickinson" (*Godey's*, Nov. 1896). Both Carmen and Koopman believed that her originality and her flouting of the genteel conventions insured her permanence, and Hughes concluded that along with Poe and Whitman she was one of the three American contributors to world lyric poetry.

The period from 1897 to 1914 was a time of great silence in Emily Dickinson criticism. Lubbers's sources list only seven articles about her in this period; and in twenty-five literary histories published between 1895 and 1913, she is mentioned in only eight. But after 1914 only Bliss Perry's *The American Spirit in Literature* (New Haven, Conn., 1918) fails to discuss Emily Dickinson. Her poems, however, appeared in eighteen anthologies between 1896 and 1914, including twenty poems in Edmund Clarence Stedman's *An American Anthology* (Boston, 1900). Stedman's use of twenty poems is misleading, because Emily Dickinson appears in his collection along with 613 other poets. Yet time was on her side, and the statement she had made in one of her letters was in the process of being demonstrated: "If fame belonged to me, I could not escape her."

When *The Single Hound* appeared in 1914, a new era in American poetry had begun. Harriet Monroe's new magazine, *Poetry*, had been in existence for two years, and Frost, Eliot, Pound, Millay, Amy Lowell, and others were already publishing. Lubbers has found only twelve reviews of this volume, but he believes that only a few review copies were sent out. Only 888 copies were issued in two small printings, and the book quickly became a collector's item. Before it went out of print Emily Dickinson was hailed as a precursor of the imagist movement that was then dominating American poetry. Elizabeth Sergeant reviewed the book for the *New Republic* (14 August 1915) under the caption "An Early Imagist" and noted that for "starkness of vision, 'quintessentialness' of expression, boldness and solidity of thought, and freedom of form" Emily Dickinson could "give the imagists 'pointers.'" Amy Lowell, the demiurge of imagism, began talking about her in lectures on the new poetry and wrote her into *A Critical Fable* (Boston, 1922). Robert Hillyer, Louis Untermeyer, and Conrad Aiken, three more young poet-critics, added their voices to the swelling chorus. Emily Dickinson's form, which had bothered even her strongest supporters in the nineties, no longer was an obstacle, and she began to be linked with Whitman as one of the liberators of American verse. She still troubled academic critics, such as the pioneer professor of American literature, Fred Lewis Pattee, who never admitted her to the pantheon, and Norman Foerster, who wrote cautiously of her in the important *Cambridge History of American Literature* (1921). Foerster felt that her "place in American letters will be inconspicuous but secure."

The most important critical essay on Emily Dickinson to appear before the centennial year was the preface that Conrad Aiken wrote to introduce his selection of the poems (1924). Both Blake-Wells and Sewall reprint it. Aiken analyzed the poetry perceptively, introduced the topics that have occupied the critics ever since, and concluded flatly that she is "among the finest poets in the language." He saw in her the "most perfect flower of New England Transcendentalism." In her mode of life she "carried the doctrine of self-sufficient individualism farther than Thoreau," and in her poetry "she carried it . . . farther than Emerson." Aiken discounted the Puritan strain in her background, a point that later writers have addressed themselves to, but he did single out the large number of poems on death as one of the remarkable things about the verse and he thought the "most characteristic and most profound" aspect of her work was "the remarkable range of metaphysical speculation and ironic introspection." Even Aiken's view of Emily Dickinson's "singular perversity, her lapses and tyrannies" is quite contemporary, and he accepts her erratic but brilliant verse "as an inevitable part of the strange and original genius she was."

One more example from the criticism written before 1930 will have to suffice for this brief survey, but it is a significant essay that looks ahead, like Aiken's, towards present-day views and shows that British opinion was moving in the same direction as the American. Susan Miles discussed with great lucidity "The Irregularities of Emily Dickinson" (*London Mercury*, Dec. 1925) in answer to an earlier essay by Harold Monro (*Criterion*, Jan. 1925) dismissing Emily Dickinson as overrated. Miss Miles argued that the "irregularities have a definite artistic significance." If a poet wishes to give expression to a world in which he believes "not a worm is cloven in vain" he does well to construct neat stanzas where *sin* rhymes with *in*, *fall* rhymes with *all*, *night* with *light*, and *ill* with *will*. And if the poet sees a world where "all discord is harmony not understood, all partial ill is universal good," he will express his view in heroic couplets of undeviating regularity. "Emily Dickinson viewed a world made up of pieces which often did not dovetail . . . and a little madness in her rhymes was part of her expression of it." The essay goes on to illustrate this point and concludes that Emily Dickinson was one of the "comparatively few poets—Thomas Hardy is another—who have achieved an aesthetic impression of a cleft and unmatching world."

Emily Dickinson and the Academicians: 1930–1955

Dividing the academic criticism of the past forty years at the year 1955 is somewhat arbitrary; but after the appearance of the Johnson variorium edition the quantity of Emily Dickinson scholarship increased sharply, and for the first time critics were able to examine the entire canon and to see it arranged, at least roughly, in chronological order. The academic critics who wrote between 1930 and 1955 worked under difficulties, although their objective in general was to define the nature of the poetry and to subject it to close analysis. The first important essay of the new era was Allan Tate's often-reprinted "New England Culture and Emily Dickinson" (*Sym*, Apr. 1932) which begins with the assumption that "Emily Dickinson is a great poet."

Tate is not at all interested in the biographical problem, "which will never give up the key to anyone's verse." Even if the seclusion had resulted from disappointment in love, "there would remain the discrepancy between what the seclusion produced and the seclusion looked at as a cause." The effect of the seclusion is the poetry, but the cause is really "the whole complex of anterior fact, which was the social and religious structure of New England." Actually, he says, "her life was one of the richest and deepest ever lived on this continent." What does interest Tate is the tension in Emily Dickinson's verse that resulted from the breaking up of the Puritan idea under the impact of Emersonian Transcendentalism. Like Shakespeare at the end of the medieval system and Donne in the seventeenth century, she lived in a time of change, in what Tate calls the perfect literary situation. "Miss Dickinson is the only Anglo-American poet of her century whose work exhibits the perfect literary situation—in which is possible the fusion of sensibility and thought." Her poetry is primarily a "poetry of ideas" and his purpose is to fit her into a tradition; for "poetry does not dispense with tradition; it probes the deficiencies of a tradition."

Whicher's *This Was A Poet* (1938) also placed Emily Dickinson firmly within her tradition, and aside from its interest as biography, it is in addition a significant work of criticism. Whicher felt obliged to counteract the enthusiastic tendency, after *The Single Hound* appeared, to see Emily Dickinson as a twentieth-century contemporary. His biographical chapters, which recreate vividly the Amherst background and the Mt. Holyoke experience, effectively contribute to this effort. Both Whicher and the poet, as Emily Dickinson put it, "see—New Englandly." Though she lived during the Gilded Age she was not a part of it. Her mental climate was much the same as Emerson's, and what she actually represents is the "last surprising bloom—the November witchhazel blossom—of New England's flowering time" (Whicher, p. 153). Three of the strongest currents of New England culture came together in her poetry: "the Puritan tradition in which she was nurtured; the Yankee or, more broadly, American humor that was just coming out of the ground; and the spiritual unrest, typified by Emerson, which everywhere was melting the frost of custom" (Ibid.)

Richard Sewall notes in the introduction to his collection of essays that one of the characteristics of academic criticism before 1955 was the "tone of grudgingness and apology on the one hand and fulsomeness and cloying unction on the other." Yvor Winters, always a prickly critic, illustrates the former tone in "Emily Dickinson and the Limits of Judgment," one of the chapters in *Maule's Curse* (Norfolk, Conn., 1938). He wrote that "no poet of comparable reputation has been guilty of so much unpardonable writing." It annoyed him that she often was praised for her worst traits, such as the silly playfulness that made "I like to see it lap the Miles" an "abominable" poem; and even her best poems, unlike those of Jonson, Herbert, or Hardy "can never be isolated certainly and defensibly from her defects." He found this state of affairs "profoundly disturbing" because she was "a poetic genius of the highest order." Winters in this essay went on to analyze a number of poems, good and bad, to accuse Emily Dickinson of an occasional "deliberate excursion into obscurity," and to quarrel with Tate because he praised a fine poem ("Because I could not stop for Death") for the wrong reasons. But when Winters called "The last Night that She lived" great poetry, despite a "badly mixed figure and at least two major grammatical blunders," his critical position was in substance not much different from Higginson's in 1890, although he conducted his analysis on a much more sophisticated level.

R. P. Blackmur's essay, "Emily Dickinson: Notes on Prejudice and

Fact" (*SoR*, Autumn 1937), was even more sophisticated and grudg-ing than Winters's.[1] He first had to clear away the undergrowth of prej-udice before he could reach the poetry to analyze it. The prejudices were several: Aiken's view that Emily Dickinson was the best woman poet in English; Mrs. Bianchi's contention that her aunt was a complete rebel and that her "slips and roughnesses" were examples of a "revolu-tionary master-craftsman"; Ludwig Lewisohn's "magnifying her intel-lectual and mystical force" in his *Expression in America* (New York, 1932); and Tate's prejudice about the poet in relation to his time "as a fatal event in cultural history." The bulk of Blackmur's essay is a detailed analysis of Emily Dickinson's language, for as he argues: "The [possible] greatness of Emily Dickinson . . . is going to be found in the words she used and in the way she put them together." What he con-cedes to his subject is that she had an aptitude for language and that this sometimes produced great poetry. He concludes, however, that "the failure and success of Emily Dickinson's poetry were uniformly acci-dental largely because of the private and eccentric nature of her relation to the business of poetry." Blackmur's view might be classed by another critic as an additional prejudice to add to the original list; but this essay is a prime example of the "new criticism" of the thirties and forties, as John Crowe Ransom pointed out in *The New Criticism* (Norfolk, Conn., 1941).

The forties produced two books on Emily Dickinson that fall into Sewall's category of "fulsomeness and cloying unction." In the first, Sister Mary Power read the poetry and discovered that though Emily Dickinson was born a latter-day New England Puritan, she actually was a Roman Catholic in spirit: *In the Name of the Bee: The Signifi-cance of Emily Dickinson* (New York, 1943). This book, which was written with the cooperation of Mrs. Bianchi, was attacked by Whicher (*NEQ*, Mar. 1944) as propaganda filled with errors of fact and inter-pretation. A more important book was H. W. Wells's *Introduction to Emily Dickinson*, which contains many perceptive comments and in-sights but makes Emily Dickinson far bigger than life size. Wells's enthu-siasm is infectious, and he is a cultivated scholar, but one is put off, for example, by such sentences as the one which begins his ten-page chapter entitled "Language of Poetry": "Emily Dickinson is one of the foremost masters of poetic English since Shakespeare, and in the severe economy of her speech comparable to Dante." For Wells, "the signifi-cance of Emily Dickinson lies in the fact that her kinship is closer to

---

1. For a later, more favorable view, see Blackmur's essay "Emily Dickinson's Notation" (*KR*, Spring 1956).

all great poets than it is to any of her contemporary New Englanders." She stands with the chief poets, seers, mystics, and visionaries, and his aim is "to deliver Emily from the claws of personal interpretation and to place her personality upon a more distinguished height, not of Amherst Hill, but of Parnassus." Both Wells and Sister Power see Emily Dickinson as a mystic, and this term occurs frequently in the earlier critical writing. Fortunately, Sister Mary Humiliata in "Emily Dickinson—Mystic Poet?" (*CE*, Dec. 1950) corrects the loose use of this term by showing that Emily Dickinson does not really belong in the company of mystics as traditionally defined.

Richard Chase's *Emily Dickinson* (1951) brought a fine critical intelligence to the reading of the poetry. The careful discriminations lacking in Wells are found here in the comparisons of Whitman, Emerson, and others with Emily Dickinson, and Chase is quite severe in limiting to about fifty the poems which "have the substance and the fineness of manner which urge us to accord them equality with much else that is excellent in the literature of lyric poetry." Chase's book also has a clear focus in seeing Emily Dickinson's poetry as possessing "one major theme, one symbolic act, one incandescent center of meaning. Expressed in the most general terms, this theme is the achievement of status through crucial experiences." He goes on to explain that experience was both narrow and profound and typically took the form of a "sudden illumination, an appalling pause in the motion of things, a seizure of an unspeakable power, an ecstatic influx." The core of this book consists of three illuminating chapters on "The Economy of Poetry," "A Poetry of Ideas," and "The Idea of Poetry." Chase agrees with Tate on the importance of Emily Dickinson's historical position, but he also believes that the "used and shopworn furniture of the bygone cultural traditions" were something of a liability and resulted in "a curious personal, poetic convention which can only be called 'rococo.'"

Emily Dickinson's aptitude for language, which Blackmur discussed in 1937, became the subject for Donald E. Thackrey's *Emily Dickinson's Approach to Poetry* (Lincoln, Neb., 1954), the last critical study before the Johnson variorum edition. Writers from Higginson on have been aware of Emily Dickinson's great preoccupation with words; in fact, she wrote Higginson that, after her first tutor died, for several years her lexicon was her only companion. Thackrey's monograph is the first to deal with this subject extensively and competently. For him, her fascination with words explains in part her method of composition. She approached poetry inductively through the "combining of words to arrive at whatever conclusion the word pattern seemed to suggest, rather than using words as subordinate instruments in expressing a total conception." Words to her had a startling vitality, some terrifying mysterious power, and her poetry is full of specific statements about language. Her intense concern with language as a means of communication no doubt accounts for the economy and frugality of her verse. At the same time it made her aware that words really could not communicate at all. "This second aspect of her experience . . . led her to a worshipful attitude toward silence," and one might have expected ultimately a withdrawal from attempts to communicate and a devotion "to a mystical experiencing of truth." But she was not a mystical type and went on writing her letter to the world.

Emily Dickinson and the Academicians: 1955–1969

Space in this essay precludes the discussion of the large number of critical articles and explications which appeared in the decade after 1955 at the rate of from ten to twenty per year and since then at a still higher rate. Many of these are significant discussions and are worth attention. It has also been impossible to deal with the forty dissertations written on Emily Dickinson, except for the eight which so far have appeared as books. Summaries of most of the unpublished dissertations may be found in *DA*. It is interesting to note, however, that the first dissertation was written at the University of Vienna in 1940, and none was produced in the United States until 1951. But since the Johnson variorum edition appeared, it has been floodtime for Dickinson dissertations.

After five years of work on the manuscripts and letters, Johnson brought out his complete edition of the poems in 1955 and in the same year issued *Emily Dickinson: An Interpretive Biography* (Boston, 1955). As criticism the biography lacks the brilliant *aperçus* of Chase's work, but it is the first book to be based on a close examination of the manuscripts arranged in approximate chronological order. Johnson was able to study the process of technical mastery as no one before had been able to do, and his discussion of "The Poet and the Muse" is a valuable contribution. He studies her prosody as it derived from Watts's *Christian Psalmody* and *The Psalms, Hymns, and Spiritual Songs*, copies of which were owned by Edward Dickinson. Her first lesson in metrics no doubt came from Watts, and Johnson's discussion of her use of common meter, long meter, and short meter is illuminating. At first she followed the hymn meters closely, but gradually she "perceived how to gain new effects by exploring the possibilities within traditional metric patterns." Her experiments continued until her "prosodic expertness was fully realized in 1862." A further study of this subject is Martha W. England, "Emily Dickinson and Isaac Watts: Puritan Hymnodists" (*BNYPL*,

Feb. 1965), which examines the Watts relationship in great detail and with a considerable knowledge of hymnology.

As has been noted, the appearance of the Johnson edition of the poetry was hailed as a momentous literary event, and the three-volume work was widely reviewed. Two interesting review-essays were written by John Crowe Ransom and Austin Warren. Ransom's pleasantly discursive "Emily Dickinson: A Poet Restored" (*Perspectives USA*, Spring 1956) surveys the work with a poet's eye and suggests that about one out of seventeen of the 1,775 poems "are destined to become a common public property." Warren's review "Emily Dickinson" (*SR*, Autumn 1957), expands this number to about three hundred, but Warren is surprised to discover that there is no "consistency of method" between the early and late poems. He had expected the "poems to grow more Dickinsonian" and not occasionally, as they do, turn back to styles not definitely hers. "Unlike Mozart and Beethoven and Hopkins and James, she had no 'late manner' so integrally held that she could not, in conscience, deviate therefrom."

The first comprehensive reading of all the poems based on the Johnson text appeared in Charles Anderson's *Emily Dickinson's Poetry: Stairway of Surprise* (New York, 1960). This is an important book that is interested solely in the poetry as art and winnows from the entire canon 103 poems for explication under several thematic groupings: "The Paradise of Art," "The Outer World," "The Inner World," and "The Other Paradise." As Anderson explains in his preface, "with a poet like Emily Dickinson who published nothing and apparently destroyed nothing, the literary remains may include the miscellaneous sweepings of the poet's workshop, ranging all the way from splendid finished creations down to absent-minded scribblings." The 103 poems, which he analyzes extensively and perceptively, represent to him the real gold of the total remains. He departs from Johnson's practice of using as basic text the earliest fair copy, and when there are variant extant texts, which often is the case, he establishes his own reading. Many of the poems Anderson includes have long been admired and often explicated, such as "Safe in their Alabaster Chambers" and "There's a certain Slant of light," but others, like "There is a Zone whose even Years" and "I went to Heaven," are much less familiar. Still others like "There came a Day at Summer's full" are surprisingly not among Anderson's selections.

About the time Anderson's book came out, three poets, Archibald MacLeish, Louise Bogan, and Richard Wilbur, appeared together at an Emily Dickinson celebration at Amherst College. Their papers were published in an interesting little book, *Emily Dickinson: Three Views*

(Amherst, Mass., 1960). MacLeish ("The Private World") believes that it is the quality of the voice in which Emily Dickinson speaks that makes her unique and important. It is "the tone rather than the words that one remembers afterwards"—a wholly "spontaneous tone" without any "literary assumption of posture or pose." And the voice "speaks to *you*," not to herself as a voice to be overheard, and it speaks with "that New England restraint which is really a self-respect which also respects others." Louise Bogan ("A Mystical Poet") revives the term mystic for Emily Dickinson but uses it as a metaphor: "We find that the progress of the mystic toward illumination, and the poet toward the full depth and richness of his insight—are much alike." She sees Emily Dickinson as belonging with the great English Romantic poets who "shared the belief that the imagination was nothing less than God as he operates in the human soul." And she elaborates the comparison with Blake that Howells and Higginson had made in 1890. Richard Wilbur's view ("Sumptuous Destitution") is of Emily Dickinson as a poet with a "sense of privation"—the "laureate and attorney of the empty-handed." She questioned God about the economy of His creation and "used her own suffering as experiential evidence about the nature of the deity." She also employed another "emotional strategy" in her "repeated assertion of the paradox that privation is more plentiful than plenty; that to renounce is to possess the more."

A book that belongs on the same shelf with Anderson's is Clark Griffith's *The Long Shadow: Emily Dickinson's Tragic Poetry* (Princeton, N.J., 1964). Griffith sets out to rescue his subject from the favorite public image of her as "an American Mrs. Browning, with a shade less preciousness and minus of course the husband, or of a feminine Walt Whitman, with the 'yawp' tuned down somewhat, and minus of course the whiskers." Anderson anticipated Griffith somewhat in rejecting the "excessively facile" poem "I never saw a Moor" and explicating instead "I know that He exists," but Griffith's book is a provocative study of more than fifty poems that define Emily Dickinson as a tragic poet. This is where her real importance lies, he believes. Her outlook was, "in the sense with which existentialism now defines these terms, an outlook suffused with *Angst*, dread, and terror." Thus Emily Dickinson belongs among her contemporaries with Melville rather than Whitman. "She shared with Melville essentially the same view of man's predicament, seeing him as a finite creature, craving order and infinity, but set down in a 'multiverse' that thwarts his cravings and remains deaf to his appeals." She tried to devise means of escaping but in her most meaningful poems the tragic vision prevails. In this book Emily Dickinson emerges as a modern tragic poet with a "sense of the discrepancy between man's potential glory and the actual horror that contains him." She is more than a tragic poet, of course, and Griffith's book needs to be supplemented by a reading of other studies such as Hyatt Waggoner's (see below).

Another writer who sees Emily Dickinson as a modern existentialist is Thomas W. Ford in *Heaven Beguiles the Tired: Death in the Poetry of Emily Dickinson* (University, Ala., 1966). It is useful to have someone isolate and organize the death poems (though he misses a few), for certainly death was one of her flood subjects; but not many Dickinson scholars will agree with Ford's thesis that "Emily Dickinson's intense interest in death was the most important single factor in shaping the contours of her poetry." Her business was circumference, as she said, and that included death among other things. Ford is simply wrong when he argues that "it can safely be assumed that the [Civil] war heightened her awareness of death still further, and that this heightened awareness was largely responsible for increased literary activities." The limitations of this book, however, lie chiefly with the failure to relate the death poems to the entire corpus of the poetry, as Griffith's book does with its chapter on "The Aesthetics of Dying." Finally, Ford's explications are far less satisfactory than those of either Anderson or Griffith.

A much more satisfactory study that deals with one facet of the poet's work is David T. Porter's *The Art of Emily Dickinson's Early Poetry* (Cambridge, Mass., 1966). Here Emily Dickinson's apprenticeship is investigated with admirable balance and thoroughness. Like Anderson, Porter is concerned only with the poetry and not at all with biography. His purpose is to plot the "boundary of the developmental period in her career" and to discover "the early stylistic habits that equipped her for the enormous flood of poetry in the year 1862." This he does ably in examining the 301 poems Johnson dated before 1862, plus the additional ones she sent Higginson during that year. In the last chapter Porter lists twenty-six early poems that he regards as superior performances. By 1862 Emily Dickinson had mastered her art and on several occasions had reached "that high level of lyric expression at which extraordinary emotional impulses are matched and dominated by even more extraordinary discipline."

Among the thirteen scholarly books on Emily Dickinson that appeared in the past five years (1965–69) are two competing studies of the poet's mind and art: Albert J. Gelpi, *Emily Dickinson: The Mind of the Poet* (Cambridge, Mass., 1965), and William R. Sherwood, *Circumference and Circumstance: Stages in the Mind and Art of Emily Dickinson* (New York, 1968). Gelpi seeks to go beyond biography and textual analysis to comprehend Emily Dickinson "fully and richly as a poet" and in addition "to suggest how central and radial a figure she is in the sweep of the American imagination." This is a very competent and comprehensive study that begins with the poet's preoccupation in an early letter to Susan Gilbert with the Emersonian problem of identity *versus* otherness, the *me* and the *not-me*. It is controlled by the metaphor of circumference throughout and returns full circle at the end to Emily Dickinson's mind as exemplifying "the paradox of the double consciousness spiraling back on itself." The complexity of her mind is not the "complexity of harmony but that of dissonance. Her peculiar burden was to be a Romantic poet with a Calvinist's sense of things: to know transitory ecstasy in a world tragically fallen and doomed." As an American poet, she occupies a pivotal position. She does not belong to the "prophetic or Dionysian strain of American poetry which derived palely from Emerson and descended lustily through Whitman to Carl Sandburg and Jeffers, and more recently to Jack Kerouac and Brother Antoninus." Rather she fits into the "Appollonian tradition which proceeds from Edward Taylor through her to Eliot, Stevens, Frost, and Marianne Moore, and thence to Robert Lowell and Elizabeth Bishop."

Sherwood's book, like Gelpi's, is a post-Johnsonian reading of all the poetry in its present ordering. Where Gelpi is mainly interested in the poet's mind as revealed in her poetry, Sherwood assumes "that poetry is a form of autobiography." He argues the Wadsworth identification again and believes that Higginson played an important part in formulating her aesthetic theory. The weight of scholarly opinion is against him on the latter subject, but nonetheless his book has a good many interesting explications. Unfortunately he does not take into account the books by Griffith, Gelpi, and Higgins, all of which deal differently with matters he treats and which appeared between the completion of his dissertation in 1964 and its publication in 1968. Emily Dickinson scholars in the sixties had to scramble to keep up to date.

Sherwood's study posits four distinct periods in Emily Dickinson's life: a period of questioning of God and immortality; a period of resentment and defiance in which she created her own god in Charles Wadsworth; a period of despair; and a period in which all her wrongs were righted by an orthodox religious conversion. The third and fourth periods occurred during the momentous year 1862 when she was composing more than a poem per day. To arrive at the conclusion that the despair and redemption both occurred in 1862, Sherwood has to reorder the 1862 poems in the Johnson edition into a coherent and logical pattern. Rearranging the poems within a given year is defensible, for Johnson's ordering is fairly arbitrary; but one cannot ever be sure that all the poems assigned to 1862 (largely on the basis of handwriting analysis) were written in that year. Sherwood's thesis, however, is provocative and possible, but what is more controversial about this book is its insistence on the importance of Puritanism in Emily Dickinson's life and the relegation of transcendentalism to an insignificant role. He writes: "Puritanism, far from being the stock from which she manufactured intellectual supports, was live, firm, and deeply rooted." In another instance he states: "Emily Dickinson's transcendentalism (or the watered-down version of it that lies behind her early poems about the intimations of nature) was a passing fancy."

A corrective to Sherwood's insistence on Puritanism's importance is a splendid chapter in Hyatt Waggoner's *American Poets: From the Puritans to the Present* (Boston, 1968). Waggoner, like Gelpi, gives Emerson a central role and places Emily Dickinson in a pivotal position in the mainstream of American poetry from Taylor to Frost: "There are very few important American poets either before or after her whose work is not suggested somewhere in hers." Waggoner also corrects Whicher's view that Emily Dickinson owed little specifically to Emerson, though she partook much of transcendentalism. If Whicher had had the Johnson editions of poems and letters, he would have seen the large Emersonian influence, but Waggoner goes on to show that Emily Dickinson eventually rejected both her father's Calvinism and Emerson's transcendentalism for the conviction that "faith was simply a 'first necessity' of our being, resting on nothing but need." Thus she redefined faith as a commitment in the manner of the later existentialists.

After eighty years of Emily Dickinson commentary one hardly expects to come across a study that breaks new ground, but such is Brita Lindberg-Seyersted's *The Voice of the Poet: Aspects of Style in the Poetry of Emily Dickinson* (Cambridge, Mass., 1968). This is a careful, lucid, abundantly documented reading of the poetry by a literary scholar with a working knowledge of modern linguistic theory.[2] It is an important addition to Emily Dickinson scholarship and answers questions previously only guessed at—often wrongly—by impressionistic critics. Mrs. Lindberg-Seyersted approaches Emily Dickinson by isolating three concepts which are realized in her language and language

2. A number of articles have treated specific topics dealt with in this book, but this is the first comprehensive literary-linguistic study. See Clendenning, Nos. 516, 578, 621, 626, 689, 785, 799, 912; also Buckingham, Nos. 6.315, 6.498, 6.599, 6.716, 6.893a, 6.924, 6.1191, 8.100.

habits: colloquialness, slantness, and privateness.[3] These are the aspects of her style that make her different from other poets, and this study investigates them on the levels of diction, metrics, and syntactic structures.

The study begins with a chapter on "The Voice and the Poet," which establishes the clear relationship between Emily Dickinson's speech and letters on the one hand and her poetry on the other: In the bulk of her poetry there is clearly a single voice speaking directly to a second person (two-fifths of all the poems are I-poems). "This contributes greatly to the prevailing impression conveyed to a reader of the character of 'spokenness' of her poetic message." Next Mrs. Lindberg-Seyersted analyzes the diction, the use of colloquial words, unique usages, shifts from one form class to another, the use of paradox and contrast, archaisms and neologisms, the mixtures of Latin roots and Anglo-Saxon words, the interplay of monosyllables and polysyllables. This is all done quite thoroughly and with ample documentation. Then the book moves on to matters of prosody and metrics, speech rhythm, and rhyme. It deals not only with traditional prosody but also with phonology and studies the interplay of linguistic and metrical rhythm. The last chapter moves on to the larger syntactic elements, which in their idiosyncratic usage contribute, just as diction and metrics do, to Emily Dickinson's colloquialness, slantness, and privateness. The book ends with an interesting explication of "Further in Summer than the Birds," using the author's literary-linguistic method.

One final note: *The Voice of the Poet* deals extensively with a problem that has vexed Emily Dickinson scholars since the manuscripts became available, the matter of punctuation and capitalization. Both Mrs. Lindberg-Seyersted and R. W. Franklin (*The Editing of Emily Dickinson*) refute Edith Perry Stamm's widely circulated article "Emily Dickinson: Poetry and Punctuation" (*SatR*, 30 March 1963) which argues that the dashes are elocution markings indicating how the poems are to be read. Franklin reproduces Emily Dickinson's recipe for coconut cake, which has the same eccentricities of punctuation and capitalization as the poems.

Arguments over how to read and interpret Emily Dickinson are likely to go on forever. Ruth Miller's *The Poetry of Emily Dickinson* (Middletown, Conn., 1965) is a case in point, for it begins by dismissing all previous Emily Dickinson scholars as either wrong or wrong-

---

3. "Slantness" is defined as a poetic technique of indirection, a term coined from the line, "Tell the truth but tell it slant"—Johnson, No. 1129. "Privateness" refers to the idiosyncratic aspects of Dickinson's style.

headed and claims that the meaning of the poems can be understood only if they are subjected to "a new kind of scrutiny." But her method is not really different from that of other explicators, and the readings are often less satisfactory than those of Anderson, Griffith, and others. Miss Miller's chief contribution, however, lies in Chapter Ten ("The Fascicles") in which she subjects the packets to intensive examination and argues that there is structure and meaning in the original arrangement of the poems. "Each is a narrative structure designed to recreate the experience of the woman" or "if the emphasis is on the poet, each fascicle records the poet's effort to understand the truth." She believes that the idea for the arrangements came from Francis Quarles's *Emblems, Divine and Moral*, which was in the Dickinson family library. The book also includes nearly two hundred pages of very useful appendices, especially the first, which tabulates the poems by fascicle in their probable original ordering (based on the work of Johnson, Leyda, and Franklin), and the third ("Emily Dickinson's Reading"), which lists the Emily Dickinson Association Books at Harvard and quotes suggestive excerpts from some of them. This listing is a valuable addition to the appendices in Capps's *Emily Dickinson's Reading*.

Two final items of minor importance will conclude the domestic portion of this survey: Dolores Dyer Lucas, *Emily Dickinson and Riddle* (DaKalb, Ill., 1969), and Marguerite Harris, compiler, *Emily Dickinson: Letters from the World* (n.p., 1970). The former is a slight study that examines Emily Dickinson's poetry in the literary and folk tradition of the riddle, arguing that the poet "consciously exploited the technique of riddle in much of her work" (p. 14) in order to allow herself "to have her say without reprisal" (p. 133). The latter collects forty-five poems on Emily Dickinson by contemporary poets, including Gregory Corso, Richard Eberhart, William Stafford, and Yvor Winters, to mention some of the more prominent.

Emily Dickinson and the World

As one might expect, Emily Dickinson's emergence as a poet of international stature in the non-English-speaking world has come lately. The Buckingham bibliography lists twenty-six separate books or pamphlet translations into ten languages, including Japanese, Polish, Czech, and Hebrew, all but one published since World War II. Samplings of the poems, however, came out in periodicals much earlier, and the bibliography lists eighteen more translations of this sort. The earliest translations appeared in a German magazine published in Chicago in 1898, but this was a unique instance; and the first translations into German published in Germany are to be found in Ewald Flügel's essay, "Die nordamerikanische Literatur" in *Geschichte der englishen Literatur* (Leipsig and Vienna, 1907). The two poems that Flügel translated may well have been the first appearances of Emily Dickinson in translation outside of the United States. One cannot be sure because the investigation of translations and foreign reception has barely begun, and neither the Buckingham nor Clendenning listing is complete. Hans Galinsky's *Wegbereiter modernen amerikanischer Lyrik: Interpretations und Rezeptionsstudien zu Emily Dickinson und William Carlos Williams* (Heidelberg, 1968) devotes a section to "Emily Dickinson in Deutschland" (pp. 47–61) and for German listings is probably complete. Also Hensley C. Woodbridge has compiled a bibliography of eleven Spanish and Portuguese translations and eighteen critical articles (*Emily Dickinson Bulletin*, Oct. 1968), which have been incorporated into Buckingham's bibliography and somewhat augmented. Three Italian bibliographies list translations, books, articles, introductions, and reviews (many brief): Marialusia Bignami, "La letteratura americana in Italia" (*Studi Americani*, 1964); Centro di Studi Americani, *Repertorio bibliografico della letteratura americana in Italia* (3 vols., Rome, 1966–69); and Paola Guidetti (see below). In any real sense Emily Dickinson began to be known abroad in the thirties when her poems first were translated into Czech, French, Italian, Hungarian, and again into German.

The appearance in 1968 of two important books by foreign scholars marks a sort of flowering of Emily Dickinson's world reputation. Klaus Lubbers (*The Critical Revolution*) is a member of the faculty at the University of Mainz, and Mrs. Lindberg-Seyersted (*The Voice of the Poet*), who is Swedish, teaches at the University of Oslo. Her book also has been published in Sweden. Interest in Emily Dickinson in both Germany and Sweden has not been extensive until recent years, but Mrs. Lindberg-Seyersted's study was preceded by two Swedish book-length translations in 1949 and 1950, the latter with an extensive introduction. Interest in Emily Dickinson in Germany, as Galinsky's study shows, has lagged, because Germans traditionally have been more interested in American fiction and drama, but there now are at least two post-Johnson selections of the poems available in translation, and Galinsky's study is a pioneering effort.

By all odds the greatest enthusiasm for Emily Dickinson outside of the United States has been shown in Italy. Not only have there been twenty-three translations of her poems into Italian, but five of them appeared in the thirties. The first book-length study of Emily Dickinson to be written in a language other than English also was in Italian,

Emilio and Giuditta Cecchi, *Emily Dickinson* (Brescia, 1939). The monograph, which began as Giuditta's thesis for the *laurea*, was reworked with the aid of her father, who, with Cesare Pavese and Elio Vittorini, was one of the pioneer introducers of American literature to Italy. Since that beginning the Italians have produced two more critical studies, Francesco Strocchetti's *Emily Dickinson* (Naples, 1957) and a more recent book by one of the most active Italian Americanists, Biancamaria Tedeschini-Lalli's *Emily Dickinson: prospettive critiche* (Florence, 1963).[4] The latter is a good introduction for Italians to the poet's cultural background, the relations of her life to her art, her poetic sensibility, and the major themes. Italian interest even has produced a detailed study of Emily Dickinson's reputation in Italy: Paola Guidetti, "La fortuna di Emily Dickinson in Italia" (*Studi Americani*, 1963). Of the two hundred-plus foreign critical pieces listed in the Buckingham bibliography, seventy-seven of them are in Italian. This compares with forty-three German items, twenty-five French, and twenty-eight from all of Spain and Latin America.

Interest in Emily Dickinson in Asia is beginning to develop, but it is a still more recent growth than in Europe and Latin America. The Japanese discovered her in 1952 and since then have produced twenty-six articles and seven translations. *A Study and Selected Poems* appeared in Tokyo in 1961, edited and translated by Toshikazu Niikura, to introduce her to non-English-speaking Japanese. The introduction of American studies to India has brought Emily Dickinson to the attention of students in that subcontinent. Two interesting chapters were devoted to her in a recent volume published in English by the U.S. Educational Foundation in India: C. D. Narasimhaiah, ed., *Indian Response to American Literature* (New Delhi, 1967). In this volume "The Poetry of Emily Dickinson" by C. Vimala Rao finds Emily Dickinson accessible to Indian readers because of the universality of her subjects: nature, love, death, immortality. In her attitude toward time he finds a special appeal for Indians, because "she appears to dwell in timelessness." Salamatullah Khan, writing on "Emily Dickinson and Death," sees parallels between her treatment of death as a suitor ("Death is the supple Suitor" and "Because I could not stop for Death") and the devotional songs of Kabir, one of the saint-poets of India.

4. An essay in Italian was published in New York in 1950: Guiseppe Tusiani, *La poesia amorosa di Emily Dickinson*.

Jonathan Edwards

EVERETT H. EMERSON

MANY SERIOUS literary students have limited their knowledge of Jonathan Edwards to the indispensible three: Clarence H. Faust and Thomas H. Johnson's volume of selections, Ola Winslow's biography, and Perry Miller's study. The problems confronting the serious student of American literature who would go significantly beyond these studies are considerable. First, obviously, is the fact that however important Edwards is as a writer (and few would deny that among early American men of letters, only he belongs in the company of Taylor and Franklin), he was primarily a theologian and philosopher—this despite Perry Miller's insistence that "theology was Edwards's medium, as blank verse was Milton's." Second, the problem of text is substantial. Until recently the most readily available edition of Edwards has been Sereno Dwight's, and though it was noted in *LHUS* as bowdlerized, it has been used as the basis of more than one serious study of Edwards. While it will not be as complete as one would wish, the Yale edition of Edwards, whose volumes will soon begin to appear regularly, will help a good deal, even if for some sermons students will still have to consult the various early editions. Third, much of the Edwards scholarship has been done by students of religion and philosophy, whose interests are often remote from those of literary scholars. (Prominent exceptions are Winslow, Miller, Alfred Owen Aldridge, Leon Howard, and Edward H. Davidson.) The recent studies of Conrad Cherry and Roland Delattre, for example, offer serious difficulties to students of Edwards not versed in modern philosophical and theological analysis.

BIBLIOGRAPHY

Thomas H. Johnson prepared a careful bibliography of Edwards's works, *The Printed Writings of Jonathan Edwards* (Princeton, N.J.,

1940). Its usefulness is somewhat limited by Johnson's decision not to indicate which sermons appear in collections nor to describe the relative value of the various collected editions. The bibliography of Edwards's writings and Edwards scholarship included in the reprint of Johnson and Clarence Faust's *Jonathan Edwards: Representative Selections* (New York, 1935; rev., 1962) covers the years through 1961; its annotations are very helpful. Another important Edwards bibliography appears in Ola Winslow's *Jonathan Edwards, 1703–1758: A Biography* (New York, 1940). Still worth consulting are the bibliographies in *CHAL* and *LHUS*, and, of course, Leary and Woodress. Thirty-one dissertations on Edwards are listed in the *Journal of Presbyterian History* (Sept. 1967).

EDITIONS

The Yale edition of *The Works of Jonathan Edwards* began with an excellent edition of *Freedom of the Will*, edited by Paul Ramsey (New Haven, Conn., 1957). This book was carefully reviewed by William S. Morris in *NEQ* (Dec. 1957), and Arthur E. Murphy has challenged Ramsey's reading of Edwards in "Jonathan Edwards on Free Will and Moral Agency" (*Philosophical Review*, Apr. 1959). The second Yale edition volume is a competent if rather lackluster *Treatise of the Religious Affections*, edited by John E. Smith (New Haven, Conn., 1959); Smith has succeeded Perry Miller as general editor of the series. The most challenging assignment is Thomas Schafer's, the editing from difficult manuscripts of the *Miscellanies*. An important account of his task and of the plans for this edition appears in Schafer's "Manuscript Problems in the Yale Edition of Jonathan Edwards" (*EAL*, Winter 1968–69).

Edwards's earlier editors found his style often incorrect and inelegant and so proceeded to improve and trim it as they saw fit. The least of the offenders, Edward Williams and Edward Parsons, published the *Works* at Leeds in eight volumes (1806–11) supplemented by two additional volumes published at Edinburgh (1847). This ten-volume edition, formerly very scarce, was reprinted recently by Burt Franklin (New York, 1968). Nearly as satisfactory is the edition of Samuel Austin published in eight volumes (Worcester, Mass., 1808). Each edition contains some materials omitted in the others, but for completeness the most valuable is the four-volume reprint of the Worcester edition "With Valuable Additions and a Copious Index" (New York, 1843). Another edition is that of Edward Hickman (London, 1833). The ten-volume edition prepared by Sereno Edwards Dwight (New York, 1829–

30) is the least valuable textually, but it contains works not otherwise available, such as the important "The Mind," not to be found among Edwards's manuscripts. All of the editions have been reprinted. For other comments on this complicated matter, see Johnson's *Writings of Edwards*, the index to which is of special value in comparing the contents of the various editions.

Many of Edwards's writings do not appear in any collected edition. A full volume of sermons, edited by Tryon Edwards as *Charity and its Fruits* (New York, 1852), was apparently prepared for publication by Edwards from sermons delivered in 1738. Many selections from the *Miscellanies* have appeared at various times, such as the thirty-six page *Observations Concerning the Scripture Oeconomy of the Trinity and Covenant of Redemption*, edited by Egbert C. Smyth (New York, 1880); "Jonathan Edwards on the Sense of the Heart," edited by Perry Miller (*HTR*, Apr. 1948), the important item No. 782, on Edwards' rhetorical theory; and, notably, *The Philosophy of Jonathan Edwards From His Private Notebooks*, edited by Harvey G. Townsend (Eugene, Oreg., 1955). Five other slim gatherings, in addition to those in the *Works*, are listed by Douglas Elwood in *The Philosophical Theology of Jonathan Edwards* (New York, 1960). Three other important publications are *An Unpublished Essay of Edwards on the Trinity*, edited by George P. Fisher (New York, 1903), with a text of sixty-six pages; *Selections from the Unpublished Writings of Jonathan Edwards of America*, edited by Alexander B. Grosart, including a "Treatise on Grace" (Edinburgh, 1865); and, more important than the above, *Images or Shadows of Divine Things*, edited by Perry Miller (New Haven, Conn., 1948). Miller's notable essay on Edwards and typology, a groundbreaker, is being superseded by the research of such scholars as Mason I. Lowance, Jr., Thomas Davis, and Ursula Brumm (*Die religiöse Typologie in amerikanischen Denken*, Leiden, 1963; translated as *American Thought & Religious Typology*, New Brunswick, N.J., 1970).

Among the most valuable editions of Edwards is Leon Howard's *"The Mind" of Jonathan Edwards* (Berkeley and Los Angeles, 1963). Howard's treatment of Edwards's early idealism, his debt to the philosophy of Descartes, and his disagreement with Locke as expressed in the youthful "Mind" has not received adequate recognition as a major contribution to the studies of the younger Edwards.

Important but briefer pieces of Edwards's writings include: seven letters and an early version of the "Faithful Narrative of the Surprising Work of God," in *Representative Selections*, edited by Faust and Johnson; eight letters and sermon notes in *Princeton University Library*

Chronicle (Winter 1954); letters, a diary, and other personal papers, in Sereno Dwight's *Life of President Edwards* (New York, 1930); two letters and two sermons, in *Puritan Sage: Collected Writings of Jonathan Edwards*, edited by Vergilius Ferm (New York, 1953); parts of three sermons that reveal Edwards's attitude toward the Great Awakening, in *NEQ* (Mar. 1948); a sermon, in *Selected Sermons of Jonathan Edwards*, edited by H. N. Gardiner (New York, 1904); six letters in *NEQ* (Apr. 1928); various letters in Winslow's *Jonathan Edwards*; and two single letters, one in *NEQ* (June 1956) and one in *Biblia Sacra* (Aug. 1844). Edwards's letters are presently being prepared for the Yale Edition by George Claghorn.

The best edition of Edwards's early essays is that of Egbert C. Smyth in *PAAS* (1896), and the best edition of his observations on flying spiders is in *Andover Review* (Jan. 1890). The best text of the important "Personal Narrative" is in Samuel Hopkins's *The Life and Character of the Late Reverend Mr. Jonathan Edwards* (Boston, 1765), reprinted in David Levin's *Jonathan Edwards: A Profile* (New York, 1969). Edwards's will appears in *Biblia Sacra* (July 1876). Convenient volumes of selections are the aforementioned excellent one by Faust and Johnson and the very full but less useful one by Vergilius Ferm. An inexpensive edition of the *Select Works* is being published in London by the Banner of Truth Trust (4 vols., 1958–). A paperback edition of *The Nature of True Virtue* (Ann Arbor, Mich., 1960) makes the whole of the brief work available.

MANUSCRIPTS

Students of Edwards will probably continue to find it necessary to consult the manuscripts, since the Yale edition will not be complete. T. A. Schafer observes that "of the more than 250 sermons spanning the first decade of Edwards's ministry, only nine have been printed" (*EAL*, Winter 1968–69). Also unpublished are a volume of notes on the book of Revelation, his Latin master's thesis, and many letters (more than 200 located so far). The largest collections of manuscripts are at Yale and at Andover-Newton Theological Seminary. Some items are at Princeton; minor items are scattered. In addition to Professor Schafer's essay, there are discussions of the manuscripts in *CHAL*; Winslow's biography; *PMHS* (1901–2 essays by Upham and Dexter); and *Littell's Living Age* (21 January 1853).

BIOGRAPHY

The first of the Edwards biographies is still one of the best. Samuel Hopkins knew Edwards well, and what he said about him has been of great use to other biographers. His *Life and Character of the Late Reverend Mr. Jonathan Edwards*, a short life, has been frequently reprinted, most recently by David Levin in *Jonathan Edwards: A Profile*. It ought to be more widely read. Among its virtues are its inclusion of the best text of Edwards's "Personal Narrative" and extracts from his diary.

Sereno Dwight thought so highly of Hopkins's work that in preparing his own biography of Edwards he remarked, "The life by Dr. Hopkins, which is the testimony of an *eye-witness*, has been incorporated." Dwight's *Life of President Edwards* is a preface to his edition of Edwards's works. Its nearly eight hundred pages include a great many important documents: letters, anecdotes, the text of "The Mind" (the only extant version), and "Notes on Natural Science." Edwards's dismissal from Northampton is fully documented; nearly one hundred pages are devoted to it. The book is a compilation, not a work of art, but it is of immense value. Largely derived from Dwight is Samuel Miller's "Life of Jonathan Edwards" in the *Library of American Biography*, edited by Jared Sparks (New York, 1839).

Primarily studies rather than biographies, the books by Allen, McGiffert, Miller, Aldridge, and Davidson are discussed below. (Aldridge provides an excellent brief biography.)

Henry B. Parkes's *Jonathan Edwards: The Fiery Puritan* (New York, 1930) gets off on the wrong foot with the title. A popular biography by a learned author, it is marred by sensationalism, condescension, and overstatement. Edwards, says Parkes, was "the father of American Puritanism." The book is full of mockery and social history. Parkes is particularly inaccurate on the early American Puritans and provides a very thin treatment of Edwards's works.

The best narrative biography is clearly Ola E. Winslow's carefully documented *Jonathan Edwards*. As Miss Winslow confesses, it was not possible, "in addition to his life story, to do more than indicate the chronology and general import of his ideas, particularly with respect to his changing fortunes." Though Perry Miller has increased our understanding of Edwards's rivals and enemies, and though Edwards's part in the Great Awakening is now clearer, little has been added to our knowledge to alter the shape of his life, although J. P. Carse (see *Criticism*, below) has indeed given it a tragic dimension. Miss Winslow's book is continually interesting and skillfully researched. If the book does not deal adequately with Edwards's ideas, neither does it distort them.

A special area of biography deserving fuller treatment than it has yet been given is Edwards's Northampton years. A valuable study that should be published is Mary Catherine Foster's dissertation, "Hampshire County, Massachusetts, 1729–1754: A Covenant Society in Transition" (University of Michigan, 1967). Based on extensive original research, the work is especially good on the Great Awakening and Edwards's dismissal from Northampton. In contrast, all but worthless to serious students is Edwin Sponseller's short monograph, *Northampton and Jonathan Edwards* (Shippensburg State College Faculty Monograph Series, Shippensburg, Pa., 1966). Sponseller, a one-time Northampton minister, rehearses the familiar. A much better study by a predecessor of Sponseller, Clement E. Holmes, exists in manuscript at the Forbes Library, Northampton. Entitled "Jonathan Edwards and Northampton," this address provides a good sense of Edwards's relationship to the town. Thomas Johnson's "Jonathan Edwards and the 'Young Folks' Bible' " (*NEQ*, Jan. 1932), is valuable for its picture of the town and Edwards's troubles over the midwife's manual.

CRITICISM

It is difficult to be fair to such older books as Arthur McGiffert's *Jonathan Edwards* (New York, 1932), for McGiffert's biography with analysis of Edwards's thought is sympathetic, intelligent, and informed, but it has been superseded by Winslow, Miller, and the books of the last ten years. Not so easy to dismiss is the pioneering work of Alexander V. G. Allen, whose *Jonathan Edwards* (Boston, 1889) remains worth reading. Like McGiffert's combination biography and critical study, Allen's book takes Edwards seriously, and though far from sympathetic, what Allen has to say is frequently penetrating. It is probably fair to call Allen's the best study before Miller's.

A brief, readable, and useful study of *Jonathan Edwards' View of Man: A Study in Eighteenth-Century Calvinism* is by Arthur B. Crabtree (Wallington, England, 1948). Although the book is not found in many libraries, it ought to be better known, for it offers a clear exposition that is not hampered by questionable generalizations. Neither a literary nor a biographical study, it is sounder than many books that attempt to offer a fresh (and usually warped) view of Edwards.

Perry Miller's *Jonathan Edwards* (New York, 1949) remains the best book on Edwards. An intellectual biography by an intellectual who found Edwards constantly stimulating, Miller's *Edwards* is appealing to students of literature partly because of its use of a literary frame of reference: for Miller, Edwards was "an artist in ideas." Scattered through the book are references to Hawthorne, Pope, Melville, and Milton, and most readers will admire Miller's effective shaping of materials, even his use of novelistic methods. Probably the peculiar merit of the book is that Miller sees Edwards as being at the same time a thinker who understood the implications of Newton and Locke and was able thereby to anticipate modern philosophical problems and approaches and also a man whose life was made difficult, by petty feuds. In fact, Miller's treatment of the Williamses, the Hawleys, and Edwards's many personal relationships is so lively that at times one forgets that much is based on conjecture, or, to put it more kindly, is interpretive.

It is easy to find fault with Miller's view of Edwards. He dramatically overstated Edwards's rejection of covenant theology. (See the relevant chapters in the books by Gerstner and Cherry, cited below, and especially Cherry's "The Puritan Notion of the Covenant in Jonathan Edwards' Doctrine of Faith," *CH*, Sept. 1965.) Miller inaccurately described Edwards's adaptation of the Lockean philosophy. (See Howard's edition of *"The Mind"* of *Jonathan Edwards* and the articles, discussed below, by Davidson and C. A. Smith.) Perhaps most unfortunate is Miller's neglect of Edwards's teachings on grace and his repeated implication and suggestion that Edwards was a philosophic naturalist.

Most of the recent books on Edwards, notably Roland Delattre's *Beauty and Sensibility in the Thought of Jonathan Edwards* (New Haven, Conn., 1968), have corrected Miller, but none provides anything comparable to his insights. Davidson offers the narrative of a Puritan mind and Carse a humanistic study in tragedy; Miller's Edwards is a man who may be a bit too much like his creator but a thoroughly fascinating creature nonetheless. An important review of Miller's book appeared in *CH* (Dec. 1951) and a cruel but lively dissection in *NEQ* (Mar. 1952). See also the very severe comments by Peter Gay in *A Loss of Mastery: Puritan Historians in Colonial America* (Berkeley and Los Angeles, 1966); Gay calls Miller's thesis absurd. A more favorable review is R. W. B. Lewis's in *Hudson Review* (Spring 1950).

Miller's other contributions include two essays, both included in *Errand into the Wilderness* (Cambridge, Mass., 1956). In a suggestive but vague study "From Edwards to Emerson" Miller notes that the mystic and pantheistic impulses felt by Edwards were in some way connected with the development of Transcendentalism. According to "The Rhetoric of Sensation," Edwards taught (as an extension of Locke's sensationalism) that for an idea to be comprehended it must affect the heart as well as the head: "an idea is a unit of experience, and experience is as much love and dread as it is logic." Grace is a new simple idea, one to be learned only from experience. (This view has been questioned by Lyttle, discussed below.)

There are many studies of Edwards's place in New England religious history. Conrad Wright's excellent *The Beginnings of Unitarianism in America* (Boston, 1955), a dissertation under Miller, provides a context for the study of Edwards's thought, or at least aspects of it. Wright's discussion of the Great Awakening, the Edwards-Chauncey debate, and especially Edwards and the Arminians on the will are of fundamental importance. Edwards's treatise on the will is shown to be an unfair attack on the Arminian position, since he ascribed to the Arminians a view of the will not really theirs. (But see Paul Ramsey, *contra* Wright, in his edition of *Freedom of the Will*.) The ironic results of Edwards's attack are amusingly described. While not the work of a masterful stylist, Wright's book is very readable. Only the first four chapters are directly concerned with Edwards.

Another valuable study of Edwards's thought is more comprehensive but less conveniently organized: Joseph Haroutunian's *Piety Versus Moralism: The Passing of the New England Theology* (New York, 1932). Haroutunian demonstrates a real comprehension of Edwards's religious position, described as "inspired by a piety which sought to glorify God and His sovereignty over man." The study describes the collapse of Edwardeanism more accurately than Frank Hugh Foster's *Genetic History of the New England Theology* (Chicago, 1907), which is, nonetheless, still a useful book. Relevant for an aspect of Edwards's theology is H. Shelton Smith's *Changing Conceptions of Original Sin* (New York, 1955). A solid, briefer study is Clarence H. Faust's "The Decline of Puritanism" in *Transitions in American Literary History*, edited by H. H. Clark (Durham, N.C., 1953). A more recent and more controversial book, Alan Heimert's long *Religion and the American Mind From the Great Awakening to the Revolution* (Cambridge, Mass., 1966), also provides an elaborate context for Edwards's thought. Heimert's thesis that "Calvinism and Edwards provided pre-Revolutionary America with a radical, even democratic, social and political ideology" has not been widely accepted. See, for example, E. S. Morgan's review in *WMQ* (July 1967). Much of the analysis of the religious history of the period has been challenged by G. J. Goodwin in "The Myth of 'Arminian-Calvinism' in Eighteenth-Century New England" (*NEQ*, June 1968).

Over the years much of the Edwards scholarship has naturally been addressed to students of philosophy and religion. Perhaps none of the valuable studies of this kind is as likely to put readers off as is John H. Gerstner's *Steps to Salvation: The Evangelistic Message of Jonathan Edwards* (Philadelphia, 1960), for it is pious, evangelical in intention and weakly documented. But it is based on a careful reading of Edwards's many unpublished sermons, and since no other full reports on them are in print, it is not to be ignored. (Gerstner is preparing a volume of sermons for the Yale edition.) The book provides a description of Edwards's teaching on a variety of topics.

Similar in some ways is Ralph G. Turnbull's *Jonathan Edwards: The Preacher* (Grand Rapids, Mich., 1958), but it is much less valuable. Conceivably one who wants to determine Edwards's views on one of Turnbull's peculiar categories, such as "Book Collecting" or "Pastoral Concern," may find the book helpful, but the tone and superficiality limit its value to students of Edwards.

Douglas Elwood's *Philosophical Theology of Jonathan Edwards* seeks to provide a general description of Edwards's thought from a sympathetic point of view. Though Elwood argues for Edwards's importance as a forward-looking thinker, the book lacks both seriousness and conviction. With the aid of many quotations, Elwood relates Edwards to some of the great philosophers and suggests that his reliance on his experience, Augustine-like, in reaching his philosophical and theological positions is what makes Edwards distinctive. For Elwood, Edwards was a panentheist: he believed in the unity of all things in God. Robert C. Whittemore has replied to Elwood's thesis in "Jonathan Edwards and the Theology of the Sixth Way" (*CH*, Mar. 1966). He argues persuasively that Edwards is better described as a Christian Neoplatonist. (Whittemore also argues, again persuasively, against Miller. He calls Edwards a medievalist in the crucial matter of his ontology: Edwards stressed "Being to the exclusion of Becoming.")

Alfred Owen Aldridge's *Jonathan Edwards* (New York, 1964) has many virtues and a few weaknesses. About two-fifths of the book consists of an excellent biography of Edwards, the best thing of its kind. Valuable also is Aldridge's familiarity with the eighteenth-century context of Edwards's thought, not surprising since Aldridge is a biographer of Franklin and Paine. But too often Aldridge looks at Edwards from a Franklinian point of view, and he is far from sympathetic with Edwards and his values. At times he shows a lack of insight into Calvinist thought, as when he cannot understand how a predestinarian can be an evangelist. Some aspects of Edwards's thought, such as his treatise on justification by faith, are slighted. Aldridge is excellent, however, on *The Nature of True Virtue.*

The Theology of Jonathan Edwards: A Reappraisal by Conrad Cherry (New York, 1966), though misnamed, is a very able work of scholarship. Cherry analyzes the concept of faith in Edwards's thought, and while he considers it central to an understanding of Edwards, the study is not quite the general study that both its title and its publication in paperback form suggest. An important chapter shows that Perry Miller had misstated the relationship of Calvin, the seventeenth-century Puritans, and Edwards on covenant theology: "Not only did Edwards retain Puritan covenant categories; inscrutability or distant mystery is not of the essence of God's saving operations in Calvin's system." This study is addressed to readers with a grounding in theology, but because Cherry is very well acquainted with Edwards and his commentators and has fresh insights, the book is an essential one.

Edward H. Davidson's *Jonathan Edwards: The Narrative of a Puritan Mind* (Boston, 1966) is more highly valued by some readers than by this one. The book seeks to provide an overview of Edwards but focuses on a few aspects of his thought. While at times Davidson is acute and perceptive (and at other times obscure), it is difficult to find a central thesis in the book, and it makes no special new contribution. For Davidson, Edwards was a Puritan, but the effort to relate Edwards to Puritanism is neither very knowledgeable nor very satisfying, and the book is marred by inaccuracies and slips: "Each Sunday," Davidson writes, Edward Taylor "penned his Preparatory Meditation in verse on the same text he had used in his sermon." There are other indications that Davidson did not know enough to write a thoroughly sound book on Edwards. The task is not an easy one; it requires much reading in both Edwards's work (Davidson unfortunately used the Dwight text) and Edwards scholarship. For another opinion of the book, see A. O. Aldridge's review in *Seventeenth-Century News* (Summer 1969).

James Carse's *Jonathan Edwards & the Visibility of God* (New York, 1967), perhaps the most attractive and stimulating study of Edwards since Miller's, is a book with a thesis about Edwards the man, which includes what Carse considers a central insight of Edwards. He begins with some valuable observations on the relationship of Edwards's thought to Locke's: he argues that for Edwards things are what they appear to be because "appearances are all there are," and "beyond what is visible there is nothing at all." Carse then considers the implications of this view in Edwards's major writings. He concludes that when seen in this light the dominant idea in *Freedom of the Will* is that "God can have no part in determining what man actually does in the world unless he becomes man's reason for doing it." After examination of Edwards's other major writings, Carse characterizes Edwards as a preacher of "a radical this-worldliness" who failed to live a life in keeping with this world view: "there was nothing in his visible mien that served as a commanding model for the 'consent of being to being.'"

One comes away from Carse's book both with a new understanding of Edwards and a recognition that to support his thesis Carse has had to disregard large facets of Edwards's thought. As Norman Grabo has pointed out in a review that is generally admiring (*EAL*, Spring 1969), Carse ignores the role of grace in Edwards's theology (much as Perry Miller did, one might add). But the book remains an exciting and thoroughly readable work.

One of the most important of recent studies of Edwards is Roland Delattre's *Beauty and Sensibility in the Thought of Jonathan Edwards*. Delattre argues that the aesthetic aspect of Edwards's thought "provides a larger purchase upon the essential and distinctive features of his thought than does any other aspect, such as the idealistic, sensationalist, Platonist, scholastic, Calvinist, or mystic," and that Edwards's peculiar contribution is his elevation of beauty to a prominent place in theology. Except for a few helpful diagrams, Delattre makes few concessions to his readers. It is a pity that a study likely to be of great interest to students of American literature should be so dense. Though the book does not lend itself to summarizing, the last two pages do set forth much of what Delattre concludes. They at least should be read by every student of Edwards, some of whom will as a result be encouraged to tackle the body of the book.

The Great Awakening and the career of Jonathan Edwards are closely identified. The standard modern study is Edwin S. Gaustad's readable *The Great Awakening in New England* (New York, 1957), but Joseph Tracy's classic *The Great Awakening* (Boston, 1841) still has much to offer. An unusually valuable collection of materials, including selections from Edwards, is *The Great Awakening: Documents Illustrating the Crisis and Its Consequences*, edited by Alan Heimert and Perry Miller (Indianapolis, Ind., and New York, 1967). It has a good introduction and a bibliography. Perry Miller's writings on the Great Awakening include an unconvincing essay on "Jonathan Edwards and the Great Awakening" in his *Errand into the Wilderness*. In it Miller relates the Awakening to the practice of "owning the covenant" and argues that the meaning of the Awakening was that ability rather than social status was to determine who was to lead. Another brief study, an excellent one, also focuses on the results of the Awakening: Robert J. Taylor's *Western Massachusetts in the Revolution* (Providence, R.I., 1954).

Readers of Perry Miller's study of Edwards have an obligation to read Peter Gay's chapter on Edwards's *History of the Work of Redemption*, a work that Miller found especially original. Gay, a historian, found the work reactionary and fundamentalist. The second half of Gay's readable essay in *A Loss of Mastery* is an analysis of Edwards as a tragic hero, with the tragedy based on "the complete incompatibility of Edwards's system of ideas with the new world of enlightened philosophy." Gay's book has had mixed reviews, despite its charm.

Many valuable general studies of Edwards have been published. One of the most celebrated is Leslie Stephen's readable essay in his *Hours in a Library*, Second Series (London, 1876). Stephen presents a sparkling denunciation of Edwards as "a kind of Spinoza-Mather" who combined "the logical keenness of the great metaphysician with the puerile superstition of the New England divine." A more sympathetic study, and one of continuing value, is that of Williston Walker in his *Ten New England Leaders* (Boston, 1901). George P. Fisher knew Edwards's writings well; his *History of Christian Doctrine* (New York, 1896) provides one of the best brief accounts of Edwards's theology.

Another thoughtful older essay is one by I. Woodbridge Riley in his *American Philosophy: The Early Schools* (New York, 1907); it argues that Edwards's chief weakness was his lack of real learning. In this essay Riley also explores the relationship of Edwards's mysticism to his idealism. Much the same view of Edwards is set forth in Riley's *American Thought from Puritanism to Pragmatism* (New York, 1915). A somewhat longer study, that of Clarence Faust in *Jonathan Edwards: Representative Selections*, edited by Faust and Thomas H. Johnson, is probably the best of all the general essays, though thirty-five years old. Here Edwards's thought is considered in the context both of his career and of eighteenth-century philosophy.

Two other general essays must be mentioned. Joseph Haroutunian's "Jonathan Edwards: A Study in Godliness" (*Journal of Religion*, July 1931) is an excellent survey of Edwards's ideas. Edward Davidson's "From Locke to Edwards" (*JHI*, July 1963) is far more useful than Davidson's book. It focuses on "Sinners in the Hands of an Angry God" as a central document for an understanding of Edwards; here Edwards "demonstrated that the world's meaning is never known except as it is experienced." Davidson sees Edwards as concerned with "the mystery of the imperilled soul forced to know first itself and then some minute and cloudy portion of the outside world."

Among literary studies of Edwards, the fundamental ones are by Thomas H. Johnson. "Jonathan Edwards's Background of Reading" (*Publications of the Colonial Society of Massachusetts*, 1930–33) provides a necessary beginning for a study of Edwards's literary milieu and influences on his writing; and "Edwards as a Man of Letters," in Faust and Johnson's volume of Edwards selections, has not been superseded. It is, however, quite brief. Another study establishes a point that may not need establishing. Paul R. Baumgartner's "Jonathan Edwards: The Theory Behind His Use of Figurative Language" (*PMLA*, Sept. 1963) argues that the "Puritan mind," especially Edwards's, was "perfectly at home with figurative language," and that there is no tension between Puritan theory and practice. One wonders if it is useful to identify Edwards with the early Puritans on such matters.

A few specialized studies make contributions to understanding, but much remains to be done. E. C. Smyth's "Some Early Writings of Jonathan Edwards, 1714–1726" (*PAAS*, 1895, 1896) considers the manuscripts on the Soul and on Natural Science and discusses their literary merits and the development of Edwards's style. Smyth considers "modesty" an important trait of the early pieces. Edwin H. Cady's "The Artistry of Jonathan Edwards" (*NEQ*, Mar. 1949) should be read along with Davidson's essay, noted above. In an analysis of "Sinners in the Hands of an Angry God" Cady shows how Edwards communicates his "excruciatingly vivid vision" to his hearers.

Daniel B. Shea's "The Art and Instruction of Jonathan Edwards's *Personal Narrative*" (*AL*, Mar. 1965) is one of two good studies of this work. Shea shows how Edwards skillfully combined spiritual autobiography and instruction. A more historical approach is provided by David C. Pierce in "Jonathan Edwards and the 'New Sense' of Glory" (*NEQ*, Mar. 1968). In an attractive essay Pierce suggests that the mysticism of the work belongs to its time, that "the 'new sense' of glory was a specific response to the rapprochement between God and nature which had been effected by the new philosophy."

Many studies deal with special aspects of Edwards's thought. William S. Morris's "The Genius of Jonathan Edwards," in *Reinterpretations in American Church History*, edited by J. C. Brauer (Chicago, 1968), argues that the logic of Burgersdicius had great influence on Edwards. Though the essay is full of philosophical and theological jargon, it makes important points. Morris calls Edwards's philosophy "spiritual realism": "God as a divine Being is alone real." Edwards is an existentialist of sorts, since for him experience is what matters, especially experience of the divine. The essay praises Edwards highly. In "Jonathan Edwards and Melancholy" (*NEQ*, June 1968) Gail T. Parker offers the view that Edwards's thought is conditioned by his attitude towards melancholy.

Among students of Edwards's theology, Thomas Schafer is unusually able. He has examined "Jonathan Edwards and Justification by Faith" (*CH*, Dec. 1951), and "Jonathan Edwards's Conception of the Church"

(*CH*, Mar. 1955). In the former he demonstrates that Edwards's treatment of justification by faith was a preliminary means of dealing with Arminianism and of defending piety against the new moralism. Later, in the treatises on the will, original sin, and true virtue, Edwards used a different approach, one that shaped American theological history. In the latter study Schafer shows that though the Great Awakening weakened the concept of the Church, Edwards's teachings strengthened it. On a related topic, Gerhard T. Alexis discusses "Jonathan Edwards and the Theocratic Ideal" (*CH*, Sept. 1966). Alexis establishes the important point that Edwards did not consider the elect, the saints, to be God's instruments, nor was he an advocate of the theocratic ideal. He took a narrower view of religion's role in society than did the early New England Puritans. And C. C. Goen, in "Jonathan Edwards: A New Departure in Eschatology" (*CH*, Mar. 1959), observes that in Edwards's view of Christian history what orthodoxy had anticipated as the difficult days were already past and the coming of the Kingdom was now imminent.

Two studies examine Edwards's ethical system. Rufus Suter's "The Concept of Morality in the Philosophy of Jonathan Edwards" (*Journal of Religion*, July 1934) provides an exposition of Edwards's system. Clyde A. Holbrook, in "Edwards and the Ethical Question" (*HTR*, Apr. 1967), notes that Edwards offers an alternative to the ethical positions of modern philosophy; for Edwards the basis of virtue is not obligation but a vision of harmony that contrasts with subjectivistic anarchy.

Richard L. Bushman has been engaged in an important fresh analysis of Edwards. In "Jonathan Edwards and Puritan Consciousness" (*Journal for the Scientific Study of Religion*, Fall 1966) he analyzes Edwards's understanding of the conversion process as a resolution of man's conflict with God. In another study, "Jonathan Edwards as Great Man: Identity, Conversion, and Leadership in the Great Awakening" (*Sound*, Spring 1969), Bushman examines Edwards's quest for identity and its relationship to his sources in the Great Awakening. This thoughtful interpretation is based on the techniques developed by Erik Erikson. It is far more profound than the older essay by Joseph H. Crooker, "Jonathan Edwards: A Psychological Study" (*NEM*, Apr. 1890), which, however, should not be ignored.

Five studies of Edwards's philosophy, each narrower than its predecessor, can be recommended. Frederick J. E. Woodbridge's "The Philosophy of Jonathan Edwards" was published in *Exercises Commemorating the Two-Hundredth Anniversary of the Birth of Jonathan Edwards* (Andover, Mass., 1904). Woodbridge notes that Edwards's influence in New England was great until about 1890, his influence not being permanent because he did not connect adequately his philosophy and his theology. It was a duality that Edwards may have become aware of toward the end of his life. The essay is of continuing importance.

Harvey G. Townsend, who edited *The Philosophy of Jonathan Edwards*, prepared a sympathetic, critical interpretation in his *Philosophical Ideas in the United States* (New York, 1934). Townsend analyzes Edwards's epistemology, ethics, and esthetics. In a more specialized study, Townsend makes clear the role of "The Will and the Understanding in the Philosophy of Jonathan Edwards" (*CH*, Dec. 1947). He summarizes: "Edwards saw quite clearly that there is a difference between propositions formulated by the understanding and strictly subject to logical processes for verification and inference on the one hand; and those willed choices which express our likes and dislikes on the other. From the latter issue all the forms of action which give men their moral and religious characters."

Two recent discussions focus on Edwards's early idealism. Wallace E. Anderson, in "Immaterialism in Jonathan Edwards's Early Philosophical Notes" (*JHI*, June 1964), observes that though Edwards's conclusions are like Berkeley's, his arguments are quite different. George Rupp's "The Idealism of Jonathan Edwards" (*HTR*, Apr. 1969) attempts to qualify the classification of Edwards as an idealist because for him resistance or solidity exists outside the mind.

The sources of Edwards's idealism have been much discussed. Its relation to Cambridge Platonism, treated by Clarence Gohdes in "Aspects of Idealism in Early New England" (*Philosophical Review*, Nov. 1930), has been exhaustively considered by Emily S. Watts in her dissertation "Jonathan Edwards and the Cambridge Platonists" (Illinois, 1963).

Edwards's sensationalism is the subject of David Lyttle's "The Sixth Sense of Jonathan Edwards" (*Church Quarterly Review*, Jan. 1966), and of C. A. Smith's "Jonathan Edwards and 'The Way of Ideas'" (*HTR*, Apr. 1966). Lyttle shows that for Edwards the experience of grace is qualitatively different from other experiences, is like a sensory experience but is not in fact empirical, though it leads to a principle of perception. Smith argues that Edwards considered man to possess "the active power of aesthetic sensitivity and that it was through this channel that man gained access to the materials of the knowledge of God."

Edwards and science is the subject of two essays. Clarence H. Faust's "Jonathan Edwards as a Scientist" (*AL*, Jan. 1930) is a fundamental study. Faust argues that: (1) Edwards was never deeply interested in science; he was always more concerned with theology and philosophy, and (2) Edwards planned the composition of theological works while at Yale as early as his sixteenth year. Theodore Hornberger in "The Effect of the New Science Upon the Thought of Jonathan Edwards" (*AL*, May 1937) suggests that Edwards's confidence in the study of nature, a confidence derived from the new science, led him to make use of it in seeking to bring men back to religion.

Two useful review articles are Vincent Buranelli's "Colonial Philosophy" (*WMQ*, July 1959) and Clyde A. Holbrook's "Jonathan Edwards and His Detractors" (*Theology Today*, Oct. 1953). Holbrook classifies Edwards's detractors as (1) those who see him as an evil force, and (2) those who see him as tragic. Both are wrongheaded, in Holbrook's view.

Fruitful work remaining to be done on Edwards by literary scholars and critics includes analyses of the more "literary" of Edwards's writings, especially of his sermons. Relatively few students of literature are, however, currently undertaking studies of Jonathan Edwards; church historians and theologians are now, as in the past, his chief students. Since their work is becoming increasingly technical, Edwards is becoming increasingly unapproachable to the responsible student of American literature. The good texts now on the way will of course help, but it is hard to be optimistic about the likelihood of an extended, up-to-date study of Edwards as a man of letters being produced in the next several years. (Norman Grabo and Daniel Shea would seem to be the scholars most likely to produce such a work.) What ought to be encouraged is a general book on Edwards's thought by one of the Yale editors, such as Thomas Schafer. A book of this kind, utilizing the work of such scholars as Delattre and Cherry, might provide what does not now exist: a reliable overview of the thought of one of America's greatest minds.

Benjamin Franklin

BRUCE GRANGER

FACED WITH the voluminous record of Franklin's careers as journalist, philomath, scientist, press agent, and statesman, it is necessary to narrow the focus. This essay will center not on scientific and state papers but on the more obviously literary writings. While Benjamin Franklin dabbled in verse early and late, it is of course as a prose writer that he made his mark in the world of American letters. His literary prose encompasses a wide range of nonfiction genres popular in the eighteenth century, notably the periodical essay, almanac, letter to the press, personal and familiar letter, bagatelle, and autobiography.

BIBLIOGRAPHY

The only formal Franklin bibliography was published over eighty years ago: Paul Leicester Ford's *Franklin Bibliography. A List of Books Written by, or Relating to Benjamin Franklin* (Brooklyn, N.Y., 1889). It lists among Franklin's own writings 600 books and pamphlets, 18 periodicals and serials in which his writings appeared, 15 state papers and treatises in the formation of which he aided, 70 works containing letters by him, and 18 writings wrongly or doubtfully ascribed to him; also 211 works relating to, written to, or dedicated to him. Ford was a conscientious bibliographer in his day, but scholarly investigation since 1889 has brought about a drastic revision and expansion of the Franklin canon and has resulted in an ever-growing library of biographical and critical studies. Two selective bibliographies that help bring Ford up to date are *Benjamin Franklin: Representative Selections*, edited by F. L. Mott and C. E. Jorgenson (Chicago and New York, 1936), and the *LHUS* and Supplement (1959). The need for a new bibliography is self-evident.

EDITIONS

Collected Works

Four important collections of Franklin's works appeared during his lifetime, all with his knowledge, several with his active help: *Experiments and Observations on Electricity* (London, 1751); *Oeuvres de M. Franklin . . . Traduites de l'anglois sur la 4 éd. Par M. Barbeu Dubourg . . .* (2 vols., Paris, 1773); *Political, Miscellaneous, and Philosophical Pieces . . .*, edited by Benjamin Vaughan (London, 1779); and *Philosophical and Miscellaneous Papers, Lately written by B. Franklin, L.L.D.*, edited by Edward Bancroft (London, 1787). Francis S. Philbrick, "Notes on Early Editions and Editors of Franklin" (*PAPS*, Oct. 1953), discusses these four collections, as well as the first two important posthumous editions, William Duane's *Works of Dr. Benjamin Franklin* (6 vols., Philadelphia, 1808–18) and William Temple Franklin's *Memoirs of the Life and Writings of Benjamin Franklin* (3 vols., London, 1817–18). There were three major editions, prior to the Yale edition now in progress: Jared Sparks's *Works of Benjamin Franklin* (10 vols., Boston, 1836–40), John Bigelow's *Complete Works of Benjamin Franklin* (10 vols., New York, 1887–88), and Albert Henry Smyth's *Writings of Benjamin Franklin* (10 vols., New York, 1905–7).

When the projected forty volumes of *The Papers of Benjamin Franklin*, edited by Leonard W. Labaree and others (New Haven, Conn., 1959–), are published, they will contain approximately 30,000 pieces by and to Franklin; fourteen volumes have appeared to date, covering the period down to December 1767. (For the years after 1767 Smyth's edition remains the most nearly definitive, though it is not always trustworthy as to either attribution or text.) Unlike earlier editions which "all had to be selective," this Yale edition is "intended to be comprehensive." In the words of the editors, it "will present the full text of every document of Franklin's career, signed or unsigned, that we can locate and establish to our satisfaction to have been written by Franklin or by Franklin with others. . . . The ultimate test to be applied in determining whether to print any document or part of a Franklin document is whether the contents are in any sense the product of his mind." It will also include letters and other communications addressed to Franklin and "third-party" letters, producing as has never before been possible a full and fair view of his very extensive correspondence. But even the Yale edition will not be complete since many of Franklin's papers were lost or destroyed, especially during the Revolution.

In trying to establish the canon of Franklin's writings the editors have erred, wisely I feel, on the side of too great conservatism. J. A.

Leo Lemay does not agree. Reviewing the first ten volumes, he finds the editors "too conservative in their attributions" and wishes that "a much larger number of essays and hoaxes [had] been included (or at least discussed) in the *Papers*" (*Eighteenth Century Studies*, 1967). Several writings not included in the Yale volumes already published have since been attributed to Franklin: A. O. Aldridge, "Benjamin Franklin and the *Pennsylvania Gazette*" (*PAPS*, Feb. 1962), attributes to him two essays that appeared in the *Pennsylvania Gazette*, a letter of a husband-hunting maid, Belinda (26 June 1732), and a discourse by "Chatterbox" on the subject of characters with the termination "box" in their names (11 January 1733), and "An Essay on Paper-Currency" in the February 1741 issue of the *General Magazine*; Aldridge, "A Religious Hoax by Benjamin Franklin" (*AL*, May 1964), argues that Franklin almost certainly wrote two pieces that appeared in the 8 August 1734 issue of the *Pennsylvania Gazette*, "companion pieces designed to ridicule a lugubrious 'Meditation on the Vanity and Brevity of Human Life, wrote in Imitation of the Psalms,' which had appeared in the preceding issue"; and Lemay, "Franklin's Suppressed 'Busy Body'" (*AL*, Nov. 1965), demonstrates that of two editions of the 27 March 1729 issue of the *American Weekly Mercury* the first, which was suppressed before distribution, "contains a hitherto unnoticed addition to Franklin's 'Busy-Body No. 8' which marks Franklin's first entry into Pennsylvania politics." In spite of such additions or possible additions to the canon, *The Papers of Benjamin Franklin*, a project prepared under the auspices of the American Philosophical Society and Yale University and supervised by Leonard Labaree until his retirement in 1969, is an editorial landmark in American literary scholarship.

Editions and Texts by Genre

In *Benjamin Franklin's Letters to the Press, 1758–1775*, edited by Verner W. Crane (Chapel Hill, N.C., 1950), a majority of the 141 documents examined are attributed to Franklin for the first time; 91 letters to the English and American press are reprinted in full for the first time. *Benjamin Franklin's Autobiographical Writings*, edited by Carl Van Doren (New York, 1945), prints, or prints in full, for the first time forty-nine Franklin pieces, chiefly letters; fifty-one of the pieces in this edition do not appear in Smyth. There have been definitive editions of three personal correspondences: *Letters and Papers of Benjamin Franklin and Richard Jackson, 1753–1785*, edited by Carl Van Doren (Philadelphia, 1947), *Benjamin Franklin and Catharine Ray Greene: Their Correspondence, 1755–1790*, edited by William G.

Roelker (Philadelphia, 1949), and *The Letters of Benjamin Franklin and Jane Mecom*, edited by Carl Van Doren (Princeton, N.J., 1950). Also Whitfield J. Bell, Jr., "'All Clear Sunshine': New Letters of Franklin and Mary Stevenson Hewson" (*PAPS*, Dec. 1956), quotes extensively from the unpublished Franklin-Stevenson correspondence. Important among editions and samplings of Franklin's familiar correspondences with French friends are *Benjamin Franklin's Letters to Madame Helvétius and Madame La Freté*, compiled by Luther S. Livingston (Cambridge, Mass., 1924); *Les amitiés américaines de madame d'Houdetot*, edited by Gilbert Chinard (Paris, 1924); and— for Franklin-Brillon letters—A. H. Smyth, "Franklin's Social Life in France" (*Putnam's Monthly Magazine*, Oct.-Dec. 1906; Jan. 1907); and W. C. Ford, "One of Franklin's Friendships" (*HM*, Sept. 1906). *Franklin's Wit and Folly: The Bagatelles*, edited by Richard E. Amacher (New Brunswick, N.J., 1953), is the most important edition of Franklin bagatelles, though it does not include any of those he wrote in Philadelphia and England and reprints two pieces, "Information to Those Who Would Remove to America" and "Remarks Concerning the Savages of North America," that are not bagatelles properly speaking. Chinard, "Random Notes on Two 'Bagatelles'" (*PAPS*, Dec. 1959), has transcribed the French text of two bagatelles from manuscript, "The Elysian Fields" and "The Ephemera."

The *Autobiography* is unfinished in two respects: Franklin brought his story only to 1760 and he did not live to revise even this long fragment to his final satisfaction. Indeed, he seems clearly to have conceived of this fragment as lying at the center of a longer autobiographical work. Part I of the *Autobiography* was written in July and August 1771, Part II in 1784, Part III in 1788, and Part IV in 1789–90. *The Autobiography of Benjamin Franklin*, edited by Leonard W. Labaree et al. (New Haven, Conn., 1964), a careful transcript of the holograph, is the most satisfactory edition for all but the specialist; the introduction is comprehensive, the notes to the text helpful and never merely gratuitous, and the biographical notes always informative. The specialist will still want to consult *Benjamin Franklin's Memoirs. Parallel Text Edition*, edited by Max Farrand (Berkeley and Los Angeles, 1949), comprising the text of the original manuscript, now at the Huntington Library; the Buisson translation of Part I, *Mémoires de la vie privée de Benjamin Franklin* (Paris, 1791); the Le Veillard version in French, which survives in manuscript at the Library of Congress; and William Temple Franklin's 1818 London edition of Parts I–III. *The Autobiography of Benjamin Franklin: A Restoration of a "Fair Copy*," edited by Max Farrand (San Marino, Calif., 1949), is an untrustworthy hybrid; Farrand, who died in 1945, was responsible only for Part I, and the edition was completed at the Huntington Library under the supervision of Godfrey Davis. Verner Crane, "Max Farrand and Benjamin Franklin's Memoirs" (*MP*, Nov. 1949), demonstrates that where MS and WTF texts differ, Farrand often exercised aesthetic judgment in choosing the version which seemed best supported by Buisson's and Le Veillard's translations and further, that since it is only in Part I that the Buisson text is available to tip the balance between the readings of MS and WTF, Davis and his staff had to be even more subjective than Farrand in completing this restoration.

MANUSCRIPTS AND LETTERS

Eight libraries own more than five hundred manuscripts by, to, or about Franklin: the American Philosophical Society, the Library of Congress, the National Archives, the Historical Society of Pennsylvania, the University of Pennsylvania, Yale University, the Massachusetts Historical Society, and the French Foreign Office. The American Philosophical Society holds by far the largest number of Franklin manuscripts, the nucleus of the collection being Mr. Charles Pemberton Fox's presentation in 1840 of 13,800 pieces in nine languages; I. Minis Hays, *Calendar of the Papers of Benjamin Franklin in the Library of the American Philosophical Society* (5 vols., Philadelphia, 1908), describes these seventy-six manuscript volumes. Of manuscripts and letters acquired by the Society since the publication of Hays's *Calendar*, the most important was the purchase in 1936 of a large collection of papers from the Bache family, descendants of Franklin's daughter Sarah. See W. E. Lingelbach, "Benjamin Franklin's Papers and the American Philosophical Society" (*PAPS*, Dec. 1955), which "treats the relations of the American Philosophical Society with Franklin's writings over a period of more than a century and a half [and] surveys the Society's relationship to" *The Papers of Benjamin Franklin*.

Second in importance is the manuscript collection at the Library of Congress, consisting principally of the 2,938 pieces in the Henry Stevens Collection; see W. C. Ford, *List of the Benjamin Franklin Papers in the Library of Congress* (Washington, D.C., 1905). Acquisitions since 1905 are described in C. W. Garrison's *List of Manuscript Collections in the Library of Congress to July, 1931* (Washington, D.C., 1932) and D. H. Mugridge's "Scientific Manuscripts of Benjamin Franklin" (*Lib. of Cong. Jour. of Current Acquisitions*, Aug. 1947). The 840 pieces held by the University of Pennsylvania are listed in an appendix to Volume 5 of Hays's *Calendar*. According to the *Guide to the Manuscript Col-*

lections of the Historical Society of Pennslyvania (Philadelphia, 1949), the "Benjamin Franklin Papers, 1747–1794" consist of about a thousand items, among them two volumes of letters and papers (1750–83) and three volumes of miscellaneous papers from his French ministry (1776–85).

The Mason-Franklin Collection at Yale University includes manuscript books and correspondence with Joseph Galloway and the Shipley family; see G. S. Eddy, "Ramble Through the Mason-Franklin Collection" (*YULG*, Apr. 1936), and D. W. Bridgewater, "Notable Additions to the Franklin Collection" (*YULG*, Oct. 1945). J. Albert Robbins with the assistance of eight regional associates is currently revising *American Literary Manuscripts* (Austin, Tex., 1960), a project which when completed will make available a more nearly definitive find-list of Franklin manuscripts than any now in existence.

BIOGRAPHY

General Studies

In "The American Image of Benjamin Franklin" (*AQ*, Summer 1957), Richard D. Miles, reviewing 150 years of Franklin biography, writes, "For three-quarters of a century following his death, Franklin appeared to most Americans as a man who, by his charm and practical sagacity, had emerged from an unpromising station to world eminence." After the Civil War, according to Miles, three forces shaped the American image of Franklin: the business ethos, xenophobia, and the works of "scholars, thinkers and creative writers" beginning with Parton. "The major task of recent serious scholarship," Miles concludes, thinking of Van Doren and Crane, "has been to reveal a more human Washington and a nobler, more heroic Franklin. The former may be the more difficult task, but the latter has more definitely been performed with success."

An early popular biography, one which emphasizes the economic and moral rather than the political significance of Franklin, is Mason L. Weems's *Life of Benjamin Franklin; with Many Choice Anecdotes and Admirable Sayings of This Great Man, Never Before Published by Any of His Biographers* (Baltimore, Md., 1815). "Parson" Weems elaborates, often fancifully, on the evidence of the *Autobiography;* thus, Abiah advises Josiah one night as they lie sleepless in bed that for fear he should go to sea instead, little Ben be allowed to go to school (ch. 5), and Ben speaks joyously of the youthful verses he has just composed (ch. 7). The first half of the book treats Franklin's life chronologically to 1730 (that is, to the end of Part I of the *Auto-*

biography). Thereafter Weems abandons strict chronology and falls back on the biographical strategy suggested in his subtitle; while some of the material is apocryphal, most of it is excerpted or given in its entirety from Franklin's own writings: sayings from *Poor Richard* (ch. 33) and anecdotes like "The Whistle" and Cotton Mather's admonition to "stoop! stoop!" (ch. 34). Some attention is given to Franklin's electrical experiments, but his political activities are scarcely mentioned and his years in France not at all. In "The Legend Maker" (*AH*, Feb. 1962) David Van Tassel speculates, "Perhaps the worldly side of Franklin was too much even for the Parson." The first important biography is James Parton's *Life and Times of Benjamin Franklin* (2 vols., New York, 1864). As the title makes clear, Parton is frequently concerned with the times of Franklin, but always in a way that is relevant; for example, there is a chapter on Old Philadelphia in the 1740s and one on electricity before Franklin. In the Revolutionary period the emphasis is heavily political and diplomatic. This is not a critical biography, though Parton unconsciously reflects the squeamishness of the age ("*Poor Richard*, at this day, would be reckoned an indecent production"). Relatively objective and by mid-nineteenth-century standards carefully researched, Parton's biography stands at the opposite end of the spectrum from Weems's.

Carl Becker's 1931 *DAB* life of Franklin—reprinted separately as *Benjamin Franklin: A Biographical Sketch by Carl L. Becker* (Ithaca, N.Y., 1946)—is precise and clear throughout its short length, striking a judicious balance between the public and the private man. Indicative of Becker's ability to catch the quintessence of his subject is the observation that Franklin "accepted the world as given with imperturbable serenity; without repining identified himself with it; and brought to the understanding and the mastery of it rare common sense, genuine disinterestedness, a fertile and imaginative curiosity, and a cool, flexible intelligence fortified by exact knowledge and chastened and humanized by practical activities." Even as he presented itemized corrections, Carl Van Doren wrote that Becker's sketch "enjoys and deserves a wide reputation as the best biography in the entire collection [*DAB*] and as the best short account of its subject in existence. Only a little over 10,000 words in length, it says more that is essential to Franklin than biographies ten times as long, and it leaves out literally nothing that is important to the understanding of that vast and versatile genius" (*WMQ*, Apr. 1947).

After more than thirty years Carl Van Doren's own *Benjamin Franklin* (New York, 1938) remains the most nearly definitive biography of its subject. It is sensitive at all times to literary nuance; thus, the proverb borrowings in *Poor Richard* are examined and the statement, "letter-writing with him was a form of art," is confirmed throughout by Van Doren's discussion of (especially) private correspondence. Like Parton, but more skillfully and less obtrusively, Van Doren presents the times behind the life. In 1940 at the "Meet Dr. Franklin" conference, his "Concluding Paper" (*JFI*, Nov. 1942) announced: "I hope in 1945 to issue a revised edition of my book, half again as long as the first." Though his interest in Franklin continued until his death in 1950, Van Doren was not able to complete the revision. Many readers will agree with Clinton Rossiter that we need a fuller biography even than Van Doren's, "something with the sweep and detail of the Freeman *Washington*" (*Seedtime of the Republic*, New York, 1953).

Verner Crane has written two slender but significant biographies. The first of these, *Benjamin Franklin, Englishman and American* (Baltimore, Md., 1936), consists of three lectures entitled "The Education of Benjamin Franklin," "Franklin as a Social Philosopher," and "Franklin and the British Empire." Franklin's life, writes Crane, has "a singular correspondence with many of the main elements of American experience in his century. . . . [He] touched in his career and in his various interests almost all of the dominant currents of American life and aspiration in his time. . . . To explore Franklin's world is largely to discover the America of the eighteenth century. It is to discover, also, of course, a larger world of European philosophy and science from which, however, America was never absolutely cut off." Crane's *Benjamin Franklin and a Rising People* (Boston, 1954) displays a comprehensive grasp of the facts of Franklin's public life, achieving a balance between history and biography. Occasionally in the first half of the book Crane engages in just enough critical analysis to make it clear that he, too, is sensitive to literary values, as in his consideration of the *Dogood* papers, *Poor Richard*, and the early letters to the English press. Although this avowedly public biography increasingly emphasizes Franklin's political and diplomatic career, the finest chapter is that on Franklin as natural philosopher.

In *Benjamin Franklin: Philosopher and Man* (Philadelphia and New York, 1965) Alfred Owen Aldridge proposes "to reveal Franklin as a man first; as a universal genius second." More than Parton and Crane, more even than Van Doren, he focuses on what Plutarch called "actions of small note." The reader puts this book down with a fuller knowledge of Franklin's private life but without any clear sense of the "complete personality" for which Aldridge was striving; which is to say, the full-length portrait of Franklin is somewhat blurred. Still, it is the most significant biography since Van Doren's, painstakingly researched and well informed.

Special Studies

Franklin's visits to Paris in 1767 and 1769 and his nine-year sojourn there (1776 to 1785) have interested biographers far more than any other period of his life. Morris Bishop calls France Franklin's "spiritual home. [There] he found intellectual companionship and social satisfactions more appropriate and welcome to his character than anything he had known in America" ("Franklin in France," *Daedalus*, May 1957). Two members of his neighbor Mme Helvétius's household, Abbé Morellet and Cabanis, left valuable recollections of Franklin, *Mémoires inédits de l'abbé Morellet* (Paris, 1822), Vol. I, chs. 9 and 15, and *Oeuvres complètes de Cabanis* (Paris, 1825), Vol. V, 219–74—recollections which not only portray the patriarchal ambassador at Passy but also add to our knowledge of Franklin's boyhood in Boston. Elsewhere a nineteenth-century Frenchman, Antoine Guillois, pictures the salon world into which Franklin stepped so effortlessly during the year of his French ministry: *Le salon de Madame Helvétius* (Paris, 1894).

In *Franklin in France* (2 vols., Boston, 1887–88) E. E. Hale and E. E. Hale, Jr., undertake "to examine anew the whole mission of Franklin to France," making use of the manuscripts at the American Philosophical Society and the Library of Congress and "printing all the more important letters of Franklin not published heretofore, and also the most important unpublished letters of his correspondents, which would throw light on the history or on his life in France." This biography, conscientious and thorough for its day, has been largely superseded. Willis Steell's *Benjamin Franklin of Paris . . . 1776–1785* (New York, 1928), although somewhat fictionalized and therefore not always trustworthy, gives a vivid account of Franklin's relations with French women of his close acquaintance. Far superior to either of these studies is Claude-Anne Lopez's superbly illustrated *Mon Cher Papa: Franklin and the Ladies of Paris* (New Haven, Conn., 1966). Mrs. Lopez, the Yale editor who will supervise publication of the material relating to Franklin and France, focuses on the pleasure he "and the French men and women of his day found in each other's company." She paints a rich and refined picture of Franklin moving among his French friends, notably Mmes Brillon and Helvétius and and Comtesse d'Houdetot. Taking exception to those who have called his written French "semi-wild" (Jusserand) and "fantaisiste" (Chinard), she maintains that "in almost every letter his unedited French had the redeeming flash of one perfect, graceful sentence."

Among shorter studies of Franklin and France two deserve special mention. J. J. Jusserand, in *Essays Offered to Herbert Putnam*, edited by W. W. Bishop and A. Keogh (New Haven, Conn., 1929), has written a well-informed, succinct account of the years 1776 to 1785, emphasizing Franklin's diplomatic activities more than his private life. At the outset Jusserand observes, "The trend of thought in France, especially since the middle of the century, had been in favor of the very ideas dear to Franklin: simpler lives, nearer to nature, the restriction of privileges, the pursuit of happiness made accessible to all, toleration, freedom of thought." In "Franklin en France" (*FR*, Feb. 1956) Gilbert Chinard surveys "l'éducation française de Benjamin Franklin" from the time he began the study of French in 1733 until the eulogies on him in 1790–91.

Since Franklin throughout a seventy-year career conceived of himself first and always as a printer, it is not surprising that this vocation has attracted considerable attention. Lawrence C. Wroth's "Benjamin Franklin: The Printer at Work" (*JFI*, Aug. 1942) is the best-informed short essay on the subject. Richard Cary, in "Benjamin Franklin, Printer-Plenipotentiary" (*Colby Library Quarterly*, Sept. 1965), traces Franklin's "professional progress as printer and publisher." "Fascinated by both the mechanical and graphic possibilities of printing," writes Cary, "Franklin early attained the skills of a master craftsman, adopted improvements to the press, experimented with inks, papermaking, engraving and stereotyping." Luther S. Livingston's *Franklin and His Press at Passy* (New York, 1914) examines in detail Franklin's experiments of this sort while in France. Julius Rodenberg shows how Franklin's printing activities interacted with his political. Of the Passy years he writes, "Der Journalismus hatte ihn zur Politik geführt, jetzt verhalf ihm die Politik zu den feinsten und schönsten Blüten im Treibhaus seines Journalismus" (*Gutenberg-Jahrbuch*, 1956).

Three other biographical studies should be mentioned at this point, the first two by J. Bennett Nolan. In *General Benjamin Franklin: The Military Career of a Philosopher* (Philadelphia, 1936) Nolan reconstructs Franklin's six-week military career in eastern Pennsylvania (December 18, 1755 to February 5, 1756), during which time he organized the Moravian settlements and built Fort Allen (or Gnaden-hütten). Nolan's book is more trustworthy than the account Franklin gives in the *Autobiography*. *Benjamin Franklin in Scotland and Ireland, 1759 and 1771* (Philadelphia, 1938) is an absorbing day-by-day account of Franklin's visits to Scotland (1759, 1771) and Ireland (1771), "the houses wherein he dwelt, the streets through which he walked, the people with whom he mingled." Finally there is C. C. Sellers's definitive *Benjamin Franklin in Portraiture* (New Haven, Conn., 1962). "My purpose in this study," he writes, "has been to define the appearance and character of Benjamin Franklin as revealed in portraiture. A secondary aim has been to show something of the historical role of the portraits themselves in spreading his fame and sustaining the philosophy, the policies, and the nation he represented. My interest has been both in the man and in the symbol." There are forty-four pages of black-and-white likenesses of Franklin, members of his family and friends, and the artists who executed them, preceded by "a general survey in nine chapters telling the story of the life portraits from young manhood to old age" and "a descriptive catalogue of them."

CRITICISM

General Estimates

In 1889 Paul Leicester Ford, in his *Franklin Bibliography*, stated that Franklin "never was a literary man in the true and common meaning of the term," a critical judgment that has been sounded again and again through the years. In "Benjamin Franklin" Paul Elmer More wrote, "There is a certain embarrassment in dealing with Franklin as a man of letters, for the simple reason that he was never, in the strict sense of the word, concerned with letters at all" (*Shelburne Essays*, Fourth Series, New York, 1906). And William C. Bruce added, "Franklin was not a conscious man of letters at all, and is not to be judged by such academic standards" (*Benjamin Franklin, Self-Revealed*, New York, 1917). Henry S. Canby, in *Classic Americans* (New York, 1931), represents the case more fairly: "as a writer from the beginning to the end [Franklin] was first of all a journalist. . . . Regarded as a man of letters—and in his capacity of prime journalist for the colonies, he must be so regarded—Franklin is, indeed, an excellent example of a phenomenon peculiarly American. In his social ideas he was ahead of his time, in his literary expression behind it." Critics who do not regard Franklin as a man of letters take too narrow a view of the prosaic and practical nature of his mind. Sainte-Beuve, for example, not comprehending the rhetorical strategy of Franklin's famous letter of January 26, 1784, to his daughter, wrote, "He brings everything down to arithmetic and strict reality, assigning no part of human imagination" (*Portraits of the Eighteenth Century*, translated by K. P. Wormeley, New York, 1905). In *The Art of Living* (New York, 1960), F. L. Lucas cautions that "one should not exaggerate Franklin's lack of the imaginative. The kind of imagination that shows itself in whimsical humour, in graceful wit, in vivid apologue and illustration, was his to a high degree."

The underlying assumption of the present essay is that Franklin is an important American man of letters. Four important critical studies, none of which is comprehensive, proceed on this assumption. The earliest by many years is the historian John Bach McMaster's *Benjamin Franklin as a Man of Letters* (Boston, 1887). Even allowing for faulty knowledge about the Franklin canon in 1887, McMaster's discussion of the writings is disturbingly uneven. The American newspaper essays and pamphlets, Prefaces to *Poor Richard*, English bagatelles, and *Autobiography* (chiefly a review of the history of its composition and publication) are stressed more than the letters to the press, personal letters, and French bagatelles. McMaster's conclusion, though, is sound: "[Franklin] could do so many things that to do one thing long was impossible. A pamphlet that could be written in the heat of the moment; a little essay or a bagatelle that could be finished at one sitting, and trimmed and polished at a couple more, was about all he had the patience and the industry to accomplish. He finished nothing. . . . Except the Bagatelles, which he wrote in his old age for the amusement of his friends, he produced little which did not serve an immediate and practical purpose, and which was not expressed in the plainest and clearest English."

Theodore Hornberger's *Benjamin Franklin* (UMPAW, Minneapolis, 1962) achieves comprehensiveness and depth in brief compass, treating in some detail *The Nature and Necessity of a Paper-Currency* (1729), *Poor Richard*, *Experiments and Observations on Electricity*, *Plain Truth* (1747), three letters to the press ("Edict," "Rules," "Sale"), and the *Autobiography*. The personal and familiar letters and the bagatelles, however, are scarcely mentioned. Hornberger's essay supports his observation that Franklin "was not as uncomplicated a man as he thought he was, nor was his literary style as simple as he believed it to be."

Richard E. Amacher's *Benjamin Franklin* (TUSAS, New York, 1962) is a very uneven book. The central chapters are loosely generic, in the sense that they deal with the *Autobiography*, *Poor Richard*, political journalism, essays, letters, scientific papers, and religious and philosophical tracts. The analysis of the *Autobiography* is largely derivative; and the argument that the work possesses organic unity is not convincing—after all, it is unfinished. Since editing *Franklin's Wit and Folly* Amacher has revised his conception of the term bagatelle to include works other than those printed on the press at Passy; and he is secure in his discussion of them. He says of Franklin's personal correspondence, "Had he written nothing else, this alone would give him claim to a high literary reputation," but the discussion that follows is disappointingly thin. The chapter on political journalism, by far the longest in the book, is steadily rewarding. Here one encounters original observations ("Certainly his twenty-five years of carefully disciplined writing and rewriting in connection with *Poor Richard* did much to weed all irrelevancies from his style.") and an examination of such letters to the press as "Rules" and "On the Slave Trade." In extenuation but not in defense of the heavy reliance on secondary sources throughout this book, it should be said that Amacher seems to have wished to familiarize the uninitiated reader with Franklin scholarship.

In *Benjamin Franklin: An American Man of Letters* (Ithaca, N.Y., 1964) Bruce Granger contends that critics like P. L. Ford who do not regard Franklin as a literary man are "guilty of applying the wrong yardstick, of measuring Franklin the writer against a definition of literature that does not accord with what we now know about colonial culture." This critical study seeks to demonstrate how Franklin, guided by a neoclassic concern for propriety, purity, perspicuity, elegance, and cadence, achieved distinctiveness and vitality through a wide range of nonfiction prose genres: periodical essay, almanac, letter to the press (or editorial), personal letter, familiar letter, bagatelle, and autobiography. The personal letter, "addressed to a single individual with no thought to publication," is to be distinguished from the familiar letter, "wherein the author poses, self-consciously revealing a side of himself, and in effect reaches beyond his audience of one to a larger public." Scientific and official papers except as they are treated incidentally have been excluded from this study.

Special Studies by Genre

Until the appearance of Martin Christadler's *Der amerikanische Essay: 1720–1820* (Heidelberg, 1968) there had been only one extensive study of the periodical essay in America, and that a dissertation by Ernest Claude Coleman, "The Influence of the Addisonian Essay in America before 1810" (Illinois, 1936). Christadler discusses the *Dogood* and *Busy-Body* papers out of a wide familiarity with the Anglo-American essay and essay serial; especially illuminating is his analysis of the persona and the angle of vision Franklin adopts in the *Dogood* serial. *The New-England Courant. A Selection of Certain*

Issues Containing Writings of Benjamin Franklin or Published by Him During His Brother's Imprisonment, edited by Perry Miller (Boston, 1956), reproduces in facsimile some fifty issues of the *Courant* between No. 1 (7 August 1722) and No. 113 (23 September 1723), thereby providing a context in which to view and evaluate the *Dogood* papers. George F. Horner, a longtime student of humor in colonial America, argues convincingly, in "Franklin's Dogood Papers Re-examined" (*SP,* July 1940), that in spite of resemblances in method, purpose, and matter, the *Dogood* papers are not merely imitative of the *Spectator;* "they show peculiar and immediate pertinence to the Boston of 1722 and exhibit significant departures from the *Spectator* convention, in style, point of view, and character-mask of the putative author." Moreover, there is "manifest a lowering of style to the level of literacy of the poorer class." Horner says finally of these earliest extant writings of Franklin: "The style, the point of view, and the character-mask, developing in them are to be his henceforth. These, it is now seen, are largely the product of practical necessity and shrewd opportunism rather than slavish imitation."

In "The Character of Poor Richard: Its Source and Alteration" (*PMLA,* Sept. 1940), John F. Ross maintains that "it has not been recognized (1) how extensively Franklin was indebted to Jonathan Swift in his hoaxing of Titan Leeds, the rival almanac-maker; (2) that the source for the characters Richard and Bridget Saunders was almost certainly Swift's Bickerstaff papers [specifically the Partridges]; and (3) that there are *two* Poor Richards—the original comic philomath of 1733 and the final American archetype, the fountain-head of shrewd prudential wisdom." My only quarrel with this steadily perceptive article is Ross's contention that "Franklin forced Richard to play a rôle"; it seems rather that insofar as the conception of Richard underwent a change between 1733 and 1758, it happened unconsciously. Harold A. Larrabee, "Poor Richard in an Age of Plenty," in a statement that is essential to a sensitive reading of *Poor Richard's Almanack,* especially the 1758 Preface (known familiarly as "The Way to Wealth"), says of Franklin: "His moral teaching—like that of John Dewey, now so much under attack—was a dynamic doctrine of 'open ends' rather than of fixed moral absolutes forcing all individuals into a single mold" (*HM,* Jan. 1956). And Robert Howard Newcomb's dissertation, "Sources of Benjamin Franklin's Sayings of Poor Richard" (Maryland, 1957), treats its subject definitively, superseding the work of earlier scholars like Stuart A. Gallacher (*JEGP,* Apr. 1949); parts of Newcomb's dissertation have been published. Newcomb demonstrates that Franklin borrowed heavily from Halifax (*PMLA,* June

1955), Montaigne (*MLN*, Nov. 1957), Richardson (*JEGP*, Jan. 1958), two English miscellanies, *Wits Recreation* and *A Collection of Epigrams* (*PQ*, Apr. 1961), and proverb collections by Thomas Fuller, George Herbert, and James Howell. Charles W. Meister, writing earlier than Newcomb (*AL*, May 1952) and not so fully aware of the sources, calls Franklin a proverb stylist. He demonstrates that in his proverb borrowings Franklin employed balance (often with alliteration), metaphor or other figures of speech (notably personification), and anticlimax; "his art was to let his sure ear select the best form of a competing lot, polish that form through pruning, adding, or supplying a lively metaphor, and then find a strategic use for the particular proverb's message."

Verner Crane's introduction to *Benjamin Franklin's Letters to the Press* is reading essential to an understanding of this popular eighteenth-century genre and Franklin's handling of it. Essential also is Crane's examination of the dominion view of empire Franklin held from 1766 to 1774. In "Dr. Franklin's Plan for America" (*Michigan Alumnus Quarterly Review*, Summer 1958) Crane writes, "From experience, from observation of American society, from his reading of the history of English colonization, sooner than others [Franklin] arrived at the equalitarian principle of empire which [American patriots] all embraced on the eve of the final crisis." There have been relatively few studies of individual letters to the press. Paul Baender, in "The Basis of Franklin's Duplicative Satires" (*AL*, Nov. 1960), explores a duplicative pattern in three of them ("Felons," "Edict," and "Slave Trade") and concludes: "In these three satires Franklin retraced the process of perception. From actual events—the transportation of felons, a tyrannical colonial policy, and pro-slavery speeches—he proceeded to analogues, as one naturally did to make experience intelligible. At the same time he put himself as well as his readers through a test of character. For his perceptions had to contain more than private values to be virtuous; they had to imply the goodness of fostering the general welfare and the viciousness of egoism. Not that Franklin needed to reassure himself; on the contrary, in returning to fundamental perceptions he was calling upon all his strength and defying his opponents to match it. They may have refused the challenge, but he was not mistaken in putting it to them." George Simson illustrates how "An Edict by the King of Prussia" follows closely the form of British parliamentary statutes and thus discloses Franklin's rhetorical strategy in this famous letter to the English press (*AL*, May 1960). In *Political Satire in the American Revolution* (Ithaca, N.Y., 1960), Bruce Granger suggests that like Swift in *A Tale of a Tub*, in "The Sale of the Hessians" Franklin "devises a situational mask the better to objectify and give bite to the satire."

Franklin's bagatelles, taken as a generic entity, have not received sufficient critical attention. Richard Amacher, in the introduction to *Franklin's Wit and Folly*, and in his discussion of "Dialogue between Franklin and the Gout," "The Whistle," and "Letter to the Royal Academy," provides incisive, if at times too ingenious, commentary on the French bagatelles. Mrs. Lopez's analysis in *Mon Cher Papa* of "The Elysian Fields" is brilliant. Aldridge describes Franklin's essay on daylight saving (usually known as "An Economical Project"), published in the *Journal de Paris*, 26 April 1784, as "a gentle parody [of] articles of practical usefulness and household hints" such as the *Journal* published. "The mild satire of this combined literary parody and moral parable resembles Swift's writings in a mellow mood. It is the type of irony Swift might have written in place of *A Modest Proposal* if he had spent five years in the company of Mmes Helvétius and Brillon" (*AL*, Mar. 1956). There have been a few source studies. Aldridge has demonstrated that "The Ephemera" is based on an essay in the *Pennsylvania Gazette*, 21 October 1731, wherein the antediluvian Pulgah warns his daughter Shual of the brevity of life; not, as is usually cited, the essay in the *Pennsylvania Gazette*, 11 December 1735, on the venerable insect vainglorious of his great age (*NEQ*, Sept. 1954). And A. S. Pitt suggests that Franklin may have derived the theory of the great chain of being, restated in the final paragraph of "An Arabian Tale," from one or more of the following acknowledged sources: Locke's *Essay Concerning Human Understanding*, III, vi, 12, *Spectator* No. 519, Pope, Thomson, Young, Buffon's *Histoire Naturelle*, or Milton's *Paradise Lost*, v, 153–204 (*PMLA*, Mar. 1942).

Max Hall, having traced in *Benjamin Franklin and Polly Baker* (Chapel Hill, N.C., 1960) the publication history of "The Speech of Miss Polly Baker," concludes that the earliest known text of this bagatelle is that printed in the London *General Advertiser*, 15 April 1747, and that the first known American printing was in the *Boston Weekly Post-Boy*, 20 July 1747. J. F. S. Smeall questions Franklin's authorship of the version of "Polly Baker" printed in the *Maryland Gazette*, 11 August 1747, seeing it "as less a bagatelle and more an ethical satire" (*NDQ*, Summer 1959). Pursuing this argument, he cautions that our reading of the text of "Polly Baker" tends to accord with a threefold preconception: its ascription to Franklin, its wit, and "its significance as a reflexion of colonial America" (*NDQ*, Winter 1960).

Far more than any other of Franklin's writings the *Autobiography* has increasingly engaged the attention of scholars. Jack C. Barnes in his dissertation, "Benjamin Franklin and His Memoirs" (Maryland, 1954), presents a convincing argument for exonerating Temple Franklin from John Bigelow's charge that he mutilated his grandfather's manuscript in his 1818 edition of the *Autobiography*. Barnes advances the hypothesis that the revisions in the Temple Franklin edition, generally attributed to him, must in fact have been the work of his grandfather. Barnes thinks it "safe to conclude that Temple was a fair, honest editor who carefully followed the copy before him." It is his contention that probably the closest we can come to an authentic text is that of the Temple Franklin version, supplemented by Part IV of the holograph—a contention voiced years earlier by Richard M. Bache in "The Two Rival Autobiographies of Franklin" (*PMHB*, 1900). In this connection it is difficult to accept Donald Mugridge's charge (*WMQ*, Oct. 1949) that Benny Bache, as he prepared the Le Veillard fair copy, reworked the original manuscript without his grandfather's knowledge. In view of the importance Franklin attached to the preparation of these fair copies, it is unlikely that he would have passed them on unread to Vaughan and Le Veillard.

There is sharp disagreement about how organic a work the *Autobiography* is. In "Form and Substance in Franklin's Autobiography" Aldridge writes: "In form Franklin's work is a virtual disaster. . . . His expository method strongly resembles that of the picaresque novel —a rambling series of events joined together by a single protagonist, but with no unity of theme or purpose except for the announced motif of chronicling the author's rise from poverty to affluence. . . . The greatest and most enduring literary value of Franklin's memoirs is psychological rather than artistic—the delight and satisfaction in fulfilling and recording a life of superior achievement," *Essays on American Literature in Honor of Jay B. Hubbell*, edited by Clarence Gohdes (Durham, N.C., 1967). Charles L. Sanford, on the other hand, calls the *Autobiography* "a great moral fable pursuing on a secular level the theme of John Bunyan's *Pilgrim's Progress*. . . . a work of imagination which, by incorporating the 'race' consciousness of a people, achieves the level of folk myth" ("An American *Pilgrim's Progress*," *AQ*, Winter 1954)—a reading which seems to assume that the *Autobiography* was a finished work, not the long fragment we know it to be. Daniel Shea's view, in *Spiritual Autobiography in Early America* (Princeton, N.J., 1968), is more convincing than Sanford's: "Neither a spiritual autobiography in the tradition of the Puritans and Quakers nor an American achievement in its formal characteristics, Franklin's *Autobiography* yet achieves a distinctly American mixture of naive perfectionism and skeptical empiricism, assuring its reader through autobiographical example that the world has yielded repeatedly to the onslaught of method, while reserving irony as a defense against hoping too much."

Point of view in the *Autobiography*, which is inseparable from form, has interested recent scholars. "Surely it must strike any reader of the *Autobiography* as curious," writes John Ward in "Who Was Benjamin Franklin?" (*ASch*, Autumn 1963), "that a character who speaks so openly should at the same time seem so difficult to define." In the *Autobiography*, says Farrand, Franklin "was not in the least morbidly introspective; if anything, he was whimsically amused" ("Self-Portraiture: The Autobiography," *JFI*, Jan. 1942). David Levin observes that "most of us overlook the crucial distinction, especially in the first half of Franklin's autobiography, between the *writer* of the book and the chief *character* he portrays. . . . Though the honest autobiographer refuses to invent fictitious incidents, he *actually creates himself as a character*" (*YR*, Winter 1964). Robert F. Sayre amplifies this observation, arguing that though the *Autobiography* as a whole is formless, Franklin's several poses give form to each of the first three parts (Part IV being too short to consider): "The first section of the *Autobiography* is the story of Franklin's building of his roles —sampling sundry occupations, hoaxes, disguises, and literary masks— and of fitting himself out in the 'plain dress' of his first and most lasting public character, flexible and adaptable as it was always to be for him, 'Benjamin Franklin of Philadelphia, Printer.' . . . the two later parts have one important thing in common: both are accounts of projects. . . . the 'Project of arriving at moral Perfection' is his French one of the *naïf* 'Philosophical Quaker.' . . . The disarming quality of the attempt to reach moral perfection was the logic of it. . . . Franklin's identity in the third part of the *Autobiography* as patriot and civic projector gives it the form of a series of lessons in 'doing good.' . . . Of all parts of the *Autobiography*, this one is most like a memoir and of most value to the descendants of early American democracy" (*The Examined Self: Benjamin Franklin, Henry Adams, Henry James*, Princeton, N.J., 1964).

In perhaps the best of the very few stylistic studies Hans Galinsky, having examined closely the first four paragraphs of the *Autobiography*, points to Franklin's partiality for participial and substantive (rather than verbal) constructions and, more broadly, three classical qualities that characterize his prose: "fast symmetrische Gliederung weiter Satzräume, Gleichgewicht in der Form des syntaktischen Gleichlaufs, Bevorzugung des Statischen vor dem Dynamischen" (*Die Neueren Sprachen*, 1957).

There have been many thematic studies of the *Autobiography*. D. H. Lawrence's well-known chapter on Franklin in his *Studies in Classic American Literature* (New York, 1923) centers its attack on the art of virtue, set forth in Part II of the *Autobiography*. "Why the soul of man is a vast forest, and all Benjamin intended was a neat back garden," he exclaims. "Think of Benjamin fencing it off! . . . He made himself a list of virtues, which he trotted inside like a grey nag in a paddock." Lawrence concludes: "And now I, at least, know why I can't stand Benjamin. He tries to take away my wholeness and my dark forest, my freedom. For how can any man be free, without an illimitable background? . . . Either we are materialistic instruments, like Benjamin or we move in the gesture of creation, from our deepest self, usually unconscious." With critics like Lawrence, he who is not with me must perforce be against me. Jesse Bier calls the *Autobiography* "the most significant book in American literature," in the sense that "it signals almost all of the chief thematic interests of the subsequent course of American letters. . . . the interest of the individual and of society, the claims of democracy and of aristocracy, the relation of Appearance and Reality, and the values of Romantic Idealism and Pragmatic Realism" (*WHR*, Winter 1958). According to Franz H. Link the *Autobiography*, "ein klassisches Dokument der Aufklärung in ihrer amerikanischen Prägung," illustrates that industry, frugality, and doing good are the means to felicity, affluence, and reputation (*DVLG*, 1961). Julian Smith argues, in "Coming of Age in America: Young Ben Franklin and Robin Molineux" (*AQ*, Fall 1965), that in writing "My Kinsman, Major Molineux" Hawthorne was probably influenced by the *Autobiography*, "especially by the twenty or so pages dealing with the period between Franklin's arrival in Philadelphia at the age of seventeen and his ill-advised voyage to England thirteen months later." Young Franklin and Robin, who "are in some way confronted with the problem of finding a place in the world, . . . desire to be exalted over their peers, and in this desire, contrary to the democratic ideals of the new country, they seek to link their fates and careers to royal officials; both are humiliated by the sudden revelation that their hopes in these officials were ill-founded; and both out of their humiliation, learn the lesson of self-reliance."

Other Special Studies

Stuart P. Sherman's characterization in *CHAL* of Franklin's style remains one of the most comprehensive and acute ever made: "It is the flexible style of a writer who has learned the craft of expression by studying and imitating the virtues of many masters: . . . His mature manner, however, is imitative of nothing but the thoroughly disciplined movement of a versatile mind which has never known a moment of languor or a moment of uncontrollable excitement. . . . the writing of his later years is marked not merely by clearness and force but also by the sovereign ease of a man who has long understood the interrelations of his ideas and has ceased to make revolutionary discoveries in any portion of his own nature. . . . He is seldom too hurried, even in a private letter, to gratify the ear by the turning and cadence of sentence and phrase; and one feels that the harmony of his periods is the right and predestined vesture of his essential blandness and suavity of temper. His stylistic drapery, however, is never so smoothed and adjusted as to obscure the sinewy vigour of his thought. His manner is steadily in the service of his matter." In contrast to Sherman's assessment stands that of Charles Angoff: "To call Franklin 'one of the greatest masters of English expression' [Faÿ] is the veriest nonsense. Almost any one of the Eighteenth Century New England theologians wrote better. Franklin, to be sure, was easier to understand, but there was far less in him worth understanding. His influence on the national letters, in the long run, was probably nil" (*A Literary History of the American People*, 2 vols., New York, 1931).

In *Franklin's Vocabulary* (Garden City, N.Y., 1928) Lois M. Mac-Laurin discovers that of approximately 4,060 words Franklin used in the period 1722 to 1751 only 19 are pure Americanisms. From which she concludes: "(1) That Franklin consciously avoided any use of 'colloquialisms' or 'Americanisms,' and that his later works show an increasing tendency in this direction. (2) That the spoken language in America must have been very closely related to the written language in England, since otherwise Franklin's vocabulary would surely have contained a larger percentage of variations, which, owing to their familiarity, would have escaped his notice when writing. Even his private letters contain practically no new words."

In *America's Coming of Age* (New York, 1915), Van Wyck Brooks claims to have discovered the basic tension in American literature, a discovery some find profoundly true and others too facile: "Not until the eighteenth century did the rift appear and with it the essential distinction between 'Highbrow' and 'Lowbrow.' It appeared in the two philosophers, Jonathan Edwards and Benjamin Franklin, who share the eighteenth century between them. . . . Were ever two views of life more incompatible than these? What indeed could Poor Richard have in common with an Angry God?" Out of this antithesis, according to Brooks, there emerged a middlebrow synthesis: ". . . it would be hard to say whether Emerson more keenly relished saintliness or shrewdness. . . . He perfectly combined the temperaments of Jonathan Edwards and

Benjamin Franklin;—the upper and lower levels of the American mind are fused in him and each becomes the sanction of the other."

A. O. Aldridge's *Benjamin Franklin and Nature's God* (Durham, N.C., 1967) is the most important study to date of Franklin's religious credo, which except for *A Dissertation on Liberty and Necessity* (1725) Aldridge finds steadily deistic, akin to "the benevolent philosophy of Shaftesbury and the English latitudinarian divines." The later chapters on Franklin's ecclesiastical associations, however, seem peripheral to the book's stated purpose, which is to concentrate on "the metaphysical and theological problems which he formulated and discussed as such in his own writings."

Reputation and Influence

Franklin's international reputation and influence originated in the correspondence, official, scientific, and social, he carried on with men of two continents over a period of sixty-five years; these documents are now scattered in repositories extending from Honolulu on the west to Leningrad and Moscow on the east. As with many another American writer, acceptance at home came later and more slowly than it did abroad. At the time of his death many Americans agreed with the Federalist critic Joseph Dennie that Franklin was "the founder of that Grubstreet sect, who have professedly attempted to degrade literature to the level of vulgar capacities, and debase the polished and current language of books, by the vile alloy of provincial idioms, and colloquial barbarism, the shame of grammar, and akin to any language, rather than English" (*The Port Folio*, 14 February 1801). More persistent than Dennie in his attempts to blacken the name of Franklin at home was John Adams. In view of Adams's indignation over Mercy Otis Warren's *History of the Rise, Progress, and Termination of the American Revolution* (1805), speculates William B. Evans, "one often wonders if Adams' ire was not stirred as much by Mrs. Warren's warmly favorable presentation of Franklin as by her somewhat cool, aloof treatment of her old friend, John Adams." Adams's antagonism toward Franklin, according to Evans, did not arise until 1780, when he sailed for Europe to negotiate treaties of peace and commerce with Britain; "regardless of how or why Adams arrived at his opinions of Franklin, he held them sincerely, and acted upon them doggedly" ("John Adams' Opinion of Benjamin Franklin," *PMHB*, Apr. 1968).

Franklin early secured his reputation abroad, nowhere earlier than in France. French contemporaries heralded him "not only as a man of letters, but also as a scientist, as a practical moralist and master of economic theory, and as a diplomat respected by the entire court," according to A. O. Aldridge, *Franklin and His French Contemporaries* (New York, 1957). "He was a double symbol," writes Morris Bishop in "Franklin in France." "He made visible and concrete the effective blending of two philosophies: Rousseau's return to Nature and Voltaire's skeptical, anticlerical rationalism" (*Daedalus*, 1957). Small wonder, then, that after his death he was widely eulogized in France. Gilbert Chinard, who has edited some of these eulogies, *L'Apothéose de Benjamin Franklin* (Paris, 1955), concludes that the apotheosis of Franklin in France "présente un phénomène qui s'est rarement manifesté et jamais, croyons-nous, avec une égale intensité," and that it "marque un moment d'espoir et d'enthousiasme dans l'histoire de la Révolution française." At the end of a long appreciative essay on Franklin's achievements by word and deed Charles Cestre says, ". . . le couronnement de sa vie de bienfaisant labeur fut l'alliance avec notre pays, qui sauva l'Amérique de la défaite et hâta l'avènement de la Révolution française" ("Franklin, homme représentatif," *Revue Anglo-Américaine*, Aug. 1928).

Franklin's fifteen-year sojourn in England (1757–62, 1764–75) and the friendships he formed there with men of varied interests made him, in the words of Leonard Labaree, "this country's first great diplomatic representative" ("Benjamin Franklin's British Friendships," *PAPS*, Oct. 1964). "The Germans," writes Alfred Vagts, "knew Franklin first as the man who had experimented with electricity. . . . Together with Washington's, his name stood for revolution. . . . To the nineteenth century German, he became the guide to winning wealth, health, happiness, friends and influence" ("Benjamin Franklin—Influence and Symbol," *American-German Review*, Dec. 1956–Jan. 1957). It is Antonio Pace's considered view in *Benjamin Franklin in Italy* (Philadelphia, 1958) that "the influence exerted by Italy upon Franklin pales into relative insignificance by comparison with the impact of Franklin upon Italy." And in the judgment of José Bataller, Franklin was the only American writer in the colonial period to make an impact in Spain where the *Autobiography* was translated as early as 1798 ("El primer libro norteamericano en España," *Filología Moderna*, 1961).

In spite of the range and quality of Franklin scholarship, especially in recent years, four major tasks need to be undertaken: a formal bibliography, a find-list of manuscripts, a definitive biography, and a comprehensive critical study. All four may have to await completion of *The Papers of Benjamin Franklin* some years hence.

Oliver Wendell Holmes

BARRY MENIKOFF

BIBLIOGRAPHY

OLIVER WENDELL HOLMES has never lacked for good bibliographies. At the present time there are three major ones: George B. Ives, *A Bibliography of Oliver Wendell Holmes* (Boston, 1907); Thomas F. Currier and Eleanor M. Tilton, *A Bibliography of Oliver Wendell Holmes* (New York, 1953); and Jacob Blanck, *BAL*. In addition to the primary bibliographical material in all three volumes, the Ives and Currier bibliographies contain extensive sections on biography and criticism. These are virtually exhaustive in their listings of reviews and essays on Holmes—Ives for the period through 1907, Currier for the years following—and are essential checklists of criticism.

A number of small and selective bibliographies remain useful. Among these are: Harry Hayden Clark, *Major American Poets* (New York, 1936); Walter F. Taylor, *A History of American Letters* (New York, 1936); S. I. Hayakawa and Howard Mumford Jones, *Oliver Wendell Holmes: Representative Selections* (New York, 1939); Lewis Leary, *Articles on American Literature, 1900–1950* (Durham, N.C., 1954); and the *LHUS* with its *Supplement* (1959).

A convenient listing of Holmes's writings on medical and scientific subjects can be found in the *Boston Medical and Surgical Journal* (11 October 1894). For additions to the Currier bibliography, see Eleanor Tilton, *PBSA* (First Quarter 1957).

EDITIONS

Although the sheer size of the Currier bibliography might suggest something of the popularity of Holmes's writings during his lifetime, the number of editions available for present-day readers is rather limited. Scholarly reprints during these past few years have made available *The Professor at the Breakfast-Table* (1860), *The Poet at the Breakfast-Table* (1872), and *Over the Teacups* (1891) (Scholarly Press, St. Clair Shores, Mich.). Literature House, an imprint of The Gregg Press (Upper Saddle River, N.J.), has reprinted *The Guardian Angel* (1867) and *A Mortal Antipathy* (1885), while Gale Research Company has reproduced *Ralph Waldo Emerson* (1884). These editions however are mainly for the benefit of library purchase. They do not satisfy the need for inexpensive and usable college texts.

The standard edition of Holmes's works remains the thirteen-volume set brought out by Houghton, Mifflin and Company, *The Complete Writings of Oliver Wendell Holmes* (Boston, 1892). This edition—also recently reprinted by Scholarly Press—has been supplemented by Albert Mordell's *The Autocrat's Miscellanies* (New York, 1959), a collection of Holmes's literary reviews and essays which were not included in the standard library edition. The most accessible single-volume edition of Holmes's poetry was edited by Horace E. Scudder, *The Complete Poetical Works of Oliver Wendell Holmes* (Boston, 1895). Selections of the poetry can be found in all good modern anthologies of American literature, as well as in Edwin Cady's *The American Poets, 1800–1900* (Glenview, Ill. 1966). Inexpensive paperback editions of *The Autocrat of the Breakfast-Table* (1858) are of course readily available, as is an edition of *Elsie Venner* (1861; New York, 1961).

MANUSCRIPTS AND LETTERS

Oliver Wendell Holmes was a prodigious letter writer. Apart from close friends like John Lothrop Motley (see *The Correspondence of John Lothrop Motley*, edited by George William Curtis, New York, 1889) and James Russell Lowell (see John T. Morse, Jr., *Life and Letters of Oliver Wendell Holmes*, Boston, 1896), Holmes's correspondents were various and numerous, causing him to complain, "I am overburdened with a correspondence which I find almost unmanageable." As long as Holmes was capable of signing his own name, however, he was meticulous in answering his "reading constituency" which he estimated at "three generations" of his own contemporaries. Many of these letters are probably irrecoverable; some are undoubtedly buried in basements and stored in attics. An occasional one, cleansed of its dust, reveals some interesting details. Roland Kent, for example, discovered a letter Holmes had written in 1875 to Kent's father in Wilmington, Delaware. In it Holmes classifies nearly a dozen of his most famous poems according to their mood and intention (*AL*, Nov. 1948). Nevertheless, a substantial body of Holmes's correspondence remains available and accounted for. All of his major biographers—Morse, Howe, Tilton, and Small—have quoted liberally from his correspondence. An appendix to the Currier bibliography provides a convenient list of all of the letters which were published in journals and books. What stands as our most pressing need, then, is a good modern edition of this correspondence.

The majority of Holmes's letters are on deposit in the Houghton Library at Harvard University. A substantial collection, donated by Justice Oliver Wendell Holmes, is in the Library of Congress; smaller collections are in the Henry E. Huntington Library (the Fields Collection) and the New York Public Library (the Berg Collection).

Eleanor Tilton describes the Holmes Collection in the Houghton Library at Harvard University as follows: "The most important items are medical lecture notes taken when Holmes was a student in Boston and Paris, medical casebooks, a bound volume of manuscripts (of which about a third are unpublished), a bound volume of letters (chiefly those written to his parents from Paris), notebooks for his major books after *The Autocrat* and *The Professor*, indexes to periodicals, and four miscellaneous notebooks." Other major repositories for manuscript materials are: the Library of Congress, the Francis A. Countway Library of Medicine in Boston, the Harvard Archives, and the Henry E. Huntington Library. Furthermore, the Oliver Wendell Holmes Library at Phillips Academy, Andover, contains the *Oliver Wendell Holmes Memorabilia Scrapbook*, a collection of notices and reviews of Holmes's books and lectures.

BIOGRAPHY

Doctor Oliver Wendell Holmes, fortunately for his biographers, lived eighty-three of his eighty-five years in Cambridge and Boston with very little to vex him. His private life was singularly without conflict, and he sustained only two antipathies in his public life, Calvinism and homeopathy. If these facts were not enough to dampen any interest biographers might have had in Holmes as a subject, then his writing itself expressed the character of the man more effectively, it seemed, than any mere biography possibly could. It was, after all, Holmes himself who added the subtitle to *The Autocrat of the Breakfast-Table*, "Every Man His Own Boswell." There were, of course, a succession of books that purported to describe the life of Holmes. These were written mainly in the years between 1880 and 1910, and they are largely encomiastic songs that possess neither wit nor point.

The first important biography was published two years after Holmes's death by his nephew, John T. Morse, Jr., *Life and Letters of Oliver Wendell Holmes*. Morse's main purpose is to provide a chronology of Holmes's career; he encloses the letters within the narrative in order to convey a sense of the personal style and tone of the author. The biography suffers, however, from an apologetic tone—Morse does not want to suggest that his subject is all *that* important—and from a fundamental lack of information. Quite simply, there were not enough letters or manuscripts available for Morse to work with. In addition, Morse himself possessed little imagination, and he tended to impose on Holmes some of his own beliefs and convictions. Thus the idea of Holmes's anti-Calvinism is given emphasis, even underlined, by Morse's own apparent hatred for the "promiscuous" doctrine. Morse summarized his impressions in "Oliver Wendell Holmes," *The Encyclopædia Britannica* (New York, 1910): "By heredity the Doctor was a theologian; no other topic enchained him more than did the stern and merciless dogmas of his Calvinist forefathers. His humanity revolted against them, his reason condemned them, and he set himself to their destruction as his task in literature." Nevertheless, *Life and Letters* remained for nearly fifty years the standard biography of Oliver Wendell Holmes. For a good critique of Morse's biography, see John White Chadwick's review in *The Nation* (11 June 1896).

The next biography of importance was written by M. A. de Wolfe Howe, *Holmes of the Breakfast-Table* (London, 1939). Although Howe depended upon Morse's earlier work, he also made use of manuscripts and letters which had been previously unavailable, particularly materials in the Harvard College Library and the Boston Medical Library. Howe's book has a simplicity of design (only five chapters), an elegance of expression, and a critical perceptiveness that reveal Holmes in his work as well as in his life. Howe recalled for his audience what Morse had barely noticed—that Holmes had been a physician, a professor of anatomy, and an active Lyceum lecturer. *Holmes of the Breakfast-Table* vividly recreates that figure. A briefer version of Howe's excellent sketch of Holmes appears in the *Dictionary of American Biography* (New York, 1932).

It was not until 1947, however, the one hundreth anniversary of Holmes's acceptance of the Parkman Professorship of Anatomy and Physiology at Harvard Medical School, that a "definitive" biography appeared: Eleanor M. Tilton's *Amiable Autocrat: A Biography of Dr. Oliver Wendell Holmes* (New York, 1947). Mentor Williams (*NEQ*,

June 1948) describes well just what the book does: "It examines Holmes against the proper socio-cultural background of his century, something the earlier biographers could not do. It evaluates Holmes's literary work from fresh viewpoints and with acute insight. It points up the Autocrat's contribution to the intellectual climate of the period." Miss Tilton's study provided readers for the first time with a detailed account of Holmes's career in Paris as a medical student: "Crowding into his two years what many of his friends acquired more leisurely in three, Holmes had summoned the necessary concentration for his heavy schedule. Never again in his life would he show such whole-hearted devotion to a single pursuit as he was showing now in his study of medicine. When Holmes wrote his family that not one among his fellow students had 'sought knowledge so ardently and courted pleasure so little,' he was taking a high tone, but he was not exaggerating." The significance of Miss Tilton's full exploration of Holmes's student days and his career as a physician and professor in America is evaluated by Miriam R. Small (*AL*, Mar. 1949): "It is time that we should see Holmes as we do here, judged as a part of his own age and its tendencies, pictured colorfully and justly as doctor, medical teacher, and anatomist as well as poet, lecturer, social wit, and Autocrat." Miss Small has herself written a critical biography, *Oliver Wendell Holmes* (New York, 1962), in which she too emphasizes Holmes's importance as a physician and "medical scholar."

Among the personal reminiscences of Holmes as a teacher, the most disarming are two accounts by his former students, David W. Cheever, "Oliver Wendell Holmes, The Anatomist" (*Harvard Graduates' Magazine*, Dec. 1894) and Thomas Dwight, "Reminiscences of Dr. Holmes as Professor of Anatomy" (*Scribner's Magazine*, Jan. 1895). Cheever's comment is typical: "As a lecturer he was accurate, punctual, precise, unvarying in patience over detail, and though not an original anatomist in the sense of a discoverer, yet a most exact descriptive lecturer; while the wealth of illustration, comparison, and simile he used was unequaled. Hence his charm; you received information, and you were amused at the same time. He was always simple and rudimentary in his instruction." For confirmation of this view, see "Oliver Wendell Holmes" in the *Boston Medical and Surgical Journal* (11 October 1894) and Charles W. Eliot, "Dr. O. W. Holmes as a Teacher of Anatomy," *Boston Medical and Surgical Journal* (28 September 1911).

An excellent portrait of Holmes as a young, practicing physician appears in Reginald Fitz's "My Dr. Oliver Wendell Holmes," *The Bulletin of the New York Academy of Medicine* (Aug. 1943). "[By 1838] Dr. Holmes was beginning to make himself felt as a doctor: not the ordinary kind of practitioner by whom small fevers were gratefully received but as a modern internist who was prepared to see only a few cases, to follow to the autopsy table those that were fatal, who wished to study disease rather than to treat it, and to advance medical knowledge, as Louis had said, by eliciting truth through the establishment of facts which were well and carefully observed." An intimate account of Holmes's role in the development of the Harvard Medical School may be found in Charles W. Eliot, "Oliver Wendell Holmes," *Harvard Graduates' Magazine* (June 1923); see also Reginald Fitz, "President Eliot and Dr Holmes Leap Forward" (*HLB*, Spring 1947).[1]

CRITICISM

It would be a convenience for this essay and my own desire for harmony to be able to say that the criticism of Oliver Wendell Holmes reflects the development of American literary criticism in general and the changing fashions in literary taste in particular. But this is not the case. In fact the criteria for judging Holmes's work have remained remarkably constant, and the criticism itself has rarely altered in its general observations. Since the publication of *The Autocrat of the Breakfast-Table* in 1858, Holmes has been extolled for his virtues and criticized for his limitations. Today, of course, his virtues seem somehow less visible while his limitations appear all the more obvious. But during his own day he was held in extremely high regard. The most brilliant conversationalist of a not undistinguished circle, for a quarter of a century he dominated New England letters.

General Estimates

Although the criticism on Holmes began as early as 1836, when he published his first volume of poems, and continued throughout his lifetime, the critical evaluations did not appear in abundance until

1. A convenient medical biography by Charles R. Bardeen can be found in *Dictionary of American Medical Biography*, edited by H. A. Kelly and W. L. Burrage (New York, 1928). Among the best literary reminiscences of Holmes are those by William Dean Howells, *Literary Friends and Acquaintance* (New York, 1900); Annie Fields, *Authors and Friends* (Boston, 1896); and M. A. de Wolfe Howe, "Dr. Holmes, the Friend and Neighbor," *YR* (Apr. 1918). Other accounts of Holmes include: J. L. Hughes, *The Canadian Magazine* (Dec. 1893); Samuel May, *Harvard Graduates' Magazine* (Dec. 1894); H. D. Sedgwick, *Century* (Aug. 1895); G. W. Smalley, *Studies of Men* (New York, 1895); E. S. Phelps Ward, *Chapters from a Life* (Boston, 1896); J. T. Trowbridge, *My Own Story* (Boston, 1903); and Sir William Osler, *An Alabama Student* (London, 1908).

the last twenty years before the turn of the century. A substantial number of these came forth in the 1890s, following Holmes's death and the publication in 1896 of Morse's *Life and Letters*. But it by no means took that long for perceptive critics to summarize the importance of Holmes's work. Early in his career, an extensive article, "Dr. Oliver Wendell Holmes and *Elsie Venner*," appeared in the *National Review* (Oct. 1861). The English have always been receptive to Holmes's writing, and he has received his most sympathetic appreciations, as well as his sharpest criticisms, from English reviewers. The *National* reviewer, who must have had one eye on the Civil War, used the occasion of *Elsie Venner* to examine the state of American literature, and the position of Dr. Oliver Wendell Holmes in that literature. First the reviewer commented on the popularity of *The Autocrat of the Breakfast-Table* and of *The Professor at the Breakfast-Table* in England: "Dr. Holmes is indisputably and above all an entertaining writer. He thinks, and he can express his thought articulately. He flashes upon you an ingenious suggestion, or a whimsical paradox, clothed in fantastic guise, and without giving you time to pause upon the truth it contains, or to reflect even whether what seems so plausible is true, presents you with another and another in endless sequence. The general effect is somewhat kaleidoscopic." Although Holmes's books appear indebted to Montaigne, Rabelais, and Sterne, they are, like Holmes himself, essentially American. And it is the American aspect which finally limits them: they are, like the culture itself, unoriginal, imitative, and intellectually "thin." Yet, despite this central criticism, the *National* reviewer details for us certain of Holmes's literary characteristics which he finds attractive: his wit and humor; his shrewd observations of life; his ingenious criticism on art, literature and philosophy; his large and humane sympathies; and especially his aversion toward any tyranny which would suppress free thought. (For an opposing view—Holmes is "un-American in style" and subject matter—as well as a thoughtful appreciation, see *Dublin University Magazine*, Sept. 1874.)

Two essays of the 1870s comment upon the humor and satire in Holmes's work. E. P. Whipple (*HM*, Mar. 1876) refers to Holmes's "fleering mockeries of folly and pretension, as in his almost Juvenalian invectives against baseness and fraud." George Stewart in *Evenings in the Library* (Toronto, 1878) emphasizes the "genial" Holmes, an emphasis which might almost be said to damn Holmes in our own day as much as it served to make him admired in his. Stewart then compares Holmes with Oliver Goldsmith: while they both appeal to "the heart and common sympathy of mankind," Holmes lacks Goldsmith's vulgarity. Thus, what the *National Review* critic saw as a weakness in 1861—

the "expurgated" or diluted tone of Holmes's essays—Stewart sees as a virtue. He places Holmes in the tradition of the nineteenth-century essayists like Lamb, Hazlitt, and Hunt. The breakfast table volumes are judged "great books" for their raillery, teasing, fun, and graceful imagery. Holmes's wit does not injure, Stewart concludes, and his writing reflects his humanity and charity.

Two major evaluations, one American and the other English, appeared in the middle eighties: E. C. Stedman's appreciative study for the *Century Magazine* (Feb. 1885) and Edward Delille's sharp critique in the *Fortnightly Review* (Aug. 1886). For Stedman, Holmes's genius reveals itself in the originality of his prose and in the excellence of his society verse. Establishing a principle that was to be repeated in later criticism, Stedman observed that the humor of the poetry and the satire of the breakfast table books had the effect of relaxing "the grimness of a Puritan constituency." In support of this observation he emphasizes Holmes's "elastic buoyant nature," his zest for life which reveals itself in all the writing, and especially in the Autocrat volumes. Stedman next makes an observation which would be echoed in all future criticism: Holmes by instinct and habit is a man rooted in the eighteenth century, a man whose proper study is mankind. Although Stedman emphasizes Holmes's own brand of contemporary conservatism, that of Cambridge and Boston, he nevertheless admires him as a progressive and speculative thinker. In addition, Stedman is the first important literary critic to insist that Holmes's primary profession was not literature, but medicine.

Edward Delille's criticism stresses the limitations that Holmes's genial temper imposes on his writing. Although his thought is not original, Delille admits, Holmes nevertheless possesses all the talent necessary for great literature. He simply lacks passion, at least the passion of a writer like Thomas Carlyle. Delille's bias seems to be a social one: he would prefer to see Holmes perform for America the kind of satiric service that he admires in the anonymous author of *Democracy*. But Holmes's very sympathy and humane feeling—his "geniality" again—prevent him from accomplishing this. Delille does find in Holmes one trait to admire without qualification—a sympathy for childhood, a sympathy which is expressed more honestly than in Dickens. Delille also rates the novels highly. He believes that "Dr. Holmes could have been . . . *the* American novelist of the century." Delille argues that Holmes had a power for depicting character that was his most genuine literary gift, a gift that is revealed to advantage in the breakfast table books which "constitute his greatest contribution to literature." Delille's final sentence, however, expresses an important reservation that was to be repeated in later criticism: "But [Holmes's] possession of all these gifts rather enhances than diminishes the regret that they should be, to a certain extent, impaired by the spirit of a *dilettante*."

During the 1890s a substantial number of general evaluations were published. The English criticisms were among the most acute and reflective. *Blackwood's Edinburgh Magazine* (Aug. 1892) commented first on the American aspect of Holmes's work, on the "frankness" and "agressive independence of attitude" with which Holmes revealed both his personality and his thought in his prose. The *Blackwood's* critic, however, expressed a minority opinion when he declared that Holmes's genius was shown to advantage first in the novels, and particularly in *Elsie Venner*. He compared the book to Hawthorne's *Transformation* (a comparison which had already become common) and admired it for its "fantastic and sensational" qualities as well as for its delightful portrait of a rural New England community. Elsewhere, James A. Noble in *Impressions and Memories* (London, 1895) felt that Holmes's "deeper thought" was revealed in the novels.

Another perceptive article (*Quarterly Review*, Jan. 1895) focused on the importance of the past, on ancestry and education in Holmes's work. The anonymous critic observed that Holmes's concern with the past was not limited to the novels—where the theme of heredity regularly appears—but also filled his prose and verse with "delightful reminiscences" of childhood. Echoing Stedman, the writer remarked that Holmes was a product of the "leisured Augustan age," a detail which was confirmed by his use of classical English measures. His conservatism revealed itself as well in his social and political convictions. But this reviewer saw another, equally important, aspect of Holmes's personality: he was the inquiring man of science, a figure engaged in the extraordinarily various activities of daily life. This side of Holmes reveals itself in the breakfast table books, those volumes of "practical philosophy" which were best suited to the Doctor's conversational gifts. If Holmes was not a man of literary genius, concludes the reviewer, he nevertheless played an essential role in his day: "No writer did more in his generation to soften the harshness of the Puritan temper, or to disperse with the cheerful warmth of innocent enjoyment the chilling gloom of its austere rule in New England. For this, even more than for his purely literary influences, he deserved, and gained, the affection of his fellow-countrymen." For confirmation of this conclusion by two American critics, see G. W. Curtis, *Literary and Social Essays* (New York, 1894) and John White Chadwick (*Forum NY*, Nov. 1894).

Leslie Stephen's sympathetic appreciation for the *National Review* (July 1896), which was reprinted in *Studies of a Biographer* (New

York, 1898), supported the general English view that Holmes was a representative of America. Unlike some of his countrymen, however, Stephen does not believe that the stamp of Boston marks Holmes as a provincial: "The New England of his day, whatever its limitations, was seething with important movements as interesting, in slightly different applications, on this side of the Atlantic as well as on the other; and the fact that Holmes looked at them from a New England point of view does not show that he did not appreciate their wider significance." Stephen did not add anything to what had already been said about Holmes; the most interesting feature of his essay, apart from its informal style, is Stephen's suggestion that Holmes had perhaps never grown to manhood. "Holmes' boyishness means the actual possession of such qualities as are attributed to boys—rashly sometimes—by loving mothers; the perfect simplicity, the confiding trustfulness of a nature which has not been soured into cynicism; and the confident assumption that their own happiness implies the general goodness of all their fellow-creatures."

Two American critics, Henry Cabot Lodge (*NAR*, Dec. 1894) and *The Nation*'s reviewer (11 October 1894), emphasized Holmes's versatility. Lodge saw Holmes as a man possessed of a creative imagination as well as a scientific habit of mind. The two traits complemented each other. "Imagination did not make his medicine or anatomy untrustworthy, nor did his scientific tendencies make either his verse or his prose cold or dry. His wit and humor, it is true, gleamed through his lectures and left behind them to a generation of students a harvest of stories and traditions. The scientific cast of thought, on the other hand, as it often supplied an image or a metaphor, may possibly have had something to do also with the unfailing correctness of the poet's verse." For Lodge, Holmes's literary talent exhibits itself to perfection in occasional verse and in *The Autocrat of the Breakfast-Table*. Continuing what had become almost a mannerism in Holmes criticism, Lodge compared the *Autocrat*, with its "exact combination of wit and humor, of pathos and wisdom, of sense and sentiment," to the best work of all the great essayists from Montaigne through Charles Lamb. *The Nation* shared Lodge's opinion regarding the richness of the *Autocrat* and the "vitality" of the breakfast table books as a group, but it stressed even more than Lodge had the belief that Holmes's "versatility" was his most exciting, and enduring, characteristic. "He must be regarded as poet, professor, and autocrat at once, if one would have a rounded conception of him, and understand what sort of personal power in him it was that extended a local reputation over a continent." But Holmes's versatility was not universally regarded as a virtue; for an adverse judgment, see the review in *The Bookman* (Sept. 1892). Finally, *The Nation*, anticipating what would become a leitmotif in Holmes criticism, assigned him a place in history: "He belongs to old Boston now—an historical period of the city that cannot be recalled without his name."

A substantial number of essays about Holmes were published at the turn of the century. But the tone of these "appreciations" differed from the earlier criticisms. Few of the critics writing in these years had known Holmes himself, and none had experienced at first hand the forceful personality of the 1860s and 1870s, the author of "Currents and Counter-Currents in Medical Science," *Elsie Venner*, "Mechanism in Thought and Morals," and *The Poet at the Breakfast-Table*. These essays maintain a certain detached attitude towards Holmes's work. They are generous in their praise, but it is a praise they seem never quite certain of. They comment almost as much on Holmes himself as they do upon his writing. The sanity and common sense which he brought to literature, his practical philosophy, his identification with the city of Boston—all are acknowledged with a sort of wistful regard for the character and person of Oliver Wendell Holmes. The writers all are conscious of an obligation to place Holmes in his proper niche in American literature. They are careful to examine his weaknesses and to explore the limitations of his talent, lest they be accused of making too strong a case for his importance.

In 1900 Barrett Wendell published his classic chapter on Holmes in *A Literary History of America*. "Among Boston lives the only other of eminence which was so uninterruptedly local is that of Cotton Mather. The intolerant Calvinistic minister typifies seventeenth-century Boston; the Unitarian physician typifies the Boston of the century just past."[2] Wendell's stress, however, was not on Holmes as a social phenomenon but on Holmes as a vigorous eighteenth-century rationalist, New England's one "uncompromising" enemy of Calvinism. "Among our men of letters this rationalist was the most sturdy, the most militant, the most pitiless enemy of a superstition whose tyranny over his childhood had left lifelong scars." Others who have recognized Holmes's antagonism toward Calvinism are Leon Vincent, *American Literary Masters* (Boston, 1906); G. K. Chesterton, "Introduction" to *The Autocrat of the Breakfast-Table* (London, 1904); and James Ormerod, *Library* (Jan. 1908). Wendell saw in Holmes a figure like Voltaire, devoted to the truth and to battling all those "delusions" which impeded the progress

2. For further discussion of Holmes as a Bostonian, see Horace Scudder, *AtM* (Dec. 1894); George Woodberry, *HM* (Feb. 1903); Richard Burton, *The Reader Magazine* (Apr. 1905); and W. G. Ballantine, *NAR* (Aug. 1909).

of men toward a better future. It is scarcely surprising that Wendell discovered in "The Deacon's Masterpiece" an allegorical satire on the inevitable destruction of Calvinism. More recently, J. S. Mattson has argued persuasively against this classic judgment on Holmes's comic *tour de force* (*NEQ*, Mar. 1968).

By 1910 the criticism of Oliver Wendell Holmes clearly had become institutionalized. His writings were the subject of an extensive, and perceptive, study in the *Edinburgh Review* (Apr. 1910); his breakfast table books were commented upon favorably by Samuel Crothers in a slim volume entitled *The Autocrat and His Fellow-Boarders* (Boston, 1909), and his prescription for life—to live to the utmost of one's powers—received a strong second, made by the reviewer for *TLS* (26 August 1909). If Holmes no longer enjoyed the popular audience that his works had commanded during his lifetime, he nevertheless appeared regularly in literary histories. William Trent and John Erskine in *Great American Writers* (New York, 1912) saluted his liberal spirit; John Macy in *The Spirit of American Literature* (New York, 1913) admired both his rationalism and his "unbroken perfection of style"; and Brander Matthews, in the most concise and judicious statement of these years (*CHAL*), praised Holmes's cleverness—a sort of Yankee ingenuity—and the civilizing influence he exerted on his time. Matthews feels that Holmes's most enduring quality is his talk: "Holmes is not only a man of science and a man of the world, he is also a humorist and a wit,—a wit who has no antipathy even to the humble but useful pun,—a humorist abounding in whimsy. And as a result of this fourfold equipment his talk is excellent merely as talk. It has the flavour of the spoken word; it is absolutely unacademic and totally devoid of pedantry. Therefore it is not only delightful but stimulating; it continually makes the reader think for himself and turn back upon himself. Despite its acuteness, its liveliness, its briskness, its vivacity, it never lacks seriousness without ever becoming ponderous."

Matthews's judgment received confirmation from an unexpected source. Henry James, reviewing the early years of the *Atlantic Monthly* in an essay on James and Annie Fields (*AtM*, July 1915), described how that celebrated magazine "was for years practically the sole organ of that admirable writer and wit, that master of almost every form of observational, of meditational, and of humorous ingenuity, the author of *The Autocrat of the Breakfast-Table* and of *Elsie Venner*." James recalled that Holmes and the Fieldses both lived on the same street. "I find myself couple together the two Charles Street houses, though even with most weight of consideration for that where *The Autocrat, The Professor, Elsie Venner*, and the long and bright succession of the unsurpassed Boston *pièces de circonstance* in verse, to say nothing of all the eagerest and easiest and funniest, all the most winged and kept-up, most illustrational and suggestional, table-talk that ever was, sprang smiling to life."

The reputation of Oliver Wendell Holmes dcelined dramatically in the 1920s. But, as I have already indicated, Holmes had never been overrated for his intrinsic literary merit. He was always seen to have limitations, and very real ones, which could never be dismissed or discounted from any honest evaluation of his work. The reaction to Holmes that one might expect in the twenties, however, surfaced only in the form of a single short essay; it was appropriately placed where it seemed designed to serve an attractive and sophisticated audience. C. Harley Grattan's article (*AM*, Jan. 1925) might almost be said to characterize our present popular conception of the debunking Jazz Age. "To have written one book of importance and a handful of occasional poems cannot make a man a figure of major significance. The impossibility appears the greater when it is recalled that the one book epitomizes the humor of a single region." Grattan chides Holmes for taking too seriously his Saturday Club friendships. He declares that the novels have no interest for modern readers. He attacks with apparent relish the reticence with which Holmes regarded sex. Grattan's criticism appears motivated mainly by a hostility towards New England regionalism and Boston gentility, and Oliver Wendell Holmes was a fitting scapegoat. "Pleasantness and fastidious conventionalism thus make up all there is of Holmes. His religious radicalism no longer scares anyone, and it didn't scare many of any intelligence in his own day. In him is summed up the humor of literary Boston—in 'The Autocrat' and a handful of poems. His life and works are materials for a footnote to the history of an epoch. The charm of his personality made his contemporaries overrate him, and the adulators of New England continued the error."

A far more judicious account of Holmes as he appeared to a critic in the twenties can be found in Vernon Parrington's *Main Currents in American Thought* (New York, 1927). Parrington, of course, finds Holmes's social conservatism uncongenial to his own egalitarian temper. He also conveys a clear Western disdain toward Holmes's belief that Boston was the freest place in America. Nevertheless he regards Holmes with a certain affection: "A radical in the field of theology where personal concern brought him to serious grappling with the problem, a tolerant rationalist in the realm of the intellect, he remained a cheerfully contented conservative in other fields. He was unconsciously insulated against the currents of social and political thought flowing all about him." For Parrington, following in the tradition of Barrett Wendell, Holmes's single most striking, indeed radical, characteristic is his militant anti-Calvinism. The only poems he admires, for example, are "The Deacon's Masterpiece," "Parson Turell's Legacy," and "The Moral Bully." Although the tone of the essay conveys a certain aloofness, it expresses at least a moderate admiration for the honesty and integrity of the "authentic Brahmin."

If the tone of writers like Harley Grattan, Vernon Parrington, and Ludwig Lewisohn (*Expression in America*, New York, 1932) tended to make us peer down on the diminutive figure of Oliver Wendell Holmes from an Olympian height, in order to see more clearly his minor place in American literature, then this tone marked only a difference in emphasis, or degree, from the earlier criticism. Most critics had agreed in evaluating Holmes's position: he was a minor figure who played a role in New England's literary history, a figure whose artistic importance, however, was rigidly limited. Even those writers who had celebrated Holmes, as E. C. Stedman and Barrett Wendell did, were conscious of the personality of the man rather than the importance of his work. But in the middle of the 1930s a radical change in the criticism of Oliver Wendell Holmes occurred. Van Wyck Brooks, Harry Hayden Clark, and S. I. Hayakawa and Howard Mumford Jones all contributed to the change in Holmes criticism.

Van Wyck Brooks's main purpose in his writing ("Dr. Holmes: Forerunner of the Moderns," *SatR*, 27 June 1963, and "Dr. Holmes's Boston," *HM*, July 1940) was to explore the nature of New England life, to find the source for modern American literature, and to uncover the impulse that kept American writing sane and whole. The figure of Oliver Wendell Holmes, "the most intelligent man in New England," seemed readymade for Brooks's task. From the outset he dismissed as absurd what had become a minor cliché in the criticism of Holmes during the 1920s, that the Doctor had intended his description of the Brahmin caste in *Elsie Venner* to reflect a "bloated Boston aristocracy." Brooks instead revived a single idea that had informed the best of the earlier criticism—Holmes as a conversationalist. In Brooks's mind, however, conversation was not merely a social gift, a talent to be cultivated for the pleasures of the Saturday Club, but a "mission," a means to expose all those "secrets" and fears which lay hidden and "twisted" within. "Fruits of the old religion of Calvinism, fruits of isolation and provincial conditions, fruits of unconscious living. Out with them, and talk them over!" Language, "expression," was New England's greatest need. "Emotions that can shape themselves in language open the gate for themselves into the great community of human affections." Holmes unfolded his wisdom for his readers—in a way offering them prescriptions for their health, both mental and physical.

Brooks turned next to "Crime and Automatism," to "Mechanism in Thought and Morals," to *Elsie Venner* and *The Guardian Angel.* In all these he saw a fundamentally modern theme: human responsibility as it related to an aberrant or disordered mind. Of course critics had always recognized the theme of limited responsibility in Holmes's work. But Brooks concentrated on that theme and drew attention to its psychological accuracy as well as to its social significance. The rattlesnake's bite in *Elsie Venner* became a metaphor for any untoward or accidental circumstance that might determine an individual's destiny. In the end the thought of Dr. Oliver Wendell Holmes, "forerunner of the moderns," led to Darwinism, Marxism, and Freudianism.

Harry Hayden Clark supported Brooks's view. His essay "Dr. Holmes: A Reinterpretation" (*NEQ,* Mar. 1939) examines in detail Holmes's literary and aesthetic ideas, his social and political ideas, and his religious and philosophical ideas. Clark discovers that Holmes was "Federalistic" and "traditional" in social, political, and literary matters; while, in his religious and philosophical thought, he was scientific, "progressive," and rational. What distinguishes the essay, however, is Clark's attempt to place Holmes in a modern setting and to find in Holmes's determinism the source for his most radical idea: a belief that pity is often the only attitude society can take toward the criminal. But Clark, like Brooks before him, placed an inordinate stress on what he regarded as the absolute determinism of Holmes. He saw in Holmes's thought the ideas that culminated in the fiction of Theodore Dreiser and the practice of Clarence Darrow.

It was left to S. I. Hayakawa and Howard Mumford Jones to provide a more restrictive, and definitive statement: "His determinism is a hopeful one because he does not make the mistake of regarding causation in the moral world as the same kind of thing as mechanical causation. Like the modern determinists, he sees the *self* as an active principle, so that the human will, while conditioned, is something more than the sum total of its conditioning agencies." The introduction which Hayakawa and Jones contributed to *Representative Selections* must be regarded as the single most comprehensive view of Holmes until that time. He was examined first in relation to his city, to the "Boston of solid mercantile culture" which he had come to represent. Holmes was faulted for his failure to understand Catholic Boston, the Boston of the Irish and the Italians, "the Boston that was undergoing profoundly significant social changes under his very eyes." He was also chided—in no uncertain terms—for his ignorance of American economic imperialism, for his inability to perceive, as Emerson and Thoreau had, the nature of American industrial development. Undoubtedly these criticisms owed a good deal of their force, as well as their impetus, to the economic depression of the 1930s. When Jones reconsidered Holmes some twenty years later, for example, in *History and the Contemporary* (Madison, Wis., 1964), his objections seem to have lost some of their sharpness.

What appeared unique and salutary about the earlier study, however, was the primary role it assigned to Holmes as a physician. Hayakawa revived the earlier judgment of writers like Stedman and Lodge and claimed that literature was never more than a "sideline" for Holmes. But he went beyond that: he studied the medical essays and declared that Holmes's "medical papers sometimes make much better reading than his literary prose," a thoroughly defensible observation. He even suggested that it was Holmes's medical knowledge that prevented his social philosophy from being thoroughly commonplace, indeed, that saved him from literary "oblivion." Mentor Williams confirmed this judgment in his review of *Representative Selections* (*NEQ*, Dec. 1941). Williams, like Hayakawa, had recently written a dissertation on Holmes and his emphasis had been similar: Holmes as a scientific thinker was more interesting than Holmes as a literary artist. Williams also commented forcefully on Holmes as a "realist" and a "hardheaded" liberal who possessed a thorough understanding of his age. He was a "pioneer of scientific humanism" as well as an "educator of the public." For Williams, the modern spirit in Holmes could be found in "Currents and Counter-Currents in Medical Science," in "Mechanism in Thought and Morals," and in "Jonathan Edwards."[3]

Poetry

Although the popularity of Holmes's poetry has diminished with the passage of time and the change in poetic taste, the criticism and evaluation of his verse has remained remarkably consistent. E. C. Stedman's *Century Magazine* study, reprinted in *Poets of America* (Boston, 1885), established the favorable feeling towards Holmes's work that prevailed in the 1880s, and it provided a sane and balanced judgment of his poetic achievement. Stedman sees Holmes's work as a "survival" of the eighteenth century, a poetry which retains the "courtesy and wit" of the Georgian age, as well as its heroic and octosyllabic measures. He finds, however, blended with the Georgian manner, a "vivacity" that

3. For useful statements on Holmes's belief in the idea of progress and his faith in science see Neal F. Doubleday, "Dr. Holmes and the Faith in the Future" (*CE*, Feb. 1943); R. W. B. Lewis, *The American Adam* (Chicago, 1955), and Don M. Wolfe, *The Image of Man in America* (Dallas, 1957). For a strong negative evaluation of Holmes's achievement see Alexander C. Kern, "Dr. Oliver Wendell Holmes Today" (*UKCR*, Spring 1948).

contributes a uniquely modern flavor to the verse. Stedman remarks that poetry for Holmes was a diversion rather than a "high endeavor." This attitude enabled him to capture the lightness and ebullience in verse that characterized his occasional poetry, a form that he mastered. Stedman was also the first to suggest that Holmes served as the unofficial poet laureate of Harvard, the heir to the tradition of Phi Beta Kappa recitationists. (See also Thomas F. Currier, "Holmes as Harvard Poet-Laureate," *PMHS*, 1945.)

S. I. Hayakawa in "The Boston Poet-Laureate: Oliver Wendell Holmes" (*SELit*, Oct. 1936) distinguishes between two forms of occasional poetry: "Private occasional poetry is essentially the same as poetry proper in its origination: a poet sees a situation, or is present at an event, and this gives rise to certain reflections or emotions which he feels constitute subject-matter for a poem." But this does not typify Holmes's work. Rather his métier is "public occasional verse," a poetry which "does not express private emotions, but emotions shared with a number of other people. The poet, under these circumstances, is the instrument of a group; he must so far as possible merge his feelings into those of the group. Consequently we properly think of this class of occasional verses as those which are written for public occasions, anniversaries, weddings, funerals, victories, and other events of public importance." In this form, of course, Oliver Wendell Holmes has no rival. Hayakawa in another essay, "Holmes's Lowell Institute Lectures" (*AL*, Nov. 1936), gathered together the newspaper accounts of Holmes's 1853 lectures on English poets.

One of the best descriptions of the poetry appears in Brander Matthews's chapter on Holmes for the *CHAL*. There Matthews argues that Holmes's poetry owes its special character to an intellectual rather than an imaginative impulse; consequently it lacks both intensity of feeling as well as breadth of vision. "It has a French felicity of fancy, a French dexterity of craftsmanship, French point and polish, and also a French inadequacy of emotion." (For additional comment on the French influence, see Rica Brenner, *Twelve American Poets Before 1900*, New York, 1933, and Gay Wilson Allen, *American Prosody*, New York, 1935.) But Holmes's serious poetry was never the serious work of his life. It is in his "familiar" verse, Matthews declares, that Holmes's distinctive gift reveals itself. For in this kind of "easy" poetry—"the lyric commingled of humour and pathos, brief and brilliant and buoyant, seemingly unaffected and unpremeditated"—Holmes has in effect found a poetic equivalent for the essay in its charm and colloquial manner.

The two most sophisticated essays on Holmes's poetic theory and practice are by William Knickerbocker and Karl Wentersdorf. In "His

Own Boswell: A Note on the Poetry of Oliver Wendell Holmes"
(*SR*, Oct.-Dec. 1933), Knickerbocker begins with an examination of
Holmes's poetic theory and declares that poetry is not the triumph of
a finished piece of work but rather the experience which the artist
himself enjoys in the process of creation, "the psychological richness
of an inner state of high emotional ecstasy in the presence of Beauty."
But Holmes recognized that he could not expect to achieve, let alone
sustain, this kind of poetic joy. Therefore he turned inward and interested himself with recording what he discovered—both for himself and
his age. "The single conception which unifies the diversity of themes in
Holmes is his frank confession that he is 'his own Boswell.' He was
bravely aware of himself, of his ancestral past, and made his chief
effort to be the versifying commentator of the emotional experiences
of a nineteenth century Yankee Brahmin. It was no slight achievement
for one of that quality to overcome the regional taboo against self-
revelation." For Knickerbocker, as for Matthews before him, Holmes's
intimate revelations in verse (akin to his "congenial table-talk" in prose)
confer upon his poetry a special strength, perhaps even durability, that
in its own way is a minor literary triumph.

Wentersdorf, on the other hand, restricts himself in "The Under-
ground Workshop of Oliver Wendell Holmes" (*AL*, Mar. 1963) to a
consideration of Holmes's view of the creative process. Drawing largely
on "Mechanism in Thought and Morals" and its "mechanistic" psychology, he argues that Holmes conceived of the creative process
as a more advanced, or deeper, form of unconscious mental activity.
The production of "genuine" poetry was therefore never "anything
but a purely mechanical process, divinely inspired, but antecedent to
the actual writing and not influenced by conscious effort." Wentersdorf diminishes the role traditionally assigned to Holmes as an expositor
of neoclassical ideas—discipline and rational effort—and focuses instead
on the contemporary accent in his aesthetic, on his belief that "automatism" affects poetic creation at least as much as it controls human
behavior. Holmes fashioned an aesthetic, the result of an artist's
"insight" and a scientist's "specialized knowledge," that "contributed
materially to the understanding of the psychological processes involved
in literary creativity. . . ."

General studies of Holmes's poetry that remain valuable are: Augus-
tus Strong, *American Poets and Their Theology* (Philadelphia, 1916);
Alfred Kreymborg, *Our Singing Strength* (New York, 1929); and
George Arms, *The Fields Were Green* (Stanford, Calif., 1953). Help-
ful studies of "The Chambered Nautilus" are: Bayard Christy (*AL*,
May 1937), Nelson Adkins (*AL*, Jan. 1938), and Cecil Eby (*ESQ*, II

Quarter 1962). Other studies demonstrate the influence of Dante, Horace, and Motley: J. Chesley Mathews (*Italica*, Sept. 1957); J. P. Pritchard, *Return to the Fountains* (Durham, N.C., 1942); *The Classical Weekly* (16 May 1932); and Eleanor Tilton (*AL*, Jan. 1965).

Novels

Although much of the best criticism of Holmes's fiction appears in general estimates of his work, a small number of special studies are nonetheless important for their independent observations. Two contemporary English reviews of *Elsie Venner*, for example, are among the most perceptive: the earlier cited *National Review* (Oct. 1861) and J. M. Ludlow's "*Elsie Venner* and *Silas Marner*: A Few Words on Two Noteworthy Novels," in *Macmillan's Magazine* (Aug. 1861). The *National* reviewer comments first on the theme of limited responsibility: "Character [for Holmes] is destiny; but organisation is character, and organisation is an affair of race and parentage and external influences, moulding the individual as clay is moulded. This is the 'destiny,' the 'romance' of which is told in *Elsie Venner*." Although the reviewer finds the doctrine uncomfortably deterministic, he objects even more to its dramatic presentation. The novel is a kind of "fantastic extravagance," a fiction whose moral lacks the clearness of an "avowed parable" and one whose main character, Elsie, lacks any reality. She is a case for the "morbid pathologist" rather than the novelist.

J. M. Ludlow agrees. He describes the manner in which Elsie assumes the characteristics of a serpent—her powers of fascination, of repulsion, her absence of human affection, and her "instinctive savagery." But what strikes Ludlow beyond all these observations is the peculiar fact that the novel could not have been written by anyone but an American. (Both writers refer to Hawthorne's *Transformation*, which had recently been published; the comparison was to become persistent in all future discussions of Holmes's fiction.) Ludlow speculates on the meaning of this fact, on why America's best writers possess such "morbid" visions: "Perhaps more than all does it come from this,—that America herself has been now for many years but a stage-effect, of which the secession crisis has shown at last the hollowness; that the lie of slavery, which has stultified from the first her Declaration of Rights, has poisoned all her art as well as all her social life. So long as the 'right to wallop one's own niggers' is considered consistent with the constitution of a free country, so long may there well be something diseased in the national mind, which inclines it to the morbid rather than to the wholesome, and which makes its highest fictions studies in human pathology, not broad representations of human life."

For less prescient and more typical contemporary reviews, see James Russell Lowell (*AtM*, Apr. 1861); Andrew Peabody (*NAR*, Apr. 1861); and *Dublin University Magazine* (Apr. 1862). For a scathing account of the fiction, see *The Nation* (14 November 1867): "His characters are figures labelled and set up to be fired at, or are names about which a love story is told, or they embody some physiologico-psychological theory; but they are never to be called characters in any true sense of the word."

The two most sophisticated modern essays on Holmes's fiction are by Edouard Roditi and Charles Boewe. Roditi, in "Oliver Wendell Holmes as Novelist" (*ArQ*, Winter 1945), begins by dismissing the notion that Holmes's novels are "psychiatric," an idea popularized by Dr. Clarence P. Oberndorf in *The Psychiatric Novels of Oliver Wendell Holmes* (New York, 1943) and "Psychic Determinism in Holmes and Freud" (*Mental Hygiene*, Apr. 1944) and pursued also by Rose Alexander in "Oliver Wendell Holmes—Psychiatrist" (*Medical Record*, Oct. 1939). Roditi argues instead that the purpose of the novels is far more philo-sophical or theological. The medical "paraphernalia" is nothing more than a rhetorical device which attempts "to achieve a persuasive veri-similitude in tales that otherwise might seem wildly romantic or drily philosophical." The psychology of the novels is no more original than that of any other nineteenth-century novelist who reveals the habits and manners of neurotic characters. And for Roditi all of Holmes's main figures—Elsie Venner, Myrtle Hazard, Maurice Kirkwood—are frus-trated and lonely individuals who from infancy have been deprived of a mother's love. What is original and striking about Roditi's essay is his suggestion that Holmes is indebted to Richard Burton and *The Anatomy of Melancholy* for his belief that emotional disturbances can be traced to the deprivation of affection during childhood.

Charles Boewe, "Reflex Action in the Novels of Oliver Wendell Holmes" (*AL*, Nov. 1954), believes that the novels can all be regarded as attacks on Calvinism. Each one is "a study of a different kind of limitation of the will, and all aim to persuade the reader that rational people cannot hold others accountable for acts over which they have no control." The determinism in the novels is dependent upon a theory of "mechanical reflex action" which Holmes derived in part from the English physician Marshall Hall.

Medical Writings

The criticism of Holmes's medical essays, written mainly by physi-cians, is not nearly as extensive as the criticism of his poetry and his fiction. Yet it is instructive for the literary critic, and for the support it offers modern writers like S. I. Hayakawa, Mentor Williams, and Eleanor Tilton in their views of Holmes's social and literary significance. As a medical writer, Holmes aligned himself with the champions of progress and opposed the forces of reaction. According to Edgar M. Bick, in "A Note on the Medical Works of Oliver Wendell Holmes," Holmes lived through medical revolutions, through "the introduction of pathology, histology, bacteriology, applied electricity, organic chemistry and modern surgery," and "stood as the whip which drove back the objectors and allowed the modern scientific concept of medicine to gain entrance" (*Annals of Medical History*, Sept. 1932). For Holmes's special role in "naming" anesthesia, see A. H. Miller, *Boston Medical and Surgical Journal* (29 December 1927). Holmes's antagonism to homeopathy was as well known among his contemporaries as was his antipathy toward Calvinism. In this too he was at the forefront of medical thought. For the principles he used in exposing homeopathy and other "kindred delusions" were derived from Pierre-Charles-Alexander Louis, the French physician who exerted such a powerful influence on all American medical students of Holmes's generation, as Henry R. Viets recalls in "Oliver Wendell Holmes, Physician" (*ASch*, Winter 1934). Holmes's essay on "Currents and Counter-Currents in Medical Science" was considered by contemporaries and later writers to be one of the finest statements ever written on the philosophy of medicine. Edward O. Otis tells us, in "The Medical Achievements of Dr. Holmes," "No medical writer of his day recognized more clearly than did he, or so persistently opposed, the evils of an inordinate use of drugs, or so insistently advocated the study of the causes of disease and the supreme importance of depending upon nature and nature's remedies for their cure" (*Boston Medical and Surgical Journal*, 30 December 1909).

But Holmes's greatest service as a medical writer, according to Otis, was that of interpreter and critic: "He was a profound student of the past and a clear-visioned prophet of the future. . . . He had an original creative mind, which had not been stifled or attenuated by too much so-called culture or education. He possessed the power of systematizing and generalizing medical knowledge in an orderly form, and, more than all, he possessed that rare ability, genius we may almost call it, of expression or style which captivates and holds fast the reader by its keenness, wealth of illustration, striking analogies, epigrammatic forms of expression and airiness of touch." His essay on the contagiousness of puerperal fever testifies more than anything else to this fact. (For confirmation of the view of Holmes as scholar, see Enoch Hale, *NAR*, July

1838, and Tracy J. Putnam, *Archives of Neurology and Psychiatry*, May 1941.) For studies of Holmes's classic essay on puerperal fever, see C. J. Cullingworth, *The British Medical Journal* (Nov. 1905); F. C. Irving, *New England Journal of Medicine* (July 1943); Henry R. Viets, *Bulletin of the Medical Library Association* (Oct. 1943); C. E. Heaton, *American Journal of Obstetrics and Gynecology* (Oct. 1943); and B. P. Watson, *Bulletin of the New York Academy of Medicine* (Aug. 1943).

From the very beginning of his career the style of Holmes's medical papers was commented upon favorably. Perhaps the best account is Neille Shoemaker's "The Contemporaneous Medical Reputation of Oliver Wendell Holmes" (*NEQ*, Dec. 1953). But what characterizes Holmes's work, even more than the brilliance of its style, and what earned Holmes the respect and love of his colleagues, is that same basic humanity which reveals itself in his literary writings. According to Andrew Peabody (*NAR*, July 1861), "What impresses us most of all in these discourses is the author's profound sense of the humane mission of the medical faculty, and his own unforced and unfeigned sympathy with the sufferings which it is his office to relieve. Some physicians treat the themes within the cognizance of their art as wholly impersonal, and as if muscles, nerves, and organs existed only for their manipulations, and for the cause of science. Dr. Holmes never forgets that he is discussing the members, liabilities, and morbid affections of a suffering body, and that his science exists for its uses, and should be cultivated for humanity's sake."[4]

4. A few reviews and essays on individual works are worth consulting. On "Mechanism in Thought and Morals": James Eliot Cabot, *The Nation* (2 March 1871); and William Dean Howells, *AtM* (May 1871). On *The Autocrat of the Breakfast-Table*: J. T. Winterich, *Publishers' Weekly* (17 January 1931); William Stetson Merrill, *Catholic World*, (Feb. 1932); and J. DeLancey Ferguson, *Col* (Feb. 1936).

William Dean Howells

GEORGE FORTENBERRY

In 1915, WILLIAM DEAN HOWELLS acknowledged that he was no longer read. Unfortunately, Howells lived only long enough to watch his first reputation fade and not long enough to see his new reputation as editor, critic, and novelist (and finally, literary symbol of the age) become firmly established. In 1971, the greatness of Howells's place in American literature could be measured by the impressive array of articles and books which have appeared since his death. Perhaps his chief monument is the Howells Edition, currently being prepared according to the editorial principles and under the auspices of the Center for Editions of American Authors of the Modern Language Association of America. Two other important testimonials to Howells's current popularity with scholars and critics are: *A Bibliography of Writing About William Dean Howells*, Part One (1860–1919) compiled by James Woodress and Part Two (1920 to the Present) compiled by Stanley P. Anderson for *American Literary Realism* (Special Number, 1969), and the William Dean Howells special number of *Modern Fiction Studies* (Autumn 1970).

BIBLIOGRAPHY

Until the 1940s *CHAL* served as a helpful listing of both primary and secondary sources on Howells. Today that volume has been superseded by various bibliographies, including Lewis Leary's *Articles on American Literature*. More specialized bibliographical coverage of Howells appeared in 1948, when William M. Gibson and George Arms published *A Bibliography of William Dean Howells* (New York Public Library, 1948; hereafter cited as Gibson-Arms) based on their 1946 and 1947 listings in *BNYPL*. This bibliography, covering about two hundred books written wholly or in part by Howells and twelve hundred of his periodical pieces, is a valuable listing of his work even though it is not a complete primary bibliography. Omissions are due in part to the restrictions on communication and travel during World War II which prohibited the coverage of English and continental editions.

The Gibson-Arms bibliography includes a checklist of works by Howells and of the works by other writers for which he wrote introductions or prefaces. It is arranged chronologically and is followed by a checklist of periodicals and newspaper contributions, plus what the editors call "departments," such as "Editor's Easy Chair." Next, there is a bibliographical description of each work, followed by an annual register of periodical publications and a selected list of secondary writing about Howells. This bibliography is especially useful because it covers Howells's early newspaper career. Also appearing in 1948 was T. H. Johnson's *LHUS* bibliography, which lists separate works, reprints, letters, and collected short essays, as well as biography and criticism. The *Supplement* (1959) by Richard M. Ludwig lists secondary articles through 1957.

A more recent Howells bibliography is included in volume IV (1963) of Jacob Blanck's *BAL*. Although it is indebted to Gibson-Arms, Blanck's bibliography contains new information on primary material, including European editions of Howells's work, and a short list of secondary books on Howells through 1962, but does not consider the wealth of newspaper material about him. A more comprehensive work than either of these is now in preparation by George Arms. Scheduled for completion in 1975, it will be the final volume of the Howells Edition. At present, the most complete and up-to-date bibliographies of secondary books and articles are those by Woodress and Anderson in the special Howells number of *ALR* (1969) and that by Maurice Beebe in the special Howells number of *Modern Fiction Studies* (Autumn 1970).

Other bibliographies of importance have appeared from time to time in books about Howells. Of special interest is James Woodress's *Howells & Italy* (Durham, N.C., 1952), which considers the manuscript sources for Howells's work and contains a long list of his articles on Italian subjects, as well as articles and reviews by other authors relating to Howells and Italy. Also helpful are the bibliographical notes by Edwin Cady in *The Road to Realism* (Syracuse, N.Y., 1956) and *The Realist at War* (Syracuse, N.Y., 1958). Olov W. Fryckstedt's *In Quest of America: A Study of Howells' Early Development as a Novelist* (Cambridge, Mass., 1958) contains a bibliography with a particularly good list of reviews and a list of Howells's early newspaper contributions.

EDITIONS

One of the problems faced by Howells scholars after his death in 1920 was the absence of an "official" or complete edition of his works. One edition, personally supervised by Howells in his later years, was called *The Writings of William Dean Howells, Library Edition* (New York and London, 1900). It was a good edition, too good in fact not to have gone beyond the six volumes published before Howells had to stop work on it. Robert Walts in "William Dean Howells and His Library Edition" (*PBSA*, Fourth Quarter 1958) takes up the problems involved in that edition, including the problem of whether the books should have been sold by subscription. The six volumes published were: *My Literary Passions* and *Criticism and Fiction; The Landlord at Lion's Head; Literature and Life; London Films* and *Certain Delightful English Towns; Literary Friends and Acquaintance* and *My Mark Twain;* and *A Hazard of New Fortunes.*

Discussions about the need for a definitive edition of Howells began in the early 1950s, but it was not until a decade later that the Howells edition got underway. In 1964 Edwin Cady was named general editor. The first volume of the projected thirty-nine volumes was John Reeves's edition of *Their Wedding Journey* (Bloomington, Ind., and London, 1968). Other completed volumes of the Howells Edition (all issued from Bloomington, Ind., and London) include *Literary Friends and Acquaintance* (1968), edited by David Hiatt and Edwin Cady; *The Altrurian Romances* (1968), edited by Clara and Rudolph Kirk; *The Shadow of a Dream* and *An Imperative Duty* (1969), edited by Martha Banta; and *The Son of Royal Langbrith* (1970), edited by David Burrows. The task of establishing other Howells texts continues in spite of the controversy aroused by Edmund Wilson's "The Fruits of the MLA: *Their Wedding Journey*" (*NY Review of Books*, 26 September 1968).

Titles and editors for the remainder of the thirty-nine volumes are as follows: *Venetian Life* and *Italian Journeys*, James Woodress; *Suburban and Other Sketches*, Jean Riviere; *Complete Poems*, Thomas O'Donnell; *A Chance Acquaintance*, Jonathan Thomas; *A Foregone Conclusion*, William Wasserstrom; *Lady of the Aroostook*, William Fischer; *The Undiscovered Country*, Olov Fryckstedt; *A Modern Instance*, George Bennett; *Indian Summer*, Scott Bennett; *The Rise of Silas Lapham* and *The Minister's Charge*, Howard Munford; *April Hopes and Private Theatricals*, Kermit Vanderbilt and Kenneth Eble; *Annie Kilburn*, Louis J. Budd; *A Hazard of New Fortunes*, Everett Carter; *The Quality of Mercy*, James P. Elliot; *The World of Chance*, J. Albert Robbins; *Selected Criticism*, Ulrich Halfmann; *Selected Criticism*, Donald Pizer; *Selected Criticism*, Ronald Gottesman; *The Landlord at Lion's Head*, William McMurray; *The Kentons*, George Carrington; *The Leatherwood God*, Eugene Pattison; *The Vacation of the Kelwyns*, John Reeves; *Selected Novelle*, Robert Walts; *Selected Short Stories*, David Frazier; *Autobiography*, David Nordloh; *English Travels*, Michael Millgate; *Selected Letters*, George Arms, Richard Ballinger, and John Reeves; and *Bibliography*, George Arms. Five volumes of the Howells Edition had been published by the end of 1970; the entire project is scheduled for completion by 1975.

As one might expect, the Howells Edition Center at Indiana University is the present Howells information center. It has a growing collection of major Howells titles, facts about the books from a Howells union catalogue, and a great deal of information not listed in either Gibson-Arms or *BAL*. This material serves as a pedigree for each text as editors prepare a listing of what is known about manuscripts of the text and first and subsequent publication. On each pedigree, for example, appears a list of the many reimpressions of Howells's works, including British and Canadian editions and the Tauchnitz editions. Work on each volume serves in effect to correct bibliographical data that will appear in the Arms bibliography, the last volume of the Howells Edition.

Howells took full advantage of the popularity of the magazine serial by publishing his books in periodical or newspaper form before their book publication. *The Vacation of the Kelwyns* (New York, 1920) was the only work to appear first in book form. Howell's writings appeared essentially in three magazines—*Harpers*, *Atlantic Monthly*, and *Century*. He published also in over sixty newspapers, most of which are mentioned in Gibson-Arms. This newspaper publication has caused a particular problem in the editing of *The Quality of Mercy* which appeared simultaneously in one Canadian and five American newspapers.

Walter J. Meserve's edition of *The Complete Plays of W. D. Howells* (New York, 1960) contains an informative general introduction as well as short introductions to thirty-six plays. For a list of texts and of matters pertaining to texts earlier than the Indiana Howells Edition, the reader should consult the selected bibliography in Clara M. and Rudolf Kirk's *William Dean Howells: Representative Selections* (New York, 1950; revised, 1961). Most of the editions on this list are single volumes, edited to serve as teaching texts.

MANUSCRIPTS AND LETTERS

With the exception of letters, there are not many extant Howells manuscripts, probably because 90 percent of Howells's work first appeared in periodicals. In some cases typescript appears, but much of the editing at the Howells Center is done from serial texts and from printer's copy. The Center holds copies of most of the available manuscripts for both the published and unpublished diaries, sketches, and poetry, as well as journals, notebooks, and some early language exercises. Many of the manuscripts are incomplete. In the following list, the manuscripts vary in length from full novels to a single leaf: "Geoffrey Winter" (unpublished), *A Foregone Conclusion, The Leatherwood God, The Landlord at Lion's Head, Literary Friends and Acquaintance, A Modern Instance, The Son of Royal Langbrith, The Vacation of the Kelwyns,* and *The World of Chance.* The portions of "Geoffrey Winter" are especially valuable as clues to Howells's beginnings as a novelist. Elsewhere, John Reeves provides the most helpful information on Howells manuscripts in two articles: "The Literary Manuscripts of William Dean Howells (*BNYPL*, June 1958) and "The Literary Manuscripts of William Dean Howells: A Supplement to the Descriptive Finding List" (*BJRL*, Sept. 1961).

Many libraries have Howells manuscripts or letters. The major holdings are at the University of California, The University of Southern California, Yale, Columbia, and Colby College. Richard Cary's "William Dean Howells to Thomas Sergeant Perry" (*Colby Library Quarterly*, Dec. 1968), describes the correspondence in the Colby College Library, 123 letters from Howells to Thomas Sergeant Perry. Other major groups of letters are addressed to Mark Twain, Henry James, John Hay, and Charles Dudley Warner. The Howells letter and manuscript collection at the University of Virginia's Barrett Library contains some 110 to 120 letters, many of which are to H. H. Boyesen, Whittier, and to Major J. B. Pond. The largest collection of letters (over seven hundred) is in the Houghton Library at Harvard. Since new letters are discovered every year, it may be some time before we have the full picture of Howells through his correspondence.

Editors of the Howells Edition letters, George Arms, Richard Ballinger, and John Reeves, plan a five-volume collection, to be called *The W. D. Howells Correspondence,* which will contain most of the letters in chronological arrangement. Their plan is to include approximately 1,700 letters, including 1,100 previously unprinted. Previously published letters will include those from Mildred Howells's *Life in Letters,* the *Mark Twain–Howells Letters,* and the *Henry James–Howells Letters,* as well as some letters previously printed in periodicals. A supplement to this edition of the letters will contain a calendar of all the letters, complete with summaries of each.

Howells's letters have appeared from time to time in published collections of his correspondents, such as Percy Lubbock's *Letters of*

Henry James (New York, 1920) and Mark Antony de Wolfe Howe's *New Letters of James Russell Lowell* (New York and London, 1932). The first large collection of letters appeared in Mildred Howells's two volume *Life in Letters of William Dean Howells* (Garden City, N.Y., 1928; reprinted, New York, 1968). Although *Life in Letters* is slanted toward biography, the letters (which cover the period from 1857 to 1920) provide insight into the character of Howells and the literary activities of the time and show the close relationship Howells enjoyed with his family. Although humor, so much a part of Howells, is seen in these volumes, this quality shows itself more clearly in his letters to Mark Twain, edited in two volumes by Henry Nash Smith and William Gibson as *Mark Twain–Howells Letters: The Correspondence of Samuel L. Clemens and William Dean Howells, 1872–1910* (Cambridge, Mass., 1960). In these letters one not only gets a clear picture of Howells as an individual but also a good understanding of Howells and Twain in collaboration, in occasional dispute, and in their different roles as editor and author. Frederick Anderson has included the best of this correspondence in a handy one-volume edition: *Selected Mark Twain–Howells Letters* (New York, 1968).

As new letters are discovered they are often reported in scholarly journals. The most significant of these reports are: George Arms's two articles, "A Novel and Two Letters" (*JRUL*, Dec. 1944) and "Ever Devotedly Yours—The Whitlock-Howells Correspondence" (*JRUL*, Dec. 1946); Edwin Cady, "Armando Palacio Valdes Writes to William Dean Howells" (*Sym*, May 1948); Bradford A. Booth, "Bret Harte Goes East: Some Unpublished Letters" (*AL*, Jan. 1948); Kjell Eksstrom, "The Cable-Howells Correspondence" (*SN*, No. 1, 1950); and Kimble C. Elkins, "Eliot, Howells, and the Courses of Graduate Instruction" (*HLB*, Winter 1956). Each article has made an interesting and informative contribution to our knowledge of Howells as a letter writer. Other discussions include Kenneth Cameron, "Literary MSS in Trinity College Library" (*ESQ*, First Quarter 1959), which describes three previously unexamined Howells letters; Baird R. Shuman, "The Howells-Lowell Correspondence: A New Item" (*AL*, Nov. 1959); James B. Stronks, "An Early Autobiographical Letter by William Dean Howells" (*NEQ*, June 1960); and Leo P. Coyle, "Restoration of a Howells Letter" (*Mark Twain Journal*, Summer 1960).

BIOGRAPHY

Edwin Cady's two-volume study, *The Road to Realism* and *The Realist at War* is the best biography to date. The first volume depicts the Ohio of Howell's boyhood and his apprenticeship in the printer's trade more effectively and more completely than any other study has done. Cady uses his resources well, including the early newspapers for which Howells wrote. As a result, *The Road to Realism* gives a special feeling for the young Howells living on the frontier, the most avid reader of a reading family. *The Road to Realism* takes Howells from his birth in 1837 to 1885, or through his periods as a young reporter and as the American Consul in Venice to his first professional home on the *Atlantic Monthly*. Cady's second volume, *The Realist at War*, is slightly less biographical in nature. It takes Howells from the first days on *Harper's Monthly* to 1920, covering his fight for realism, his period of dark spiritual depression, his interest in social reform, and the last days of his life, when he was no longer a moving force in American literature. Cady has made more of Howells's psychological problems than have most other writers, and he has provided the best picture of the man and writer.

Van Wyck Brooks, in *Howells: His Life and World* (New York, 1959), did not attempt to produce a work comparable in scope to Cady's; nevertheless, he has given us a good life of Howells by keeping within his announced intention of making Howells come alive through a study of his relations with his contemporaries. Brooks devotes little time to criticism of Howells's work; he chooses rather to describe life as (in Brooks's view) it was for Howells. Brooks finds no difficulty in making Howells a combination of theoretical socialist and practical aristocrat, one who enjoyed the society life of Boston and New York. Finally, Brooks shows a stoic and placid Howells faced with the hostilities of the critics after having grown old in the service of a literary art that passed him by.

Edward Wagenknecht's *William Dean Howells: The Friendly Eye* (New York, 1969) presents a broader view of Howells's intellectual life. Although Wagenknecht prefers the term "psychography" to biography, his book recounts the small details that made up the day-to-day facts of Howell's life. Wagenknecht makes us aware of Howells's personal life by revealing such things as a choice of surname and his feeling about the sport of hunting. Howells's only real sport and his greatest joy was reading, and Wagenknecht describes carefully his reading habits and the great range of subjects which engaged his attention. Howells had a great appetite for the literatures of many nations, but he limited his reading mostly to modern writers. He liked nearly everything except the detective story and the historical novel, and, of course, he was not fond of romantic literature. Wagenknecht tries harder than most writers to get at the meaning behind the overworked labels (such as "smiling aspects") in Howells studies. Wagenknecht's book is some-what overloaded with details; on the other hand, he knows his subject well, and overall he pays tribute to Howells as writer and man.

CRITICISM

Critical interest in Howells has grown steadily with but one period of decline since the appearance of Alexander Harvey's *William Dean Howells: A Study of the Literary Artist* (New York, 1917). From that time to the present, scholars have been learning more about this domi-nant literary figure of the period from 1860 to 1910. Harvey's work, however, has not been too useful to Howells scholars because of its obvious deficiency in thoroughness of method. Its one claim to our attention is its high estimate of *The Rise of Silas Lapham*.

A few key expressions have always been popular in Howells criticism. Through the 1920s and 1930s, the terms "realism" and "social con-science" were prominent. The latter was used as early as Cooke's study of Howells in 1922 and became even more a speical term in Howells studies thereafter. Later books and articles suggesting a change in Howells studies featured such words as "pragmatism," "pastoral," and "myth." Attempts are still being made to arrive at a generally accept-able definition of realism, and such attempts invariably lead to some discussion of Howells. Our age has not completely agreed with H. L. Mencken's opinion that Howells says nothing but says it with a great deal of charm, but Mencken's influence was certainly felt in the 1930s and early 1940s. A present-day undergraduate is probably able to detect more value in a Howells novel than Mencken saw there.

Delmar Cooke's *William Dean Howells: A Critical Study* (New York, 1922) marks the first appearance of a genuine critical book, or at least the first to indicate the depth of Howells's social conscience and the firmness of his attachment to the novel form as an important force for socialization. Cooke approaches the body of Howells's work with an honest desire to discriminate between the novelist's weaknesses and his strengths. Cooke saw Howells as a mediator between moral art and the acceptance of art for art's sake. And he noted what he believed to be Howells's faulty judgment in his attitude toward women.

A third early work, Oscar W. Firkins's *William Dean Howells: A Study* (New York, 1924), presents Howells in a broader scope, bringing a wealth of material to bear upon Howells's life and work. This book may be valued more today for its inclusiveness than for its critical value. Firkins's comments on the novels are difficult to follow, but this work, as well as Cooke's, shows an awareness of Howells's value as a writer.

A lull in the appearance of book-length studies followed these first three books, although Howells continued to be discussed in general studies such as Vernon L. Parrington's "The Development of Realism" in his *Reinterpretation of American Literature* (New York, 1928). Parrington finds Howells's work to be important to realism but unsuited to his later ideas about social justice. Another discussion by Parrington, "William Dean Howells and the Realism of the Commonplace" in his *Main Currents in American Thought* (3 vols., New York, 1930), gives no indication of understanding Howells as a novelist. Arthur H. Quinn, in *American Fiction* (New York, 1936), deals adequately with the novels and recognizes the large world which Howells creates. During the years of sharp political interest when Howells's socialism seemed too mild for the serious intellectual, his cause was helped by all these commentaries, but especially by the attentions of Parrington.

The appearance in 1948 of the Gibson-Arms bibliography marked a resurgence of interest in Howells that has carried steadily to the present. Book-length studies of Howells began to appear in the 1950s, a decade quite fruitful for Howells scholarship. First was Clara M. and Rudolf Kirk's *William Dean Howells: Representative Selections*, which is important both for its thorough introduction and its carefully chosen selections. Published the same year was Henry Steele Commager's edition, *Selected Writings of William Dean Howells* (New York, 1950). Commager had championed Howells two years earlier in "The Return of Howells" (*Spectator*, 28 May 1948), and in his introduction to this book he makes it clear that Howells should not be forgotten.

James Woodress's important study, *Howells & Italy* (1952), shows the influence of Italy on Howells's later career. His Italian experiences furnished much of the subject matter for his later travel writings and novels, affected his change from poet to writer of fiction, formed his taste for realistic writing through his study of Goldoni, and strengthened his ties with Lowell and Longfellow through his study of Dante.

By 1954, scholars were depicting Howells more and more as the central figure of his age. Everett Carter, *Howells and the Age of Realism* (Philadelphia and New York, 1954), was the first to place Howells in such prominence. Carter considers Howells's attack on sentimentalism, the influence of Taine on the realists, and the age's use of autobiography as realism, as well as the importance of pragmatism to realism. Carter has helped many readers understand Howells's relationship to his time and to other realists. The best combination of biographical and critical study is found in Edwin Cady's *The Road to Realism* and *The Realist at War*. *The Realist at War* follows Howells's career through his battle for realism into a period of deep concern for his country, leading finally to *Altruria* for his readers but to a period of lost leadership for Howells himself. Cady reveals the battle for realism as more than a squabble between an old realist and prudish, tea-sipping romantics.

Prefaces to Contemporaries, a collection of previously unpublished Howells prefaces, edited by George Arms, William Gibson, and Frederick C. Marston (Gainesville, Fla., 1957), illustrates the range and depth of Howells's interest in the literature of his age. Olov W. Fryckstedt's *In Quest of America* presents Howells as an important writer and critic, at home not only on the American but also on the international scene. Fryckstedt cites the year 1882 as marking the end of Howells's early development as a novelist. With *A Modern Instance* Howells reached the peak of his artistic development; and in spite of the fact that Howells was not popular in his later years, he had established a tradition within which younger writers worked. Part of that tradition was concerned with moral and ethical questions, a subject Robert L. Hough discusses in *The Quiet Rebel* (Lincoln, Neb., 1959). Hough, who is more interested in Howells's social than his belletristic writing, points out the importance of Howells's social and economic thought in relation to later ideas on reform by showing that his work in the national magazines was read widely. Howells, in short, had a definite impact on liberal thinking in this country.

More concerned with Howells the artist than with Howells the social critic is George N. Bennett in *William Dean Howells: The Development of a Novelist* (Norman, Okla., 1959). Bennett surveys Howells's complete range as a novelist, discussing more of the novels than any other critic and showing the effects of Howells's editorial activities on *The Atlantic Monthly* upon his literary career. Although Bennett's book makes no great claims for Howells as an artist, it does show his importance as a novelist. The years from 1950 to 1960 were not only productive in numbers of books, they were also productive in terms of contributing to our understanding of Howells, especially as they revealed the subtlety and the depth of his works.

The 1960s equalled the preceding decade in the production of books on Howells. Rudolf and Clara Kirk added works singly and jointly. beginning with her *W. D. Howells, Traveler From Altruria* (New Brunswick, N.J., 1962). This book explains much not covered in Hough's *The Quiet Rebel* about Howell's social thought; it includes, in particular, material concerning Howells's move to *Cosmopolitan* and his relationship with various Christian socialists. In 1962 the. Kirks wrote *William Dean Howells* (New York, 1962) for TUSAS. This volume, distinct in its use of Howells's own work as its chief source, touches upon all aspects of his work. The Kirks present Howells in the company of Mark Twain and Henry James. He emerges as a writer whose years spent in editing helped to sharpen his critical faculties and to make him a better artist. Howells, when he worked as a novelist, had a definite creed and stayed well within its limits, even when another editor rejected one of his novels. After he had studied Tolstoy, this creed led him to a doctrine of complicity. By concentrating upon American subjects (rather than following Henry James's lead toward international themes), Howells was able to set a pattern for Drieser, Lewis, Marquand, and other American writers. The Kirks show that Howells, unlike James, found enough material to make himself a complete artist in the American vein.

Howells himself did not place a high value on criticism, although he once edited a volume of critical writings by his contemporaries. Today he might see irony in the fact that two volumes of critical articles on him are readily available when most of his literary works are out of print. The first of these, edited by Edwin H. Cady and David Frazier, *The War of the Critics over William Dean Howells* (Evanston, Ill., 1962), is a reprinting of sixty-eight previously printed articles and reviews, selected to illustrate conflicting views about Howells as a realist. The materials are also well selected to give the reader a view of the cultural history of Howells's time. A similar volume, edited by Kenneth Eble, is *Howells: A Century of Criticism* (Dallas, Tex., 1962). Eble, who includes only a few of the pieces printed in *The War of the Critics*, presents editorial commentary at the beginning of each of his divisions. Each of these volumes is helpful to students of Howells.

Clara M. Kirk's *W. D. Howells and Art in His Time* (New Brunswick, N.J., 1965) adds valuable information about an almost unknown side of Howells by illustrating the influence of painting and sculpture on his theory of realism. In addition to knowing many artists and using their work in his own writing, Howells was concerned with the relation of the artist to society, as he shows especially in *The Landlord at Lion's Head*. Mrs. Kirk explains the place of both Howells and James in the Whistler-Ruskin controversy and shows that Howells was quite sensitive to new movements in art. This book opens another significant dimension of Howells's thought.

Another approach to Howells's fictional art appeared in George C. Carrington's *The Immense Complex Drama* (Columbus, Ohio, 1966), which promises in its introduction to deliver something entirely new in Howells criticism. In fact, Carrington attempts to accomplish in his criticism what Howells wanted to accomplish in fiction: to give the reader a truthful treatment of relevant materials. The results of this study are interesting and to a certain extent controversial. Carrington discusses the idea of the alienation of the artist as it appears in Howells's work; the use of demonic characters culminating in the character of Dylks in *The Leatherwood God;* and the importance of perception as Howells's most compelling theme. Carrington asserts that critics have found Howells guilty of the wrong things, such as not being a different writer than he was. Howells can be criticized for his lack of control and for not always being true to his own method of writing. He wrote too much and he sometimes lacked the power to create; but according to Carrington, he rightfully belongs in the tradition of Melville and Hawthorne.

William McMurray's *The Literary Realism of William Dean Howells* (Minneapolis, Minn., 1967), in addition to contributing a careful reading of twelve of Howells's novels, shows the relationship between his realism and the pragmatism of William James. Each of the twelve interpretations demonstrates in some way that the characters undergo a certain amount of suffering before finally coming to terms with the world or settling for what works best for them. William M. Gibson, *William Dean Howells* (Minneapolis, Minn., 1967), also offers interesting readings of the novels; moreover, Gibson points out the need for a thorough study of Howells's criticism apart from that found in *Criticism and Fiction*. Gibson gives Howells credit for being "the architect of the revolution" of language in American literature, a revolution carried to a conclusion by Mark Twain. In this sense Howells fits into a tradition running from Emerson to Hemingway.

The newer critics of Howells—Carrington, McMurray, and others—have been freer to direct their efforts toward interpretation, since the older Howells scholars set in place the important biographical and critical details. Kermit Vanderbilt takes full advantage of this situation in *The Achievement of William Dean Howells* (Princeton, N.J., 1968), which is primarily interpretive. Vanderbilt, who feels that Howells has been made "the victim of the biographical approach in its most irresponsible form," is concerned, among other things, with showing how *The Undiscovered Country* is a pastoral which must be related to Latin myth. This novel was Howells's first "broad treatment" of America; in it he dramatizes social dislocation through a use of pastoral motifs. Vanderbilt studies Howells's background reading and reviewing very carefully. In the case of *A Modern Instance* Vanderbilt shows that Howells had been reading Greek tragedy before beginning the novel, and that he saw a performance of *Medea* during the time he was writing it. Vanderbilt sees *A Modern Instance* as anti-pastoral. His discussions of *The Rise of Silas Lapham, A Hazard of New Fortunes,* and *The Undiscovered Country* are strong and original, and the book as a whole is one of the best pieces of criticism on Howells in several years.

While it is yet too early to tell what the '70s will produce, a new study by James L. Dean, *Howells' Travels Toward Art* (Albuquerque, N.M., 1970), suggests that the promise is good. Dean has probed still another Howells interest, that of travel writing; he shows that Howells worked out a theory of travel literature which was modified in his later travel books. Dean offers convincing arguments for the fact that Howells's travel literature can be placed alongside the best in this genre.

The literary career of William Dean Howells has been well described in periodical articles and in chapters of books as well as in book-length works. Among the former, Newton Arvin's "The Usableness of Howells" (*NR,* 30 June 1937) has the virtue of being prophetic about the change in critical attitude toward Howells. Arvin found an emerging warmth for Howells and contended that he was indeed usable, especially for the critics.

By far the most popular topics in Howells criticism are those involving some aspect of realism. The vitality of interest in realism is seen in the fact that the battles about realism fought in the periodicals in Howells's time are still being fought. Carl Van Doren, "Howells and Realism" in his *The American Novel, 1789–1939* (New York, 1921), sees Howells as using his own special brand of realism. During the next twenty years critics came to believe that realism went further than Howells did. Alfred Kazin in *On Native Grounds* (New York, 1942), shows Howells's limited realism as the trap that places him between old and new forces in literature. Frederick Hoffman sees Howellsian realism as part of developing naturalism in "Henry James, William Dean Howells and the Art of Fiction" in his *The Modern Novel in America, 1900–1950* (Chicago, 1950). John K. Reeves's "The Way of a Realist: A Study of Howells's Use of the Saratoga Scene" (*PMLA,* Dec. 1950) is another attempt to show how Howellsian realism worked. Sections of two other books in the 1950s were devoted to the discussion of realism. Clarence Gohdes's "Realism for the Middle Class" in *The Literature of the American People,* edited by Arthur Hobson Quinn (New York, 1951), indicates that Howells's demand for realism called for simplicity in art. Robert Falk's "The Rise of Realism," in *Transitions in American Literary History,* edited by Harry H. Clark (Durham, N.C., 1953), considers the rise of realism a general cultural movement and discusses the role Howells played in that movement.

As with the term "romanticism," critics used the term "realism" for many years without trying to define it. Howells's own concept of realism was as difficult to define as other concepts, although there have been critics who preferred to oversimplify it. Articles like John K. Reeves's "The Limited Realism of Howells' *Their Wedding Journey*" (*PMLA*, Dec. 1962) attempt to demonstrate something about Howells's method. For H. Wayne Morgan, Howells's "realism was neither pretentious nor hard to define. As the name implied, it insisted on fidelity to life as it really was, not as it might be in some cuckooland" (*American Writers in Rebellion*, New York, 1965). The best coverage of the subject of realism, Howellsian and otherwise, suggests that realism is difficult to define. Harold H. Kolb's *The Illusion of Life: American Realism as a Literary Form* (Charlottesville, Va., 1969), handily shows that the clichés of the past break down under a thorough examination. By drawing upon the areas of philosophy, subject matter, morality, and style for his definition, Kolb comes closer to defining the realism of the 1880s than anyone else has.

A number of studies of American literature in general have been concerned with Howells's work as a comment on industrial America, the growth of our economy, and the rise of the city. Morton G. and Lucia White, *The Intellectual Versus the City* (Cambridge, Mass., 1962), reveal Howells as an accurate chronicler of urban life. John G. Cawelti, "The Self-Made Man and Industrial America: The Portrayal of Mobility in the Nineteenth Century Novel" in his *Apostles of the Self-Made Man* (Chicago and London, 1965), treats the manner in which Howells's male characters meet the challenge in a growing and industrial America. Articles dealing with Howells's response to industrial America have been relatively few in number, but this has been a popular theme for book-length studies which include Howells.

Several studies have shown the influence of Tolstoy on the growth of Howells's social conscience. An early but oversimplified study is Russell Blankenship's *American Literature as an Expression of the National Mind* (New York, 1931). George Arms has contributed numerous articles concerned with Howells's social criticism, one of the best of which is "The Literary Background of Howells' Social Criticism" (*AL*, Nov. 1942). Instead of giving Tolstoy full credit for Howells's intensified interest in social affairs, Arms traces four other influences on his thought. He discusses Howells's debt to Gronlund and the literary influences of the *Atlantic* coterie on Howells's writing. This article and two by Louis J. Budd, "Howells and the *Atlantic* and

Republicanism" (*AL*, May 1952) and "Altruism Arrives in America" (*AQ*, Spring 1956), have supplied especially interesting material. By tracing Howells's activities as a Republican, Budd shows that he did not suddenly become aware of things political but had grown up in the tradition of the *Atlantic Monthly*'s social criticism. In the second article Budd traces the origins of the word *altruism* and then shows Howells's literary interest in the subject. Another valuable article, Marc L. Ratner's "Howells and Boyesen: Two Views of Realism" (*NEQ*, Sept. 1962), shows how Howells's brand of realism, instead of following that of Europe, became a social realism.

While a great deal of study has been devoted to such subjects as the commonplace, Howells and gentility, and Howells and neo-Puritanism, not enough attention has been given to Howells's influence as an editor who worked to bring North, South, East, and West together after the Civil War; and certainly not enough attention has been given to Howells's attempts to help create a truly American style of writing. And although more attention has been devoted to his literary criticism in general than to general matters of style, probably too much consideration has been given *Criticism and Fiction* and not enough to his other critical writing.

Among essays devoted to Howells as a critic, Alexander Cowie's "William Dean Howells" in his *The Rise of the American Novel* (New York, 1948) contains a good discussion of Howells's literary creed, and John Paul Pritchard's *Criticism in America* (Norman, Okla., 1956) evaluates Howells as a kindly realist who is paternal enough to spare his country the pain of a harsher realism. Somewhat more useful is Pritchard's "William Dean Howells" in his *Return to the Fountains* (Durham, N.C., 1942), which takes up Howells's use of classical themes. A good article on Howells's criticism is Donald Pizer's "The Evolutionary Foundation of William Dean Howells' *Criticism and Fiction*" (*PQ*, Jan. 1961), which gives Howells credit for thinking through his critical theory in a systematic way.

Other significant essays which have appeared since 1960 are: James L. Woodress's "The Dean's Comeback: Four Decades of Howells Scholarship" (*TSLL*, Spring 1960), which places Howells studies in perspective and shows how important Howells had become to American literature; William G. McMurray, "Point of View in Howells' *The Landlord at Lions Head*" (*AL*, May 1962), which emphasizes Howells as a conscious artist; Kermit Vanderbilt, "*The Undiscovered Country;* Howells' Version of American Pastoral" (*AQ*, Winter 1965), which shows a richness in this novel that had eluded many readers; and G. Thomas Tanselle, "The Architecture of *The Rise of Silas Lapham"* (*AL*, Jan. 1966), which gives us the best analysis yet of the structure in this important novel.

Although William Dean Howells may have been the least important figure in the triad which included Mark Twain and Henry James, scholarship has already shown that as an editor and literary sponsor of other writers he is without peer in American letters. And his reputation as a literary artist is growing. Scholars are now beginning to think of Howells not simply as the man who fought for realism, but as the man who also gave us good novels to read. Even though many of these same novels were dismissed as having no thought or depth after World War I, when courses in American literature were becoming popular in colleges and universities, present-day critics are examining Howells's work in a clearer light and are finding artistry along with social comment.

Washington Irving

HENRY A. POCHMANN

INSOFAR AS biographers, critics, editors, and publishers can make or break authors' reputations, Irving fared rather better than his immediate compeers Cooper and Bryant. Winning the distinction of being the "first" in several areas of literary activity, he also achieved, by his own foresight and the cooperation of an enterprising publisher, the honor of being the first major American man of letters to have his writings collected, revised, and edited by himself in what then passed current for a complete, uniform edition.

The "Author's Revised Edition" in fifteen volumes published by George P. Putnam in 1848–1851, originally put the "Father of American Literature" in a favored position—barely ahead of Cooper (whose twelve-volume edition of 1849–1850, however, was far from complete) but decades before other major nineteenth-century authors were enshrined in "complete" or "collected" authorized editions, when near the turn of the century Houghton Mifflin sought to consolidate its authors' and their own position. Meanwhile Pierre Munro Irving's four-volume biography (1862–1864), printed a score of years before Irving's contemporaries became the subject of official biographies, set the tone, style, and scope for others to follow in preparing "standard" lives of the major nineteenth-century figures.

But to be the first in a field is not always an unmixed blessing. For example, although Pierre M. Irving quoted liberally from his uncle's journals and letters, their separate collection lagged far behind what was being done for Irving's contemporaries, presumably on the supposition that the samplings which the official biography provided were sufficient for most purposes. And so they were until the demands of twentieth-century scholarship encouraged a first generation of serious Irving students to supply some of the more significant lacunae in Irving's journals and notebooks and special collections of his letters.

Good as these were, they followed varying standards and methods of transcription and editing, besides leaving large gaps—in the case of the journals and notebooks, some two dozen manuscripts or volumes, while hundreds of letters remained uncollected and unedited, and still others remain unlocated. To rectify this anomalous situation a half-dozen students of Irving met informally during the 1959 sessions of the Modern Language Association of America and projected a complete edition of the journals and letters, to be prepared uniformly and in accord with modern editorial standards. When the Center for Editions of American Authors was formed, the Irving project was included in the editions sponsored by the Center, and expanded to twenty-eight volumes—five of journals, four of letters, eighteen of works, and one of bibliography —to comprise *The Complete Works of Washington Irving*, and to be published by the University of Wisconsin Press. Of this edition, two volumes of journals and one of works have appeared, and more are scheduled for publication.

BIBLIOGRAPHY

Bibliographically, Irving has fared very well, comparatively speaking. Besides the better-than-average representation in *CHAL*, Henry A. Pochmann's briefly annotated "Selected Bibliography" in the American Writers Series edition of *Selections* (New York, 1934), and Thomas H. Johnson's succinct bibliographical essay in volume III of *LHUS*, Irving attracted four competent scholars who prepared two bibliographies from very different but complementary points of view. The first is primarily a collector's bibliography compiled by William R. Langfeld and Philip C. Blackburn, originally published in the *BNYPL* (June to Dec. 1932) and in book form the year after. While confined largely to first American and English editions, it is a detailed descriptive bibliography (though without precise collational formulae or strict observance of bibliographical terms that have become standardized since then), citing in many cases data on issues and conditions most useful for purposes of identification. The information about the locations of copies described is very helpful. The *Bibliography* prepared by Stanley T. Williams and Mary Allen Edge (New York, 1936), properly a third-volume addition to Williams's authoritative two-volume *Life of Washington Irving* of the year before, casts a much wider net, being in the nature of a checklist. Listing as it does titles and editions of Irving's writings, in English and other languages, published here and abroad, that appeared during his lifetime and afterwards, as well as the biographical and critical literature concerning Irving, it becomes an index to his contemporary as well as posthumous reputation not merely as essayist and story writer, but as historian, biographer, and contributor to periodicals. Titles personally examined by the compilers are asterisked to distinguish them from others gleaned from printed sources.

The treatment of Irving, in the fifth volume (1970) of Jacob N. Blanck's indispensable *BAL*, which often distinguishes between states, issues, and impressions for first editions and, in some instances, between significant later editions, verified Williams's claim made on the appearance of the Williams-Edge compilation that Irving had achieved "the most complete bibliographical record of any American literary figure." This claim was reemphasized by the appearance in the *BNYPL* (Jan. 1964) of Herbert L. Kleinfield's "A Census of Washington Irving Manuscripts," which laid the necessary groundwork for the Wisconsin edition. Several lesser bibliographical contributions, usually in the form of articles, are not particularized here because they are cited by either Blanck or Kleinfield, or in such annual bibliographical surveys as *American Literary Scholarship* and the listings in *AL* and *PMLA*.

MANUSCRIPTS AND LETTERS

Especially revelatory of Irving's long and multiform connections with the NYPL is Andrew B. Myers's "Washington Irving and the Astor Library" (*BNYPL*, June 1968). Noteworthy reports on Irving exhibits and Irving collections in the NYPL are in *BNYPL* (Nov. 1914; May 1920; Feb. 1926; Apr. 1929; Feb. 1943; Mar. 1964). Lesser collections are described in the *Library of Congress Quarterly* (Feb. 1948) and *YULG* (Apr. 1966; Oct. 1966; Jan. 1967). While the NYPL remains the largest depository of Irving MSS (see especially *The Seligman Collection of Irvingiana*, New York, 1926, and *Catalogue of the Hellman Collection of Irvingiana*, New York, 1929), the Yale, Huntington, and Harvard libraries contain noteworthy collections, and in recent years the gifts of Clifton Waller Barrett to the University of Virginia library have made its holdings of prime importance. Irving's extensive diplomatic correspondence in the Library of Congress and in the files of the National Archives in Washington will become generally available when the four volumes of letters in the Wisconsin edition are published.

Perhaps as many as one-half of Irving's extant letters have been published in one form or another. One of the earliest collections appeared shortly after Irving's death in Evert A. Duyckinck's *Irvingiana: A Memorial to Washington Irving* (New York, 1860), and another, in Charles R. Leslie's *Autobiographical Recollections* (Boston, 1860). The next, and the most considerable body of letters is reproduced, or extracted, by

Pierre M. Irving in *The Life and Letters of Washington Irving* (4 vols., New York, 1862–1864). George S. Hellman's *Washington Irving, Esquire: Ambassador at Large from the New World to the Old* (New York, 1925) added some more, chiefly from the 1840s. Among the more special collections are the correspondence of Irving and John Howard Payne in *Scribner's Magazine* (Oct., Nov. 1910); Irving and the Renwicks (New York, 1910); Irving and Henry Brevoort, edited by G. S. Hellman (2 vols., New York, 1918); Stanley T. Williams's editions of *Letters from Sunnyside and Spain* (New Haven, Conn., 1928), and *Washington Irving and the Storrows* . . . (Cambridge, Mass., 1933); S. T. Williams and Leonard B. Beach, "Washington Irving's Letters to Mary Kennedy," *AL* (Mar. 1934); Barbara D. Simison, "Letters to Sarah Storrow from Spain . . . ," in *Papers in Honor of Andrew Keogh, Librarian of Yale University, by the Staff of the Library* (New Haven, Conn., 1938); Clara and Rudolf Kirk, "Seven Letters of Washington Irving [1804–1805]," *JRUL* (Dec. 1945 and June 1946); Clara L. Penney, "Washington Irving in Spain: Unpublished Letters Chiefly to Mrs. Henry O'Shea, 1845–1854," *BNYPL* (Dec., 1958); and Everett H. and Katherine T. Emerson, "Some Letters of Washington Irving, 1833–1843," *AL* (May 1963). Lesser collections are itemized in *LHUS* and *Supplement*, or listed in more recent bibliographies.

EDITIONS

Irving has been fortunate in his publishers and editors, so that his works have been almost constantly available for a century and a half. Before the appearance in 1848–1851 of the collected Author's Revised Edition, prepared by himself, his popularity was such that virtually all of his individual titles were in print, in either authorized or pirated editions. Since then, for well over a century, the Putnam firm kept his books in print in a great variety of editions, beginning with the original fifteen volumes of 1848–1851. These were supplemented in 1860 by Vol. XVI: *Salmagundi* (which Irving had purposely omitted, along with the Jonathan Oldstyle Letters, as juvenilia), and the five volumes of *George Washington* were added in 1860, to make twenty-one volumes in the New Author's Revised Edition. All subsequent Putnam editions, including the Riverside (21 vols., 1850–1860), Kinderhook (28 vols. in 14, 1850–1880), Sunnyside (28 vols., 1860), National (21 vols., 1860), Knickerbocker (27 vols., 1869), Geoffrey Crayon (27 vols., 1880–1883), Spuyten Duyvil (12 vols., 1881), Hudson (27 vols., 1882), another Knickerbocker (40 vols., 1891), Autograph (40 vols., 1895), People's (23 vols., 1901), and such other twentieth-century reissues as the Hudson, Nepperhan, Stuyvesant, Knickerbocker, Sunnyside, Pocantico, and Popular, are all based on the original Author's Revised Edition, as are most of the unauthorized editions issued by a great number of publishers in America, England, France, and Germany—sometimes in translation. The quantity and variety of selected works and of single titles appearing at home and abroad throughout the years are simply staggering. A mere listing of them occupies some 150 pages in the Williams-Edge checklist. That many of these volumes are available today is owing chiefly to the long-excellent collections in the New York Public Library and the acquisition in recent years of Stanley T. Williams's books by the Miriam Lutcher Stark Library of the University of Texas. The Wisconsin edition collates all relevant editions antecedent to the Author's Revised and later ones that appeared during Irving's lifetime, but is still basically the text of 1848–1851, the printing of which was supervised by Irving himself and which, generally speaking, incorporated his latest wishes.

For the rest, in 1866 Pierre M. Irving edited some essays on Spanish subjects and other stray pieces in two volumes of *Spanish Papers and Other Miscellanies*, all of which are reproduced in the more comprehensive Putnam editions. Irving's contributions to the operatic stage, *Abu Hassan* and *The Wild Huntsman*, were edited by George S. Hellman (New York, 1924), and William R. Langfeld edited *The Poems of Washington Irving* for the *BNYPL* (Nov. 1930). A stray but interesting item is Stanley T. Williams and Ernest E. Leisy's edition of " 'Polly Holman's Wedding': Notes by Washington Irving" in *Southwest Review* (July 1934), typifying one of Irving's more realistic pieces of writing; and Martin Roth's *Washington Irving's Contributions to "The Corrector"* (Minneapolis, Minn., 1968) supplements our knowledge of Irving's early journalistic writings. A good deal more of fugitive material will form the last volume of works in the Wisconsin edition.

The selection of journals, notebooks, and diaries for publication has hitherto depended largely on the availability of the manuscripts and on the particular interests of the collector or editor. One editorial project that aimed at greater comprehensiveness is *The Journals of Washington Irving, from July, 1815, to July, 1842*, prepared by William P. Trent and George S. Hellman in three volumes (Boston, 1919), but its gaps and omissions are legion, and essential annotation is lacking. Other special editions (arranged in chronological order) include *Journal, 1803*, edited by Stanley T. Williams (New York, 1934); *Notes and Journal of Travel, 1804–1805*, edited by William P. Trent (3 vols., New York, 1921); Stanley T. Williams, "Washington Irving's First Stay in Paris [1805]" (*AL*, Mar. 1930); Barbara D. Simison, "Washington Irving's Notebook of 1810" (*YULG*, July and Oct. 1949); *Notes While Preparing Sketch Book, &c. . . . 1817*, and *Tour in Scotland, 1817, and Other Manuscript Notes*, both edited by S. T. Williams (New Haven, Conn., 1927); *Journal of Washington Irving, 1823–1828*, edited by S. T. Williams (Cambridge, Mass., 1931); Andrew B. Myers, "Washington Irving's Madrid Journal, 1827–1828" (*BNYPL*, May to Aug. 1958); *Journal of Washington Irving, 1828*, edited by S. T. Williams (New York, 1927); *Washington Irving's Diary: Spain 1828–1829*, edited by Clara L. Penney (New York, 1926); *The Western Journals of Washington Irving* [1832–1833], edited by John F. McDermott (Norman, Okla., 1944); and Barbara D. Simison, "Some Autobiographical Notes of Washington Irving" (*YULG*, July 1933), consisting of "random anecdotes and stray facts" written in Spain about 1843–1845. The Wisconsin edition of the journals and notebooks, of which volumes covering the years 1803 to 1806 (edited by Nathalia Wright) and 1819 to 1827 (edited by Walter A. Reichart) have appeared, is uniformly edited and will present all the eighty-eight separate journals currently known to be extant, about a third of which have never been published.

BIOGRAPHY

Like the life of Irving, the history of his biography is a remarkably placid one. Unlike Cooper, or Poe, or Whitman, whose lives provoked controversies from the first, the four-volume *Life and Letters* by his nephew, Pierre Munro Irving, in 1862–1864 stood unchallenged for many years. Succeeding biographies by Charles Adams (New York, 1870), David J. Hill (New York, 1879), Charles Dudley Warner (Boston, 1881), Daniel Wise (New York, 1883), Richard H. Stoddard (New York, 1886), Francis H. Underwood (Philadelphia, 1890), George W. Curtis (New York, 1891), Henry W. Boynton (Boston, 1901), and a respectable two-volume German study by Adolf Laun (Berlin, 1870) added little more than biographical minutiae and occasional critical insights into Irving's writings, which for the most part Pierre M. Irving had eschewed, but they added virtually nothing to alter the overall picture. Generally revered, Irving had fallen into a comfortable and respectable niche, where he seemed to rest secure from even the debunking and plain-speaking of the 1920s and 1930s. When a new, more critical approach to literary biography did finally reach him, it was altogether fitting that it should come from an admirer who had long been an avid collector of Irvingiana—the editor of the Irving-Brevoort correspondence and coeditor with W. P. Trent of Irving's journals from 1815 to 1842. Thus prepared, George S. Hellman wrote his *Washington*

Irving Esquire: Ambassador at Large from the New World to the Old,
in 1925, the first book since Pierre M. Irving's official biography to
draw in any marked degree upon the new source materials, some of
which apparently had hitherto not been available, even to Irving's
nephew Pierre.

Without pretensions to profundity of scholarship, Hellman nevertheless wrote both an informed and an engaging book that filled a gap
here, elucidated a new point there, and documented the whole with
colorful bits from journals and letters not previously utilized. The style
is informal and anecdotal. Without strict attention to chronology or
precise dates, the book moves forward rapidly, hitting the more interesting high points, embellished with aptly chosen quotations, and as a
result comes a good deal nearer painting a lifelike portrait than that of
the formal "Mr. Irving" which the nephew-biographer had drawn.

The point at which Hellman provoked controversy was his assertion,
based on a partially erased passage in Irving's Dresden journal, that
Irving had proposed marriage to Emily Foster in March 1823, and was
rejected—thus attacking the sentimental story Pierre M. Irving had
labored to construct about Irving's remaining all his life true to his
first tragic love for Matilda Hoffman—never mentioning her name,
"not even to his most intimate friends," and preserving to the end of
his days a miniature of her and a lock of her hair.

In his edition of Irving's Dresden journal, Stanley T. Williams
pointed out that while Hellman's contention seemed plausible, it
remained an unproved assumption and must be considered conjectural.
Hellman replied in *MLN* (May 1932), and Williams returned to his
position in "Washington Irving, Matilda Hoffman, and Emily Foster"
(*MLN*, Mar. 1933). Other pertinent contributions include Walter A.
Reichart's "Washington Irving, the Fosters, and the Forsters" (*MLN*,
Jan. 1935), pointing out that in some instances Hellman had confused
the Foster and Forster families; Francis P. Smith, "Washington Irving,
the Fosters, and Some Poetry" (*AL*, May 1937), and Reichart, "Baron
Von Gumppenberg, Emily Foster, and Washington Irving" (*MLN*,
May 1945). The publication in 1938 of the *Journal of Emily Foster*,
edited by Williams and Leonard Beach, did little to resolve the matter
one way or the other.

As a matter of fact, Hellman was not the first to consider Irving to
have been in love with Emily Foster and to have proposed marriage.
Emily's younger sister, Flora Foster Dawson, believed as much and said
so at the time when Pierre M. Irving's biography was going through
the press. She supported her claim with quotations from the Fosters'
Dresden diaries (including her own), which Richard Bentley, Pierre

M. Irving's British publisher, incorporated into the third volume of the English edition of the *Life and Letters* without consulting the author. This high-handed procedure provoked Pierre M. Irving's righteous anger and led him to refute the claim in the appendix to the English edition and elsewhere in the American edition, with a vigor that led Hellman to conclude that he "doth protest too much."

It appears that Hellman misread the partially erased word "Evening" as "Emily" in a passage of Irving's Dresden diary upon which he based much of his hypothesis, and that, as Williams pointed out, he misinterpreted the word "triste." The complete rendition of Irving's journals for 1819 to 1827, as presented by Walter A. Reichart, demonstrates the fact that Irving used the word "triste" as often when referring to the state of his mind as when commenting on the state of the weather. What there is no longer any doubt about, as Hellman was the first to document, is that Irving was powerfully drawn to women both before and after Matilda's death; and now that much more corroborative evidence on Irving's emotional involvements has appeared, Hellman's interpretation has gained general though not absolute acceptance. Indeed, evidence recently adduced makes the presumption strong that so early as 1815, barely six years after Matilda's death, Irving was sufficiently touched by love for Serena Livingston, daughter of John R. Livingston, to have at least contemplated marriage, but he delayed because of his then precarious financial position and the meddling interference of Major Henry (Black Horse Harry) Lee, the "unsteady" son of Light Horse Harry (see M. A. Weatherspoon, "1815–1819: Prelude to Irving's *Sketch Book*," *AL*, Jan. 1970).

This tempest-in-a-teapot controversy has obscured the most noteworthy contribution that Hellman's book made in the last four chapters, to which the preceding thirteen are chiefly prelude: that is, Irving's role, officially and unofficially, as Ambassador at Large from the New World to the Old. Hellman's reproduction, chiefly from the governmental archives in Washington, of Irving's correspondence with Martin Van Buren, John Tyler, Daniel Webster, Hugh S. Legaré, John C. Calhoun, and James Buchanan provides the climax, as it were, to the thesis of the book as expressed in the subtitle.

When Stanley T. Williams's two-volume *Life* appeared in 1935, it was acclaimed as both "judicial" and "authoritative." One reviewer summed it up by saying: "The service that Professor Williams has performed for American biography is not unlike the service Irving himself performed for American literature: for as *The Sketch Book* marked the point of departure from a derivative, and announced the advent of an original, American literature, so this work marks the arrival at maturity of American biography." Thus Irving achieved another "first"—the first American man of letters to be honored by a full-length, modern, critical biography—for which Poe, Emerson, Hawthorne, Melville, Whitman, and others had to wait some years longer.

The fullness of Williams's inquiries and researches is indicated by his relegation to an appendix of his more intensive and specialized studies of the origins and sources of Irving's writings, lest these more special treatments disrupt the thread of biography. Here he broke new ground and pointed out paths that later researchers have followed to explore still other areas of investigation—not only in the traditional ones of literary inquiry and critical evaluation but in what has come to be the latest rediscovery, namely, that Irving did more than merely dabble in folklore and myth.

The most recent critical biography is Edward Wagenknecht's *Washington Irving: Moderation Displayed* (New York, 1962), that is, the Irving who, as the author puts it, "consistently inhabited a middle region which he surveyed and described with a winning, companionable charm." The idea is not a new one, but it is presented in tellingly new terms and seemingly with an eye to those of Irving's critics who have, as Wagenknecht feels, treated the gentle Irving too harshly. Thus he wonders how Williams could devote so much of his life to the study of an author of whom he was so often very critical. Nonetheless, he pays tribute to his predecessor's work by admitting that a new biography "could not be much more than a paraphrase of Williams," and accordingly contents himself with painting a "portrait" of Irving. This he does superbly, especially in the middle and by far the longest section of the book, entitled "The Man." Occasional errors of fact and an unhappy and inadequate metaphor on which the entire book is constructed do not materially detract from its overriding virtue —the author's transparently sincere empathy with Irving as a man and his intelligent reading of him as a writer. Besides offering numerous insights into Irving's character not previously emphasized, Wagenknecht's portrait is a beautiful example of how hard-won but often prosaically presented data of investigation as they appear in doctoral dissertations can be put to use by a skillful hand. He particularly mines and polishes the nuggets found in five dissertations: Francis Prescott Smith, "Washington Irving and France" (Ph.D., Harvard, 1937), Marguerite Mallet Raymond, "Washington Irving and the Theater" (M.A., Wellesley, 1940), Pete Kyle McCarter, "The Literary, Political, and Social Theories of Washington Irving" (Ph.D., Wisconsin, 1939), Robert Stevens Osborne, "A Study of Washington Irving's Development as a Man of Letters to 1825" (Ph.D., North

Carolina, 1947), and William L. Hedges, "The Fiction of History: Washington Irving Against a Romantic Transition" (Ph.D., Harvard, 1954). The last three especially are turned to excellent use. This is not to detract from Wagenknecht's own researches in the several repositories of Irving manuscripts and among other primary materials, for which his succinct notes provide an adequate index.

LITERARY HISTORY AND CRITICISM

For Irving more than for most American writers, it seems, literary history is inseparable from literary criticism, and until recently there was very little of the latter *per se*. Even the "new critics" have not found Irving as discutable as, for example, Hawthorne and Melville. So Irving, like Cooper, has remained in the special domain of the critical biographers and the literary historians. Much of what they have written is concerned with Irving's place in American literary annals, with historical data concerning persons and places related to his literary career, with his sources, and with the vogue and influence of his writings.

Among efforts at a general treatment is the introduction of nearly a hundred pages in Henry A. Pochmann's *Washington Irving: Representative Selections* . . . in the American Writers Series (New York, 1934)—a book reviewed by Stanley T. Williams as "On the whole . . . the most informative volume in existence concerning Washington Irving" (*AL*, Jan. 1935). It presents a rounded appraisal of Irving as conditioned by his social milieu, his political stance, his literary development, and his philosophical and religious views. Now somewhat dated, the book has a useful supplement in Lewis Leary's forty-eight-page booklet on Irving, written *con amore*, in the University of Minnesota Pamphlets on American Writers, No. 25 (Minneapolis, Minn., 1963). Saxe Commins's twelve-page introduction to the Modern Library edition of *Selected Writings of Washington Irving* (New York, 1945) is perfunctory.

At the head of book-length studies of special subjects stands William L. Hedges's *Washington Irving: An American Study, 1802–1832* (Baltimore, Md., 1965). The main corrective effort Hedges makes is to modify the hitherto widely held view of Irving as the gentle, affable soul of geniality, by emphasizing those persistent strains of moodiness, self-depreciation, indirection, insecurity, depression, and negativism that were also very much a part of him. The result is that we see in this book some of Irving's frustrations and failures, both as man and as artist; he becomes more alive and real—and infinitely more complex.

What particularly contributes toward this new picture is the depth it acquires through Hedges's adroit explanation of several important themes: how Irving fits into his times, how he was influenced by those who preceded him, and how, in turn, he was received by those who followed. So we travel backward and forward tracing affinities with Swift, Addison, Charles Brockden Brown, Cooper, Poe, Hawthorne, Emerson, Thoreau, Melville, Mark Twain, and Howells. What is demonstrated, without laboring the point, is the tremendous influence that Irving exerted on his successors, especially Poe, Hawthorne, and Melville.

Not primarily a study of sources or of influences, the analysis neglects no important formative influence in Irving's literary development that comes to mind. The chief value of the book lies in its telling analysis of the manner in which motifs such as the following allowed Irving to achieve his peculiar literary identity: the imagery of estrangement, sensibility, melancholy, whimsey, the picturesque, Rabelaisianism, dilettantism, antiquarianism and primitivism, Gothicism, mutability, involvement and alienation, fantasy and dream, and conscious and "unconscious" sex symbolism. On the last head, Hedges is tentative, generally avoiding the extremes of the new psychoanalytic interpretations (while dutifully mentioning them in footnotes) but occasionally suggesting sexual overtones and symbolisms not in keeping with Irving's well-known instinctive reticences.

Of equally high caliber are two other book-length studies of a special nature: Walter A. Reichart's *Washington Irving in Germany* (Ann Arbor, Mich., 1957) and Ben Harris McClary's *Washington Irving and the House of Murray* (Knoxville, Tenn., 1969). The first is a full-bodied treatment of the subject barely sketched by Henry A. Pochmann in "Irving's German Sources in *The Sketch Book*" (*SP*, July 1930) and "Irving's German Tour and Its Influence on His Tales" (*PMLA*, Dec. 1930). (See also Pochmann's *German Culture in America*, Madison, Wis., 1957.) Besides presenting an exhaustive discussion of Irving's literary affairs as they related to Germany, Reichart's treatment of the Emily Foster episode is as judicious a statement as is possible on the basis of the available evidence. McClary's access to the Murray archives enabled him to write as full and engaging an account as we have of an American author's relations with his principal English publisher, and of the contacts Irving formed, largely through John Murray, with English notables like Byron, Campbell, D'Israeli, Gifford, Hallam, Lockhart, Moore, Rogers, Southey, and Scott.

A good deal of pertinent criticism has appeared in books not devoted exclusively to Irving—for example, Daniel G. Hoffman's *Form and*

Fable in American Fiction (New York, 1961), in which "The Legend of Sleepy Hollow" is credited with enabling Irving to bring "into belles lettres for the first time the comic mythology and folk belief of his native region . . . which would soon become a major theme in our literature, as well as a continuing motif in a century and a half of folk-tales, and in our national history."

Not to be overlooked is the chapter on Irving in Henry Seidel Canby's *Classic Americans* (New York, 1931), which, as we look back on it now, possibly overemphasized or oversimplified Federalism, making it the mainspring of Irving's thinking as well as writing, but which nonetheless encouraged students of the Williams-Pochmann generation to search more diligently for other fundamental bases that made Irving more than a literary dilettante.

Van Wyck Brooks's *The World of Washington Irving* (New York, 1944) is a chatty, popular portrayal of the period of American literature from 1800 to about 1840, for which Irving's name provided Brooks with a convenient title. Irving as Irving gets short shrift.

Articles dealing with Irving's haunts and facts relating to his visits to various places at home and abroad are legion, many of them of questionable accuracy and slight significance. Those dealing with Irving at Sunnyside are especially numerous, many of them based on hearsay or local myth—composites of fact and fancy. Well above the average are *Washington Irving and His Circle: A Loan Exhibition Observing the Restoration of "Sunnyside," October 8 through October 26, 1946*, with an introduction by Stanley T. Williams (New York, 1946), and *Washington Irving at Sunnyside*, prepared by Harold Dean Cater, the first research director of the Rockefeller Sleepy Hollow Restorations (Tarrytown, N.Y., 1957). Also above the ordinary for authenticity are the recollections of Irving's friends and traveling companions, for example, M. C. Yarborough's "Rambles with Washington Irving: Quotations from an Unpublished Autobiography by William C. Preston" (*SAQ*, Oct. 1930), which records Preston's observations while touring Scotland with Irving in 1817. Others of a similar nature are V. H. Palsits's "Washington Irving and Frederick Saunders" (*BNYPL*, Apr. 1932); Richard Beale Davis's "James Ogilvie and Washington Irving" (*Americana*, July 1941), and his "Washington Irving and Joseph C. Cabell," in *English Studies in Honor of J. Southall Wilson* (Charlottesville, Va., 1951).

Of special interest are the journals of Peter Irving, Washington's older brother, who was his closest confidant during much of the time Irving spent abroad. They are competently edited by Leonard Beach, Theodore Hornberger, and Wyllis E. Wright for the *BNYPL* (Aug.-

Dec. 1943). Unfortunately they record only Peter's tour of Europe in 1807 and tell us nothing of the years he and his brother spent together in France and Spain during the younger brother's most active years as a writer.

For Irving in Spain, the basic information is to be found in John DeLancey Ferguson, *American Literature in Spain*, chap. II (New York, 1916); Claude G. Bowers, *The Spanish Adventures of Washington Irving* (Boston, 1940); and Stanley T. Williams, *The Spanish Background of American Literature* (2 vols., New Haven, Conn., 1955). (See also Williams's essay on the earliest appearances of Irving's writings in Spain in *MP*, Nov. 1930.) For Irving in Italy, there are essays by E. Goggio in *RR* (Jan.-Mar. 1930; Oct.-Dec. 1931) and in Nathalia Wright's *American Novelists in Italy* (Philadelphia, 1965). The exhaustive treatment of Irving in Germany is Walter A. Reichart's *Washington Irving in Germany*. Special topics are treated by Reichart in *BNYPL* (Oct. 1957), *Anglia Zeitschrift für Englische Philologie*, (Third Quarter 1956), *MLR* (Oct. 1957), *PMLA* (July 1941), and *Maske und Kothurn* (Graz-Wien, 1968). Little has appeared on the important topic of Washington Irving in England beyond Robert E. Spiller's *The American in England during the First Half Century of Independence* (New York, 1926) and Ferdinand Künzig's older study, *Washington Irving und seine Beziehungen zur englishen Literatur des 18. Jahrhunderts* (Heidelberg, 1911). One topic that has been widely discussed for as much as a century, with no man's knowing the straight of it, is the Dickens-Irving relationship. Whether Irving, who was obviously on intimate terms with Dickens during the latter's American tour early in 1842, was sufficiently offended soon afterwards by Old Boz's strictures on America in *American Notes* (1842) and *Martin Chuzzlewit* (1843) or by the "vulgar display" of Dickens's "tavern manners" when they dined together in Madrid in 1844 to cut him on his later visits to England has been argued pro and con, most recently by Ernest Boll, "Charles Dickens and Washington Irving" (*MLQ*, Dec. 1944), Christof Wegelin, "Dickens and Irving: The Problem of Influence" (*MLQ*, Mar. 1946), and W. C. Desmond Pacey, "Washington Irving and Charles Dickens" (*AL*, Jan. 1945). Williams accepted Maunsell F. Field's story, first told in *Memories of Many Men and Some Women* (New York, 1874), about the gentle, sensitive Irving's disaffection because of Dickens's table manners; Wagenknecht doubts it. What seems not to have been sufficiently considered is that when Irving, lately appointed Minister to Spain, last saw John Murray on May 10, 1842, Dickens was not among the guests assembled at 50 Albemarle Street. On his later brief visits to London he may have regarded himself enough the Ambassador at Large to think it imprudent to visit the man who had just given great offense to many of his countrymen. What's more, when later in 1845 he was summoned to help with the Oregon boundary dispute, he was preoccupied with diplomatic duties; and in the late summer of 1846, on his way home, he stopped in London too briefly to see even Leslie and others of the "Old Lads" who had long anticipated a last reunion. In short, his failure to renew the friendship with Charles Dickens may be owing to nothing more than the natural exigencies of time and occasion.

The important subject of Irving in France, especially Paris, remains unexplored except for John P. Young's *Washington Irving à Bordeaux* (Niagara Falls, Ont., 1946) and the unpublished Harvard Ph.D. dissertation of 1937 by Francis Prescott Smith, "Washington Irving in France."

A subject hitherto given scant attention is illuminatingly treated in James T. Callow's *Kindred Spirits: Knickerbocker Writers and American Artists, 1807–1855* (Chapel Hill, N.C., 1967). Irving, along with Cooper, figures prominently in this study of mutually beneficial relationships.

Among articles that attempt general analysis or reevaluation of Irving are Ernest E. Leisy, "Irving and the Genteel Tradition" (*SR*, Sept. 1947); George Snell, "Washington Irving: a Revaluation" (*MLQ*, Sept. 1946); Leonard Beach, "Washington Irving: The Artist in a Changing World" (*UKCR*, Summer 1948); Donald E. Ringe, "New York and New England: Irving's Criticism of American Society" (*AL*, Jan. 1967); Allen Guttmann, "Washington Irving and the Creative Imagination" (*AL*, May 1964); and Henry A. Pochmann, "Washington Irving: Amateur or Professional?" in *Essays on American Literature in Honor of Jay B. Hubbell*, edited by Clarence Gohdes (Durham, N.C., 1967). The last, drawing on rapidly accumulating new data as the Wisconsin edition is being prepared, suggests that Irving's literary successes were owing less to luck or fortuitous circumstances, as has often been supposed, than to careful calculation of his potentials as an artist, so that he is to be regarded less the divine amateur "toying with esoteric aspirations beyond his reach than the canny professional gauging his grasp by his reach."

For the rest, significant individual works are arranged below in chronological order. Critical discussion on "The Letters of Jonathan Oldstyle" and on *Salmagundi*, among Irving's earliest literary efforts, is virtually nonexistent, except for Jacob N. Blanck's bibliographical studies of the latter in *PBSA* (First Quarter 1947; see also *BAL*, 10097, and *Publishers' Weekly*, 28 November 1936); but for *Diedrich Knickerbocker's History of New York* there are reprintings of the 1809 and the

1812 editions, together with enlightening commentary (the first by S. T. Williams and Tremaine McDowell, New York, 1917, and the second by Edwin T. Bowden, New York, 1964) and independent studies beginning with Edwin A. Greenlaw's "Washington Irving's Comedy of Politics" (*Texas Review*, Apr. 1916). Greenlaw was the first to point out anew what had been obvious to every reader in 1809 but had been obscured by the passage of a hundred years, namely, Diedrich Knickerbocker's satire on Jefferson and Republicanism. Other significant aspects of *Knickerbocker* are treated by Clarence Webster, "Irving's Expurgation of the 1809 *History of New York*" (*AL*, Nov. 1932); Charlton G. Laird, "Tragedy and Irony in *Knickerbocker's History*" (*AL*, May 1940); Henry M. Lydenberg, "Irving's *Knickerbocker* and Some of Its Sources" (*BNYPL*, Nov.–Dec. 1952); Charles W. Jones, "Knickerbocker Santa Claus" (*New York Historical Society Quarterly*, Oct. 1954); W. L. Hedges, "Knickerbocker, Bolingbroke, and the Fiction of History" (*JHI*, June to Sept. 1959); Tremaine McDowell, "General James Wilkinson in *Knickerbocker's History of New York*" (*MLN*, June 1926); Wayne R. Kime, "The Satiric Use of Names in Irving's *History of New York*" (*Names*, Fourth Quarter 1968); and Michael L. Black, "Bibliographical Problems in Irving's Early Works" (*EAL*, Winter 1968–1969).

The Sketch Book, of course, has received as much critical attention as the rest of Irving's titles put together, "Rip Van Winkle" and "The Legend of Sleepy Hollow" naturally drawing the lion's share. The effort to identify the prototype for Ichabod has elicited four articles: Herbert Reed, *The Staten Island Historian* (1963); Truman Strobridge and Edwin Turnblath, *PNJHS* (1966); Patrick Conley, *AL* (Mar. 1968); and Ben Harris McClary, *N&Q* (Jan. 1968). Beyond that, interest in Ichabod has centered on his mythological significance, as typified by Daniel G. Hoffman's essay on "Irving's Use of American Folklore in 'The Legend of Sleepy Hollow'" (*PMLA*, June 1953), and Marjorie Bruner's "The Legend of Sleepy Hollow: A Mythological Parody" (*CE*, Jan. 1964). Rip Van Winkle continues to interest the influence seekers: Louis Le Fevre, *YR* (Sept. 1946), Elmer Brooks, *AL* (Jan. 1954), John T. Krumpelmann, *Archiv* (1956), and Walter A. Reichart, *Monatshefte* (Jan. 1956), also *Archiv* (1957); and the mythologizers have also taken note of him (see Kenneth Cameron, *ESQ*, Second Quarter 1960, and Philip Young, *KR*, Autumn 1960). Ichabod and Brom Bones have been identified as representing the imaginative versus material values, the pastoral ideal versus technological progress, by Robert A. Bone, *AQ* (Summer 1963), and by Leo Marx in *The Machine and the Garden* (New York, 1964). See also

Terence Martin, "Rip, Ichabod, and the American Imagination" (*AL*, May 1959).

Bracebridge Hall has been passed over, and *Tales of a Traveller* has fared little better, Nathalia Wright's "Irving's Use of His Italian Experiences in *Tales of a Traveller*: The Beginning of an American Tradition" in *AL* (May 1959) representing the sole recent scholarly concern with the book.

Irving's books dealing with Spanish subjects, or having their inception in Spain, have fared better, *Columbus* being the subject of a significant essay by William L. Hedges, "Irving's *Columbus*: The Problem of Romantic Biography" (*Américas* [Pan American Union], Oct. 1956), and *Granada*, by Louise Hoffman's "Irving's Use of Spanish Sources in The Conquest of Granada" (*Hispania*, Nov. 1945), and Earl N. Harbert's "Fray Antonio Agapida and Washington Irving's Romance with History" (*TSE*, 1969). Oddly enough, *The Alhambra* has gone generally unstudied, as have also Irving's last three biographies: *Goldsmith*, *Mahomet*, and *Washington*. Even *Wolfert's Roost*, Irving's last work of fiction published during his lifetime, has received no separate treatment apart from occasional mention in more general discussions of Irving's total literary output.

His western books, on the other hand, have all appeared in modern scholarly editions: *A Tour on the Prairies*, edited by John F. McDermott (Norman, Okla., 1956), *Astoria* (Norman, Okla., 1964) and *Bonneville* (Norman, Okla., 1961), both edited by Edgeley W. Todd. Further documentation appears in Henry Leavitt Ellsworth's *Washington Irving on the Prairie or A Narrative of a Tour of the Southwest in the Year 1832*, edited by Stanley T. Wiliams and Barbara D. Simison (New York, 1937); [Charles Joseph] *Latrobe's Tour with Washington Irving. From Letters in The Rambler in North America* (*London, 1835*), edited and annotated by Muriel H. Wright and George H. Stirk (Oklahoma City, Okla., 1955); and George E. Spaulding's *On the Western Tour with Washington Irving: The Journal and Letters of Count de Pourtales*, translated by Seymour Feiler (Norman, Okla., 1968).

Irving shares with Poe the dubious honor of having his origins or sources most thoroughly investigated—Poe probably because of his extravagant claims of originality, and Irving possibly because he was reputed to have been the first in so many areas. In addition to the more important book-length studies already cited, there are some forty articles, many of them representing bit-work, that can hardly be even listed. The student bent on source hunting does best to consult the available bibliographies, special and annual.

Among the clearest indications of a healthy revival of scholarly interest in Irving are two symposiums. One, commemorating the 150th anniversary of the publication of *The Sketch Book*, and comprising seven papers read at a meeting sponsored jointly by the Metropolitan New York Chapter of the American Studies Association and Sleepy Hollow Restorations on October 31, 1970, will be published in the autumn of 1971 by the latter and edited by Andrew B. Myers, under the title, *Washington Irving Symposium, a Salute to "The Sketch Book."* The other is the publication, in two parts of No. 5 (First Quarter, 1970) of the *American Transcendental Quarterly*, of a dozen significant articles presenting new viewpoints on Irving, and collected by Ralph M. Aderman under the title *Washington Irving Reconsidered* (Hartford, 1969).[1] Nine of them are by editors of volumes in the Wisconsin Edition, and the authors of two others are associated with that undertaking. Each of the essays is an outgrowth of the writer's intensive work on the text of his volume. This is as it should be, for basic textual studies have traditionally inspired new critical analysis and appraisal.

1. This renewed interest is reflected also in a spate of dissertations during the past decade, among the more considerable of which (besides those already cited) are the following: Martin Roth, "Satire and Humor in the Early Writings of Washington Irving" (Chicago, 1965); Elsie L. West, "Gentle Flute: Washington Irving as Biographer" (Columbia, 1965); Thomas C. Buell, "The Professional Idler: Washington Irving's European Years" (Washington, 1965); Michael L. Black, "Washington Irving's *History of New York*, with Emphasis on the 1848 Revision" (Columbia, 1967); Helen M. Loschky, "Washington Irving's *Knickerbocker's History of New York*: Folk History as a Literary Form" (Brown, 1970); Richard Cracroft, "The American West of Washington Irving: The Quest for a National Tradition" (Wisconsin, 1969); Haskell S. Springer, "Washington Irving's *Sketch Book*: A Critical Edition" (Indiana, 1968); Andrew B. Myers, "Washington Irving, Fur Trade Chronicler: An Analysis of *Astoria* with Notes for a Corrected Edition" (Columbia, 1964); Wayne R. Kime, "Washington Irving's *Astoria*: A Critical Study" (Delaware, 1968); Dahlia Terrell, "A Textual Study of Washington Irving's *A Tour on the Prairies*" (Texas, 1966); Jill Cohn, "The Short Fiction of Washington Irving" (Michigan State, 1971); and James Louis Gray, "The Development of the American Short Story to Washington Irving" (Duke, 1971).

Henry Wadsworth Longfellow

RICHARD DILWORTH RUST

As the chief American poet of his time, Henry Wadsworth Longfellow has been included in practically every discussion of American
literature of the nineteenth century. Furthermore, many of the literary
elite of Longfellow's era who were also his friends or acquaintances left
their reminiscences and evaluations of him. Despite the hundreds of
books, articles, and reviews from the 1830s through the 1910s, it was
not until approximately fifty years after Longfellow's death that there
was serious consultation of manuscripts and letters at the Craigie-
Longfellow House, and approximately seventy-five years until the first
impartial full-length biography appeared.

Longfellow criticism is especially interesting as an index to changing
aesthetic tastes. The man whom Hawthorne considered "the head of
our list of native poets" was disparaged by some in the 1920s and '30s as
the epitome of Victorianism, didacticism, Brahminism, and the genteel
tradition. Critical interest in Longfellow has increased since that time,
yet not in any widespread manner. In the last ten years (as represented
in the *PMLA* bibliographies for 1959 through 1968) there were forty-
seven articles, five books, four scholarly editions, and two doctoral
dissertations on Longfellow—hardly an average year's output on Longfellow's friend Hawthorne. Nevertheless, several of the most significant
books on Longfellow were published in the 1960s, and the next decade promises further reexaminations stimulated by the appearance of
carefully edited letters and journals.

BIBLIOGRAPHY

With the publication of volume 5 of Jacob Blanck's *BAL*, we have
the first full Longfellow bibliography of primary books and reprints
and the first listing of Longfellow material in books by authors other

263

than Longfellow, sheet music with lyrics derived from Longfellow, and some secondary criticism and biographies. Blanck's material supersedes Luther S. Livingston's *A Bibliography of the First Editions in Book Form of the Writings of Henry Wadsworth Longfellow* (New York, 1908; reprinted, 1968), which still has value for its notes accompanying some entries.

The earliest Longfellow bibliography appeared in the *Literary World*, 26 February 1882, and was revised and enlarged to form an appendix to Samuel Longfellow's *Final Memorials of Henry Wadsworth Longfellow* (Boston, 1887). (In 1891, *Final Memorials* was in turn integrated into the earlier *Life of Henry Wadsworth Longfellow* to form a three-volume biography, reprinted, Grosse Point, Mich., 1968.) To this bibliography of books, translations, and reviews, Samuel Longfellow added a list of Longfellow's poems and dates of composition. The original *Literary World* bibliography is further expanded by a lengthy list of contemporary reviews at the end of Eric S. Robertson's *Life of Henry Wadsworth Longfellow* (London, 1887) and by Thomas Wentworth Higginson's additions to the list of translations, in an appendix to his *Henry Wadsworth Longfellow* (Boston, 1902).

The most complete bibliography of books on Longfellow in foreign languages is Paul Morin's *Les Sources de l'Oeuvre de Henry Wadsworth Longfellow* (Paris, 1913), in which Morin lists 145 biographies and critical writings and 320 reviews and appreciations. A more accessible list of foreign and English language biographies and criticism is found at the end of Volume 2 of *CHAL*. This bibliography on Longfellow, prepared by H. W. L. Dana, also includes periodical contributions not contained in the *Complete Works*.

An annotated bibliography is found in Harry H. Clark's *Major American Poets* (New York, 1936), an excellent anthology which also has extensive notes on selected poems. This is complemented by the annotated bibliography in Odell Shepard's *Henry Wadsworth Longfellow: Representative Selections, with Introduction, Bibliography, and Notes* (New York, 1934). More exhaustive and up-to-date bibliographies are in Edward Wagenknecht's *Longfellow: A Full-Length Portrait* (New York, 1955); the *LHUS* and *Supplement*; and Lewis Leary's *Articles on American Literature, 1900–1950* and *Articles on American Literature, 1950–1967*.

EDITIONS

Editions of Longfellow's complete works, single works, selections, and translations are legion. The Library of Congress lists 384 editions of Longfellow; the British Museum in its 1962 printed catalog lists 531.

Blanck's section on Longfellow is thus far the longest on any author treated in *BAL*. As Henry Pochmann and Gay Wilson Allen note in their *Introduction to Masters of American Literature* (Carbondale, Ill., 1969), Longfellow's writings have been translated into Russian, Hebrew, Dutch, French, German, Italian, Spanish, Portuguese, Swedish, Norwegian, Danish, Pennsylvania-Dutch, Yiddish, and Icelandic (and, they might have added, Latin, Polish, and Persian).

Many separate and collected Longfellow works appeared during his lifetime, the most significant of which are listed in the *LHUS* bibliography. Four years after his death, the Houghton Mifflin Company published an authorized Riverside Edition of Longfellow's works (11 vols., Boston, 1886). Five years later, Samuel Longfellow's three-volume *Life* was added to form the Standard Library Edition of *The Works of Henry Wadsworth Longfellow* (Boston, 1891; now available in reprint from AMS Press). This edition is divided into two volumes of prose works, six of poetical works, three of the *Divine Comedy*, and the biography. Two years later, and in many reprintings thereafter, appeared a one-volume edition of *The Complete Poetical Works of Henry W. Longfellow*, edited by Horace E. Scudder (Boston, 1893).

Judicious selections of both poetry and prose are in Odell Shepard's *Longfellow: Representative Selections*. A current edition of a Longfellow novel is *Kavanagh, A Tale*, edited, with an introduction surveying critical reception of the book, by Jean Downey (New Haven, Conn., 1965). Useful collections of poetry are: *The Poems of Henry Wadsworth Longfellow*, edited by Louis Untermeyer (New York, 1943); the Modern Library edition of *The Poems of Longfellow* (New York, 1945), which includes the four major narrative poems but excludes the best sonnets; *Longfellow: Selected Poetry*, edited by Howard Nemerov (New York, 1959); *The Essential Longfellow*, edited by Lewis Leary (New York, 1963); *Favorite Poems*, edited by H. S. Canby (Garden City, N.Y., 1967); and *Poems*, edited by Edmund Fuller (New York, 1967). In addition to these, the 1969 *Books in Print* lists numerous editions of individual poems, including five of *Evangeline* and five of *Hiawatha*. Perusal of current book lists would suggest, in fact, that Longfellow's poetry continues to be a staple of elementary and junior high school reading.

MANUSCRIPTS AND LETTERS

The majority of Longfellow manuscripts and letters belong to the Henry Wadsworth Longfellow Trust and are on deposit in the Houghton Library at Harvard University. Located there are 242 volumes of papers by or pertaining to Longfellow, including manuscripts of his works, lectures, and journals. Also on deposit are 2,789 letters from Longfellow to various persons and letters from 6,228 identified persons to Longfellow. Harvard has many volumes from Longfellow's personal library, part of which were donated by Alice Longfellow about 1905, and the remainder of which were deposited by the Longfellow Trust.

The Bowdoin College Library has 17 Longfellow manuscripts and 61 letters by Longfellow and 80 to him. In addition, the library has over a thousand volumes of Longfellow's works and more than seven hundred musical scores of Longfellow poems. Parts of this collection are described very attractively in Richard Harwell's *Hawthorne and Longfellow: A Guide to an Exhibit* (Brunswick, Maine, 1966), with commentary on Longfellow's college years and some letters and documents pertaining to Longfellow at Bowdoin.

Although Longfellow letters and manuscripts are scattered throughout the country, the following libraries account for the remaining bulk of them. The Massachusetts Historical Society has about 175 letters written by Longfellow to various correspondents. The Boston Public Library has 10 manuscripts and 85 letters. At Yale University, the Sterling Memorial Library has 10 letters by Longfellow and the Beinecke Rare Book and Manuscript Library has 7 manuscripts and 42 letters. The Clifton Waller Barrett Library at the University of Virginia has 7 manuscripts of Longfellow's prose, 45 of verse, and 318 letters. At the Henry E. Huntington Library and Art Gallery are 14 Longfellow manuscripts, 203 letters by Longfellow, and 173 letters to him. And Longfellow materials at the Pierpont Morgan Library, as described by George K. Boyce in "Modern Literary Manuscripts in the Morgan Library" (*PMLA*, Feb. 1952), include 11 manuscripts and 75 letters (with four more letters having been added since 1952).

Although the 5,000 or so extant letters present a formidable mass, Andrew Hilen has taken upon himself the task of editing a selection from them in an accurate and readable format. The first two volumes of *The Letters of Henry Wadsworth Longfellow* were published by Harvard Press (Cambridge, Mass., 1966) and cover the period from 1814 to 1843. The completed edition will run to six or seven volumes of letters, with volumes III and IV to be published in 1972. In each of the volumes published, Hilen provides an informative biographical introduction and thorough notes. His purpose, as he states in "The Longfellow Letters" (*Manuscripts*, Summer 1955), is "to rescue Longfellow through the publication of authentic texts of his best letters, from the morass of Victorian misinterpretation and modern misunderstanding into which he has fallen."

For Longfellow letters after 1843 we have to depend primarily on

Samuel Longfellow's *Life*, although Hilen in the *Letters* warns us that "equipped with scissors and paste and a divinity-school training," Samuel Longfellow tampered with the manuscripts at his disposal and "created a portrait in soft tones of a saint without force, a man without troubles or anger or sex." T. W. Higginson's biography provides quotations from previously unpublished letters, mainly those from Longfellow to the Potter family in Portland. J. T. Hatfield has published "The Longfellow-Freiligrath Correspondence" (*PMLA*, Dec. 1933). John Van Schaick, Jr., has ten pages of letters appended to his *Characters in "Tales of a Wayside Inn"* (Boston, 1939). And Carl Johnson in *Professor Longfellow of Harvard* (Eugene, Ore., 1944) prints various letters pertaining mainly to Longfellow's relations with the Harvard administration. For a listing of additional Longfellow letters, which often have been published one or two at a time, the reader is referred to Wagenknecht's *Longfellow: A Full-Length Portrait*.

Along with the accurate printing of the letters, the publication of Longfellow's journals in their original form is essential for a more thorough understanding of his character and conflicts. To date we have to rely almost solely on Samuel Longfellow's extensive but altered versions of the journals in his *Life*. Fortunately, Robert S. Ward is presently editing the journals, having finished the first two volumes (as yet not in print) which correspond in time with Hilen's editions of letters (1814 to 1843). Segments of journals pertaining to Longfellow's visits in Spain, Scandinavia, and France are in Andrew Hilen's *Longfellow and Scandinavia: A Study of the Poet's Relationship with the Northern Languages and Literature* (New Haven, Conn., 1947); Iris Lilian Whitman's *Longfellow and Spain* (New York, 1927); and C. L. Johnson's "Longfellow's Journey along the Loire, 1826" (*FR*, Oct. 1966).

BIOGRAPHY

Longfellow's letters and journals, reminiscences of his family and friends, autobiographical novels, and standard biographies provide an abundance of material on Longfellow's life. Three books of the last sort appeared shortly after his death: William Sloane Kennedy's *Henry W. Longfellow* (Cambridge, Mass., 1882); Francis H. Underwood's *Henry Wadsworth Longfellow: A Biographical Sketch* (Boston, 1882); and George Lowell Austin's *Henry Wadsworth Longfellow: His Life, His Works, His Friendships* (Boston, 1883). Although Kennedy sought out reminiscences from Longfellow's friends, he turned mostly to printed reviews in newspapers and journals to produce his disjointed and second-hand work. Underwood's biography likewise is derivative, although he pays more attention than other biographers of the 1880s to Longfellow as poet. In 1876, Austin started gathering memoranda from Longfellow himself, but postponed this work until Longfellow's death terminated the project. Regretting his failure to complete what would have been the closest thing to an authorized biography, Austin later enlisted the help of John Owen, Longfellow's cousin, to finish his partial biography and collection of anecdotes.

Despite its weaknesses, Samuel Longfellow's *Life of Henry Wadsworth Longfellow* remains the standard biography. The body of the *Life* consists of selections from Longfellow's journals and letters which allow Longfellow to "tell his own story as far as possible" and thus show "how a man of letters spends his time, and what occupies his thoughts." Filling in his portrait with segments of letters and favorable reviews as well as his own reminiscences, Samuel Longfellow delineates his brother as "the good son, devoted husband, affectionate father; the generous, faithful friend; the urbane and cultivated host; the lover of children; the lover of his country; the lover of liberty and of peace."

Samuel Longfellow's opinion of Longfellow the man is echoed in Annie Fields's *Authors and Friends* (Boston, 1893). She writes from the vantage point of the daughter of Longfellow's publisher, James T. Fields, and embellishes her highly anecdotal and slightly naive account with information from correspondence between Fields and Longfellow. Holding a similarly high opinion of Longfellow but tempering his enthusiasm with critical acuity, Thomas Wentworth Higginson gives us fresh and readable accounts of Longfellow in *Old Cambridge* (New York, 1899) and *Henry Wadsworth Longfellow*. The latter biography contrasts markedly with the biographies of the eighties and nineties in its smooth-flowing narrative; moreover, it introduces new material from unpublished letters, Harvard records, and uncollected early writings.

The most notorious Longfellow biography is Herbert S. Gorman's *A Victorian American, Henry Wadsworth Longfellow* (New York, 1926; reprinted, Port Washington, N.Y., 1967). Lacking in original information, slightly condescending in tone, and burdened by a thesis, Gorman's book presents Longfellow as "a sort of American Queen Victoria" who had "a total lack of moralistic analysis and an eminently 'safe' observation of life." Gorman's subthesis is that the greater part of Longfellow's mental and intellectual sustenance was drawn from the Old World; yet he undercuts the positive aspect of this thesis by saying that the "facile and kindly" sage used European culture only as a prop.

In contrast with Gorman's derivative work, the biographies of the thirties and forties contain new insights by scholars who returned to the original sources, especially the letters and journals at the Longfellow-Craigie House. Entitling his book *New Light on Longfellow* (Boston, 1933), James Taft Hatfield concerns himself more with Longfellow's temperament than with his poetic achievement. Hatfield does provide some "new light," particularly regarding Longfellow's relations to Europe and his mastery of European languages and poetic forms; yet his insights are limited by his uncritical rating of Longfellow's position as "worthy of Apollo."

Lawrance Thompson's *Young Longfellow (1807–1843)* (New York, 1938; reprinted, 1969) is an important milestone in Longfellow biography. Reacting against the Samuel Longfellow stereotype of Henry Wadsworth Longfellow, Thompson emphasizes the human elements in Longfellow's life and concentrates on "the conflicting problems which confronted Longfellow as a young man," particularly a strain of Yankee opportunism in him which was at odds with his dominantly romantic attitude toward life. Thompson's narrative is coherently written and well documented; moreover, by its close attention to original documents and dispassionate scrutiny of Longfellow's early life it provides a significant reinterpretation of him.

Any biographical study of Longfellow the poet must of necessity be accompanied by an examination of Longfellow the professor who devoted twenty-four years of his life to teaching languages and literature. Thompson is thorough in his treatment of the Bowdoin years and early Harvard years. Carl L. Johnson's *Professor Longfellow of Harvard* focuses somewhat narrowly on Longfellow's professional responsibilities as Smith Professor of Modern Languages and on his dealings with the Harvard administration. Rounding out the portrait of Longfellow as teacher are the Bowdoin and Harvard lectures printed at the end of Robert Stafford Ward's dissertation, "Longfellow's Lehrjahre" (Boston Univ., 1951), and E. C. Dunn's "Longfellow the Teacher" (*NAR*, Feb. 1920) in which Longfellow is considered as a fighter against Philistinism in America and as a bold innovator in the teaching of French.

Edward Wagenknecht combines the explorative spirit of Hatfield and Thompson and the narrative sense of Higginson in his major critical biography, *Longfellow: A Full-Length Portrait*, which he rewrote in modified and shortened form as *Henry Wadsworth Longfellow: Portrait of an American Humanist* (New York, 1966). Based on painstaking and exhaustive study of manuscript materials as well as published sources, Wagenknecht's biography presents Longfellow in an illuminating historical perspective. Instead of simply following a strict chronology, Wagenknecht explores diverse aspects of Longfellow's life such as his reading, friendships, family relationships, and artistic theory and practice. The result is a finely balanced view of Longfellow, the man and the artist, which resolves many of the misconceptions concerning him. As just one example, Wagenknecht finds that Longfellow's conventionalism is overstressed and that Longfellow achieved in his poetry a "combination of spontaneity and careful craftsmanship."

Two ancillary contributions to Longfellow biography are Wagenknecht's edition of *Mrs. Longfellow: Selected Letters and Journals of Fanny Appleton Longfellow (1817–1861)* (New York, 1956) and *Clara Crowninshield's Diary: A European Tour with Longfellow, 1835–1836,* edited by Andrew Hilen (Seattle, Wash., 1956). The latter is an "artless and unpretentious" journal which provides a glimpse into the private life of the Longfellows before Henry achieved his popularity as a poet. Three Longfellow critical biographies of the 1960s which I intend to discuss in detail later are Newton Arvin's *Longfellow: His Life and Work* (Boston, 1963), Edward L. Hirsh's *Henry Wadsworth Longfellow* (Minneapolis, Minn., 1964), and Cecil Brown Williams's *Henry Wadsworth Longfellow* (New York, 1964).

CRITICISM

Three dominant modes of evaluating Longfellow are found in the early criticisms by Nathaniel Hawthorne, Edgar Allan Poe, and Margaret Fuller, and have continued to the present. Hawthorne represents those who admire Longfellow the man and comment, sometimes extravagantly, on the virtues they find in his writings. Thus, in his letter of December 26, 1839 (quoted by Samuel Longfellow), Hawthorne says concerning Longfellow's poems, "Nothing equal to some of them was ever written in this world, this western world, I mean; and it would not hurt my conscience much to include the other hemisphere." Again, in his review of *Evangeline*, reprinted by Randall Stewart in "Hawthorne's Contributions to *The Salem Advertiser*" (*AL*, Jan. 1934) and discussed by H. H. Hoeltje in "Hawthorne's Review of *Evangeline*" (*NEQ*, June 1950), Hawthorne praises the poem for the "simplicity of high and exquisite art" with which it is told.

Poe's criticisms of Longfellow are often brilliant and incisive, yet they demonstrate what Longfellow called "the irritation of a sensitive nature chafed by some indefinite sense of wrong." Poe represents critics whose evaluations are negatively biased by their seeing Longfellow as a representative of imitative poetry, superficiality, sentimentality, and the like. Poe's reviews, collected in *The Complete Works of Edgar Allan Poe* (New York, 1902), contain guarded praise for several poems but are in the main disparaging. Reviewing *Hyperion* in 1839, Poe

considers Longfellow "singularly deficient in all those important faculties which give artistical power, and without which never was immortality effected. He has no combining or binding force." Reviewing *Ballads and Other Poems*, Poe criticizes the theory of poetry which regards
the inculcation of a moral as essential. Then, in reviewing *The Waif*
in 1845, Poe started "the Longfellow war" by charging Longfellow
with plagiarism—a charge he repeated later that year. (For a summary
of Poe's criticisms, see Wagenknecht, *Longfellow: A Full-Length
Portrait*, and Perry Miller, *The Raven and the Whale*, New York,
1956.)

Margaret Fuller, like Poe, resented the excessive praise given Longfellow, but nevertheless demonstrated a kind of balancing of strengths
and weaknesses which is found in the most penetrating Longfellow
criticism. In *Papers on Literature and Art* (London, 1846) and in *The
Writings of Margaret Fuller*, edited by Mason Wade (New York,
1941), she says: "Longfellow is artificial and imitative. He borrows
incessantly, and . . . is very faulty in using broken or mixed metaphors.
The ethical part of his writing has a hollow, secondhand sound. He
has, however, elegance, a love of the beautiful, and a fancy for what is
large and manly, if not a full sympathy with it. His verse breathes at
times much sweetness; and if not allowed to supersede what is better,
may promote a taste for good poetry. Though imitative, he is not
mechanical." Again, his work is "of little original poetic power, but
of much poetic taste and sensibility."

Reputation

Longfellow's readership and popularity during his lifetime was
immense in the United States (as indicated by Wagenknecht and by
L. E. Hart, "The Beginnings of Longfellow's Fame," *NEQ*, Mar. 1963)
and was unequalled by any other writer of the period throughout the
world (as noted by Clarence Gohdes in *American Literature in Nineteenth Century England*, New York, 1944). Gohdes says that in England Longfellow was better known than Tennyson or Browning; critical
reviews there mixed harsh criticism with extravagant praise. In Russia,
according to David Hecht, "Longfellow in Russia" (*NEQ*, Dec. 1946),
Longfellow was one of the first American poets who was widely read.
Hecht cites ten Russian translators of Longfellow before 1900, and notes
that from 1918 to 1935 the appearance of seven editions of his poems
indicated Longfellow's popularity under the Soviet regime. And in
South America, Longfellow has had the largest number of poems translated by the greatest number of South American translators, although
he lost ground in the twentieth century to Poe and Whitman, as J. E.

Englekirk tells us in "Notes on Longfellow in South America" (*Hispania* [Stanford], Oct. 1942). (For an overview of Longfellow's reputation in Latin America, see Robert S. Ward's introductory note to Ernest J. Moyne's "The Origin and Development of Longfellow's *Song of Hiawatha*," *Journal of Inter-American Studies*, Jan. 1966.)

Longfellow's position and popularity reached a peak in the 1880s and remained high through the Longfellow centennial in 1907. Expressing a widely held opinion, Charles Eliot Norton in *Tributes to Longfellow and Emerson by The Massachusetts Historical Society* (Boston, 1882) states: "It was not by depth of thought or by original views of nature that he won his place in the world's regard; but it was by sympathy with the feelings common to good men and women everywhere, and by the simple, direct, sincere, and delicate expression of them, that he gained the affection of mankind." Longfellow's appeal to Eric S. Robertson, as shown in his *Life of Henry Wadsworth Longfellow* (London, 1887), was his ability to embellish the common and to produce "a wealth of tender and beautiful sayings that in every civilized land . . . became household favorites." And William Dean Howells, in *Literary Friends and Acquaintance* (New York, 1900) and in "The Art of Longfellow" (*NAR*, Mar. 1907), praises Longfellow as a poet who saw beyond his native New England to express the universal in the sense that "the poet has nothing to tell, except from what is actually or potentially common to the race."

A sampling of criticism during or near the Longfellow centennial finds Longfellow lauded for his moral purpose (R. B. Steele, "The Poetry of Longfellow," *SR*, Apr. 1905), his "trustworthy and graceful" translations (Leon H. Vincent, *American Literary Masters*, Boston, 1906), his popularizing "our scant store of American traditions" (M. C. Crawford, "Longfellow: Poet of Places," *Putnam's Monthly Magazine*, Feb. 1907), his simplicity, reverence, and grace which appeals to the "intellectual middle class" (Bliss Perry, "The Centenary of Longfellow," *AtM*, Mar. 1907), his interpreting to his generation "the hitherto alien treasures of European culture" (Bliss Perry, *Park-Street Papers*, Boston, 1908), and his mastery of the sonnet (Paul Elmer More in *Shelburne Essays, Fifth Series*, New York, 1908, and H. W. Mabie, "Sonnets from the *Divine Comedy*," *Outlook*, Jan. 1909). Summing up Longfellow's reputation at the turn of the century, Thomas Wentworth Higginson in *Henry Wadsworth Longfellow* affirms that "he is a classic" who "will never be read for the profoundest stirring, or for the unlocking of the deepest mysteries" but "will always be read for invigoration, for comfort, for content."

Paradoxically, it was often the elements praised by Norton, Higginson, Perry, Stedman, and others that were deprecated by later critics. Thus Longfellow's ability to reach all levels of society is dismissed by Gamaliel Bradford as mere commonplace ("Portraits of American Authors," *Bookman*, Nov. 1915) or is considered by John Macy to be an appeal to "simple minds" (*The Spirit of American Literature*, New York, 1913). Instead of Longfellow's being an adaptor of "the beauty and sentiment of other lands to the convictions of his people" (E. C. Stedman, *Poets of America*, Boston, 1913), he is considered a grizzled old man to whom "the world was a German picture-book, never detaching itself from the softly colored pages" (Van Wyck Brooks in *America's Coming-of-Age*, New York, 1915, reprinted in Philip Rahv, *Literature in America*, Cleveland, 1957). And rather than a "storyteller in verse" with "power to transplant to American literature some of the colour and melody and romantic charm of the complex European literature he had studied" (William P. Trent, "Longfellow," *CHAL*), Longfellow is considered "bounded by his books and he cannot see beyond them" (Gorman, *A Victorian American*).

That Longfellow ceased to appeal to certain moderns of the twenties and thirties is illustrated by I. A. Richards's experiment, described in *Practical Criticism* (New York, 1929), in which 92 percent of his students judged Longfellow's "In the Churchyard at Cambridge" unfavorably—"by far the most disliked" of the thirteen poems they criticized. And Ludwig Lewisohn in *Expression in America* (New York, 1932) says: "Who, except wretched schoolchildren, now reads Longfellow? . . . He never touches poetry. He borrows form and accepts content from without. . . . To minds concerned with the imaginative interpretation of man, of nature and of human life, Longfellow has nothing left to say."

Responding to the type of disparagement found in Lewisohn and others (such as V. L. Parrington) who found "little intellect" and "little creative originality" in Longfellow, G. R. Elliot in "Gentle Shades of Longfellow," in *The Cycle of Modern Poetry* (Princeton, N.J., 1929), argues persuasively that the modern taste is too caught up in aesthetic dogmas to recognize Longfellow's vital place in the mainstream of American poetry. Saying that the academics have "a fatal aversion for American naïveté," Elliott proposes a literary-historical study of American literature which views its past growth "more largely and more organically." Commenting on Longfellow's simplicity, George Saintsbury in *Prefaces and Essays* (London, 1933) asserts that while one never has to question Longfellow's meaning, his meaning is never contemptible and is sometimes very admirable. Saintsbury advocates selectivity in evaluating Longfellow's poetry—which already had been a practice of Longfellow's most discerning critics but which allowed a hasty discounting, in Saintsbury's case, of *Evangeline*, "The Arsenal at Springfield," and the sonnets.

An important contribution to the revaluation of Longfellow during the thirties was Odell Shepard's introduction to *Representative Selections* of Longfellow's writings. Discussing Longfellow's environment, opinions, limitations, and popularity, Shepard notes weaknesses such as Longfellow's uncritical temper, incomprehensive grasp of contemporary fact, self-indulgent romanticism, escape to the past, and flinching "from all violence, satire, and stern denunciation"; yet he balances these by praising Longfellow's success in "saying what all have thought and in singing what all have felt," his "harmony and unity of the whole composition," and his deepening "our sense of the American past," thereby providing a link with what we have been. In the same vein as Shepard, Howard Mumford Jones called for a revaluation of Longfellow, first in "The Longfellow Nobody Knows" (*Outlook*, 8 August 1928) and later in *American Writers on American Literature*, edited by John A. Macy (New York, 1934). While recognizing that Longfellow lacks depth and sharpness of philosophy, Jones esteems his narrative talent, sense of humor, and command of the sonnet, and considers "lucidity, gentleness, musicality" his essential qualities. It was also in the midthirties that Van Wyck Brooks in *The Flowering of New England* (New York, 1936) revised his earlier opinion and asserted that while "Longfellow's flaccidity debarred him from the front rank," his work possessed "a quality, a unity of feeling and tone, that gave him a place apart among popular poets."

Three of the most disinterested views of Longfellow's place in literature appeared approximately a century after the publication of *Evangeline* and *The Song of Hiawatha*, thus harmonizing with Samuel Johnson's test of literary merit. Norman Holmes Pearson writes about Longfellow's function as "laureate of the common man" and as poet "of the castle and the court" in "Both Longfellows" (*University Review*, Summer 1950). In justifying Longfellow's fame, Pearson emphasizes his powers in myth-making by which he helps restore to a nation a "past function of poetry." George Arms in *The Fields Were Green: A New View of Bryant, Whittier, Holmes, Lowell, and Longfellow* (Stanford, Calif., 1953) says the "schoolroom poets" are unpopular with twentieth-century moderns because of differences in conceptions of poetry or aesthetic taste. "Longfellow's age took comfort in extensive moral explanation and was uneasy when wit was forced to its attention; our age is hot for wit and boggles at direct moral intent." Arms sums up his succinct and fair-minded evaluation by asserting that "though Longfellow does not go deeply into human experience, he sees with a good deal of clarity and poise that life which comes to his view." And Howard Nemerov in his introduction to *Longfellow: Selected Poetry* affirms that Longfellow is a genuine, though minor poet who employs allegory, personification, and anecdote rather than symbol, metaphor, and myth. Recognizing that Longfellow stretched his modest gifts too far, Nemerov nevertheless defends Longfellow's didacticism and clarity against the now-current fashion for obscurity and implication. Longfellow's moralizing is often "poetically just"; that is, it grows organically from the body of the poem and has "the force of a formal close" which brings the measure and the meaning to a resolution together. Arms is not so generous with the didactic element, and he suggests the improvement of several poems by excluding certain lines and stanzas—particularly the moral at the end. It is interesting that William Dean Howells similarly suggested in "The Art of Longfellow" that "The Village Blacksmith" would be improved by omitting the last two stanzas "which make it a homily."

Critical views in the sixties which diminish Longfellow's reputation are found in Roy Harvey Pearce's *The Continuity of American Poetry* (Princeton, N.J., 1961); Marcus Cunliffe's *The Literature of the United States* (Baltimore, Md., 1964); Richard Ruland's "Longfellow and the Modern Reader" (*EJ*, Sept. 1966); and Hyatt H. Waggoner's *American Poets: From the Puritans to the Present* (Boston, 1968). Pearce says that Longfellow "glosses over hard fact and harder motivation," and that "desiring the universal, he failed to see that it could be achieved only through a meticulous attention to the particular." Indicating his dislike of priggishness in Longfellow's novels and unreality in *Hiawatha*, Cunliffe is of the opinion that Longfellow's reputation has declined not because of his Brahminism, but because of "an inability to transcend the requirements of his generation which he so admirably met." Ruland attributes Longfellow's decline to the limited conception held by the nineteenth-century writer and audience alike that the poet's role is to state the values of his culture in language and forms which are both acceptable and beautiful. And, contrary to his stated desire to rehabilitate the "schoolroom poets," Waggoner comes down hard on Longfellow. He severely criticizes "The Psalm of Life" and "Excelsior"—horses which already had been beaten to death—and by selecting a few lines expressing Longfellow's "true" inner doubts and feeling, concludes that Longfellow "was a very sad poet who became not simply banal but incoherent and confused when he tried to cheer himself or others."

There is an element of truth in Waggoner's conclusion—Longfellow did have inner doubts and troubles and was not simply a facile optimist; yet to take Waggoner's view exclusively means to discount much of Longfellow's poetry as hypocritical and false. A clearer perspective on this question is found in William Charvat's previously unpublished essay, "Longfellow," in *The Profession of Authorship in America, 1800–1870* (Columbus, Ohio, 1968).[1] Separating Longfellow the "public poet" from "private poets" such as Emily Dickinson and "mass poets" such as James Whitcomb Riley, Charvat declares that Longfellow recognized the unpleasant realities of frustration, failure, weariness, deprival, and death in the life of the average citizen, and taught in his poetry the acceptance of life's labors and sorrows. Robert S. Ward in "The Integrity of Longfellow's Philosophic Perspective" (*Carrell*, Dec. 1960) also argues against the point of view held by Waggoner. By comparing the early "Psalm of Life" with "Two Rivers," a poem representative of Longfellow's final period, Ward affirms that Longfellow maintained a consistent system of beliefs from 1838 to his death in 1882 and that his changes in attitude over the years "are not inconsistent with his former views but developments out of them."

The most recent book-length studies of Longfellow are Edward L. Hirsh's *Henry Wadsworth Longfellow*, Cecil Brown Williams's *Henry Wadsworth Longfellow*, and Newton Arvin's *Longfellow: His Life and Work*. Hirsh's brief but compact UMPAW study presents a generally sympathetic yet objective analysis of Longfellow's prose and poetry. Longfellow's chief faults, according to Hirsh, are an "inability to probe life's dark or sordid aspects," fondness for literary diction, and "explication of the already-evident"; yet Longfellow has an "impressive tonal range," and "within the age's literary conventions, Longfellow used language skillfully and sensitively." Williams divides his TUSAS book into biography and criticism, the latter being mainly appreciative. Considering Longfellow not a major poet but not a minor one either, Williams calls for a reappraisal of Longfellow—produced by objectively seeing him in terms of biography and literary history.

Arvin's critical biography is by far the most thorough critical study of Longfellow. Written in his usual well-modulated style, Arvin's study

---

1. Printed along with "Longfellow" is Charvat's essay "Longfellow's Income from His Writings, 1840–1852," which first appeared in *PBSA* (First Quarter 1944). This essay shows Longfellow's business acuity in getting the greatest financial return from his poems and prose by publishing first in periodicals, then collecting poems in a small volume, reassembling small volumes into a collected edition, and then making each collection outmoded by publishing new, separate volumes of verse, which in turn formed the basis for a new collected edition.

provides in-depth analyses of Longfellow's major works and of numerous minor poems. Following the method of balancing strengths and
weaknesses (sometimes too apologetically), Arvin finds Longfellow was
at times "facile and flaccid" and "could fall a victim to the bad sentimental taste of his age"; yet "at his best he is an accomplished, sometimes an exquisite, craftsman" who had the strain of the folk poet in
his make-up. In his epilogue, Arvin sums up the various critical attitudes held regarding Longfellow. His conclusion is that Longfellow
was a minor writer who suffered in the twentieth century from a shift
in taste, yet as a demotic poet, he should have an enduring place in
our esteem. Certainly critics of stature such as Arvin, Wagenknecht,
Thompson, and Charvat have through their perceptive and thorough
studies helped ensure that esteem.

Sources and Influences

Given Longfellow's eclectic reading and his methods of composition,
it is obvious there is an important place in Longfellow criticism for
examination of his sources and influences. An extremely narrow way to
look at the subject is to see Longfellow as being mainly a plagiarist.
Since Poe's time, however, few have faulted Longfellow for plagiarism.
Nor have they generally criticized him for being simply derivative, as
did Margaret Fuller in her left-handed defense of Longfellow (*Writings*): "We have been surprised that anyone should have been anxious
to fasten special charges [of plagiarism] upon him, when we had supposed it so obvious that the greater part of his mental stores were derived
from the works of others." Rather, the large number of persons who
have written about Longfellow sources, parallels, echoes, and influences have usually taken Margaret Fuller's premise without her caustic
tone and have recognized Longfellow's indebtedness to writings from
many countries which he transmuted artistically into his own work.

The most complete study in this last category is Paul Morin's *Les
Sources de l'Oeuvre de Henry Wadsworth Longfellow*. Morin begins
his 637-page work by asserting it was natural for Longfellow to assimilate—sometimes unconsciously—writings of European authors into his
own poetry or prose. In defense of Longfellow, Morin affirms that literary borrowing was no more a sin for Longfellow than it was for Chaucer or Shakespeare. Morin's method for the most part is to rely greatly
on parallel texts, although for major works he lists definite sources and
possible sources—finding for *Evangeline*, for example, fifteen books of
the former type and twenty-eight of the latter. Another general treatment of Longfellow's sources is Francesco Viglione's *La Critica Literaria di Henry Wadsworth Longfellow* (2 vols., Florence, 1934) which

examines extensively Longfellow's relationships with various people
and places in America and Europe—with the information being digested
mainly from Viglione's wide reading in secondary works. And Edward
Wagenknecht surveys "Longfellow's Reading" both in an article by
that title (*Boston Public Library Quarterly*, Apr. 1955) and in his
biography.

Although Robert S. Ward argues in "Longfellow's Roots in Yankee
Soil" (*NEQ*, June 1968) that Yankee folklore, especially oral tradition,
was important in Longfellow's works, the mass of studies of this sort
deal almost exclusively with European sources and influences. A suc-
cinct and comprehensive survey of these commentaries is made by
Arvin in his critical biography. For a discussion of French influences,
Edmond Estève in his Bowdoin lecture, *Longfellow et la France* (Brunswick, N.J., 1925), gives a limited but interesting overview; Carl L.
Johnson treats the subject much more extensively in his dissertation,
"Longfellow and France" (Harvard, 1933). In regard to Italy, Emilio
Goggio in "Italian Influences on Longfellow's Works" (*RR*, July 1925)
shows that Longfellow's Italian scholarship was both intensive (in the
case of Dante) and extensive (in the case of the more minor figures).
And as for Spain, Iris Lilian Whitman's *Longfellow and Spain* contains
many extracts from Longfellow's writings which show his practical and
academic grasp of Spanish materials, leading her to conclude that
Spain broadened his appreciation of life and helped him as much as
other European countries to form his literary career. Taking a more
scholarly and objective approach than Whitman, Stanley T. Williams
adds to her examination in *The Spanish Background of American Literature* (2 vols., New Haven, Conn., 1955), in which he points to
Longfellow's comprehension of the Spanish spirit and his "long service
of introducing to America the literature of Spain"—most remarkably
through his translations or adaptations.

A great deal has been written about the influence of Germany and
German literature on Longfellow, beginning with a series of doctoral
dissertations emerging from German universities. Two examples of this
sort which cite Longfellow's references to Germany and German subjects and which suggest his work is infused with the German spirit are
J. Perry Worden's *Über Longfellows Beziehungen zur Deutschen Lit-
teratur* (Halle, 1900) and Friedrich Kratz's *Das Deutsche Element in
den Werken H. W. Longfellow* (Wasserburg, 1920). J. T. Hatfield's
subtitle to *New Light on Longfellow—With Special Reference to His
Relations to Germany*—indicates his special focus. Hatfield discounts
some of the German borrowings and influences earlier ascribed to Longfellow, yet still finds the German influence to be large. Hatfield's study

is especially valuable in its account of Longfellow's friendship with Bernard Rolker, Ferdinand Freiligrath, and others, and in its lists of Longfellow's German friends and correspondents and German studies and reading. Orie W. Long's *Literary Pioneers: Early American Explorers of European Culture* (Cambridge, Mass., 1935) has a chapter on Longfellow derived in part from examination of letters and journals at the Craigie-Longfellow House. Long considers Longfellow the most important of the early "ambassadors of learning" who "made Goethe a living figure in academic halls." In a balanced article on "Longfellow and Germany" (*DN*, 1952), Anna J. DeArmond concludes that while the German influence broadened Longfellow, it also encouraged his tendency to formlessness and softness. And Henry A. Pochmann in *German Culture in America: Philosophical and Literary Influences, 1600–1900* (Madison, Wis., 1957) believes that Longfellow was most influenced by the German spirit because of his natural sympathy for German literature, his stays in Germany, and his work with German literature after his returns to America.

Longfellow's relationship with Scandinavia is examined by Andrew R. Hilen in *Longfellow and Scandinavia: A Study of the Poet's Relationship with the Northern Languages and Literature*. Hilen is especially good in tracing the influence of Tegnér and concludes that Longfellow's relationship with Scandinavia "was essentially the product not of scholarly inquisitiveness but of his interest as a romanticist in remote and unfamiliar scenes."

Much of what has been written about the long narratives deals with influences and sources. In regard to *Evangeline*, Edward Thostenberg in "Is Longfellow's *Evangeline* a Product of Swedish Influence?" (*Poet-Lore*, Autumn 1908) first pointed out the parallels between Longfellow's Nova Scotia and the Swedish landscape described in his article on Tegnér's *Frithiof's Saga*. Similarities or a "rapprochement" between *Jocelyn* and *Evangeline* are illustrated by Mario Mormile in *L'idylle épique de Lamartine et Longfellow: Étude de Jocelyn et d'Evangeline* (Rome, 1967). M. G. Hill in "Some of Longfellow's Sources for the Second Part of *Evangeline*" (*PMLA*, Nov. 1916) examines as source material Fremont's *Expedition to the Rocky Mountains*, Sealsfield's *Life in the New World*, and Kip's *Early Jesuit Missions*. And Manning Hawthorne and H. W. L. Dana in *The Origin and Development of Longfellow's "Evangeline"* (Portland, Maine, 1947) consider anew the historical background, genesis, and inception of Longfellow's work. They also suggest that *Evangeline* undoubtedly has stimulated the production of more than 250 books and articles on the subject of the Acadians since the poem was published.

The Song of Hiawatha has been the subject of intense source studies ever since Thomas C. Porter in the *Washington National Intelligencer* (26 November 1855) charged that Longfellow borrowed "the entire form, spirit, and many of the most striking incidents" of *Kalevala*. This began a series of attacks and responses, discussed thoroughly by Ernest J. Moyne in *Hiawatha and Kalevala: A Study of the Relationship between Longfellow's "Indian Edda" and the Finnish Epic* (Helsinki, 1963). Moyne exonerates Longfellow of plagiarism, but shows how Longfellow used Anton Schiefner's translation of the *Kalevala* as a model for the meter and form of *Hiawatha*. Although proven wrong in his thesis that Longfellow did not borrow from the *Kalevala*, Waino Nyland in "*Kalevala* as a Reputed Source of Longfellow's *Song of Hiawatha*" (*AL*, Mar. 1950) does point, in his attention to Indian songs, to an interesting area of related study. The subject of Indian folklore elements in *Hiawatha* has in fact been discussed perceptively by Christabel F. Fiske, "Mercerized Folklore in *Hiawatha*" (*Poet-Lore*, Dec. 1920); Stith Thompson, "The Indian Legend of Hiawatha" (*PMLA*, Mar. 1922); Albert Keiser, *The Indian in American Literature* (New York, 1933); and R. M. Davis, "How Indian is *Hiawatha*?" (*MF*, Spring 1957). Fiske shows how in *Hiawatha* the fabric of primitive myths was "mercerized"; that is, "its fibers were shrunken, its surface more lustrous, its colors more vivid or pastel-like than of old." Thompson notes Longfellow's erroneous identification of Hiawatha with Manabozho (which was Schoolcraft's error as well) and then says that Longfellow humanizes Manabozho and emphasizes romantic and poetic elements, thereby departing greatly from the spirit of the myth. Keiser also observes these discrepancies but partially justifies them as stemming from the poet's "kind and delicate nature" and to his tailoring the poem for his contemporaries. Davis, with Fiske and Thompson, says that Longfellow does not grasp the animistic modes of thought behind Indian myths. Despite the validity of these criticisms, we should remind ourselves that Longfellow did not have access to twentieth-century information about Indian anthropology, but rather derived most of his material from George Catlin, J. G. E. Heckewelder, and particularly from Henry Rowe Schoolcraft. These sources, especially the last, are discussed at great length but disjointedly by Chase S. and Stellanova Osborn in *Schoolcraft-Longfellow-Hiawatha* (Lancaster, Pa., 1942).

Sources for *Tales of a Wayside Inn* and *The Golden Legend* are fairly obvious and have not been subjects of controversy. Besides Arvin, W. E. A. Axon, "On the Sources of Longfellow's *Tales of a Wayside Inn*" (*Royal Society Literary Transactions*, 1911), and John Van Schaick, *The Characters in "Tales of a Wayside Inn*," have discussed sources of the *Tales*; the latter book is devoted mainly to biographical sketches of Longfellow's real-life models. Hartmann von Aue's *Der arme Heinrich* as the main source for *The Golden Legend* is discussed superficially in Friedrich Münzner's *Die Quellen zu Longfellows Golden Legend* (Dresden, 1898). By contrast, Carl Hammer, Jr.'s *"Golden Legend" and Goethe's "Faust"* (Baton Rouge, La., 1952) is a carefully documented examination of the many echoes of *Faust*. More important than single correspondences, though, "is the impression that Longfellow's poem derives much of its afflatus" from *Faust*.

Poetic Forms and Methods

Longfellow's poetics have always interested critics, with the best and most expansive discussions being those by Gay Wilson Allen, *American Prosody* (New York, 1935), George Arms, and Newton Arvin. Earlier critics often focused on narrow aspects of Longfellow's poetry, with a disproportionate amount of energy in the nineteenth century and the first decade of this century spent in debating the appropriateness of his hexameters. A learned article which stands above the others of the time is Cornelius C. Felton's review of *Ballads and Other Poems* (*NAR*, July 1842) which places Longfellow's hexameters in the context of the history of the hexameter from the early Greek poetry to the modern-day English and American poetry. In such a context, Felton concludes, Longfellow's is not a true hexameter. Modern criticism, though, is considerably more pragmatic. Allen, for example, analyzes varieties of Longfellow's forms and meters in terms of their effectiveness, and concludes, "On the whole, Longfellow's hexameters are appropriate for his purposes." Likewise, Arvin in discussing *Evangeline* says, "At its most successful, the verse has a kind of grave, slow-paced, mellifluous quality, like a slightly monotonous but not unmusical chant, which is genuinely expressive of its mournful and minor theme."

Poetic matters more closely related to Longfellow's current and future reputation as a poet are his handling of diverse forms of poetry, the technical and lyrical qualities of his nondidactic poems—particularly the sonnets, and his translations. Allen exemplifies a current critical viewpoint when he says Longfellow's translations and imitations of foreign forms directed attention to systems of versification unfamiliar to America and gave us "a wide acquaintance with the chief poetic techniques of the world." Rich possibilities still exist for close readings of his poems, two admirable examples being G. Thomas Tanselle's "Longfellow's 'Serenade' (*The Spanish Student*)," (*Expl*, Feb. 1965) and Michael Zimmerman's "War and Peace: Longfellow's 'The Occultation of Orion'" (*AL*, Jan. 1967). Tanselle's method is to show the poem's movement from the remote to the near and from the concrete to the abstract, reflecting the lover's state of mind. Zimmerman pays close attention to allusions and ambiguities in the poem and to the milieu in which the poem was written to demonstrate Longfellow's "ability to impress upon us a significant, more or less complex feeling by means of metaphor and image, tone, and dramatic situation." In regard to the sonnets, one reason for their success and continuing interest for modern readers, according to Arms, is that they limit the poet to a two-stage movement (scene and analogy) and thus omit a third stage—frequently found in Longfellow's poems—of statement or homily.

As for Longfellow's translations, they continue to receive generally high praise. Whitman (*Longfellow and Spain*) finds that Longfellow's translations from the Spanish hold fairly true to his ideal of "rendering literally the words of a foreign author while at the same time [preserving] the spirit of the original" (Longfellow's "Preface" to the *Coplas*, 1833). Stanley T. Williams (*Spanish Background*) agrees with this thesis and proposes that Longfellow is a good translator because of his gift with words, his facility in verse, and his respect for the original. Longfellow's translations of Dante were held in esteem by his contemporaries; John Fiske in *The Unseen World and Other Essays* (Boston, 1876) declares that Longfellow's translation rises to "something like the grandeur of the original." A more temperate view is held by Angelina La Piana (*Dante's American Pilgrimage*, New Haven, Conn., 1948) who says that general response to Longfellow's translation was favorable, although adverse criticism focused on his literalness, latinate diction, excessive inversions, and rhythmical irregularities. Finally, Arvin somewhat equivocally illustrates that Longfellow's translation of the *Divine Comedy* compares favorably with those by Henry F. Cary and Laurence Binyon. Yet he concludes by esteeming Longfellow as a translator who could preserve the meaning and form of the original lines because "he was a poet himself, because his feeling for languages was so intuitive, and because, for some sorts of poetry, his resources in his own language were so adequate."

Future studies of Longfellow undoubtedly will continue along lines pursued in the 1960s. An indication of this is found in the titles of articles in the Longfellow symposium published in *ESQ* (First Quarter 1970). In the category of biography we find "Voices of Longfellow: *Kavanagh* as Autobiography" by Steven Allaback; "Longfellow and Music" by Robert L. Volz; and "Librarian Longfellow" by Richard Harwell. Longfellow's reputation is treated in Edward Wagenknecht's "Longfellow and Howells," which illustrates Howells's favorable criticisms of Longfellow. Longfellow's poetics is the subject of Evelyn Thomas Helmick's "Longfellow's Lyric Poetry." The relatively untouched area of Longfellow's themes is probed by Phyllis Franklin in "The Importance of Time in Longfellow's Works." And the study of sources and influences—which has been prominent in Longfellow criticism since the mid-nineteenth century—continues with new information from Carl L. Johnson in "Longfellow Studies in France"; Ernest J. Moyne in "Longfellow and Kah-ge-ga-gah-bowh" (Longfellow's American Indian acquaintance who lectured in the United States and Europe); and Robert Stafford Ward in "The Influence of [Giambattista] Vico upon Longfellow." As was the case with these writers, it seems likely that in the next decade or so, critics will cease to debate Longfellow's relative rank as an American poet and will go on to evaluate his best literary output in terms of traditional literary criticism. Ironically, it may be that the best criticism will be by persons such as Tanselle and Zimmerman who use some of the methods of the "new critics" who had so harshly dismissed Longfellow. And it is almost certain that the biographical materials being made widely available by Hilen, Ward, Moyne, and others will help provide new bases for interesting reinterpretations of Longfellow's works.

James Russell Lowell

ROBERT A. REES

> He will doubtless cease to be one of our superstitions, but he
> will always remain one of our chief glories.
>
> William C. Brownell (1909)

HOLMES SAID of Lowell, "He was alive, alive all over." Not an isolated poet nor an inward-oriented artist patiently growing toward perfection, Lowell blossomed early in direct relationship to his individual background and the general atmosphere and issues of his time—and he blossomed perennially, but in many varieties of bloom. In studying Lowell, one must keep in mind his versatility, his interaction with his milieu, and his vitality.

Some writers can be studied in their texts alone; others are understood far better by resorting also to biographical and historical aids. Lowell, an enormously talented man of letters who never had a real mentor and who was not divinely endowed with patience or self-criticism, is one of the latter. Although his talent was not efficiently channeled, it may have been greater than that of contemporaries who have —deservedly—fared better with the critics.

BIBLIOGRAPHY

There is no modern, fully cumulative Lowell bibliography. However, a primary bibliography will be available in 1972 or 1973 with the publication of Vol. 6 of Jacob Blanck's *Bibliography of American Literature*. According to Blanck, "The Lowell list will contain approximately 250 primary entries; about 200 additional entries in the section of Lowell reprints (*i.e.*, books bearing Lowell's name on the title-page but containing no first edition material); and a large number of books by authors other than Lowell which contain material by him, none of which is first book appearance."[1]

---

1. Letter from Jacob Blanck to Robert A. Rees, 15 October 1970. Quoted with permission.

The earliest bibliography of value is the one at the end of volume
II of Horace E. Scudder's biography, *James Russell Lowell* (2 vols., Boston, 1901). The works are arranged chronologically in order of appearance and the listings include the place of first publication. The first
Lowell bibliography in book form was George W. Cooke's *A Bibliography of James Russell Lowell* (Boston, 1906). It contains primary and
secondary bibliography, each separated into useful categories, and it is
still the only bibliography dealing extensively with nineteenth-century
critical literature. Although some entries are inaccurate and the volume is now badly out of date, it is unique and valuable. It provides
relatively few references to periodical literature before 1870.

Careful scholarship within a limited area is available in Luther S.
Livingston's *A Bibliography of the First Editions in Book Form of the
Writings of James Russell Lowell* (New York, 1914), which is based to
a large extent on a collection of Jacob C. Chamberlain (and is therefore sometimes called the "Chamberlain Bibliography"). In spite of
the title, it includes a few of the Lowell biographies written after his
death and describes items of the broadside or souvenir type. Fewer
than fifty primary items are in book form. Although more limited in
its coverage than Cooke's, Livingston's collection contains more information on certain entries and is generally more reliable.

The selective bibliography of the 1917–1921 edition of *CHAL* lists
35 primary works, 19 works which Lowell edited or to which he contributed, and about 120 biographical and critical items.

Since the publication of Cooke's and Livingston's bibliographies, a
number of articles, notes, dissertations, and books have added new
items which have helped to clarify and refine certain aspects of the
Lowell canon.

Although nominally devoted to history, Grace Griffin's *Writings on
American History* (Washington, D.C., 1936) cites "representative"
works in many areas and provides leads which do not appear in other
bibliographies and guides. The annotated bibliography in Harry
Hayden Clark and Norman Foerster's *James Russell Lowell: Representative Selections* (New York, 1947) is a valuable guide to the most
significant Lowell scholarship before 1946. It supersedes an earlier and
slightly shorter version in Clark's *Major American Poets* (New York,
1936).

The chapter notes to Leon Howard's *Victorian Knight-Errant: The
Early Literary Career of James Russell Lowell* (Berkeley, Calif.,
1952) provide some useful bibliographic information on material covering Lowell's career up to the Civil War.

Martin Duberman's *James Russell Lowell* (Boston, 1966) was written chiefly from manuscript sources and its bibliography is not intended to include all previous scholarship. However, the explanatory remarks on pp. 373–380 and the categorically arranged bibliographies evaluate certain titles and provide an excellent orientation to a number of earlier works.

TEXTS AND EDITIONS

The standard edition is *Writings of James Russell Lowell,* published by Houghton, Mifflin & Co., in 1890 (Boston and New York). This edition, known as the Riverside edition, is preferred by most scholars because the selections for the ten volumes (six of prose and four of poetry) were made by Lowell himself. An eleventh volume, published after Lowell's death, includes essays selected by Charles Eliot Norton, Lowell's literary executor. The Elmwood edition of 1904 is almost identical to the Riverside, but includes three volumes of letters edited by Norton, which had been published separately ten years earlier. In this edition, Norton added new letters, corrected errors, and identified additional addressees in the earlier letters.

Many Lowell writings excluded in these editions appeared in collections published subsequently. The most important of these are: *The Function of the Poet and Other Essays,* early essays and reviews edited by Albert Mordell (Boston, 1920); *Lectures on the English Poets,* Lowell's 1855 lectures at the Lowell Institute (Cleveland, Ohio, 1897); and *The Anti-Slavery Papers of James Russell Lowell* (Boston, 1902), two volumes of essays from the *Pennsylvania Freeman* (1844) and the *National Anti-Slavery Standard* (1845–1850).

The Cambridge edition of *The Complete Poetical Works of James Russell Lowell* (Boston, 1897; "sixth printing," 1968) is the only comprehensive anthology of Lowell's poetry. It includes the poetry from the Riverside edition plus a small group of poems published in C. E. Norton's edition of *Last Poems of James Russell Lowell* (Boston, 1895). This volume contains a biographical sketch, headnotes, and a chronological list of Lowells' poems—all by Horace Scudder.

The only new volume of poetry to appear in the twentieth century is the *Uncollected Poems of James Russell Lowell* (Philadelphia, 1950), edited by Thelma Smith and based on her 1945 University of Pennsylvania dissertation. Miss Smith's volume includes 135 poems printed originally in newspapers and magazines, which were omitted from the Elmwood edition but not specifically rejected by Lowell. While admitting that Lowell's best poems "are still to be found among those selected by the poet for his collected works," Miss Smith nevertheless feels that these additional poems, which span Lowell's lifetime, are necessary for a full view of the poet. She thinks Lowell would have included some of these in the Riverside edition had he remembered them. Miss Smith's annotated edition identifies available manuscript sources and provides bibliographic information about the publication of each poem. She mistakenly attributes a poem by Arthur Hugh Clough to Lowell.

Clark and Foerster's *James Russell Lowell: Representative Selections* includes a carefully balanced collection of poems, letters, and prose. *Lowell: Essays, Poems and Letters*, edited by William Smith Clark II (New York, 1948), is the only other modern anthology devoted exclusively to Lowell.

Of special interest is Scully Bradley's facsimile edition of the *Pioneer* (New York, 1947), the journal edited by Lowell and Robert Carter in 1843. Bradley's introduction is excellent and his footnotes are extensive.

The only single volume of Lowell material to appear recently and the only Lowell volume presently available in paperback is Herbert F. Smith's edition of the *Literary Criticism of James Russell Lowell* (Lincoln, Neb., 1969).

The work of Lowell's which has been reprinted most often is *The Vision of Sir Launfal*, probably because it lent itself to moralistic interpretations, which were popular in schools until recent decades. With the advent of the reprint houses, most of Lowell's works, as well as many works about him, are now available, including the Elmwood edition and Norton's edition of the *Letters*.

MANUSCRIPTS AND LETTERS

Lowell's early recognition and a long, creative life suggest that his manuscripts would be found in quantity and in diverse places. *American Literary Manuscripts* (Austin, Tex., 1960) lists sixty-two depositories of Lowell manuscripts and letters.

As Lowell was a Harvard alumnus (by the skin of his teeth) and a Harvard professor, it is not surprising that many collections of his manuscripts and letters are to be found at Harvard; the Houghton Library contains the largest collections of Lowell material. Other significant collections are in the following public and private libraries: Boston Public, Colby College, Harvard University Archives, Hispanic Society (New York), Huntington, Library of Congress, Massachusetts Historical Society, Morgan Library, New York Public, University of

Pennsylvania, University of Texas, University of Virginia, and Yale University.

The best guide to manuscript sources is by Duberman, who provides a detailed list of the holdings in public and private libraries as well as in eleven privately owned collections. Duberman also includes a list of auction house catalogues, some of which describe manuscripts now lost.

The first collection of Lowell's letters was edited by Charles Eliot Norton, who brought out his two-volume *Letters of James Russell Lowell* in 1894. Like many nineteenth-century letter collections, Norton's has limited value. While acknowledging that "few writers have given in their letters a more faithful representation of themselves, and of few men is the epistolary record more complete from youth to age," Norton gives a bowdlerized version of the letters with the justification that "portions of every man's life are essentially private, and knowledge of them belongs by right only to those intimates whom he himself may see fit to trust with his entire confidence" (that is, Norton). After stating that "there was nothing in Mr. Lowell's life to be concealed and excused," Norton makes considerable use of ellipses, saying, "Nothing will, I hope, be found in these volumes which [Lowell] himself might have regretted to see in print." A literary executor has many difficult choices, but to the modern reader it seems unnecessary for the private Lowell to have been multilated to preserve the formal public image. Norton's excising and clipping seem especially unfortunate because many of the letters to which he had access have since been lost or destroyed. As an early critic remarked, "The result is like a photograph from which the retoucher has taken all lines that give strength and character to the face. . . . For the greater part of the thousand pages we ponder over the asterisks of omission, and wonder, in no spirit of idle curiosity, what Lowell really wrote" (William B. Cairns, "James Russell Lowell: A Centenary View," *Nation*, 22 February 1919).

The only other published volume of Lowell letters is M. A. de Wolfe Howe's *New Letters of James Russell Lowell* (New York, 1932). These letters, most of them to Lowell's daughter, are edited more honestly than those presented by Norton, and from them a clearer picture of Lowell emerges.

In addition to small groups of letters published in scholarly journals (such as those from Lowell to Nathan Hale, Jr., edited by Philip Graham for *TSLL*, Winter 1962), Lowell letters have appeared in volumes of published correspondence of his friends: *Letters of John Holmes to James Russell Lowell and Others* (Boston, 1917); *The Scholar Friends: Letters of Francis James Child and James Russell*

Lowell, edited by M. A. de Wolfe Howe and G. W. Cottrell, Jr. (Cambridge, Mass., 1952); and *Browning to His American Friends: Letters Between the Brownings, the Storys and James Russell Lowell*, edited by Gertrude Reese Hudson (London, 1965). Also of interest is Ada Nisbet's dissertation, "Some Letters of Thomas Hughes to James Russell Lowell: A Chapter in Anglo-Americana" (U.C.L.A., 1947), and Quentin G. Johnston's M.A. thesis, "The Letters of James Russell Lowell to Robert Carter, 1842–1876" (Oregon, 1956). Miss Nisbet's notes documenting the Hughes letters quote extensively from unpublished Lowell letters. The forty-seven letters from Lowell to Carter are now in the Berg Collection of the New York Public Library.

Some of Lowell's diplomatic correspondence as Minister to Spain is published in *Impressions of Spain* [by] *James Russell Lowell*, compiled by J. B. Gilder and with an introduction by A. A. Adee (Boston, 1899).

Since Lowell was one of the greatest letter writers in American literature and since his letters have been so inadequately edited, a new scholarly edition of his correspondence is long overdue.

BIOGRAPHY

Though Lowell is extensively discussed in literary histories and critical works and though he is mentioned in biographies of other great men of his time, there are relatively few biographies of Lowell. Of these only two qualify as full-scale historical biographies: Horace Scudder's *James Russell Lowell: A Biography* and Martin Duberman's *James Russell Lowell*.

Scudder's book was preceded by such works as Francis H. Underwood's *The Poet and the Man: Recollections and Appreciations of James Russell Lowell* (Boston, 1892) and Edward Everett Hale, Jr.'s *James Russell Lowell and His Friends* (Boston, 1899). Written shortly after his death by those who saw him as the dominant literary figure of America, these books have little to recommend them to the modern scholar. Both authors are more interested in praising than in portraying and evaluating Lowell. An anonymous reviewer lamented particularly the superficiality of Hale's biography since Hale was "perhaps the one surviving man best acquainted with Lowell and his career from the brilliant start to the honored close." He saw Hale's book as "a series of gossipy reminiscences" which were "interesting . . . but also disappointing" ("Littérateur, Ambassador, Patriot, Cosmopolite," *Academy*, 29 July, 1899).

Two noteworthy views by Lowell's later contemporaries are those of

Henry James and William Dean Howells, both of whom had long and intimate associations with Lowell. In his "Studies of Lowell" (a reprint of an essay in the September 1900 issue of *Scribner's*) in *Literary Friends and Acquaintance* (New York, 1900), Howells warmly recalls many visits with Lowell, especially at Elmwood. He concludes, "I believe neither in heroes nor in saints; but I believe in great and good men, and among such men Lowell was the richest nature I have known. His nature was not always serene and pellucid; it was sometimes roiled by the currents that counter and cross in all of us; but it was without the least alloy of insincerity, and it was never darkened by the shadow of a selfish fear. His genius was an instrument that responded in affluent harmony to the power that made him a humorist and that made him a poet, and appointed him rarely to be quite either alone."

Henry James recalled his long friendship with Lowell in two *Atlantic Monthly* essays (Jan. 1892 and Jan. 1897; the first was reprinted in *Essays in London and Elsewhere*, New York, 1893). James, who certainly was not blind to Lowell's shortcomings, considered him "completely representative." After rereading Lowell, James says, "He looms, in such a renewed impression, very large and ripe and sane, and if he was an admirable man of letters there should be no want of emphasis on the first term of the title." He concludes, "He was strong without narrowness; he was wise without bitterness and bright without folly. That appears for the most part the clearest ideal of those who handle the English form, and he was altogether in the straight tradition. This tradition will surely not forfeit its great part in the world so long as we continue occasionally to know it by what is so solid in performance and so stainless in character."

Scudder's two-volume study is a surprisingly competent work for its time. Scudder was the first scholar to use letters and manuscripts in telling the story of Lowell's life, and he is the first to suggest the complexities of the man. While Scudder, like Norton, is cautious and conservative when it comes to the proprieties of biography, one must credit him at least with an attempt at objectivity. It is a tribute to Scudder that subsequent biographers have been indebted to him and that his work was the standard biography for over sixty years.

Ferris Greenslet, *James Russell Lowell: His Life and Work* (Boston, 1905), proposed to write "a biography of the mind," but Greenslet, like others before him in the nineteenth century, set limitations which precluded any presentation of a viable image of the mind or the man. In his introduction Greenslet says, "In this narrative . . . there will be little occasion to adduce any piece of 'bare truth' that the man himself in his essays, his poems, and his letters has not made a part of the record." In spite of these limitations, and in spite of the fact that his work is derivative, Greenslet is at times accurate and perceptive about some aspects of Lowell's life. His chapter on Lowell's poetry is especially penetrating. Greenslet's later study, *The Lowells and Their Seven Worlds* (Boston, 1946), which is devoted to the Lowell family, adds little to his picture of Lowell. Perhaps the best brief biography of Lowell was that written for the *DAB* (1933) by M. A. de Wolfe Howe, who makes a masterful summary of Lowell's life and an estimate of his place in American literature.

Only two major biographical studies of Lowell appeared between Greenslet's work and Duberman's: Richmond Croom Beatty's *James Russell Lowell* (Nashville, Tenn., 1942) and Leon Howard's *Victorian Knight-Errant: A Study of the Early Literary Career of James Russell Lowell*. Both studies are limited. In his preface Beatty admits to a bias ("almost everybody appears to have one") and then proceeds to manifest that bias on almost every page. As a southerner, Beatty seems incapable of forgiving Lowell for being a northerner and an abolitionist. He says Lowell "never understood history, . . . never comprehended politics. . . . Moreover, Harvard scholar though he was, he never made any effort worth mentioning to understand the civilization of the South. He proved himself, from his undergraduate days, a dupe of the most irresponsible propaganda his age afforded." Nor does Beatty give Lowell much credit as a thinker and a critic: "For the central facts about [Lowell's] mind were its discursiveness, its self-conscious irrelevance, and inner certainty, the compulsion of which was always present to disperse his meditations. . . . The evidence is unmistakable that any basic coherence in his thinking about literature appears to have come to him only at intervals, and by happy though sadly infrequent accidents." At times Beatty shows enough insight into Lowell to suggest he might have written a far better book.

Beatty's view on Lowell and the South does not jibe with that of Howells, who said of Lowell, in his reminiscence mentioned above (*Scribner's*, Sept. 1900): "He had a great tenderness for the broken and ruined South, whose sins he felt that he had had his share in visiting upon her, and he was willing to do what he could to ease her sorrows in the case of any particular Southerner." Howells's view is supported by Max L. Griffin's "Lowell and the South" (*TSE*, 1950). Griffin feels that Lowell's abolitionism was moral and philosophical rather than political and sectional, and that it did not affect his personal friendships with southerners.

Leon Howard's study is limited by design. Howard did not intend to write a full or a conventional biography; instead he wanted "to discover the extent to which a meticulous examination of an individual's entire literary output, within the human context of its origin, could improve one's understanding of the individual himself and of the age in which he lived." Howard's book is an interesting study in literary research; it is also the most comprehensive view we have of Lowell's life and times through his literature. Howard may give more information than some readers would wish, but he draws extensively and intelligently upon the canon of Lowell's creative work to provide us with many new biographical insights. One should not quibble with the limits stipulated by Howard, but one cannot help but wish he had carried his study past the year 1857 when, for him, Lowell reached a state of arrested development; the success of Howard's approach to the early Lowell makes us want to see all of Lowell in such a context.

Although written earlier than Howard's book, H. H. Clark's biographical introduction to *James Russell Lowell: Representative Selections* presents an interesting view that differs from Howard's premise. For Clark, Lowell's life underwent progressive change from beginning to end. Clark traces the development of Lowell's life and career through three major stages—the Humanitarian (to 1850), the Nationalist (1850 to 1867), and the Natural Aristocrat (1867 to 1891)—and makes a convincing argument that the evolution from one to the other was organic. This argument is based on Clark's earlier study, "Lowell— Humanitarian, Nationalist, or Humanist?" (*SP*, July 1930), in which he argued that Lowell's life was "an essentially progressive and symmetrical expansion from a center, a steady widening of circles."

Duberman's intended scope was all-inclusive, and he had access to practically every manuscript relevant to Lowell's life. He made good use of those materials in filling in the gaps and fleshing out the details of Lowell's life and in correcting errors that have accumulated over the years. Duberman states that his purpose in writing the book was not "to restore Lowell's stature as a Renaissance figure or a literary giant" (he feels that Lowell was neither), but "to restore him as a man." Duberman is interested in Lowell as a virtuous man, as a man of character, and not as a man of letters. One has the feeling that part of the real Lowell is still missing and that Duberman's easy dismissal of Lowell as an artist ("There are many moments in his poetry, long sections in his essays, which deserve respect, . . . but they remain incidental; rather than high-lighting a consolidated achievement, they call attention to its absence.") suggests that he does not fully understand Lowell. But Duberman's study is likely to be the best that we will have for some time. Perhaps it need disappoint only those who still consider Lowell primarily as a litterateur, as a man who gave American letters a dignity that it has seldom had in our history.

A biographical study of Lowell which has appeared since Duberman's, Claire McGlinchee's TUSAS *James Russell Lowell* (New York, 1967), is hardly worthy of mention. A glib and superficial study, it contributes nothing to our understanding of Lowell.

One of the difficulties that have faced his biographers and one of the reasons why the essential Lowell has in one way or another eluded all of his biographers, is that he was so diverse and so versatile. If comparison often places him second in some category of literary or other endeavors, rarely has one man demonstrated excellence in so many facets. He was: poet, essayist, humorist, letter-writer, linguist, critic. He was also: abolitionist, journalist, crusader for political and other reform, diplomat, teacher of modern foreign languages and literatures, public lecturer, after-dinner speaker, and editor (*The Pioneer, The Atlantic Monthly,* and *The North American Review*). As Frank R. Stockton said in a "Personal Tribute to Lowell" written at the time of Lowell's death, "Without occupying the highest rank in any of his vocations, he stood in front of his fellow citizens because he held so high a rank in so many of them" (*The Writer,* Sept. 1891).

There are areas of Lowell's life which need further attention. Though a great deal is known of Lowell and Lowell's thinking from the time of his youth, his letters are revelatory on some matters and carefully silent on others. These areas of reverberating silence involve his relationships with his family and his feeling about his mother's insanity. The silence is entirely in keeping with nineteenth-century reticence; it indicates no scandal, but it cuts off a means of insight into Lowell as a creative artist. That he had a morbid streak far deeper than his contemporaries realized or reported can be deduced from many *passim* remarks. And no one has satisfactorily come to terms with Lowell's mysticism, an aspect of his life on which there is a good deal of divided opinion. Psychoanalysis, applied through the veil of over a century and based on fragmentary evidence, would be foolish and dangerous, but some new attempt to evaluate and to interpret all of Lowell's character and personality is needed.

Another area that needs further exploration is the influence of Lowell's wives upon his moral and intellectual patterns. There is speculation that Maria was more devoted to abolition than he was and that she was more creative. There are also indications that Frances did not like Lowell's dialect poetry; since moderns consider this one of his strongest areas, did she inhibit him from developing further along this line?

Perhaps there are parts of the Lowell puzzle which we will never find, but until we understand more about the complexities of his personality we will never completely understand him as a creative artist. Perhaps the key to the puzzle lies in the works themselves. And until a biographer comes along who has a greater interest in Lowell's total creative output—bad as well as good—we are not likely to get the story of Lowell's life which we need and which he deserves.

CRITICISM

James Russell Lowell's critical reputation has never been very secure. In almost every decade since he started writing, he has been praised by some critics and damned by others—sometimes for the same thing. One could generalize, however, that before his death Lowell was praised for things that were not true of him and after his death damned for things that were.

Lowell's critics seem always to lament that he was not something other than he was: a more disciplined poet, less a dilettante, more patriotic, less a Puritan, more a scholar, less an Anglophile, more an abolitionist, and so on. Critics wishing that Lowell were not himself seem to reflect Poe's sentiment on first meeting Lowell: "He is not half the noble looking person I expected to see."

While a good deal of nineteenth-century criticism is essentially effusive and of little critical worth to modern readers, there have been from the beginning a few critics who have tried to be objective about Lowell. Of Lowell's early contemporaries, perhaps the views of Edgar Allan Poe and Margaret Fuller are most significant. Poe felt that Lowell was the best poet in America with the exception of Longfellow and "perhaps one other" (presumably Poe himself), essentially because of the vigor of Lowell's imagination. Poe, however, felt that Lowell's ear for rhythm was imperfect and his artistic ability of second rank. Poe was less than enthusiastic about *A Fable for Critics*, which he found "essentially 'loose'—ill conceived and feebly executed as well in detail as in general" and lacking polish (*Southern Literary Messenger*, Mar. 1849). Poe's estimate may have been colored by Lowell's finding him "two-fifths sheer fudge" in the *Fable*.

Margaret Fuller was more sharply critical of Lowell and, in her estimate of his reputation, almost prophetic. Speaking of Longfellow, she says, "Though imitative, his [poetry] is not mechanical. We cannot say as much for Lowell, who, we must declare it, though to the grief of some friends, and the disgust of more, is absolutely wanting in the true spirit and tone of poesy. His interest in the moral questions of the day has supplied the want of vitality in himself; his great facility at versification has enabled him to fill the ear with a copious stream of pleasant sound. But his verse is stereotyped; his thought sounds no depth, and posterity will not remember him." In retaliation, Lowell painted a most unflattering portrait of Miss Fuller in the *Fable* and refused to remove or soften it in later editions.

Lowell's death in 1891 stimulated some of the most vigorous criticism of him in the nineteenth century. Thomas Wentworth Higginson is perhaps representative of those who were extravagant in their evaluations of Lowell. Higginson (*Nation*, 13 August 1891) called the "Commemoration Ode" "the finest single poem yet produced in this country"; and Lowell himself "our foremost critic." If Higginson is close to the mark in these estimates, he was clearly off the mark in stating that "no American author, unless it be Emerson, has achieved a securer hold upon a lasting fame."

An opposite, almost violent reaction to Lowell is found in an anonymous review of his *Last Poems* (1895) in the *Athenaeum* (4 January 1896). The reviewer considers Lowell a third-rate poet primarily because of his inability to use metaphor properly: "The figure of speech was to him speech at its finest elevation; and he laid violent and indiscriminate hands on everything that could be compared to anything else." He adds, "But after all it is not the prevalence of bad lines, of false metaphors, of any other external blemish, that forbids us to assign Lowell any place among the conspicuous poets of his time; it is his radically prosaic attitude of mind and his radically prosaic construction of verse. . . . He gets the right number of syllables in his lines, but he seems to get them by counting on his fingers." He concludes, "That he should ever have seemed to the American critic or the American public a poet of national importance is, perhaps, the severest criticism on itself that the American nation has ever made."

A more rational and perceptive English view is that in "An English Estimate of Lowell" (*ForumNY*, Oct. 1891) by Frederic William Farrar. Farrar points out that Lowell "might have been greater, had he in some respects been less. He might have done more, had he not known so much." Farrar felt that *A Fable for Critics* had been underestimated, that it had "a very unusual power of seeing the real men through the glamour of temporary popularity and the cloud of passing dislike." Farrar is just as perceptive when it comes to Lowell's poetry: "The chief element of his strength, and not of his weakness, was the intensity of that moral sympathy which makes his best poetry distinctly didactic. The best chords of his lyre are exactly those in which he means to preach." Farrar sees Lowell's poetry as being too imitative;

"sometimes defective in distinctness, and sometimes in symmetry, as well as sometimes in melody"; and lacking "a clear, definite impression."

A final nineteenth-century estimate worthy of mention is that of Henry James in Charles Dudley Warner's edition of *A Library of the World's Best Literature, Ancient and Modern* (New York, 1897). James was impressed with Lowell's learning and his versatility, which gave him "among Americans of his time, the supreme right to wear the title of a man of letters." James praises *The Biglow Papers* as "an extraordinary performance and a rare work of art" which established Lowell as "the master and the real authority" of dialect and colloquial writing. Of Lowell's poetry, James remarks, "The chords of his lyre were of the precious metal, but not perhaps always of the last lyric tenuity. He struck them with a hand not idle enough for mere moods, and yet not impulsive enough for the great reverberations. He was sometimes too ingenious, as well as too reasonable and responsible."

While others criticized Lowell for his Puritanism, James praised him for it: "It is the recognition of the eternal difference between right and wrong that gives the ring to his earliest melodies, the point to his satire, the standard to his critical judgments, the sublimity to his Commemoration Ode" (*AtM*, Jan. 1897).

Ferris Greenslet's biography of Lowell did not add much to Scudder's in terms of biographical fact, but he far surpassed Scudder in his critical evaluation of Lowell as a writer. In speaking of Lowell's weakness as a poet, Greenslet observes, "The expression of his views and opinions meant more to him—in all save his most ecstatic poetic moods—than the production of a perfect poem; and he was never steadily able to distinguish between the stress of opinions seeking utterance and the pure poetic impulse." In spite of these shortcomings, Greenslet feels that much of Lowell's poetry succeeds because of "the utter and fervent sincerity of the moods expressed in it"; "the amount of mind that lay back of it"; and "the constant ideality, which was both root and branch of his sincerity and of his abounding intellectual life."

Like others before and after him, Greenslet found the best and the worst of Lowell's prose related to Lowell's conversational style. It is loosely structured and lacking in intellectual unity, but full of learning and emotionally convincing.

An important early twentieth-century essay on Lowell was that by William C. Brownell in his *American Prose Masters* (New York, 1909).[2] For Brownell, Lowell had a "representative rather than individual

2. A new edition of Brownell's study was edited by Howard Mumford Jones in 1963 (Cambridge, Mass.). Jones's introduction to the text is valuable for the information it provides on Brownell as a literary critic.

turn of mind" and "was not an original but an independent thinker" whose chief qualities were his poise; his passion for patriotism, books, and nature; his "ingrained cleverness" and "his extraordinary personal charm." Brownell feels that, although Lowell's prose "has the piquancy of Pegasus in harness, . . . at least it is never prose poetry. It is masculine, direct, flexible, and energetic prose." While he feels that Lowell wrote "a good deal too much verse," Brownell believes that "a great deal of it is very fine, very noble and at times very beautiful, and it discloses the distinctly poetic faculty of which rhythmic and figurative is native expression." Brownell is of the opinion that Lowell's "patriotic poetry is altogether unmatched—even unrivalled."

Bliss Perry took the occasion of the commemoration of the centenary of Lowell's birth to answer some of Brownell's charges against Lowell. In "James Russell Lowell" (*Harvard Graduate Magazine*, June 1919), Perry felt that Brownell failed to answer the question as to why, in spite of his defects, Lowell's essays were read "with such pleasure by so many intelligent" people. Perry felt that Lowell's greatness was due to the fact that he wrote in a great tradition of literary essays and that he was so much a man of learning and culture. If Lowell was not a great poet, Perry feels, it was because "his was a divided nature, so variously endowed that complete integration was difficult."

In *The Spirit of American Literature* (Garden City, N.Y., 1913), John Albert Macy states that, with the exception of *The Biglow Papers*, Lowell's poetry is not successful, "the music simply does not happen." *The Biglow Papers*, however, "have no rivals. . . . Occasional poems, they have wings that lift them above occasion to immortality. In them Lowell is possessed by his genius, by a genius that never visited anyone else in the same shape." Macy is one of the few who considers the second series of *The Biglow Papers* superior to the first.

Further praise of *The Biglow Papers* is found in Edward M. Chapman's "*The Biglow Papers* Fifty Years After" (*YR*, Oct. 1916). Chapman sees *The Biglow Papers* as Lowell's chief contribution to literature because they are written "in a field [humorous wit] where his learning was most profound and his heart most enlisted."

The most extravagant praise of *The Biglow Papers* is found in Lewis H. Chrisman's "Permanent Values in *The Biglow Papers*" in his *John Ruskin, Preacher, and Other Essays* (New York, 1921). Chrisman feels that "in American literature in the field of satire we have nothing better to show than Lowell's Biglow Papers." He adds, "No other writer has written in dialect lines so pathetically beautiful and enchantingly melodious." *The Biglow Papers* contain "some of the ripest, richest, and most virile thoughts in American literature." Less hyperbolic but as appreciative is Jenette Reid Tandy's estimate in her *Crackerbox Philosophers in American Humor and Satire* (New York, 1925): "Lowell's range and penetration in satirical portraiture are unsurpassed in America. As a piece of sustained irony *The Biglow Papers* has escaped the careful study of present-day critics. We have no other satirist at once so witty and so racy."

An opposite view of *The Biglow Papers* is seen in V. L. Parrington's *The Romantic Revolution in America* (New York, 1927). Parrington says, "The native clutter of Lowell's mind is there laid bare—the grotesque mixture of homely satire, moral aphorisms, Yankee linguistics, literary criticism—an unwieldy mass that he could neither simplify nor reduce to order. The machinery spoils the propaganda and weighs down the satire." This is characteristic of Parrington's entire estimate of Lowell. He sees Lowell as limited by his Brahmin and Puritan background and to the last "extraordinarily parochial." For Parrington, Lowell "never speculated widely or analyzed critically. Ideas, systems of thought, intellectual and social movements, he had no interest in; he was content to remain a bookish amateur in letters, loitering over old volumes for the pleasure of finding apt phrases and verbal curiosities. With all his reading, history remained a blank to him; and science he would have none of."

H. H. Clark offered another view of Lowell's Puritanism in his essay on "Lowell's Criticism of Romantic Literature" (*PMLA*, Mar. 1925): "Lowell's refusal to divorce art from ethics goes far deeper than puritanism; it is part of the humanistic creed. Although Lowell appears to stress the ethical side of art, he is very far from slighting beauty; he simply asks that beauty be disciplined to some centre of universal human experience."

In his essay on Lowell in *Nature in American Literature* (New York, 1923), Norman Foerster says that "although nature is the theme or background of most of the poems, [Lowell] never writes of her with sustained spontaneity." Foerster ponders why Lowell's poetry of nature is not better than it is and concludes that it is due to Lowell's failure as an artist to revise and polish his verse and to "the paralyzing effect of the spirit of the times" which confused Lowell's heart and mind.

In the thirties and forties there was a general critical reaction against Lowell. Writing with a definite Marxist bias, Granville Hicks, in *The Great Tradition* (New York, 1933), sees Lowell as inexorably locked into his Brahminism to the extent that he always looked backwards. For Hicks, Lowell belonged to a class of writers who were "kindly men, well-informed, well-intentioned, full of eloquent professions of patriotic and literary zeal, but they were nevertheless parasites—parasites upon the past, upon foreign culture, upon an industrial order that they did not try to understand, did not think of reforming, and did not even venture to defend and advance."

Hicks's point of view is echoed in Percy Boynton's *Literature and American Life* (Boston, 1936) and, to a lesser extent, in Van Wyck Brooks's *The Flowering of New England* (New York, 1936).

In his *American Prosody* (New York, 1935), Gay Wilson Allen found no system or theory of prosody in Lowell's poetry. He concludes, "We must decide that Lowell made no direct contribution to American prosodic thought, but his versification introduced into American poetry the freedom which we find in the first two or three decades of nineteenth-century English poetry."

The anti-Lowell sentiment of the thirties and forties can perhaps best be summarized by quoting the conclusion of Arthur W. M. Voss's 1949 essay on "James Russell Lowell" (*UKCR*, Spring 1949): "He was a significant force in furthering our cultural development and is therefore a worthy subject of study for the literary scholar and historian. But he wrote no books which have true literary power. A volume of considerable literary merit might be culled from his writings, but it would be made up of passages and parts, not wholes. Lowell served the cause of humane letters well, but whoever holds that only the best of intellects, the greatest of literary artists, are worthy of the reader's serious attention may ignore him."

Although Leon Howard's interest in Lowell's writings is essentially biographical, his study nevertheless contains a good deal of astute critical commentary. For Howard, the main value of the poems and essays is not in the literary merit they possess, but in the insight they give into Lowell's life and the age he lived in: "Lowell never achieved the quality of excellence which makes some literature so great that it possesses a life of its own, independent of time and place. He was intimately a part of nineteenth-century America, and his importance is determined by that intimacy rather than by the inherent quality of his writings."

Howard sees Lowell's early poetry as his best because Lowell was "fighting wholeheartedly for a poet's place in a difficult world." For Howard, Lowell became less a true poet in middle and later life, because he confused the role of the poet with that of the preacher or moralist and because he "accepted the wisdom of the market place instead of pursuing something less tangible. . . . As a poet, he applied his craftsmanship to writing up to the occasion which called forth his verses, instead of trying to compete with the best that had been thought and said in the world before him."

In spite of such sentiments, Lowell has continued to have his defenders. In his *The Conservative Mind from Burke to Santayana* (Chicago, 1953), Russell Kirk notes that it had become fashionable to belittle Lowell. Kirk answers such critics as Parrington and Harold Laski (*The American Democracy*, New York, 1948) in saying of Lowell: "But how civilized a man, and how versatile! Whoever reads Lowell's letters is not likely to dismiss him summarily. . . . Lowell founded the major American school of literary criticism; he was a poet of high, if limited talent; and he represented the best in Brahmin culture."

George Arms believes that part of the decline in Lowell's reputation is related to the fact that he has been so poorly represented in anthologies, something Arms attempts to correct in the selections of Lowell's poetry he includes in *The Fields Were Green* (Stanford, Calif., 1953). Though Arms feels that Lowell is essentially a failure as a poet ("These closing pages are not written with the hope of making the reader forget the enormously disheartening effect that Lowell's verses as a whole produce."), he feels his best poetry has been wrongly judged by association with his worst. For Arms, Lowell "had a real genius for a certain kind of poem" and Lowell's reputation as a poet must rest on a handful of poems (in addition to *The Biglow Papers* and *A Fable for Critics*): "Agassiz," "Fitz Adam's Story," "To the Dandelion," "Auspex," "The Cathedral," and "Ode Recited at the Harvard Commemoration."

In *The Continuity of American Poetry* (Princeton, N.J., 1961), Roy Harvey Pearce sees Lowell as the poet of the ideal, who wrote poetry "to give direction and coherence to men living in the real world and save them from their temptation to take seriously the natural world." As such, Lowell is the "poet as patriarch" and preacher, who writes good public but not good private poems, who sings Songs of Ourselves, but no Song of Myself.

In "The Craftsmanship of Lowell: Revisions in *The Cathedral*" (*BNYPL*, Jan. 1966), G. Thomas Tanselle demonstrates that Lowell was a better craftsman than he is usually accounted.

The matter of Lowell's reputation as a critic deserves special mention if for no other reason than that it has been given special attention by critics and literary historians. Lowell was considered by his contemporaries to be the foremost critic in American letters. This was undoubtedly due in part to his astute appraisal of his contemporaries (and himself) in *A Fable for Critics* and to the fact that he expressed his critical views on a variety of subjects over a long period of time.

Although Lowell's reputation as a critic was relatively more secure in the nineteenth century, there were those who belittled that reputation. Two early essays point to the weaknesses that twentieth-century critics were to emphasize. In "Professor Lowell as Critic" (*Lippincott's*

Monthly Magazine, June 1871), John Foster Kirk feels that Lowell is "narrow, shallow, and hard, destitute of the insight, the comprehension, the sympathy, by which the true critic, the true poet, searches the domain of thought and the recesses of the mind, illumines the emotions and kindles them." In a long article on "Mr. Lowell's Prose" (*Scribner's*, May, June, July 1872), William Cleaver Wilkinson grants Lowell the wide literary background, the ability to empathize with other writers, and the artistry requisite to the good critic, but feels that Lowell fails as a critic because he has no basic and systematic critical position.

While admiring Lowell as a scholar and man of culture, William C. Brownell, in *American Prose Masters*, feels that Lowell was deficient as a critic because "he occupied himself mainly with genius. As a subject . . . the best was good enough for him." This, according to Brownell, led to Lowell's proclivity to rank poets rather than to evaluate and describe them. Lowell's failure as critic was related to three characteristics, according to Brownell: his criticism grew out of his reading and not out of his thought; he was insensitive to the plastic arts; and he had "no philosophic view to advocate or express."

In the first comprehensive treatment of Lowell as critic (*James Russell Lowell as A Critic*, New York, 1915), Joseph J. Reilly expands on Brownell's view. He considers Lowell a failure because he was limited in his critical interest; he was deficient in his knowledge of art and history; he lacked sympathy for science and classical art; and he had little interest in drama and fiction. According to Reilly, "If Lowell is to survive, it must be frankly as an impressionist, for so far as criticism approaches a science, so far as it depends to any serious extent on ultimate principles, so far, in a word, as it is something more fundamental and abiding than the *ipse dixit* of an appreciator, Lowell is not a critic."

George E. De Mille in "The Critic from Cambridge" (*SR*, Oct. 1924) does not try to determine how good a critic Lowell is, but what kind of critic. If Lowell is measured by the standards of the scientific critic "we can hardly say that Lowell is a critic at all. If, on the other hand, we accept Professor Brewster's definition . . . that criticism is simply 'talk about books,' . . . Lowell takes a very high rank indeed."

In *The Romantic Revolution in America* V. L. Parrington takes Reilly's first definition and finds Lowell sorely wanting: "He had no standards other than ethical, only likes and dislikes; no interest in ideas, only a pottering concern for the text; no historical backgrounds, only isolated figures dwelling in a vacuum. He was puzzled over new schools and unfamiliar technic, and was at ease only in praising established reputations and confirming approved judgments."

The best defense of Lowell as critic has been made by Norman Foerster. In "The Creed of Lowell as Literary Critic" (*SP*, July 1927), Foerster counters Brownell's contention that Lowell's criticism "lacks the unity of a body of doctrine." In a fuller treatment published the following year in his *American Criticism: A Study in Literary Theory from Poe to the Present* (Boston and New York, 1928), Foerster calls Lowell "our most distinguished literary critic," and defends him against the charge of being merely an impressionist. Foerster feels that Lowell had a "comprehensive vision of the task of the critic. It involves sensitiveness to impressions, historical understanding, and an aesthetic-ethical judgment." If Foerster's views seem at times too much influenced by New Humanism, his defense of Lowell helped to pave the way for a more balanced view of Lowell as critic.

Although generally appreciative of Lowell's critical ability, Bernard Smith (*Forces in American Criticism*, New York, 1939) points out that Lowell did not understand or sympathize with contemporary literary movements after the Civil War. He had nothing to say about Twain and little about James, Howells, or Whitman. Nevertheless, Smith feels Lowell is the "*beau idéal* of gentlemanly critics."

Richard D. Altick defends Lowell against earlier critics (Reilly, Clark, Parrington, and others) who charged that Lowell was unaware of the importance of historical perspective in formulating his critical judgment. In fact, Altick accuses these critics with the same charges they had raised against Lowell, for they failed to evaluate correctly the resources available to Lowell and thus judged him by modern standards. According to Altick, Lowell "was by no means ignorant of the value or the nature of historical criticism, and . . . his critical essays abound with evidences of his awareness of the power exerted by contemporary circumstance upon the literature of a given era" ("Was Lowell an Historical Critic?" *AL*, Nov. 1942).

In "Lowell's Criticism of Romantic Literature" (*PMLA*, Mar. 1925), H. H. Clark says that Lowell did not like romantic literature "because it failed to fulfill the requirements of his poetic creed." C. M. Lombard argues that Clark and others were incorrect in their judgment of Lowell's attitude toward the Romantics and that Lowell gave the Romantics reasonable praise ("Lowell and French Romanticism," *Revue de Littérature Comparée*, Oct.–Dec. 1964). In "Lowell on Thoreau" (*SP*, July 1930), Austin Warren feels that in his infamous essay Lowell as humanist reacts more to romanticism than to Thoreau.

The culmination of the discussion of Lowell as critic is seen in two well-balanced views. Although John Paul Pritchard (*Criticism in America*, Norman, Okla., 1965) is realistic about Lowell's shortcomings as critic—"His ignorance of America south of Philadelphia and west of the Alleghenies narrowed considerably his capacity to speak for and of the whole country; his aristocratic point of view . . . made him unable to *feel* the nobility of toil; his inability to adapt himself to the age of science restricted his understanding of later writers; and he was too much Man Reading"—he still sees him as at times surprisingly modern, as in his theory of the lyric: "Here eighty years before the relation of poetic texture and structure were discussed by John Crowe Ransom and Allen Tate, Lowell adumbrated the approach to lyric poetry which these well-known New Critics have amplified."

Richard H. Fogle in "Organic Form in American Criticism: 1840–1870" (in *The Development of American Literary Criticism*, edited by Floyd Stovall, Chapel Hill, N.C., 1955) sees Lowell's conservatism and his inhospitality to new writers as having two causes: "He comes at the end of a *great tradition* [the organic tradition of Herder, Goethe, and Coleridge], which at the last failed in energy to revitalize itself; and there really was much in the new generations which Lowell did well to reject." Fogle feels that "Lowell's criticism is eclectic, but organicist in its very eclecticism. . . . He shows the organicist willingness to sympathize, to assimilate, to absorb before he passes judgment. And his judgments generally stand up well. His essay on Keats, for example, written in 1854, contains in the germ all that modern scholarship has fathomed of Keats's identity, his unique fusion of experience and thought, his sensuous power and his idealism."

Influence on Lowell's thinking and writing have been traced by a number of scholars. In his chapter on Lowell in *Return to the Fountains* (Durham, N.C., 1942), John Paul Pritchard finds a significant indebtedness to classical literature, an indebtedness he explored in two earlier essays, "Lowell's Debt to Horace's *Ars Poetica*" (*AL*, Nov. 1931) and "James Russell Lowell and Aristotle's Poetics" (*Classical Weekly*, 15 January 1934). Of Aristotle's influence on Lowell, Pritchard says, "It is not too much to say that Lowell's important position in American letters and criticism is based largely upon his knowledge of the principles advocated by Aristotle in the Poetics and his adherence to them." In two later studies, "Lowell and Longinus" (*Transactions of the American Philological Association*, 1945) and "A Glance at Lowell's Classical Reading" (*AL*, Jan. 1950), Pritchard adds Longinus, Plato, and Plutarch to the list of Lowell's classical mentors.

Related to Pritchard's work is George P. Clark's Ph.D. dissertation on "Classical Influences and Background in the Writings of James Russell Lowell" (Yale, 1948), and his "James Russell Lowell's Study of the Classics Before Entering Harvard" (*JA*, 1963).

In "James Russell Lowell's Interest in Dante," J. Chesley Mathews documents Lowell's lifelong preoccupation with Dante but concludes that Dante's influence on Lowell's poetry was slight (*Italica*, June 1959). According to Lawrence H. Klibbe, the Spanish influence on Lowell was not great except for Cervantes and Calderón, both of whom "are vital to the analysis of Lowell's literary theories" (*James Russell Lowell's Residence in Spain, 1877–1880*, New York, 1964). The Spanish influence on Lowell is further explored by Stanley T. Williams in *The Spanish Background of American Literature* (2 vols., New Haven, Conn., 1955).

Charles Oran Stewart's *Lowell and France* (Nashville, Tenn., 1951) examines the influence of French culture and literature in a number of Lowell's works, showing that they provided him with both subject matter and inspiration.

Like many of his contemporaries, Lowell rejected the Bible as a religious text early, but used it extensively in his writing throughout his life. William J. De Saegher concludes his study of "James Russell Lowell and the Bible" (Ph.D. dissertation, U.C.L.A., 1964) by remarking that Lowell understood the Bible well and used it often and variously in his writing, so that "biblical material pervades every facet of his work."

The winds of criticism, notoriously capricious, have left Lowell becalmed in the decade of the sixties, when others of his contemporaries enjoyed revivals of interest. Judging from present trends, it seems ironically unlikely that the Modern Language Association's new annual "James Russell Lowell Prize" for outstanding literary studies will soon be awarded for a study on Lowell, in spite of the fact that the definitive study of Lowell has not yet been written. But no one as richly versatile and influential as Lowell will forever remain unattractive or unrewarding to scholars. The years to come may produce the biographer and critic who will give us the whole artist and the whole man.

Frank Norris

WILLIAM B. DILLINGHAM

BIBLIOGRAPHY

UNTIL 1959 the student of Frank Norris was greatly hampered by the absence of a definitive bibliography. An early mimeographed bibliography by Joseph Gaer (California Literary Research Project, 1934) was brief and unreliable. With the publication of *Frank Norris: A Bibliography* (Los Gatos, Calif., 1959), Kenneth A. Lohf and Eugene P. Sheehy filled the need. Lohf and Sheehy's bibliography includes sections on Norris's collected works, individual works, dramatizations, film adaptations, translations, and—of special value—Norris's contributions to periodicals. Another section is devoted to writings about Norris, including reviews. William White's "Frank Norris: Bibliographical Addenda" (*BB*, Sept.-Dec. 1959) lists forty-six additional items (of slight significance) not found in Lohf and Sheehy. Ernest Marchand's *Frank Norris: A Study* (Stanford, Calif., 1942) contains a bibliographical essay (Chapter Six) which is particularly valuable for a survey of contemporary reviews. An excellent bibliographical essay is also to be found in Warren French, *Frank Norris* (New York, 1962). French also published an abbreviated bibliography on Norris in *ALR* (Fall 1967). For a checklist of Norris's literary criticism, the bibliography in Donald Pizer's edition of *The Literary Criticism of Frank Norris* (Austin, Tex., 1964) is useful. A selected bibliography of Norris's works and of principal works about him is included in Pizer's *The Novels of Frank Norris* (Bloomington, Ind., 1966). The most recent annotated bibliography of works about Norris is in William B. Dillingham, *Frank Norris: Instinct and Art* (Lincoln, Neb., 1969).

EDITIONS

Both Collier and Son's *The Complete Works of Frank Norris* (4 vols., 1898–1903) and Doubleday, Page and Company's *The Complete*

Works of Frank Norris (7 vols., 1903) omit *Vandover and the Brute*, which was not published until 1914. The standard edition is *The Complete Edition of Frank Norris* (Garden City, N.Y., 1928) in ten volumes. Actually released in the early part of 1929, this edition is dated 1928. Although it is better than the early editions of many writers, the *Complete Edition* is not complete. Notable is the omission of some of Norris's critical essays. Norris scholars would welcome a new edition of the quality of those sponsored by the Modern Language Association's Center for Editions of American Authors.

The only collections of Norris's writings published after the *Complete Edition* are *Frank Norris of "The Wave"* (San Francisco, 1931, now very rare), with an introduction by Oscar Lewis, and Donald Pizer's edition of *The Literary Criticism of Frank Norris*, which superseded *The Responsibilities of the Novelist* (New York, 1903), the first collection of Norris's essays.

Clothbound editions of *McTeague, The Pit,* and *The Responsibilities of the Novelist* are in print as are several paperback editions of *McTeague* and *The Octopus*. One paperback edition of *The Pit* is available. *Vandover and the Brute* is at this moment no longer listed as being in print in any edition. Norris's potboilers, *Moran of the Lady Letty, Blix,* and *A Man's Woman*, have not been in print for several years.

MANUSCRIPTS AND LETTERS

Norris's manuscripts and letters are scarce. The most important single collection is in the Bancroft Library of the University of California at Berkeley. Many of the manuscripts for the novels have been lost, but through persistent effort, James D. Hart of the University of California has managed to collect much of the manuscript of *McTeague*. The first volume of each set of the *Argonaut Manuscript Limited Edition of Frank Norris's Works* (Garden City, N.Y., 1928), a more expensive (but otherwise identical) version of *The Complete Edition of Frank Norris*, contained a full or half page of the manuscript of *McTeague*. The 245 sets of this edition were scattered over the world when Hart began collecting the manuscript. He recorded his experiences in reassembling this manuscript and in obtaining several other valuable papers for the Bancroft Library in a fascinating article, "Search and Research: The Librarian and the Scholar" (*College and Research Libraries*, Sept. 1958). Hart also discovered the themes which Norris wrote in Lewis Gates's course at Harvard. In addition the Norris collection at the Bancroft includes in addition Franklin Walker's interview notes for his biography on Norris, several books owned by Norris, various clippings, notes by Norris, letters, and scrapbooks.

A slim volume of Norris's letters was edited by Franklin Walker (*The Letters of Frank Norris*, San Francisco, 1956), and "Ten Letters by Frank Norris" which Walker did not include were edited and published by Donald Pizer (*Quarterly News-Letter* of the Book Club of California, Summer 1962).

BIOGRAPHY

As little is known about Frank Norris the man as about any novelist of importance in American literature. He lived only thirty-two years, and his whereabouts can easily be accounted for in each one of those years—Chicago, San Francisco, Paris, Berkeley, Harvard, South Africa, New York, Cuba, and trips between New York and San Francisco. We know who his parents were, where he went to school, what he studied, what grades he made, where he worked, whom he married, what he wrote, and where and how he died. We can read reports of what he was like from his friends and acquaintances: Harry M. Wright's reminiscence, "In Memoriam—Frank Norris, 1870–1902" (University of California *Chronicle*, Oct. 1902); Isaac Marcosson's account of his friendship with Norris in *Adventures in Interviewing* (London, 1920); Wallace W. Everett's anecdotal treatment of Norris the fraternity man in "Frank Norris in His Chapter" (*The Phi Gamma Delta*, Apr. 1930); Grant Richards's sparkling account of how Norris defended Dreiser's *Sister Carrie* in *Author Hunting By an Old Literary Sportsman* (New York, 1934); and comments about Norris by his lifelong close friend Ernest Peixotto in "Romanticist Under the Skin" (*SatR*, 27 May 1933). Despite all these articles by those who apparently knew him best, Frank Norris remains elusive. One strongly suspects that he could not have been as uncomplicated, boyish, and superficial as these reminiscences depict him and still have written books like *Vandover and the Brute*, *McTeague*, and *The Octopus*.

Probably the most influential article yet published about Norris's life is Charles C. Dobie's "Frank Norris, or Up From Culture" (*AM*, Apr. 1928, reprinted as the introduction to vol. 7 of the *Complete Edition*). It is the source of several ideas about Norris, some of them doubtful or erroneous, that have been expressed through the years. Written for a wide audience, this article is more popular than scholarly. Sensational aspects of Norris's life are dramatized throughout: the difference between Mr. Norris, the down to earth businessman, and Frank, the sensitive son; the avid desire of Mrs. Norris, an ex-actress and a socialite, for a career in the arts for her sensitive son against the wishes of her husband; Norris's "lead soldier stage," when he made up stories to please his younger brother; Dwight L. Moody's choirmaster talking Mr. Norris into letting Frank study art in London at the "Kensington School of Art," and then in Paris; Frank's indifference to his art studies; Mr. Norris's discovering some installments of a romantic novel Frank was writing and sending home to his brother Charles and his subsequent cabling to Frank to return home at once. Many of these stories cannot stand close scrutiny. Norris's father, for example, was a far more complicated person than Dobie suggested. No one had to persuade him to escort Norris to Europe, and probably it was more Frank's decision than his father's to return home. Norris was not nearly so cavalier about painting as Dobie claimed, and, incidentally, if one sets out seriously to retrace Norris in London and to find "the Kensington School of Art," failure awaits. The school in London which Norris probably attended was the National Art Training School, but biographers and critics have continued for a generation to repeat Dobie's error in this as well as in most of his other oversimplifications or inaccuracies.

Norris's younger brother, Charles G. Norris, himself a minor novelist, was responsible to a large extent for the smoke screen one must get through to get at the real Frank Norris. Most of what has been written about Norris's life either came directly from Charles Norris or had his stamp of approval. He was understandably concerned about protecting his brother from too intimate a probing. His memory sometimes made honest errors; a few times he simply gave misinformation. In his foreword to the *Complete Edition* volume of *Vandover and the Brute*, for example, he concocted the story which has been repeated countless times by biographers and critics that the manuscript of *Vandover* had been temporarily packed away in a crate and stored in a warehouse in San Francisco after Norris's death. When the fire and earthquake occurred, the warehouse burned, and it was assumed *Vandover* was lost forever. Then years later a letter was received from the storage company stating that the crate had been moved just before the fire and was safe. Since the manuscript did not have the author's name on it, however, more years went by before someone recognized Norris's style. Then the novel was at last published. When Franklin Walker questioned Charles Norris about this matter in 1930, Charles admitted that he had made up the entire story, that the manuscript had actually been in the hands of Norris's widow all along, and that he did it to explain the long delay before the novel was published.

Walker had a great deal more information about Norris than he used in his *Frank Norris: A Biography* (Garden City, N.Y., 1932), the only full-length biography yet published. His interview notes are extremely important to anyone seriously interested in Norris's life. Considering the fact that Walker worked very closely with Charles and Jeannette Norris (Frank's widow), the biography is amazingly good. In fact, it is so judiciously balanced that it has had, ironically, an adverse effect. Few new facts about Norris's life have come to light since it was written, and its competence discourages would-be biographers. Consequently, no new biography has appeared in almost forty years, an extraordinary situation for a writer of Norris's importance, especially when one counts the biographies of Crane (whose life was even shorter) and Dreiser, Norris's fellow naturalists.

As sound as Walker's biography is, it is clear that he exercised a certain restraint in dealing with the more intimate questions of Norris's life such as his marriage, which may not have been quite the made-in-heaven match usually pictured, and with his general psychological make-up. Charles Norris was greatly pleased with the Walker biography, and wrote the foreword to it, stating that "in other hands the personality of my brother might have suffered." Walker was also unquestionably influenced by Dobie's article, from which he sometimes quoted. That a generally accurate and useful biography emerged is much to Walker's credit, but the fact is that biographical work on Norris is now lagging far behind criticism of his fiction. What is urgently needed is a new appraisal of Norris, a look at the inner man. While provocative new ideas are being expressed about his work, all biographical discussion, to paraphrase Hemingway, comes from one book by Franklin Walker. There was nothing before. There has been nothing as good since.

William B. Dillingham's two biographical chapters in his *Frank Norris: Instinct and Art* make a start in the right direction. Dillingham explores to some extent Norris's fear of failure, corrects some previous biographical mistakes, and deals with the much neglected area of French painting as an influence on his life and writings. Still, a fuller portrait of Norris is needed. Since new facts are difficult to come by and since his life has been so long shrouded in a cloak of "boyishness," the task will be a most difficult undertaking.

CRITICISM

From the death of Norris in 1902 until 1930, he received little critical attention.[1] The situation is illustrated in a 1911 statement by Frederic

1. For surveys of contemporary reviews of Norris's works, see Paul H. Bixler, "Frank Norris's Literary Reputation" (*AL*, May 1934) and Ernest Marchand's concluding chapter in *Frank Norris: A Study*.

Taber Cooper: "The work of Norris, taken as a whole, has been thrown into an unjust and misleading remoteness. We are apt to think of him as belonging to a bygone generation, as an influence which after showing a brief potentiality suddenly withered once and for all." During Norris's lifetime and shortly thereafter, William Dean Howells was one of his strongest supporters. He paid high tribute to Norris in his reviews of *McTeague* (*Literature*, 24 March 1899) and *The Pit* (*Harper's Weekly*, 14 March 1903) and in an essay which was occasioned by Norris's sudden death (*NAR*, Dec. 1902). After this, however, even Howells seemed all but to forget the young author who has been called by one critic "the last and most powerful of Howells's protégés."

Cooper's essay in *Some American Story Tellers* (New York, 1911) was the first serious and sustained scholarly estimate of Norris's work. In pointing out Norris's literary split personality—the realist and the romantic—Cooper struck a note still heard today in Norris criticism. "It is impossible to read Norris's works," Cooper wrote, "without perceiving that from first to last there was within him an instinct continually at war with his chosen realistic methods; an unconquerable and exasperating vein of romanticism that led him frequently into palpable absurdities—not because romanticism in itself is a literary crime, but because it has its own proper place in literature, and that place is assuredly not in a realistic novel." Through the years this question has been the single most controversial issue in writings about Norris. The inability to see Norris's work for what it is, whole, coherent, and cohesive, has been perhaps the greatest failure of numerous critics from Cooper onward. Cooper's commentary also launched another perennial question: how good is *The Pit?* Like a few recent critics, Cooper preferred it to most of Norris's other novels, including *The Octopus*, but for the unusual and tenuous reason that "the symbolism is kept further in the background."

If Cooper felt that Norris's romantic tendency was his greatest shortcoming, John Curtis Underwood saw it as a typical American trait and Norris as the very best America had to offer. In *Literature and Insurgency* (New York, 1914), Underwood set Norris up as "unrivaled, unassailed and unassailable" for the reason that Norris loved and wrote for "the Plain People" and dealt with "the material of our common national life." Full of lengthy, tedious plot summaries and indiscriminate praise, Underwood's essay is valuable today chiefly as a dramatic means of seeing how far criticism on Norris has come.

A much briefer but far more illuminating early commentary is that by Theodore Dreiser, which he wrote as an introduction to *McTeague* in the *Complete Edition*. It is illuminating both for what it says about Norris and for what it suggests about Dreiser. The strongest link between these two giants of American literary naturalism was their uncanny talent for capturing a moment in American culture. Dreiser admired Norris most of all for his ability to depict scenes like Polk Street, a phenomenon wholly "indigenous to America, and California, and San Francisco—a brilliant and accurate picture of a certain phase of life in this most amazing of new lands." Norris had that same awareness of the historical moment which Robert Penn Warren has praised Dreiser for possessing.

The decade of the thirties was the Dark Age of criticism. Ideological critics found truths where they did not exist, and dogmatic literary historians were too prudish or too opinionated (or both) to offer objective evaluations. Considering the perils of the time, Norris fared very well. Vernon Louis Parrington did not live to complete his third volume of *Main Currents in American Thought* (New York, 1930), but his notes indicate that he found Norris "the most stimulating and militant of our early naturalists." Even that guardian of literary good taste, Fred Lewis Pattee, had warmed to Norris somewhat by 1930. In an earlier volume, *A History of American Literature Since 1870* (New York, 1915), he gave Norris only summary treatment. But in Pattee's *The New American Literature, 1890–1930* (New York, 1930), Norris is awarded an entire chapter, and *The Octopus* heralded as being almost "the great American novel." Reviewing the new *Complete Edition* of Norris's work, Edward Wagenknecht in "Frank Norris in Retrospect" (*VQR*, Apr. 1930) was probably the only critic who has aimed his praise and admiration particularly at Norris's "fundamental decency and sanity," a position eminently justified.

One of the most wrongheaded but persistent theories about Norris's work is that it was moving steadily in the direction of social protest when his death occurred. *The Octopus*, of course, is the book such theorists have in mind. The most recent of college desk dictionaries, a thoroughly reliable one in most respects, labels Norris "Author of novels of social protest." This label became indelibly stamped upon him in the 1930s. By misreading *The Octopus* and then making the further mistake of ignoring most of Norris's other work, a critic like Russell Blankenship in *American Literature as an Expression of the National Mind* (New York, 1931) could conclude that "from *The Octopus* to the soap-box and the indignant, perfervid eloquence of Upton Sinclair is only a step" and could make the astounding statement that *The Pit* "must stand as an example of what a naturalist can produce when he becomes too much interested in sociology." Arthur Hobson

Quinn in *American Fiction* (New York, 1936) voiced a similar but quieter objection to *The Octopus* when he complained that Norris "made the railroad so completely black" that the book is not convincing. In *The Foreground of American Fiction* (New York, 1934), Harry Hartwick wrote accurate plot summaries but dubious generalizations, one of which was that Norris was on his way to socialism.

Norris did not go far enough for Granville Hicks, who was in those days a card-carrying Communist. Instead of ending with a clear-cut Marxist position, Norris, in Hicks's view, sadly went into philosophical fibrillation. The year before Hicks's *The Great Tradition* (New York, 1933) appeared, John Chamberlain in *Farewell to Reform* (New York, 1932) laid the groundwork for the controversy on philosophical inconsistency in *The Octopus*, a problem over which Norris's tireless critics are still butting their heads. Chamberlain questioned whether the "good" which Norris wrote of at the end of *The Octopus* is supported by the facts of the plot. Hicks picked up the argument and made it popular. He charged that Norris never really understood the philosophical implications of determinism. What bothered him most, however, was that Norris admired the giants of industry at the same time that he expressed sympathy for the common people. Hicks's co-Marxist, V. F. Calverton, emphasized what he considered Norris's inherent and justified pessimism in *The Liberation of American Literature* (New York, 1932); and in *Expression in America* (New York, 1932), Ludwig Lewisohn offered the highly original but profoundly tenuous notion that Norris was influenced deeply by Octave Mirbeau. In Lewisohn's opinion, only *McTeague* was worth preserving of all Norris's work.

The 1930s also ushered in the first serious studies of Norris's sources and of influences upon his writing. The earliest extended treatment of Zola's influence upon Norris was Marius Biencourt's *Une Influence du Naturalisme Française en Amérique: Frank Norris* (Paris, 1933). In "Frank Norris's Reading at Harvard College" (*AL*, May 1935), Willard E. Martin, Jr., used the borrower's record of the Harvard College Library to reveal books Norris checked out while he was a student there in 1894–95 and writing both *Vandover and the Brute* and *McTeague*.

Only two other commentaries on Norris from the thirties deserve mention. In *Companions on the Trail* (New York, 1931), Hamlin Garland reminisced about Norris and his reaction to Norris's death ("Nothing of late has so stirred me and grieved me"). This essay also included the text of an earlier critical estimate of Norris's work which Garland had published in *The Critic* (Mar. 1930). Alfred Kazin in

"Three Pioneer Realists" (*SatR*, 8 July 1939) stressed the point that Norris "was the product of many diverse influences, and to the end betrayed them all often simultaneously." What seemed to impress Kazin most about Norris was his "unquenchable joy in life that one finds only in the younger Elizabethan poets, a joy that is like the first discovery of the world, splendid in its freshness and eager to absorb every flicker of life." Kazin corrected factual errors in this essay (such as his statement that Norris was once a student at the University of Southern California), revised it slightly, and included it three years later in his book *On Native Grounds*.

Criticism of the 1940s focused largely upon *The Octopus*. The controversy over philosophical inconsistency which Chamberlain and Hicks had inaugurated some years before now raged with stalwarts on both sides of the issue. The beginning of the decade found H. Willard Reninger attempting to answer the charges of Hicks and others. In "Norris Explains *The Octopus*: A Correlation of His Theory and Practice" (*AL*, May 1940), Reninger took the position that Norris was following his own literary theory as set out in *The Responsibilities of the Novelist*, a set of philosophical and aesthetic values which Reninger considered coherent. Unfortunately, the article was not a convincing answer to Chamberlain, Hicks, and others because it overrated Norris as a literary critic. *The Responsibilities of the Novelist*, Reninger wrote, "is a far more penetrating volume than any student of American criticism has yet revealed." And, further, "*The Responsibilities* stands as the climax of American critical theory of the novel in the nineteenth century."

In a brief note, "Frank Norris on Realism and Naturalism" (*AL*, Mar. 1941), Charles Child Walcutt, who was a few years later to become one of the most important critics of Norris and American literary naturalism, answered Reninger by revealing an obvious error in one of his key quotations and by pointing out a glaring flaw in the logic of his position: "The relation of theory and practice in his [Norris's] work is to be determined not by a study of his own critical *dicta*—for authors have been notoriously prone to rationalize their works into a theoretical consistency—but by careful analysis of his novels in relation to the ideas which they pretend to express and to which they attempt to give significant form."

In his long intellectual history, *Intellectual America: Ideas on the March* (New York, 1941), Oscar Cargill surveyed Norris's career and his writings and found *The Octopus* to be "Frank Norris at his best." Cargill quarreled with Norris's characterization of Presley, Behrman, and Shelgrim, but seemed to detect no inconsistency in the theme.

Walter Fuller Taylor generally agreed with Walcutt. In *The Economic Novel in America* (Chapel Hill, N.C., 1942), he credited Norris with having lifted the "romance of economic conflict," which was being depicted by inferior authors, to a new "literary level." Furthermore, Norris showed that the philosophy of naturalistic determinism was "peculiarly appropriate" to stories which have as "the principal human value the thrill of successful struggle for survival." Nevertheless, "the survival in his work of moral themes and attitudes, the mingling of deterministic and undeterministic strains of thought, shows to what extent the contradictory leadings of two widely divergent views of life left him confused." Taylor felt that "in any discriminating judgment of Norris's worth, this confusion of mind must necessarily be remembered to his detriment." Perhaps an even severer charge, however, was that Norris did not possess "a certain 'fusing' quality of imagination," which would make the elements of his stories seem organic "as if they had grown together naturally and of themselves." After spending a great deal of time in supporting these arguments of philosophical inconsistency, especially as revealed in *The Octopus*, and of structural and stylistic defects, Taylor concludes his consideration of Norris with the astounding thought that the objections he raised were not very important after all "when weighed against the solid worth" of Norris's writing. The failure in philosophical consistency and in style are merely "failures in certain useful accessories of fiction, not in its absolute essentials." Critics as well as novelists can indulge in philosophical confusion.

The first really effective defense of *The Octopus* was George W. Meyer's "A New Interpretation of *The Octopus*" (*CE*, Mar. 1943). In showing the thematic unity of *The Octopus*, Meyer was the first critic to make it plain that the wheat ranchers of the San Joaquin Valley were themselves partly responsible for their defeat, that they were in the business of making money, and that they were scarcely less selfish than the railroad. Meyer further pointed out that Shelgrim's speech did not necessarily reflect Norris's beliefs, nor did Presley always represent Norris. Meyer's chief contribution, however, was his suggestion that nature in *The Octopus* was neither malevolent nor benevolent, but a great force which could seem benevolent if man aligned himself with it instead of against it. Only when Meyer attempted to discuss the subject of moral blame and to establish a subtle distinction between determinism and fatalism did he falter, for Norris then looks too much like a didactic moralist, and more questions about the nature of human responsibility are raised than could possibly be answered.

Meyer's case for *The Octopus* seemed to go unheard by three other critics who echoed earlier objections to the novel. Malcolm Cowley in "Naturalism's Terrible McTeague" (*New Republic*, 5 May 1947) expressed his preference for *McTeague*, and of *The Octopus* he wrote: "At the end it declined into muzzy sentiments and fine writing." Describing and evaluating Norris's writing in *The Shapers of American Fiction, 1798–1947* (New York, 1947), George Snell accepted what had become the majority opinion of *The Octopus*—that it contained too many antithetical elements and that thematically it was disorderly, diverse, and distracting. By this time, critical analyses of *The Octopus* began to sound strangely like the early reviews of *Moby-Dick*. Robert E. Spiller called *The Octopus* "the most ambitious novel of its generation," but he echoed the old charge of inconsistency: "The book finally fails as tragic drama because Norris has no consistent position on the vast economic and metaphysical problems he raises" (*LHUS*). One commentary on *The Octopus* which did not confront this long-standing controversy was Irving McKee's "Notable Memorials to Mussel Slough" (*PHR*, Feb. 1948), which recounted the details of the Mussel Slough incident of 1880 and indicated how Norris utilized the event in his novel.

With the exception of Lars Åhnebrink's *The Influence of Émile Zola on Frank Norris* (Cambridge, Mass., 1947), which was superseded by his later book (discussed below), the only book to be published on Norris during the decade of the 1940s was Ernest Marchand's *Frank Norris: A Study* (Stanford, Calif., 1942). Marchand read Norris with a level head and with much more care than many previous critics. He thoroughly digested Norris's critical writings, and furthermore he read and evaluated most carefully most of the reviews and articles on Norris. In his treatment of Norris's fiction, Marchand is eminently sound in his evaluations and accurately descriptive. What is missing is a probing of depth into the methods and motives of Norris, the literary artist. Marchand does not take us very deep; he does not tell us *why* Norris felt it so essential, for example, to use detail so extensively, or what fundamentally he was trying to achieve as a symbolist. Nevertheless, as a pioneering critical study, it is admirable, especially in comparison with initial books on many authors.

A critic is always impressive when he takes upon himself the enormous task of describing and analyzing an entire group of writers, whether they be the classicists, the neoclassicists, the romantics, the realists, the naturalists, the lost generation, the beats, or any others who have been grouped and labeled chiefly for convenience by literary historians. When such an attempt fails, as it does more often than not, the failure seems abysmal. Such, precisely, is the case with Malcolm

Cowley's ambitious attempt to characterize the naturalistic movement in America, " 'Not Men': A Natural History of American Naturalism" (*KR*, Summer 1947). Using outmoded generalizations about literary naturalism, Cowley treated Norris, Dreiser, and Crane, three very different kinds of writers, as if they all believed the same things and wrote the same way.[2] Of greater significance are two articles on Norris by Charles C. Walcutt, "Frank Norris and the Search for Form" (*UKCR*, Winter 1947) and "The Naturalism of *Vandover and the Brute*" (in *Forms of Modern Fiction*, Minneapolis, Minn., 1948). Revised versions of both articles were incorporated later into Walcutt's book, which will be discussed below.

The next ten years saw nearly as many critical commentaries published on Norris as had been produced in the forty-eight years from his death to 1950. Many of these are significant enough to constitute both a substantial upsurge of interest in Norris and a thoughtful reconsideration of his place in American literature. By this period Norris's stature had been determined: he would not be regarded as a minor writer like his contemporaries Robert Herrick, David Graham Phillips, or even Harold Frederic. He had risen far above Jack London and had taken his place beside Crane, Dreiser, Howells, and many others just below the highest rank of such American novelists as Hawthorne, Melville, and James. The most unfortunate aspect of this particular rank is that it leaves a critic somewhat uncertain about how much he can take for granted in dealing with such a writer's works. He cannot, that is, assume that the reader had read the works of Norris or Howells with the same confidence that he could assume a reader's knowledge of the novels of Hawthorne or Melville. As a result, the reader who wishes to acquaint himself adequately with the criticism must wade through plot summary after plot summary.

A book which illustrates this point well is Lars Åhnebrink's celebrated work, *The Beginnings of Naturalism in American Fiction* (Cambridge, Mass., 1950). A substantial portion of Åhnebrink's discussion of Norris is taken up with plot summaries and with biographical information which contributes nothing at all new. Insofar as criticism on Norris is concerned, the most important part of the book is the third section of Chapter Ten, which deals with the influence of Zola. It establishes once and for all the extent of Zola's influence with more

2. A revised and expanded version of Cowley's essay (which was originally delivered as a lecture at Princeton) was published as "Naturalism in American Literature" in *Evolutionary Thought in America*, edited by Stow Persons (New Haven, Conn., 1950).

than enough evidence and example. When Åhnebrink leaves Zola for other possible influences, he is frequently unconvincing. His case for Huysman's influence, for example, is shaky at best, and when he gets to Turgenev and Ibsen, he seems to be clutching at straws. In Chapter Twelve, he indicates that no scholar has suggested that Turgenev might have had a direct influence on Norris, admits that "there is no reference whatever to Turgenev in Norris's works," and then proceeds to show parallels. It becomes clear that in this part of his book, Åhnebrink is discussing *resemblance*, not direct influence, and the results are not fruitful. Of *The Octopus* he writes: "The atmosphere of anarchism, conspiracy, and revolt which pervades the latter part of *The Octopus* is *somewhat reminiscent* [italics mine] of that of *Virgin Soil*." In the inevitable "summing up" that concludes each chapter, Åhnebrink sometimes sums up more than he has proved, as in the case of Turgenev: "Norris's debt to Turgenev can be traced in at least two novels: *The Octopus* and *The Pit*." In trying to show Ibsen's influence, Åhnebrink makes the following statement: "In the autobiographical *Blix*, the heroine is a young, independent, modern woman, reminiscent of Nora in *A Doll's House*." Such tenuous comparisons are all too frequent in this book.

The interest in Norris's sources continued with Charles Kaplan's "Norris's Use of Sources in *The Pit*" (*AL*, Mar. 1953), in which he discusses Curtis Jadwin's similarity to Joseph Leiter, who tried to corner the wheat market in 1897, and "Fact into Fiction in *McTeague*" (*HLB*, Autumn 1954), an enlightening treatment of Norris's extensive reliance on Thomas Fillebrown's *A Text-book of Operative Dentistry* for technical details in *McTeague*. Even minor novels were examined for their possible sources, as in John C. Sherwood's "Norris and the *Jeannette*" (*PQ*, Apr. 1958), which shows how the early scenes of *A Man's Woman* follow the published records of an actual expedition, Commander De Long's *The Voyage of the Jeannette* (1884) and Chief Engineer Melville's *In the Lena Delta* (1884).

A different kind of influence was pointed out by Joseph J. Kwiat in "The Newspaper Experience: Crane, Norris, and Dreiser" (*NCF*, Sept. 1953). Kwiat suggests that several of the typical aspects of these three naturalistic writers can be traced to their experience as newspaper men: "All three . . . discovered that their value to a newspaper depended upon the cultivation of technical facility and an awareness of the human interest angle. All three attempted to be 'detached' observers who accepted life as it was for its facts and drama."

One of the most significant contributions to the study of Norris in the fifties was a doctoral dissertation, Robert D. Lundy's "The Making of *McTeague* and *The Octopus*" (University of California, 1956), which should have been published but has not been. Lundy convincingly established the chronology of composition of these two novels and discussed the important themes which Norris wrote for Gates at Harvard. He was the first to show in some detail how much *The Octopus* owed in its philosophy to Norris's science professor at the University of California, Joseph Le Conte. Lundy's brief introduction to *The Octopus* (New York: American Century Series, 1957) argues that Norris borrowed techniques from Zola but not materialistic determinism. Norris's own position Lundy calls "evolutionary transcendentalism."

The influence Norris might have had on later writers has been greatly neglected. Perhaps because Norris was so heavily indebted to Zola, critics have not had much inclination to explore the mark he might have made on others. Henry Dan Piper's "Frank Norris and Scott Fitzgerald" (*HLQ*, Aug. 1956) should have set critics off on a new kind of search, but it has not. Piper pointed out the influence of Norris's work, especially *Vandover*, on Fitzgerald.

If the 1950s began with Åhnebrink's attempt to fit Norris into the European stream of literary naturalism, much of the remainder of the decade was spent trying to denaturalize him. He began to be treated more as an individual and less as an example of a literary trend. One way of doing this was through utilizing the tools of Freudian psychology. Norris's psychoanalyst of the fifties was Maxwell Geismar. His *Rebels and Ancestors: The American Novel, 1890–1915* (Boston, 1953) opened with a lengthy chapter on Norris. In his preface, Geismar explained: "Because Frank Norris illustrates the impact of the new age upon the old so clearly in the meeting of the Angel and the Brute in our fiction at the turn of the century, I have used him to open this volume and to serve as a figurehead for the period." Geismar's penetratingly interesting essay probes beneath the boyish surface of Frank Norris and discovers a man afraid of drives within himself that he did not understand—the "obsessive preoccupation of a spirit in the grip of what is considered to be a destructive physical or psychological process." Geismar finds, however, that Norris's "wound was also a source of his power; the animal instincts were the origin of his most human insights; and even the tormented rites of reversionary emotions became a path of liberation in the works of art." Geismar's persistent use of the jargon of psychology is annoying, but his essay is one of the most original and incisive discussions yet to be published on Norris.

Not so incisive is Kenneth S. Lynn's attempt to examine Norris's work in terms of a mother-father conflict (*The Dream of Success*, Boston, 1955). Lynn's argument involves him in a tremendous amount of guessing, some of it wide of the mark. "There is no doubt," he writes of young Norris's broken arm, "that Norris's failure to prove himself to his father on the playing field was a crucial event in his life." Or, referring to Norris's fascination with Froissart's *Chronicles*: it was "another way his [the father's] son took to hide his naked hero worship of his father." Norris's heroines, Lynn claims, are all tall and strong because they represent his mother: "It is not so much that they are of abnormal size, but that the viewpoint from which they are described is that of a small boy looking at his mother." In the end, Lynn asserts, Norris finally cast off the mother influence. Whereas Geismar, despite all his talk of morbidity, oedipal relationships, and castration complexes, has contributed significantly to an understanding of Norris and his work, Lynn seems to have performed an exercise in futile conjecture. More perceptive is Lynn's introduction to *The Octopus* (Boston: Riverside Editions, 1958), although his analysis of Presley as "Norris's intellectual" does not take enough into account the important role of instinct in the novel.

Two articles in 1955 were of particular interest in the new attempt to understand Norris's work not merely as naturalistic fiction but for what it is. Charles G. Hoffmann in "Norris and the Responsibility of the Novelist" (*SAQ*, Oct. 1955) argued that "by the time Norris came to write *The Octopus* and *The Pit*, he explored the power of love as man's saving element in a world of impersonal forces. Thus the regenerative power of love seems to be Norris's solution to the dilemma presented by the interaction of deterministic forces and social responsibilities on his characters. The solution is fundamentally a moral one." Therefore, Hoffmann rightly concluded, "the key to Norris's literary practice lies not in his adherence to any one theory of the novel such as 'naturalism.' " Donald Pizer, in the first of several important articles on Norris, reconsidered the charge of philosophical inconsistency so often leveled against Norris. In "Another Look at *The Octopus*" (*NCF*, Dec. 1955), Pizer made clear what had for some reason remained fuzzy in the minds of many previous critics, that much of the ostensible inconsistency in *The Octopus* was not Norris's wavering between positions of free will and determinism but the character Presley's, through whom much of the story is told. If Presley's role is understood, the problem of thematic fragmentation is largely solved. Pizer also pointed out that *The Octopus* owed as much to the transcendentalists as to naturalism.

For students of American naturalistic writing, the most important book to be published in the fifties was Charles Child Walcutt's *American Literary Naturalism, A Divided Stream* (Minneapolis, Minn., 1956). Walcutt thoughtfully surveyed the work not only of Norris,

Crane, London, and Dreiser but also that of certain important realists such as Harold Frederic, Hamlin Garland, and Winston Churchill. In addition, he related the naturalism of the older authors to more recent writers like Anderson, Farrell, Steinbeck, Hemingway, and Dos Passos. Walcutt's chapter on Norris is uneven; it includes most of the ideas expressed in his previously published articles and thus in some ways reflects an earlier critical position. At a time that critics were beginning to move away from the idea that Norris was a muddled thinker in *The Octopus*, for example, Walcutt stuck to the position taken by Chamberlain and Hicks twenty years before, that "the wheat books, magnificently conceived, fail structurally because they contain conflicting and contradictory sets of ideas." Walcutt's most thoughtful contribution is in his discussion of *Vandover and the Brute*, which he says narrowly misses being a modern tragedy. In reexamining the characteristics of literary naturalism, Walcutt made the long overdue point that naturalism was not a world-view which was new and terrible but a new pronouncement of old truths: "In short, so long as it is essentially transcendental, naturalism will give full recognition to the power and immensity of the physical world but will also assume a meaning in it that is akin to and ideally accessible to the mind of man; so that man achieves tragic dignity as he strives to penetrate and master his own nature and the physical universe. . . . Seen in this light, naturalism is no revolutionary departure from the world-view of Shakespearian tragedy. It is rather a mode of presenting in realistic 'modern' terms the forces, microcosmic and macrocosmic, against which man has always tragically contended. Naturalism is the modern approach to Fate." The oversimplifications of literary historians about naturalism as an ogre-offspring of Darwin should have been answered once and for all by this clarification.

If all of the old and tired generalizations about Norris and naturalism were not completely silenced, at least they were not heard so frequently as in the past. Norris was being examined in new ways and by discriminating and thoughtful critics. Richard Chase, for example, gave Norris a chapter in *The American Novel and its Tradition* (Garden City, N.Y., 1957) among the exclusive company of Hawthorne, Melville, James, Twain, and Faulkner. Although Chase's treatment of Norris is provocative, some of his ideas are questionable. Seeing Norris as being in deep sympathy "with the doctrines of American Populism, the movement of agrarian protest and revolt which was in its heyday when Norris was forming his ideas in the 1880's and 1890's," Chase is led to conclude that Norris hated the city. "The City (even San Francisco) is the abode of evil and decay, like the East, in Norris's

Populist mythology." What Chase overlooks is that Norris's attitude toward big centers of population was ambivalent—there was, to be sure, evil and decay there, but there was also vitality, force, in a word, Life. San Francisco never failed to fascinate Norris because he considered it a cross section of all that was vigorous and exciting in American life. Chase is undoubtedly correct, however, in his observation that "there is all through his work a tension between Norris the liberal humanist and ardent democrat and Norris the protofascist, complete with a racist view of Anglo-Saxon supremacy . . . and a portentous nihilism. . . ." This was a restatement in fresh terms of an old idea, the split between Norris the romantic and Norris the naturalist. Chase was the first to call Norris what he no doubt was, "a classic case of the modern lowbrow novelist, something of an intellectual himself to be sure, and yet a lowbrow because of his native temperament and conviction—but also because . . . lowbrowism is one of the most successful literary poses in modern America," and to fit him into a tradition of "anti- or non-intellectualism shown by most of the important modern novelists except those who belong to the school of James and Howells."

Three other essays of this period took another look at Norris's world view. Arnold L. Goldsmith in "The Development of Frank Norris's Philosophy" (*Studies in Honor of John Wilcox*, Detroit, Mich., 1958) traced Norris's vacillation between positions of determinism and free will, concluding that he was neither romantic nor naturalist: "It is this optimistic world view which places his complete works on the literary bridge between romanticism and naturalism." In "Romantic Individualism in Garland, Norris and Crane" (*AQ*, Winter 1958), Donald Pizer defined Norris's final position as "an imaginative and emotional reliance upon self in the presence of nature." And in "Frank Norris and the Werewolf of Guilt" (*MLQ*, Sept. 1959), Stanley Cooperman argued that "Frank Norris, in *McTeague* and *Vandover*, was motivated far more directly by Calvinist-Christian guilt than by scientific naturalism." By now, it was becoming extremely difficult to consider Frank Norris in the simplistic terms of "naturalist" or "determinist" which at one time had been so freely used to sum him up.

The several literary histories of the fifties reflected this growing trend to view Norris in a more complex light. In his crisply written essay, "Facts of Life *versus* Pleasant Reading" (*The Literature of the American People*, New York, 1951), Clarence Gohdes commented that "*The Octopus* shows how the author had learned to mix Zola and Hugo, Tolstoi and Dickens, with perhaps a dash of Stevenson, into a palatable literary cocktail all his own." Grant C. Knight surveyed most of Norris's work in his two volumes, *The Critical Period in American Lit-*

erature (Chapel Hill, N.C., 1951) and *The Strenuous Age in American Literature* (Chapel Hill, N.C., 1954). He pointed out the extent to which Norris brought American life vividly to the reading public. Only Van Wyck Brooks, who deplored Norris's "confused" naturalism, reverted atavistically to the stale arguments of yesteryear in his *The Confident Years: 1885–1915* (New York, 1952). Norris also received brief attention in more specialized literary histories such as Everett Carter's *Howells and the Age of Realism* (Philadelphia, 1954) and Frederick J. Hoffman's *The Modern Novel in America, 1900–1950* (Chicago, 1951). Edward Wagenknecht, who had written a sensitive estimate of Norris's work over twenty years earlier, reexamined it in *Cavalcade of the American Novel* (New York, 1952). Taking note of the long-standing argument over philosophical inconsistency in *The Octopus*, Wagenknecht raised a new point: "Whether it is artistically unified would seem to be a more important consideration."

By 1960 very few critical assumptions about Norris's work had gone unchallenged. Above all, it was no longer meaningful (or even intelligent) to categorize Norris as a "naturalist" without important qualifications or, indeed, to talk about naturalism in the old simplistic terms. In "Frank Norris and the Genteel Tradition" (*TSL*, 1960), William B. Dillingham cautioned against overemphasizing Norris's break with the fiction of polite society, for in retrospect his differences with the genteel tradition can be seen as far less pronounced than they appeared to readers of his time and a few decades thereafter.

One critical viewpoint which had been expressed repeatedly throughout previous years by numerous critics without serious dissent was that *McTeague* was flawed by the "romantic" subplot involving the old people, Grannis and Miss Baker. In "The Old Folks of *McTeague*" (*NCF*, Sept. 1961), William B. Dillingham pointed out that there are no fundamental differences between the forces that bring Old Grannis and Miss Baker together and those that destroy McTeague and Trina. The issue is a broad one, for the tendency to see everything in Norris's work which is pleasant and ends happily as "romantic" and everything which is unpleasant and destructive as "naturalistic" constitutes a failure to understand Norris's most basic belief—that the forces to which man is subjected, especially his deepest instinctive drives, may lead to fulfillment and happiness as well as to destruction.

George W. Johnson's article on "Frank Norris and Romance" (*AL*, Mar. 1961) places Norris, as did Stanley Cooperman a few years earlier, in the Calvinist tradition "of spiritual antinomies in a cosmos whose causation was ordered yet inscrutable." According to Johnson, Norris was attempting "to reconstitute romance in American letters" on the basis of "a precarious balance between the centrifugal pull of large abstractions [romance] and a centripetal interest in careful observation [realism]." Johnson's otherwise provocative article is blemished by his insistence that McTeague is a sort of agrarian hero: "Gullible, mute, and unmalicious, McTeague is an Anglo-Saxon country boy, a figure of archetypal innocence destroyed by an evil objectified in the city." Johnson presented fundamentally the same argument in "The Frontier Behind Frank Norris' *McTeague* (*HLQ*, Nov. 1962), where he described McTeague as something of a frontiersman out of place in civilization, "a debased version of the folkloristic mountain man, like a muted Mike Fink." In stressing Norris's Populist bent, Johnson was following the lead of Richard Chase, and in doing so he made fundamentally the same error in overemphasizing the purity of McTeague and the evil of the city. In formulations like the following, however, he goes much further than Chase: "*McTeague* does reflect the agrarian distrust of urban life as parasitic, corrupting, and degenerate. In Trina's unexplained pallor, we find the Populist conception of the city girl's vitiation; in McTeague's perversion we find the Populist conviction that trade was a harlot and the metropolis a Babylon. The overwrought emphasis on gold in the novel mirrors the agrarian preoccupation with the money power, and in McTeague's victimization by the law, one might argue, there is worked out the Populist melodrama of the struggle between the only two urban classes, the robbers and the robbed."

That McTeague is not simply a good-natured country boy driven to crime by urban evil was pointed out concurrently by William B. Dillingham in "Themes and Literary Techniques in the Fiction of Frank Norris" (University of Pennsylvania doctoral dissertation, 1961) and by Donald Pizer in "Evolutionary Ethical Dualism in Frank Norris' *Vandover and the Brute* and *McTeague*" (*PMLA*, Dec. 1961). Dillingham and Pizer argued that in his characterization of McTeague, Norris was following to a large extent the theories of the popular Italian criminologist Cesare Lombroso and that McTeague is a clear representative of a type Lombroso termed the born criminal. Even though McTeague was not meant to represent a typical Anglo-Saxon with healthy heritage, it is still possible for the reader to feel sympathy for him as a human being. Indeed, Pizer further pointed out in "Nineteenth-Century American Naturalism: An Essay in Definition" (*BuR*, Dec. 1965) that the essence of American literary naturalism is partly the tension between the forces that determine a character's life and his own individual suffering and striving. Another tension completed Pizer's definition of naturalism: that between the common and ordinary on the one hand and the sensational and extraordinary on the other hand. Pizer convincingly examined *McTeague, Sister Carrie,* and *The Red Badge of Courage* with these two sets of contrasts in mind. His contention was that traditional definitions of naturalism have "handicapped thinking both about the movement as a whole and about individual works within the movement. It has resulted in much condescension toward those writers who are supposed to be naturalists yet whose fictional sensationalism (an aspect of romanticism) and moral ambiguity (a quality inconsistent with the absolutes of determinism) appear to make their work flawed specimens of the mode."

Pizer's thoughtful work on the theory of American naturalism has added immensely to our understanding of that complicated literary movement. Several of his previously published articles were collected and reprinted as *Realism and Naturalism in Nineteenth-Century American Literature* (Carbondale, Ill., 1966), an indispensable volume to the student of this period. Not only is Pizer's analysis of what constitutes a naturalistic novel original and penetrating, but his argument about the relevance of naturalistic fiction lifts it from the barrenness of the cold Darwinian winter to the realm of human values: "It involves a belief that life on its lowest levels is not so simple as it seems to be from higher levels. It suggests that even the least significant human being can feel and strive powerfully and can suffer the extraordinary consequences of his emotions, and that no range of human experience is free of the moral complexities and ambiguities which Milton set his fallen angels to debating. Naturalism reflects an affirmative ethical conception of life, for it asserts the value of all life by endowing the lowest character with emotion and defeat and with moral ambiguity, no matter how poor or ignoble he may seem."

An important assumption underlying most of Pizer's work on Norris is that "the naturalistic novel is . . . not so superficial or reductive as it implicitly appears to be in its conventional definition." In "Synthetic Criticism and Frank Norris; Or, Mr. Marx, Mr. Taylor, and *The Octopus*" (*AL*, Jan. 1963, reprinted as Chapter Thirteen of *Realism and Naturalism*), Pizer objected to oversimplification and distortion by critics who try to make a literary work fit a pre-established pattern. He particularly objected to Leo Marx's analysis of *The Octopus*, which, he charged, does not take into account the intrinsic pattern of the novel but attempts to superimpose an extrinsic pattern upon it. Pizer's own approach to *The Octopus* can be seen in "The Concept of Nature in Frank Norris' *The Octopus*" (*AQ*, Spring 1962). In his continuing effort to show the artistic integrity of Norris's work, Pizer examined *The Octopus* from the standpoint of evolutionary theism, that eclectic view of the late nineteenth century which attempted to reconcile religion with the new theories about evolution. Norris's teacher in this area was Joseph Le Conte at Berkeley, who combined in the manner of John Fiske "Spencerianism, transcendentalism and utilitarianism" into a philosophical brew that could take care of almost any conflicting problems. Evolution could be viewed as both scientific and theistic; evil could be seen as real but temporary; God and Force could be identified. It is this view, Pizer argued, which accounts for the optimistic ending of *The Octopus*, and to this coherent system of ideas the novel is true from beginning to end. Those who complain of philosophical inconsistency are actually quarreling "with such basic Christian paradoxes as the coexistence of free will and determinism, the eternity of life despite death and the emergence of good out of evil."

A much different and less convincing interpretation of *The Octopus* was offered by James K. Folsom. In "Social Darwinism or Social Protest? The 'Philosophy' of *The Octopus*" (*MFS*, Winter 1962–63), Folsom found the novel's optimistic ending ironic and reverted to the muckraking interpretation of the book which had not been offered in several years. *The Octopus*, Folsom concluded, was clearly a novel of social protest and not otherwise philosophical in its content. Most serious readers of Norris's work will find this interpretation untenable.

Oscar Cargill agreed that Norris began his novel as an out and out protest against the Southern Pacific Railroad but contended that the writer's plans were drastically altered when he interviewed Collis P. Huntington. This essay is one of the few places where one may find an accurate and concise summary of the Mussel Slough incident, the model for the pitched battle at the irrigation ditch in *The Octopus*. Although Cargill's essay, which appeared as the afterword to the Signet Classics edition of *The Octopus* (1964) and as a chapter in his volume *Toward a Pluralistic Criticism* (Carbondale, Ill., 1965), is admittedly based upon speculation, it is fascinating reading. According to Cargill, Norris was greatly impressed by Huntington, who told Norris something he had not heard before, namely that the wheat farmers had tried to "pack" the state rate-fixing commission. The surprised Norris then found it difficult to see the conflict in the same terms as before, with the railroad as the villain and the farmers as victims. He then set to work and shifted the emphasis of the book. The interview, argued Cargill, "took the heart out of Norris and . . . this explains the flatulence of *The Pit*."

It has been fashionable since Norris's death to speculate as to what kind of fiction he might have written had he lived beyond his short thirty-two years. Michael Millgate, unlike most recent critics, feels that the two volumes of Norris's proposed wheat trilogy seem so unalike and rife with inconsistencies because they represent a partial job. In *American Social Fiction: James to Cozzens* (London, 1964), Millgate wrote: "Had Norris lived, it is conceivable that he might have been able, in *The Wolf*, to round off the trilogy into a satisfactory whole, making the apparent inconsistencies within individual works fully comprehensible as parts of an overall pattern." As is, Millgate does not rate Norris very high, but shows how his work, especially *The Pit*, fulfills what James had stated the American novel of business might be: "The epic heroism, the 'wounds of the market,' the 'ferocity of battle,' the imagery of war and the aura of romance, the central importance of the relationship between the businessman and his 'immitigable womankind.'"

Various kinds of literary histories in the sixties surveyed Norris's work. H. Wayne Morgan in *American Writers in Rebellion from Mark Twain to Dreiser* (New York, 1965) praised Norris highly but added little that was new to a critical interpretation of his work. Robert W. Schneider's *Five Novelists of the Progressive Era* (New York, 1965) likewise covered ground that had already been well covered. In *The American 1890s: Life and Times of a Lost Generation* (New York, 1966), Larzer Ziff argued that though Le Conte's influence on Norris may have been in some ways beneficial, *The Octopus* would have been better without it: "In short, the realism of the scene works powerfully to make *The Octopus* a first-rate novel, while the LeContian theory, used as a Zolaesque organizing principle, drags it back into the confusing and the second-rate." Nevertheless, Ziff concluded, "the genius which was released, once this handle to the world [popular Darwinism] was grasped, brought into American literature not only a new cast of characters but a closer observation and shrewder delineation of the problems they shared with their fellows—not the least of which was sexuality."

This thesis was developed further by Gordon O. Taylor in *The Passages of Thought: Psychological Representation in the American Novel 1870–1900* (New York, 1969). Taylor indicated that in *McTeague* sex "is more clearly acknowledged as psychological fact" than in earlier American novels. Norris treated sex, argued Taylor, as a "process which is physiologically determined, unconsciously experienced by the character, and detachedly observed by the author." Yet the influence of Le Conte is apparent, for the force behind the process "is an abstract conception removed from the action and from the passage of time, and positing a moral consciousness or a moral instinct to struggle with purely physical urges."

One of the most provocative comments from a literary history of this period came from Jay Martin's *Harvests of Change: American Literature, 1865–1914* (Englewood Cliffs, N.J., 1967). Martin saw the real subject of *The Octopus* as the writing of an American epic: "Presley is a writer preparing, at the conclusion of the novel, to write the epic he has lived; the novel is in a sense hung upon his growing insight into the nature of an American epic, as he has lived through it. During the book, he rejects most of the genteel notions of the epic." Presley, then, has undergone the basic training of heart and mind and has at the end been brought through several steps to the point of being able to begin the epic he wanted to write in the beginning, and "the quest for the epic becomes the subject of the epic."

Three commentaries on Norris from this period were largely unsympathetic. Warner Berthoff, in *The Ferment of Realism: American Literature, 1884–1919* (New York, 1965), admitted that "Frank Norris may be the writer this history will be most unjust to." Berthoff found it difficult to account for Norris's "continuing reputation as a serious figure in American literature"; dismissed *The Octopus* as "preposterous"; and described Norris's style "as if Cole Porter had written novels." Philip Walker complained in "*The Octopus* and Zola: A New Look" (*Sym*, Summer 1967) that Norris's "most Zolaesque" novel, *The Octopus*, falls far short of Zola's work because of heavy-handedness in the use of metaphor, obtrusive "romantic wishfulfillment," and "metaphysical anxiety," which becomes in the concluding pages "shrill, dominant, infinitely disturbing." A like objection is expressed by W. M. Frohock (*Frank Norris*, UMPAW, Minneapolis, 1968), who argued that *The Octopus* is greatly indebted to Zola but much inferior to the master's work. The thesis of Frohock's essay is that Norris "emerges as an instinctive melodramatist working with naturalist materials." Frohock's discussion of Norris's life and work is unfortunately pervaded by a tone of somewhat amused condescension. Frohock writing about Norris reminds one of Norris writing about McTeague. In Frohock's appraisal, Norris suffers greatly from not having written like Henry James, who "has reformed our notion of the novel."

At no other time in the history of criticism on Norris has there been so much interest in his essays as in the 1960s. The posthumously published collection *The Responsibilities of the Novelist* (1903) was for many years the only source of Norris's literary criticism. Willard E. Martin published "Two Uncollected Essays by Frank Norris" (*AL*, May 1936), but it was not until 1964 that a new collection of Norris's essays on literature appeared. Much more comprehensive than the earlier *Responsibilities* (which Norris had no hand in putting together), Donald Pizer's edition of *The Literary Criticism of Frank Norris* includes articles which Norris wrote for the San Francisco *Wave*, as well as several of the "Weekly Letters" from the *Chicago American Literary and Art Review*, all of which were omitted from the earlier volume. In contrast to *Responsibilities*, Pizer's edition is arranged carefully, with Norris's essays on literary theory coming first, followed by numerous articles that reveal Norris applying these theories to specific works or problems. Pizer is one of few critics who have considered Norris seriously as a literary critic. The result is a thoughtful, comprehensive, and logically presented body of editorial comment in this volume. In every respect, Pizer's work supersedes *Responsibilities* as the definitive edition of Norris's literary criticism. The remaining seven letters which Norris had written for the *Chicago American* and which Pizer did not include in his edition were edited and published by Richard Allan Davison (*ALR*, Summer 1968).

Both the editorial commentary in *The Literary Criticism of Frank Norris*[3] and Pizer's earlier "Frank Norris' Definition of Naturalism" (*MFS*, Winter 1962–63) admit that the critical essays are "poorly written, repetitious, and occasionally plain silly," but Pizer is able to see that despite their crudity they "contain a coherent critical attitude of some importance." As Pizer sees it, Norris "conceived of naturalism as a fictional mode which illustrated some fundamental truth of life within a detailed presentation of the sensational and low." Such a concept resolved the differences between romanticism and realism by taking from the one the idea of "philosophical depth," from the other the technique of "detailed accuracy," and adding a third ingredient which both romanticism and realism neglect, the use of the "sensational and low" as subject matter.

After examining Norris's criticism on literature and his opinions about social responsibility, Joseph J. Kwiat concluded that the two strains were separate and conflicting. In "Frank Norris: The Novelist as Social Critic and Literary Theorist" (*ArQ*, Winter 1962), Kwiat stated that "any attempt to reconcile completely Norris' aesthetic theories with his social theories is an ill-fated venture." Nevertheless, Kwiat argued that in his essays Norris reflected the same intellectual struggle experienced by several other important American writers, including Melville, Twain, Stephen Crane, Dreiser, Hemingway, Steinbeck, Dos Passos, and Farrell.

After Ernest Marchand's critical study appeared in 1942, another

---

3. Certain paragraphs from Pizer's introduction were republished as "The Significance of Frank Norris's Literary Criticism," Chapter Nine in *Realism and Naturalism*.

book-length work on Norris was not published until the 1960s, when three appeared. Warren French's lively *Frank Norris* (TUSAS, New York, 1962) summarizes Norris's life in a chapter and then surveys his work chronologically. French's contention is that Norris was not so much a naturalist in the French tradition as he was "a scion of the transcendentalists." Although this thesis is certainly tenable, French tends to carry it too far. As a transcendentalist, Norris must hate urban civilization, find nature benevolent, and be optimistic in all of his works. To make him so, French has to perform a number of critical contortions. To get around Norris's comment in *The Octopus* that nature is indifferent, for example, French argues that Norris did not really mean indifferent but "unconscious": "Nature, he [Norris] feels, does good without thinking about it—but it does do good in the long run." French rates *The Octopus* and *McTeague* somewhat lower than usual and considers *The Pit* "the only work in which Norris shows promise of achieving intellectual maturity."

Donald Pizer's *The Novels of Frank Norris* (Bloomington, Ind., 1966) uses the foundation that he had established in several previously published articles to show that "Norris' novels are philosophical novels in the sense that they contain coherent systems of belief and value." Although some readers will feel that Pizer somewhat overemphasizes the influence of Joseph Le Conte on Norris and attributes too much in Norris's work to his belief in "evolutionary theism," this book represents an enormous contribution to criticism on Frank Norris. Its greatest strength is that it considers Norris in a new context, in fresh terms, and avoids entrapment in the tired generalizations that had been piling up for years.

William B. Dillingham's *Frank Norris: Instinct and Art* deals with both Norris's life (see *Biography*, above) and writings. Dillingham views Norris as being similar to D. H. Lawrence, who insisted on the gods within "that come and go." The gods for Norris were man's instinctive drives, sometimes creative, sometimes destructive, but always the primary force of life. No external influence upon Norris was as important as his own instincts (and the source of those will remain an eternal mystery). Dillingham argues that although much of what Norris wrote was not successful, his attempt was extremely ambitious, especially in the area of literary symbolism.

The several decades of criticism on Norris have by no means exhausted the possibilities for study. Long categorized with the tag *Naturalism* (and in a Death Valley of literary history), Norris has in recent years been viewed from new and provocative angles. Still, it has not been fully appreciated that Norris's works are a mine of Americana and that he himself is an ideal subject to study for an understanding of the culture and thought of late nineteenth-century America. In Norris the principal American myths and national contradictions of his time are reflected with rare clarity. He was both roughrider and velvet-jacketed gentleman, racist and liberal, traditionalist and progressive, artist and lowbrow. Like F. Scott Fitzgerald, who read and admired him, Norris was of that unusual breed of writers who seem totally fused with the dominant spirit of their time and yet manage to see life from a larger perspective with a clear, honest vision. He also needs further consideration as an extremely ambitious literary artist whose failures in art are nearly as interesting and instructive as his accomplishments.

Edward Taylor

NORMAN S. GRABO

THE DISCOVERY of Edward Taylor's poetry signifies considerably more than the recovery of yet another minor poet of the seventeenth century, though that alone might justify the attention he has received since 1937, for he is not a bad poet, and sometimes startlingly good. Its significance is inextricably bound into the circumstances and conditions that generated the poetry in the first place. Here is a real toad in the garden of scholarly explanations, justifications, rationalizations—a real (if limited) poet in the midst of a culture absolutely inimical to real poetry. American scholarship had by 1937 explained thoroughly, inventively, and admirably why, for social, political, theological, and aesthetic reasons, virtually no real poetry had been created by New England Puritans—by the dominant culture of the first century of American civilization. The appearance of Taylor has thus proved a greater shock than his intrinsic poetic merit might warrant. But if, as Thomas H. Johnson believed from the beginning and as I believe with him, Taylor's presence must significantly alter the map of American literature, it must yet be confessed that that potential remains essentially unrealized. Indeed, and quite properly, the first thirty years of Taylor criticism have attempted to grasp Taylor's work on its own terms, to define a new and unexpected phenomenon. There is much more to do, but the beginnings are very promising.

BIBLIOGRAPHY

No single comprehensive and complete bibliography of Taylor exists, primarily because of the recentness of scholarly concern with Taylor, the continued discovery of new materials, and the rapid increase in Taylor scholarship and criticism in the 1960s. Thomas H. Johnson described the Yale manuscript "Poetical Works" in detail in *The Poetical*

Works of Edward Taylor (New York, 1939). He also listed the other manuscripts in Taylor's hand at Yale and at the Westfield Athenaeum, Westfield, Massachusetts; two known printed works from nineteenth-century issues of *CMHS* (a letter to Increase Mather and the "Diary"); and twenty-nine "Secondary Works," necessarily biographical.

Donald E. Stanford expanded the number of bibliographical sources to thirty-five in his doctoral dissertation, "An Edition of the Complete Poetical Works of Edward Taylor" (Stanford, 1953). Although that bibliography was not retained in Stanford's *The Poems of Edward Taylor* (New Haven, Conn., 1960), two excellent analytical appendices appear there. The first is a detailed description of all the previous printings of Taylor's poems, diary, and letters. The second appendix is an annotated description of manuscripts in the Yale University Library, the Massachusetts Historical Society, and the Westfield Athenaeum. Stanford also describes for the first time three manuscript books in the Redwood Library and Athenaeum at Newport, Rhode Island (see *Manuscripts and Letters*, below). These appendices do not appear in the second edition of *Poems* (1963), issued in paperback.

The Prince Library: A Catalogue of the Collection of Books and Manuscripts which formerly belonged to the Reverend Thomas Prince (Boston, 1870) describes somewhat inaccurately the Taylor manuscripts in the Boston Public Library. Some of these materials are listed in Norman S. Grabo, *Edward Taylor* (New York, 1961) in a briefly annotated "Selected Bibliography" of primary and secondary sources. Donald Stanford's UMPAW pamphlet entitled *Edward Taylor* (Minneapolis, 1965) provides a brief selected bibliography usefully subdivided into "Selected and Collected Editions," "Poems in Magazines," "Bibliography," and "Biographical and Critical Studies."

Apart from doctoral dissertations which undertake a review of extant scholarship and criticism, there are only four attempts to survey secondary material. The bibliography volume of *LHUS* lists critical studies of Taylor only up to 1956. Carol Ann Hoffman provides a list of ten primary sources and forty-two secondary items, including some notes, reviews, and dissertations up to 1960, in "Edward Taylor: A Selected Bibliography" (*BB*, Jan.-Apr. 1961), limited to work appearing prior to the publication of Stanford's *Poems*. More up to date is the section on Taylor in J. A. Leo Lemay's "Seventeenth-Century American Poetry: A Bibliography of the Scholarship, 1943 to 1966" (*EALN*, Winter 1966), where the most recent item is dated 1966. Lemay includes doctoral dissertations announced in *DA*, as well as published books, articles, and anthologies. And the most recent survey is Mary Jane Elkins's "Edward Taylor: A Checklist" (*EAL*, Summer 1969) which is limited to published writings and lists by date 126 books, articles, and notes through the early months of 1969. Omissions, some minor misinformation, and inconsistent procedures make it difficult to perceive the logic of this unrefined checklist, but it stands now as the most complete single guide to Taylor scholarship. Not the least interesting fact reflected here is that ninety-one of these items are products of the last decade.

Doctoral dissertations devoted to Taylor are listed in James Woodress, *Dissertations in American Literature 1891–1966* (Durham, N.C., 1968). And Richard Beale Davis makes telling appraisals of current scholarship and criticism in *American Literary Scholarship*, edited by James Woodress, under the heading "Literature to 1800." One special bibliography deserves attention. From the inventory of Taylor's estate, made about two months after his death, Thomas H. Johnson compiled a list of 192 titles in Taylor's library for his edition of *The Poetical Works*. The list has some minor errors, but considering the meager evidence provided in the inventory and the lack at that time of all of Taylor's manuscripts, Johnson's identifications are remarkably astute. The list still represents a relatively untapped source of information about the development of Taylor's thought.

EDITIONS

There is no collected edition of Taylor's works and no complete edition of his poems, all of which, but for two stanzas from "Upon Wedlock and Death of Children" included in Cotton Mather's *Right Thoughts in Sad Hours* (London, 1689), remained in manuscript until the 1930s. After announcing the significance of the manuscript "Poetical Works" (at a meeting of the Modern Language Association in 1936), Thomas H. Johnson, in "Edward Taylor: A Puritan 'Sacred Poet'" (*NEQ*, June 1937), published "Huswifery," "Upon Wedlock and Death of Children," "The Ebb and Flow," four poems and some shorter excerpts from *Gods Determinations*, nine meditations, and a short excerpt from "My Last Declamation in the Colledg Hall."

Response to the poems was swift and favorable. Norman Holmes Pearson and William Rose Benét printed eight selections in the very successful *Oxford Anthology of American Literature* (New York, 1938), Perry Miller incorporated references to Taylor's manuscript poems in the now classic *The New England Mind: The Seventeenth Century* (Cambridge, Mass., 1939), and Miller and Johnson made room for several poems in *The Puritans: A Sourcebook of Their Writing* (New York, 1938).

Johnson then published a very ample selection of the poems in a limited edition of 925 copies under the title, *The Poetical Works of Edward Taylor* (New York: Rockland Editions, 1939). This volume was reissued in 1943 by the Princeton University Press, and released yet again in paperback by Princeton in 1966. The standard edition for twenty years, it includes a brief biography and descriptive evaluation of the poetry, a glossary, notes, a list of Taylor's library, a description of the manuscript, a bibliography, and the following poems: all of *Gods Determinations*, "An Address to the Soul Occasioned by a Rain," "Upon a Spider Catching a Fly," "Huswifery," "Upon Wedlock and Death of Children," "The Ebb and Flow," and thirty-one meditations. The quality of Johnson's selections may be indicated by the fact that no subsequent anthology of the period ignores Taylor, and there is hardly an anthologized poem that did not first appear here. Johnson's texts, however, are not reliable.

In 1942 Johnson also published "The Topical Verses of Edward Taylor" (*Publications of the Colonial Society of Massachusetts*, Feb. 1942), including the following poems: "Elegy on Mr. Sims," "Elegy on Francis Willoughby," "Declamation in the Colledg Hall," "Elegy on Mr. John Allen," "Elegy on Mr. Charles Chauncey," "Acrostic Love Poem to Elizabeth Fitch," "Elegy on Mrs. Elizabeth Taylor," "Elegy on Mr. Sam Hooker," "Elegy on Mrs. Mehetabel Woodbridge," "Elegy on Dr. Increase Mather," and "Verses made upon Pope Joan." The following year, in "Some Edward Taylor Gleanings" (*NEQ*, June 1943), Johnson edited "Upon a Wasp Child with Cold," "Huswifery II," "Upon the Sweeping Flood," and eight previously unpublished meditations. Several additional poems from the "Poetical Works" were published between then and 1960 (all listed in Stanford, *Poems*).

In 1953, Donald E. Stanford transcribed all the poems from the Yale manuscript in his dissertation, "An Edition of the Complete Poetical Works of Edward Taylor." Done before the discovery of the Redwood Library manuscripts, this is the closest approach to date to a complete edition of the poems. Although its texts are not as exact as those of the printed *Poems* (1960), they are still an improvement over Johnson's, and are the basis for the Yale edition. Stanford's 189-page introduction is the fullest discussion thus far of Taylor's biography, theology, and poetry, and Stanford also transcribes Taylor's diary and his letter to Increase Mather.

In 1960, Stanford's texts, refined from their dissertation state but not representing all the poems in the manuscript "Poetical Works," were published as *The Poems of Edward Taylor*, with a foreword by Louis L. Martz; a twenty-four page introduction by Stanford on Taylor's biography, theology, previous editions, and the texts of the poems; a bibliographical appendix on previous editions; another detailed appendix on the Taylor manuscripts (see *Manuscripts and Letters*, below); a glossary of technical, theological, and dialectal terms (essentially the same as the glossary of the 1953 dissertation); and the following poems: all 217 *Preparatory Meditations*, all of *Gods Determinations*, "When Let by Rain," "Upon a Spider Catching a Fly," "Upon a Wasp Child with Cold," "Huswifery" and "Another upon the Same," "Upon Wedlock and Death of Children," "The Ebb and Flow," "Upon the Sweeping Flood," "A Funeral Poem [upon his wife Elizabeth]," "An Elegy upon the Death of . . . Mr. Samuel Hooker," "A Fig for Thee Oh! Death," and extracts from the *Metrical History of Christianity*. This edition was reissued, abridged, in 1963, as a Yale Paperbound. It deletes both the foreword and introduction, replacing them with a new introduction by Donald Stanford, and deletes the excerpt from the *Metrical History*, both elegies, "A Fig for Thee Oh! Death," both bibliographical appendices, and sixty-six meditations.

Stanford published his typescript of the whole 21,500-line *Edward Taylor's Metrical History of Christianity* (Cleveland, Ohio: Micro Photo, Inc.) in 1962, from the Redwood Library collection, and from that same collection, "The Earliest Poems of Edward Taylor" (*AL*, May 1960), selecting "A Letter sent to his Brother Joseph Taylor and his wife after a visit," "The Lay-Mans Lamentation," "an epigram on the Archbishop of Canterbury," "A dialogue in verse between the writer and a Maypole dresser," "this in a letter I sent to my schoolfellow, W. M.," and "Another Answer [to a Popish Pamphlet]," as verses originally by Taylor, presumably before his emigration to America.

Until the discovery of the Redwood Library cache, it was assumed that Taylor's diary, first published in *PMHS* (1880), had been lost. Since then, the diary, which covers Taylor's expedition from England, his college years at Harvard, and his final settlement in Westfield, has been reedited with an introduction by Francis Murphy in *The Diary of Edward Taylor* (Springfield, Mass., 1964).

Norman S. Grabo edited a diplomatic text of *Edward Taylor's Christographia* (New Haven, Conn., 1962), with an introduction arguing that these fourteen sacrament-day sermons preached between 1701 and 1703 constitute a kind of poetic workbook for the *Preparatory Meditations* (Second Series, 42–56), since the poems were "Chiefly upon the Doctrin preached," and therefore presumably followed the sacramental sermons in order of composition, in structure, and in controlling logic and imagery. The full title of the Yale manuscript is "CHRISTOGRAPHIA. or A Discourse touching Christs Person, Natures, the Personall Union of the Natures, Qualifications, and Operations Opened,

Confirmed, and Practically improoved in Severall Sermons delivered upon Certain Sacrament Dayes unto the Church and people of God in *Westfield*."

Eight more sermons—these from the Prince Collection of the Boston Public Library, and untitled by Taylor—were edited by Norman S. Grabo as *Edward Taylor's Treatise Concerning the Lord's Supper* (East Lansing, Mich., 1965). The editor's introduction argues that these sermons belong to the ecclesiastical and theological Stoddardean controversy over qualifications for admission to the sacrament of the Lord's Supper, and moreover, to the developing theories of "signs" or knowable marks of God's grace as they were expounded by Thomas Shepard and Jonathan Edwards. A practical rather than a definitive text, modernizing and regularizing some usage, this edition lacks adequate textual notes regarding substantive emendations and readings, but the "Explanatory Notes" are exceptionally full, making considerable use of the sources Taylor used in composing the sermons.

MANUSCRIPTS AND LETTERS

In the sketch of Edward Taylor supplied for William Sprague's *Annals of the American Pulpit* (1866), the Hon. Henry W. Taylor wrote that most of the books Taylor used were manuscript copies transcribed by Taylor: "His manuscripts were all handsomely bound in parchment by himself, of which tradition says he left, at his death, more than a hundred volumes." Detailed description of fourteen of these may be found in Stanford's *Poems*. The manuscripts described by Stanford, with their location, are:

1. "Poetical Works" (Yale University Library). Several brief or incomplete or simply very bad poems have not yet been printed; they are, however, all transcribed in Stanford's dissertation, "An Edition of the Complete Poetical Works of Edward Taylor."
2. "Poems found in the Binding of 'Poetical Works'" (Yale University Library); these are described in more detail and evaluated in Donald Junkins, "Edward Taylor's Revisions" (*AL*, May 1965).
3. "Manuscript Book" (Yale University Library).
4. "China's Description and Commonplace Book" (Yale University Library).
5. "Metallographia" (Yale University Library).
6. "Dispensatory" (Yale University Library).
7. "Christographia" (Yale University Library). These are fully

published and described in Norman S. Grabo, ed., *Edward Taylor's Christographia*.

8. "The Public Records of the Church at Westfield" (Westfield Athenaeum). John Hoyt Lockwood relied heavily upon this material, quoting portions of it in passing, in *Westfield and Its Historical Influences, 1669–1919: The Life of an Early Town* (Springfield, Mass., 1922). Part of the manuscript is printed in Donald Stanford, "Edward Taylor's 'Spiritual Relation' " (*AL*, Jan. 1964); this document is discussed in the context of "Traditional Patterns in Puritan Autobiography" by Daniel B. Shea in *Spiritual Autobiography in Early America* (Princeton, N.J., 1968). A microfilm of the entire manuscript was prepared by the Genealogical Society, Salt Lake City, Utah.

9. "Copy Book of the Council of Trent" (Westfield Athenaeum).

10. "Origen's *Contra Celsus* and *De Principiis*" (Westfield Athenaeum); described in Francis E. X. Murphy, "An Edward Taylor Manuscript Book" (*AL*, May 1959).

11. "Commonplace Book" (The Massachusetts Historical Society); two of the forty-two items—an exchange of letters—are published in Norman S. Grabo, "The Poet to the Pope: Edward Taylor to Solomon Stoddard" (*AL*, May 1960).

12. "Diary, Theological Notes, and Poems" (Redwood Library and Athenaeum). The diary has been twice published, and the poems appeared in Donald Stanford, "The Earliest Poems of Edward Taylor" (see *Editions*, above).

13. "A Metrical History of Christianity" (Redwood Library and Athenaeum); described fully in Donald E. Stanford, "Edward Taylor's Metrical History of Christianity" (*AL*, Nov. 1961).

14. "Harmony of the Gospels" (Redwood Library and Athenaeum).

  Charles W. Mignon discusses several of these manuscripts in "Some Notes on the History of the Edward Taylor Manuscripts" (*YULG*, Apr. 1965), also mentioning an additional manuscript:

15. "Notes on Divinity" (Yale University Library).

  One other manuscript collection has been mentioned previously:

16. "Extracts, by Rev. Edward Taylor, Westfield" (Boston Public Library); see *The Prince Library: A Catalogue* for a description of the contents. Of this material, Taylor's expanded foundation sermon, "A Particular Church Is God's House" (1679), the original of which is in Item 8 above, is described in Norman S. Grabo, "Edward Taylor on the Lord's Supper" (*Boston Public Library Quarterly*, Jan. 1960). Eight sermons delivered at Westfield in

1693–94 are published as *Edward Taylor's Treatise Concerning the Lord's Supper*, ed. Norman S. Grabo (East Lansing, Mich., 1965). Another item from this manuscript is described in Norman S. Grabo, " 'The Appeale Tried': Another Edward Taylor Manuscript" (*AL*, Nov. 1962).

Until recently a manuscript owned by Mr. Lewis S. Gannett escaped listing:

17. "Commonplace Book" (Yale University Library); Charles W. Mignon describes this book in "Another Taylor Manuscript at Yale" (*YULG*, Oct. 1966).

The manuscript letters of Taylor are all listed in Stanford, *Poems* (1960); he also lists all the letters previously printed, with the exception of the letter to Stoddard, cited above, Item 11. For manuscripts pertaining to Taylor, see Thomas H. Johnson, "Secondary Works," in *The Poetical Works*, and Alexander Medlicott, "Notes on Edward Taylor from the Diaries of Stephen Williams" (*AL*, May 1962).

BIOGRAPHY

Despite the fact that Taylor's relative obscurity has led to numerous biographical comments since his poetry first came to light, there is so far nothing approaching a full, authoritative, and reliable, not to say definitive, biography. While a good number of facts have by now been accumulated, they have mostly been put to the service of explaining episodes in Taylor's long poetic career. The central biographical problems have been these: When was he born? Was he by training and faith theologically orthodox by his contemporary standards? If he was, how could he have composed such sensuous poetry in an Anglo-Catholic and "Metaphysical" manner? And why did he suppress the publication of his poetry?

The fullest printed outline of Taylor's life is by Norman S. Grabo, *Edward Taylor*, based primarily upon previously published information. Grabo argues for Taylor's

social and theological orthodoxy, his involvement in the intellectual life of his times, his commitment to all that colonial New England represents. Except for the accidents of place and event that distinguish any individual, Taylor's upbringing, education, and vocation were typical. He was a learned man in an age of many learned men, a frontiersman when the entire continent was yet a wilderness, and a man of God in a land swarming with ministers. He detested monarchy, but he played the despot in his own congregation. He denounced Quakers and hated Roman Catholics. He knew there were devils and witches. He believed God exerted His providence in all minutiae of nature. He thought he was among God's chosen few and that by God's great design the mass of men skidded to everlasting and inescapable damnation. Viewed from the outside, from his "activities"—even his habit of versifying—Edward Taylor was a typical Puritan.

Grabo tries to record Taylor's inward biography as revealed in his prose and poetry and by the social occasions that provided the context for Taylor's writing. As critical and theoretical concerns gain the ascendancy, biographical considerations wane.

Briefer, less interpretative (and in tone more temperate) are Donald E. Stanford's several biographical sketches. The first appeared in his introduction to the 1960 edition of the *Poems*, a much reduced, lightly documented version of the life that appeared in his dissertation. For the second edition of the *Poems* (1963), Stanford prepared a new introductory essay. It incorporates new evidence regarding Taylor's parentage and birth, and his earliest poetry, concluding that

> Taylor, then, seems to have been endowed with most of those qualities usually connoted by the word *puritan*. He was learned, grave, severe, stubborn, and stiff-necked. He was very, very pious. But his piety was sincere. It was fed by a long continuous spiritual experience arising, so he felt, from a mystical communion with Christ. The reality and depth of this experience is amply witnessed by his poetry.

Another and expanded essay covering essentially the same factual material, but now interlarded with comments and judgments upon the documents, designed to emphasize that "Taylor is an anomaly," was published by Stanford in *Edward Taylor*. This 46-page pamphlet is presently the most up-to-date and authoritative guide to the public record of Taylor's life. It makes evident the fact that the question of Taylor's birth date cannot be established with certainty because no official record of his birth has been discovered and because "the baptismal entries of the Taylor family in the parish church of Burbage, England, are incomplete." But Stanford decides that it must have been 1642, ignoring other hypothetical dates as late as 1646 on the grounds of circumstantial evidence and the long-held family tradition supporting the early date.

When Thomas H. Johnson announced Taylor's poetry in 1937, he inadvertently raised a question that has plagued Taylor scholar-critics ever since. In "Edward Taylor: A Puritan 'Sacred Poet,'" Johnson clearly indicated "Taylor's artistry in stating orthodox covenant theology in terms of sensuous imagery," but in his emphatic conclusion he suggested that Taylor belonged to the tradition of Ango-Catholic conceitists and that he "turned to Anglican and, perhaps, to Catholic poets for example." Two years later, and much more circumspect in his introduction to the *Poetical Works*, Johnson insisted that the "reader need not search afield for analogues among the verses of the seventeenth-century conceitists to explain Taylor's choice of subject," and again that "the *Meditations* need no analogues among Anglo-Catholic sacramentalists to explain their adoration of Christ." He then went on to discriminate very carefully and accurately the points at which Congregational, Calvinist, Anglican, and Roman Catholic sacramental theology coincided, in order to explain the "orthodoxy" of Taylor's poetic expression. But the damage had already been done; the issue of Taylor's orthodoxy has only recently abated.

The importance of Taylor's personal religious orthodoxy to American literary history can only be appreciated if one compares him to the other known poets of the period—Wigglesworth, Bradstreet, Tompson —upon whose work had been elaborately constructed a seemingly satisfactory explanation for the dreariness of colonial poetry. As Puritans, it was argued, they saw mainly mnemonic and utilitarian value in verse, they admired plainness and were suspicious of figurative language, and if not religiously averse to all forms of earthly beauty, they nonetheless detested all sensuality, all imagery (especially in a religious context), all eroticism, and certainly such objects as altars, censers, crosses, and vestments. And yet Taylor, a "stiff-necked" New England minister, seemed to violate every assumption about American Puritans, presenting a highly artificial, mannered, sensual, even erotic poetry abounding in imagery drawn from ancient Christian, and therefore Catholic, rituals. He so obviously did not fit the picture that the easiest explanation must be that he was not, truly, a Puritan.

This explanation proved attractive to a number of influential writers: Kenneth B. Murdock, in *Literature & Theology in Colonial New England* (Cambridge, Mass., 1949), suggested that although Taylor "was an orthodox Puritan, he felt as a poet a sense of constraint within the bounds of the ordinary plainness and sobriety of Puritan literary style," adding that his contemporaries would probably have found his "erotically suggestive imagery" offensive, a suggestion he repeats again in *The Literature of the American People*, edited by A. H. Quinn (New York, 1951). In two essays Willie T. Weathers implied that Taylor's theology was a fundamentally pagan and Platonic conception flimsily covered with Calvinistic trappings—"Edward Taylor: Hellenistic Puritan" (*AL*, Mar. 1946) and "Edward Taylor and the Cambridge Platonists" (*AL*, Mar. 1954). Perry Miller shifted the argument somewhat by suggesting that Taylor's verse technique itself was one that "Puritans

considered suitable only to the sensualities of the Church of England,"
The New England Mind: From Colony to Province (Cambridge, Mass.,
1953). And Samuel Eliot Morison posited, albeit rhetorically, that
"Such intensity of devotion, such richness in color and imagery, one
looks for in the Anglo-Catholic poets rather than among puritans," *The
Intellectual Life of Colonial New England* (New York, 1956). Morison
goes on to deny the implication, but the suggestion is stronger than
his rebuttal of it.

An obvious alternative explanation for Taylor's unusualness is simply that prevailing theories of Puritan aesthetics were wrong. But
that argument has been slow in coming. Instead, the response to such
charges has been primarily biographical. Donald E. Stanford, not per-
suaded by these hints of unorthodoxy and maintaining that orthodoxy
was not an aesthetic or poetic question but strictly a doctrinal one,
argued vigorously in his dissertation that Taylor was a thoroughly
orthodox Calvinist and not a deviant New England covenant theologian. But that seems to have been an unprofitable line of argument,
and it has never been developed in print. More to the point was his
description of Taylor's "orthodoxy" in the long-lasting argument with
Solomon Stoddard, especially as the issues are encountered in Taylor's
Meditations II: 102–111, where Stanford mentions the disagreement
with the Johnson-Miller Covenant/Calvinist distinction, but does not
press it, "Edward Taylor and the Lord's Supper" (*AL*, May 1955).
Taylor's orthodoxy, both theological and ecclesiastical, in this running
battle with Stoddard, is discussed in much greater detail in Grabo's
Edward Taylor; "Edward Taylor on the Lord's Supper"; and his introduction and notes to *Edward Taylor's Treatise Concerning the Lord's
Supper*. Grabo concludes that on matters of church polity Taylor was
so strong a covenant theologian that Perry Miller could have constructed "The Marrow of Puritan Divinity" from Taylor's writing
alone, but that in purely theological matters—the Eucharist or Chris-
tology in particular—the covenant theology coincided almost exactly
with Calvin and Calvin's sources among the early Church Fathers.

In "Catholic Tradition, Puritan Literature, and Edward Taylor"
(*PMASAL*, 1960), Grabo also made a case for the Puritan acceptance
of essentially Catholic devotional procedures, suggesting that Taylor's
contemporaries would not have been as surprised or shocked by his
practices as earlier critics supposed. But the weakest point in this argument, and the strongest for the proponents of Taylor's unorthodoxy,
whether doctrinal or poetic, was Taylor's prohibition of the publication of his poems. This prohibition was reported in a letter written in
1851 by Taylor's great grandson Henry Wyllys Taylor, a New York

judge, to William B. Sprague who was then collecting information for his *Annals of the American Pulpit*, which appeared in 1857. Edward Taylor, reported the Judge, previous to his death "enjoined it upon his heirs never to publish any of his writings." The remark was repeated in Sprague's entry for Edward Taylor, and echoed again in John L. Sibley's *Biographical Sketches of Graduates of Harvard College*, vol. II (Cambridge, Mass., 1881). When Johnson announced and published his selections of Taylor's poetry in 1937 and 1939, he carefully repeated Sibley's phrasing, that Taylor "gave orders that his heirs should never publish any of his writings." But when S. Foster Damon reviewed Johnson's *Poetical Works* in *NEQ* (Dec. 1939), he remarked that Taylor's "large library contained a manuscript volume of his poems, the publication of which he forbade."

Thus began to form a kind of mystery—why did Taylor forbid the publication of his poems? While the "fact" of his injunction (now particularized to cover only the poetry) received constant reinforcement in anthologies, in critical essays, and in historical reviews, its significance took a new turn after Richard D. Altick popularized the story of the recovery of Taylor's poetry in *The Scholar Adventurers* (New York, 1950), and Perry Miller insinuated that Taylor must have had something to hide by keeping his lyrics "secretive" (*The New England Mind: From Colony to Province*). He asserts this interpretation most strongly in the introduction to Taylor in his anthology, *The American Puritans: Their Prose and Poetry* (New York, 1956). Quietly contesting this interpretation, Stanford nonetheless recorded in his 1960 edition of the *Poems* that "Taylor did not publish his poems and he forbade his heirs to publish them," and Grabo, returning to the language reported in Sprague and Johnson, reminded readers of *Edward Taylor* (1961) that "actually Taylor forbade the publication of any of his writing, though this fact tends to be overlooked by critics wishing to further the myth that Taylor's poetry would have been considered evil by his contemporaries."

But not everyone was fooled. Shortly after Emmy Shepard in "Edward Taylor's Injunction Against Publication" (*AL*, Jan. 1962) suggested that perhaps Taylor's motive in forbidding publication "was simple, genuine humility, touched by self-respect and pride in his work and perhaps—lightly—by the perversity of the aged," Francis Murphy pointed out that curiously "no questions have ever been raised concerning the basis of authority for this controversy." Murphy declares flatly and convincingly, in "Edward Taylor's Attitude Toward Publication: A Question Concerning Authority" (*AL*, Nov. 1962), that "there is no documentary evidence whatsoever regarding Edward Taylor's final intention toward his work. Henry Taylor's remark can only be based on some family tradition, and whether it grew up early or late, we shall never know. The major point to be made is that in the absence of any documentary evidence all serious consideration of this question is impossible." So ended a regrettable, but not entirely useless controversy.

CRITICISM

The pattern Taylor criticism has assumed in its three decades since the publication of Johnson's *Poetical Works* is almost suspiciously pat. Each decade seems dominated by a different kind of interest or method, partly perhaps a reflection of critical interests and fads in literary criticism, but more probably a reflection of the primary problem of characterizing, describing, indeed identifying this rare poet in a poetic desert. What primarily distinguished criticism of the forties from that of the fifties and sixties was the critical context that then seemed most relevant to and instructive regarding Taylor's poetry. In the forties the most relevant context seemed to be poetic history, and critics pointed to Taylor's dependence upon or similarities with various poetic traditions— Metaphysical, Baroque, the medieval morality plays, or a variety of Greek and Roman classics. The fifties saw a definite shift in emphasis. It began with Sidney Lind's protest that Taylor did not deserve the dignity the comparisons of the forties implied because of his religious culture, and was reinforced by Roy Harvey Pearce's insistence that Taylor's poetic accomplishment must be understood and measured by his own Puritan culture. Criticism in this decade addressed the questions of Taylor's theological and intellectual background with increased emphasis, without entirely ignoring contextual questions raised by the first decade of Taylor critics. At the end of this decade, Donald E. Stanford's ample edition of the *Poems* (1960) provided a basis for renewed and deeper consideration of both the poetic and intellectual traditions to which Taylor's poetry belongs, but more important, turned attention to the poetic qualities of the poems themselves. The sixties have therefore seen an increasing interest in the explication of single poems, in the details of Taylor's poetic technique, and in the quality of his poetic accomplishment. The movement since 1939 has been, then—and not surprisingly—from understanding to evaluation.

Poetic Traditions

All Taylor criticism has deepened, without changing the essential contours of Thomas H. Johnson's earliest appraisals. Johnson, in "Edward Taylor: A Puritan 'Sacred Poet,' " maintained from the beginning that Taylor was a completely orthodox New England Puritan who was also "a poet of real, not merely historic, importance"; that he was "not indifferent to poetry as an art"; and that if one must seek "parallels or analogues for Taylor's verse," one will find them naturally in the seventeenth-century conceitists, especially Herbert, Quarles, and Crashaw. With the kind of overstatement that has marked Taylor criticism until very recently, the publishers of *Poetical Works* predicted in 1939 that "a re-evaluation of early American letters will be made in the light of this publication." In 1966, when the *Poetical Works* was reissued, Johnson could quite rightly say, "Indeed it is no exaggeration to say that the twentieth-century reassessment of Puritanism, especially in those aspects which reveal the Puritan's feeling for beauty in his hungry search for Heaven, has been given impetus by the appearance of Taylor's poetry."

Austin Warren, with deft analysis and informed perceptions, began the history of modifications that Johnson's judgments would undergo for thirty years. In "Edward Taylor's Poetry: Colonial Baroque" (*KR*, Summer 1941), Warren argued that Taylor's verse belongs to the seventeenth-century tradition that would have been described as "false wit" by late seventeenth-century critics such as Addison. Metaphysical in neither the cosmic sense of Du Bartas nor the psychological sense of Donne, it nonetheless performed the "humble baroque ingenuities" that other New England poetasters found so attractive. A poet of wit whose chief instrument was "the homely conceit," Taylor was largely unaware of the intellectual implications of his method, associating his devices, "in baroque fashion, about surprises." The effects, illustrated in Taylor's "Meditation Eight" and "The Reflexion"—both analyzed very sensitively—may be amateurish, but still powerful, though Warren's final judgment is that "Taylor is sometimes a neat little artisan but more often an unsteady enthusiast, a naïve original, an intermittently inspired Primitive." Slightly altered, this essay was reprinted as "Edward Taylor" in Warren's *Rage for Order* (Ann Arbor, Mich., 1948).

Wallace Cable Brown disagreed sharply with Warren, arguing that at his best Taylor went beyond baroque devices "and became a full-fledged, if minor, metaphysical poet" in "Edward Taylor: An American 'Metaphysical'" (*AL*, Nov. 1944). He supported this argument by tracing a variety of characteristics Taylor's poetry shared with Donne's and Herbert's: kinds of metrical roughness, syntactic complexity, wit, heterogeneous ideas, "the peculiar effect on the imagination of the great distances between focal points of the imagery," the "sensuous apprehension of thought," and the tight logical structure or "intellectuality in the presence of strong personal emotion." Brown concludes that with "the exception of tight logical structure, which he does not always manage to achieve, Taylor's work exhibits all the 'earmarks' (as he himself would say) of the metaphysical esthetic."

In *The First Century of New England Verse*, printed originally in *PAAS* (Oct. 1943) and issued the following year under separate cover (Worcester, Mass., 1944), Harold S. Jantz rejected Brown's characterization in favor of Warren's: "Taylor employs his treasure of images in a typically late Baroque manner: lavishly but purposefully and consequentially, in an ordered, well-disposed intricacy." But Jantz's remarks are general rather than analytical, proceeding in part from the larger purpose of his study and in part from his unwillingness to grant so much to Taylor's poetic quality or significance as was at least implied by earlier critics.

Undaunted by Jantz's cautious approach, two writers discovered somewhat more remote literary alliances in the same issue of *American Literature* (Mar. 1946). Nathalia Wright, beginning by observing the "flair for drama" that runs through all of Taylor's verse, developed one set of parallels in "The Morality Tradition in the Poetry of Edward Taylor." She focuses on *Gods Determinations* to demonstrate points in common with four well-known morality plays: the *Coventry XI* pageant, the *Castle of Perseverance*, *Mary Magdalen*, and *Wisdom*. Plot, stock themes, hints of costuming, the use of various verse forms, allegorical devices, and tricks of characterization all contribute to the medieval character of Taylor's poem. Professor Wright concludes: "Taylor may thus have been led to the morality tradition, not by one, but by a combination of influences: a keen dramatic sense, a congeniality with the thought of the Middle Ages, and long habits of theological speculation." Early in her essay, however, distinguishing Taylor from other Renaissance poets who used morality elements, she remarked that Taylor "lacks the classical background upon which they constantly drew." But Willie T. Weathers maintained that "Miss Wright is clearly mistaken" about this, in "Edward Taylor, Hellenistic Puritan." Pointing to the six volumes of classical poetry in Taylor's library, Professor Weathers compiles a series of "cursory findings" revealing Taylor's debt to Theocritan song-contests and bits and passages that seem to owe their inspiration to Greek and Latin sources. The analogies become very tenuous, however, as the crippled man of *Gods Determinations* suggests "the hero of Oedipus," or Taylor's line, "As Spot barks back the sheep again," prompts the interpretation that "Spot is obviously the 'flock-dog' often mentioned in Theocritan pastorals, and by one shepherd given the name 'White-Tail.'"

Intellectual and Theological Traditions

Sidney E. Lind, obviously irked by the amount of critical attention paid Taylor, "as though he were a poet of high merit whose resurrection has added significantly to the cultural hoard of America," argued to the contrary, in "Edward Taylor: A Revaluation" (*AL*, Dec. 1948), that "he is at best a mediocre poet, as he was doomed to be, whatever his inherent poetic gifts, by reason of his station in life." Lind's point is that New England Puritan culture—a "highly codified theologico-cultural system" fully and accurately described by Perry Miller's *New England Mind*—provided too narrow a basis for the production of "sustained passages of real beauty" or for "the flawless blending of communication and art." Taylor only occasionally lapsed from the Puritan standards of doctrinal primacy, utility, and intelligibility, into poetry, and the criticism that ignores the Puritan limits of Taylor's culture is an exercise in empty rhetoric.

Despite Lind's questionable assumptions regarding the nature of Puritan culture, his insistence that Taylor must be related to it did not go unattended. Without sharing Lind's evaluation of Taylor's poetic worth, Roy Harvey Pearce in "Edward Taylor: The Poet as Puritan" (*NEQ*, Mar. 1950) agreed that critics had been reluctant to read Taylor simply as a colonial poet. For Pearce this meant that Taylor's culture limited his achievement to "one of discovery, most often the discovery of God-informed unity in man's experience in and of his world. Whatever struggle is involved in making such a discovery, however, is not in the poem; it is external, anterior to the poem." Taylor's method and purpose are therefore characterized as essentially Ramistic. This Pearce demonstrates in comments upon "Huswifery," "Meditation Six," *Gods Determinations*, and "Meditation Eight." All show that "for Taylor technique is little or nothing," and that the poetry of discovery is essentially undramatic. The Puritan culture that made his poetry what it is "indeed, cut Taylor down (or should one say, built Taylor up?) to its size. However adequate that culture might have been for major religious experience, it was yet inadequate for major poetry; for it allowed for little play of the individual will—in the last analysis for little real human drama." But however much Pearce and Lind agreed, one senses none of Lind's superficial assumptions about New England Puritanism and its desiderata in Pearce's remarks.

Kenneth Murdock's treatment of Taylor in "A Little Recreation of Poetry," in *Literature & Theology in Colonial New England*, was sympathetic, but like Jantz's, cautious in its claims, and did not much advance upon critical discriminations already made, although it also treated Taylor primarily in terms of his colonial culture. But Herbert Blau's "Heaven's Sugar Cake: Theology and Imagery in the Poetry of Edward Taylor" (*NEQ*, Sept. 1953) brought a new sensibility to bear upon Taylor's poems, and one that focused upon his theology. Blau believed that at his best Taylor was the equal of Donne and Crashaw, but when locked (as Pearce had pointed out) in the game of "discovery," his search for signs of grace often led him poetically astray. Blau shows that Taylor profoundly accepted a Calvinist paradox that allowed him to argue as if repentance were possible despite the doctrine of absolute predestination. Rejecting *Gods Determinations* as "fairly tedious, inconsistent theologically, and neither a good narrative nor a good *débat*," Blau concentrates upon the *Meditations* and analyzes their diction, prosody, and syntax in greater depth and with a finer eye for detail than any previous critic. His comparisons range from Gascoigne and Greville through Donne, Herbert, and the other metaphysicals to Blake, Dickinson, T. S. Eliot, and Ezra Pound—both unexpectedly and justly. Blau is especially sharp-sighted in defining and illustrating Taylor's most persistent fault—lapses in taste and decorum.

The following year, Willie T. Weathers again argued for Taylor's Classicism, but this time centered on Taylor's relationships with seventeenth-century Platonists who were also eminent theologians, in "Edward Taylor and the Cambridge Platonists." Weathers points to the exceptional lapses from colonial Puritanism that Lind had acknowledged, but sees them as manifestations of Taylor's "personal Platonism," which opened for him mystical, erotic, aesthetic, and imaginative possibilities that the public doctrines of Puritanism seemed to deny. Weathers distinguishes at length this liberal, Platonic temperament from the dominant authoritarian and scholastic one, defining seven precise areas in which Neoplatonism differed from orthodox Puritanism—in each of which Taylor sides with the Neoplatonists. But Weathers misreads *Gods Determinations*—from which the bulk of her evidence comes—rather badly. Evidence not fully available when she wrote disproves every major point, indicating that what she calls Taylor's "ingenuity" is rather her own. But to the extent that Platonic thought and imagery permeated Renaissance religious writing and were thus available to Taylor, these speculations are very suggestive and deserve reexamination in the light of subsequent findings.

Donald E. Stanford pulled both Blau and Weathers back to earth by explaining that Taylor's mystical response to the Lord's Supper was perfectly orthodox in Puritan terms, in "Edward Taylor and the Lord's Supper." Regrettably, Mindele Black seems not to have availed herself of Stanford's work; her otherwise excellent "Edward Taylor: Heaven's Sugar Cake" (*NEQ*, June 1956) would have been even better. Black begins by pointing out Taylor's affinity with pre-Restoration English poets—particularly Herbert—as somewhat inconsistent, but reasons that "the seeming inconsistency lies not so much in Taylor himself as in the devotional tradition to which he belongs." That tradition Black identifies primarily with the sacramental writings of Increase Mather, Thomas Doolittle, and Samuel Willard, agreeing with E. I. Watkin that "this side of Puritan devotion, as opposed to the theological, was not a genuine Protestant development but an influx of direct or indirect borrowings from Catholic spirituality." This view permits her acceptance of Taylor's proximity with Herbert and Crashaw, despite their differences theologically, and she bolsters her argument with quotations from Taylor's *Christographia* sermons. But again this is a case of intuition exceeding careful reading: Black assumes, for example, that *Gods Determinations* is, like Wigglesworth's *Day of Doom*, about Judgment Day. Nonetheless, Mindele Black distinctly narrowed the circle of relevant traditions, and brought the decade's search for intellectual contexts into its most appropriate limits to date.

Notes and articles of a historical or explicatory nature were published before the decade ended, but few were of any critical significance. In the year 1960 an even dozen articles and reviews appeared, mostly occasioned by the publication of Stanford's edition of the *Poems*, opening a new era of Taylor criticism.

The Poetry Itself

The most important critical essay of 1960 was Louis L. Martz's foreword to the *Poems*. In *The Poetry of Meditation* (New Haven, Conn., 1954), Professor Martz had provided the rationale behind Mindele Black's argument for a specific devotional tradition. Martz argued that the devotional methods of Ignatius of Loyola, modified by later Jesuits, provided models first for Anglican adaptation in the work of Joseph Hall and then for adaptation by Presbyterian and Independent churchmen through Richard Baxter's *Saints Everlasting Rest*. Moreover, he demonstrated most persuasively that Donne, Herbert, and Crashaw, among others, showed the effects of formal Ignatian meditation in their poems, and mentioned Taylor in passing. In the foreword, therefore, it is no accident that Taylor is closely related to the "metaphysical" poets, particularly Herbert, and that the meditative tradition is peculiarly appropriate for Taylor: "In Baxter's arguments for the use of sensory images in meditation we have, I believe, the grounds of justification for Taylor's bold and often unseemly use of common imagery."

Often with very particular and acute examples and analytical comments, Martz accentuated the metaphysical-meditational qualities of Taylor's verse.

Norman S. Grabo was the most enthusiastic follower of Martz's suggestions in "Catholic Tradition, Puritan Literature, and Edward Taylor," arguing like Mindele Black that Taylor's contemporaries were not at all averse to Catholic devotional practices and, like Martz, that the method of Ignatian meditation was known to them and favored by some of them. In 1961 Grabo expanded the implications of this principle into what still remains the only book-length survey of Taylor's work, *Edward Taylor*. There Grabo surveys Taylor's active life and characterizes his inward or contemplative life as recorded in his writings to conclude that Taylor was essentially a mystic, that his meditative procedures reflect the various stages of Western Christian mysticism while remaining thoroughly within the orthodox teaching of New England Calvinism, and that his poetry was the natural result of his mysticism. This is demonstrated by showing the extent to which Taylor's sacramental preaching—especially in the *Christographia* sermons for which there are corresponding meditations—determined the structure, themes, images, and general development of Taylor's poems. Two final chapters consider the early poems as Taylor's apprenticeship to poetry, and his major accomplishment in the *Preparatory Meditations* and *Gods Determinations*. The questions raised about Taylor's art are not particularly new, but the scope of the book allows for more particular analyses of Taylor's techniques and significance than had been afforded earlier. Grabo's emphasis upon Taylor's personal mysticism has proved the most objectionable and least tenable part of the study.

Since then there have been several good general definitions of Taylor's accomplishment, the best being Donald E. Stanford's introduction to the second edition of the *Poems* and his pamphlet, *Edward Taylor*, both of which penetrate deeper into the area of Taylor's own reading. Grabo's introduction and explanatory notes to *Edward Taylor's Christographia* contribute to this general intellectual history and explicate in detail the thesis that Taylor's *Preparatory Meditations* are determined by his sacrament-day sermons. Likewise, his introduction and notes to *Edward Taylor's Treatise Concerning the Lord's Supper* explore Taylor's use of theological and ecclesiastical polemics as they relate to the poems, locating Taylor's sacramentalism in a literary-theological tradition that runs from Shepard to Edwards and seeks to determine the extent to which a man's spiritual condition may be judged from his observable behavior. Several essays in the sixties explore these implications.

But the major change in Taylor criticism since 1960 has been an intensified examination of particular poems or devices, by asking questions narrower in scope and pursuing them more deeply, while at the same time attending to the poetic surface more exactly than before. Johannes Hedberg began this effort with a ludicrously heavy-handed dismantling of a Taylor poem in "Meditations Linguistic and Literary on 'Meditation Twenty-Nine' by Edward Taylor" (*Moderna Språk*, 1960). First appears the poem, then a glossary, a section on Taylor's "Rhyme, Rhythm and Sense," an "Interpretative Paraphrase," then some "Facts and Opinions" about Taylor, and some final definitions of terms. William R. Manierre II discusses the presence and significance of "polyptotonic play," in "Verbal Patterns in the Poetry of Edward Taylor" (*CE*, Jan. 1962), focusing on the effectiveness of *ploce* and *polyptoton* in the "Preface" to *Gods Determinations*. John Clendenning, arguing that "We now need a deepened understanding of particular poems, a task which few of Taylor's critics have adequately attempted," provides a close reading of "The Reflexion," tracing the four basic images that control the poem—food, light, flowers, and sex—in "Piety and Imagery in Edward Taylor's 'The Reflexion'" (*AQ*, Summer 1964). And Norman S. Grabo explores the meaning of Taylor's "Huswifery" by examining the use of spinning, weaving, and clothing imagery throughout his poetry and prose in "Edward Taylor's Spiritual Huswifery" (*PMLA*, Dec. 1964).

With a wholly different approach, Donald Junkins tests previous critical generalizations by a careful look at Taylor's manuscript for indications of his artistry. In "Edward Taylor's Revisions," he concludes that "all the evidence shows that he wrote, re-wrote, crossed out, and incorporated, that he revised painstakingly, and that his process was artistically sound." This sense of Taylor's artistic self-consciousness is also supported by Charles W. Mignon's "Diction in Edward Taylor's 'Preparatory Meditations'" (*AS*, Dec. 1966) which analyzes Taylor's "difficult words"—obsolete, dialect, Americanisms, and special terms. Mignon shows that Taylor's "*Meditations* have a higher incidence of difficult words per page than any random sampling selected from the published verse of Taylor's contemporaries of New England," suggesting that this relative obscurity substantiates Taylor's privateness and "reflects Taylor's desire to write for no one but himself."

Somewhat more conventional is the series of articles on Taylor's images that appeared around mid-decade. Cecilia Halbert discussed "Tree of Life Imagery in the Poetry of Edward Taylor" (*AL*, Mar. 1966). Although it is misinformed, the main value of this discussion is that it provoked Ursula Brumm to establish the theological tradition of that image as Taylor would most probably have known and used it, in "The 'Tree of Life' in Edward Taylor's Meditations" (*EAL*, Fall 1968), a translation of her earlier article cited below, and one of the more sophisticated contributions to Taylor scholarship in recent years. Thomas Werge emphasizes the Puritan use of this image in "The Tree of Life in Edward Taylor's Poetry: The Sources of a Puritan Image" (*EAL*, Winter 1968–69), but though he usefully associates Thomas Shepard and Jonathan Edwards with the image, he does not avail himself of Brumm's more thoroughgoing and suggestive discussion. Werge does underline Taylor's own reading, however, and that is likewise the emphasis of Jean L. Thomas's "Drama and Doctrine in *Gods Determinations*" (*AL*, Jan. 1965), particularly his reading in homiletic and devotional literature. Thomas E. Johnston, Jr., dwells on yet another line of devotional imagery in "Edward Taylor: An American Emblematist" (*EAL*, Winter 1968–69).

Inevitably, emphasis upon Taylor's own reading as a source for ideas and images leads away from the poetry and towards intellectual history. Stephen Fender, a British scholar, in "Edward Taylor and 'The Application of Redemption'" (*MLR*, July 1964), emphasizes the parallel aspects of Taylor's poetic-meditative method and that developed by Thomas Hooker. Robert M. Benton challenges Grabo's interpretation that the poems followed the sermons in compositon and therefore developed the "doctrine" of the sermons rather than the scriptural texts by showing how Meditations ii:47 and ii:43 use images from the scriptural contexts rather than from the sermons, in "Edward Taylor's Use of His Text" (*AL*, Mar. 1967). And Allen Richard Penner argues that, understood in terms of Taylor's theology and method, "Meditation One" escapes the facile critical descriptions of early Taylor critics. We must, Penner says in "Edward Taylor's Meditation One" (*AL*, May 1967), "re-create as well as we are able the intensity and significance of the theology which inspired those meditations," in order to appreciate them fully. But this line of inquiry is essentially a continuation of the criticism of the fifties, though in many respects more particular.

Another continuation is evident in the foreign attention paid to Taylor. General introductions to Taylor have appeared in Italy, Germany, and Japan. Biancamaria Tedeschini Lalli's introduction to what was then known of Taylor appeared in *Studi Americani*, 1956. Very like it, but better informed, is Ken Akiyama's in *Studies in Humanities* (Doshisha University, 1963). And there are signs of appreciation of Taylor's mysticism by Indian scholars. But it is so far only in Germany that Taylor has received serious critical examination. The general and derivative comments in Henry Lüdeke's *Geschichte der amerikanischen*

Literatur (Bern, 1954) and Alfred Weber's review of Stanford's edition of the *Poems* (*JA*, 1962) only prepared the way for the intensive studies of Ursula Brumm and Peter Nicolaisen. Brumm devotes a chapter to Taylor in her very well received *Die religiöse Typologie im amerikanischen Denken* (Leiden, 1963), entitled "Edward Taylor's Meditationen über das Abendmahl" (that is, on the Lord's Supper), in which she analyzes Taylor's use of types, emblems, signs, and metaphors to place him in a tradition that reaches through Jonathan Edwards to Emerson and thus into the main tradition of American writing through Faulkner. In "Der 'Baum des Lebens' in den Meditationen Edward Taylors" (*JA*, 1967) Brumm presents the background to Taylor's Tree of Life imagery as developed in English a year later. Both studies emphasize Taylor's reliance on the Bible and on traditional ways of explicating and applying biblical material.

Somewhat different is Peter Nicolaisen's excellent monograph on Taylor's imagery, *Die Bildlichkeit in der Dichtung Edward Taylors* (Neumünster, 1966). Nicolaisen's is the first printed examination of this most irresistible aspect of Taylor's art. American dissertations by Thomas Wack, Elizabeth Wiley, and Emma L. Shepard at the beginning of the decade elaborately categorized and analyzed Taylor's images, but Nicolaisen goes beyond such studies by fitting his analysis to a controlling thesis—that Taylor uses images, especially images of amplification, to support his sense that the attempt of the human understanding and imagination to comprehend God is doomed to failure. Thus the poems do not express achieved union of man and God but only testify to its desirable impossibility. Nicolaisen emphasizes the biblical sources of Taylor's imagery and minimizes origins in Taylor's personal experience, especially in the *Preparatory Meditations*, using the Anglican Herbert as a foil to help define the peculiar nature of Taylor's art. A good five-page English abstract declares the general thesis at the end of the book.

Since mid-decade, commentary has been increasingly general. Acknowledging that Taylor's poems do indeed work, critics seek to explain more exactly just how they do so. Clark Griffith, in "Edward Taylor and the Momentum of Metaphor" (*ELH*, Dec. 1966), maintains in comments on "Meditation Eight," "Huswifery," and the "Preface," that Taylor's poems move from allegorical, rational images and tropes to increasingly idiosyncratic conceits, thereby generating the energy that is so striking in the poems. Peter Force, on the other hand, in "Edward Taylor as a Poet" (*NEQ*, Sept. 1966), contends that it is exactly at those points of potential hindrance to appreciation of Taylor's poetry that the elevating force of poems frequently originates. He illustrates with examples of troubling diction, punctuation, syntax, sound-sense relationships, imagery, and structure.

A good number of quite competent studies have appeared since 1967, especially in the pages of *EAL*, but three essays of very recent vintage seem to me to epitomize the direction of Taylor studies in the sixties, and perhaps to suggest the direction of studies to come. With an uncommonly rich knowledge of all of Taylor's work and previous Taylor criticism, E. F. Carlisle writes very elegantly of "The Puritan Structure of Edward Taylor's Poetry" (*AQ*, Summer 1968). Carlisle reasons that behind, or beneath the evident form of Taylor's sermons and poems there is a personalized and intense "deep form" determined by Taylor's personal response to his Puritan faith. Like several previous critics, he sees the crucial root of Taylor's work in a "fundamental sense of vast difference" between the world of human experience and the transcendent realm of godly ideals. But Carlisle sees four "formal"—in a sense structural—principles inherent in this sense and basic to the movement of several poems, including the "Prologue," Meditation I: 6, Meditation II: 46, and "Huswifery." These principles of contrast, ascension, question-and-answer, and metaphor or symbol both clarify the difference between the public and private qualities of Edward Taylor's verse, and bring "the Puritan minister, man and poet together in the underlying structure of the poetry." Charles Mignon's similar interest in Taylor's privateness also finds support in the "Prologue," "The Reflexion," and Meditation II:77, in "Edward Taylor's *Preparatory Meditations*: A Decorum of Imperfection" (*PMLA*, Oct. 1968). Like Carlisle, he sees the vast disparity between man's fallen condition and his high poetic purpose at the root of Taylor's aesthetic, which first diminishes man by meiosis and then amplifies God by hyperbole drawn from the scriptures. Mignon concludes that "Taylor has a decorum peculiar to himself with subjects recognizable in their general outlines as Puritan: the ineffectiveness of fallen rhetoric itself, and the impossibility of successfully praising God with this rhetoric." Coincidentally, the same subject occupies Donald Junkins in "'Should Stars Wooe Lobster Claws?': A Study of Edward Taylor's Poetic Practice and Theory" (*EAL*, Fall 1968). Junkins argues that Taylor's anguished sense of his own spiritual imperfections is embodied in his numerous images of writing. Poetry is thus a metaphor of his spiritual condition, especially clear in images of self-abasement cast as criticism of his own poetic incompetence: "The poem, then, is the medium through which he experiences both art and religion." Faith and poetic intention are indistinguishably intertwined in what Junkins calls a "religio-Aesthetic process," delineating an orginal sense of the relationship of religion and art in Taylor's work. The focus of examination in these three essays, one notes, is very similar to Nicolaisen's thesis, and all four address with varying degrees of consciousness the challenge issued by Sidney Lind in 1948 to put Taylor into the context of his Puritanism—not, however, by going to second-hand intellectual history, but by examining the dynamics of the poems themselves.

By 1970, then, Taylor scholarship and criticism have reached a fairly complicated and postadolescent, if not entirely mature, state. A full biography remains the most crucial need, but perhaps could not be adequately accomplished until more work is done on particular historical and critical matters. Despite a good essay, for example, like Michael J. Colacurcio's "God's Determinations Touching Half-Way Membership: Occasion and Audience in Edward Taylor" (*AL*, Nov. 1967), and despite the frequency of its mentions, *Gods Determinations* still needs an exhaustive reading and interpretation. The Taylor issue of *EAL* (Winter 1969) testifies to the growing interest and intensity of Taylor criticism, and publication of Gene Russell's concordance to the poems will certainly suggest new directions for these critical energies. But only the surface of Taylor's own reading and his use of centuries of theological and biblical commentary have been tapped. And the implications of Taylor's accomplishment for our understanding of the Puritan mind and its artistic potential still await serious examination.

John Greenleaf Whittier

KARL KELLER

JOHN GREENLEAF WHITTIER has been first of all important as a personality and as a historical force but only minimally important to literary
criticism. Affection has at most points taken the place of analysis and
documentation the place of discussion. Whittier has been a writer to
love, not to belabor. Though more attention has been shown him than
most other schoolroom poets, he has suffered more than most at the
hands of his biographers and critics.

BIBLIOGRAPHY

Students of Whittier have a superb bibliography in the work of
Thomas F. Currier, *A Bibliography of John Greenleaf Whittier* (Cambridge, Mass., 1937). Currier has accurately identified and described
most of Whittier's works—the poetry, the essays and tales, letters to the
press, and contributions to the newspapers, anthologies, and tracts
which Whittier edited. Included in Currier's volume is Pauline F. Pulsifer's bibliography of the biographical and critical writings on Whittier up to 1936. It is the most comprehensive bibliography on Whittier.
Lewis Leary's *Articles on American Literature, 1900–1950* (Durham,
N.C., 1954) serves as a supplement to Pulsifer but it is quite incomplete. Much more significant is the selective critical bibliography in
Edward Wagenknecht's *John Greenleaf Whittier: A Portrait in Paradox*
(New York, 1967); here the most important scholarship on Whittier
since 1936 is brought carefully up to date. Although subsumed in large
part by the Currier and Wagenknecht lists, of bibliographical interest
are the *Stephen H. Wakeman Collection of Books of Nineteenth-
Century American Writers* issued by the American Art Association
(New York, 1924) and *Thirteen Author Collections of the Nineteenth-
Century*, vol. II, compiled by Jean C. Wilson and David A. Randall

357

(New York, 1950). Less significant but accessible bibliographies are by Harry H. Clark in *Major American Poets* (Cincinnati, Ohio, 1936) and by Harry Hartwick in Walter F. Taylor's *History of American Letters* (Boston, 1936). Currier's list of Whittier first editions is supplemented by Merle Johnson, *American First Editions* (New York, 1965) and by C. Marshall Taylor, "Some [Whittier] First Editions Published in the British Isles" (*Journal of the Friends Historical Association*, No. 2, 1950). A *Whittier Newsletter* is published (Amesbury, Mass.) by John B. Pickard for bibliographical and review purposes.

EDITIONS

Fortunately, Whittier is one of America's most accessible poets. The first collection of Whittier's poems was the Boston edition of 1837 and the first collection of his prose was the Boston edition of 1866. Since 1857 Houghton Mifflin has held the copyrights to all editions of Whittier's works, the most comprehensive of which is *The Writings of John Greenleaf Whittier*, the Riverside Edition of 1888 (7 volumes), edited by Horace E. Scudder with Whittier's assistance. All editions—including such admirable reprintings as the Artists' Edition of 1892, the Cambridge Edition of 1895, and the Household Edition of 1873—derive from the Riverside Edition. In "Making Whittier Definitive" (*NEQ*, June 1939), Eleanor M. Tilton describes the exchange between Scudder and Whittier that made the Riverside Edition accurate and full.

Still, many items were lost before the Riverside Edition or were rejected by Whittier in the course of the work with Scudder, and as unearthed since have been published in scattered places, often in inaccurate form. *Whittier on Writers and Writing*, edited by Harry H. Clark and Edwin H. Cady (Syracuse, N.Y., 1950), is a gathering of literary reviews and criticism by Whittier from various periodicals of his day; other fugitive prose is reprinted in the *Boston Evening Transcript*, 7 February 1925 (*NEQ*, Dec. 1933), and in a collection of Whittier columns by John M. Moran, Jr., "Editor Whittier and the *New England Weekly Review*" (*ESQ*, First Quarter 1968). The complete *Legends of New England*, as edited by J. B. Pickard, has been reissued (Gainesville, Fla., 1965), as has *The Supernaturalism of New England*, as edited by Edward Wagenknecht (Norman, Okla., 1969). Yet unfortunately only a small portion of Whittier's prose has been reprinted.

On the other hand, the search for Whittier's unpublished poems—particularly the earliest ones—has been productive. These are published in *The Independent* (Nov. 1893), *NEM* (Nov. 1903; Feb. 1904),

Whittier-Land by Samuel T. Pickard (Boston, 1904), *Congregationalist and Christian World* (Dec. 1907), *AL* (May 1932), *BFHA* (Spring 1936), *American Collector* (Dec. 1926), *JRUL* (June 1944), *NEQ* (Dec. 1937; Mar. 1949; Mar. 1961), *EIHC* (Apr. 1955), and *ESQ* (Third Quarter 1965). Two collections of previously uncollected Whittier verse, with commentaries on sources and secrets of the search, are Frances M. Pray's *A Study of Whittier's Apprenticeship as a Poet, 1825–1835* (Bristol, N.H., 1930) and a thesis by Edward F. Grier, "The Uncollected Periodical Poems of John Greenleaf Whittier" (Columbia, 1938). Thomas F. Currier discusses peculiar problems of editing Whittier's early verse in "The Whittier Leaflet 'Pericles'" (*Library Quarterly*, Apr. 1934). But no definitive edition of the poetry has been attempted since 1888. As a result, a large body of Whittier's writings remains inaccessible. Mainly because there is so much uncollected material in newspapers, a new edition of Whittier is needed.

The Household Edition is still the most usable one-volume selection of Whittier's poems; both the Household Edition and the seven-volume Riverside Edition are currently in print. Louis Untermeyer's edition of poems (New York, 1945) is generally available but does not have an adequate introduction or notes and lacks full representation of Whittier's thinking and activity. The most recent edition of poems is that by Donald Hall for Dell (New York, 1960); Hall's introduction argues Whittier's relevance effectively but the selection of poems is too frugal.

MANUSCRIPTS AND LETTERS

The Whittier manuscripts are at the Haverhill Public Library; at the Whittier homestead at Oak Knoll, Haverhill, Mass.; at the Morgan Library; and at the Essex Institute in Salem—all of which are described by Harriet S. Tapley in *EIHC* (Apr. 1931) and in *A Descriptive Exhibition of Rare Whittierana*, edited by D. K. Campbell and Pauline F. Pulsifer (Haverhill, Mass., 1938). There are important manuscripts in the Quaker Collection at Haverford College, which are described by Edward D. Snyder in two articles: "Whittier Returns to Philadelphia after a Hundred Years" (*PMHB*, Apr. 1938) and "Notes on Whittier and Haverford College" (*BFHA*, Spring 1936). Still other manuscripts are in the Friends Historical Library at Swarthmore College, at the Harvard Library, the Boston Public Library, the Longfellow House in Cambridge, and at the Thomas B. Aldrich Library in Portsmouth, New Hampshire.

Superior collections of works by and about Whittier can be found at the Haverhill Public Library, at the Library of Haverford College, at the Essex Institute, and at Yale University.

Much of Whittier's life was lived in his correspondence. At times of literary value in themselves because of their wit and charm and concern for style, his letters give us as much of Whittier's mind as he ever revealed at any time. More important, though, like the letters of William Lloyd Garrison and Wendell Phillips, they are primary documents in the history of the pre–Civil War period; indeed, they made the history of the times.

J. B. Pickard is at work on a collected edition of letters selected from Whittier's 4,500 known letters, scheduled to appear in three volumes in 1971 from Harvard University Press. By and large, however, collectors have thus far used his correspondence to document a particular relationship or an individual idea but have had little interest in giving us the whole man.

An attempt was made by Samuel T. Pickard in his *Life and Letters of John Greenleaf Whittier* (Boston, 1894) to form a life around some of Whittier's letters, though some of them had to be altered for Pickard's purposes. Most of them were selected to show Whittier's problems of publishing or part of his abolition work, and few reveal personal matters or the full range of his social conscience. Several other small collections have helped to fill such gaps: John Albree's edition of *Whittier Correspondence from the Oak Knoll Collections* (Salem, Mass., 1911), made up of letters showing the life of the Whittier family and their Quaker friends; M. V. Denervaud's edition of the letters to Whittier's first sweetheart, Elizabeth Lloyd, in *Whittier's Unknown Romance* (Boston, 1922), expanded by Thomas F. Currier in *Elizabeth Lloyd and the Whittiers* (Cambridge, Mass., 1939); "Letters of John Greenleaf Whittier in the Roberts Collection at Haverford College," edited by Edward D. Snyder and Anna B. Hewitt for *BFHA* (Spring 1936), which has thirteen letters on Whittier's family life and abolitionist worries; and Martha H. Shackford's picture of family relationships in the Quaker world of the Whittier's, *Whittier and the Cartlands: Letters and Comments* (Wakefield, Mass., 1950). These collections, along with the biographies of Whittier, have been to date the main purveyors of Whittier's correspondence. Yet other letters have been published in widely scattered places.

For more than sixty years Whittier waged a difficult but successful war against slavery and discrimination—with his verse, his newspapers, and his profuse correspondence. Most of his correspondence in the service of abolition is lost but what remains shows his force of mind and the great force of his influence. In 1900 Samuel T. Pickard collected

Whittier's letters to a fellow Quaker abolitionist, Elizur Wright, Jr., in *Whittier as a Politician* (Boston, 1900), and he has published letters showing Whittier's influence on the British abolitionist John Bright (*Independent*, Jan. 1899; *NEQ*, Dec. 1935). Other abolitionists with whom Whittier had a significant exchange of letters are William Francis Channing, the son of William Ellery Channing (*AL*, Nov. 1930); Thomas Clarkson, the British abolitionist (*AL*, Jan. 1936); Henry B. Stanton (*JRUL*, Dec. 1945), and Gerrit Smith (*AL*, May 1950)—the last of these having importance because they document Whittier's shift from Garrisonian abolitionism to the abolitionism of the Liberty Party in 1840. Another letter on this schism is in *NEQ* (June 1964). Of special significance is the correspondence between Whittier and Henry Clay in 1837 on the relation between slavery and the annexation of Texas, discussed in the *Kentucky Historical Society Register* (1953). But no doubt the single abolitionist letter most important to the history of American literature is Whittier's 1845 letter to Emerson attempting to enlist him in the cause of abolition and the Liberty Party, edited and discussed by Roland H. Woodwell in *EIHC* (Oct. 1957). An important debate on the subject of abolition is constructed from the letters exchanged during and after the Civil War between Whittier and Paul Hamilton Hayne—two partisans of the slavery question, North and South, pro and con—edited by Max L. Griffin in *AL* (Mar. 1947). J. B. Pickard has published a Whittier letter (*NEQ*, June 1964) showing Whittier's concern over the split in the ranks of the abolitionists, and Elizabeth L. Adams has published a letter showing Whittier's attempt to influence abolitionists to run for Congress (*More Books*, Nov. 1943).

A number of the published Whittier letters document his relations with other writers of the period. They show not only the wide range of Whittier's reputation and influence but also some of his esthetic principles and literary judgments. Whittier's most important literary relationship was with James T. Fields of the *Atlantic* between 1861 and 1881; this relationship is documented by letters in James C. Austin's *Fields of the Atlantic Monthly* (San Marino, Calif., 1953). Whittier's relation with the editors Willis G. and Lewis G. Clark is documented by new letters edited by John C. Hepler in *BNYPL* (Nov. 1966). Other letters of literary-historical import are the ones to George Washington Cable (*NEQ*, Mar. 1949), to Oliver Wendell Holmes about the poetry of Walt Whitman (*Walt Whitman Review*, Mar. 1958), and to Paul Hamilton Hayne about the poetry of Henry Timrod (in *The Last Years of Henry Timrod*, edited by Jay B. Hubbell, Durham, N.C., 1941). There are also letters that show that Whittier was important to the emerging careers of a series of minor writers of the period: the poet

Lydia Maria Child (in her *Letters*, Boston, 1883); Rose Terry Cooke, a local-colorist of Connecticut (*QH*, Spring 1963); Harriet Prescott Spofford and Sarah Orne Jewett (*Dial*, Dec. 1907); the novelist Richard Henry Stoddard (in his *Recollections Personal and Literary*, New York, 1903); William J. Allinson, a young Quaker writer (*BFHA*, Spring 1948); Harriet McEwen Kimball, an aspiring young poet (*EIHC*, Jan. 1959); and the popular short-story writer S. R. Crockett (*Independent*, Oct. 1899). Richard Cary has edited further letters to Sarah Orne Jewett for *ESQ* (First Quarter 1968). Joseph M. Ernest's dissertation "Whittier and the American Writers" (Tennessee, 1952) lists hundreds of letters written by Whittier to writers of the time who sought both to learn from and do honor to him as a poet.

Additional published letters show Whittier's literary, political and religious influence among Quakers in the Midwest. These have been edited by Charles A. Hawley (*EIHC*, Oct. 1931; *IJHP*, Apr. 1937; *Palimpsest*, Sept. 1937; and *BFHA*, Autumn 1939; Spring 1941). Still others record personal and family matters (*BFHA*, Autumn 1940, Autumn 1960; *EIHC*, Jan. 1933, Oct. 1939, Oct. 1940; *LHJ*, Dec. 1899, Jan. 1900). Whittier's letters to Mary Emerson Smith, an early sweetheart, edited by J. B. Pickard (*AL*, Jan. 1967), suggest a more passionate Whittier than has been suspected by most of his biographers.

The corrupting of Whittier's letters to make him fit a particular religious or political bias is discussed by Richard Cary, "Whittier Regained" (*NEQ*, June 1941). Cary has in mind in particular the letters on Whittier's faith doctored by Charlotte F. Bates for *McClure's Magazine* (Jan. 1894). Edward D. Snyder is also concerned with the recovery of Whittier's original intent in his letters in "Whittier MS. Discovered 'to Order' " (*The Friend*, 12 December 1936).

There are five main manuscript collections of Whittier letters. Swarthmore has over six hundred in manuscript, mainly from the early years. The Houghton Library at Harvard has a useful collection of four hundred from the early period and has well over a thousand in its Pickard-Whittier collection. The Essex Institute houses the famous Oak Knoll Collection of over five hundred letters, plus hundreds written to Whittier, most of these from the period after 1860. The Huntington Library has about three hundred and fifty from Whittier's correspondence with James T. Fields and Thomas Wentworth Higginson. And Central Michigan University has over five hundred by and to Whittier from the Oak Knoll period; John Hepler of Central Michigan has an unpublished manuscript which includes the best of these.

The edition of letters that J. B. Pickard is editing includes all the extant letters from the important years 1828 to 1860 and all the letters after 1860 of biographical, literary, social, or political significance. This edition will be a major contribution to the understanding of Whittier for a number of reasons: it will recover the newspaper correspondence that made up Whittier's historically significant personal warfare on behalf of abolition; it will document the almost daily progress of Whittier from farm boy to national reformer as an example of The American Dream; and it will assist in reconciling the paradox of lyric poet and didactic reformer that has troubled Whittier's biographers.

BIOGRAPHY

Whittier is unusual in American literary history in that he is important as a writer mainly because of his life, rather than the other way around. That fact puts him in a class with, say, Winthrop, Jefferson, Lincoln, and John Kennedy. As with these others, the writing of Whittier's life has evolved from the fondling of his memory to a kind of hagiography and then to critical reaction against legend. By and large, the Whittier Lives succeed in being a justification of part of the history of the nation (as microcosm, as myth, as example), more than a contribution to the life of the mind in America.

Edward D. Snyder attempted an overview of "Seventy Years of Whittier Biographies, 1882–1952" (*BFHA*, Spring 1954), but its sectarian prejudice makes it a disappointing account of the regard paid Whittier over the years. Another, closer look is needed.

The first biography of Whittier was William Sloane Kennedy's *John Greenleaf Whittier: His Life, Genius, and Writings* (Boston, 1882). Whittier had not authorized it and disliked it intensely. Published at the height of the veneration of Whittier, the view of his life and work is remarkable for its objectivity. Kennedy clearly loved the man and saw an intimacy between his personality and his work. But what he finds to praise in Whittier—his piety, his passion, and his politics—to him only degraded his art: "He has three crazes that have nearly ruined the mass of his poetry. They are the reform craze, the religious craze, and the rhyme craze." In this Kennedy identified the key problem for biographers of Whittier: the disparity between the passionate man and the pale poet. Heroic as Kennedy finds Whittier's life, he finds the reasons for the pale poet in the qualities of the passionate man: he was for Kennedy too much the Quaker, too much the militant for the good of his art. Kennedy finds Whittier's life so much dominated by the Puritan strain of his Quaker faith that he could not love beauty for its own sake. Whittier's triteness, lack of originality in form or idea, and ultimately his tameness are to Kennedy due to "the subdued and art-chilling atmosphere of his Quaker religion." This view of his life, a view that Kennedy expanded in his 1892 biography, *John Greenleaf Whittier: The Poet of Freedom* (New York, 1892), no doubt cut Whittier to the quick.

On the other hand, Francis H. Underwood's *John Greenleaf Whittier: A Biography* (Boston, 1884) was undertaken with the approval though not with the cooperation of Whittier and was "not intended as a critical study, but as a friendly guide and interpreter." The portrait of Whittier therefore glows: the background is fortunate, the motives are just right, the actions heroic, the poetry pure, the interest in reform and the interest in literature perfectly united. Everything is magnified so as to be incomparable, and the process of mythologizing Whittier was begun. "Some imperfection clings to all souls," Underwood writes, "but few have been observed in our time so well poised, so pure, and so stainless as his." This formed the pattern for the inflated level of most discussions of Whittier's life since.

The biography that Whittier authorized as the picture he wanted painted of himself was Samuel T. Pickard's *Life and Letters of John Greenleaf Whittier*. Because of Pickard's personal affection for Whittier, it is often sentimental in championing the purity of Whittier's homelife, the intimacy of his poetry with his life, the sincerity of his journalism, the devotion of Whittier to the various causes of reform, and the genuineness of Whittier's literary and political success in his own time. Pickard's central argument in the biography is that Whittier's political ambition gradually overwhelmed his literary ambition, both strengthening and temporizing his art. Pickard's *Life* was based on the broadest survey of Whittier letters ever attempted and done with thousands of personal interviews and contacts, but it is an idealization of Whittier that we get, even an attempt at mythologizing him. For most purposes, it remains the standard biography, however, and the basis for most biographies that followed.

Those that followed almost kill Whittier with indiscriminate sentimentality. Such is the case in B. O. Flower's *Whittier: Prophet, Seer and Man* (Boston, 1896). Though an attempt is made to show him as barefoot boy, prophet of freedom, and modern spiritual apostle, Whittier loses his toughness in the process. This is true too in the Lives of Whittier published in England, all of them derivative and all of them sentimentalizations—Wilfred Whitten, *John G. Whittier* (London, 1892), and W. J. Linton, *Life of John Greenleaf Whittier* (London, 1893), both deriving from Kennedy and Underwood; G. K. Lewis, *John Greenleaf Whittier: His Life and Work* (London, 1913), a Christian Life; Henry Hudson, *Whittier and His Poetry* (London, 1918), the best of the British Lives; Arthur Rowntree, *Whittier: Crusader and Prophet* (London, 1944), in which Whittier is pictured as one of the pilgrims sustaining Christianity through the whole of a godless century. The worst of this kind is Fredrika S. Smith's *John Greenleaf Whittier: Friend and Defender of Freedom* (Boston, 1948), a Horatio Alger success story in fiction form in which Whittier is a simple country boy who conquers the century with his verse.

The long tradition of loving and laudatory reminiscences of Whittier is best represented by Mary B. Claflin's *Personal Recollections of John G. Whittier* (New York, 1893) and Annie Fields's *Whittier: Notes of His Life and of His Friendships* (New York, 1893). It is easy to forget that in the nineteenth century the reminiscence was a widely accepted form of literary criticism. Used on Whittier, the form is standard: the general sketch of a background of hardship, the randomly selected anecdotes that make a list of virtues, the few quoted lines of verse to imply a life of the mind, the attention to the uniqueness of wit, and the deep feeling for the poet that is intended to suggest his own deep feeling for life.

Many such personal reminiscences found their way into print, most of them recalling visits to Whittier in his later years that upon reflection take on the stature of pilgrimages, with anecdotes that teach his example. They were for the most part sensational fodder for the press. Caroline Cadbury makes "A Visit to Whittier in 1881" (*BFHA*, Autumn 1957). Ellen E. Dickinson recalls "A Morning with the Poet Whittier" (*Churchman*, June 1882). Walter M. Merrill makes a delightful summary discussion of many who claimed, "We Talked with Whittier" (*EIHC*, Apr. 1958). Samuel J. Cappen reports "A Visit to John Greenleaf Whittier" (*Leisure Hour*, Sept. 1888). Charles H. Battey remembers finding "Whittier at Home" (*Friend's Intelligence and Journal*, Nov. 1891). Sarah E. Palmer, in "A Memory of Whittier" (*Century*, Nov. 1893), tells the events of an evening visit with Whittier shortly before his death. In her "Personal Recollections of Whittier" (*NEM*, June 1893), Charlotte Grimke tells of several visits to Whittier to express the gratitude of the Negro race for Whittier's abolition work. Isaac Wilson tells of his "Visit to John Greenleaf Whittier" (*Friend's Intelligence and Journal*, June 1894) and Helen Burt of a summer spent with Whittier in 1880 in West Ossippee, in "Reminiscences of the Poet Whittier" (*Bookman*, June 1895). Robert S. Rantoul tells about Whittier's simplicity, practicality, and self-assurance in "Some Reminiscences of the Poet Whittier" (*EIHC*, Apr. 1901). Wyatt Eaton tells in his "Recollections of American Poets" of Whittier's homey personality during the painting of a portrait (*Century*, Oct. 1902). Among his "Reminiscences of a Long Life," Carl Schurz recalls a visit to the "kindly" Whittier (*McClure's*, Jan. 1907). J. Warren Thyng's *Reminiscences of the Poet Whittier* (Manchester, N.H., 1908) is a collection of memories of Whittier in his home setting. In his "Reminiscence of Whittier," W. H. Beckford retells a conversation (*Book News Monthly*, Sept. 1914). Caroline Ticknor, in *Glimpses of Authors* (New York, 1922), recalls memories of problems in publishing Whittier's works. Others remember Whittier for his humor—Josiah L. Pickard, "The Humor of Whittier" (*Midland Monthly*, May 1897); Elizabeth Stuart Phelps, "Whittier's Sense of Humor" (*McClure's Magazine*, July 1896); Samuel T. Pickard, "Whittier's Sense of Humor," in his *Whittier-Land*. The last in this long line of personal reminiscences was Emily B. Smith's *Whittier* (Amesbury, Mass., 1935). Many of these memory pieces were no doubt written out of genuine affection for the man; others were mere obsequiousness or attempts at promoting Quakerism.

The collections of anecdotes about Whittier are only a little less annoying. George Stewart tells "Bits of Gossip" about Whittier in *Belford's Monthly Magazine* (Oct. 1877). In her *Chapters from a Life* (Boston, 1897), Elizabeth Stuart Phelps tells stories showing Whittier's sense of humor. The anecdotes that Charlotte F. Bates remembers about Whittier make up her "Whittier Desultoria" (*Cosmopolitan*, Jan. 1894). G. F. Carter reprints "Some Little-known Whittierana" in *Literary Collector* (July 1904). Anecdotes from his life, selected to make Whittier a hero and saint, make up F. C. Sparhawk's *Whittier at Close-Range* (Boston, 1925).

Kennedy's more serious view of Whittier as a man larger than his work was revived by Richard Burton in his *John Greenleaf Whittier* (Boston, 1901). "What we are," he quotes Whittier as saying, "will then be more important than what we have done or said in prose or rhyme." But Burton finds an irony in this, for it was because of his work as reformer, though he was for so much of his life rejected in that role, that Whittier became known as a representative American poet. The religiosity of his life turned him quite naturally into a reformer and his obsession with reform turned him quite naturally into a didactic poet. So his life and his work became one.

Pickard had challenged that position before the turn of the century by arguing that the strong qualities of Whittier's character had made his verse strong. T. W. Higginson took up that same challenge against Kennedy and Burton in his *John Greenleaf Whittier* (New York, 1902), written for the English Men of Letters series. To Higginson, Whittier was more man than reformer or writer. Whittier's strong personal qualities—his simplicity, his intimacy, his life lived "near the people," and above all his Quaker quietism—were important creative forces. It was because of these qualities that as a reformer he preferred legislative change and nonresistance to violence, and because of these that as a writer he preferred to work on the public conscience rather than confronting the enemy more directly as in politics or debate. It was these qualities, more than the events around him, that transformed a young man of little promise into "the leading bard of the greatest moral movement of the age." To Higginson, an ardent literary nationalist, Whittier was the epitome of those ethical values fundamental to a democracy.

George R. Carpenter was selected to write the biography of Whittier for the American Men of Letters series, *John Greenleaf Whittier* (Boston, 1903), even though he had little sympathy for the moral idealism and social reform of Whittier and the period. To Carpenter the main interest in Whittier's life was politics rather than poetry. But because of his poor health, poverty, and quietism, Whittier was disappointed in his political ambitions, and so came to write a kind of poetry of politics—that is, a poetry of public occasions, local history, and humanitarian interests. Carpenter feels that Whittier was essentially an inner rather than an outer man and so was ineffective in public affairs. Indeed, according to Carpenter, from Whittier's abolitionism and involvement in other public matters came his poetry's narrow range, its lack of wide human sympathy, its esthetic poverty. Occasions gave his writings an importance wholly out of proportion to their artistic merits. Yet though the reformer in him killed the poet in him, he was more effective as journalist, pamphleteer, and poet than he could have been as a politician; reform poetry and tracts made it possible for him to be the man of action he could not otherwise have been.

Bliss Perry, in his *John Greenleaf Whittier: A Sketch of His Life* (Boston, 1907), argues further against Kennedy's thesis about the poet made bad by his piety, passion, and politics. To Perry, Whittier's passion for justice, especially in the dangerous business of abolitionism, purged his verse of melancholy, provincialism, and triteness, or at least made these characteristics negligible. The saintliness of Whittier's life came from his strong social conscience, and without a storm to strengthen his lines, his writings were merely occasional, though effectively so. It was issues, after all, that made Whittier a poet and so his attention to "the great interests of humanity" saved him from literary oblivion.

A repudiation of the Whittier legend built by all the biographers from Kennedy to Perry, Albert Mordell's *Quaker Militant: John*

Greenleaf Whittier (Boston, 1933) was the first psychoanalytic study of Whittier. In it the modest, mild, and sexless saint gives way to a militant and radical but sexually repressed agitator. The young man that Mordell found was one devoured by desire for worldly success but frustrated in his political ambition by his idealism. Similarly, the "natural man" that Mordell felt he found under Whittier's skin was one obsessed with a love of women but frustrated by a puritan conscience. In all cases his idealism controlled everything he did, leaving his life with a psychic impotence, his personal poetry without warmth, and his reform work centering more around propaganda than active involvement. His prolonged virginity was to Mordell the source of the nervous condition that limited his political ambitions, it had a ruinous effect artistically upon his poems, and it left Whittier a philandering celibate in his less radical years.

Fascinating as Whittier's sexual repression is to Mordell as an explanation for Whittier's limitations, he is much more interested in Whittier as a radical. He finds Whittier unique in poeticizing the cause of social justice (this makes his reform poetry superior to his domestic and pious poetry), and finds him effective in manipulating men and agitating masses in the cause of abolition. Though his Quaker idealism dampened much of his fire, it also made him militant against worldliness. A number of Mordell's arguments are suspect, yet they succeeded in moving Whittier criticism to a different plane—away from mythology and toward analysis.

Whitman Bennett was infuriated by Mordell's Freudianized Whittier and so wrote his *Whittier, Bard of Freedom* (Chapel Hill, N.C., 1941) in reply. What Mordell called a wound of passion in Whittier, Bennett found to be little more than a dramatized series of casual platonic crushes. What Mordell called sublimation of sexuality into the channels of reform work, Bennett found to be simply a soul on fire. Bennett's interest in Whittier is much simpler and more reasonable: Whittier exerted a dynamic influence throughout the nation, not because he was a man of genius, but because he was enormously devoted to a significant cause. A weak body kept Whittier's strong soul from involvement in the reform work, journalism, and political activity that he loved, but produced a mind sensitive to nature and spirit. Bennett's is a good sketch of the nation-shaking political and reformist events into which Whittier fit and which Bennett finds him affecting mightily with his pen.

Though John A. Pollard's intent in *John Greenleaf Whittier, Friend of Man* (New York, 1949) was to show Whittier as a well-balanced man with a broad range of interests, experiences, and abilities, it is, like most of the biographical studies since the 1930s, mainly a political life—one in which the politician is a prophet of the people and the prophet is a poet. To Pollard, Whittier's importance was his concern with the whole life of man in the world rather than with literary art merely. He wanted to be known in a more socially relevant capacity than as a maker of rhymes; so his poetry was written mainly in the service of his various social roles—as politician, as propagandist, as reformer, as moralist. Great movements exalted him and with his pen he became a kind of prophet of an age. Like Amos he lived within a small radius but with his voice he remade the age in his own image. Pollard documents Whittier's important place in American history better than anyone else, showing his influence on humanitarian reforms, his creation of a national conscience over slavery, his construction of a new national morality. Whittier's home life, love life, and religion all seem incidental over against Pollard's magnification of Whittier's public life.

Lewis Leary's *John Greenleaf Whittier* (New York, 1961) is the antithesis of the political lives. Forced to fit the format of the TUSAS, the biography is but an overview of Whittier's life and work, yet the emphasis is clear: Leary's Whittier is a man of peaceful nature, a gentle man, a man of simple faith and compassionate humility. He is a man of sense among violently emotional issues; a man of passive resistance in the face of militance; a man who drew quietly into himself when war threatened; a man of holiness in materialistic times. Yet to Leary, Whittier was not primarily a personality but a poet, or rather a personality turned into an important poet by popularity, by the course of events, and by his holy regard for the world around him.

The best critical biography of Whittier (and it is a temptation to say the only sensitively analytical biography) is Edward Wagenknecht's *John Greenleaf Whittier: A Portrait in Paradox.* By identifying the paradoxes of Whittier's life, Wagenknecht is able to destroy most of the stereotypes. The result is the fullest and most humane view of Whittier's temperament and mind. The paradoxes that Wagenknecht finds in Whittier make him a complex man: the fact that he lived celebate and yet was strongly attracted to women; his desire for fame as opposed to his moral obligation to the work of reform; his desire for power amid his love of man; his interest in reform as opposed to his interest in poetry; the fact that he was a pacifist and yet militant; his view of beauty as grace though also as a snare; his Quaker cosmology vs. his nature worship.

With the exception of Wagenknecht's study, the Whittier biographies appear to have been written either to create the hero-saint or to explain Whittier's severe limitations as a writer. Roland H. Wood-well is currently at work on a definitive life, the point of view of which he reveals in *The* [Whittier-College] *Rock* (1968). One hopes that it will avoid both mythologizing and rationalization.

The hero-worship of Whittier led to an inordinate interest in the stock he came from. The Whittier genealogy is discussed in D. B. Whittier's *Genealogy of Two Branches of the Whittier Family from 1620 to 1873* (Boston, 1873) and Charles C. Whittier's *Genealogy of the Whittier Family, 1622–1882* (Boston, 1882). Two other branches of Whittier's genealogy are discussed in James E. Greenleaf's *Genealogy of the Greenleaf Family* (Boston, 1896); in Alonzo H. Quint, "The Hussey Ancestry of the Poet Whittier" (*NEHGR*, 1896); and in Roland H. Woodwell and Martha H. Dureen, "The Hussey Ancestry of the Poet Whittier" (*EIHC*, Jan. 1934). A tribute to Whittier's sister and her services in furthering his literary efforts is Annie R. Marble, "Elizabeth Whittier and the Amesbury Home" (*Outlook*, Sept. 1907). Lloyd W. Griffin has pointed out the importance to literary history of Whittier's brother, Matthew Franklin Whittier, known in the humorist circles of Artemus Ward and Mark Twain as "Ethan Spike" (*NEQ*, Dec. 1941).

Whittier lived most of his life in one place and out of devotion to the area became one of our literature's first regionalists. The fascination with Whittier's locale led Samuel T. Pickard to compile his handbook of North Essex, *Whittier-Land*, an illustrated guide. George M. White attempts to identify "The Local Associations of Whittier's Poems" (*HM*, Feb. 1883). A great deal of fuss has been made about Whittier's moves between Amesbury and Oak Knoll in Danvers, Mass. Abby J. Woodman attempts to describe his daily life in her *Reminiscences of John Greenleaf Whittier at Oak Knoll* (Salem, Mass., 1908). Other fuss is made by S. W. Phillips, "Further Light on the Question of the Residence of John Greenleaf Whittier" (*EIHC*, Jan. 1933) and by Roland H. Woodwell, "Whittier's Place of Residence from 1876 to 1892" (*EIHC*, Oct. 1932). The efforts to preserve Whittier's birthplace are told by Edmund C. Stedman, "The Whittier Home Association" (*Independent*, May 1902). Donald P. Wright has made a photographic documentary of Whittier's life in his *John Greenleaf Whittier: A Profile in Pictures* (Haverhill, Mass., 1967). Another collection of pictures is in J. B. Pickard, *Memorabilia of John Greenleaf Whittier* (Hartford, Conn., 1968, reprinted from *ESQ*, First Quarter 1968).

One of the special problems in Whittier's biography is his influence as a young newspaperman in Philadelphia. Thomas F. Currier writes on the events and people in his life at this time, in "Whittier's Philadelphia Friends in 1838" (*BFHA*, Autumn 1938), and Arthur H. Reede documents the political influence of Whittier in Pennsylvania in "Whittier's Pennsylvania Years, 1837–1840" (*Pennsylvania History*, Oct. 1958).

The special problem raised by Mordell's biography—the facts of Whittier's various romances—is discussed effectively by Norman Foerster in "Whittier as Lover" (*Freeman*, Feb. 1923). Foerster's concern is especially with Whittier's ill-fated romance with Elizabeth Lloyd. Whittier's romance with Evelina Bray is discussed by M. M. Barrows, "The Love Story of Whittier's Life" (*NEM*, Apr. 1905). Albert Mordell has two additional notes to support his argument on Whittier's romance with Lucy Hooper, both in *NEQ* (June 1934).

Perhaps the single most contradictory event in Whittier's later life was the occasion of his seventieth birthday, when tributes were mixed with satire of the old poet. The great praise that came to Whittier can be seen in *The Literary World*, 1 December 1877, and George H. Brownell documents the differing reactions to "Mark Twain's Speech at the Whittier Banquet" (*American Book Collector*, Aug. 1933). Bernard De Voto's account in *Mark Twain's America* (Boston, 1932) is a justification of Twain's attack on Whittier on esthetic grounds. Henry Nash Smith, in "That Hideous Mistake of Poor Clemens's" (*HLB*, Spring 1955) and in "The Backwoods Bull in the Boston China Shop" (*AH*, Aug. 1961), tells why Twain turned the dinner into a public scandal; Twain was daring to suggest that the cult of the writers taking Whittier as a model was an elaborate fraud.

Whittier's life as an unceasing struggle to overcome his pride and to achieve a life that was modest, meek, selfless, and serene is argued by J. J. McAleer, "Whittier's Quest for Humility" (*QH*, Spring 1961). This is one of the most attractive views of Whittier proposed, for it resolves what other biographers have abandoned as paradoxes of his life and mind.

Unfortunately, there have not been any specialized studies of significant stretches of Whittier's life—say, the young Whittier, Whittier's abolitionist years, or the later domestic Whittier. Nor do we have separate studies of Whittier's love life, reform activities, or life as a Quaker. Whittier's biographers have desired instead to see him whole.

As should be evident, the Whittier Lives have been a gradual recognition of what H. E. Hurd calls "The Paradoxes in the Life and Poetry of John Greenleaf Whittier" (*Poetry Review* [London], Aug. 1926). Hurd, in summary, lists the main paradoxes as these: (1) Whittier was a man of limited culture and opportunity, yet he captured the affections of educated men; (2) violating the conventions of verse, he became a poet; (3) he was an ardent lover who never married; (4) Whittier spiritualized the hard life that crushed him; (5) he was a dreamer who could scheme; (6) Whittier, a prophet of peace, sharpened the swords of the North for the Civil War; (7) even without a pulpit, he was a powerful preacher.

CRITICISM

The shape of Whittier criticism from the middle of the nineteenth century to the middle of this century has been discussed by Lewis E. Weeks, "Whittier Criticism Over the Years" (*EIHC*, July 1964). Weeks has found two phases in the critical fortunes of Whittier. The first phase (up to Whittier's death in 1892) is characterized by a double attitude: he is the kindly, honest Quaker and the dreaded, vigorous abolitionist; he is violently loved (because he is loyally American, domestic, public, and a simple, earnest, sincere writer) and violently hated (because he is an anarchist, an overpassionate libertarian, overweeningly didactic, and a poet without adequate technique or range). Beginning in mistrust, the criticism becomes increasingly elegiac toward the end of the century. But because Whittier was such a personal force, there was difficulty in assessing his work esthetically. The second phase (the twentieth century) is concerned mainly with placing Whittier in perspective. The result by and large is a minor rank for him, yet not obscurity. His morality is worth rescuing but not his moralizing, his courage but not his voice, his passion for writing but not the poems that he wrote passionately. Our concern has therefore turned in this century from his substance to his reputation.

Although Whittier was noticed almost everywhere during his lifetime, only a few of the notices now seem very important. One of the earliest serious assessments of Whittier was Rufus Griswold's *Poets and Poetry of America* (Philadelphia, 1842). Whittier's *Supernaturalism in New England* appeared in 1847 and it was one of literary history's "shocks of recognition" when Hawthorne reviewed it in *The Literary World* (reprinted in *NEQ*, Sept. 1936); Hawthorne saw Whittier as too practical-minded to "believe his ghost-story while he is telling it," too pedantic and fussy, too far removed from the folk life from which New England legends spring; Whittier, Hawthorne said, "did not care much for literature." Orestes Brownson, in a review of Whittier's *Songs of Labor* in *Brownson's Quarterly Review* (Oct. 1850), went further and saw Whittier as the devil incarnate; to Brownson, Whittier sought to undermine faith, eradicate loyalty, break down authority, and establish the reign of anarchy: "He is a Quaker, an infidel, an abolitionist, a philanthropist, a peace man, a Red Republican, a nonresistant, a revolutionist, all characters we hold in horror and detestation, and his poems are the echo of himself." In contrast, David Wasson, representative of the period's Transcendentalists, thought of Whittier as a kind of Biblical poet-prophet (*AM*, Mar. 1864); like a prophet, Whittier spoke plainly to plain men, had a firm "moral sentiment," and was a reformer of the world around him.

Near the end of his life and immediately following his death, as Currier and Pulsifer have noted in the Whittier bibliography, discussions of Whittier, most of them by Friends and friends, ran into the hundreds. Harriet Prescott Spofford's is typical of these (*HM*, Jan. 1884); because he is democratic, simple, rustic, moral, a man of broad interests and natural esthetic sense, Whittier is promoted as the ideal American poet, the nation's poet laureate. Edmund Gosse's *Portraits and Sketches* (London, 1912) is also typical; like Gosse, many found his personality "sweet" and "Quakerly" but his verse "primitive" and "redundant." Yet interestingly enough, the first assessment of Whittier from a nearly esthetic point of view was not made until 1881 when Richard Henry Stoddard wrote *The Homes and Haunts of Our Elder Poets* (New York) and until 1885 when Edmund C. Stedman wrote *Poets of America* (Boston). Both found that the power of Whittier's poetry comes not from the man so much as from his background (the Colonial past, the injustices in the society around him) and yet both also attempt to account for his failings as a poet: he is too naive, too moralistic, too simplistic. Unfortunately, most of the critical comments on Whittier at his death serve better as nostalgia than as literary criticism.

Whittier's reputation in America during his lifetime has been discussed by T. W. Higginson, "The Place of Whittier among the Poets" (*Reader*, Feb. 1905), and his reputation abroad by John A. Pollard, "Whittier's Esteem in Great Britain" (*BFHA*, Spring 1949). A brief note on Whittier's reputation is C. Marshall Taylor, "The 1849 Best Seller" (*BFHA*, Autumn 1950). The problem of keeping Whittier's reputation alive is discussed by C. Waller Barrett, "John Greenleaf Whittier: The 100th Anniversary of His Birth" (*American Antiquarian Society Proceedings*, 1957) and by Donald C. Freeman, "The History of the Haverhill Whittier Club" (*ESQ*, First Quarter 1968).

As Weeks has mentioned, almost all of the Whittier criticism since the turn of the century is concerned essentially with Whittier's reputation, rather than with his thought or art. Three attempts to account for Whittier's universal appeal in the nineteenth century but neglect in the twentieth are Rica Brenner, *Twelve American Poets before 1900* (New York, 1932); Desmond Powell, "Whittier" (*AL*, Nov. 1937); and W. Harvey-Jellie, "A Forgotten Poet" (*Dalhousie Review*, Apr. 1939).

There are almost formidable problems in reading Whittier in the twentieth century. Stanley Kunitz has articulated best, in *American Authors, 1600–1900* (New York, 1938), how invalid Whittier's assumptions about life and art and how irrelevant his writings now seem. He was "the voice of the middle nineteenth-century New England farmer and small town dweller," but ours is a different world. In *The Fields Were Green* (Stanford, Calif., 1953), George Arms, while defending him as a poet, sees Whittier's single-mindedness as the central problem in reading him today. To Arms, Whittier was a personal poet, a poet of personal experience, who tended to have only one motif, the Quaker view of man, even going so far as to identify English Romanticism with Quaker cosmology. As a result Whittier was uneasy as a poet; he could not accept art as an essential expression of life. Like Arms, Howard Mumford Jones, in "Whittier Reconsidered," in his *History and the Contemporary* (Madison, Wis., 1964), bemoans the inattention given Whittier's values and Christian gentlemanliness in our own time, but sees that the central problems for us are the superficiality of Whittier's indignation and his monotony and sentimentality.

Yet for all the problems in reading Whittier, much of the Whittier criticism has attempted to find what is redeemable in the man and his art. One of the most balanced early views is that by John Vance Cheney, *That Dome in Air* (Chicago, 1895); Cheney feels that though Whittier is stiff and provincial, what he has left to generations after him is the idea of the poet as lover of man. Like this view is Paul Elmer More's, in *Shelburne Essays, Third Series* (Boston, 1906): for all Whittier's faults of taste, he had an indisputable, simple grace. To More, Whittier is the poet who brought the quiet affections of the home into our literature; his poetry is unmatched in the genre of "poetry of the hearth." Bliss Perry, in "Whittier for Today" (*AtM*, Dec. 1907), explains Whittier's relevance on other grounds—his courage and humanity, his involvement in social affairs. To Perry, there are two issues on which Whittier is always right: his insistence that there must not be any race issue and his demand for international peace. An extension of Perry's claim for Whittier is Ernest D. Lee's argument, in "John Greenleaf Whittier" (*The Westminister Review*, Jan. 1908), that Whittier should be preserved as an example of the phenomenon of a national poet.

Winfield Townley Scott, in his excellent essay "A New Consideration of Whittier's Verse" (*NEQ*, June 1934) and in his poem "Mr. Whittier," deplores the schoolroom use to which Whittier has been put and argues that Whittier can be restored to eminence if emphasis is placed on the poetry written after the Civil War, especially the religious verse. Hyatt H. Waggoner, in his *American Poets from the Puritans to the Present* (Boston, 1967) and in "What I Had I Gave: Another Look at Whittier" (*EIHC*, Jan. 1959), also finds Whittier's religious verse that which should recommend him to our own time. Waggoner shows how Whittier moved from moralizing and propagandizing to symbolizing and spiritualizing the world as he knew it, making him one of our literature's few Christian poets. To Waggoner there is value in relearning how to read Whittier; his contemporaries read him as a religious poet, as a poet of universal and humane causes, as a poet documenting God's part in the progress of The American Dream, and we must do so too.

Yet to read Whittier today, as Donald Hall has argued in "Whittier" (*Texas Quarterly*, Autumn 1960), requires an effort of the historical imagination. To Hall it is the nineteenth-century themes of goodness and optimism that give Whittier a firm place in our literary history. George E. Woodberry, in his essay on Whittier in *Makers of Literature* (New York, 1901), was one of the first to see how representative Whittier was of his time. John Macy, in *The Spirit of American Literature* (New York, 1913), saw Whittier as the poet who best represents the crudeness, banality, and prejudices, but also the idealism and exaltation, of the nineteenth century. To William M. Payne, writing in *CHAL*, Whittier was the representative man of "the epic days" preceding the war. Yet as Daniel W. Smythe has pointed out in "Whittier and the New Critics" (*ESQ*, First Quarter 1968), Whittier continues to suffer disparagement under contemporary critical methods.

Whittier's development as an artist has been discussed best by H. H. Clark, J. B. Pickard, and Edward Wagenknecht. Clark, in an essay, "The Growth of Whittier's Mind" (*ESQ*, First Quarter 1968), assigns Whittier's work to the three conventional phases of his life: up to 1833, Whittier was interested mainly in sensational local legend; from 1833 to 1857 his mind was preoccupied with outward reformism; and from 1857 until his death he turned to the inward life. Pickard, in the critical essays in *John Greenleaf Whittier: An Introduction and Interpretion* (New York, 1961), sees his growth not so much in subject matter as in movement between genres, that is, from folk forms to protest forms and finally to nature poems and religious lyrics. Wagenknecht, on the other hand, sees, in *John Greenleaf Whittier: A Portrait in Paradox*, the growth of Whittier's mind in terms of coming to grips with the contradictions in his thinking; that is, the resolution of his fears, his pride, his senses (all of which conflicted with his otherworldly interests) into a sense of grace.

The earliest work on Whittier's esthetics and literary theory was done by Samuel T. Pickard, "Whittier's Literary Methods" (*Independent*, Sept. 1897) and by Harry H. Clark, in his notes on Whittier in *Major American Poets*. J. B. Pickard's work on the artistry of Whittier (especially in an essay, "Poetic Creed and Practice," in his *John Greenleaf Whittier*) shows that Whittier's views on art and beauty are dominated by a conflict between the lure of external natural beauty and the strict plainness of the Quaker life-style. Confusing religion with esthetics, Whittier's view of the purpose of art remained obscured throughout his life. Edward Wagenknecht's life, like Pickard's, is mainly a concern for Whittier's esthetics, and like Pickard he finds Whittier torn between regarding beauty as grace and beauty as a snare. Wagenknecht's discussion of Whittier's worship of nature, "The Light That Is Light Indeed," is excellent in reconciling Whittier's regard for art with his regard for religion. Lewis Leary, in his *John Greenleaf Whittier*, finds Whittier's literary principles centered around the idea of "the beauty of holiness, of purity, of that inward grace which passeth show," as opposed to the idea of the holiness of beauty of his Romantic contemporaries. Like Emerson, he felt that a high seriousness made language poetic, and though he lacked that esthetic education which might have provided the literary counterbalance to the moralist in him, he compensated for it with sincerity, devotion, humor, and stinging words. Though Leary is often more interested in Whittier's performance than in his poetics, he does demonstrate how a sense of the past, a consciousness of life being lived, and the meditating on one's own pride and humility were to Whittier more important parts of the poet's esthetics than his prosody or imagery. Roy Harvey Pearce, in discussing the esthetics of the Fireside Poets in *The Continuity of American Poetry* (Princeton, N.J., 1961), distorts Whittier in arguing that his literary principles were dominated by a fantasy principle, that is, by the belief that the poet has special access to the common man's dreams and fantasies. Whittier's poems, Pearce maintains, are therefore dominated by visions, dreams, nostalgia, idealistic indulgence, romanticizing of the past, and blind faith in the future.

With regard to Whittier's literary theory, what is lacking in the criticism is an extended discussion of Whittier's concern for form. We have Gay Wilson Allen's discussion of rhythm and stanza form in his *American Prosody* (New York, 1935) and two notes on "Whittier's Rhymes" by Kathryn A. McEuen and S. T. Byington (*AS*, Feb. 1945;

Feb. 1946), but Whittier's use of conventions and his many innovations have gone largely unexplored.

Whittier himself promoted the popular legend that he was not a well-read man, but scholars have gone to great pains to prove otherwise. The closest we have to a list of Whittier's reading is "The Library of John G. Whittier" (*ESQ*, First Quarter 1964). Alwin Thaler, in "Whittier and the English Poets" (*NEQ*, Mar. 1951; *ESQ*, First Quarter 1968), lists all of the British writers that Whittier knew. Thaler persuasively argues Whittier's wide reading and frequent use of his reading in his poems, especially Elizabethan and Romantic writings.

Whittier's legend also excluded the problem of literary influence, but the writers who influenced Whittier the most are revealed in an unpublished dissertation, Joseph M. Ernest's "Whittier and the American Writers" (Tennessee, 1952). As with other New England writers of the period, some of the strongest influences on Whittier were Elizabethan, German, and Oriental—all of which Whittier in his strict Quaker orthodoxy was able largely to resist. Iola K. Eastburn shows Whittier's catholic interests and wide reading in *Whittier's Relation to German Life and Thought* (Philadelphia, 1915); though Whittier was interested in German legends and reform movements, the German influence on him was not strong. Whittier was not a mystic, either, not a promoter of faith in the transcendent, and yet his Oriental interests were strong. Arthur E. Christy, "The Orientalism in Whittier" (*AL*, Jan. 1930; Nov. 1933), found that what appealed to the orthodox Quaker was mainly the moral tone and the general ethical principles of Eastern thought; Whittier's was not a spiritual and philosophical affinity with the Orient like Emerson's, for he was blind to distinctions between Christian and Oriental principles.

That Whittier was a borrower from his readings is shown by J. Chesley Matthews's study of "Whittier's Knowledge of Dante" (*Italica*, 1957), by Jack Stillinger's notice of "Whittier's Early Imitation of Thomas Campbell" (*PQ*, Oct. 1959), by Theodore Garrison's account of "The Influence of Robert Ginsmore ['the Rustic Bard of Windham, N. H.'] upon Whittier" (*ESQ*, First Quarter 1968), and by Nelson F. Adkins, "Sources of Some of Whittier's Lines" (*NEQ*, June 1933).

As a critic, as Edwin H. Cady and H. H. Clark show in their collection *Whittier on Writers and Writing*, Whittier was much more interested in the moral, the sublime, the antiquarian, and that which would reform society than he was in technical skill. The best discussions of Whittier's critical principles are two unpublished dissertations: C. P. Marcy, "The Literary Criticism of John Greenleaf Whittier" (Boston University, 1945) and J. M. Ernest, "Whittier and the American

Writers." Marcy outlines the formative influences on Whittier's critical thought—his homelife, his education, his religion and politics—and finds Whittier most concerned with a writer's morality, the sensitivity of his response to nature, and the functionality of his imagination. Marcy's conclusion is that Whittier was not a discriminating critic of literature, and what limited him most severely was his idea that literature should conform to the conventions of a society controlled by Quaker tenets of morality and simplicity. Ernest, on the other hand, is interested mainly in showing how Whittier was one of the great promoters of American literature. He had a deep interest in seventeenth-century American writings and he kept abreast of the literary movements of his time by meeting and corresponding with, reading and reviewing most of the authors of his day. But as a critic, because his interests were primarily ethical rather than esthetic, he did not usually consider the work as distinct from the author. Not until he was older did his esthetic sense outgrow his crusading zeal.

Whittier's relationships with writers who were his contemporaries have been taken up separately to show what John J. McAleer calls "Whittier's Selective Tolerance" (*ESQ*, First Quarter 1968). McAleer finds Whittier both consoling and severe in his work with other writers. While the relationship between Whittier and Tennyson, as William J. Fowler (*Arena*, Dec. 1892) and Alwin Thaler (*PQ*, Oct. 1949) have both found, was one of mutual admiration, Whittier's regard for Carlyle, discussed by Roland H. Woodwell in *ESQ* (First Quarter 1968), was one of growing disgust because of Carlyle's refusal to support humanitarian causes important to Whittier.

The regard that Whittier and Bryant had for one another is discussed by Charles D. Deshler, *Afternoon with the Poets* (New York, 1879), and by Charles I. Glicksberg, "Bryant and Whittier" (*EIHC*, Apr. 1936); what they had in common was the cause of human freedom and an ardent patriotism. Longfellow's indebtedness to Whittier is discussed by Frank B. Sanborn, "Whittier and Longfellow Compared as Poets of New England" (*Boston Evening Transcript*, 24 July 1902), and by O. S. Coad, "The Bride of the Sea" (*AL*, Mar. 1937). His indebtedness to Bayard Taylor is discussed by Joseph M. Ernest in *Friend's Intelligencer* (Sept. 1952). Ernest has also documented Whittier's influence on American women writers in the latter half of the century in "Whittier and the 'Feminine Fifties'" (*AL*, May 1956). Ernest gives credit to Whittier for the phenomenon of so many women writers in the period; more than anyone else, Whittier gave them practical help and encouragement in their liberal causes. This important influence is documented further by Rudolph Kirk, "Whittier and Miss Piatt" (*JRUL*,

June 1944), and by Carl J. Weber, "Whittier and Sarah Orne Jewett" (*NEQ*, Sept. 1945).

Whittier's thorniest relationship was with Whitman. Joseph M. Ernest, in "Whittier and Whitman: Uncongenial Personalities" (*BFHA*, Autumn 1953), blames Whittier for this. Whittier threw his copy of *Leaves of Grass* into the fire, would not mention Whitman's name, and then publicly denounced him in 1885. Lewis E. Weeks's documentation of the relationship, "Whittier and Whitman" (*ESQ*, First Quarter 1968), finds great similarity between them but also inevitable incompatibility.

Whittier is one of the pioneer regionalists in our literature. The attention to nation, region, land, and folk called for by Emerson was already appearing, though from a different, less self-conscious, less programmatic perspective than Emerson's, in the writings of Whittier. Mamoru Ohmori has written of this in "J. G. Whittier and American National Literature" in his *Essays in English and American Literature* (New York, 1961). The causes that led Whittier to use folk materials in his poems are discussed by George C. Carey, "Whittier's Place in New England Folklore" (*ESQ*, First Quarter 1968) and "Whittier's Roots in a Folk Culture" (*EIHC*, Jan. 1968). Carey shows that Whittier was the product of a folk milieu, born and raised in the context of rural New England story-telling. So where most of the writers of the time were patricians, Whittier was a new phenomenon to our literature, the peasant poet. Henry W. Wells, in "Cambridge Culture and Folk Poetry," in his *The American Way of Poetry* (New York, 1943), sees Whittier as a type—"the New England Quaker," a role Whittier played so well that he gave us a form of folk poetry. In "Whittier's Ballads: The Making of an Artist" (*EIHC*, Jan. 1960), J. B. Pickard discusses Whittier's ballads as the best re-creation of native folklore and legend written in the nineteenth century. A special study of a folktale type is Harry Oster, "Whittier's Use of the *Sage* in His Ballads," in *Studies in American Literature*, edited by Waldo McNeir and Leo B. Levy (Baton Rouge, La., 1960).

The attention to New England folk ways and history resulted in an early if sometimes awkward and sentimental form of regional writing, as has been shown by Albert Mordell in his biography *Quaker Militant* and by Theodore R. Garrison in a dissertation, "John Greenleaf Whittier: Pioneer Regionalist and Folklorist" (Wisconsin, 1960). The use to which Whittier put New England history is given general treatment by Thomas F. Waters, "Whittier, the Poet, as Historian" (*Massachusetts Magazine*, Jan. 1908) and M. Jane Griswold, "American Quaker History in the Works of Whittier, Hawthorne, and Longfellow"

(*Americana*, 1940). How willing a contributor to the Puritan legend Whittier was—and in this regard as a forerunner of Hawthorne and Melville—is discussed by Louis C. Schaedler, "Whittier's Attitude toward Colonial Puritanism" (*NEQ*, Sept. 1948). Though Whittier's attitude turned initially from impartiality to hostility, the more he dealt with Puritan materials the more appreciative he became. Cecil B. Williams, in a work devoted entirely to Whittier's regionalism, *Whittier's Use of Historical Material in "Margaret Smith's Journal"* (Chicago, 1936), shows the care with which Whittier used colonial records and New England historians in the construction of his prose legend. The quality of Whittier's imagination is seen in his use of the legend genre to turn historical material into protest literature. This approach inspired much of the local color writing toward the end of the century. The skillful construction of this work is discussed further by Lewis Leary, "A Note on Whittier's Margaret Smith" (*ESQ*, First Quarter 1968).

The best argument against Whittier as being merely a regionalist is Cora Dolbee, "Kansas and 'The Prairied West' of John G. Whittier" (*EIHC*, Oct. 1945). Although intended as a survey of Whittier's contribution to freedom in Kansas, from 1827 to 1891, the discussion demonstrates Whittier's ability to deal with local issues and local color of areas outside New England.

Discussions of individual works by Whittier are for the most part attempts either at checking Whittier's facts and sources or making one aware of Whittier's values. Whittier's poem "Barbara Frietchie" and his poems on John Brown ("Brown of Ossawatomie") and Daniel Webster ("Ichabod") are cases in point. As early as 1875, historians began questioning Whittier's use of the Revolutionary War story of Barbara Frietchie; see especially Jubal Early, "Barbara Frietchie: The Poet's Base of Facts" (*Boston Daily Advertiser*, 8 May 1875) and "Letter on the Barbara Frietchie Myth" (*Southern Historical Society Papers*, 1879), and Henry M. Nixdorff, *Life of Whittier's Heroine, Barbara Frietchie* (Frederick, Md., 1887). Others, however, have rushed to Whittier's defense with information from Maryland history: Caroline H. Dall, *Barbara Frietchie, a Study* (Boston, 1892); R. M. Cheshire, "More About Barbara Frietchie" (*Book of the Royal Blue*, July 1903); D. M. and W. R. Quynn, "Barbara Frietchie," *Maryland Historical Magazine*, Sept. 1942; Dec. 1942).

In the case of the John Brown poem, Cecil D. Eby has tried to prove the accuracy of Whittier's information, first in "Whittier's 'Brown of Ossawatomie'" (*NEQ*, Dec. 1960) and then in "John Brown's Kiss" (*Virginia Cavalcade*, May, 1961). In the case of the Webster poem, two brief notes have tried to show the features of Webster's life and personality that Whittier uses in his poem: Margaret H. Gangewer, "Whittier's Poem 'Ichabod' " (*AN&Q*, Mar. 1889) and Motley S. Maddox, "Whittier's 'Ichabod' " (*Expl*, Apr. 1960).

Even with more explicable poems like "Skipper Ireson's Ride" and "Snow-Bound," the critical comments have had more to do with historical and biographical background than with art. There are a number of notes identifying the characters in "Snow-Bound" and these show how personal the poem was: Nathaniel L. Sayles, "A Note on Whittier's 'Snow-Bound' " (*AL*, Nov. 1934); Helen L. Drew, "The Schoolmaster in 'Snow-Bound' " (*AL*, May 1937); Elizabeth F. Hoxie, "Harriet Livermore: 'Vixen and Devotee' " (*NEQ*, June 1945); W. Gary Groat, "Harriet Livermore: A Whittier Recollection" (*AN&Q*, May 1966). But there are two long discussions of the poem (the only two real explications among all of the comments on Whittier's individual poems) which are excellent: J. B. Pickard, "Imagistic and Structural Unity in 'Snow-Bound' " (*CE*, Mar. 1960), and Elizabeth V. Pickett, " 'Snow-Bound' and the New Critics" (*ESQ*, First Quarter 1968). These two essays show that the greatest need in Whittier criticism is for full discussions of individual poems.

Most Whittier criticism has had to deal in one way or another with Whittier's faith, which was important personally and culturally. "In Whittier," wrote Whitman, "lives the zeal, the moral energy that founded New England." Whittier's place in American religious literature in the nineteenth century is explored by Augustus H. Strong, *American Poets and Their Theology* (Philadelphia, 1916), and Elmer J. Bailey, *Religious Thought in the Greater American Poets* (Boston, 1922). Whittier's Quaker contribution to our literature is examined by Howard W. Hintz, *The Quaker Influence in American Literature* (New York, 1940). Three essays in Howard H. Brinton's *Byways in Quaker History* (Wallinford, Pa., 1944) are a good introduction to the three major concerns about Whittier's faith. Rufus M. Jones, in "Whittier's Fundamental Religious Faith," agrees that Whittier's faith leaned neither to the orthodox nor to the unitarian side of nineteenth-century American Quakerism, but as the result of the influence of Coleridge and Emerson, it was unique in its strong Platonism, and as such is the finest expression of Quaker beliefs in American life. Henry J. Cadbury, in "Whittier as Historian of Quakerism," shows how Whittier found in historic Quakerism the full expression of his social philosophy and therefore tried to protect it from misrepresentation or abuse. C. Marshall Taylor, in "Whittier, the Quaker Politician," shows Whittier's faith as the main force behind his interest in social reform.

The broad religious interests of Whittier—Biblical, Quaker, Oriental—are discussed in a dissertation by Charles R. Tegen, "The Religious Poetry of John Greenleaf Whittier" (Central Wesleyan, 1968). Whittier's specific principles are discussed by Luella Wright, "Whittier on the Dignity of Man" (*The Friend*, Dec. 1945) and by Elfriede Fecalek in an unpublished work, "Die Wertwelt John Greenleaf Whittiers" (Vienna, 1946). His general morality is commented on by C. M. Severance, F. M. Larkin, and J. C. Carr in a Whittier symposium in *Pacific Monthly* (Spring 1891).

Whittier was seen, by Friends and others, as an important religious force in his time. Early comments like Henry Blanchard's "The Theology of Whittier" (*The Friend*, May 1866) and G. R. Baker's "John Greenleaf Whittier" (*Friends Quarterly Examiner*, Oct. 1871), show how important he was to Quakers on both sides of the Atlantic as a purveyor of the faith. Estimates like those of Mrs. James T. Fields, "The Inner Life of John Greenleaf Whittier" (*The Chautauquan*, Nov. 1899), and Oliver Wendell Holmes, "Whittier's Religion" (*Unity*, Dec. 1892), show how important he was to writers of the time as a sustainer of Christian thought. Other brief comments emphasizing how much Whittier's Quaker ancestry, environment, and faith meant to him are John W. Chadwick, "Whittier's Spiritual Career" (*New World*, Mar. 1893); William H. Savage, "Whittier's Religion" (*Arena*, July 1894); and Will D. Howe, "Whittier," in *American Writers on American Literature*, edited by John Macy (New York, 1931).

A number of the separate titles on Whittier are merely Quaker tracts, in which the Quaker life is celebrated as much as Whittier's orthodoxy: Julius W. Atwood, *The Spiritual Influence of John Greenleaf Whittier* (Providence, R.I., 1894); Ernest E. Taylor, *John Greenleaf Whittier, the Quaker* (New York, 1954); and Benjamin F. Trueblood, *The Faith of John Greenleaf Whittier* (Amesbury, Mass., 1957). The significance of Whittier's poetry in transmitting Quaker ideas to the common man is emphasized by T. T. Munger, "The Religious Influence of Whittier" (*Christian Union*, 24 September 1892), and by Frederick M. Meek, "Whittier the Religious Man" (*ESQ*, First Quarter 1968).

Yet for all of the faith in Whittier's faith, a battle has raged over whether he was really orthodox. His leanings toward New England Puritanism are discussed by James Mudge in "The Quaker Laureate of Puritanism" (*Methodist Review*, Jan. 1908) and by M. E. Kingsley in "A Quaker Poet in Puritan New England" (*Poet-Lore*, Oct. 1910). On the other side of the nineteenth-century Quaker spectrum, it is argued that Whittier inclined toward Unitarianism, an accusation Whittier fought all his life. Richard H. Thomas, "Was Whittier Unitarian?" (*Friends' Review*, 17 November 1892), and Edward D. Snyder, "Whittier and the Unitarians" (*BFHA*, Autumn 1960), attempt to show that though he was not Unitarian, Whittier had mild pro-Unitarian feelings that made him a man of interdenominational good will. Lewis H. Chrisman argues, in "The Spiritual Message of Whittier" (in his *John Ruskin, Preacher and Other Essays*, Cincinnati, Ohio, 1921), that Whittier's fundamentalism was a reaction against the popularity of a nebulous Unitarianism.

Other defenses of Whittier's orthodoxy have been made on the basis of the principle of the Inner Light. Chauncey J. Hawkins, in *The Mind of Whittier: A Study of Whittier's Fundamental Religious Ideas* (New York, 1904), shows how Whittier's faith depended on the concept of the immanence of God; hope and humanitarianism were to Whittier man's main courses of action, but both spring from the conviction of immanence in self and others. Edward Wagenknecht, in "Whittier and the Supernatural—a Test Case" (*ESQ*, First Quarter 1968), is also able to defend Whittier's orthodoxy on the basis of his belief in immanence; Whittier survived nineteenth-century religious currents because he took the Inner Light, rather than the Bible, tradition, or superstition, as the supreme authority in his life.

This does not mean, however, that Whittier was a mystic, as some have carelessly labeled him: S. M. Crothers, "Whittier the Mystic" (*Unity*, Dec. 1892); Rufus M. Jones, "Whittier the Mystic" (*American Friend*, Dec. 1907); and Lyman Abbott, "John G. Whittier, Mystic" (*Outlook*, Jan. 1921). The role of nature in Whittier's religious outlook is discussed by Norman Foerster, *Nature in American Literature* (New York, 1923), a role disputed by Percy H. Boynton, *American Poetry* (New York, 1921). As Arthur E. Christy has shown in his discussions of Whittier's Oriental interests in "The Orientalism in Whittier," Whittier was not so much resistant to other religious systems as he was selective of those values from them which coincided with his own.

Still, Whittier has been looked at from a wide variety of sectarian positions, perhaps indicating the universality of his values. For a Roman Catholic view, see John L. Spalding, "John Greenleaf Whittier" (*Catholic World*, Jan. 1877); for a Universalist view, W. T. Stowe, "Whittier" (*University Quarterly*, July 1867); for a Presbyterian view, A. MacLeod, "The Great Poets of America: Whittier" (*Catholic Presbyterian*, July 1882); for a Unitarian view, Edward Everett Hale, "Curtis, Whittier, and Longfellow" (in his *Five Prophets of To-day*, Boston, 1892); for a Methodist view, Camden M. Cobern, "The Religious Beliefs of John Greenleaf Whittier" (*Methodist Re-*

view, Mar. 1895); for a Congregational view, J. W. Buckham, "Whittier Face to Face" (*Congregational Quarterly*, Sept. 1935); and for a Disciples of Christ view, Henry J. Cadbury, "Whittier's Religion" (*Christian Century*, 5 February 1958).

There are two studies of Whittier and the Bible: S. Trevena Jackson, "Whittier's Use of the Bible" (*Christian Advocate*, Dec. 1907) and James S. Stevens, *Whittier's Use of the Bible* (Orono, Maine, 1930), both showing Whittier to be a literalist. This literal use resulted in a large body of religious verse, as Edward D. Snyder had pointed out in "Whittier's Religious Poetry" (*Friends Quarterly Examiner*, Apr. 1934). Whittier as a writer of religious verse for hymns has been discussed by William C. Gannett, "Whittier in Our Hymn Books" (*Unity*, Dec. 1892), and by C. Marshall Taylor, "Whittier Set to Music" (*EIHC*, Jan. 1952).

Unfortunately, most of the commentary on Whittier's faith deals with the phenomenon of Quaker theology and says little about Whittier himself in this regard. Two studies that are enlightening on the religious Whittier are by Philip C. Moon and Perry Miller. Moon, in "Observations on the Religious Philosophy and Method of Whittier in *Voices of Freedom*" (*EIHC*, Oct. 1957), demonstrates that it was the influence of Garrison, not Quakerism, that gave Whittier his messianic humanitarianism, his conscientious devotion, and his religious-reformist zeal. But Miller, in "John Greenleaf Whittier: The Conscience in Poetry" (*Harvard Review*, Spring 1964), identifies Whittier's Quaker role as a method of self-defense, a convenience, a life-long act; beneath his quietism was a ferocity that characterized the real Whittier.

The regard for Whittier as abolitionist could not have been higher in his lifetime. As Samuel J. May put it, in *Some Recollections of Our Anti-Slavery Conflict* (Boston, 1869), "Of all our American poets, John G. Whittier has from first to last done most for the abolition of slavery. All my anti-slavery bretheren, I doubt not, will unite with me to crown him our laureate." The anti-slavery movement and Whittier's place in it are discussed effectively in Gilbert H. Barnes, *The Anti-Slavery Impulse* (New York, 1933), and in *The Anti-Slavery Vanguard*, edited by Martin Duberman (Princeton, N.J. 1965). Whittier's part in the reconciliation of North and South after the war is discussed in Paul H. Beck, *The Road to Reunion* (Boston, 1937).

Many other contemporaries celebrated Whittier as a poetic prophet of the movement—David V. Barlett, *Modern Agitators* (New York, 1855); William Lloyd Garrison II, *John Greenleaf Whittier* (Brooklyn, N.Y., 1892); T. W. Higginson, "Whittier as a Combatant" (*Book News Monthly*, Dec. 1907); Frank B. Sanborn, "Whittier as Man,

Poet, and Reformer" (*Biblia Sacra*, Apr. 1908). Seldom did anyone take issue, as William Dean Howells did in his *Literary Friends and Acquaintance* (New York, 1900), with those who considered him a great reformer. The most extensive treatment of Whittier's antislavery ideas and activities is an unpublished work, Siegfried Krugmann's "John Greenleaf Whittiers Kampf gegen die Sklaverei" (Erlangen, 1953).

However, Whittier's abolition poetry, roughly one-third of the canon, has seldom been discussed critically. Most comments are like John V. Cheney's "Whittier" (*Chautauquan*, Dec. 1892), arguing that Whittier is the ideal poet for democracy and that his antislavery poems are central to that position, or like Alfred Kreymborg's "A Rustic Quaker Goes to War" in his *Our Singing Strength* (New York, 1928), arguing that Whittier's poetry is autobiographical and that his best poetry resulted from his abolition work. The only discussion of artistic qualities of the poetry is in J. B. Pickard's "Whittier's Abolitionist Poetry" (*ESQ*, First Quarter 1968). "At best," Pickard concludes, "their earnest simplicity and religious intensity redeemed their topical nature, simplified their digressive tendency, and toughened their derivative phrasing."

The wide range of Whittier's social conscience has been celebrated best by V. L. Parrington, *Main Currents in American Thought* (New York, 1927), but many others have cited his historical significance for liberalism. J. Wilfred Holmes shows this wide range in his collection, *Whittier's Prose on Reforms Other than Abolition* (Pittsburgh, Pa., 1945). Whittier's work against capital punishment is discussed in David Brion Davis, "The Movement to Abolish Capital Punishment in America, 1787–1861" (*AHR*, Oct. 1957). His concern for laborers and labor conditions is discussed in Thomas F. Currier, "Whittier and the Amesbury-Salisbury Strike" (*NEQ*, Mar. 1935), and John A. Pollard, "Whittier on Labor Unions" (*NEQ*, Mar. 1939). That Whittier belongs to the tradition of Hawthorne and Melville in reacting against the advance of technology is argued by Richard Olson, "Whittier and the Machine Age" (*ESQ*, First Quarter 1968); in the conflict, Whittier preferred the garden, that is, the idyllic and humane, to the machine.

Whittier's relationships with other reformers, political or abolitionist, reveal the uniqueness and limitations of his thinking. His political idealism resulted in an intimate friendship like that with Charles Sumner, as J. Wilfred Holmes claims in "Whittier and Sumner: A Political Friendship" (*NEQ*, Mar. 1957), though a number of differences were dictated by Whittier's Quakerism. The same is true of his relation with Thomas Clarkson, as C. Marshall Taylor notes (*BFHA*, Autumn 1954).

The relation with William Lloyd Garrison was more of a test, however. Philip C. Moon, in "Observations on the Religious Philosophy and Method of Whittier in *Voices of Freedom*," argues that Garrison was the main creative influence in Whittier's life, and Cecil B. Williams, in "Whittier's Relation to Garrison and the *Liberator*" (*NEQ*, June 1952), shows how Garrison helped Whittier's career as poet and journalist. T. W. Higginson's was perhaps the earliest serious comparison of the two, "Garrison and Whittier" (*Independent*, Dec. 1905); to him the men complemented each other. C. Marshall Taylor's comparison, "Whittier vs. Garrison" (*EIHC*, July 1946), though heavily biased in favor of Whittier's pacifism, patience, idealism, and faith, identifies the cause of their differences in Whittier's heavy sense of sin. Other discussions of Whittier as an editor of abolitionist periodicals are Bertha-Monica Stearns, "John Greenleaf Whittier, Editor" (*NEQ*, June 1940), and Thomas F. Currier,"Whittier and the *New England Weekly Review*" (*NEQ*, Sept. 1933).

The Negro view of Whittier as an abolitionist is shown by Beatrice J. Fleming, "John G. Whittier, Abolition Poet" (*Negro History Bulletin*, Dec. 1942). J. Wilfred Holmes, in "Whittier's Friends among the Lowly" (*ESQ*, First Quarter 1968), discusses Whittier's association with and attitude toward Negroes. Even though he finds Whittier's poems to have been evoked more by specific events than by humanitarian values, Osborn T. Smallwood, in "The Historical Significance of Whittier's Anti-Slavery Poems as Reflected in Their Political and Social Background" (*Journal of Negro History*, Apr. 1950), recognizes that Whittier's poems are an important part of the protest literature that molded public opinion and finally elected Lincoln.

Whittier's abolitionist influence extended to the Midwest, where through his correspondence he worked to keep new states free; these were among his most successful political moves. Whittier's influence on affairs in Iowa and Nebraska is discussed by Charles A. Hawley in *IJHP* (Apr. 1936) and in *BFHA* (Autumn 1939; Spring 1941). Whittier's concern over freedom abroad is discussed by Livio Jannattoni, "Whittier e la Beecher Stowe d'accordo su Garibaldi" (*La Fiera Letteraria*, Oct. 1951), and by Francis B. Dedmond, "A Note on Whittier and Italian Freedom" (*BFHA*, Autumn 1951).

In conclusion it must be said that, in depth, the Whittier criticism leaves much to be desired. Though Whittier does not fit easily into any mode of criticism, he has been dealt with honestly (and it is a temptation to say excessively) if not fully. In the criticism, we have much of Whittier's life, mind, soul, and times, but not yet all of the life and liveliness that may be hidden in the poetry itself.

The Literature of the Old South

C. HUGH HOLMAN

THE SOUTHEASTERN STATES—those that in 1861 united to form the Confederacy—represented in the first half of the nineteenth century a substantial portion of the land area and of the population of the United States. Bound together by a steadily growing defense of their agricultural economy and in particular by the institution of slavery on which it rested, they formed a self-conscious political, intellectual, and social unit, one which placed a very high premium on public service, especially in politics and law, and on an aesthetic which found its clearest expression more often in a way of gracious living than in the more enduring art forms. It was a culture that usually expressed itself in essays, polemical pamphlets, occasional poems, and ardent oratory when it took recourse to the arts of the written language. Its formal fiction paid Sir Walter Scott the highest of tributes, that of imitation, and it continued to admire and imitate him long after the rest of the nation had shifted its literary allegiance to such writers as Dickens and Thackeray. Only on its rampaging frontier did the Old South fashion a literature sufficiently fresh and vital to speak very powerfully to us today. During the first six decades of the nineteenth century, it produced few literary figures of any enduring stature: perhaps only Edgar Allan Poe, William Gilmore Simms, and Henry Timrod.

In this essay, which differs substantially in the type of subject matter and in purpose from others in this volume, I shall attempt to give the literary student some guidance through the general literary and cultural materials on the Old South and to indicate special studies which have some special value for him. I have consciously avoided reference to very many periodical essays, partly because there are too many of them and most are on highly specialized subjects, and partly because the present essay does not attempt such particularized approaches (if it had it would have been far too long). I have attempted to guide the student to bibliographies and discussions that will lead him on to more detailed treatments. Edgar Allan Poe, the only truly major figure, is covered in detail in an excellent essay by Jay B. Hubbell in *Eight American Authors*, and therefore is not treated here. Other southern writers of the antebellum period I shall treat in segments of the special studies sections.

BIBLIOGRAPHY

The student of southern literature is fortunate in having thorough and carefully prepared bibliographical tools. *A Bibliographical Guide to the Study of Southern Literature*, edited by Louis D. Rubin, Jr., a cooperative venture of one hundred scholars, covers the writing done in the southeastern United States from its beginnings to the present. In addition to detailed treatments of over 130 writers from the nineteenth and twentieth centuries, it contains sections on sixty-eight colonial southern writers, most of whom are also briefly discussed in bibliographical headnotes. Of especial value are twenty-three essays and listings on general topics, including "General Works on the South," "General Works on Southern Literature," "The Colonial Period," "The Negro in Southern Literature," "Humorists of the Old Southwest," "Local Color," "Southern Literary Periodicals," "Folklore," and "Southern Speech." This work, perhaps the most detailed and serious contemporary guide to the scholarship on the literary work of any region, is an indispensable tool and should be the hourly companion of any serious student of the literature of the southeastern United States.

The discursive bibliographical essay in Jay B. Hubbell, *The South in American Literature, 1607–1900* (Durham, N.C., 1954), remains of great usefulness. It is the fruit of a half-century of committed and exhaustive study of the literature of the region by the dean of southern literary scholars. Professor Hubbell's bibliography is divided into three main parts: "General Studies," which surveys and evaluates the treatment of the South in various kinds of literary and cultural history; "Important Topics," which lists a great variety of works in many areas, including "Authorship in the South," "Cities and Towns," "The Civil War," "Education," "Fiction," "The Fine Arts," "The Humorists," "Intersectional Literary Relations," "Libraries, Reading, and Literary Taste," "Magazines," "Newspapers," "Poetry," "Political and Economic Thought," "Printing and Publishing," "Religion," "Scholarly Interests," "Social Life," "Theater and Drama," "Travelers," "Women Writers"; and a final section, "Individual Writers," where over one hundred colonial and nineteenth-century southern writers are treated. For material published through 1953, Professor Hubbell is of great value. His comments are pertinent and informed, and a wealth of information from unusual and sometimes unexpected sources is presented.

Two anthologies contain excellent bibliographies: Edd Winfield Parks, *Southern Poets: Representative Selections* (New York, 1936), and Gregory L. Paine, *Southern Prose Writers: Representative Selections* (New York, 1947). Professor Paine's bibliography is particularly rich in items dealing with cultural history. The listing on the southern region in *Literature and Theater of the States and Regions of the U.S.A.: An Historical Bibliography*, by Clarence Gohdes (Durham, N.C., 1967), is detailed and accurate. There is also bibliographical data with cultural and historical emphasis and with some evaluative commentary in Rollin G. Osterweis, *Romanticism and Nationalism in the Old South* (New Haven, Conn., 1949; Baton Rouge, La., 1967), and in C. Hugh Holman, *Three Modes of Modern Southern Fiction: Ellen Glasgow, William Faulkner, Thomas Wolfe* (Athens, Ga., 1966). The bibliographical data in Volume I of *LHUS* is uneven, but that in Volume II and the *Supplement* is valuable. The bibliography in *Humor of the Old Southwest*, edited by Hennig Cohen and William B. Dillingham (Boston, 1964), is excellent, both on its general subject and on individual writers.

TEXTS

The most inclusive collection of southern literary materials remains the *Library of Southern Literature*, edited by Edwin A. Alderman, Joel Chandler Harris, and Charles W. Kent (17 vols., Atlanta, Ga., 1908–1923). It contains generous and generally judicious selections from southern writers, but its critical and biographical apparatus is dated, inadequate, and often naive. The two volumes in the American Writers Series, edited by Edd Winfield Parks and Gregory L. Paine, respectively, *Southern Poets* and *Southern Prose Writers*, are excellent though comparatively brief selections of southern writing; Professor Parks's collection of southern poetry is particularly valuable; Professor Paine's selections are confined largely to the nineteenth century. *The Literature of the South*, edited by Richmond Croom Beatty, Floyd C. Watkins, and T. Daniel Young (Chicago, 1952; rev., 1968) is a large collection made for the student, with its major emphasis on twentieth century writing. *Humor of the Old Southwest*, edited by Cohen and Dillingham is a generous and judicious selection of material with informed and accurate introductions. *A Southern Reader*, edited by Willard Thorp (New York, 1955), is a generous selection of southern materials of all kinds, much of it nonliterary, by a nonsoutherner in love with the region. Professor Thorp's introductions and headnotes are particularly illuminating. *Southern Stories*, edited by Arlin Turner (New York, 1960), is a good selection of short fiction, with a sensible introduction. The most detailed selection of colonial and nineteenth-century southern writing is in the anthology *Southern Writing, 1585–1920*, edited by Richard Beale Davis, C. Hugh Holman, and Louis D. Rubin, Jr. (New York, 1970).

GENERAL STUDIES

The basic work on the literature of the Old South is Jay B. Hubbell's monumental study, *The South in American Literature, 1607–1900*. This study, the result of a lifetime of scholarly endeavor, deals thoroughly with the writers and writings of the South to 1865, devoting the first 170 of its closely printed pages to the colonial and early national period and the next 525 pages to the Age of the Federalists and the Old South. Its treatment of the last third of the nineteenth century is briefer and much more selective, comprising only 135 pages. In dealing with the period between 1789 and 1865, Professor Hubbell examines the general cultural history of the region, the chief literary movements, and the special issues, and he treats over sixty writers in biographical-critical essays, as well as dealing with special groups such as "The Humorists," "Women Writers," and "Southern Antislavery Writers." No other work assembles so much useful information about the writing of the Old South and also about the South as a subject for nonsouthern writers. If its tendency to fall into a collection of separate essays discourages the reader of the work as a whole, it still is helpful as a reference work; and if Professor Hubbell's unadventurous critical approach may sometimes shut him off from truly fresh insights, it also saves the user the problem of finding his stance in a field of critical speculations.

Of the several attempts at a literary history of the South before Hubbell, a few are still of some merit to the student. Montrose J. Moses, *The Literature of the South* (New York, 1910), is still useful, although it is sometimes eccentric and always seems dated. Its treatment is often more social than literary—a not uncommon failing of works on southern writing. Carl Holliday, *A History of Southern Literature* (New York, 1906), although often inaccurate and superficial, is a readable book. Samuel Albert Link's *Literary Pioneers of the South* (2 vols., Nashville, Tenn., 1899–1900) has sketches of the major writers before the Civil War, although it contains little not readily available elsewhere. C. Alphonso Smith's *Southern Literary Studies: A Collection of*

Literary, Biographical, and Other Sketches (Chapel Hill, N.C., 1927), by a pioneer scholar in the field, is made up of essays, some of which deal with the antebellum period. But the long introductions to Parks's *Southern Poets* and Paine's *Southern Prose Writers* taken together form a careful, well-documented, and astute literary history of the region— after Hubbell the best purely historical treatment. Paine is particularly useful on the cultural history of the region and its relation to literature.

The most inclusive treatment of antebellum southern writers is James Wood Davidson, *The Living Writers of the South* (New York, 1869), which gives brief biographical and critical statements and selective bibliographies of the works of more than two hundred southern writers living in 1869. However, Davidson's information is often inaccurate, his judgments prejudiced, and his bibliographies incomplete. Yet his work is still important for the minor figures. The *Cyclopædia of American Literature*, edited by Evert A. and George L. Duyckinck (2 vols., New York, 1856; rev., 1875), is unusually rich in materials about southern writers, much of it supplied by William Gilmore Simms, and it should be consulted for most writers of the Old South. Its biographical sketches are reasonably accurate; it gives intelligent contemporary judgments; and it often presents brief selections from the writer's work. The revised edition corrects some of the errors of the earlier edition.

Several books on the culture and the intellectual life of the region contain chapters that are pertinent commentaries on the literature of the Old South. Vernon Louis Parrington, in *Main Currents in American Thought* (3 vols., New York, 1927–1930), made a major cultural reassessment of the South. His treatment of southern literary figures has been a germinating force for much that has followed, and he has been strongly instrumental in refocusing attention on such figures as John Taylor of Caroline, William Wirt, Nathaniel Beverley Tucker, John Pendleton Kennedy, John Caldwell Calhoun, Hugh Swinton Legaré, and William Gilmore Simms. W. J. Cash deals with literature extensively in his important reevaluation of the southern experience, *The Mind of the South* (New York, 1941). C. Vann Woodward, in *The Burden of Southern History* (Baton Rouge, La., 1960; rev., 1968), a group of incisive essays, states the most stimulating current thesis about southern history and its relation to the national experience, with some emphasis on literary materials. Rollin G. Osterweis, *Romanticism and Nationalism in the Old South*, is a provocative although oversimplified treatment of antebellum southern culture as resting on a romanticism compounded of the plantation system, Negro slavery, and the cult of chivalry. Much of his evidence is drawn from literature and from periodicals. William R. Taylor's *Cavalier and Yankee: The Old*

South and American National Character (New York, 1961) is a brilliant study dealing with the ideational and historical qualities of southern aristocracy before the Civil War. Taylor sees the cultural history of the Old South as the record of the failure of the Cavalier ideal both in life and literature, and he emphasizes sectional differences. Operating from a different assumption, *The Southerner as American*, edited by Charles G. Sellers, Jr. (Chapel Hill, N.C., 1960; New York, 1966), is the effort of nine writers to define the South in terms of its American rather than regional qualities, although only one of its essays, "The Southerner as American Writer" by C. Hugh Holman, is specifically on literature.

The historians Clement Eaton and Francis B. Simkins have paid unusually great attention to the writing of the Old South—Eaton in *The Growth of Southern Civilization, 1790–1860* (New York, 1961), *The Mind of the Old South* (Baton Rouge, La., 1964; rev., 1967), and *The Waning of the Old South Civilization* (Athens, Ga., 1968); Simkins in *A History of the South* (New York, 1953; rev., 1963). Both writers should be consulted on the cultural history of the region.

Formal literary histories have tended to give the Old South short shrift, as the *LHUS* did. A notable exception has been Van Wyck Brooks's five-volume *Makers and Finders: A History of the Writer in America, 1900–1915* (New York, 1936–1952), particularly the volume, *The World of Washington Irving* (New York, 1944). Most of the southern material from Brooks's large work has been assembled in *A Chilmark Miscellany* (New York, 1948). Brooks's portrayals of southern writers in their time and place are graceful and surprisingly appreciative. Edmund Wilson's *Patriotic Gore: Studies in the Literature of the American Civil War* (New York, 1962) has excellent material on southern writers, notably in Chapters Twelve and Thirteen.

SPECIAL STUDIES

Fiction

There is a useful but sketchy *History of Southern Fiction* by Edwin Mims in volume VIII of *The South in the Building of the Nation*, edited by John Bell Henneman et al. (13 vols., Richmond, Va., 1909–1913), but most of the work on southern fiction is concentrated on individual writers or on themes or subjects. Francis Pendleton Gaines, *The Southern Plantation: A Study in the Development and the Accuracy of a Tradition* (New York, 1924), is a landmark in such studies, but relatively little of it is devoted to the antebellum period. Shields McIlwaine, in *The Southern Poor-White from Lubberland to Tobacco*

Road (Norman, Okla., 1939), examines the other extreme in social standing and devotes a considerable amount of space to the earlier periods. McIlwaine's study is an illuminating and often amusing counterpoise to the monolith of the South of magnolias and tall white columns. Robert A. Lively, in *Fiction Fights the Civil War* (Chapel Hill, N.C., 1957), deals briefly with the very end of the period in a book remarkable for the concision of its treatment of over 550 novels. C. Hugh Holman, in *Three Modes of Modern Southern Fiction*, postulates that the differing subject matters of southern fiction are related to geographical and historical differences, but treats the Old South only cursorily in moving to his examination of twentieth-century writing. Jay B. Hubbell, in *Southern Life in Fiction* (Athens, Ga., 1960), deals casually with the Old South. His published dissertation (Columbia, 1922), *Virginia Life in Fiction* (Dallas, Tex., 1922), is a more detailed treatment, but only of Virginia, which, it is true, was the state producing much of the antebellum fiction.

Special treatments of American fiction sometimes give some emphasis to southern fiction. Two are particularly noteworthy: Herbert Ross Brown, in *The Sentimental Novel in America, 1789–1860* (Durham, N.C., 1940), deals gracefully and accurately with the several southern replies to *Uncle Tom's Cabin* in his chapter, "Uncle Tom's and Other Cabins." Ima Honaker Herron, in *The Small Town in American Literature* (Durham, N.C., 1939), gives an unusual amount of space to southern fiction, as also does Albert Keiser in *The Indian in American Literature* (New York, 1933).

The best work on antebellum southern fiction is in studies of individual writers. Curtis Carroll Davis, in *Chronicler of the Cavaliers: A Life of the Virginia Novelist, Dr. William A. Caruthers* (Richmond, Va., 1953), has dealt thoroughly with Caruthers and his novels. Davis's introduction to Caruthers's novel, *The Knights of the Golden Horseshoe* (Chapel Hill, N.C., 1970), is a good presentation of an unjustly neglected writer. The only book-length treatment of John Esten Cooke is the critical biography *John Esten Cooke, Virginian* by John O. Beaty (New York, 1922), but the best treatment of him is in Hubbell's *The South in American Literature*. There have been three studies of John Pendleton Kennedy: the early "official" study by Henry T. Tuckerman, *The Life of John Pendleton Kennedy* (New York, 1871); Charles H. Bohner, *John Pendleton Kennedy: Gentleman from Baltimore* (Baltimore, Md., 1961), a thorough and careful biography; and J. V. Ridgely's study of his novels, *John Pendleton Kennedy* (New York, 1966). There are good bibliographies in the Bohner and Ridgely volumes and also in the Goldentree bibliography of *The American Novel*

Through Henry James by C. Hugh Holman (New York, 1966). An edition of *Horse-Shoe Robinson* (New York, 1937, 1962), edited by Ernest E. Leisy, has much valuable material.

William Gilmore Simms, the major novelist of the Old South, has so far not received adequate book-length treatment. The only biography is still William Peterfield Trent's study in the old American Men of Letters series, *William Gilmore Simms* (Boston, 1892), which is dated in its critical judgment and is written from a marked social bias. Joseph V. Ridgely's *William Gilmore Simms* (New York, 1962) is a study of the novels in the Border Romance series as portrayals of an ideal of southern society. An indispensable tool is *The Letters of William Gilmore Simms*, edited by Mary C. Simms Oliphant, A. T. Odell, and T. C. Duncan Eaves (5 vols., Columbia, S.C., 1952–1956), a monumental scholarly work, rich in information and essential to an understanding both of Simms and of the literary life of the Old South. Of the shorter-than-book-length general treatments, the most inclusive and in many respects the best is that of Alexander Cowie in *The Rise of the American Novel* (New York, 1948, 1951), although Jay B. Hubbell's chapter in *The South in American Literature, 1607–1900* is detailed and excellent. Clement Eaton's "The Romantic Mind: William Gilmore Simms," in his *The Mind of the Old South*, and William R. Taylor's "Revolution in South Carolina," in his *Cavalier and Yankee*, are thoughtful studies of Simms's place in southern culture and history. Vernon L. Parrington's treatment of Simms in *Main Currents in American Thought* is a provocative appreciation and the most significant single statement about Simms of this century, although its central thesis that he was the victim of Charleston's patrician snobbishness has been seriously questioned. Van Wyck Brooks, in *The World of Washington Irving*, writes charmingly and sympathetically of Simms. Donald Davidson's appreciation of Simms's work, in the introduction to *The Letters*, will appear to most readers to overpraise Simms. A bibliographical guide to Simms is in C. Hugh Holman's note and checklist in Rubin's *Bibliographical Guide to the Study of Southern Literature* and in his section on Simms in the Goldentree bibliography of *The American Novel Through Henry James*. Three editions of *The Yemassee* contain editorial data and introductory essays: one edited by Alexander Cowie (New York, 1937) which has a good introduction and bibliography; one by C. Hugh Holman (Boston, 1961), with an essay introduction that sketches a thesis about Simms's novelistic career and attributes his dimunition as a novelist to his growing sectionalism; and one edited by J. V. Ridgely, with an introduction (New York, 1964). Richmond Croom Beatty edited *Woodcraft; or, Hawks About the Dovecote* (New

York, 1961), with a brief introduction. The first appearance in book form of *Voltmeier* (Columbia, S.C., 1969) was edited by James B. Meriwether, with an introduction by Mrs. Oliphant and Donald Davidson. It is volume I of the University of South Carolina's *Centennial Simms*, a projected fifteen-volume edition that will not reprint the "standard" Simms books which are readily available although not in print. The somewhat surprising exception is *The Yemassee*, which will be included. The *Catalogue of the* [A. S.] *Salley Collection of the Works of Wm. Gilmore Simms*, compiled by A. S. Salley (Columbia, S.C., 1943), remains the closest thing to an adequate bibliography, rivaled only by the sometimes inaccurate *A Bibliography of the Separate Writings of William Gilmore Simms, 1806–1870* by Oscar Wegelin (Hattiesburg, Miss., 1941).

George Tucker, the author of *The Valley of Shenandoah; or, Memoirs of the Graysons* (New York, 1824), is the subject of a good scholarly biography by Robert Colin McLean, *George Tucker: Moral Philosopher and Man of Letters* (Chapel Hill, N.C., 1961). Tucker is also treated in some detail in Richard Beale Davis's important study, *Intellectual Life in Jefferson's Virginia, 1790–1830* (Chapel Hill, N.C., 1964). A new edition of *The Valley of Shenandoah*, edited by Donald Noble (Chapel Hill, N.C., 1970), makes an important early novel again available. Nathaniel Beverley Tucker, author of *George Balcombe*, which Poe praised, and *The Partisan Leader*, lacks adequate treatment. The best thing on him is Carl Bridenbaugh's introduction to the 1933 edition of *The Partisan Leader* (New York, 1933), now out of print. A new edition (Chapel Hill, N.C., 1971) has an introduction by C. Hugh Holman, which relates it to the political currents of its time. Rhoda Coleman Ellison's introduction to her edition of *The Planter's Northern Bride* by Caroline Lee Hentz (Chapel Hill, N.C., 1970) reintroduces a popular woman novelist of the Old South, one who was notorious for her replies to *Uncle Tom's Cabin*.

Poetry

The most useful volume on southern poetry is Edd Winfield Parks, *Southern Poets: Representative Selections*. Its introduction represents a scholarly effort to deal with southern poetry and poetic theory. Its concepts are elaborated in two essays in Parks, *Segments of Southern Thought* (Athens, Ga., 1938). Henry Nelson Snyder's early essay, "Characteristics of Southern Poetry from the Beginning to 1865," in volume VII of *The South in the Building of the Nation*, is still useful. Collections of poetry by states have been made by Philip Graham, *Early Texas Verse* (Austin, Tex., 1936), by Armistead C. Gordon, Jr.,

Virginian Writers of Fugitive Verse (New York, 1923), and by Richard Walser, *North Carolina Poetry* (Richmond, Va., 1941; rev., 1951).

Individual poets have faired a little better. Thomas Holley Chivers was the subject of an important study, S. Foster Damon's *Thomas Holley Chivers: Friend of Poe* (New York, 1930), which suffers from an overemphasis of Chivers's influence on Poe, a questionable issue. Charles Henry Watts II, *Thomas Holley Chivers: His Literary Career and His Poetry* (Athens, Ga., 1956), is a careful critical study. *The Correspondence of Thomas Holley Chivers*, edited by Emma Lester Chase and Lois Ferry Parks (Providence, R.I., 1957), was announced as the first volume of a *Complete Works*, but additional volumes have not appeared.

Philip Pendleton Cooke receives biographical and critical treatment in John D. Allen, *Philip Pendleton Cooke* (Chapel Hill, N.C., 1942), and in an essay "Philip Pendleton Cooke: Virginia Gentleman, Lawyer, Hunter, and Poet" by David K. Jackson in his *American Studies in Honor of William Kenneth Boyd* (Durham, N.C., 1940). *Philip Pendleton Cooke: Poet, Critic, Novelist* is a volume of selections edited with an introduction by John D. Allen (Johnson City, Tenn., 1969).

Paul Hamilton Hayne is treated in a critical study by Rayburn S. Moore, *Paul Hamilton Hayne* (New York, 1971). His correspondence has been edited by Daniel M. McKeithen, *A Collection of Hayne Letters* (Austin, Tex., 1944), and Charles Duffy, *The Correspondence of Bayard Taylor and Paul Hamilton Hayne* (Baton Rouge, La., 1945), but the needed full-scale, biographical-critical study and a modern edition of his work remain undone.

The Texas poet Mirabeau B. Lamar is well represented in a study by Philip Graham, *The Life and Poems of Mirabeau B. Lamar* (Chapel Hill, N.C., 1938), which contains the eighty-seven extant poems and a definitive biography. There is also a biography by Herbert P. Gambrell, *Mirabeau Buonaparte Lamar, Troubadour and Crusader* (Dallas, Tex., 1934). Herman C. Nixon, *Alexander Beaufort Meek: Poet, Orator, Journalist, Historian, Statesman* (Auburn, Ala., 1910), reprints some of Meek's poems and is still the fullest treatment. The absence of any serious work on Edward Coote Pinkney, a minor though true poetic voice, except for the indispensable T. O. Mabbott and Frank Lester Pleadwell, *The Life and Works of Edward Coote Pinkney* (New York, 1926), is a telling commentary on the neglect of antebellum southern poetry.

William Gilmore Simms, a prolific and lifelong poet, has fared little better. The study of his verse has been casual and no collection is in print, although one is promised, to be edited by C. Hugh Holman, in the *Centennial Simms*. This neglect would have astounded Simms's contemporaries, even the unfriendly ones. Richard Henry Wilde is adequately represented in Edward L. Tucker, *Richard Henry Wilde: His Life and Selected Poems* (Athens, Ga., 1966), which contains many of his poems and translations and a biographical study. On the other hand, Wilde's *Hesperia*, published posthumously in 1867, one of the few long antebellum southern poems, is practically impossible to secure.

Henry Timrod, the one poet of the Old South, other than Poe, who has received adequate treatment, is certainly, after Poe, the best of the antebellum southern poets. Paul Hamilton Hayne's edition of *The Poems of Henry Timrod* (New York, 1873) is good, and the biographical sketch it contains is indispensable as the record made by Timrod's closest friend. Guy A. Cardwell, Jr., published a fine text of *The Uncollected Poems of Henry Timrod* (Athens, Ga., 1942) with a valuable introduction. Edd Winfield Parks and Aileen Wells Parks have edited a variorum edition of *The Collected Poems of Henry Timrod* (Athens, Ga., 1965). George A. Wauchope's *Henry Timrod: Man and Poet* (Columbia S.C., 1915) is a perceptive critical study. Henry T. Thompson, *Henry Timrod: Laureate of the Confederacy* (Columbia, S.C., 1928), is a biography by the son of a close friend of Timrod. Edd Winfield Parks, *Henry Timrod* (New York, 1964), is a sound critical study. Jay B. Hubbell, *The Last Years of Henry Timrod* (Durham, N.C., 1941), reprints much correspondence and has important biographical commentary.

Literary Criticism

Despite the fact that Edgar Allan Poe, perhaps the greatest literary critic of the antebellum period, was a southerner, and that certain of his attitudes have persisted among southern writers down through the New Critics, there has been relatively little done on the literary criticism produced in the Old South, aside from that of Poe. The major work is Edd Winfield Parks, *Ante-Bellum Southern Literary Critics* (Athens, Ga., 1962), in which the critical writings of Jefferson, Legaré, Wilde, Simms, Philip Pendleton Cooke, Chivers, Grayson, Timrod, and Hayne are examined and the critical intent of the humorists and the novelists explored. Professor Parks has done a major job of exploring these neglected areas and his extensive footnotes constitute a virtual guide to critical thinking in the Old South. His separate monograph, *William Gilmore Simms as Literary Critic* (Athens, Ga., 1961), explores the most prolific of antebellum literary critics with care. *Views and Reviews in American Literature, History and Fiction*, First Series, by William Gilmore Simms (1845), has been reprinted in the John

Harvard Library with notes and an introduction by C. Hugh Holman
(Cambridge, Mass., 1962). The introduction attempts to place Simms
in the national literary movements of his time. The third southern literary critic, after Poe and Simms, is represented in Edd Winfield Parks's
excellently edited collection of Timrod's critical essays, *The Essays of
Henry Timrod* (Athens, Ga., 1942).

The Humorists

The modern scholarly and critical assessment of the humorists of the
Old Southwest began with Franklin J. Meine's anthology, *Tall Tales of
the Southwest: An Anthology of Southern and Southwestern Humor,
1830–1860* (New York, 1930). It was followed by Constance Rourke's
American Humor: A Study of the National Character (New York,
(1931), a seminal work that has not yet been superseded. Walter Blair,
in his long introduction and in his generous southern selections in
Native American Humor, 1800–1900 (New York, 1937; rev., San Francisco, 1960), wrote virtually an illustrated history with substantial
attention to the southern antebellum humorists. Blair (with Franklin
J. Meine) has also done extensive work on Mike Fink, in *Mike Fink,
King of Mississippi Keelboatmen* (New York, 1933), and in *Half
Horse, Half Alligator: The Growth of the Mike Fink Legend* (Chi-
cago, 1956). Both Bernard De Voto, in *Mark Twain's America* (Boston,
1932), and Kenneth Lynn, in *Mark Twain and Southwestern Humor*
(Boston, 1959), have substantial material on the antebellum humorists
in their treatments of Mark Twain's literary backgrounds. Thomas D.
Clark made a historical survey in *The Rampaging Frontier: Manners
and Humors of Pioneer Days in the South and the Middle West* (New
York, 1939). Arthur Palmer Hudson's Anthology, *Humor of the Old
Deep South* (New York, 1936), is both rich in its selections and in the
information in its introduction. James R. Masterson's *Tall Tales of
Arkansaw* (Boston, 1943) has similar value. Willard Thorp's pamphlet *American Humorists* (Minneapolis, Minn., 1964) is a brief,
graceful introduction. There is a wealth of information in the anthology *Humor of the Old Southwest*, edited by Cohen and Dillingham,
and its bibliographies on individual writers are indispensable.

The Negro

Relatively little has been done on the Negro in the literature of the
Old South, and most of what has been done has centered on his representation in antebellum southern fiction. Pioneer studies such as Sterling Brown's *The Negro in American Fiction* (Washington, D.C.,
1937) and John Herbert Nelson's *The Negro Character in American*

Literature (Lawrence, Kans., 1926) are primarily concerned with accuracy in fictional portrayal. Robert A. Bone, *The Negro Novel in America* (New Haven, Conn., 1958; rev., 1965), the standard work, has little on the antebellum period (William Wells Brown's *Clotel*, the first novel by an American Negro, was published in 1853). *Clotelle* (the spelling of the 1864 edition) has been reprinted with an excellent introduction by W. Edward Farrison (New York, 1970). Farrison's biography, *William Wells Brown: Author and Reformer* (Chicago, 1969), is definitive and important. The most significant single volume is *Images of the Negro in American Literature*, edited by Seymour L. Gross and John Edward Hardy (Chicago, 1966), an anthology of critical essays. The bibliography, by Seymour Gross, is excellent, as is his long introduction. Tremaine McDowell's essay, "The Negro in the Southern Novel Prior to 1850" (originally printed in *JEGP*, 1926), is included.

Drama and Theater

The number of antebellum southern playwrights was small and, because of peculiarities of the copyright law, relatively few of their works survive. Most of these plays are listed in Charles S. Watson's section on "Eighteenth and Nineteenth Century Drama" in *A Bibliographical Guide to the Study of Southern Literature*. Rodney M. Baine's *Robert Munford; America's First Comic Dramatist* (Athens, Ga., 1967) is the only adequate critical-biographical study of any of these playwrights. On the other hand, the theater was a significant and important institution in southern life and culture, from the appearance of the "Virginia Comedians" under Lewis Hallam's direction at Williamsburg in 1763 to the Civil War. The history of the theater in the South has been described in detail by two historians: Hugh F. Rankin, *The Theater in Colonial America* (Chapel Hill, N.C., 1965), and James H. Dormon, Jr., *Theater in the Antebellum South 1815–1861* (Chapel Hill, N.C., 1967).

The theater of specific locales has also been treated. W. Stanley Hoole has dealt with the most energetic of the antebellum theaters in the *The Ante-Bellum Charleston Theatre* (University, Ala., 1946). John S. Kendall has recorded the history of *The Golden Age of the New Orleans Theatre* (Baton Rouge, La., 1952). J. Max Patrick described the early Savannah stage in *Savannah's Pioneer Theater from Its Origins to 1810* (Athens, Ga., 1953). Douglas L. Hunt described a period in Nashville's stage history in *The Nashville Theater, 1830–1840 (Birmingham-Southern Coll. Bull.*, May 1935). Henry W. Adams did a comparable job for Montgomery, Alabama, in *Montgomery Theater,*

1822–1835 (University, Ala., 1955). Two bibliographies are of particular note: O. B. Brockett, "The Theatre of the Southern United States from the Beginnings Through 1865: A Bibliographical Essay" (*Theatre Research, II, 1960*) and Clarence Gohdes, *Literature and Theatre of the States and Regions of the U.S.A.: An Historical Bibliography.*

The Literature of the New South

LOUIS D. RUBIN, JR.

THE DEMAND for a distinctive literature that would image the unique circumstances of life in the southern states of the American Union arose out of the separatist, nationalistic drive of the antebellum period. The impulse toward southern nationalism climaxed in secession, the creation of the Confederate States of America, and the Civil War. The loss of the war abruptly ended both the hope and even the desire for separate nationhood. It did not, however, terminate a self-conscious sectionalism, and for a century to come the South would consider itself —and with some reason—a unique region with a unique kind of culture. Its literature would reflect that attitude.

Because of this heritage of aborted nationalism and self-conscious sectionalism, literature in the South has been tied in with all manner of social and political loyalties. The southern writer was expected— and generally he himself desired—to defend the Confederate heritage and the purity and legitimacy of the section's motives during the years before secession. Such demands as these made it difficult for the post– Civil War southern author to explore and portray the deepest concerns of the society in which he lived. And these demands also conditioned and limited to a great degree the development of a genuinely critical body of literary scholarship that would give order and definition to the study of that literature. The result is that a great deal of what has been written about southern literature of the latter years of the nineteenth century has been defensive and shallow, tending toward appreciation rather than evaluation.

The term *New South* can be used to signify either the South that followed Appomattox Court House, that is, the successor to the plantation-dominated Old South; or it can be used to describe the economic, political, and intellectual movement of the 1880s and 1890s, whose best spokesman was Henry W. Grady. This movement sought a "New South" that would be industrial, commercial, and forward-looking, one that would no longer be held back by the dead hand of the Confederate past. Throughout this essay the term *New South* will be used in the latter sense, to denote not merely a time and place, but an ideology.

The discussion that follows, therefore, is an effort to sketch the nature and extent of the available scholarship on the period from 1865 to 1900. No attempt has been made to cover individual authors. Such truncated coverage would not be representative or useful, and a reader interested in particular writers should consult the more complete checklists available elsewhere. Following is a list of the more important bibliographical compilations for some of the leading southern writers of the period who are not covered in Floyd Stovall, *Eight American Writers*, or in this volume. In addition to the items given below, students should consult the checklists on individual authors in *A Bibliographical Guide to the Study of Southern Literature*, edited by Louis D. Rubin, Jr. (Baton Rouge, La., 1969); Lewis Leary, *Articles in American Literature, 1900–1950* and *1950–1967* (see Preface); and the annual checklists of "Scholarship in Southern Literature" in the spring issues of *Mississippi Quarterly* for 1969 and successive years.

James Lane Allen: William K. Bottorff, *James Lane Allen* (New York, 1964); Grant C. Knight, *James Lane Allen and the Genteel Tradition* (Chapel Hill, N.C., 1935).

George Washington Cable: *LHUS* (3rd ed., rev., New York, 1963); Jay B. Hubbell, *The South in American Literature, 1607–1900* (Durham, N.C., 1954); Philip Butcher, "George Washington Cable" (*ALR*, Fall 1969); Butcher, *George W. Cable* (New York, 1962); Jacob L. Blanck, *BAL*, ii (New Haven, Conn., 1955–); Louis D. Rubin, Jr., *George W. Cable: The Life and Times of a Southern Heretic* (New York, 1969); Arlin Turner, *George W. Cable* (Durham, N.C., 1955).

Charles W. Chesnutt: Dean H. Keller, "Charles Waddell Chesnutt" (*ALR*, Summer 1968).

Kate Chopin: Lewis Leary, ed., *Kate Chopin: The Awakening and Other Stories* (New York, 1970); Daniel S. Rankin, *Kate Chopin and Her Creole Stories* (Philadelphia, 1932); Per Seyersted, *Kate Chopin* (Baton Rouge, La., 1969).

Joel Chandler Harris: Jay B. Hubbell, *The South in American Literature; LHUS;* Paul M. Cousins, *Joel Chandler Harris* (Baton Rouge, La., 1968); Arlin Turner, "Joel Chandler Harris" (*ALR*,

Summer 1968); Robert L. Wiggins, *The Life of Joel Chandler Harris* (Nashville, Tenn., 1918).

Sidney Lanier: Hubbell, *The South in American Literature; LHUS;* Charles R. Anderson, ed., *The Centennial Edition of the Works of Sidney Lanier,* VI (Baltimore, Md., 1945); Aubrey H. Starke, *Sidney Lanier* (Chapel Hill, N.C., 1933).

Mary Noailles Murfree: *LHUS;* Richard Cary, *Mary N. Murfree (Charles Egbert Craddock)* (New York, 1967); Cary, "Mary Noailles Murfree" *(ALR,* Fall 1967); Edd Winfield Parks, *Charles Egbert Craddock (Mary Noailles Murfree)* (Chapel Hill, N.C., 1941).

Thomas Nelson Page: Hubbell, *The South in American Literature; LHUS;* Theodore Gross, *Thomas Nelson Page* (New York, 1967); Gross, "Thomas Nelson Page" *(ALR,* Fall 1967); Harriet Holman, "The Literary Career of Thomas Nelson Page: 1884–1900" (Ph.D. diss., Duke, 1947; available on Microcards).

Similarly, any outline of the existing scholarship on southern literature from 1865 to 1900 should be prefaced with a warning about its shortcomings and failures. Otherwise, a mere survey of what has been written about southern literature of the period is certain to provide a false picture. What is most striking about the scholarship of this period is not what has been done, but what has not been done. Except for Mark Twain, the sole important author who may be said to have been covered with any degree of thoroughness is George W. Cable. As for Clemens, who is the only major southern writer between Poe and Faulkner, in spite of all the vast and often brilliant body of critical work that has been done on him, he has not really been looked at in terms of the crucial relationship between his life and art and the slaveholding, small-town society from which he came. The truth of this relationship may be summed up by the implications lying unexamined in the remark that Howells made about Mark Twain: "He was the most desouthernized Southerner I ever knew." There is no good biography or full-scale critical study of Thomas Nelson Page. No existing study of Joel Chandler Harris gets beneath the surface of his complex personality or his deceptive and often implicitly subversive art. Almost all the scholarship on Lanier has been essentially uncritical (which may be just as well). Of the lesser figures, only Kate Chopin (if indeed she is a "lesser figure") and Mary Noailles Murfree have been competently handled. Nor is the picture much better with regard to overall studies. No one has examined the phenomenon of the southern local color movement in detail. And although we now know much more about the economic history and social implications of the southern plantation than when the book was written, Francis Pendleton Gaines's *The Southern Plantation* (New York, 1924) is still the only extended examination of this literary image. There is not even a reliable survey history of the literature of the period; the chapters that Jay B. Hubbell included in his *The South in American Literature, 1865–1900,* a book that makes no pretense at thorough coverage subsequent to 1865, are the best that can be found. The literary manifestations of such themes as the changing role and worsening lot of the Negro, the emerging democracy of the up-country white South, the spread of fundamentalist religion, the delayed impact of industrialism, the emergence of the New South ideal, to name a few possibilities, have been explored imperfectly or not at all.

The survey of available scholarship that follows, therefore, is significant as much for what is not available as for what is.

BIBLIOGRAPHICAL WORKS

Whatever the gaps in the scholarship itself, there exists an abundance of bibliographical information about southern literature from 1865 to 1900.

A recent publication, *A Bibliographical Guide to the Study of Southern Literature,* edited by Louis D. Rubin, Jr., (see above and Preface), is a joint effort of some one hundred scholars who have provided twenty-three general checklists and selective individual checklists of some two hundred and fifty southern writers. The existing scholarship on dozens of writers active during the period 1865 to 1900 is cited, along with general checklists on such subjects as The New South, Local Color, The Negro in Southern Literature, Southern Literary Periodicals, Southern Popular Literature, Manuscript Holdings, and Southern Bibliography.

Volume II of *LHUS* comprises the rather uneven general and the valuable individual bibliographies originally contained in volume III of the 1948 edition, together with Richard M. Ludwig's 1959 *Supplement.* Editions of various southern writers of the period are included in the successive volumes of Jacob Blanck, *Bibliography of American Literature,* of which five have thus far appeared. An invaluable index of dissertations and theses is Clyde H. Cantrell and Walton R. Patrick's *Southern Literary Culture: A Bibliography of Masters' and Doctors' Theses* (University, Ala., 1955), currently being revised to include material after 1948. The bibliographical listings in Jay B. Hubbell, *The South in American Literature, 1607–1900,* are indispensable. Clarence Gohdes, *Literature and Theater of the States and Regions of the U.SA.: An Historical Bibliography* (Durham, N.C., 1967), is a detailed, comprehensive work.

Still useful are the checklists by Dudley Miles, "The New South," and C. Alphonso Smith, "The Dialect Writers," both in Vol. II of *CHAL*. Excellent annotated bibliographies are included in *Southern Prose Writers*, edited by G. L. Paine (New York, 1947), and *Southern Poets*, edited by Edd W. Parks (New York, 1936). Arthur Hobson Quinn, *American Fiction: An Historical and Critical Survey* (New York, 1936), and *The Literature of the American People*, edited by Quinn (New York, 1951), contain useful compilations. There is a good bibliography also in C. Vann Woodward, *Origins of the New South, 1877–1913* (Baton Rouge, La., 1951).

Such standard compilations as Lewis Leary, *Articles on American Literature, 1950–1967* (Durham, N.C., 1970); James L. Woodress, *Dissertations in American Literature, 1891–1965* (Durham, N.C., 1969); Lyle Henry Wright, *American Fiction, 1876–1900: A Contribution Toward a Bibliography* (San Marino, Calif., 1966); Merle De Vore Johnson, *American First Editions* (4th ed., Cambridge, Mass., 1962); Roy P. Basler et al., *A Guide to the Study of the United States of America* (Washington, D.C., 1960); and *The Union List of Serials in Libraries of the United States and Canada* (5 vols., 3rd ed., New York, 1965), are valuable for their relevant listings.

Beginning with a checklist for 1968, published in the Summer 1969 issue, the *Mississippi Quarterly* is providing an annual annotated checklist of scholarship in the field of southern literature. Thus far three have appeared. This checklist will complement the listings in *American Literature* and in the *MLA International Bibliography*. The Annual volumes entitled *American Literary Scholarship*, edited by James Woodress, survey and evaluate new material. Successive issues of *American Literary Realism* (1967–) have contained checklists for a number of the southern authors of the period.

There are in addition various specialized bibliographical listings. The bibliography by Seymour L. Gross, in *Images of the Negro in American Literature*, edited by Gross and John Edward Hardy (Chicago, 1966), is an excellent listing of material relevant to the Negro as writer and as subject. Darwin T. Turner, *Afro-American Writers* (New York, 1970), is a well-planned review. Other useful sources include: Carvel E. Collins, "Nineteenth-Century Fiction of the Southern Appalachians" (*BB*, Sept.-Dec. 1942); Edward Graham Roberts, *A Southern Supplement to the Union List of Serials* (Atlanta, Ga., 1959); Louis R. Wilson and Robert B. Downs, "Special Collections for the Study of History and Literature in the Southeast" (*PBSA*, Nov.

1934); and S. H. Kessler, "American Negro Literature: A Bibliographic Guide" (*BB*, Sept.-Dec. 1955).

SCHOLARSHIP

In attempting to describe some of the scholarship available on southern literature of the period of 1865 to 1900, I find it convenient to divide the discussion into two parts. One part concerns scholarship—historical, appreciative, not normally overly critical or deficient in sectional pride—produced either during the period or shortly thereafter, and the other part considers the scholarship that has been done since (roughly) World War I. The difference between the earlier and the later work is not merely chronological. Suffice it to say that the esteem in which the literature of the local color period (and after) was held by the scholars and critics of that time was for the most part very high indeed, while the judgment of a later day has been considerably less charitable. The southern critic of southern literature who wrote during the 1880s and 1890s considered it his duty to extol the excellences of southern writing and frequently to show its allegiance to the spirit of purpose exemplified in the New South ideal. Critics of a later time have felt considerably less obligation of this kind.

A sizable body of critical, historical, and biographical work about southern literature was produced during the latter years of the nineteenth century. This period of activity culminated in the multivolumed collection, *A Library of Southern Literature*, edited by Edwin A. Alderman, Charles W. Kent, and (formally at least) Joel Chandler Harris (17 vols., Atlanta, Ga., 1908–23). Any student of southern literature will find this collection helpful, but it should be used with considerable care. It consists of biographical sketches of numerous authors, followed by selections from their works; and finally there are supplementary volumes of various kinds. (Volume xiv, for example, contains a good bibliography.) The short biographies were written by various hands, and most were executed in a spirit of commendation rather than criticism. Another multivolume work of the period, *The South in the Building of a Nation*, edited by John Bell Henneman et al. (13 vols., Richmond, Va., 1909–13), contains much material about the New South; volume viii, *History of Southern Fiction*, is prefaced with a useful introduction by Edwin Mims.

Among numerous other writings about southern literature produced during the period 1865 to 1900 and shortly thereafter, by far the most impressive is William Malone Baskervill's *Southern Writers: Biographical and Critical Sketches* (2 vols., vol. 1, Nashville, Tenn.,

1897; vol. 2, Dallas, Tex., 1903). The first volume, written entirely by Baskervill, offers critical and appreciative essays on a group of leading southern writers of the late nineteenth century; the second was published after Baskervill's death, and only one essay was written by him. In 1910 Montrose J. Moses published *The Literature of the South* (New York), a sometimes useful though discursive volume, now very much dated in its judgments. Carl Holliday's *A History of Southern Literature* (New York, 1906) is not reliable in its factual material. Other useful contemporary works are C. Alphonso Smith, *Southern Literary Studies* (Chapel Hill, N.C., 1927), which contains several of Smith's essays about the New South and its writers; Henry N. Snyder, "The Reconstruction of Southern Literary Thought" (*SAQ*, Apr. 1902) and "The Matter of 'Southern Literature'" (*SR*, Apr. 1907); Thomas Nelson Page, "Literature in the South Since the War" (*Lippincott's*, July 1891); John Spencer Bassett, "The Problems of the Author in the South" (*SAQ*, July 1902); Hamilton Wright Mabie, "The Poetry of the South" (*International Monthly*, Jan.-June 1902); Charles W. Coleman, Jr., "The Recent Movement in Southern Literature" (*HM*, May 1887); John Bell Hennemann, "The National Element in Southern Literature" (*SR*, July 1903); Edwin Mims, "The Function of Criticism in the South" (*SAQ*, Oct. 1903); and John R. Ormond, "Some Recent Products of the New School of Southern Fiction" (*SAQ*, July 1904).

Albion W. Tourgee's often-cited essay, "The South as a Field of Fiction" (*ForumNY*, Dec. 1888), is a significant and informative response by a northern writer and former Abolitionist to the political implications of the popularity of southern local color literature. Less politically astute, but showing considerably more literary sophistication, is William Dean Howells's "American Letter: The Southern States in Recent American Literature" (*Literature* [London], Sept. 10, 17, 24, 1898).

Among numerous other studies of the period, none of them especially useful today except as specimen material, may be listed the following: Caroline M. Brevard, *Literature of the South* (New York, 1908); James Wood Davidson, *Living Writers of the South* (New York, 1869); Samuel Albert Link, *Literary Pioneers of the South* (2 vols., Nashville, Tenn., 1899–1900); Louise Manly, *Southern Literature from 1597 to 1895* (Richmond, Va., 1895); LaSalle C. Pickett, *Literary Hearthstones of Dixie* (Philadelphia, 1912); and Mildred L. Rutherford, *The South in History and Literature* (Atlanta, Ga., 1907).

In attempting to understand the intellectual and social milieu of the southern writers of the period, memoirs written by the writers themselves, and by later writers who grew up during the 1880s and 1890s, can be of considerable help. *Memories of a Southern Woman of Letters,* by the novelist Grace King (New York, 1932), conveys a feeling for the New Orleans scene and the forces at work there that so bedeviled George W. Cable's career. Another interesting work is Lizette Woodworth Reese's *A Victorian Village: Reminiscences of Other Days* (New York, 1929). In *Let Me Lie* (New York, 1947), James Branch Cabell recalls the Richmond scene in the gaslight era with much insight and amusement. Ellen Glasgow, both in her autobiographical work, *The Woman Within* (New York, 1954), and in the volume of prefaces, *A Certain Measure* (New York, 1943), has much to say about life and letters of the period. A memoir by an editor who worked with a number of southern local color writers is Robert Underwood Johnson's *Remembered Yesterdays* (Boston, 1925), interesting both for what it says of the southern writers and for the insight it offers into the values and the attitudes of a leading magazine editor of the Genteel Tradition. One of the richest of all American autobiographies is James Weldon Johnson's *Along This Way* (New York, 1933), which affords a matchless portrait of the South of the period. Charles Chesnutt has recorded his memories of his early literary career in an essay, "Post-Bellum—Pre-Harlem" (*Col,* Part 5, 1931).

The most influential work of literary scholarship written during the period is the biography of an antebellum writer, *William Gilmore Simms,* by William Peterfield Trent (Boston, 1892). The attitudes of Trent, an "emancipated" southerner of the New South era, shed light on the literary climate of his own time as well as of Simms's—the more so in that the volume was bitterly resented and attacked by less progressive-minded southerners.

There has been no overall literary history of the South written during the past four decades. Not even Jay B. Hubbell's monumental *The South in American Literature, 1607–1900* will quite serve the purpose for the period 1865 to 1900; for though that work contains some excellent general chapters and takes up a half-dozen authors in detail, its primary emphasis is on southern literature up to the Civil War. A recent study which deals extensively with the post–Civil War writers is Richard M. Weaver, *The Southern Tradition at Bay: A History of Postbellum Thought,* edited by George Core and M. E. Bradford (New Rochelle, N.Y., 1968), which examines most of the principal southern writers of the period 1865 to 1900 in terms of the survival of Confederate values and the rise of New South ideology. A new study, Paul M. Gaston's *The New South: A Study in Southern Mythmaking* (New York, 1970), discusses the work of some New South authors. F. Garvin

Davenport's *The Myth of Southern Writing* (Nashville, Tenn., 1970) deals briefly with the New South. Various general studies of American literature touch on the period. The *LHUS* devotes parts of several chapters to post–Civil War southern literature, but with no great thoroughness or distinction. A much better analysis, though limited in coverage, is that in Jay Martin, *Harvests of Change: American Literature, 1865–1914* (Englewood Cliffs, N.J., 1967), which treats the literary South as providing an image of a pastoral paradise, used to sustain the nostalgia of a recently industrialized America. Other studies include Warner Berthoff, *The Ferment of Realism* (New York, 1965); Donald Pizer, *Realism and Naturalism in Nineteenth-Century American Literature* (Carbondale, Ill., 1966); Van Wyck Brooks, *The Times of Melville and Whitman* (New York, 1947) and *The Confident Years, 1885–1915* (New York, 1952); Alexander Cowie, *The Rise of the American Novel* (New York, 1949); Arthur Hobson Quinn, *American Fiction: An Historical and Critical Survey*; Fred Lewis Pattee, *The Development of the American Short Story* (New York, 1923) and *A History of American Literature Since 1870* (New York, 1915); and Carl Van Doren, *The American Novel* (New York, 1940). In addition, the works of two historians, Paul S. Buck's *The Road to Reunion, 1865–1900* (Boston, 1937) and C. Vann Woodward's *Origins of the New South, 1876–1913* (Baton Rouge, La., 1951), contain excellent general chapters on southern literature.

The student will find much of value throughout Edmund Wilson, *Patriotic Gore: Studies in the Literature of the American Civil War* (New York, 1962). The general and author introductions in a textbook anthology, edited by Thomas Daniel Young, Floyd C. Watkins, and Richmond Croom Beatty, *Literature of the South* (rev. ed., New York, 1968), contain much helpful material, as do those in *Southern Writing, 1585–1920*, edited by Richard Beale Davis, C. Hugh Holman, and Louis D. Rubin, Jr. (New York, 1970; see especially Section III, "Southern Writing, 1865–1920"). Among good general essays are C. Hugh Holman, "A Cycle of Change in Southern Literature," in *The South in Continuity and Change*, edited by John C. McKinney and Edgar T. Thompson (Durham, N.C., 1965); Claud B. Green, "The Rise and Fall of Local Color in Southern Literature" (*MissQ*, Winter 1964–65); and Theodore L. Gross, "The South in the Literature of Reconstruction" (*MissQ*, Spring 1961). Two introductions to anthologies of American local color writings contain useful material: Claude M. Simpson, *The Local Colorists: American Short Stories, 1857–1900* (New York, 1960) and (of considerably less critical perception) Harry R. Warfel and G. Harrison Orians, *American Local Color Stories*

(New York, 1941). Also of much value are the introductions to Edd Winfield Parks, *Southern Poets*, and Gregory L. Paine, *Southern Prose Writers*. Louis J. Budd, Richard P. Adams, Darwin T. Turner, and Paschal Reeves, "The Forgotten Decades of Southern Writing, 1890–1920" (*MissQ*, Fall 1968), survey writings of the turn of the century.

For discussions of the Negro in southern literature during the latter half of the century, there are early accounts such as B. M. Drake, *The Negro in American Literature* (Nashville, Tenn., 1898); John H. Nelson, *The Negro Character in American Literature* (Lawrence, Kans., 1926); and more recent estimates such as Theodore Gross's "The Negro in the Literature of the Reconstruction," in *Images of the Negro in American Literature*, and Margaret Just Butcher's *The Negro in American Culture* (New York, 1956). Discussions of numerous Negro authors, including some from the period 1865 to 1900, may be found in Benjamin Brawley, *The Negro in Literature and Art* (New York, 1929); Brawley, *The Negro Genius* (New York, 1937); Herman Dreer, *American Literature by Negro Authors* (New York, 1950); Vernon Loggins, *The Negro Author: His Development in America to 1900* (New York, 1931); Benjamin Mays, *The Negro's God, as Reflected in His Literature* (Boston, 1938); and Jay Saunders Redding, *To Make a Poet Black* (Chapel Hill, N.C., 1939). Biographical information on numerous Negro writers may be found in collections such as those edited by the following: Sylvester C. Watkins, *Anthology of American Negro Literature* (New York, 1944); James Weldon Johnson, *The Book of American Negro Poetry* (New York, 1922; rev., 1931); Sterling A. Brown, Arthur P. Davis, and Ulysses Lee, *The Negro Caravan* (New York, 1941); and Newman I. White and Walter C. Jackson, *An Anthology of Verse by American Negroes* (Durham, N.C., 1924). Among relevant periodical essays are the following by Sterling Brown: "Negro Character as Seen by White Authors" (*Journal of Negro Education*, 1933), "The American Race Problem as Reflected in Negro Literature" (*Journal of Negro Education*, 1939), and "Century of Negro Portraiture in American Literature" (*Massachusetts Review*, Winter 1966). Other studies deserving of attention are Penelope Bullock's "The Mulatto in American Fiction" (*Phylon*, First Quarter 1945); Francis Pendleton Gaines's "The Racial Bar Sinister in American Romance" (*SAQ*, Jan. 1926); and Louis D. Rubin, Jr., "Southern Local Color and the Black Man" (*SoR*, Oct. 1970).

There are various specialized investigations of southern literature in the period. Of these, perhaps the most valuable is Francis Pendleton Gaines, *The Southern Plantation: A Study in the Development and*

Accuracy of a Tradition. This seminal work chronicles and intreprets the development of the antebellum plantation myth in southern literature, and it focuses extensively on the local color period. There is a pressing need for a revision and extension of Gaines's investigation both in the light of modern southern literature and of the significant change that has taken place in our evaluation of many of the problems involved in this study. Another useful book is Shields McIlwaine, *The Southern Poor White from Lubberland to Tobacco Road* (Norman, Okla., 1939), which contains considerable commentary on post-Reconstruction fiction. Wade Hall, *The Smiling Phoenix: Southern Humor from 1865 to 1914* (Gainesville, Fla., 1965), is more impressive in scope than in judgment. A specialized study dealing with one field of southern local color writing is Lorice C. Boger, *The Southern Mountaineer in Literature* (Morgantown, W.Va., 1964).

The southern historical costume romance is exhaustively treated in Robert A. Lively, *Fiction Fights the Civil War* (Chapel Hill, N.C., 1957), while Ernest E. Leisy, *The American Historical Novel* (Norman, Okla., 1950), discusses southern historical novels in various periods. James D. Hart, *The Popular Book: A History of America's Literary Taste* (New York, 1950), involves southern popular literature, as does Frank Luther Mott, *Golden Multitudes* (New York, 1947), a history of best sellers in America.

What little southern drama exists for the period is discussed in *Provincial Drama in America, 1870–1916*, edited by Paul T. Nolan (Metuchen, N.J., 1967).

From the brief survey given, it should be clear that much critical scholarship needs to be done in post–Civil War southern literature. Now that interest in the period seems to be on the increase, one would hope that some of the major shortcomings can be remedied. We need good critical biographies of such figures as Harris, Page, Chesnutt, and Lanier. We need a much more thoroughgoing and imaginative assessment of the relationship of the literature of local color to the history, politics, and culture of the late nineteenth-century South. We need to consider the function of such literature as American pastorale in the Gilded Age, the crucial role of the black man as a focus for such pastorale, the relationship of southern local color to critical realism; we need to view the literature of this period both in relationship to what came before it and what came afterwards. As it is, one tends to look upon the literature of the post–World War I Renascence of southern writing as if it had come out of nowhere, with no important antecedents in the literature of an earlier South. Yet in one way or another every one of the most important themes of the literature of Faulkner, Wolfe, Welty, the Nashville Fugitives, and the host of other important twentieth-century southern writers was present in the work of the late nineteenth-century writers. We need to ask what there was in the time and place that inhibited those writers from producing, out of much the same materials, literature of the stature and significance that later southern writers would achieve. Above all, I think, we need to study the role and the example of Mark Twain in relation to the country of his origins and of his greatest literature. For until the literature of the post–Civil War American South is viewed in a context larger than that of sectional self-defense, and the definition of what it involves is expanded to include those authors whose work transcended its imme-diate social, political, and geographical concerns—to include, in short, the South's greatest writer of the nineteenth century—the study of the literature of the nineteenth-century American South will remain narrowly sectional and relatively unimportant.

Notes on Contributors

JAMES FRANKLIN BEARD, born in Memphis, Tennessee, in 1919, is Professor of English at Clark University. Educated at Columbia College (A.B.), Columbia University (M.A.), and Princeton University (Ph.D.), he has taught at Princeton, at Dartmouth, and since 1955 at Clark. Among other awards, he has held Guggenheim Fellowships, 1952–53, 1958–59, and a Senior Fellowship of the National Endowment for the Humanities, 1967–68. Author of numerous articles, reviews, and introductions, his major work to date is the six-volume *Letters and Journals of James Fenimore Cooper* (1960–1968). He is at present coordinating efforts to initiate a definitive edition of Cooper's writings and preparing a critical biography. He is a member of the Executive Committee of the Center for American Authors of the Modern Language Association and a member of the Advisory Committee of the Imprint Society.

WILLIAM B. DILLINGHAM is Professor of English at Emory University, where he has taught (with appropriate interruptions) since 1956. Born in Atlanta in 1930, he holds degrees from Emory (A.B. and M.A.) and the University of Pennsylvania (Ph.D.). He was a Fulbright-Hays lecturer in American literature at the American Institute, University of Oslo, Norway, 1964–65. His books include *Frank Norris: Instinct and Art* (1969) and *Humor of the Old Southwest*, edited with Hennig Cohen (1964). His essays on American literature have appeared in *College English, Nineteenth-Century Fiction, Philological Quarterly, American Literature, English Studies*, and other journals.

EVERETT H. EMERSON, Professor of English and director of the Honors Program at the University of Massachusetts, was born in 1925. He holds degrees from Harvard (A.B.), Duke (M.A.), and Louisiana State University (Ph.D.). He has made early American literature his specialty. He served as the first chairman of the Modern Language Association's Early American Literature Group and is now editor of the group's journal,

413

Early American Literature. In addition to many articles, he is the author of *John Cotton* (1964), *English Puritanism from John Hooper to John Milton,* and a forthcoming study of Captain John Smith. Currently he is editing a volume called *Essays on Early American Literature* and preparing a study of American Puritanism from John Winthrop to Jonathan Edwards. He has twice held a Folger Library Fellowship.

GEORGE FORTENBERRY is Associate Professor of English at the University of Texas at Arlington. A native of Texas, he holds an M.A. degree from T.C.U. and a Ph.D. degree from the University of Arkansas. He is Associate Editor of *American Literary Realism* and Advisory Editor of *The Arlington Quarterly.*

NORMAN S. GRABO was born in Chicago in 1930, educated at Elmhurst College (B.A.) and the University of California at Los Angeles (M.A. and Ph.D.). He has taught at Michigan State University and U.C.L.A., and is now Professor of English at the University of California, Berkeley. A Fellow of the Folger Shakespeare Library (1959), the Society for Religion in Higher Education (1966–67), and the Guggenheim Memorial Foundation (1970–71), he is the author of *Edward Taylor* (1961) and editor of *Edward Taylor's Christographia* (1963), *Edward Taylor's Treatise Concerning the Lord's Supper* (1965), *American Thought and Writing* (1965), and *American Poetry and Prose* (1970). His essays on Taylor and other colonial writers have appeared in a number of academic journals.

BRUCE INGHAM GRANGER, Professor of English at the University of Oklahoma, was born in Philadelphia in 1920 and educated at Cornell (A.B., M.A., Ph.D.). He has taught at the University of Wisconsin, the University of Denver, and the University of Oklahoma as well as at the University of Vienna as a Fulbright Lecturer. He is the author of *Political Satire in the American Revolution* (1960) and *Benjamin Franklin: An American Man of Letters* (1964); currently he is editing Washington Irving's *Oldstyle—Salmagundi* for the University of Wisconsin Press.

EARL N. HARBERT, Associate Professor of English at Tulane University, was born in Cleveland, Ohio, in 1934. He received a B.A. from Hamilton College, an M.A. from Johns Hopkins University, and the Ph.D. from the University of Wisconsin. He served as Fulbright-Hays Lecturer at the University of Deusto, Bilbao, Spain. He has contributed to *American Literature, American Transcendental Quarterly, Studies in Short Fiction,* and *Tulane Studies in English.* At present he is working on a book-length study of the Adams family and a critical edition of Washington Irving's *A Chronicle of the Conquest of Granada,* for the University of Wisconsin Press.

C. HUGH HOLMAN is Kenan Professor of English at the University of North Carolina at Chapel Hill, where he has also served as Dean of the College of Arts and Sciences, Dean of the Graduate School, and Provost. He was born in Cross Anchor, South Carolina, in 1914, and was educated at Presbyterian College and the University of North Carolina, where he received the Ph.D. He received an honorary D.Litt degree from Presbyterian College in 1963 and an honorary L.H.D. degree from Clemson University in 1969. In 1968–69 he was a John Simon Guggenheim Memorial Fellow. He is the author of *Thomas Wolfe* (1960), *John P. Marquand* (1965), *The American Novel Through Henry James: A Goldentree Bibliography* (1966), and *Three Modes of Modern Southern Fiction* (1966). He is the co-author of *A Handbook to Literature* (1960) and *Southern Fiction Today* (1969). He has edited *The Short Novels of Thomas Wolfe* (1961), *The World of Thomas Wolfe* (1962), *The Thomas Wolfe Reader* (1962), and *Views and Reviews, by W. G. Simms* (1962). He is co-editor, with Sue F. Ross, of a new edition of *The Letters of Thomas Wolfe to His Mother* (1968), and is co-editor of *Southern Writing, 1585–1920* (1970). Currently he is working on a biographical study of Simms and on an edition of Irving's late American Journals.

KARL KELLER is Associate Professor of English at San Diego State College. He took his B.A. and M.A. at the University of Utah and his Ph.D. at the University of Minnesota. He has taught at the University of Minnesota, the State University College at Cortland, New York, and at San Diego State. He has published essays on Edward Taylor, Emerson, Thoreau, Melville, and Robinson Jeffers, and has just finished a book, *The Example of Edward Taylor*. He has co-authored a text, *American Literature: Post 1945*, for the College of Individual Learning, is editor of an eighteenth-century novel, *Amelia; or, The Faithless Briton*, and is on the Board of Editors of the journal *Dialogue* and on the bibliography staff of *American Literature*.

BARRY MENIKOFF, Associate Professor of English at the University of Hawaii, was born in Brooklyn, New York, in 1939. He received his B.A. from Brooklyn College and his M.A. and Ph.D. from the University of Wisconsin. He served as a Fulbright Lecturer at the University of Santiago, Santiago de Compostela, Spain. He is co-editor of *The Short Story: An Introductory Anthology* and has published articles and reviews on Henry James.

DONALD PIZER, who was born in New York City in 1929, received his B.A., M.A., and Ph.D. from the University of California, Los Angeles. After service in the Army, he joined the faculty of Newcomb College, Tulane University, in 1957, where he is now Professor of English. He is a Guggenheim Fellow (1962) and has also received research awards from the

Huntington Library and the American Philosophical Society. During 1967–68 he was a Fulbright Lecturer at the University of Hamburg. Among his books are *Hamlin Garland's Early Work and Career* (1960), *Realism and Naturalism in Nineteenth-Century American Literature* (1966), *The Novels of Frank Norris* (1966), and editions of works by Hamlin Garland, Frank Norris, Theodore Dreiser, and Stephen Crane.

HENRY A. POCHMANN is Professor of English at the University of Wisconsin, where he has been a member of the faculty since 1938. He was born in Round Top, Texas, in 1901, and was educated at Southwest Texas State University, the University of Texas, and the University of North Carolina, where he received a Ph.D. He taught at Austin State University, Louisiana State University, The University of Mississippi, and Mississippi State University, where he served as Chairman of the English Department and Dean of the Graduate School, before coming to Wisconsin. He has been a Rockefeller Foundation Fellow and a Huntington Library Fellow and in 1970–71 was Senior Faculty Fellow at the University of Wisconsin Institute for Research in the Humanities. He is the author of numerous studies of American Literature and culture, including *German Culture in America, 1600–1900* (1957) which was awarded the Loubat Prize (1958). Currently he is General Editor of *The Complete Works of Washington Irving* (28 volumes), in which series his own *Mahomet and His Successors* appeared in 1970.

ROBERT A. REES is Assistant Professor of English at U.C.L.A. He was born in Los Angeles in 1935 and educated at Brigham Young University (B.A.) and the University of Wisconsin (M.A., Ph.D.). He has published articles, essays and bibliographies on various aspects of American Literature and is currently preparing an edition of Washington Irving's *The Adventures of Captain Bonneville* for the University of Wisconsin Press's Irving Project.

JAMES E. ROCKS has been an Assistant Professor of English at Tulane University since 1965. Born in Cleveland, Ohio, in 1939, he received his A.B. in 1961 from Western Reserve University. His M.A. (1962) and Ph.D. (1966) are from Duke University, where he was a James B. Duke Fellow for two years. Mr. Rocks teaches courses in nineteenth-century American literature and in southern literature at Tulane. His essays on Camus, Hawthorne, and Caroline Gordon have appeared in *Tulane Studies in English* and *Mississippi Quarterly*. He is presently working in the area of modern southern literature.

LOUIS D. RUBIN, JR., is Professor of English at the University of North Carolina at Chapel Hill. Previously, he taught for ten years at Hollins College, Virginia. He was born in Charleston, South Carolina, and holds degrees from the University of Richmond (B.A.) and Johns Hopkins University (M.A., Ph.D.). He has been a *Sewanee Review*, Guggenheim, and American Council of Learned Societies fellow. Among his books are *Thomas Wolfe: The Weather of His Youth* (1955), *The Golden Weather: a Novel* (1961), *The Faraway Country: Writers of the Modern South* (1963), *The Curious Death of the Novel* (1967), *The Teller in the Tale* (1967), and *George W. Cable: The Life and Times of a Southern Heretic* (1969).

RICHARD DILWORTH RUST is Associate Professor of English at the University of North Carolina. He was born in Provo, Utah, in 1937, and was educated at Brigham Young University and the University of Wisconsin, where he received his Ph.D. in 1966. He has published articles on Herman Melville, Mark Twain, and Eugene O'Neill, and has edited *Glory and Pathos: Responses of Nineteenth-Century American Authors to the Civil War* (1970). At present he is completing work on an edition of *Astoria, or Anecdotes of an Enterprize Beyond the Rocky Mountains,* to be published by the University of Wisconsin Press as part of *The Complete Works of Washington Irving.*

JAMES WOODRESS, Professor of English and Chairman of the English Department at the University of California at Davis, was born in Webster Groves, Missouri, in 1916. He was educated at Amherst (A.B.), N.Y.U. (M.A.), and Duke (Ph.D.). He is the author of biographies of Booth Tarkington, Joel Barlow, and Willa Cather and a study of Howells in Italy. He has been a Guggenheim Fellow and Fulbright Lecturer in France and Italy. He was the founder and editor for five years of *American Literary Scholarship*. He is one of the editors of the Indiana University Howells edition.

Index

419